MORE PRAISE FROM ~~[illegible]~~
FOR THE JOB~~[illegible]~~

"I've been very impressed by the high caliber of candidates referred to our agency via *The Metropolitan New York JobBank*."
-**Jeannette A. Henry, CPC, President**
Huntington Personnel Consultants

"For those graduates whose parents are pacing the floor, conspicuously placing circled want ads around the house and typing up resumes, [*The Carolina JobBank*] answers job-search questions."
-*Greensboro News and Record*

"A timely book for Chicago job hunters follows books from the same publisher that were well received in New York and Boston ... A fine tool for job hunters ..."
-**Clarence Peterson,** *Chicago Tribune*

"I refer all jobseekers to *The Chicago JobBank*. It is on my must-have list--whether you live in Chicago or are relocating from another city."
-**Alice Huntsha,**
Pahlman, Murphy, and Attridge, Inc./Tempfleet, Inc.

"Because our listing is seen by people across the nation it generates lots of resumes for us. We encourage unsolicited resumes. We'll always be listed [in *The Chicago JobBank*] as long as I'm in this career."
-**Tom Fitzpatrick, Director of Human Resources**
Merchandise Mart Properties, Inc.

"In my business, referrals are essential to me. I receive more telephone calls, and receive more resumes, from people who have found me in [*The Chicago JobBank*] than from any other single source, including the Yellow Pages. [*The Chicago JobBank*] is a constant, quality source of candidates for my office."
-**Victor Persico, President**
Management Recruiters of Chicago - SW

"Job hunters can't afford to waste time. *The Minneapolis-St. Paul JobBank* contains information that used to require hours of research in the library."
-**Carmella Zagone**
Minneapolis-based Human Resources Administrator

"*The Florida JobBank* is an invaluable job-search reference tool. It provides the most up-to-date information and contact names available for companies in Florida. I should know--it worked for me!"
        -Rhonda Cody, Human Resources Consultant
        Aetna Life and Casualty

"A powerful resume, *The Boston JobBank,* an aggressive job-search strategy, and a positive attitude are the keys to landing the job you want."
        -Anne M. Savas, Principal
        The Competitive Edge

"*The Boston JobBank* series is a unique and effective tool, necessary in today's competitive marketplace, for job seekers of all levels. I wouldn't hesitate to recommend it highly to those seeking quality results."
        -M. Nofal, President
        TARGET Career Center

"*The Boston JobBank* provides a handy map of employment possibilities in Greater Boston. This book can help in the initial steps of a job search by locating major employers, describing their business activities, and for most firms, by naming the contact person and listing typical professional positions. For recent college graduates, as well as experienced professionals, *The Boston JobBank* is an excellent place to begin a job search."
        -Juliet F. Brudney, Career Columnist
        Boston Globe

"No longer can jobseekers feel secure about finding employment just through want ads. With the tough competition in the job market, particularly in the Boston area, they need much more help. For this reason, *The Boston JobBank* will have a wide and appreciative audience of new graduates, job changers, and people relocating to Boston. It provides a good place to start a search for entry-level professional positions."
        -Journal of College Placement

"*The Phoenix JobBank* provides the most convenient information source available to professionals with tight budgets and little time to waste."
        -Jerry Mosqueda, President
        Mosqueda & Mijas

"*The Phoenix JobBank* is a first-class publication. The information provided is useful and current."
        -Lyndon Denton
        Director of Human Resources and Materials Management

What makes the JobBank series the nation's premier line of employment guides?

With vital employment information on thousands of employers across the nation, the JobBank series is the most comprehensive and authoritative set of career directories available today.

Each book in the series provides information on **dozens of different industries** in a given city or area, with the primary employer listings providing contact information, telephone numbers, addresses, a summary of the firm's business, and in many cases descriptions of the firm's typical professional job categories, the principal educational backgrounds sought, and the fringe benefits offered.

In addition to the **detailed primary employer listings,** the 1996 JobBank books give telephone numbers and addresses for **thousands of additional employers.**

All of the reference information in the JobBank series is as up-to-date and accurate as possible. Every year, the entire database is thoroughly researched and verified by mail and by telephone. Adams Media Corporation publishes **more local employment guides more often** than any other publisher of career directories.

In addition, the JobBank series features important information about the local job scene -- **forecasts on which industries are the hottest, overviews of local economic trends,** and **lists of regional professional associations,** so you can get your job hunt started off right.

Hundreds of discussions with job hunters show that they prefer information organized geographically, because most people look for jobs in specific areas. The JobBank series offers **20 regional titles,** from Minneapolis to Houston, and from Boston to San Francisco. Jobseekers moving to a particular area can review the local employment data not only for information on the type of industry most common to that region, but also for names of specific companies.

A condensed, but thorough, review of the entire job search process is presented in the chapter **The Basics of Job Winning**, a feature which has received many compliments from career counselors. In addition, each JobBank directory includes a section on **resumes and cover letters** the *New York Times* has acclaimed as "excellent."

The JobBank series gives job hunters the most comprehensive, timely, and accurate career information, organized and indexed to facilitate the job search. An entire career reference library, JobBank books are the consummate employment guides.

Published by Adams Media Corporation
260 Center Street, Holbrook, MA 02343

Manufactured in the United States of America.

Copyright © 1996 by Adams Media Corporation. All rights reserved. No part of the material printed may be reproduced or used in any form or by any means, electronic or mechanical, including photocopying, recording, or by any information storage retrieval system without permission from the publisher.

The Metropolitan Washington JobBank, 1996 and its cover design are trademarks of Adams Media Corporation.

Brand name products in the employer listings are proprietary property of the applicable firm, subject to trademark protection, and registered with government offices.

Because addresses and telephone numbers of smaller companies change rapidly, we recommend you call each company and verify the information before mailing to the employers listed in this book. Mass mailings are not recommended.

While the publisher has made every reasonable effort to obtain and verify accurate information, occasional errors are inevitable due to the magnitude of the database. Should you discover an error, or if a company is missing, please write the editors at the above address so that we may update future editions.

"This publication is designed to provide accurate and authoritative information with regard to the subject matter covered. It is sold with the understanding that the publisher is not engaged in rendering legal, accounting, or other professional advice. If legal advice or other expert assistance is required, the services of a competent professional person should be sought."
--From a *Declaration of Principles* jointly adopted by a Committee of the American Bar Association and a Committee of Publishers and Associations

The appearance of a listing in the book does not constitute an endorsement from the publisher.

Cover photo courtesy of the DC Convention and Visitors Association.

ISBN: 1-55850-571-7

*This book is available at quantity discounts for bulk purchases.
For information, call 800/872-5627.*

Visit our home page at http://www.adamsonline.com

The Metropolitan Washington JobBank 1996

Managing Editor
Carter Smith

Series Editor
Steven Graber

Associate Editors
Kenny Brooks
Marcie DiPietro
Jennifer B. Greene
Jennifer J. Pfalzgraf

Editorial Assistants
Kathryn Couzens
Lissa Harnish
Ernest Minks

ADAMS PUBLISHING
Holbrook, Massachusetts

Top career publications from Adams Media Corporation

The Atlanta JobBank, 1996 ($15.95)
The Boston JobBank, 1996 ($15.95)
The Carolina JobBank, 3rd Ed. ($15.95)
The Chicago JobBank, 1996 ($15.95)
The Dallas-Ft. Worth JobBank, 1996 ($15.95)
The Denver JobBank, 7th Ed. ($15.95)
The Detroit JobBank, 5th Ed. ($15.95)
The Florida JobBank, 1996 ($15.95)
The Houston JobBank, 1996 ($15.95)
The Los Angeles JobBank, 1996 ($15.95)
The Minneapolis-St. Paul JobBank, 1996 ($15.95)
The Metropolitan New York JobBank, 1996 ($15.95)
The Ohio JobBank, 1996 ($15.95)
The Greater Philadelphia JobBank, 1996 ($15.95)
The Phoenix JobBank, 5th Ed. ($15.95)
The St. Louis JobBank, 6th Ed. ($15.95)
The San Francisco Bay Area JobBank, 1996 ($15.95)
The Seattle JobBank, 1996 ($15.95)
The Tennessee JobBank, 2nd Ed. ($15.95)
The Metropolitan Washington JobBank, 1996 ($15.95)

The National JobBank, 1996 (Covers the entire U.S.: $270.00)

The JobBank Guide to Employment Services, 1996-1997 (Covers the entire U.S.: $160.00)

Other Career Titles:

The Adams Cover Letter Almanac ($10.95)
The Adams Jobs Almanac, 1996 ($15.95)
The Adams Resume Almanac ($10.95)
America's Fastest Growing Employers, 2nd Ed.($16.00)
Career Shifting ($9.95)
Careers and the College Grad ($12.95)
Careers and the Engineer ($12.95)
Careers and the MBA ($12.95)

Cold Calling Techniques (That Really Work!), 3rd Ed. ($7.95)
The Complete Resume & Job Search Book for College Students ($9.95)
Cover Letters That Knock 'em Dead, 2nd Ed. ($10.95)
Every Woman's Essential Job Hunting & Resume Book ($10.95)
The Harvard Guide to Careers in the Mass Media ($7.95)
High Impact Telephone Networking for Job Hunters ($6.95)
How to Become Successfully Self-Employed, 2nd Ed. ($9.95)
The Job Hunter's Checklist ($5.95)
The Job Search Handbook ($6.95)
Knock 'em Dead, The Ultimate Jobseeker's Handbook, 1996 ($12.95)
The Lifetime Career Manager ($20.00)
The MBA Advantage ($12.95)
The Minority Career Book ($9.95)
The National Jobline Directory ($7.95)
The New Rules of the Job Search Game ($10.00)
Outplace Yourself ($25.00 hc) ($15.95 pb)
Over 40 and Looking for Work? ($7.95)
Reengineering Yourself ($12.95)
The Resume Handbook, 2nd Ed. ($5.95)
Resumes That Knock 'em Dead, 2nd Ed. ($10.95)
300 New Ways to Get a Better Job ($7.95)

To order these books or additional copies of this book, send check or money order (including $4.50 for postage) to:

Adams Media Corporation
260 Center Street
Holbrook MA 02343

Ordering by credit card?
Just call 800/USA-JOBS
(In Massachusetts, call 617/767-8100).
Please check your local bookstore first.

TABLE OF CONTENTS

SECTION ONE: INTRODUCTION

How to Use This Book/10
An introduction to the most effective way to use The Metropolitan Washington JobBank.

The Metropolitan Washington Job Market/15
An informative economic overview designed to help you understand all of the forces shaping the metropolitan Washington job market.

SECTION TWO: THE JOB SEARCH

The Basics of Job Winning/22
A condensed review of the basic elements of a successful job search campaign. Includes advice on developing an effective strategy, time planning, preparing for interviews, interview techniques, etc. Special sections address unique situations faced by those jobseekers who are currently employed, those who have lost a job, and college students conducting their first job search.

Resumes and Cover Letters/39
Advice on creating a strong resume. Includes sample resumes and cover letters.

SECTION THREE: PRIMARY EMPLOYERS

The Employers/56
The Metropolitan Washington JobBank *is organized according to industry. Many listings include the address and phone number of each major firm listed, along with a description of the company's basic product lines and services, and, in many cases, a contact name and other relevant hiring information. Also included are hundreds of secondary listings providing addresses and phone numbers for small- and medium-sized employers.*

  Accounting and Management Consulting/56
  Advertising, Marketing and Public Relations/64
  Aerospace/68
  Apparel and Textiles/71
  Architecture, Construction and Engineering/75
  Arts and Entertainment/Recreation/85
  Automotive/90
  Banking/Savings and Loans/93
  Biotechnology, Pharmaceuticals, and Scientific R&D/104
  Business Services and Non-Scientific Research/110
  Charities and Social Services/122
  Chemicals/Rubber and Plastics/126
  Communications: Telecommunications and Broadcasting/134
  Computer Hardware, Software, and Services/144
  Educational Services/156
  Electronic/Industrial Electrical Equipment/164

Environmental Services/172
Fabricated/Primary Metals and Products/175
Financial Services/178
Food and Beverages/Agriculture/184
Government/191
Health Care: Services, Equipment and Products/202
Hotels and Restaurants/218
Insurance/226
Legal Services/231
Manufacturing and Wholesaling: Miscellaneous Consumer/234
Manufacturing and Wholesaling: Miscellaneous Industrial/238
Mining/Gas/Petroleum/Energy Related/247
Paper and Wood Products/249
Printing and Publishing/252
Real Estate/265
Retail/270
Stone, Clay, Glass and Concrete Products/283
Transportation/286
Utilities: Electric/Gas/Sanitation/292

SECTION FOUR: GOVERNMENT JOBS

Working For The Federal Government/296
Everything you need to know to find a job with the federal government.

SECTION FIVE: EMPLOYMENT SERVICES

Temporary Services and Employment Agencies/309
Includes addresses, phone numbers, and descriptions of companies specializing in temporary placement of clients. Also includes contact names, specializations, and a list of positions commonly filled.

Executive Search Firms/316
Includes addresses, phone numbers, and descriptions of companies specializing in permanent placement of executive-level clients. Also includes contact names, specializations, and a list of positions commonly filled.

Resume and Career Counseling Services/316
Includes addresses, phone numbers, and descriptions of companies offering resume and career counseling services..

SECTION SIX: INDEX

Alphabetical Index of Primary Employers/324
Includes larger employer listings only. Does not include employers that fall under the headings "Additional Employers."

INTRODUCTION

HOW TO USE THIS BOOK

Right now, you hold in your hands one of the most effective job hunting tools available anywhere. In *The Metropolitan Washington JobBank*, you will find a wide array of valuable information to help you launch or continue a rewarding career. But before you open to the book's employer listings and start calling about current job openings, take a few minutes to learn how best to put the resources presented in *The Metropolitan Washington JobBank* to work for you.

The Metropolitan Washington JobBank will help you to stand out from other jobseekers. While many people looking for a new job rely solely on newspaper help-wanted ads, this book offers you a much more effective job-search method -- direct contact. The direct contact method has been proven twice as effective as scanning the help-wanted ads. Instead of waiting for employers to come looking for you, you'll be far more effective going to them. While many of your competitors will use trial and error methods in trying to set up interviews, you'll learn not only how to get interviews, but what to expect once you've got them.

In the next few pages, we'll take you through each section of the book so you'll be prepared to get a jump-start on your competition:

The Metropolitan Washington Job Market: An Overview

To get a feel for the state of the local job scene, read the introductory section called *The Metropolitan Washington Job Market*. In it, we'll recap the economy's recent performance and the steps that local governments and business leaders are taking to bring new jobs to the area.

Even more importantly, you'll learn where the local economy is headed. What are the prospects for the industries that form the core of the region's economy? Which industries are growing fastest and which ones are laying off? Are there any companies or industries that are especially hot?

To answer these questions for you, we've pored over local business journals and newspapers and interviewed local business leaders and labor analysts. Whether you are new to the area and need a source of regional information, or are a life-long resident just looking for a fresh start in a new job, you'll find this section to be a concise thumbnail sketch of where the jobs are.

This type of information is potent ammunition to bring into an interview. Showing that you're well versed in current industry trends helps give you an edge over job applicants who haven't done their homework.

Basics of Job Winning

Preparation. Strategy. Time-Management. These are three of the most important elements of a successful job search. *Basics of Job Winning* helps you address these and all the other elements needed to find the right job.

How to Use This Book/11

One of your first priorities should be to define your personal career objectives. What qualities make a job desirable to you? Creativity? High pay? Prestige? Use *Basics of Job Winning* to weigh these questions. Then use the rest of the chapter to design a strategy to find a job that matches your criteria.

In *Basics of Job Winning*, you'll learn which job-hunting techniques work, and which don't. We've reviewed the pros and cons of mass mailings, help-wanted ads and direct contact. We'll show you how to develop and approach contacts in your field; how to research a prospective employer; and how to use that information to get an interview and the job.

Also included in *Basics of Job Winning*: interview dress code and etiquette, the "do's and don'ts" of interviewing, sample interview questions, and the often forgotten art of what to do after the interview. We also deal with some of the unique problems faced by those jobseekers who are currently employed, those who have lost a job, and college students conducting their first job search.

Resumes and Cover Letters

The approach you take to writing your resume and cover letter can often mean the difference between getting an interview and never being noticed. In this section, we discuss different formats, as well as what to put on (and what to leave off) your resume. We review the benefits and drawbacks of professional resume writers, and the importance of a follow-up letter. Also included in this section are sample resumes and cover letters which you can use as models.

The Employer Listings

Employers are listed alphabetically by industry, and within each industry, by company names. When a company does business under a person's name, like "John Smith & Co.", the company is usually listed by the surname's spelling (in this case "S"). Exceptions occur when a company's name is widely recognized, like "JCPenney" or "Howard Johnson Motor Lodge." In those cases, the company's first name is the key ("J" and "H" respectively).

The Metropolitan Washington JobBank covers a very wide range of industries. Each company profile is assigned to one of the industry chapters listed below.

Accounting and Management Consulting
Advertising/Marketing and Public Relations
Aerospace
Apparel and Textiles
Architecture, Construction, and Engineering
Arts and Entertainment/Recreation
Automotive
Banking/Savings and Loans

Biotechnology, Pharmaceuticals and Scientific R&D
Business Services and Non-Scientific Research
Charities and Social Services
Chemicals/Rubber and Plastics
Communications: Telecommunications and Broadcasting
Computer Hardware, Software and Services

Educational Services
Electronic/Industrial Electrical
   Equipment
Environmental Services
Fabricated/Primary Metals and Products
Financial Services
Food and Beverage/Agriculture
Government
Health Care: Services, Equipment and
   Products
Hotels and Restaurants
Insurance
Legal Services
Manufacturing and Wholesaling: Misc.
   Consumer
Manufacturing and Wholesaling: Misc.
   Industrial
Mining/Gas/Petroleum/Energy Related
Paper and Wood Products
Printing and Publishing
Real Estate
Retail
Stone, Clay, Glass and Concrete Products
Transportation
Utilities: Electric/Gas/Sanitation

Many of the company listings offer detailed company profiles. In addition to company names, addresses, and phone numbers, these listings also include contact names or hiring departments, and descriptions of each company's products and/or services. Many of these listings also include a variety of additional information including:

Common positions - A list of job titles that the company commonly fills when it is hiring, organized in alphabetical order from Accountant to X-ray Technician. Note: Keep in mind that *The Metropolitan Washington JobBank* is a directory of major employers in the area, not a directory of openings currently available. Many of the companies listed will be hiring, others will not. However, since most professional job openings are filled without the placement of help-wanted ads, contacting the employers in this book directly is still a more effective method than browsing the Sunday papers.

Educational backgrounds sought - A list of educational backgrounds that companies seek when hiring.

Benefits - What kind of benefits packages are available from these employers? Here you'll find a broad range of benefits, from the relatively common (medical insurance) to those that are much more rare (health club membership; child daycare assistance).

Special programs - Does the company offer training programs, internships or apprenticeships? These programs can be important to first time jobseekers and college students looking for practical work experience. Many employer profiles will include information on these programs.

Parent company - If an employer is a subsidiary of a larger company, the name of that parent company will often be listed here. Use this information to supplement your company research before contacting the employer.

Number of employees - The number of workers a company employs.

How to Use This Book/13

Companies may also include information on other U.S. locations and any stock exchange the firm may be listed on.

Because so many job openings are with small and mid-sized employers, we've also included the addresses and phone numbers of such employers. While none of these listings include any additional hiring information, many of them do offer rewarding career opportunities. These companies are found under each industry heading. Within each industry, they are organized by the type of product or service offered.

A note on all employer listings that appear in *The Metropolitan Washington JobBank*. This book is intended as a starting point. It is not intended to replace any effort that you, the jobseeker, should devote to your job hunt. Keep in mind that while a great deal of effort has been put into collecting and verifying the company profiles provided in this book, addresses and contact names change regularly. Inevitably, some contact names listed herein have changed even before you read this. We recommend you contact a company before mailing your resume to ensure nothing has changed.

At the end of each industry section, we have included a directory of other industry-specific resources to help you in your job search. These include: professional and industrial associations, many of which can provide employment advice and job search help; magazines that cover the industry; and additional directories that may supplement the employer listings in this book.

Working for the Federal Government
This section offers information on application procedures for federal employment. It will tell you everything you need to know to get a job with the federal government.

Employment Services
Many jobseekers supplement their own efforts by contracting "temp" services, head hunters, and other employment services firms to generate potential job opportunities. The employment services section is a comprehensive listing of such firms, arranged alphabetically under the headings Employment Agencies, Temporary Agencies, and Executive Search Firms. Each listing includes the firm's name, address, telephone number and contact person. Most listings also include the industries the firm specializes in, the type of positions commonly filled, and the number of jobs filled annually.

Index
The Metropolitan Washington JobBank index is a straight alphabetical listing.

The Metropolitan Washington Job Market: An Overview

If you're considering a career as a Washington bureaucrat, right now might be the time to rethink your plans. Since the Republican Revolution hit town in January 1995, well-paying federal jobs have been slashed faster than you can say "Freddy Krueger." And it's not just the Republicans wielding the knife: the Clinton Administration has already proposed the elimination of 34,000 federal jobs by the year 2000.

The picture for local District government workers is even bleaker. The District of Columbia has long supported a severely bloated bureaucracy. According to researchers at George Washington University, the city government has paid for its largesse by levying heavy taxes that have forced many leading employers -- and middle-class residents -- to head for suburban Maryland and Virginia. In fact, since 1986, when the District's population reached its all-time high, the number of DC residents has plunged more than 10 percent, to 570,000. In 1994 alone, the city's population dropped by 17,000. That's a 3 percent drop in population in a single year.

This kind of statistic spells both short- and long-term trouble for the city's job market. Today, Washington's biggest strength is foreign tourism. As one of the world's leading tourist attractions, the city draws legions of foreign tourists each year -- tourists whose heavy shopping supports retail sales and creates jobs in the hotel business. But while the number of jobs in Washington's hotels and restaurants has been increasing -- 1,500 new restaurant jobs and 300 new hotel jobs between March '94 and March '95 -- no other industries can be considered strong. Aside from hotel and restaurant jobs, the entire remainder of the city's private sector added only another 3,100 jobs. In fact, out of the 27 largest cities in the country, Washington DC's February unemployment rate of 8.1 percent was the seventh highest. While that rate is somewhat better than the February, 1994 rate of 8.8 percent, clearly the District continues to lag behind the national average of 5.4 percent.

To find most of the job growth in metro Washington, one needs to look beyond the borders of the city. The Washington suburbs added 52,000 new workers between March, 1994 and February, 1995. Jobseekers should keep in mind that federal cutbacks don't mean that the U.S. government will stop being the area's biggest consumer of products and services. It does mean that many area businesses must rethink what services or products they can still market to the government.

Many regional firms have been arriving upon creative solutions. The minority-owned **Technautics**, of Arlington, named by *Inc.* as one of the nation's fastest-growing private firms, was founded as a provider of engineering and technical support for weapons programs. However, the company began to feel the pinch as many federal minority and small business programs that helped garner government contracts began to be phased out. Much of the company's defense work has now been taken over by larger competitors. In response, Technautics has expanded new directions, snatching up tech support and engineering accounts from the National Institute of Health and the Federal Highway Administration. Now, defense-related work accounts for just 35 to 40 percent of sales.

H.J. Ford Associates, another engineering and technical services firm, took a similar tactic. The firm now receives business from a healthy mix of non-defense agencies including the General Services Administration, the IRS, and the Departments of Energy and Transportation.

What does all this mean for jobseekers? Flexibility, diversity, and skills are important traits in an environment where a company's primary client, and therefore product, may change at any given time. Workers should be prepared to apply basic skills to a variety of applications. Jobseekers should also investigate small companies, which have the flexibility to react to dynamic market forces that many large companies do not.

Services and Retail

As in the rest of the country, the bulk of all jobs in metro Washington will be in service industries. *Among the hottest service sectors:* business, health care, and engineering and management services. *Among the hottest firms:* **Fastrak Training**, of Columbia, MD, a software training services firm whose sales grew by 797 percent between 1988 and 1992; **Payroll 1 Mid Atlantic** of McLean, VA, a payroll and payroll tax services company; and **MVM**, of Falls Church, VA, a company that provides security and investigative services, guarding embassies and military bases for which government security doesn't have the resources.

Job openings in the retail sector also abound in metro DC, fueled by population growth in the suburbs. **Pet Ventures** of Arlington is one example. The company sells pet food and supplies, combining two current trends -- the growing popularity of pampering pets and the appeal of warehouse-style stores.

High-Tech

Metro Washington has recently emerged as one of the important centers for technology, taking its place next to Silicon Valley, Route 128 outside of Boston, and the Research Triangle of North Carolina. Dubbed the "Netplex" by *Fortune* magazine, the area has led the world in creating and managing high-speed data communications networks. The metro region now has over 180,000 employees working in high-tech jobs.

As home to federal data networks, such as those operated by NASA and the Department of Defense, Washington has always been a communications leader. Many of the heavyweights of the private sector maintain large presences here, including both **MCI** and **Sprint**. Other large employers are the local telephone service, **Bell Atlantic**; **AT&T Paradyne**, a data communications subsidiary of AT&T; **Cable and Wireless**, a British long-distance and data services firm; and **Metropolitan Fiber Systems**, another long-distance telephone company.

Virtually all of these firms are linked both figuratively and literally on the Internet, which connects more than 25,000 computer networks. Any of its 20 million users can send messages, files, software, and other data to any other computer on the Net. Originally created by the Pentagon as a Cold War communications network, it has come into general use over the past two years and is now the fastest-growing communications medium in history, doubling its number of users annually.

The good news for Washington jobseekers: there are a multitude of new and rapidly growing employers related to the Internet. Sprint and MCI not only provide long-distance services, but also build, sell, and rent out high-speed lines. Metropolitan Fiber Systems operates a fiber line that runs between Falls Church, VA and College Park, MD, connecting the Internet to Europe. Sprint is also an Internet access provider. Other businesses that have cropped up as providers of Internet services include **Performance Systems International**, of Herndon, VA, and **UUNET**, of Falls Church, VA. Both are primary providers of Internet connections to thousands of companies and organizations. Two of the four major on-line services in the nation, **GEnie**, owned by GE Information Services, and **America Online**, are also located in the Netplex region.

The Internet has already given rise to a substantial industry to build and manage its circuits and link up customers from corporations to government agencies to individuals. Some of the companies that make a living from internetworking: **Network Solutions**, of Herndon, VA, manages the military's Defense Data Network, and assigns addresses to networks as they join the Internet. Two other Herndon companies are **Intercon Systems**, the biggest producer of Internet software for Macintosh users, and **Newbridge Networks**, which sells more than $230 million a year in networking hardware.

Health Care

The health services industry is expected to continue to grow in metro DC, with doctors' offices, nursing and personal care facilities, and hospitals as the leading contributors. The growing elderly population will increase the need for geriatric care. **Integrated Health Services** provides non-hospital health care in twenty-one states. The pioneer of low-cost mini-hospitals within nursing homes, Integrated Health Services qualified as a *Fortune* 100 fastest-growing company. **Mid Atlantic Medical Services**, of Rockville, MD, operates three HMOs, a preferred provider organization (PPO), and a mental health care subsidiary. **CMG Health**, of Owings Mills, MD, manages health and benefits for substance abuse treatment programs for HMOs and has been classified by *Inc.* as a fastest-growing company. By specializing in that field, CMG feels it can work more efficiently than HMOs do themselves.

Media

As the nation's capital and the hub of the country's political activity, there are a multitude of media companies in Washington, although competition for media jobs is always fierce. However, media is one of the markets more sensitive to the economy, so opportunities will keep in time with the recovery. The two largest employers are the **Washington Post Company**, a major communications and media company which publishes *The Washington Post*, *Newsweek*, and a host of other publications, and **Gannett Company Inc.**, the multi-media conglomerate with interests in news and information, book and newspaper publishing, broadcasting, and advertising. Gannett is best known for its newspaper, *USA Today*. In July, 1995, it was announced that the company would purchase Multimedia Inc., one of the nation's largest broadcasting and newspaper companies.

Manufacturing

Manufacturing in the metropolitan Washington area has shown more consistent growth than the rest of the nation -- at least outside the District itself. It remains one of the most important segments in the area's economy. Industries with the greatest employment are transportation equipment, textiles, food processing, printing, electronic and other electrical equipment, apparel, chemicals, lumber and wood products, industrial machinery and equipment, and furniture. Leading the pack of top employers for the Washington area are **General Dynamics**, the aerospace manufacturer of Arlington, VA, and **Black and Decker Corporation**, the well-known manufacturer and distributor of power tools and small household appliances.

The Environment

Environmental services is an industry coming into its own in metro Washington, fueled by stricter EPA requirements and a growing national concern for the environment. **Air Cure Environmental** is moving its headquarters to Annapolis, MD from Minneapolis, MN. This company engineers and provides air pollution control equipment to industrial customers worldwide. **Environmental Restoration**, in Fredericksburg, VA, an environmental consulting services company, and **HTS Environmental Group** and **Bruce Company**, of DC, are three of the smaller companies that were classified by *Inc.* as fastest-growing companies. And in Annapolis, MD an Environmental Science Center is planned for construction by the **Environmental Protection Agency**, due to be completed in 1996.

Other sources for employment information:

Arlington Chamber of Commerce
1 Annapolis Street
Annapolis MD 21401

Baltimore Chamber of Commerce
204 East Lombard Street, Suite 300
Baltimore MD 21202

DC Department of Employment Services
500 C Street NW, Suite 201
Washington DC 20001

Washington DC Chamber of Commerce
1301 Pennsylvania Avenue NW, Suite 309
Washington DC 20004

THE JOB SEARCH

THE BASICS OF JOB WINNING: A CONDENSED REVIEW

This chapter is divided into four sections. The first section explains the fundamentals that every jobseeker should know, especially first-time jobseekers. The following three sections deal with special situations faced by specific types of jobseekers: those who are currently employed, those who have lost a job, and college students.

THE BASICS:
Things Everyone Needs To Know

Career Planning The first step to finding your ideal job is to clearly define your objectives. This is better known as career planning (or life planning if you wish to emphasize the importance of combining the two). Career planning has become a field of study in and of itself.

If you are thinking of choosing or switching careers, we particularly emphasize two things. First, choose a career where you will enjoy most of the day-to-day tasks. This sounds obvious, but most of us have at one point or another been attracted by a glamour industry or a prestigious job title without thinking of the most important consideration: Would we enjoy performing the everyday tasks the position entails?

> **The first step in beginning your job search is to clearly define your objectives.**

The second key consideration is that you are not merely choosing a career, but also a lifestyle. Career counselors indicate that one of the most common problems people encounter in job-seeking is that they fail to consider how well-suited they are for a particular position or career. For example, some people, attracted to management consulting by good salaries, early responsibility, and high-level corporate exposure, do not adapt well to the long hours, heavy travel demands, and constant pressure to produce. Be sure to ask yourself how you might adapt to not only the day-to-day duties and working environment that a specific position entails, but also how you might adapt to the demands of that career or industry choice as a whole.

Assuming that you've established your career objectives, the next step of the job search is to develop a strategy. If you don't take the time to develop a strategy and lay out a plan, you may find yourself going in circles after several weeks of randomly searching for opportunities that always seem just beyond your reach. **Choosing Your Strategy**

The most common job-seeking techniques are:

- following up on help-wanted advertisements
- using employment services
- relying on personal contacts
- contacting employers directly (the Direct Contact method)

Many professionals have been successful in finding better jobs using each one of these approaches. However, the Direct Contact method boasts twice the success rate of the others. So unless you have specific reasons to believe that other strategies would work best for you, Direct Contact should form the foundation of your job search.

If you prefer to use other methods as well, try to expend at least half your effort on Direct Contact, spending the rest on all of the other methods combined. Millions of other jobseekers have already proven that Direct Contact has been twice as effective in obtaining employment, so why not benefit from their experience?

With your strategy in mind, the next step is to work out the details of your search. The most important detail is setting up a schedule. Of course, since job searches aren't something most people do regularly, it may be hard to estimate how long each step will take. Nonetheless, it is important to have a plan so that you can monitor your progress. **Setting Your Schedule**

> Job hunting is intellectually demanding work that requires you to be at your best. So don't tire yourself out working around the clock.

When outlining your job search schedule, have a realistic time frame in mind. If you will be job-searching full-time, your search could take at least two months or more. If you can only devote part-time effort, it will probably take at least four months.

You probably know a few currently employed people who seem to spend their whole lives searching for a better job in their spare time. Don't be one of them. If you are presently working and don't feel like devoting a lot of energy to job-seeking right now, then wait. Focus on enjoying your present position, performing your best on the job, and storing up energy for when you are really ready to begin your job search.

Those of you who are currently unemployed should remember that job-hunting is tough work physically and emotionally. It is also intellectually demanding work that requires you to be at your best. So don't tire yourself out by working on your job campaign around the clock. At the same time, be sure to discipline yourself. The most logical way to manage your time while looking for a job is to keep your regular working hours.

> **The more you know about a company, the more likely you are to catch an interviewer's eye. (You'll also face fewer surprises once you get the job!)**

If you are searching full-time and have decided to choose several different contact methods, we recommend that you divide up each week, designating some time for each method. By trying several approaches at once, you can evaluate how promising each seems and alter your schedule accordingly. But be careful -- don't judge the success of a particular technique just by the sheer number of interviews you obtain. Positions advertised in the newspaper, for instance, are likely to generate many more interviews per opening than positions that are filled without being advertised.

If you are searching part-time and decide to try several different contact methods, we recommend that you try them sequentially. You simply won't have enough time to put a meaningful amount of effort into more than one method at once. Estimate the length of your job search, and then allocate so many weeks or months for each contact method, beginning with Direct Contact.

And remember that all schedules are meant to be broken. The purpose of setting a schedule is not to rush you to your goal but to help you periodically evaluate how you're progressing.

The Direct Contact Method

Once you have scheduled your time, you are ready to begin your search in earnest. If you decide to begin with the Direct Contact method, the first step is to develop a check list for categorizing the types of firms for which you'd like to work. You might categorize firms by product line, size, customer-type (such as industrial or consumer), growth prospects, or geographical location. Your list of important criteria might be very short. If it is, good! The shorter it is, the easier it will be to locate a company that is right for you.

Now you will want to use this *JobBank* book to assemble your list of potential employers. Choose firms where *you* are most likely to be able to find a job. Try matching your skills with those that a specific job demands. Consider where your skills might be in demand, the degree of competition for employment, and the employment outlook at each company.

Separate your prospect list into three groups. The first 25 percent will be your primary target group, the next 25 percent will be your secondary group, and the remaining names you can keep in reserve.

After you form your prospect list, begin work on your resume. Refer to the Resumes and Cover Letters section following this chapter to get ideas.

DEVELOPING YOUR CONTACTS: NETWORKING

Some career counselors feel that the best route to a better job is through somebody you already know or through somebody to whom you can be introduced. These counselors recommend that you build your contact base beyond your current acquaintances by asking each one to introduce you, or refer you, to additional people in your field of interest.

The theory goes like this: You might start with 15 personal contacts, each of whom introduces you to three additional people, for a total of 45 additional contacts. Then each of these people introduces you to three additional people, which adds 135 additional contacts. Theoretically, you will soon know every person in the industry.

Of course, developing your personal contacts does not work quite as smoothly as the theory suggests because some people will not be able to introduce you to anyone. The further you stray from your initial contact base, the weaker your references may be. So, if you do try developing your own contacts, try to begin with as many people that you know personally as you can. Dig into your personal phone book and your holiday greeting card list and locate old classmates from school. Be particularly sure to approach people who perform your personal business such as your lawyer, accountant, banker, doctor, stockbroker, and insurance agent. These people develop a very broad contact base due to the nature of their professions.

Once your resume is complete, begin researching your first batch of prospective employers. You will want to determine whether you would be happy working at the firms you are researching and to get a better idea of what their employment needs might be. You also need to obtain enough information to sound highly informed about the company during phone conversations and in mail correspondence. But don't go all out on your research yet! You probably won't be able to arrange interviews with some of these firms, so save your big research effort until you start to arrange interviews. Nevertheless, you should plan to spend several hours researching each firm. Do your research in batches to save time and energy. Start with this book, and find out what you can about each of the firms in your primary target group. Contact any pertinent professional associations that may be able to help you learn more about an employer. Read industry publications looking for articles on the firm. (Addresses of associations and names of important publications are listed after each industrial section of employer listings in this book.) Then try additional resources at your local library. Keep organized, and maintain a folder on each firm.

> It is said that the personnel office never hires people; they screen candidates.

If you discover something that really disturbs you about the firm (they are about to close their only local office), or if you discover that your chances of getting a job there are practically nil (they have just instituted a hiring freeze), then cross them off your prospect list. If possible, supplement your research efforts by contacting individuals who know the firm well. Ideally you should make an informal contact with someone at that particular firm, but often a direct competitor, or a major supplier or customer, will be able to supply you with just as much information. At the very least, try to obtain whatever printed information the company has available -- not just annual reports, but product brochures and any other printed materials that the firm may have to offer, either about its operations or about career opportunities.

Getting The Interview Now it is time to arrange an interview, time to make the Direct Contact. If you have read many books on job-searching, you may have noticed that most of these books tell you to avoid the personnel office like the plague. It is said that the personnel office never hires people; they screen candidates. Unfortunately, this is often the case. If you can identify the appropriate manager with the authority to hire you, you should try to contact that person directly. However, this will take a lot of time in each case, and often you'll be bounced back to personnel despite your efforts. So we suggest that initially you begin your Direct Contact campaign through personnel offices. If it seems that the firms on your prospect list do little hiring through personnel, you might consider some alternative courses of action.

DON'T BOTHER WITH MASS MAILINGS OR BARRAGES OF PHONE CALLS

Direct Contact does not mean burying every firm within a hundred miles with mail and phone calls. Mass mailings rarely work in the job hunt. This also applies to those letters that are personalized -- but dehumanized -- on an automatic typewriter or computer. Don't waste your time or money on such a project; you will fool no one but yourself.

The worst part of sending out mass mailings, or making unplanned phone calls to companies you have not researched, is that you are likely to be remembered as someone with little genuine interest in the firm, who lacks sincerity -- somebody that nobody wants to hire.

HELP WANTED ADVERTISEMENTS

Only a small fraction of professional job openings are advertised. Yet the majority of jobseekers -- and quite a few people not in the job market -- spend a lot of time studying the help wanted ads. As a result, the competition for advertised openings is often very severe.

A moderate-sized employer told us about their experience advertising in the help wanted section of a major Sunday newspaper:

It was a disaster. We had over 500 responses from this relatively small ad in just one week. We have only two phone lines in this office and one was totally knocked out. We'll never advertise for professional help again.

If you insist on following up on help wanted ads, then research a firm before you reply to an ad. Preliminary research might help to separate you from all of the other professionals responding to that ad, many of whom will have only a passing interest in the opportunity. It will also give you insight about a particular firm, to help you determine if it is potentially a good match. That said, your chances of obtaining a job through the want ads are still much smaller than they are with the Direct Contact method.

The three obvious means of initiating Direct Contact are:

- Showing up unannounced
- Mail
- Phone calls

Cross out the first one right away. You should never show up to seek a professional position without an appointment. Even if you are somehow lucky enough to obtain an interview, you will appear so unprofessional that you will not be seriously considered.

> **Always include a cover letter if you are asked to send a resume.**

Mail contact seems to be a good choice if you have not been in the job market for a while. You can take your time to prepare a letter, say exactly what you want, and of course include your resume. Remember that employers receive many resumes every day. Don't be surprised if you do not get a response to your inquiry, and don't spend weeks waiting for responses that may never come. If you do send a letter, follow it up (or precede it) with a phone call. This will increase your impact, and because of the initial research you did, will underscore both your familiarity with and your interest in the firm.

Another alternative is to make a "Cover Call." Your Cover Call should be just like your cover letter: concise. Your first statement should interest the employer in you. Then try to subtly mention your familiarity with the firm. Don't be overbearing; keep your introduction to three sentences or less. Be pleasant, self-confident, and relaxed. This will greatly increase the chances of the person at the other end of the line developing the conversation. But don't press. When you are asked to follow up "with something in the mail," don't try to prolong the conversation once it has ended. Don't ask what they want to receive in the mail. Always send your resume and a highly personalized follow-up letter, reminding the addressee of the phone conversation. Always include a cover letter if you are asked to send a resume.

Unless you are in telephone sales, making smooth and relaxed cover calls will probably not come easily. Practice them on your own, and then with your friends or relatives.

If you obtain an interview as a result of a telephone conversation, be sure to send a thank-you note reiterating the points you made during the conversation. You will appear more professional and increase your impact. However, unless specifically requested, don't mail your resume once an interview has been arranged. Take it with you to the interview instead.

Preparing For The Interview

Once the interview has been arranged, begin your in-depth research. You should arrive at an interview knowing the company upside-down and inside-out. You need to know the company's products, types of customers, subsidiaries, parent company, principal locations, rank in the industry, sales and profit trends, type of ownership, size, current plans, and much more. By this time you have probably narrowed your job search to one industry. Even if you haven't, you should still be familiar with the trends in the firm's industry, the firm's principal competitors and their relative performance, and the direction in which the industry leaders are headed.

BE PREPARED:
Some Common Interview Questions

Tell me about yourself...

Why did you leave your last job?

What excites you in your current job?

Where would you like to be in five years?

How much overtime are you willing to work?

What would your previous/present employer tell me about you?

Tell me about a difficult situation that you faced at your previous/present job.

What are your greatest strengths?

What are your greatest weaknesses?

Describe a work situation where you took initiative and went beyond your normal responsibilities.

Why do you wish to work for this firm?

Why should we hire you?

Dig into every resource you can! Read the company literature, the trade press, the business press, and if the company is public, call your stockbroker (if you have one) and ask for additional information. If possible, speak to someone at the firm before the interview, or if not, speak to someone at a competing firm. The more time you spend, the better. Even if you feel extremely pressed for time, you should set aside several hours for pre-interview research.

> **You should arrive at an interview knowing the company upside-down and inside-out.**

If you have been out of the job market for some time, don't be surprised if you find yourself tense during your first few interviews. It will probably happen every time you re-enter the market, not just when you seek your first job after getting out of school.

Tension is natural during an interview, but knowing you have done a thorough research job should put you more at ease. Make a list of questions that you think might be asked in each interview. Think out your answers carefully and practice them with a friend. Tape record your responses to the problem questions. If you feel particularly unsure of your interviewing skills, arrange your first interviews at firms you are not as interested in. (But remember it is common courtesy to seem enthusiastic about the possibility of working for any firm at which you interview.) Practice again on your own after these first few interviews. Go over the difficult questions that you were asked.

Interview Attire

How important is the proper dress for a job interview? Buying a complete wardrobe of Brooks Brothers pinstripes or Donna Karan suits, donning new wing tips or pumps, and having your hair styled every morning are not enough to guarantee you a career position as an investment banker. But on the other hand, if you can't find a clean, conservative suit or won't take the time to wash your hair, then you are just wasting your time by interviewing at all.

Top personal grooming is as important as finding appropriate clothes for a job interview. Careful grooming indicates both a sense of thoroughness and self-confidence. This is not the time to make a statement -- take out the extra earrings and avoid any garish hair colors not found in nature. Women should not wear excessive makeup, and both men and women should refrain from wearing any perfume or cologne (it only takes a small spritz to leave an allergic interviewer with a fit of sneezing and a bad impression of your meeting). Men should be freshly shaven, even if the interview is late in the day, and men with long hair should have it pulled back and neat.

Men applying for any professional position should wear a suit, preferably in a conservative color such as navy or charcoal gray. It is easy to get away with wearing the same dark suit to consecutive interviews at the same company; just be sure to wear a different shirt and tie for each interview.

Women should also wear a businesslike suit. Professionalism still dictates a suit with a skirt, rather than slacks, as proper interview garb for women. This is usually true even at companies where pants are acceptable attire for female employees. As much as you may disagree with this guideline, the more prudent time to fight this standard is after you land the job.

> **SKIRT VS. PANTS:**
> **An Interview Dilemma**
>
> For those women who are still convinced that pants are acceptable interview attire, listen to the words of one career counselor from a prestigious New England college:
>
> *I had a student who told me that since she knew women in her industry often wore pants to work, she was going to wear pants to her interviews. Almost every recruiter commented on how she was wearing pants, and even referred to her as "the one with the pants." The funny thing was that one of the recruiters who commented on her pants had been wearing jeans!*

The final selection of candidates for a job opening won't be determined by dress, of course. However, inappropriate dress can quickly eliminate a first-round candidate. So while you shouldn't spend a fortune on a new wardrobe, you should be sure that your clothes are adequate. The key is to dress at least as formally or slightly more formally and more conservatively than the position would suggest.

What To Bring

Be complete. Everyone needs a watch, a pen, and a notepad. Finally, a briefcase or a leather-bound folder (containing extra, *unfolded*, copies of your resume) will help complete the look of professionalism.

Sometimes the interviewer will be running behind schedule. Don't be upset, be sympathetic. There is often pressure to interview a lot of candidates and to quickly fill a demanding position. So be sure to come to your interview with good reading material to keep yourself occupied and relaxed.

The Interview

The very beginning of the interview is the most important part because it determines the tone for the rest of it. Those first few moments are especially crucial. Do you smile when you meet? Do you establish enough eye contact, but not too much? Do you walk into the office with a self-assured and confident stride? Do you shake hands firmly? Do you make small talk easily without being garrulous? It is human nature to judge people by that first impression, so make sure it is a good one. But most of all, try to be yourself.

Often the interviewer will begin, after the small talk, by telling you about the company, the division, the department, or perhaps, the position. Because of your detailed research, the information about the company should be repetitive for you, and the interviewer would probably like nothing better than to avoid this regurgitation of the company biography. So if you can do so tactfully, indicate to the interviewer that you are very familiar with the firm. If he or she seems intent on providing you with background information, despite your hints, then acquiesce.

But be sure to remain attentive. If you can manage to generate a brief discussion of the company or the industry at this point, without being forceful, great. It will help to further build rapport, underscore your interests, and increase your impact.

Soon (if it didn't begin that way) the interviewer will begin the questions, many of which you will have already practiced. This period of the interview usually falls into one of two categories (or somewhere in between): either a structured interview, where the interviewer has a prescribed set of questions to ask; or an unstructured interview, where the interviewer will ask only leading questions to get you to talk about yourself, your experiences, and your goals. Try to sense as quickly as possible in which direction the interviewer wishes to proceed. This will make the interviewer feel more relaxed and in control of the situation.

> **The interviewer's job is to find a reason to turn you down; your job is to not provide that reason.**
>
> -John L. LaFevre, author,
> *How You Really Get Hired*
>
> Reprinted from the 1989/90 *CPC Annual*, with permission of the National Association of Colleges and Employers (formerly College Placement Council, Inc.), copyright holder.

Remember to keep attuned to the interviewer and make the length of your answers appropriate to the situation. If you are really unsure as to how detailed a response the interviewer is seeking, then ask.

As the interview progresses, the interviewer will probably mention some of the most important responsibilities of the position. If applicable, draw parallels between your experience and the demands of the position as detailed by the interviewer. Describe your past experience in the same manner that you do on your resume: emphasizing results and achievements and not merely describing activities. But don't exaggerate. Be on the level about your abilities.

The first interview is often the toughest, where many candidates are screened out. If you are interviewing for a very competitive position, you will have to make an impression that will last. Focus on a few of your greatest strengths that are relevant to the position. Develop these points carefully, state them again in different words, and then try to summarize them briefly at the end of the interview.

Often the interviewer will pause toward the end and ask if you have any questions. Particularly in a structured interview, this might be the one chance to really show your knowledge of and interest in the firm. Have a list prepared of specific questions that are of real interest to you. Let your questions subtly show your research and your knowledge of the firm's activities. It is wise to have an extensive list of questions, as several of them may be answered during the interview.

> Often the interviewer will pause toward the end and ask if you have any questions. Have a list prepared of specific questions that are of real interest to you.

Do not turn your opportunity to ask questions into an interrogation. Avoid reading directly from your list of questions, and ask questions that you are fairly certain the interviewer can answer (remember how you feel when you cannot answer a question during an interview).

Even if you are unable to determine the salary range beforehand, do not ask about it during the first interview. You can always ask about it later. Above all, don't ask about fringe benefits until you have been offered a position. (Then be sure to get all the details.)

Try not to be negative about anything during the interview (particularly any past employer or any previous job). Be cheerful. Everyone likes to work with someone who seems to be happy.

Don't let a tough question throw you off base. If you don't know the answer to a question, simply say so -- do not apologize. Just smile. Nobody can answer every question -- particularly some of the questions that are asked in job interviews.

Before your first interview, you may be able to determine how many rounds of interviews there usually are for positions at your level. (Of course it may differ quite a bit even within the different levels of one firm.) Usually you can count on attending at least two or three interviews, although some firms, such as some of the professional partnerships, are known to give a minimum of six interviews for all professional positions. While you should be more relaxed as you return for subsequent interviews, the pressure will be on. The more prepared you are, the better.

Depending on what information you are able to obtain, you might want to vary your strategy quite a bit from interview to interview. For instance, if the first interview is a screening interview, then be sure a few of your strengths really stand out. On the other hand, if later interviews are primarily with people who are in a position to veto your hiring, but not to push it forward, then you should primarily focus on building rapport as opposed to reiterating and developing your key strengths.

If it looks as though your skills and background do not match the position the interviewer was hoping to fill, ask him or her if there is another division or subsidiary that perhaps could profit from your talents.

After The Interview

Write a follow-up letter immediately after the interview, while it is still fresh in the interviewer's mind (see the sample follow-up letter format found in the Resumes and Cover Letters chapter). Then, if you haven't heard from the interviewer within a week, call to stress your continued interest in the firm, and the position, and request a second interview.

> Getting a job offer is a lot like getting a marriage proposal. Someone is not going to offer it unless they're pretty sure you're going to accept it.
>
> -Marilyn Hill, Associate Director, Career Center, Carleton College

THE BALANCING ACT:
Looking For A New Job While Currently Employed

For those of you who are still employed, job-searching will be particularly tiring because it must be done in addition to your normal work responsibilities. So don't overwork yourself to the point where you show up to interviews looking exhausted and start to slip behind at your current job. On the other hand, don't be tempted to quit your present job! The long hours are worth it. Searching for a job while you have one puts you in a position of strength.

Making Contact

If you're expected to be in your office during the business day, then you have an additional problem to deal with. How can you work interviews into the business day? And if you work in an open office, how can you even call to set up interviews? As much as possible you should keep up the effort and the appearances on your present job. So maximize your use of the lunch hour, early mornings, and late afternoons for calling. If you keep trying, you'll be surprised how often you will be able to reach the executive you are trying to contact during your out-of-office hours. You can catch people as early as 8 a.m. and as late as 6 p.m. on frequent occasions.

Scheduling Interviews

Your inability to interview at any time other than lunch just might work to your advantage. If you can, try to set up as many interviews as possible for your lunch hour. This will go a long way to creating a relaxed atmosphere. (Who isn't happy when eating?) But be sure the interviews don't stray too far from the agenda on hand.

Lunchtime interviews are much easier to obtain if you have substantial career experience. People with less experience will often find no alternative to taking time off for interviews. If you have to take time off, you have to take time off. But try to do this as little as possible. Try to take the whole day off in order to avoid being blatantly obvious about your job search, and try to schedule two to three interviews for the same day. (It is very difficult to maintain an optimum level of energy at more than three interviews in one day.) Explain to the interviewer why you might have to juggle your interview schedule -- he/she should honor the respect you're showing your current employer by minimizing your days off and will probably appreciate the fact that another prospective employer is interested in you.

> Try calling as early as 8 a.m. and as late as 6 p.m. You'll be surprised how often you will be able to reach the executive you want during these times of the day

References

What do you tell an interviewer who asks for references? Just say that while you are happy to have your former employers contacted, you are trying to keep your job search confidential and would rather that your current employer not be contacted until you have been given a firm offer.

IF YOU'RE FIRED OR LAID OFF:
Picking Yourself Up and Dusting Yourself Off

If you've been fired or laid off, you are not the first and will not be the last to go through this traumatic experience. In today's changing economy, thousands of professionals lose their jobs every year. Even if you were terminated with just cause, do not lose heart. Remember, being fired is not a reflection on you as a person. It is usually a reflection of your company's staffing needs and its perception of your recent job performance and attitude. And if you were not performing up to par or enjoying your work, then you will probably be better off at another company anyway.

A thorough job search could take months, so be sure to negotiate a reasonable severance package, if possible, and determine what benefits, such as health insurance, you are still legally entitled to. Also, register for unemployment compensation immediately. Don't be surprised to find other professionals collecting unemployment compensation -- it is for everyone who has lost their job.

> Be prepared for the question, "Why were you fired?", during job interviews.

Don't start your job search with a flurry of unplanned activity. Start by choosing a strategy and working out a plan. Now is not the time for major changes in your life. If possible, remain in the same career and in the same geographical location, at least until you have been working again for a while. On the other hand, if the only industry for which you are trained is leaving, or is severely depressed in your area, then you should give prompt consideration to moving or switching careers.

Avoid mentioning you were fired when arranging interviews, but be prepared for the question, "Why were you fired?", during an interview. If you were laid off as a result of downsizing, briefly explain, being sure to reinforce that your job loss was not due to performance. If you were in fact fired, be honest, but try to detail the reason as favorably as possible and portray what you have learned from your mistakes. If you are confident one of your past managers will give you a good reference, tell the interviewer to contact that person. Do not to speak negatively of your past employer and try not to sound particularly worried about your status of being temporarily unemployed.

Finally, don't spend too much time reflecting on why you were let go or how you might have avoided it. Think positively, look to the future, and be sure to follow a careful plan during your job search.

THE COLLEGE STUDENT:
How To Conduct Your First Job Search

While you will be able to apply many of the basics covered earlier in this chapter to your job search, there are some situations unique to the college student's job search.

Gaining Experience   Perhaps the biggest problem college students face is lack of experience. Many schools have internship programs designed to give students exposure to the field of their choice, as well as the opportunity to make valuable contacts. Check out your school's career services department to see what internships are available. If your school does not have a formal internship program, or if there are no available internships that appeal to you, try contacting local businesses and offering your services -- often, businesses will be more than willing to have any extra pair of hands (especially if those hands are unpaid!) for a day or two each week. Or try contacting school alumni to see if you can "shadow" them for a few days, and see what their day-to-day duties are like. Either way, try to begin building experience as early as possible in your college career.

What do you do if, for whatever reason, you weren't able to get experience directly relating to your desired career? First, look at your previous jobs and see if there's anything you can highlight. Did your duties include supervising or training other employees? Did you reorganize the accounting system, or come up with a new way to boost productivity? Accomplishments like these demonstrate leadership, responsibility, and innovation -- qualities that most companies look for in employees. And don't forget volunteer activities and school clubs, which can also showcase these traits.

On-Campus Recruiting

Companies will often send recruiters to interview on-site at various colleges. This gives students a chance to get interviews at companies that may not have interviewed them otherwise, particularly if the company schedules "open" interviews, in which the only screening process is who is first in line at the sign-ups. Of course, since many more applicants gain interviews in this format, this also means that many more people are rejected. The on-campus interview is generally a screening interview, to see if it is worth the company's time to invite you in for a second interview. So do everything possible to make yourself stand out from the crowd.

The first step, of course, is to check out any and all information your school's career center has on the company. If the information seems out of date, call the company's headquarters and ask to be sent the latest annual report, or any other printed information.

THE GPA QUESTION

You are interviewing for the job of your dreams. Everything is going well: you've established a good rapport, the interviewer seems impressed with your qualifications, and you're almost positive the job is yours. Then you're asked about your GPA, which is pitifully low. Do you tell the truth and watch your dream job fly out the window?

Never lie about your GPA (they may request your transcript, and no company will hire a liar). You can, however, explain if there is a reason you don't feel your grades reflect your abilities, and mention any other impressive statistics. For example, if you have a high GPA in your major, or in the last few semesters (as opposed to your cumulative college career), you can use that fact to your advantage.

Many companies will host an informational meeting for interviewees, often the evening before interviews are scheduled to take place. DO NOT MISS THIS MEETING. The recruiter will almost certainly ask if you attended. Make an effort to stay after the meeting and talk with the company's representatives. Not only does this give you an opportunity to find out more information about both the company and the position, it also makes you stand out in the recruiter's mind. If there's a particular company that you had your heart set on, but you weren't able to get an interview with them, attend the information session anyway. You may be able to convince the recruiter to squeeze you into the schedule. (Or you may discover that the company really isn't suited for you after all.)

Try to check out the interview site beforehand. Some colleges may conduct "mock" interviews that take place in one of the standard interview rooms. Or you may be able to convince a career counselor (or even a custodian) to let you sneak a peek during off-hours. Either way, having an idea of the room's setup will help you to mentally prepare.

Be sure to be at least 15 minutes early to the interview. The recruiter may be running ahead of schedule, and might like to take you early. But don't be surprised if previous interviews have run over, resulting in your 30-minute slot being reduced to 20 minutes (or less). Don't complain; just use whatever time you do have as efficiently as possible to showcase the reasons *you* are the ideal candidate.

LAST WORDS

A parting word of advice. Again and again during your job search you will be rejected. You will be rejected when you apply for interviews. You will be rejected after interviews. For every job offer you finally receive, you probably will have been rejected a multitude of times. Don't let rejections slow you down. Keep reminding yourself that the sooner you go out and get started on your job search, and get those rejections flowing in, the closer you will be to obtaining the job you want.

RESUMES AND COVER LETTERS

When filling a position, a recruiter will often have 100-plus applicants, but time to interview only a handful of the most promising ones. As a result, he or she will reject most applicants after only briefly skimming their resumes.

Unless you have phoned and talked to the recruiter -- which you should do whenever you can -- you will be chosen or rejected for an interview entirely on the basis of your resume and cover letter. Your cover letter must catch the recruiter's attention, and your resume must hold it. (But remember -- a resume is no substitute for a job search campaign. *You* must seek a job. Your resume is only one tool.)

RESUME FORMAT:
Mechanics of a First Impression

The Basics

Recruiters dislike long resumes, so unless you have an unusually strong background with many years of experience and a diversity of outstanding achievements, keep your resume length to one page. If you must squeeze in more information than would otherwise fit, try using a smaller typeface or changing the margins.

Keep your resume on standard 8-1/2" x 11" paper. Since recruiters often get resumes in batches of hundreds, a smaller-sized resume may get lost in the pile. Oversized resumes are likely to get crumpled at the edges, and won't fit easily in their files.

First impressions matter, so make sure the recruiter's first impression of your resume is a good one. Print your resume on quality paper that has weight and texture, in a conservative color such as white, ivory, or pale gray. Use matching paper and envelopes for both your resume and cover letter.

Getting It On Paper

Modern photocomposition typesetting gives you the clearest, sharpest image, a wide variety of type styles, and effects such as italics, boldfacing, and book-like justified margins. It is also much too expensive for many jobseekers. And improvements in laser printers mean that a computer-generated resume can look just as impressive as one that has been professionally typeset.

A computer or word processor is the most flexible way to type your resume. This will allow you to make changes almost instantly and to store different drafts on disk. Word processing and desktop publishing systems also offer many different fonts to choose from, each taking up different amounts of space. (It is generally best to stay between 9-point and 12-point font size.) Many other options are also available, such as bold-facing for emphasis, justified margins, and the ability to change and manipulate spacing.

The end result, however, will be largely determined by the quality of the printer you use. You need at least "letter quality" type for your resume. Do not use a "near letter quality" or dot matrix printer. Laser printers will generally provide the best quality.

Household typewriters and office typewriters with nylon or other cloth ribbons are *not* good enough for typing your resume. If you don't have access to a quality word processor, hire a professional who can prepare your resume with a word processor or typesetting machine.

Don't make your copies on an office photocopier. Only the personnel office may see the resume you mail. Everyone else may see only a copy of it, and copies of copies quickly become unreadable. Either print out each copy individually, or take your resume to a professional copy shop, which generally use professionally-maintained, extra-high-quality photocopiers and charge fairly reasonable prices.

Proof With Care Whether you typed it yourself or paid to have it produced professionally, mistakes on resumes are not only embarrassing, but will usually remove you from further consideration (particularly if something obvious such as your name is misspelled). No matter how much you paid someone else to type, write, or typeset your resume, *you* lose if there is a mistake. So proofread it as carefully as possible. Get a friend to help you. Read your draft aloud as your friend checks the proof copy. Then have your friend read aloud while you check. Next, read it letter by letter to check spelling and punctuation.

If you are having it typed or typeset by a resume service or a printer, and you can't bring a friend or take the time during the day to proof it, pay for it and take it home. Proof it there and bring it back later to get it corrected and printed.

> **The one piece of advice I give to everyone about their resume is: show it to people, show it to people, show it to people. Before you ever send out a resume, show it to at least a dozen people.**
>
> -Cate Talbot Ashton,
> Associate Director,
> Career Services,
> Colby College

If you wrote your resume on a word processing program, also use that program's built-in spell checker to double-check for spelling errors. But keep in mind that a spell checker will not find errors such as "to" for "two" or "wok" for "work." It's important that you still proofread your resume, even after it has been spell-checked.

Types Of Resumes

The two most common resume formats are the functional resume and the chronological resume (examples of both types can be found at the end of this chapter). A functional resume focuses on skills and de-emphasizes job titles, employers, etc. A functional resume is best if you have been out of the work force for a long time and/or if you want to highlight specific skills and strengths that your most recent jobs don't necessarily reflect.

Choose a chronological format if you are currently working or were working recently, and if your most recent experiences relate to your desired field. Use reverse chronological order. To a recruiter your last job and your latest schooling are the most important, so put the last first and list the rest going back in time.

Organization

Your name, phone number, and a complete address should be at the top of your resume. Try to make your name stand out by using a slightly larger font size or all capital letters. Be sure to spell out everything -- never abbreviate St. for Street or Rd. for Road. If you are a college student, you should also put your home address and phone number at the top.

Next, list your experience, then your education. If you are a recent graduate, list your education first, unless your experience is more important than your education. (For example, if you have just graduated from a teaching school, have some business experience, and are applying for a job in business, you would list your business experience first.)

Keep everything easy to find. Put the dates of your employment and education on the left of the page. Put the names of the companies you worked for and the schools you attended a few spaces to the right of the dates. Put the city and state, or the city and country, where you studied or worked to the right of the page.

This is just one suggestion that may work for you. The important thing is simply to break up the text in some way that makes your resume visually attractive and easy to scan, so experiment to see which layout works best for your resume. However you set it up, stay consistent. Inconsistencies in fonts, spacing, or tenses will make your resume look sloppy. Also, be sure to use tabs to keep your information vertically lined up, rather than the less precise space bar.

RESUME CONTENT:
Say It With Style

Sell Yourself

You are selling your skills and accomplishments in your resume, so it is important to inventory yourself and know yourself. If you have achieved something, say so. Put it in the best possible light. But avoid subjective statements, such as "I am a hard worker" or "I get along well with my coworkers." Just stick to the facts.

While you shouldn't hold back or be modest, don't exaggerate your achievements to the point of misrepresentation. Be honest. Many companies will immediately drop an applicant from consideration (or fire a current employee) if inaccurate information is discovered on a resume or other application material.

Keep It Brief

Write down the important (and pertinent) things you have done, but do it in as few words as possible. Your resume will be scanned, not read, and short, concise phrases are much more effective than long-winded sentences. Avoid the use of "I" when emphasizing your accomplishments. Instead, use brief phrases beginning with action verbs.

While some technical terms will be unavoidable, you should try to avoid excessive "technicalese." Keep in mind that the first person to see your resume may be a human resources person who won't necessarily know all the jargon -- and how can they be impressed by something they don't understand?

Also, try to keep your paragraphs at six lines or shorter. If you have more than six lines of information about one job or school, put it in two or more paragraphs. The shorter your resume is, the more carefully it will be examined. Remember: your resume usually has between eight and 45 seconds to catch an employer's eye. So make every second count.

Job Objective

A functional resume may require a job objective to give it focus. One or two sentences describing the job you are seeking can clarify in what capacity your skills will be best put to use.

> *Examples:* An entry-level position in the publishing industry.
> A challenging position requiring analytical thought and excellent writing skills.

Don't include a job objective in a chronological resume. Even if you are certain of exactly what type of job you desire, the presence of a job objective might eliminate you from consideration for other positions that a recruiter feels are a better match for your qualifications. But even though you may not put an objective on paper, having a career goal in mind as you write can help give your resume a sense of focus.

Work Experience

Some jobseekers may choose to include both "Relevant Experience" and "Additional Experience" sections. This can be useful, as it allows the jobseeker to place more emphasis on certain experiences and to de-emphasize others.

Emphasize continued experience in a particular job area or continued interest in a particular industry. De-emphasize irrelevant positions. Delete positions that you held for less than four months (unless you are a very recent college grad or still in school).

USE ACTION VERBS

How you write your resume is just as important as *what* you write. The strongest resumes use short phrases beginning with action verbs. Below, we've listed a few of the action verbs you may want to use. (This list is not all-inclusive.)

accelerated	determined	interpreted	recorded
achieved	developed	interviewed	recruited
administered	devised	invented	reduced
advised	directed	launched	referred
analyzed	discovered	maintained	regulated
arranged	distributed	managed	reorganized
assembled	edited	marketed	represented
assisted	eliminated	mediated	researched
attained	established	monitored	resolved
budgeted	evaluated	motivated	restored
built	examined	negotiated	restructured
calculated	executed	obtained	reviewed
cataloged	expanded	operated	revised
charted	expedited	ordered	scheduled
circulated	facilitated	organized	selected
collaborated	formulated	oversaw	served
collected	founded	participated	sold
compiled	generated	performed	solved
completed	headed	persuaded	streamlined
computed	identified	planned	studied
conducted	implemented	prepared	summarized
consolidated	improved	presented	supervised
constructed	increased	processed	supplied
consulted	initiated	produced	supported
controlled	innovated	programmed	tested
coordinated	inspired	promoted	trained
counseled	installed	proposed	updated
created	instituted	provided	upgraded
designed	instructed	published	worked
detected	integrated	purchased	wrote

Stress your results, elaborating on how you contributed in your previous jobs. Did you increase sales, reduce costs, improve a product, implement a new program? Were you promoted? Use specific numbers (i.e., quantities, percentages, dollar amounts) whenever possible.

Mention all relevant responsibilities. Be specific, and slant your past accomplishments toward the position that you hope to obtain. For example, do you hope to supervise people? If so, then state how many people, performing what function, you have supervised.

Education

Keep it brief if you have more than two years of career experience. Elaborate more if you have less experience. If you are a recent grad with two or more years of college, you may choose to include any high school activities that are directly relevant to your career. If you've been out of school for awhile, list post-secondary education only.

Mention degrees received and any honors or special awards. Note individual courses or research projects you participated in that might be relevant for employers. For example, if you are an English major applying for a position as a business writer, be sure to mention any business or economics courses.

> Those things [marital status, church affiliations, etc.] have no place on a resume. Those are illegal questions, so why even put that information on your resume?
>
> -Becky Hayes, Career Counselor
> Career Services, Rice University

Highlight Impressive Skills

Be sure to mention any computer skills you may have. You may wish to include a section entitled "Additional Skills" or "Computer Skills," in which you list any software programs you know. An additional skills section is also an ideal place to mention fluency in a foreign language.

Personal Data

This section is optional, but if you choose to include it, keep it very brief (two lines maximum). A one-word mention of hobbies such as fishing, chess, baseball, cooking, etc., can give the person who will interview you a good way to open up the conversation. It doesn't hurt to include activities that are unusual (fencing, bungee jumping, snake-charming) or that somehow relate to the position or the company you're applying to (for instance, if you are a member of a professional organization in your industry). Never include information about your age, health, physical characteristics, marital status, or religious affiliation.

References

The most that is needed is the sentence, "References available upon request," at the bottom of your resume. If you choose to leave it out, that's fine.

HIRING A RESUME WRITER:
Is It The Right Choice for You?

If you write reasonably well, it is to your advantage to write your own resume. Writing your resume forces you to review your experience and figure out how to explain your accomplishments in clear, brief phrases. This will help you when you explain your work to interviewers.

If you write your resume, everything will be in your own words -- it will sound like you. It will say what you want it to say. If you are a good writer, know yourself well, and have a good idea of what parts of your background employers are looking for, you should be able to write your own resume better than anyone else can. If you decide to write your resume yourself, have as many people review and proofread it as possible. Welcome objective opinions and other perspectives.

When To Get Help

If you have difficulty writing in "resume style" (which is quite unlike normal written language), if you are unsure of which parts of your background you should emphasize, or if you think your resume would make your case better if it did not follow one of the standard forms outlined either here or in a book on resumes, then you should consider having it professionally written.

There are two reasons even some professional resume writers we know have had their resumes written with the help of fellow professionals. First, they may need the help of someone who can be objective about their background, and second, they may want an experienced sounding board to help focus their thoughts.

If You Hire A Pro

The best way to choose a writer is by reputation -- the recommendation of a friend, a personnel director, your school placement officer, or someone else knowledgeable in the field.

Important questions:
- "How long have you been writing resumes?"
- "If I'm not satisfied with what you write, will you go over it with me and change it?"
- "Do you charge by the hour or a flat rate?"

There is no sure relation between price and quality, except that you are unlikely to get a good writer for less than $50 for an uncomplicated resume and you shouldn't have to pay more than $300 unless your experience is very extensive or complicated. There will be additional charges for printing.

Few resume services will give you a firm price over the phone, simply because some resumes are too complicated and take too long to do for a predetermined price. Some services will quote you a price that applies to almost all of their customers. Once you decide to use a specific writer, you should insist on a firm price quote before engaging their services. Also, find out how expensive minor changes will be.

COVER LETTERS:
Quick, Clear, and Concise

Always mail a cover letter with your resume. In a cover letter you can show an interest in the company that you can't show in a resume. You can also point out one or two skills or accomplishments the company can put to good use.

Make It Personal The more personal you can get, the better. If someone known to the person you are writing has recommended that you contact the company, get permission to include his/her name in the letter. If you have the name of a person to send the letter to, address it directly to that person (after first calling the company to verify the spelling of the person's name, correct title, and mailing address). Be sure to put the person's name and title on both the letter and the envelope. This will ensure that your letter will get through to the proper person, even if a new person now occupies this position. But even if you don't have a contact name and are simply addressing it to the "Personnel Director" or the "Hiring Partner," definitely send a letter.

Type cover letters in full. Don't try the cheap and easy ways, like using a computer mail merge program, or photocopying the body of your letter and typing in the inside address and salutation. You will give the impression that you are mailing to a host of companies and have no particular interest in any one.

Cover letter dos and don'ts

- *Do* keep your cover letter brief and to the point.
- *Do* be sure it is error-free.
- *Don't* just repeat information verbatim from your resume.
- *Don't* overuse the personal pronoun "I."
- *Don't* send a generic cover letter -- show your personal knowledge of and interest in that particular company.
- *Do* accentuate what you can offer the company, not what you hope to gain from them.

FUNCTIONAL RESUME
(Prepared on a word processor and laser printed.)

PENELOPE FRANCES PANZ
430 Miller's Crossing
Essex Junction VT 05452
802/555-9354

Objective
A position as a graphic designer commensurate with my acquired skills and expertise.

Summary
Extensive experience in plate making, separations, color matching, background definition, printing, mechanicals, color corrections, and personnel supervision. A highly motivated manager and effective communicator. Proven ability to:

- Create Commercial Graphics
- Produce Embossed Drawings
- Color Separate
- Control Quality
- Resolve Printing Problems
- Analyze Customer Satisfaction

Qualifications

Printing:
Knowledgeable in black and white as well as color printing. Excellent judgment in determining acceptability of color reproduction through comparison with original. Proficient at producing four or five color corrections on all media, as well as restyling previously reproduced four-color artwork.

Customer Relations:
Routinely work closely with customers to ensure specifications are met. Capable of striking a balance between technical printing capabilities and need for customer satisfaction through entire production process.

Specialties:
Practiced at creating silk screen overlays for a multitude of processes including velo bind, GBC bind, and perfect bind. Creative design and timely preparation of posters, flyers, and personalized stationery.

Personnel Supervision:
Skillful at fostering atmosphere that encourages highly talented artists to balance high-level creativity with maximum production. Consistently meet or beat production deadlines. Instruct new employees, apprentices, and students in both artistry and technical operations.

Experience
Graphic Arts Professor, University of Vermont, Burlington VT (1987-1993).
Manager, Design Graphics, Barre VT (1993-present).

Education
Massachusetts Conservatory of Art, Ph.D. 1987
University of Massachusetts, B.A. 1984

CHRONOLOGICAL RESUME
(Prepared on a word processor and laser printed.)

MAURICE DUPETREAUX
412 Maple Court
Seattle, WA 98404
(206) 555-6584

EXPERIENCE

THE CENTER COMPANY   Seattle, WA
Systems Programmer   1993-present
- Develop and maintain over 100 assembler modules.
- Create screen manager programs, using Assembler and Natural languages, to trace input and output to the VTAM buffer.
- Install and customize Omegamon 695 and 700 on IBM mainframes.
- Develop programs to monitor complete security control blocks, using Assembler and Natural.
- Produce stand alone IPLs and create backrests on IBM 3380 DASD.

INFO TECH, INC.   Seattle, WA
Technical Manager   1991-1993
- Designed and managed the implementation of a network providing the legal community with a direct line to Supreme Court cases, using Clipper on IBM 386s.
- Developed a system which catalogued entire library inventory, using Turbo Pascal on IBM AT.
- Used C to create a registration system for university registrar on IBM AT.

EDUCATION

SALEM STATE UNIVERSITY   Salem, OR
   B.S. in Computer Science.   1989
   M.S. in Computer Science.   1991

COMPUTER SKILLS

- Programming Languages: C, C++, Assembler, COBOL, Natural, Turbo Pascal, dBASE III+, and Clipper.
- Software: VTAM, Complete, TSO, JES 2, ACF 2, Omegamon 695 and 700, and Adabas.
- Operating Systems: MVS/XA, MVS/SP, MS-DOS, AND VMS.

FUNCTIONAL RESUME
(Prepared on an office-quality typewriter)

LORRAINE AVAKIAN
70 Monback Avenue
Oshkosh, WI 54901
(608) 586-1243

OBJECTIVE:
To contribute over eight years experience in promotion, communications, and administration to an entry-level position in advertising.

SUMMARY OF QUALIFICATIONS:
- Performed advertising duties for small business.
- Experience in business writing and communications skills.
- General knowledge of office management.
- Demonstrated ability to work well with others, in both supervisory and support staff roles.
- Type 75 words per minute.

SELECTED ACHIEVEMENTS AND RESULTS:

Promotion:
Composing, editing, and proofreading correspondence and PR materials for own catering service. Large-scale mailings.

Communication:
Instruction; curriculum and lesson planning; student evaluation; parent-teacher conferences; development of educational materials. Training and supervising clerks.

Computer Skills:
Proficient in MS Word, Lotus 1-2-3, Excel, and Filemaker Pro.

Administration:
Record-keeping and file maintenance. Data processing and computer operations, accounts receivable, accounts payable, inventory control, and customer relations. Scheduling, office management, and telephone reception.

WORK HISTORY:
Teacher; Self-Employed (owner of catering service); Floor Manager; Administrative Assistant; Accounting Clerk.

EDUCATION:
Beloit College, Beloit, WI, BA in Education, 1986

CHRONOLOGICAL RESUME
(Prepared on a word processor and laser printed)

T. WILLIAM MAGUIRE
16 Charles Street #3
Marlborough CT 06447
203/555-9641

EDUCATION Keene State College, Keene NH
Bachelor of Arts in Elementary Education, 1994
- Graduated *magna cum laude*
- English minor
- Kappa Delta Pi member, inducted 1991

EXPERIENCE
September 1994-
Present

Elmer T. Thienes Elementary School, Marlborough CT
Part-time Kindergarten Teacher
- Instruct kindergartners in reading, spelling, language arts, and music.
- Participate in the selection of textbooks and learning aids.
- Organize and supervise class field trips and coordinate in-class presentations.

Summers
1992-1994

Keene YMCA, Youth Division, Keene NH
Child-care Counselor
- Oversaw summer program for low-income youth.
- Budgeted and coordinated special events and field trips, working with Program Director to initiate variations in the program.
- Served as Youth Advocate in cooperation with social worker to address the social needs and problems of participants.

Spring 1994

Wheelock Elementary School, Keene NH
Student Teacher
- Taught third-grade class in all elementary subjects.
- Designed and implemented a two-week unit on Native Americans.
- Assisted in revision of third-grade curriculum.

Fall 1993

Child Development Center, Keene NH
Daycare Worker
- Supervised preschool children on the playground and during art activities.
- Created a "Peter Rabbit Corner," where children could quietly look at books or take a voluntary "time-out."

ADDITIONAL INTERESTS
Martial arts, skiing, politics, reading, writing.

GENERAL MODEL FOR A COVER LETTER

Your mailing address
Date

Contact's name
Contact's title
Company
Company's mailing address

Dear Mr./Ms. _____:

Immediately explain why your background makes you the best candidate for the position that you are applying for. Describe what prompted you to write (want ad, article you read about the company, networking contact, etc.). Keep the first paragraph short and hard-hitting.

Detail what you could contribute to this company. Show how your qualifications will benefit this firm. Describe your interest in the corporation. Subtly emphasizing your knowledge about this firm and your familiarity with the industry will set you apart from other candidates. Remember to keep this letter short; few recruiters will read a cover letter longer than half a page.

If possible, your closing paragraph should request specific action on the part of the reader. Include your phone number and the hours when you can be reached. Mention that if you do not hear from the reader by a specific date, you will follow up with a phone call. Lastly, thank the reader for their time, consideration, etc.

Sincerely,

(signature)

Your full name (typed)

Enclosure (use this if there are other materials, such as your resume, that are included in the same envelope)

COVER LETTER SAMPLE

16 Charles Street
Marlborough CT 06447
November 16, 1995

Ms. Lia Marcusson
Assistant Principal
Jonathon Daniels Elementary School
43 Mayflower Drive
Keene NH 03431

Dear Ms. Marcusson:

Janet Newell recently informed me of a possible opening for a third grade teacher at Jonathon Daniels Elementary School. With my experience instructing third-graders, both in schools and in summer programs, I feel I would be an ideal candidate for the position. Please accept this letter and the enclosed resume as my application.

Jonathon Daniels' educational philosophy that every child can learn and succeed interests me, since it mirrors my own. My current position at Elmer T. Thienes Elementary has reinforced this philosophy, heightening my awareness of the different styles and paces of learning and increasing my sensitivity toward special needs children. Furthermore, as a direct result of my student teaching experience at Wheelock Elementary School, I am comfortable, confident, and knowledgeable working with third-graders.

I look forward to discussing the position and my qualifications for it in more detail. I can be reached at 203/555-9641 evenings or 203/555-0248 weekdays. If I do not hear from you before Tuesday of next week, I will call to see if we can schedule a time to meet. Thank you for your time and consideration.

Sincerely,

T. William Maguire

T. William Maguire

GENERAL MODEL FOR A FOLLOW-UP LETTER

Your mailing address
Date

Contact's name
Contact's title
Company
Company's mailing address

Dear Mr./Ms._____:

Remind the interviewer of the reason (i.e., a specific opening, an informational interview, etc.) you were interviewed, as well as the date. Thank him/her for the interview, and try to personalize your thanks by mentioning some specific aspect of the interview.

Confirm your interest in the organization (and in the opening, if you were interviewing for a particular position). Use specifics to re-emphasize that you have researched the firm in detail and have considered how you would fit into the company and the position. This is a good time to say anything you wish you had said in the initial meeting. Be sure to keep this letter brief; a half-page is plenty.

If appropriate, close with a suggestion for further action, such as a desire to have an additional interview, if possible. Mention your phone number and the hours that you can be reached. Alternatively, you may prefer to mention that you will follow up with a phone call in several days. Once again, thank the person for meeting with you, and state that you would be happy to provide any additional information about your qualifications.

Sincerely,

(signature)

Your full name (typed)

PRIMARY EMPLOYERS

ACCOUNTING AND MANAGEMENT CONSULTING

As the number of accounting grads drops and the economy strengthens, all kinds of accounting professionals will benefit. According to the BLS, the number of accounting jobs may grow by as much as 40 percent by 2005. In fact, a recent survey conducted by Robert Half International found that the best opportunities for accountants were in the financial, insurance, and real estate sector, followed by the retail and wholesale industries. The best states in the country for accountants are Arkansas, Louisiana, Oklahoma, and Texas.

Even faster growth is projected for the management consulting industry, where the number of jobs is expected to grow almost three times faster than the rate for all industries. The increasing complexity of business will contribute to industry growth. Among other things, today's managers must worry about rapid technological innovations, changes in government regulation, growing environmental concerns, continuing reduction of trade barriers, and globalization of markets. Because it has become difficult to keep abreast of these changes, corporations, institutions, and governments will increasingly need the aid of well-trained, well-informed management consulting professionals.

ADIA INFORMATION TECHNOLOGIES
210 West Pennsylvania Avenue, Suite 650, Townsend MD 21204-4532. 410/821-0435. **Contact:** Melenie Porter, Director of Human Resources. **Description:** Providers of information consulting services. **Common positions include:** Information Systems Consultant; Software Engineer. **Educational backgrounds include:** Data Processing. **Parent company:** Adia Services, Inc.

AMERICAN INSTITUTE OF CERTIFIED PUBLIC ACCOUNTANTS
1455 Pennsylvania Avenue NW, Washington DC 20004. 202/737-6600. **Contact:** Office Manager. **Description:** A leading professional organization, dedicated to serving the needs of the certified public accounting industry.

ARTHUR ANDERSEN & COMPANY
1666 K Street NW, Washington DC 20006. 202/862-3100. **Contact:** Catherine Hope, Assistant Director/Recruiting. **Description:** One of the Big Six worldwide accounting firms. This location is the coordinating entity of The Arthur Andersen Worldwide Organization which includes all member firms and their related entities. Serves clients through two business units: Arthur Andersen, whose service lines include audit and business advisory services, as well as tax and corporate specialty services; and Andersen Consulting, whose service lines include systems building and systems integration; change management services; technology services; strategic services; software products; and computer operations management and systems support. Member firms provide uniform professional training, share practice methodologies and technology; and coordinate their operations to eliminate barriers to serving clients. It is one of the Big Six professional services organizations, operating offices in more than 72 countries. **Other U.S. locations include:** all major U.S. cities. **Common positions include:** Accountant/Auditor; Information Systems Consultant; Tax Specialist. **Educational backgrounds include:** Accounting; Business Administration; Computer Science; Engineering. **Benefits:** Dental Insurance; Disability Coverage; Employee

Discounts; Life Insurance; Medical Insurance; Profit Sharing; Savings Plan. **Special Programs:** Internships; Training Programs. **Corporate headquarters location:** Chicago IL. **Operations at this facility include:** Service. **Number of employees at this location:** 1,500.

ARTHUR ANDERSEN & COMPANY
120 East Baltimore Street, 20th Floor, Baltimore MD 21202. 410/727-5800. **Contact:** Recruiting Coordinator. **Description:** Serves clients through two business units: Arthur Andersen, whose service lines include audit and business advisory services, as well as tax and corporate specialty services; and Andersen Consulting, whose service lines include systems building and systems integration; change management services; technology services; strategic services; software products; and computer operations management and systems support. Member firms provide uniform professional training, share practice methodologies and technology; and coordinate their operations to eliminate barriers to serving clients. It is one of the Big Six professional services organizations, operating offices in more than 72 countries. **Other U.S. locations include:** all major U.S. cities. **Corporate headquarters location:** Chicago IL.

ARINC RESEARCH CORPORATION
2551 Riva Road, Annapolis MD 21401. 410/266-4000. **Fax:** 410/573-3201. **Contact:** Director of Human Resources. **Description:** An engineering and management consulting firm providing technical studies, analyses, and evaluations of aircraft, ship systems, communications, and information systems. Arinc Research Corporation's customers include: DoD, DoE, DoT, and FAA. **Common positions include:** Aerospace Engineer; Budget Analyst; Ceramics Engineer; Computer Programmer; Computer Systems Analyst; Draftsperson; Electrical/Electronics Engineer; Financial Analyst; Materials Engineer; Mechanical Engineer; Metallurgical Engineer; Software Engineer; Technical Writer/Editor. **Educational backgrounds include:** Communications; Computer Science; Engineering; Mathematics; Physics. **Benefits:** 401K; Daycare Assistance; Dental Insurance; Disability Coverage; Employee Discounts; Life Insurance; Medical Insurance; Pension Plan; Tuition Assistance. **Special Programs:** Internships. **Corporate headquarters location:** This Location. **Other U.S. locations:** Fountain Valley CA; San Diego CA; Colorado Springs CO; Washington DC; Panama City FL; Pensacola FL; Warner Robins GA; Boston MA; Ft. Monmouth NJ; Dayton OH; Oklahoma City OK; San Antonio TX. **Operations at this facility include:** Administration; Research and Development; Sales. **Listed on:** Privately held. **Number of employees at this location:** 1,000. **Number of employees nationwide:** 2,000.

ARITEC INC.
5530 Wisconsin, Chevy Chase MD 20815. 301/656-1047. **Contact:** Human Resources. **Description:** Providers of management services.

ARONSON, FETRIDGE & WIEGLE
6116 Executive Boulevard, 5th Floor, Rockville MD 20852. 301/231-6200. **Contact:** Sharon Kulesa, Director of Personnel. **Description:** An accounting firm. **Number of employees at this location:** 100.

BEATTY, SATCHELL COMPANY
17 South Washington Street, P.O. Box 1187, Easton MD 21601. 410/822-0045. **Contact:** John D. Keen, CPA, Partner. **Description:** An accounting firm. **Common positions include:** Accountant/Auditor. **Benefits:** 401K; Life Insurance; Medical Insurance; Pension Plan. **Corporate headquarters location:** Salisbury MD. **Number of employees at this location:** 10. **Number of employees nationwide:** 60.

BOOZ-ALLEN & HAMILTON, INC.
8283 Greensboro Drive, McLean VA 20814. 703/902-5000. **Fax:** 703/902-3620. **Recorded Jobline:** 703/902-5400. **Contact:** Sheila Carney, Recruiting Services Manager. **Description:** Booz-Allen's Technology Center provides systems development and technology services in the areas of defense, space, computing, communications, transportation, environment, and management sciences to government and industry. **Common positions include:** Budget Analyst; Computer Programmer; Computer Systems Analyst; Electrical/Electronics Engineer; Operations Research Analyst; Secretary; Software Engineer; Systems Analyst; Transportation/Traffic Specialist. **Educational backgrounds include:** Computer Science; Engineering; Finance. **Benefits:** Dental Insurance; Disability Coverage; Life Insurance; Medical Insurance; Pension Plan; Savings Plan; Tuition Assistance. **Special Programs:** Training Programs. **Corporate headquarters location:** This Location. **Operations at this facility include:** Service.

PAUL BROWNER, CHARTERED
932 #17 Hungerford Drive, Rockville MD 20850. 301/340-3340. **Contact:** Paul Browner, President. **Description:** An accounting firm.

CLIFTON GUNDERSON & COMPANY
412 The Exchange Building, 1122 Kenilworth, Towson MD 21204. 410/337-3830. **Contact:** Mr. Terry Hancock, Hiring Partner. **Description:** An accounting firm.

COOPERS & LYBRAND
1800 M Street NW, 4th Floor, Washington DC 20036-4339. 202/822-4191. **Contact:** Gene Clark, Director of Administration. **Description:** One of the Big Six certified public accounting firms, providing a broad range of services in the areas of accounting and auditing, taxation, management consulting and actuarial, and benefits and compensation consulting. Operates over 100 offices in the United States; and 735 offices in 117 foreign locations. Coopers & Lybrand has 67,000 employees worldwide. **Common positions include:** Accountant/Auditor; Actuary; Attorney; Computer Programmer; Economist/Market Research Analyst; Human Resources Specialist; Marketing Specialist. **Educational backgrounds include:** Accounting; Computer Science. **Benefits:** Dental Insurance; Disability Coverage; Life Insurance; Medical Insurance; Pension Plan; Savings Plan; Tuition Assistance. **Special Programs:** Internships. **Corporate headquarters location:** New York NY. **Number of employees at this location:** 700.

COOPERS & LYBRAND
217 East Redwood Street, Baltimore MD 21202. 410/783-7653. **Contact:** Patricia Sobin, Human Resources Manager. **Description:** One of the Big Six certified public accounting firms, providing a broad range of services in the areas of accounting and auditing, taxation, management consulting and actuarial, and benefits and compensation consulting. Operates over 100 offices in the United States; and 735 offices in 117 foreign locations. Coopers & Lybrand has 67,000 employees worldwide. **Common positions include:** Accountant/Auditor. **Educational backgrounds include:** Accounting. **Benefits:** Dental Insurance; Disability Coverage; Life Insurance; Medical Insurance; Pension Plan; Savings Plan. **Corporate headquarters location:** New York NY.

DELOITTE & TOUCHE
1001 Pennsylvania Avenue NW, Suite 350 North, Washington DC 20004. 202/879-5600. **Contact:** Human Resources Department. **Description:** An international firm of certified public accountants, providing professional accounting, auditing, tax, and management consulting services to widely diversified clients. The company operates through more than 500 offices throughout the world and has a specialized program consisting of some 25 national industry groups and 50 functional (technical) groups that cross industry lines. Groups are involved in various disciplines, including accounting, auditing, taxation management advisory services, small and growing businesses, mergers and acquisitions, and computer applications.

ERNST & YOUNG
1225 Connecticut Avenue NW, Washington DC 20036. 202/327-6000. **Contact:** Employment. **Description:** One of the world's largest professional services firms providing clients with auditing, accounting, tax, and management consulting services. Offices are located in most major U.S. metropolitan areas and in numerous international locations. **Corporate headquarters location:** New York NY.

ERNST & YOUNG
One North Charles Street, Baltimore MD 21201. 410/539-7940. **Contact:** Hiring Partner. **Description:** One of the world's largest professional services firms providing clients with auditing, accounting, tax, and management consulting services. Offices are located in most major U.S. metropolitan areas and in numerous international locations. **Corporate headquarters location:** New York NY.

GBS CORPORATION
8320 Giford Road, Suite A, Columbia MD 21042. 410/381-2250. **Contact:** Director/Human Resources. **Description:** Provides a broad range of small business consulting services, data processing services, record systems, and income tax advisory consulting services. **Common positions include:** Accountant/Auditor; Administrator; Department Manager; Human Resources Specialist; Marketing Specialist; Operations/Production Manager; Systems Analyst; Technical Writer/Editor. **Educational backgrounds include:** Accounting; Business Administration;

Clerical/Secretarial; Computer Science; Data Processing; Marketing. **Benefits:** Disability Coverage; Life Insurance; Medical Insurance; Paid Vacation; Pension Plan; Tuition Assistance. **Corporate headquarters location:** This Location. **Operations at this facility include:** Administration; Research and Development; Sales; Service.

GENERAL ACCOUNTING OFFICE
441 G Street NW, Washington DC 20548. 202/512-3000. **Recorded Jobline:** 202/512-6092. **Contact:** Human Resources. **Description:** Government office examining all accounting-related issues of public funds for Congress.

GRANT THORNTON
1850 M Street NW, Suite 300, Washington DC 20036. 202/296-7800. **Contact:** Personnel Department. **Description:** An accounting firm. **NOTE:** Please direct inquiries to a specific department.

GRANT THORNTON
2 Hopkins Plaza, Suite 700, Baltimore MD 21201-2998. 410/685-4000. **Contact:** Melanie Fuss, Recruiting Coordinator. **Description:** An accounting firm.

HARITON, MANCUSO & JONES, P.C.
11140 Rockville Pike, Suite 340, North Bethesda MD 20852. 301/984-6400. **Fax:** 301/984-0028. **Contact:** Personnel Director. **Description:** An accounting firm. **Common positions include:** Accountant/Auditor. **Educational backgrounds include:** Accounting. **Benefits:** 401K; Dental Insurance; Life Insurance; Medical Insurance. **Listed on:** Privately held. **Number of employees at this location:** 30.

KPMG PEAT MARWICK
2001 M Street NW, Washington DC 20036. 202/467-3000. **Contact:** Human Resources Department. **Description:** An accounting and management consulting firm. **Corporate headquarters location:** New York NY.

KPMG PEAT MARWICK
111 South Calvert Street, Baltimore MD 21202. 410/783-8300. **Contact:** Kate Strempek, Director of Administration. **Description:** An accounting and management consulting firm. **Common positions include:** Accountant/Auditor; Administrator; Attorney; Biomedical Engineer; Economist/Market Research Analyst; Editor; Financial Analyst; Health Services Worker; Human Resources Specialist; Marketing Specialist; Purchasing Agent and Manager; Reporter; Systems Analyst; Tax Specialist; Technical Writer/Editor. **Educational backgrounds include:** Accounting; Banking; Biology; Business Administration; Chemistry; Communications; Computer Science; Economics; Engineering; Health Care; Information Systems; Law/Pre-Law; Marketing; Mathematics; Real Estate; Tax. **Benefits:** 401K; Dental Insurance; Disability Coverage; Life Insurance; Medical Insurance; Pension Plan; Savings Plan. **Corporate headquarters location:** New York NY. **Operations at this facility include:** Service.

KAMANITZ UHLFELDER PERMISON
Four Reservoir Circle, Suite 200, Baltimore MD 21208. 410/484-8700. **Contact:** Personnel Department. **Description:** An accounting firm.

KENNETH LEVENTHAL & COMPANY
1150 18th Street NW, Suite 500, Washington DC 20036. 202/775-1880. **Contact:** Alan Gittelson, Managing Partner. **Description:** An accounting firm.

ARTHUR D. LITTLE, INC.
955 L'Enfant Plaza Southwest, Suite 4200, Washington DC 20024-2119. 202/268-6700. **Contact:** Human Resources. **Description:** Founded in 1886, Arthur D. Little is an employee-owned international management and technology consulting firm. The company offers services in three distinct but complementary areas: management consulting, technology and product development, and environmental, health and safety consulting. Services include cost reduction, total quality management consulting, market assessments, logistics management, telecommunications management, auditing, safety programs, software development, and toxicology. The company conducts operations through 34 offices and laboratories in North America, Asia, Europe, Latin America, and the Middle East. Clients operate in a variety of industries, including aerospace, automotive, telecommunications, electronics, and consumer products.

MERCER MANAGEMENT CONSULTING
2300 N Street NW, 8th Floor, Washington DC 20037. 202/778-7000. **Contact:** Personnel. **Description:** Company provides strategy and management consulting services.

MITCHELL/TITUS & CO.
1825 K Street NW, Suite 515, Washington DC 20006. 202/293-5713. **Contact:** Personnel. **Description:** An accounting firm. **Common positions include:** Accountant/Auditor. **Educational backgrounds include:** Accounting. **Benefits:** Disability Coverage; Employee Discounts; Life Insurance; Medical Insurance; Pension Plan; Tuition Assistance. **Corporate headquarters location:** New York NY.

NATIVE AMERICAN CONSULTANTS INC.
725 Second Street Northeast, Washington DC 20002. 202/547-0576. **Contact:** Rebecca Samler, Director of Administration. **Description:** Consultants for governmental agencies engaged in research for Native Americans. **Common positions include:** Civil Engineer; Computer Programmer; General Manager; Industrial Engineer; Mechanical Engineer; Systems Analyst; Technical Writer/Editor. **Educational backgrounds include:** Business Administration; Computer Science; Economics; Engineering; Liberal Arts. **Benefits:** Disability Coverage; Life Insurance; Medical Insurance; Pension Plan. **Corporate headquarters location:** This Location. **Operations at this facility include:** Administration; Regional Headquarters; Service.

PENSION BENEFIT GUARANTEE CORP.
1200 K Street NW, Suite 120, Washington DC 20005. 202/326-4110. **Recorded Jobline:** 202/326-4111. **Contact:** Human Resources. **Description:** Guarantees payment of pension benefits in private-sector pension plans.

PRICE WATERHOUSE
1301 K Street NW, 800 West, Washington DC 20005-3333. 202/414-1313. **Contact:** H. Charles Loew, Director/Human Resources. **Description:** An international certified public accounting firm with nearly 300 offices internationally and 100 offices in the United States. Price Waterhouse's professional employment reaches 28,000 in 100 countries worldwide. Services include accounting, auditing, business advisory services, tax consulting, and all areas of management consulting. **Corporate headquarters location:** New York NY.

STEGMAN & COMPANY
405 East Joppa Road, Suite 200, Towson MD 21286. 410/685-1700. **Contact:** William E. Clark, Personnel Director. **Description:** An accounting firm. **Common positions include:** Accountant/Auditor. **Educational backgrounds include:** Accounting.

VSE CORPORATION
2550 Huntington Avenue, Alexandria VA 22303. 703/329-4220. **Fax:** 703/329-4623. **Recorded Jobline:** 703/329-4784. **Contact:** Jim McFarland, Personnel Administrator. **Description:** Offers engineering services, logistical support services, and data processing services. **Common positions include:** Administrative Services Manager; Aerospace Engineer; Chemical Engineer; Civil Engineer; Computer Programmer; Computer Systems Analyst; Designer; Draftsperson; Economist/Market Research Analyst; Editor; Electrical/Electronics Engineer; Electrician; Financial Analyst; Industrial Engineer; Management Trainee; Mechanical Engineer; Purchasing Agent and Manager; Technical Writer/Editor. **Benefits:** 401K; Dental Insurance; Disability Coverage; Medical Insurance; Pension Plan; Savings Plan; Tuition Assistance. **Other U.S. locations:** Nationwide. **Number of employees at this location:** 200. **Number of employees nationwide:** 1,800.

WOODEN & BENSON
100 West Pennsylvania Avenue, Towson MD 21204. 410/825-4860. **Contact:** Manager. **Description:** An accounting firm.

Note: Because addresses and telephone numbers of smaller companies change rapidly, we recommend you call each company to verify the information below before inquiring about job opportunities. Mass mailings are not recommended.

Accounting and Management Consulting/61

Additional employers with under 250 employees:

ACCOUNTING, AUDITING, AND BOOKKEEPING SERVICES

C W Amos & Company
2 N Charles St Ste 210, Baltimore MD 21201-3754. 410/727-5341.

Legi-Slate Inc.
777 N Capitol St NE Ste 900, Washington DC 20002-4239. 202/898-2300.

Reznick Fedder & Silverman
4520 E West Hwy, Bethesda MD 20814-3319. 301/652-9100.

Wolpoff and Co.
200 Saint Paul Pl Ste 2300, Baltimore MD 21202-2004. 410/837-3770.

Central Credit Control
300 Hospital Dr, Glen Burnie MD 21061-5770. 410/760-1925.

MANAGEMENT SERVICES

Aurora Associates
1015 18th St NW Ste 400, Washington DC 20036-5203. 202/463-0950.

Rcg/Hagler Bailly Inc.
1530 Wilson Blvd Ste 900, Arlington VA 22209-2447. 703/351-0300.

Washington Service Bureau Inc.
655 15th St NW Ste 270, Washington DC 20005-5701. 202/883-9200.

Zeiders Enterprises
3182 Golansky Blvd, Woodbridge VA 22192-4221. 703/878-2007.

Coppi-Lindsey Associates
6665 Old Dominion Dr, Mc Lean VA 22101-4518. 703/506-8226.

Corman Construction
12001 Guilford Rd, Jessup MD 20794. 410/792-9400.

David Orr Associates
8629 Sudley Rd, Manassas VA 22110-4590. 703/335-5497.

Hanscomb Association
1600 Duke St, Alexandria VA 22314-3421. 703/684-6550.

Heery International
8201 Corporate Dr, Landover MD 20785-2230. 301/577-9408.

Heery Program Management Inc.
1460 Ritchie Hwy, Arnold MD 21012-2730. 410/757-1122.

Woodstock Construction Mgmt.
10623 Saint Paul Ave, Woodstock MD 21163-1011. 410/461-5217.

Brantley Enterprises
3887 Plaza Dr, Fairfax VA 22030-2512. 703/385-3603.

Mardeck Ltd.
1700 Rockville Pike Ste 200, Rockville MD 20852-1631. 301/468-0707.

Plamondon Enterprises
4 McCain Dr, Frederick MD 21702. 301/695-5051.

BUSINESS CONSULTING SERVICES

Apco Associates
1155 21st St Nw, Washington DC 20036-3302. 202/778-1000.

Applied Management Systems Inc.
9175 Guilford Rd, Columbia MD 21046-1844. 301/317-6002.

Cassidy and Associates
700 13th St Nw, Washington DC 20005-3960. 202/347-0773.

Development Associates
1730 N Lynn St, Arlington VA 22209-2004. 703/276-0677.

Development Mgmt. Systems Inc.
1700 N Moore St Ste 720, Arlington VA 22209-1903. 703/525-1489.

Format Associates
7504 Hancock Ave, Takoma Park MD 20912-5732. 301/270-1562.

Futron Corporation
7315 Wisconsin Ave Ste 1250 W, Bethesda MD 20814-3211. 301/657-7732.

Hay Systems Inc.
4301 Fairfax Dr Ste 500, Arlington VA 22203-1627. 703/841-0079.

Information Spectrum
1235 Jefferson Davis Hwy, Arlington VA 22202-3283. 703/892-5500.

Interlog Inc.
5203 Leesburg Pike Ste 501, Falls Church VA 22041-3401. 703/845-8441.

LSA Inc.
1215 Jefferson Davis Hwy Ste 1, Arlington VA 22202-4302. 703/979-4600.

Management Technology
7700 Old Branch Ave # D-201, Clinton MD 20735-1628. 301/856-4840.

McKinsey & Co.
1101 Pennsylvania Ave NW Ste 7, Washington DC 20004-2514. 202/662-3100.

Meta
2000 14th St N Ste 450, Arlington VA 22201-2573. 703/243-3608.

National Systems Management
4600 H Pinecrest Ofc Pk Dr, Alexandria VA 22312-1441. 703/941-9021.

Performance Partners
15 Montgomery Ave, Takoma Park MD 20912-4614. 301/270-0558.

Ralph B. Rothstein Enterprises
1100 E West Hwy, Silver Spring MD 20912-5930. 301/565-0909.

Robert Bell & Co. Inc.
513 Benfield Rd, Severna Park MD 21146-2519. 410/544-4445.

Team Research
1200 Prospect Ave, Takoma Park MD 20912-7314. 301/434-9299.

The Three Sigma Group
9302 Lee Hwy, Fairfax VA 22031-1214. 703/385-9815.

University Research Corporation
7200 Wisconsin Ave Ste 600, Bethesda MD 20814-4811. 301/654-8338.

Washington Consulting Group
11 Dupont Cir NW Ste 8, Washington DC 20036-1207. 202/797-7800.

Wurzbacher & Associates
7305 Wildwood Dr, Takoma Park MD 20912-6928. 301/439-5324.

62/The Metropolitan Washington JobBank

A H Interviewing Service
7 Lydia Ct, Pikesville MD 21208-2027. 410/655-5892.

Aware Inc.
7007 Carroll Ave, Takoma Park MD 20912-4429. 301/270-1920.

The JBG Companies
1250 Connecticut Ave Nw, Washington DC 20036-2603. 202/364-6200.

Development Alternatives
7250 Woodmont Ave Ste 200, Bethesda MD 20814-2960. 301/718-8699.

World Trade Associates
7320 Carroll Ave, Silver Spring MD 20912-4514. 301/270-4898.

Chemonics
2000 M St Nw, Washington DC 20036-3307. 202/466-5340.

Dames & Moore Inc.
7101 Wisconsin Ave Ste 700, Bethesda MD 20814-4805. 301/652-2215.

National Guardian Systems Inc.
8980 Old Annapolis Rd, Columbia MD 21045. 410/715-1770.

Rolf Jensen & Associates
3040 Williams Dr Ste 400, Fairfax VA 22031-4618. 703/641-4600.

Asset Growth Partners
222 Severn Ave, Annapolis MD 21403-2531. 410/267-8660.

Bell Atl. Tricon Lease Corporation
110 West Rd, Baltimore MD 21204-2316. 410/821-0550.

Octagon Group
7927 Jones Branch Dr, Mc Lean VA 22102-3322. 703/556-6101.

For more information on career opportunities in accounting and management consulting:

Associations

AMERICAN ACCOUNTING ASSOCIATION
5717 Bessie Drive, Sarasota FL 34233. 813/921-7747. An academically-oriented accounting association that offers two quarterly journals, a semi-annual journal, a newsletter, and a wide variety of continuing education programs.

AMERICAN INSTITUTE OF CERTIFIED PUBLIC ACCOUNTANTS
1211 Avenue of the Americas, New York NY 10036. 212/596-6200. A national professional organization for all CPAs. AICPA offers a comprehensive career package to students.

AMERICAN MANAGEMENT ASSOCIATION
Management Information Service, 135 West 50th Street, New York NY 10020. 212/586-8100. Provides a variety of publications, training videos, and courses, as well as an Information Resource Center, which provides management information, and a library service.

ASSOCIATION OF GOVERNMENT ACCOUNTANTS
2200 Mount Vernon Avenue, Alexandria VA 22301. 703/684-6931.

ASSOCIATION OF MANAGEMENT CONSULTING FIRMS
521 Fifth Avenue, 35th Floor, New York NY 10175. 212/697-9693. Offers certification programs.

INSTITUTE OF MANAGEMENT CONSULTANTS
521 Fifth Avenue, 35th Floor, New York NY 10175. 212/697-8262. Offers certification and professional development and a directory of members.

FEDERATION OF TAX ADMINISTRATORS
444 North Capital Street NW, Washington DC 20001. 202/624-5890.

INSTITUTE OF INTERNAL AUDITORS
49 Maitland Avenue, Altamont Springs FL 32701. 407/830-7600. Publishes magazines and newsletters. Provides information on current issues, a network of more than 50,000 members in 100 countries, and professional development and research services.

INSTITUTE OF MANAGEMENT ACCOUNTANTS
10 Paragon Drive, Box 433, Montvale NJ 07645-1760. 201/573-9000. Offers a Certified Management Accountant Program, periodicals, seminars, educational programs, a research program, a financial management network, and networking services.

NATIONAL ASSOCIATION OF TAX CONSULTORS
454 North 13th Street, San Jose CA 95112. 408/298-1458.

NATIONAL ASSOCIATION OF TAX PRACTITIONERS
720 Association Drive, Appleton WI 54914. 414/749-1040. Offers seminars, research, newsletters, preparer worksheets, state chapters, insurance, and other tax-related services.

NATIONAL SOCIETY OF PUBLIC ACCOUNTANTS
1010 North Fairfax Street, Alexandria VA 22314. 703/549-6400. Offers professional development services, government representation, a variety of publications, practice aids, low-cost group insurance, and annual seminars.

Directories

AICPA DIRECTORY OF ACCOUNTING EDUCATION
American Institute of Certified Public Accountants, 1211 Avenue of the Americas, New York NY 10036. 212/596-6200. $150.00. Only available to AICPA members.

ACCOUNTING FIRMS AND PRACTITIONERS
American Institute of Certified Public Accountants, 1211 Avenue of the Americas, New York NY 10036. 212/596-

6200. $150.00. Only available to AICPA members.

Magazines

CPA JOURNAL
530 Fifth Avenue, New York NY 10136. 212/719-8300. Published monthly by The New York State Society.

CPA LETTER
American Institute of Certified Public Accountants, 1211 Avenue of the Americas, New York NY 10036. 212/596-6200.

JOURNAL OF ACCOUNTANCY
American Institute of Certified Public Accountants, 1211 Avenue of the Americas, New York NY 10036. 212/596-6200.

MANAGEMENT ACCOUNTING
Institute of Management Accounting, 10 Paragon Drive, Montvale NJ 07645. 201/573-9000.

WENDELL'S REPORT FOR CONTROLLERS
Warren, Gorham, and Lamont, Inc., 210 South Street, Boston MA 02111. 617/423-2020.

ADVERTISING, MARKETING AND PUBLIC RELATIONS

Due to several trends shaping the industry, finding a job in advertising is as tough today as it ever has been. To remain competitive, the industry's largest firms are downsizing to save money for larger campaigns. On the other hand, smaller agencies are increasingly specializing in fields such as direct marketing and public relations in order to gain a stronger presence in the market. Meanwhile, the growing cable industry has opened the door to new business opportunities, as has the Internet. Increasingly, advertisers are using the Information Highway to conduct business, as well as to target specific "digital" audiences.

In the public relations field, there has been an explosion in the number and range of consultants in the marketplace. Partially as a result of the recession of the early '90s, many senior executives who were released from their contacts at major firms have launched companies of their own.

ABRAMSON ERLICH MANES
1275 K Street NW, #300, Washington DC 20005. 202/289-6900. **Contact:** Human Resources. **Description:** An advertising agency. **Common positions include:** Advertising Clerk; Commercial Artist; Marketing Specialist; Public Relations Specialist. **Educational backgrounds include:** Liberal Arts; Marketing. **Benefits:** Dental Insurance; Disability Coverage; Life Insurance; Medical Insurance; Profit Sharing. **Special Programs:** Internships. **Corporate headquarters location:** This Location.

ALLIED ADVERTISING
1156 15th Street NW, Suite 1220, Washington DC 20005. 202/223-3660. **Contact:** Managing Director/Promotion and Publicity. **Description:** An advertising agency. **Common positions include:** Advertising Clerk; Marketing Specialist. **Educational backgrounds include:** Art/Design; Business Administration; Communications; Computer Science; Liberal Arts; Marketing. **Operations at this facility include:** Service.

ARBITRON COMPANY
9705 Patuxent Woods Drive, Columbia MD 21046. 410/312-8000. **Contact:** Wanda Kemp, Professional Recruiter. **Description:** Engaged in the field of broadcast audience measurement. The field staff of more than 3,000 interviewers contact more than 2 million households, representing a cross-section of Americans in every country, to obtain television viewing and radio listening information. The company produces the Arbitron Television and Radio Reports, which describes television viewing or radio listening patterns in more than 200 marketing areas in the United States. Advertisers and their agencies use these reports when planning, buying, or evaluating their advertising schedules to determine the cost-efficiency of their campaigns. More than 2,000 radio stations, 580 television stations, and 3,500 advertisers and their agencies and buying services use the reports. **Other U.S. locations:** Los Angeles CA; San Francisco CA; Washington DC; Atlanta GA; Chicago IL.

BALTIMORE SIGN COMPANY
201 North Haven Street, Baltimore MD 21224-1621. 410/276-1500. **Contact:** Human Resources. **Description:** A manufacturer of advertising signs.

EARLE PALMER BROWN
6935 Arlington Road, Bethesda MD 20814. 301/986-0510. **Fax:** 301/657-2590. **Recorded Jobline:** 301/961-3502. **Contact:** Polly Burkert, Human Resources Manager. **Description:** A full-service advertising agency. **Common positions include:** Account Executive; Account Manager; Accountant/Auditor; Advertising Clerk; Artist; Computer

Programmer; Computer Systems Analyst; Copywriter; Financial Analyst; Public Relations Specialist. **Educational backgrounds include:** Accounting; Art/Design; Communications; Marketing. **Benefits:** 401K; Dental Insurance; Disability Coverage; EAP; Employee Discounts; Life Insurance; Medical Insurance; Tuition Assistance; Vision Insurance. **Special Programs:** Internships. **Corporate headquarters location:** Greenwich CT. **Other U.S. locations:** St. Petersburg FL; New York NY; Philadelphia PA; Richmond VA. **Operations at this facility include:** Administration. **Listed on:** Privately held. **Number of employees at this location:** 130. **Number of employees nationwide:** 350.

EISNER & ASSOCIATES, INC.
12 West Madison Street, Baltimore MD 21201. 410/685-3390. **Fax:** 410/685-0387. **Contact:** Sue Holland, Director of Personnel. **Description:** An advertising and public relations company. **Common positions include:** Advertising Clerk. **Educational backgrounds include:** Accounting; Art/Design; Business Administration; Communications; Liberal Arts; Marketing. **Benefits:** 401K; Dental Insurance; Disability Coverage; Life Insurance; Medical Insurance. **Special Programs:** Internships. **Corporate headquarters location:** This Location. **Operations at this facility include:** Administration. **Listed on:** Privately held. **Number of employees at this location:** 58.

GOLDBERG, MARCHESANO, KOHLMAN
1700 Wisconsin Avenue NW, Washington DC 20007. 202/337-0700. **Fax:** 202/298-3477. **Contact:** Linda Roper, Office Manager. **Description:** A full-service advertising agency. **Common positions include:** Account Executive; Accountant/Auditor; Administrative Worker/Clerk; Administrator; Buyer; Commercial Artist; Marketing Specialist; Media Planner/Specialist; Operations/Production Manager; Typist/Word Processor. **Educational backgrounds include:** Accounting; Art/Design; Business Administration; Communications; Finance; Liberal Arts; Marketing. **Benefits:** Dental Insurance; Medical Insurance; Pension Plan. **Special Programs:** Internships; Training Programs. **Corporate headquarters location:** This Location. **Operations at this facility include:** Administration; Service. **Number of employees at this location:** 50.

HILL AND KNOWLTON
901 31st NW, Washington DC 20007. 202/333-7400. **Contact:** Rose Parker, Personnel Manager. **Description:** Provides clients with public relations services.

IMAGE DYNAMICS, INC.
1101 North Calvert Street, Suite 1400, Baltimore MD 21202. 410/539-7730. **Contact:** Phyllis Brotman, CEO/President. **Description:** An advertising and public relations agency.

HENRY J. KAUFMAN AND ASSOCIATES, INC.
2233 Wisconsin Avenue NW, Suite 500, Washington DC 20007. 202/333-0700. **Contact:** Maxine Siegel, Personnel Director. **Description:** An advertising, public relations and marketing firm. **Common positions include:** Advertising Clerk; Commercial Artist; Marketing Specialist; Public Relations Specialist. **Educational backgrounds include:** Art/Design; Liberal Arts; Marketing. **Benefits:** Daycare Assistance; Dental Insurance; Disability Coverage; Life Insurance; Medical Insurance; Pension Plan; Savings Plan; Tuition Assistance. **Special Programs:** Internships. **Corporate headquarters location:** This Location. **Number of employees at this location:** 60.

PORTER/NOVELLI
1120 Connecticut Avenue NW, Suite 1100, Washington DC 20036. **Contact:** Jill Fitzsimmons, Personnel Director. **Description:** A public relations agency. **Common positions include:** Graphic Artist; Public Relations Specialist; Secretary. **Educational backgrounds include:** Communications; English; Journalism; Public Relations. **Benefits:** Dental Insurance; Disability Coverage; Life Insurance; Medical Insurance; Pension Plan; Profit Sharing; Savings Plan; Tuition Assistance. **Special Programs:** Internships. **Corporate headquarters location:** New York NY. **Other U.S. locations:** Los Angeles CA; Chicago IL; Boston MA; New York NY. **Operations at this facility include:** Service. **Number of employees at this location:** 65.

THE SMITH COMPANY
4455 Connecticut Avenue NW, Suite B600, Washington DC 20008. 202/895-0900. **Contact:** Human Resources. **Description:** A telemarketing company.

Note: Because addresses and telephone numbers of smaller companies change rapidly, we recommend you call each company to verify the information below before inquiring about job opportunities. Mass mailings are not recommended.

Additional employers with under 250 employees:

PUBLIC RELATIONS SERVICES

Dorf & Stanton Communications Inc.
1025 Thomas Jefferson St Nw, Washington DC 20007-5201. 202/625-6930.

Sawyer Miller Group Bozell
1818 N St Nw, Washington DC 20036-2406. 202/223-1300.

The Chelsea Group
4266 E Capitol St Ne, Washington DC 20019-4489. 202/399-4276.

MISC. ADVERTISING SERVICES

The Viguerie Association
7777 Leesburg Pike, Falls Church VA 22043-2403. 703/356-0440.

W B Doner & Company
400 E Pratt St # 9, Baltimore MD 21202-3116. 410/338-1600.

The One Book
1850 York Rd, Timonium MD 21093-5122. 410/339-4100.

DIRECT MAIL ADVERTISING SERVICES

DDD Co.
8000 Corp Dr, Landover MD 20785. 301/731-4595.

Direct Mail Management
201 Skipjack Rd, Prnc Frederck MD 20678-3411. 301/855-1600.

Diversified Mailing Service Inc.
4333 Davenport Rd, Fredericksbrg VA 22408-8716. 703/898-6245.

KCMS Inc.
3401 Eastwest Highway, Hyattsville MD 20782. 301/853-6601.

Mail Marketing Systems
8318 Sherwick Ct, Jessup MD 20794-3102. 301/953-7202.

Sisk Mailing Service
203 Logcanoe Circle, Stevensville MD 21666. 410/643-7900.

Advo-Systems Inc.
9420 Gerwig Ln, Columbia MD 21046-1500. 410/290-3700.

Pennysaver
1057 Saint Ignatius Dr, Waldorf MD 20602-1836. 301/884-8288.

Rockville Mailing Service Co.
711 E Gude Dr, Rockville MD 20850-1387. 301/279-0606.

For more information on career opportunities in advertising, marketing, and public relations:

Associations

ADVERTISING RESEARCH FOUNDATION
641 Lexington Avenue, New York NY 10022. 212/751-5656.

AFFILIATED ADVERTISING AGENCIES INTERNATIONAL
2280 South Xanadu Way, Suite 300, Aurora CO 80014. 303/671-8551.

AMERICAN ASSOCIATION OF ADVERTISING AGENCIES
666 Third Avenue, New York NY 10017. 212/682-2500. Offers educational and enrichment benefits such as publications, videos, and conferences.

AMERICAN MARKETING ASSOCIATION
250 South Wacker Drive, Suite 200, Chicago IL 60606. 312/648-0536.

DIRECT MARKETING ASSOCIATION
1120 Avenue of Americas, New York NY 10036-6700. 212/768-7277. Offers monthly newsletters and seminars and conferences.

INTERNATIONAL ADVERTISING ASSOCIATION
521 Fifth Avenue, Suite 1807, New York NY 10075. 212/557-1133.

LEAGUE OF ADVERTISING AGENCIES
2 South End Avenue #4C, New York NY 10280. 212/945-4991. Seminars available.

MARKETING RESEARCH ASSOCIATION
2189 Silas Deane Highway, Suite #5, Rocky Hill CT 06067. 203/257-4008. Publishes several magazines and newsletters.

PUBLIC RELATIONS SOCIETY OF AMERICA
33 Irving Place, New York NY 10003. 212/995-2230. Publishes three magazines for public relations professionals.

TELEVISION BUREAU OF ADVERTISING
850 3rd Avenue, 10th Floor, New York NY 10022-5892. 212/486-1111.

Directories

AAAA ROSTER AND ORGANIZATION
American Association of Advertising Agencies, 666 Third Avenue, 13th Floor, New York NY 10017. 212/682-2500.

DIRECTORY OF MINORITY PUBLIC RELATIONS PROFESSIONALS
Public Relations Society of America, 33 Irving Place, New York NY 10003. 212/995-2230.

O'DWYER'S DIRECTORY OF PUBLIC RELATIONS FIRMS
J. R. O'Dwyer Co., 271 Madison Avenue, Room 600, New York NY 10016. 212/679-2471.

PUBLIC RELATIONS CONSULTANTS DIRECTORY
American Business Directories, Division of American Business Lists, 5711 South 86th Circle, Omaha NE 68127. 402/593-4500.

PUBLIC RELATIONS JOURNAL -- REGISTER ISSUE
Public Relations Society of America, 33 Irving Place, New York NY 10003. 212/995-2230.

STANDARD DIRECTORY OF ADVERTISING AGENCIES
Reed Reference Publishing Company, P.O. Box 31, New Providence NJ 07974. 800/521-8110.

Magazines

ADVERTISING AGE
Crain Communications, 740 North Rush Street, Chicago IL 60611. 312/649-5316.

ADWEEK
BPI, 1515 Broadway, 12th Floor, New York NY 10036-8986. 212/536-5336.

BUSINESS MARKETING
Crain Communications, 740 North Rush Street, Chicago IL 60611. 312/649-5260.

JOURNAL OF MARKETING
American Marketing Association, 250 South Wacker Drive, Suite 200, Chicago IL 60606. 312/648-0536.

THE MARKETING NEWS
American Marketing Association, 250 South Wacker Drive, Suite 200, Chicago IL 60606. 312/648-0536.

PR REPORTER
PR Publishing Co., P.O. Box 600, Exeter NH 03833. 603/778-0514.

PUBLIC RELATIONS JOURNAL
Public Relations Society of America, 33 Irving Place, New York NY 10003. 212/995-2230.

PUBLIC RELATIONS NEWS
Phillips Publishing Inc., 1202 Seven Locks Road, Suite 300, Potomac MD 20854. 301/340-1520.

AEROSPACE

The aerospace industry, which was wracked by layoffs throughout the early '90s, has yet to pull out of its tailspin. As ever, the slump is being fueled by declining commercial aircraft orders and further defense cuts. As a result, research and development dollars have been trimmed and more industry mergers are expected. Many companies are trying to shift to commercial production, reducing their dependence on dwindling defense contracts.

Although the industry depends less on defense spending than in the past, defense purchases still support a significant number of aerospace workers. Employment in aerospace production occupations are projected to decline in the next few years, as manufacturers increase productivity by improving organizational and manufacturing techniques. Over the long haul, the industry's focus on advanced technology will mean more professional and technical positions -- with engineers leading the way.

AEROSPACE INDUSTRIES ASSOCIATION OF AMERICA
1250 I Street NW, Suite 1100, Washington DC 20005. 202/371-8400. **Fax:** 202/289-6024. **Contact:** Jane Weeden, Personnel Manager. **Description:** An organization representing companies involved in aerospace research, development and manufacturing. **NOTE:** E-mail address for Jane Weeden is aia@millkern.com. **Common positions include:** Accountant/Auditor; Aerospace Engineer; Ceramics Engineer; Computer Programmer; Computer Systems Analyst; Economist/Market Research Analyst; Editor; Electrical/Electronics Engineer; Librarian; Materials Engineer; Metallurgical Engineer; Operations/Production Manager; Secretary; Statistician; Technical Writer/Editor. **Educational backgrounds include:** Accounting; Art/Design; Business Administration; Communications; Computer Science; Engineering; Finance; Liberal Arts. **Benefits:** Life Insurance; Medical Insurance; Pension Plan. **Corporate headquarters location:** This Location. **Operations at this facility include:** Administration. **Number of employees at this location:** 60.

BANNER AEROSPACE, INC.
300 West Service Road, Washington DC 20041. 703/478-5790. **Contact:** Human Resources. **Description:** Banner Aerospace distributes a broad range of aircraft parts such as jet engines and engine components, avionic, hydraulic and electrical systems, fasteners, bearings and other airframe components. The company also provides support services, and processes and sells insulated electrical wire for the aerospace/aviation market; sells refurbished corporate aircraft, such as helicopters, jet and turboprop airplanes; and repairs aircraft engines.

BRITISH AEROSPACE
22070 Broderick Drive, Sterling VA 20166. 703/406-1328. **Fax:** 703/406-1330. **Contact:** Frank Sterrett, Director of Human Resources. **Description:** Engaged in aircraft marketing and customer support. **Common positions include:** Accountant/Auditor; Attorney; Budget Analyst; Buyer; Computer Programmer; Computer Systems Analyst; Construction and Building Inspector; Customer Service Representative; Financial Analyst; Public Relations Specialist; Purchasing Agent and Manager; Quality Control Supervisor. **Educational backgrounds include:** Accounting; Business Administration; Computer Science; Finance; Marketing. **Benefits:** 401K; Dental Insurance; Disability Coverage; Life Insurance; Medical Insurance; Pension Plan; Tuition Assistance. **Special Programs:** Internships. **Corporate headquarters location:** This Location. **Parent company:** British Aerospace PLC. **Operations at this facility include:** Administration; Sales; Service. **Number of employees at this location:** 350.

Aerospace/69

C.R. DANIELS, INC.
3451 Ellicott Center Drive, Ellicott City MD 21043. 410/461-2100. **Fax:** 410/461-2987. **Contact:** John E. Frangos, Senior Vice President of Manufacturing. **Description:** Produces a wide range of aviation accessory products, including seats, nets, and cushions; material handling containers; industrial fabrics and other premium fabric products; canvas and synthetic tarpaulins; and conveyor belting. **Common positions include:** Accountant/Auditor; Administrator; Blue-Collar Worker Supervisor; Buyer; Credit Manager; Customer Service Representative; Draftsperson; Industrial Engineer; Industrial Production Manager; Manufacturer's/Wholesaler's Sales Rep.; Mechanical Engineer; Purchasing Agent and Manager; Quality Control Supervisor. **Educational backgrounds include:** Business Administration; Engineering. **Benefits:** Dental Insurance; Disability Coverage; Life Insurance; Medical Insurance; Pension Plan; Profit Sharing. **Special Programs:** Training Programs. **Corporate headquarters location:** This Location. **Other U.S. locations:** Rutledge TN. **Operations at this facility include:** Administration; Manufacturing; Research and Development; Sales. **Number of employees at this location:** 170.

FAIRCHILD SPACE & DEFENSE CORPORATION
20301 Century Boulevard, Germantown MD 20874. 800/368-2812. **Contact:** James Jutzin, Manager, Human Resources. **Description:** Designs, develops and produces space electronics and other spacecraft systems, digital avionics equipment, communication and intelligence systems, and components and subsystems for aerospace applications. **Common positions include:** Accountant/Auditor; Administrator; Aerospace Engineer; Blue-Collar Worker Supervisor; Budget Analyst; Buyer; Computer Programmer; Computer Systems Analyst; Cost Estimator; Department Manager; Designer; Draftsperson; Electrical/Electronics Engineer; Electrician; Financial Analyst; Human Resources Specialist; Industrial Engineer; Industrial Production Manager; Instructor/Trainer; Marketing Specialist; Mechanical Engineer; Metallurgical Engineer; Operations/Production Manager; Purchasing Agent and Manager; Quality Control Supervisor; Software Engineer; Systems Analyst. **Educational backgrounds include:** Accounting; Business Administration; Computer Science; Economics; Engineering; Finance; Marketing; Physics. **Benefits:** Dental Insurance; Disability Coverage; Life Insurance; Medical Insurance; Profit Sharing; Savings Plan; Tuition Assistance. **Special Programs:** Internships. **Corporate headquarters location:** Dulles VA. **Other U.S. locations:** Pomona CA; Boulder CO. **Parent company:** Orbital Sciences Corporation. **Operations at this facility include:** Administration; Manufacturing; Research and Development; Service. **Listed on:** New York Stock Exchange. **Number of employees at this location:** 1,000. **Number of employees nationwide:** 2,000.

LOCKHEED MARTIN CORPORATION
400 Virginia Avenue, Washington DC 20024. 202/646-2000. **Contact:** Tom Perry, Human Resources. **Description:** An aerospace and technology company engaged in the design, manufacture, and management of systems and products in the fields of space, defense, electronics, communications, information management, energy, and materials. **Number of employees nationwide:** 62,800.

LORAL AEROSYS
7375 Executive Place, Seabrook MD 20706. 301/805-0300. **Fax:** 301/805-0517. **Contact:** Human Resources. **Description:** Provides turnkey systems development, engineering services, and spaceflight mission support for civil and commercial space programs worldwide. Supports both space and ground-based systems, with emphasis on command and control and data storage and processing systems.

MARTIN MARIETTA CORPORATION
6801 Rockledge Drive, Bethesda MD 20817. 301/897-6237. **Contact:** Ken Brown, Senior Human Resources Representative. **Description:** An aerospace and technology company.

NATIONAL AERONAUTICS AND SPACE ADMINISTRATION
GODDARD SPACE FLIGHT CENTER
Building 1, Room 160, Greenbelt MD 20771. 301/286-7918. **Recorded Jobline:** 301/286-5326. **Contact:** Human Resources. **Description:** Conducts developments and flight operations for spacecraft.

ORBITAL SCIENCES CORPORATION
21700 Atlantic Boulevard, Dulles VA 20166-3729. 703/406-5000. **Contact:** Human Resources. **Description:** Designs, manufactures, operates, and markets a broad range of space products. Products include: space transportation systems (space and

suborbital launch vehicles and orbit transfer vehicles); spacecraft systems and payloads (spacecraft systems and subsystems, and space sensors and instruments); and satellite-based services and space support products (satellite-based data communications services and environmental and remote sensing services). **Number of employees at this location:** 350. **Number of employees nationwide:** 1,165.

TELEDYNE
10707 Gilroy Road, Hunt Valley MD 21031. 410/771-8600. **Contact:** Sandra Brown, Personnel Manager. **Description:** Engaged in space and terrestrial thermoelectric generator development and production. **Corporate headquarters location:** Beverly Hills CA. **Listed on:** New York Stock Exchange.

Note: Because addresses and telephone numbers of smaller companies change rapidly, we recommend you call each company to verify the information below before inquiring about job opportunities. Mass mailings are not recommended.

Additional employers with over 100 employees:

AIRCRAFT

Fokker Aircraft USA Inc.
1199 N Fairfax St Ste 500, Alexandria VA 22314-1437. 703/838-0100.

Rohr Inds. Inc.
18238 Showalter Rd, Hagerstown MD 21742-1345. 301/790-9500.

Twenty First Century Technology
733 15th St NW Ste 700, Washington DC 20005-2112. 202/393-3243.

AEROSPACE PRODUCTS

Aerotech Management
7802 Worthing Ct, Alexandria VA 22310-4032. 703/971-3409.

Arianespace Inc.
700 13th St NW Ste 230, Washington DC 20005-3960. 202/628-3936.

Lunacorp
9100 White Chimney Ln, Great Falls VA 22066-2321. 703/759-0700.

Standard Space Platforms Corp.
1364 Beverly Rd, Mc Lean VA 22101-3627. 703/883-0218.

Yamada International
1235 Jefferson Davis Hwy, Arlington VA 22202. 703/486-0490.

For more information on career opportunities in aerospace:

Associations

AIR TRANSPORT ASSOCIATION OF AMERICA
1301 Pennsylvania Avenue NW, Suite 1100, Washington DC 20004. 202/626-4000.

AMERICAN INSTITUTE OF AERONAUTICS AND ASTRONAUTICS
85 John Street, 4th Floor, New York NY 10038. 212/349-1120. Membership required. Publishes six journals and books.

FUTURE AVIATION PROFESSIONALS OF AMERICA
4959 Massachusetts Boulevard, Atlanta GA 30337. 404/997-8097. Publishes monthly newsletter which monitors the job market for flying jobs; a pilot employment guide, outlining what is required to become a pilot; and a directory of aviation employers.

NATIONAL AERONAUTIC ASSOCIATION OF USA
1815 North Fort Meyer Drive, Suite 700, Arlington VA 22209. 703/527-0226. Publishes a magazine. Membership required.

PROFESSIONAL AVIATION MAINTENANCE ASSOCIATION
500 NW Plaza, Suite 1016, St. Ann MO 63074. 314/739-2580. Members' resumes are distributed to companies who advise the organization of employment opportunities. Many local chapters also provide job referrals. Members also can have access to the Worldwide Membership Directory.

APPAREL AND TEXTILES

The apparel industry is looking toward an uncertain future. Women's apparel prices dropped 4.4 percent in 1994, and many experts expect continued deflation through 1996. Consumers have remained uninterested in new fashions and refuse to pay higher prices. Textile and apparel mills are under pressure from the other end of the supply chain as well -- the cost of cotton and other raw materials has remained at close-to-record highs, with raw cotton prices jumping 35 percent in 1994. As a result, many textile producers have recently reported significant drops in earnings. However, improved consumer confidence, more attractive fashions, and lower prices may prod consumers into buying after going without for the past four years, and this will eventually increase business for mills. Also, the sales of men's suits soared by 20 percent in 1994, and this trend is expected to continue, though at a somewhat slower pace, as men look for upscale casual wear to accommodate more relaxed dress codes. The highest demand in both men's and women's apparel will probably be for lower priced clothing produced for discount stores.

ALPHA INDUSTRIES INC.
1600 Spring Hill Road, Suite 220, Vienna VA 22182. 703/506-2482. **Fax:** 703/506-2487. **Contact:** Human Resources. **Description:** Founded in 1959 in a leased building with forty employees, Alpha Industries Inc. has grown to become one of the largest military clothing manufacturers in the United States. More than thirty-seven years ago Alpha Industries received it first U.S. Department of Defense contract for field jackets and has produced them continuously since then. In 1961 Alpha Industries landed its first U.S. Government contract for MA-1 flight jackets and, since that time, Alpha has supplied virtually all of the MA-1's to the U.S. Military. Alpha Industries' manufacturing facilities, in Knoxville, TN, utilize modern equipment and manufacturing techniques to produce the technical, specialized military clothing required by the world's sophisticated military forces as well as civilians seeking cold weather clothing.

BATA SHOE COMPANY, INC.
4501 Pulaski Highway, Belcamp MD 21017. 410/272-2000. **Fax:** 410/272-3346. **Contact:** Barbara Higgins, Vice President of Human Resources. **Description:** A manufacturer and marketer of industrial protective footwear and related products. Also manufactures safety boots for all market segments. **Common positions include:** Accountant/Auditor; Blue-Collar Worker Supervisor; Buyer; Cashier; Chemist; Clinical Lab Technician; Computer Operator; Computer Programmer; Cost Estimator; Credit Manager; Customer Service Representative; Electrical/Electronics Engineer; Electrician; Financial Manager; Human Resources Specialist; Industrial Engineer; Industrial Production Manager; Machinist; Manufacturer's/Wholesaler's Sales Rep.; Mechanical Engineer; Order Clerk; Payroll Clerk; Purchasing Agent and Manager; Receptionist; Secretary; Stock Clerk; Transportation/Traffic Specialist. **Educational backgrounds include:** Chemistry; Engineering. **Benefits:** Dental Insurance; Disability Coverage; Employee Discounts; Life Insurance; Medical Insurance; Pension Plan; Tuition Assistance. **Special Programs:** Training Programs. **Corporate headquarters location:** Toronto, Canada. **Operations at this facility include:** Administration; Manufacturing; Sales. **Listed on:** Privately held. **Number of employees at this location:** 170.

ENGLISH AMERICAN TAILORING COMPANY
411 North Cranberry Road, Westminster MD 21157. 410/857-5774. **Contact:** Human Resources. **Description:** A manufacturer of men's coats and suits.

HARTZ & COMPANY, INC.
1341 Hughes Ford Road, Frederick MD 21701. 301/662-7500. **Fax:** 301/662-0800. **Contact:** Jane L. Pollack, Director of Human Resources. **Description:** A manufacturer of men's clothing. **Common positions include:** Accountant/Auditor; Clerical Supervisor; Computer Programmer; Computer Systems Analyst; Cost Estimator; Credit Manager; Customer Service Representative; Designer; Draftsperson; Electrician; Financial Analyst; General Manager; Human Resources Specialist; Industrial Engineer; Industrial Production Manager; Management Analyst/Consultant; Operations/Production Manager; Purchasing Agent and Manager; Quality Control Supervisor; Restaurant/Food Service Manager; Services Sales Representative; Wholesale and Retail Buyer. **Educational backgrounds include:** Art/Design; Business Administration; Engineering; Liberal Arts. **Benefits:** 401K; Dental Insurance; Disability Coverage; Employee Discounts; Life Insurance; Medical Insurance. **Corporate headquarters location:** This Location. **Other U.S. locations:** Broadway VA. **Operations at this facility include:** Administration; Divisional Headquarters; Manufacturing; Sales. **Listed on:** Privately held. **Number of employees at this location:** 350. **Number of employees nationwide:** 650.

I.C. ISAACS & COMPANY
3840 Bank Street, Baltimore MD 21224. 410/342-8200. **Contact:** Human Resources Department. **Description:** A women's outerwear company.

LEVI STRAUSS & COMPANY
P.O. Box 580, Warsaw VA 22572. 804/333-4007. **Contact:** Human Resources Department. **Description:** Manufactures men's and boys' outerwear and sportswear. Levi Strauss is particularly known for its jeans. Also manufactures women's outerwear.

LIBERTY FABRICS INC.
One Cleveland Street, P.O. Box 308, Gordonsville VA 22942. 703/832-2261. **Fax:** 703/832-7145. **Contact:** Laura M. Byrnes, Personnel Manager/Training Administrator. **Description:** One of the largest producers of lace in the country. Liberty Fabrics Inc. also produces knit fabrics, and this facility is responsible for dyeing and finishing the products. **Common positions include:** Accountant/Auditor; Budget Analyst; Buyer; Customer Service Representative; Human Resources Specialist; Industrial Engineer; Industrial Production Manager; Operations/Production Manager; Services Sales Representative; Textile Manager. **Educational backgrounds include:** Chemistry; Textiles. **Benefits:** 401K; Disability Coverage; Life Insurance; Medical Insurance; Profit Sharing; Spending Account; Tuition Assistance. **Corporate headquarters location:** New York NY. **Other U.S. locations:** Janesville NC; North Bergen NJ; Woolwine VA. **Parent company:** Courtaulds Textiles. **Operations at this facility include:** Administration; Manufacturing; Research and Development; Sales. **Number of employees at this location:** 250. **Number of employees nationwide:** 1,200.

LONDON FOG INDUSTRIES
1332 Londontown Boulevard, Eldersburg MD 21784. 410/795-5900. **Fax:** 410/549-8019. **Contact:** Denise Youngs, Employment Specialist. **Description:** Founded in Baltimore, MD in 1923, London Fog is a progressive manufacturer and retailer of traditional and contemporary top quality men's and women's rainwear. Also a manufacturer and retailer of men's, women's, and children's outerwear and sportswear with well over 100 outlet stores nationwide. **Common positions include:** Accountant/Auditor; Adjuster; Administrative Services Manager; Attorney; Blue-Collar Worker Supervisor; Buyer; Clerical Supervisor; Credit Manager; Customer Service Representative; Designer; Electrician; Financial Analyst; Health Services Manager; Human Resources Specialist; Industrial Engineer; Management Trainee; Operations/Production Manager; Purchasing Agent and Manager; Transportation/Traffic Specialist. **Educational backgrounds include:** Accounting; Art/Design; Business Administration; Communications; Computer Science; Economics; Engineering; Finance; Liberal Arts; Marketing. **Benefits:** 401K; Dental Insurance; Disability Coverage; Employee Discounts; Life Insurance; Meal Plan; Pension Plan; Savings Plan; Tuition Assistance. **Corporate headquarters location:** Darien CT. **Other U.S. locations:** Nationwide; Baltimore MD; Boonsboro MD; Hagerstown MD; Hancock MD. **Operations at this facility include:** Administration; Divisional Headquarters; Manufacturing. **Listed on:** Privately held. **Number of employees at this location:** 500. **Number of employees nationwide:** 2,400.

Apparel and Textiles/73

THE SCHWAB COMPANY
P.O. Box 1742, Cumberland MD 21501-1742. 301/729-4488. **Contact:** Human Resources. **Description:** Manufacturer of Little Me and Ralph Lauren children's playwear.

H. WARSHOW & SONS INC.
P.O. Box 488, Tappahannock VA 22560. 804/443-3391. **Contact:** Human Resources Department. **Description:** A textile mill.

Note: Because addresses and telephone numbers of smaller companies change rapidly, we recommend you call each company to verify the information below before inquiring about job opportunities. Mass mailings are not recommended.

Additional employers with under 250 employees:

APPAREL WHOLESALE

L'Eggs Products Inc.
6679 Santa Barbara Rd, Baltimore MD 21227-5846. 410/796-1204.

MEN'S AND BOYS' CLOTHING

Haas Tailoring Co.
3425 Sinclair Ln, Baltimore MD 21213-2080. 410/732-3800.

New Maryland Clothing Manufacturers
3023 E Madison St, Baltimore MD 21205-1700. 410/675-8800.

Oakloom Clothes Inc.
1800 Johnson St, Baltimore MD 21230-4940. 410/837-6763.

A Schreter & Sons
600 S Pulaski St, Baltimore MD 21223-3409. 410/945-3600.

Wrangler Inc.
Washington St, Madison VA 22727. 703/948-4504.

Head Sports Wear International Inc.
9189 Red Branch Rd, Columbia MD 21045-2013. 410/730-8300.

Katzenberg Brothers
3500 Parkdale Ave, Baltimore MD 21211-1479. 410/669-4400.

Yale Sportswear Corporation
215 N Washington St, Easton MD 21601-3150. 410/822-0720.

Aileen Inc.
Old Brandy Rd, Culpeper VA 22701. 703/825-8363.

FOOTWEAR

Thurmont Shoe Co
31 Apples Church Rd, Thurmont MD 21788-1711. 301/271-7335.

For more information on career opportunities in the apparel and textiles industries:

Associations

AMERICAN APPAREL MANUFACTURERS ASSOCIATION
2500 Wilson Boulevard, Suite 301, Arlington VA 22201. 703/524-1864. Publishes numerous magazines, newsletters, and bulletins for the benefit of employees in the apparel manufacturing industry.

AMERICAN TEXTILE MANUFACTURERS INSTITUTE
Office of the Chief Economist, 1801 K Street NW, Suite 900, Washington DC 20006. 202/862-0500.

THE FASHION GROUP
597 5th Avenue, 8th Floor, New York NY 10017. 212/593-1715. A nonprofit organization for professional women in the fashion industries (apparel, accessories, beauty, and home). Offers career counseling workshops 18 times per year.

INTERNATIONAL ASSOCIATION OF CLOTHING DESIGNERS
475 Park Avenue South, 17th Floor, New York NY 10016. 212/685-6602.

Directories

AAMA DIRECTORY
American Apparel Manufacturers Association, 2500 Wilson Boulevard, Suite 301, Arlington VA 22201. 703/524-1864. A directory of publications distributed by the American Apparel Manufacturers Association.

APPAREL TRADES BOOK
Dun & Bradstreet Inc., 430 Mountain Avenue, New Providence NJ 07974. 908/665-5000.

FAIRCHILD'S MARKET DIRECTORY OF WOMEN'S AND CHILDREN'S APPAREL
Fairchild Publications, 7 West 34th Street, New York NY 10001. 212/630-4000.

Magazines

ACCESSORIES
Business Journals, 50 Day Street, P.O. Box 5550, Norwalk CT 06856. 203/853-6015.

AMERICA'S TEXTILES
Billiam Publishing, 37 Villa Road, Suite 111, P.O. Box 103 Greenville SC 29615. 803/242-5300.

APPAREL INDUSTRY MAGAZINE
Shore Communications Inc., 6255 Barfield Road, Suite 200, Atlanta GA 30328-4893. 404/252-8831.

BOBBIN
Bobbin Publications, P.O. Box 1986, 1110 Shop Road, Columbia SC 29202. 803/771-7500.

TEXTILE HILIGHTS
American Textile Manufacturers Institute, Office of the Chief Economist, 1801 K Street NW, Suite 900, Washington DC 20006.

WOMEN'S WEAR DAILY (WWD)
Fairchild Publications, 7 West 34th Street, New York NY 10001. 212/630-4000.

ARCHITECTURE, CONSTRUCTION AND ENGINEERING

The U.S. Department of Labor anticipates 1.2 million new construction jobs from 1992 through 2005, due to the need to replace aging experienced workers. Residential construction will grow slowly, as a result of the expected decline in population growth. Industrial construction, however, will be stronger because of an increase in exports by manufacturers. Heavy construction is growing faster than the industry average, with much activity in highway, bridge, and street construction.

Job prospects for engineers have been good for a number of years, and will continue to improve into the next century. Employers will need more engineers as they increase investment in equipment in order to expand output. In addition, engineers will find work improving the nation's deteriorating infrastructure.

AEPA ARCHITECTS ENGINEERS
2421 Pennsylvania Avenue NW, Washington DC 20037. 202/822-8320. **Contact:** Ms. C.M. Liu, Director of Operations. **Description:** An architecture and engineering firm. **Corporate headquarters location:** This Location.

ALLIEDSIGNAL TECHNICAL SERVICES CORPORATION
1 Bendix Road, Columbia MD 21045. 410/964-7000. **Contact:** Human Resources. **Description:** An integrated management and field engineering services company. **Parent company:** AlliedSignal.

ATEC ASSOCIATES, INC.
8918 Hermann Drive, Columbia MD 21045. 410/381-0210. **Contact:** Human Resources. **Description:** Provides engineering services.

MICHAEL BAKER JR., INC.
CIVIL AND WATER RESOURCES DIVISION
3601 Eisenhower Avenue, Suite 600, Alexandria VA 22304. 703/960-8800. **Fax:** 703/960-9125. **Contact:** Human Resources. **Description:** Michael Baker Jr., Inc., is a professional services company that provides engineering consulting and design services, construction services, and operations and maintenance services. Established in 1940 as the company's core business, the engineering group encompasses a broad range of disciplines required to plan, design, and inspect the construction of architectural and engineering projects and other facilities. Baker's construction group consists of: construction management and design, heavy and highway construction, and general construction.

BALTIMORE AIRCOIL COMPANY
P.O. Box 7322, Baltimore MD 21227. 410/799-6204. **Contact:** Marian Thompson, Manager of Human Resources. **Description:** A specialist in the design and manufacture of evaporative cooling equipment, producing cooling towers, evaporative condensers, and closed circuit cooling systems at 11 manufacturing plants worldwide. **Common positions include:** Accountant/Auditor; Air Quality Scientist; Chemical Engineer; Design Engineer; Financial Analyst; Industrial Engineer; Marketing Specialist; Mechanical Engineer; Research Scientist; Sales Representative.

BARBER & ROSS COMPANY
P.O. Box 1294, 110 Catoctin Circle, Leesburg VA 22075. 703/478-1970. **Contact:** Dan Reeves, Personnel. **Description:** Manufactures window units, interior/exterior door

units, door entrance features, and other door and sash products. **Corporate headquarters location:** This Location.

BLAKE CONSTRUCTION COMPANY
1120 Connecticut Avenue NW, Suite 1200, Washington DC 20036. 202/828-9000. **Contact:** Cindy Daley, Office Manager. **Description:** A contractor engaged primarily in commercial construction activities.

CECO CONCRETE CONSTRUCTION
10738 Baltimore Avenue, Beltsville MD 20785. 301/595-3941. **Fax:** 301/595-2093. **Contact:** Pat Blowe, Executive Secretary. **Description:** A supplier of construction products and services to the industry for 80 years. **Common positions include:** Attorney; Branch Manager; Civil Engineer; Clerical Supervisor; Computer Programmer; Construction Contractor and Manager; Cost Estimator; Draftsperson; General Manager. **Educational backgrounds include:** Business Administration; Engineering; Marketing. **Benefits:** 401K; Dental Insurance; Disability Coverage; Employee Discounts; Life Insurance; Medical Insurance; Tuition Assistance. **Corporate headquarters location:** Kansas City KS. **Other U.S. locations:** Denver CO; Hartford CT; Tampa FL; Boston MA; Detroit MI; Dallas TX; San Antonio TX. **Parent company:** Pettibone Corporation. **Operations at this facility include:** Administration; Divisional Headquarters; Regional Headquarters; Sales. **Listed on:** New York Stock Exchange. **Number of employees at this location:** 12.

CENTURY ENGINEERING, INC.
32 West Road, Towson MD 21204. 410/823-8070. **Contact:** Human Resources. **Description:** Provides electrical, mechanical, civil, structural, and geotechnical engineering.

COMPLETE BUILDING SERVICES INC.
2101 Wisconsin Avenue NW, Washington DC 20007. 202/333-4977. **Contact:** Joseph Widmayer, President. **Description:** Offers a wide range of commercial and industrial management and maintenance services, including automatic temperature control and pneumatic and electrical installation.

DAVENPORT INSULATION INC.
15445 Depot Lane, Upper Marlboro MD 20772. **Contact:** Carolyn Sprinkle, Personnel. **Description:** A contracting and retail operation specializing in the installation and servicing of insulation and related products.

DEWBERRY & DAVIS
200 Harry Truman Parkway, Annapolis MD 21401. 410/841-6812. **Contact:** Human Resources. **Description:** A full-service architectural and engineering firm. Dewberry & Davis has been included in the top 50 of *Engineering News-Record's* (ENR) Top 500 Design Firms for the past several years. Operations include water resources, environmental engineering, transportation engineering, mechanical/electrical and structural engineering, planning, landscape architecture, architecture, program management, and digitized mapping services, as well as land development engineering and surveying. **Subsidiaries include:** Goodkind & O'Dea, Inc. in New York NY; Rutherford NJ, North Haven CT, Boston MA, and Dillsburg PA; TOLK, Inc.; Dewberry & Davis Service Operations, Inc.; Dewberry & Davis Risk Management, Inc.; and American Digital Systems. **Corporate headquarters location:** Fairfax VA. **Other U.S. locations:** Gaithersburg MD; Lanham MD; Raleigh NC; Danville VA; Leesburg VA; Manassas VA; Marion VA; Richmond VA.

THE DONOHOE COMPANIES, INC.
2101 Wisconsin Avenue NW, Washington DC 20007. 202/333-0880. **Contact:** Deirdre Robinson, Human Resources Manager. **Description:** A real estate construction and development company. **Common positions include:** Accountant/Auditor; Civil Engineer; Construction and Building Inspector; Construction Contractor and Manager; Construction Trade Worker; Cost Estimator; Heating/AC/Refrigeration Technician; Property and Real Estate Manager; Secretary. **Educational backgrounds include:** Accounting; Engineering. **Benefits:** Dental Insurance; Disability Coverage; Employee Discounts; Life Insurance; Medical Insurance; Profit Sharing; Savings Plan; Tuition Assistance. **Corporate headquarters location:** This Location. **Operations at this facility include:** Administration; Divisional Headquarters; Regional Headquarters; Sales; Service. **Number of employees at this location:** 300. **Number of employees nationwide:** 300.

Architecture, Construction and Engineering/77

THE DRIGGS CORPORATION
8700 Ashwood Drive, Capital Heights MD 20743. 301/499-1950. **Contact:** Personnel Director. **Description:** A paving contractor/consultant. **Common positions include:** Accountant/Auditor; Administrator; Blue-Collar Worker Supervisor; Energy Engineer; Purchasing Agent and Manager; Services Sales Representative; Transportation/Traffic Specialist. **Educational backgrounds include:** Business Administration; Marketing. **Benefits:** Life Insurance; Medical Insurance; Profit Sharing.

P. FLANIGAN & SONS INC.
2444 Loch Raven Road, Baltimore MD 21217. 410/669-6300. **Contact:** Human Resources Department. **Description:** A general contractor specializing in asphalt and concrete paving.

FORT MYER CONSTRUCTION CORPORATION
2237 33rd Street Northeast, Washington DC 20018. 202/636-9535. **Contact:** Human Resources Department. **Description:** A building construction general contractor.

HADRON INC.
9990 Lee Highway, Fairfax VA 22030. 703/359-6404. **Contact:** Human Resources. **Description:** Offers engineering services.

HALLIBURTON/NUS ENVIRONMENTAL CORPORATION
910 Clopper Road, Gaithersburg MD 20878-1399. **Contact:** Employment. **Description:** Halliburton Company, operating in 100 countries, is one of the world's largest diversified energy services and engineering and construction companies. Halliburton Energy Services provides methods of drilling and production operations. Some of the products and services Halliburton offers include pressure pumping, well logging, drilling systems and well completion equipment and services. Brown & Root is a provider of engineering, construction, project management, facilities operations and maintenance and environmental services.

HAMILTON & SPIEGEL, INC.
P.O. Box 288, Bladensburg MD 20710. 301/322-3150. **Contact:** Mr. Odea, Owner. **Description:** Sheet metal and roofing constructors. Also engaged in stainless steel fabrication. **Corporate headquarters location:** This Location.

JOHN H. HAMPSHIRE INC.
320 West 24th Street, Baltimore MD 21211. 410/366-8900. **Contact:** Human Resources. **Description:** A construction company.

HORNING BROTHERS
1350 Connecticut Avenue NW, Suite 800, Washington DC 20036. 202/659-0700. **Contact:** Mr. Casby Coffey, Payroll Administrator. **Description:** A residential and commercial development, construction, and management company. **Common positions include:** Accountant/Auditor; Construction Contractor and Manager; Groundskeeper; Maintenance Worker; Property and Real Estate Manager. **Educational backgrounds include:** Business Administration; Marketing. **Benefits:** 401K; Dental Insurance; Disability Coverage; Life Insurance; Pension Plan; Profit Sharing; Tuition Assistance. **Corporate headquarters location:** This Location. **Operations at this facility include:** Administration; Divisional Headquarters. **Number of employees at this location:** 15. **Number of employees nationwide:** 100.

THE GEORGE HYMAN CONSTRUCTION COMPANY
7500 Old Georgetown Road, Bethesda MD 20814. 301/986-8300. **Contact:** Director of Personnel. **Description:** One of the metropolitan area's largest general contractors.

KCI TECHNOLOGIES
10 North Park Drive, Hunt Valley MD 21030. 410/316-7800. **Contact:** Director of Personnel. **Description:** Provides planning, engineering, surveying, geotechnical testing, and construction inspection services. **Common positions include:** Accountant/Auditor; Architect; Civil Engineer; Computer Programmer; Credit Manager; Draftsperson; Electrical/Electronics Engineer; Industrial Engineer; Mechanical Engineer; Technical Writer/Editor. **Educational backgrounds include:** Accounting; Computer Science; Engineering. **Benefits:** Dental Insurance; Disability Coverage; Employee Discounts; Life Insurance; Medical Insurance; Pension Plan; Profit Sharing; Savings Plan; Tuition Assistance. **Corporate headquarters location:** Saddlebrook NJ. **Parent company:** Kidde, Inc. **Listed on:** New York Stock Exchange.

JOHN J. KIRLIN, INC.
643 Lofstrand Lane, Rockville MD 20850. 301/424-3410. **Contact:** Human Resources. **Description:** A construction special trade contractor.

C.J. LANGENFELDER & SONS, INC.
8427 Pulaski Highway, Baltimore MD 21237. 410/682-2000. **Contact:** Human Resources. **Description:** A highway and street construction contractor.

R. MARINUCCI & SONS
11217 Maryland Avenue, Beltsville MD 20705. 301/595-5800. **Contact:** Personnel. **Description:** A contracting firm engaged in sewer and water construction projects.

MILLER & LONG COMPANY, INC.
4824 Rugby Avenue, Bethesda MD 20814. 301/657-8000. **Contact:** Miles Gladstone, Personnel Director. **Description:** A construction firm, specializing in high-rise concrete construction, and other large-scale projects. **Corporate headquarters location:** This Location.

PIERCE ASSOCIATES
4216 Wheeler Avenue, Alexandria VA 22304. 703/751-2400. **Fax:** 703/751-2479. **Contact:** Robert N. Keyser, Senior Vice President. **Description:** A special trades contractor in mechanical construction (H.V.A.C., plumbing, and fire protection). **Common positions include:** Mechanical Engineer. **Benefits:** 401K; Dental Insurance; Life Insurance; Medical Insurance. **Corporate headquarters location:** This Location. **Listed on:** Privately held. **Number of employees at this location:** 40.

DOUGLAS PORETZ LTD.
916 Helga Place, Vienna VA 22102. 703/506-1778. **Contact:** Human Resources. **Description:** A construction company.

QUANTA SYSTEMS CORPORATION
213 Perry Parkway, Gaithersburg MD 20877-2145. 301/590-3334. **Contact:** Personnel Manager. **Description:** A research and development engineering company. Also manufactures high-technology products and commercial communications equipment. **Parent company:** Compudyne Corporation.

RUST ENVIRONMENTAL & INFRASTRUCTURE
11240 Waples Mill Road, Suite 100, Fairfax VA 22030. 703/385-3566. **Contact:** Human Resources Department. **Description:** A consulting engineering firm.

RYAN HOMES, INC.
7601 Lewinsville Road, Suite 300, McLean VA 22102. 703/761-2255. **Fax:** 703/761-2259. **Contact:** Joseph Madigan, Director, Human Resources. **Description:** Ryan Homes (and sister company NV Homes) are both wholly-owned subsidiaries of NVR, Inc., one of the nation's leading homebuilders. **Common positions include:** Accountant/Auditor; Construction Contractor and Manager; Customer Service Representative; Economist/Market Research Analyst; Financial Analyst; Services Sales Representative. **Educational backgrounds include:** Accounting; Business Administration; Communications; Economics; Finance; Liberal Arts; Marketing; Mathematics. **Benefits:** 401K; Dental Insurance; Disability Coverage; Employee Discounts; Life Insurance; Medical Insurance; Profit Sharing. **Other U.S. locations:** DE; MD; NC; NY; PA; VA. **Operations at this facility include:** Divisional Headquarters; Regional Headquarters; Sales; Service. **Listed on:** American Stock Exchange. **Number of employees at this location:** 500. **Number of employees nationwide:** 2,000.

THE RYLAND GROUP, INC.
11000 Broken Land Parkway, Columbia MD 21044. 410/715-7000. **Contact:** Human Resources. **Description:** Ryland is one of the nation's largest homebuilders and is a leading mortgage-finance company. From the company's initial sale of 48 homes in Columbia, Maryland, in 1967, Ryland has expanded selectively across the nation and now builds homes in six regions and more than 25 cities. Operations of the Ryland Group, Inc. and subsidiaries consist of three business segments: homebuilding, financial services, and limited-purpose subsidiaries. Ryland Homes specializes in the on-site construction of single-family attached and detached homes, priced from $80,000 to more than $300,000. Since its founding, Ryland has built more than 120,000 homes. Operating out of 34 retail and four wholesale branches, Ryland Mortgage's work directly with Ryland homebuyers. Since 1978, Ryland has provided mortgage-financing for more than 115,000 families. **Corporate headquarters location:**

This Location. **Other U.S. locations:** nationwide. **Listed on:** New York Stock Exchange. **Number of employees at this location:** 600. **Number of employees nationwide:** 3,200.

STV GROUP
21 Governor's Court, Baltimore MD 21244. 410/944-9112. **Contact:** Joseph A. Morrone, Vice President. **Description:** A full-service architecture and engineering firm engaged in planning, architecture, and engineering. **Common positions include:** Architect; Civil Engineer; Computer Programmer; Computer Systems Analyst; Construction and Building Inspector; Construction Contractor and Manager; Cost Estimator; Designer; Draftsperson; Electrical/Electronics Engineer; Environmental Engineer; Geologist/Geophysicist; Landscape Architect; Materials Engineer; Mechanical Engineer; Structural Engineer; Surgical Technician; Technical Writer/Editor; Transportation/Traffic Specialist. **Benefits:** 401K; Disability Coverage; Life Insurance; Medical Insurance; Pension Plan; Tuition Assistance. **Corporate headquarters location:** Pottstown PA. **Other U.S. locations:** Nationwide. **Parent company:** STV Inc. **Listed on:** NASDAQ. **Number of employees at this location:** 120. **Number of employees nationwide:** 1,000.

A.J. SACKETT & SONS COMPANY
1701 South Highland, Baltimore MD 21224. 410/276-4466. **Contact:** Ruth Sroka, Personnel. **Description:** An engineering services company which also manufactures handling and processing equipment.

CHARLES H. TOMPKINS COMPANY
1333 H Street NW, Suite 200, Washington DC 20005. 202/789-0770. **Contact:** Jean Sutton, Manager. **Description:** A general construction contractor.

TRULAND SYSTEMS CORPORATION
3330 Washington Boulevard, Arlington VA 22201. 703/524-4900. **Contact:** Human Resources. **Description:** An electrical contractor.

UNITED STATES GYPSUM COMPANY
5500 Quarantine Road, Baltimore MD 21226. 410/355-6600. **Contact:** Tom Foley, Human Resources Manager. **Description:** Produces a wide range of gypsum building products. Nationally, United States Gypsum Company is a manufacturer of building materials, producing a complete range of products for use in new building construction, repair, remodeling, and in many industry processes. Operates more than 110 plants in the United States, Canada, Mexico, and Great Britain. **Corporate headquarters location:** Chicago IL. **Listed on:** New York Stock Exchange.

WHITING-TURNER CONTRACTING COMPANY
300 East Joppa Road, Towson MD 21286. 410/821-1100. **Contact:** Human Resources. **Description:** A general contracting and construction management company.

WILLIAMS INDUSTRIES INC.
2849 Meadow View Road, Falls Church VA 22042. **Contact:** Human Resources. **Description:** A construction company. **Common positions include:** Accountant/Auditor; Adjuster; Attorney; Civil Engineer; Computer Programmer; Construction and Building Inspector; Construction Contractor and Manager; Cost Estimator; Industrial Engineer. **Educational backgrounds include:** Accounting; Energy. **Benefits:** 401K; Dental Insurance; Life Insurance; Medical Insurance. **Corporate headquarters location:** This Location. **Operations at this facility include:** Administration; Sales. **Listed on:** NASDAQ.

Note: Because addresses and telephone numbers of smaller companies change rapidly, we recommend you call each company to verify the information below before inquiring about job opportunities. Mass mailings are not recommended.

Additional employers with under 250 employees:

CONSTRUCTION MATERIALS WHOLESALE

J J Haines & Company
6950 Aviation Blvd, Glen Burnie MD 21061-2531.
410/760-4040.

Blue Circle Atlantic
2411 Crofton Ln, Crofton MD 21114-1304. 410/721-4904.

Standard Supplies Inc.
14 Meem Ave, Gaithersburg MD 20877-2115. 301/948-2690.

W E Campbell Co. Inc.
4390 Lottsford Vista Rd,
Lanham MD 20706-4817.
301/937-5700.

PLUMBING, HEATING, AND A/C EQUIPMENT WHOLESALE

Aireco Supply Inc.
4124 Walney Rd # J,
Chantilly VA 22021-2922.
703/378-0300.

Baltimore Refrigeration
1102 Russell St # A,
Baltimore MD 21230-2622.
410/783-9220.

ENGINEERING SERVICES

Aepco Inc.
15800 Crabbs Branch Way
#300, Rockville MD 20855-2604. 301/670-6770.

Cexec Inc.
8618 Westwood Center Dr #
100, Vienna VA 22182-2222. 703/893-3220.

Compliance Corporation
34 Essex Dr S, Lexingtn Park
MD 20653-1151. 301/863-8070.

Comsis Corporation
8737 Colesville Rd Ste
1100, Silver Spring MD
20910-3921. 301/588-0800.

DDL Omni Engineering Corporation
8260 Greensboro Dr Ste
600, Mc Lean VA 22102-3806. 703/903-9759.

Dual Inc.
2101 Wilson Blvd Ste 600,
Arlington VA 22201-3062.
703/527-3500.

Eagan McAllister Associates
300 Three Notch Rd N,
Lexingtn Park MD 20653-1514. 301/863-2192.

EBA Engineering Inc.
5800 Metro Dr, Baltimore
MD 21215-3223. 410/358-7171.

Executive Resource Associates
2011 Crystal Dr, Arlington
VA 22202-3709. 703/920-5200.

Forensic Technologies Internat
2021 Research Dr, Annapolis
MD 21401-3083. 410/224-8770.

Henkels & McCoy
PO Box 1507, Newington VA
22122-1507. 703/550-0450.

JJH Inc.
5400 Shawnee Rd,
Alexandria VA 22312-2300.
703/642-3152.

John J. McMullen Associates Inc.
2341 Jefferson Davis Hwy,
Arlington VA 22202-3809.
703/418-0100.

Mantech Services Corporation
12015 Lee Jackson
Memorial Hwy, Fairfax VA
22033-3300. 703/218-6400.

Peer Consultants Pc
5125 MacArthur Blvd NW
Ste 32, Washington DC
20016-3300. 202/966-3300.

Person-System Integration Ltd.
2401 Huntington Ave,
Alexandria VA 22303-1531.
703/960-5555.

PRB Associates Inc.
47 Airport View Dr,
Hollywood MD 20636-9760.
301/373-2360.

Raytheon Service Co. Nasa Logistics
9060 Junction Dr, Annapolis
Jct MD 20701-1123.
301/497-0600.

Rummel Klepper & Kahl
81 W Mosher St, Baltimore
MD 21217-4250. 410/728-2900.

Schnabel Engrg. Associates Inc.
10215 Fernwood Rd Ste
250, Bethesda MD 20817-1106. 301/564-9355.

Summit Technologies
6551 Loisdale Ct Ste 600,
Springfield VA 22150-1808.
703/922-5226.

Techmatics Inc.
12450 Fair Lakes Cir, Fairfax
VA 22033-3810. 703/802-8300.

Whitney Bailey Cox & Magnani
1850 York Rd, Luthvle
Timon MD 21093-5122.
410/252-6060.

Wilson Hill Associates
8401 Arlington Blvd Ste
500, Fairfax VA 22031-4619. 703/207-3100.

Dames & Moore
170 Jennifer Rd Ste 230,
Annapolis MD 21401-3064.
410/224-5640.

Harding Lawson Associates
3175 21st St N, Arlington
VA 22201-5107. 703/528-5809.

Saic
7600 Leesburg Pike, Falls
Church VA 22043-2004.
703/821-4600.

Stearns & Wheler
4201 Northview Dr, Bowie
MD 20716-2604. 301/805-5629.

American Society Mechl. Engineers
8996 Burke Lake Rd, Burke
VA 22015-1607. 703/978-5000.

Jackson & Tull
7501 Forbes Blvd, Lanham
MD 20706-2253. 301/805-6090.

Law Engineering
8940-A Rt 108, Columbia
MD 21045. 410/995-1552.

Wilbur Smith Associates
2921 Telestar Ct, Falls
Church VA 22042-1205.
703/698-9780.

Andrews Bettigole & Clark Inc.
522 Rock Spring Rd, Bel Air
MD 21014-2941. 410/879-2512.

Camp Dresser & McKee
7535 Little River Tpke,
Annandale VA 22003-6609.
703/642-5500.

National Tech Associates
2075 Great Mills Rd,
Lexingtn Park MD 20653-1319. 301/863-6512.

Symbiotic Technologies
5711 Sarvis Ave, Riverdale
MD 20737-1394. 301/951-7000.

Volt Information Sciences
3800 Concorde Pky,
Chantilly VA 22021-1127.
703/802-3000.

Engineering Science
10521 Rosehaven St, Fairfax
VA 22030-2837. 703/591-7575.

ARCHITECTURAL SERVICES

Delon Hampton & Associates
800 K St NW Ste 720,
Washington DC 20001-8000. 202/898-1999.

Ellerbe Becket
1875 Connecticut Ave NW
Ste 60, Washington DC
20009-5728. 202/986-2000.

Architecture, Construction and Engineering/81

Greiner Inc.
2219 York Rd Ste 200,
Timonium MD 21093-3118.
410/561-0100.

Henningson Durham & Richardson
103 Oronoco St, Alexandria VA 22314-2015. 703/683-3400.

Lyon Associates Inc.
21 Government Ct, Baltimore MD 21244. 410/944-9112.

M Rosenblatt & Son
2341 Jefferson Davis Hwy, Arlington VA 22202-3809. 703/415-7800.

SURVEYING SERVICES

Greenhorne & O'Mara
5444 Jefferson Davis Hwy, Fredericksbrg VA 22407-2627. 703/891-1600.

GENERAL CONTRACTORS

Brown & Root Inc.
20935 Belmont Ridge Rd, Ashburn VA 22011-4311. 703/729-5195.

Centennial Contractors
1801 Alexander Bell Dr Ste 100, Reston VA 22091-4344. 703/264-0235.

Centex-Simpson Construction Co.
PO Box 427, Merrifield VA 22116-0427. 703/273-3311.

Columbia Construction
9600 Martin Luther King Jr Hwy, Lanham MD 20706-1838. 301/459-0808.

Diversified Homes
10015 Old Columbia Rd, Columbia MD 21046-1703. 410/381-6696.

Facchina Construction
9320 W & W Industrial Rd, La Plata MD 20646. 301/753-3369.

George Hyman Construction Co.
5245 Greenbelt Rd, College Park MD 20740-2243. 301/220-1560.

Gilbane Building Co.
7901 Sandy Spring Rd Ste 500, Laurel MD 20707-3589. 301/317-6100.

Hitt Contracting Inc.
2704 Dorr Ave, Fairfax VA 22031-4901. 703/846-9000.

Kasco Chesapeake Builders
25 Main St, Reisterstown

MD 21136-1215. 410/526-4404.

Kenbridge Construction Regional Office
6585 Merchant Pl, Gainesville VA 22065-2307. 703/349-9585.

Long Enterprises Inc.
8253 Backlick Rd # J, Lorton VA 22079-1416. 703/339-0330.

Manhattan Construction
6905 Crain Hwy, La Plata MD 20646-3956. 301/934-2352.

Minkoff Company Inc.
14310 Sullyfield Cir, Chantilly VA 22021-1629. 703/802-8711.

Reinsch Construction Corporation
2040 Columbia Pike, Arlington VA 22204-4605. 703/920-3600.

Richmarr Construction Corporation
5301 Wisconsin Ave Nw, Washington DC 20015-2015. 202/686-8000.

Specialty General Contractors
3817 Ady Rd, Street MD 21154-1429. 410/838-7738.

Toll Brothers Inc.
15097 Stillfield Pl # T, Centreville VA 22020-1145. 703/450-0461.

Twigg Corporation
15100 Buck Ln, Uppr Marlboro MD 20772-7854. 301/952-9400.

Washington Homes
1802 Brightseat Rd, Landover MD 20785-4232. 301/772-8900.

William Prince Construction Co.
9599 Hawkins Dr, Manassas VA 22110-3907. 703/361-1005.

Bozzuto & Associates
6401 Golden Triangle Dr # 200, Greenbelt MD 20770-3200. 301/220-0100.

Heckingers Owings Mills
11610 Reisterstown Rd, Reisterstown MD 21136-3702. 410/526-5592.

Mitchell & Best Homes
11650 Glen Rd, Potomac MD 20854-1210. 301/299-2009.

Q D I
57 W Timonium Rd, Luthvle Timon MD 21093-3125. 410/252-6222.

Q D I
216 Dorchester Ave, Cambridge MD 21613-2445. 410/228-8700.

Better Living Patio Rooms MD
9592 Deereco Rd, Timonium MD 21093-2119. 410/561-0177.

MI Homes
44040 Bruceton Mills Cir, Ashburn VA 22011-4808. 703/478-8330.

Montgomery Meadows Homes
5105 Morningside Ln, Ellicott City MD 21043-7912. 410/461-8432.

Randolph D Rouse
6407 Wilson Blvd, Arlington VA 22205-1506. 703/532-2257.

Washington Homes
11123 Drumsheugh, Uppr Marlboro MD 20772. 301/499-4657.

E A Baker Co. Inc.
6482 Sligo Mill Rd, Takoma Park MD 20912-4700. 301/270-2121.

OPERATIVE BUILDERS

Stanley-Martin Companies Inc.
8000 Towers Crescent Dr # 800, Vienna VA 22182-2700. 703/760-8100.

Winchester Homes Inc.
6305 Ivy Loan Ste 800, Greenbelt MD 20770-1474. 301/595-0080.

GENERAL INDUSTRIAL CONTRACTORS

G&C Construction Corporation
8550 Lee Hwy Ste 500, Fairfax VA 22031-1515. 703/849-8100.

Jones Artis Construction Co.
704 T St Ne, Washington DC 20018-1012. 202/529-5588.

Morton Buildings
1918 Industrial Dr, Culpeper VA 22701-4114. 703/825-3633.

Chas H Tompkins Co.
1333 H St NW Ste 200, Washington DC 20005-4707. 202/789-0770.

Demar Inc.
702 Russell Ave,
Gaithersburg MD 20877-2682. 301/590-0200.

Falls Church Construction Corporation VA
11244 Waples Mill Rd,
Fairfax VA 22030-6040.
703/591-0600.

James G Davis Construction Corporation
12500 Parklawn Dr # 2227,
Rockville MD 20852-1702.
301/881-2990.

Jowett Incorporated
9106 Brandywine Rd, Clinton
MD 20735-2501. 301/868-2880.

Leapley Co.
1724 Kalorama Rd Nw,
Washington DC 20009-2636. 202/483-1800.

Somyr Contractors
1605 Kenilworth Ave Ne,
Washington DC 20019-2010. 202/396-7781.

William Schlosser Co.
2400 51st Pl, Hyattsville MD
20781-1396. 301/773-1300.

Cossentino Contracting Co. Inc.
8505 Contractors Rd,
Baltimore MD 21237-3085.
410/574-5800.

Della Ratta Inc.
1370 Lamberton Dr, Silver
Spring MD 20902-3427.
410/792-7936.

John W Brawner Cntrctng Co. Inc.
3312 Paper Mill Rd, Phoenix
MD 21131-1428. 410/666-2500.

ROAD CONSTRUCTION

Baltimore Asphalt Paving Co.
1320 N Monroe St,
Baltimore MD 21217-1594.
410/669-6300.

David A Bramble Inc.
705 Morgnec Rd,
Chestertown MD 21620-3105. 410/778-3023.

Flippo Construction Co.
3820 Penn Belt Pl, Forestville
MD 20747-4748. 301/736-7996.

Haverhill Contracting Co. Inc.
8100 Lynhurst Rd, Baltimore
MD 21222-3615. 410/388-1400.

Parametric Inc.
5625 Allentown Rd Ste 104,
Suitland MD 20746-4521.
301/702-9651.

Ratrie Robbins & Schweizer
803 Glen Eagles Ct,
Baltimore MD 21286-2201.
410/821-3400.

Francis O Day Co. Inc.
8700 Darcy Rd, Forestville
MD 20747-2610. 301/350-3700.

Slurry Pavers Inc.
8738 Vulcan Ln, Manassas
VA 22110-3951. 703/369-1326.

HEAVY CONSTRUCTION

Rockingham Construction
220 Spring St, Herndon VA
22070-5209. 703/435-0028.

PLUMBING, HEATING, AND A/C

Knott-Coakley & Associates
433 Hahn Rd, Westminster
MD 21157-4658. 410/876-0600.

Maryland Environmental Systems
PO Box 219, Columbia MD
21045-0219. 410/997-3363.

R M Thornton Inc.
120 W Hampton Ave,
Capitol Hts MD 20743-3516. 301/350-5000.

James Vito Inc.
14004 Willard Rd, Chantilly
VA 22021-2929. 703/802-2268.

Poole & Kent Corporation
2457 Linden Ln, Silver
Spring MD 20910-1230.
301/587-1640.

Warner Corporation
6100 Livingston, Oxon Hill
MD 20745. 301/567-2300.

Warner Corporation
10528 Saint Paul St,
Kensington MD 20895-2613. 301/654-0727.

Hess Mechanical Corporation
9600 Fallard Ct, Uppr
Marlboro MD 20772-6718.
301/856-4700.

McShane Inc.
701 W Ostend St, Baltimore
MD 21230-2696. 410/659-9400.

B&B AC & Heating Service Co. Inc.
Calvert, Prnc Frederck MD
20678. 410/535-4327.

Cornell-Aec
3520 Bladensburg Rd,
Brentwood MD 20722-1806.
301/779-8200.

Smith Service Company
2811 Old Lee Hwy, Fairfax
VA 22031-4303. 703/207-0100.

PAINTING AND PAPER HANGING

The House Doctor
2022 Kilgore Rd, Falls
Church VA 22043-1353.
703/893-7811.

ELECTRICAL WORK

Cydell Corporation
9157 Whiskey Bottom Rd,
Laurel MD 20723-1354.
301/595-0165.

Glen Industrial Communications
979 Rollins Ave, Rockville
MD 20852-1636. 301/231-8750.

John W Tieder Inc.
PO Box 653, Cambridge MD
21613-0653. 410/228-5262.

Commerce Electric Supply Inc.
230 Gateway Dr # A, Bel Air
MD 21014-4200. 410/838-2600.

Commerce Electric Supply Inc.
21 Fontana Ln, Baltimore MD
21237-4605. 410/574-0550.

L C Allen Enterprise
2102 Lirio Ct, Reston VA
22091-1308. 703/758-9209.

L T Bowden Inc.
13944 Willard Rd # F,
Chantilly VA 22021-2935.
703/631-1100.

Proctor Electric Inc.
4438 Lottsford Vista Rd,
Lanham MD 20706-4824.
301/341-2039.

MASONRY, STONEWORK, AND PLASTERING

Banner Masonry Corporation
6729 Dogwood Rd,
Baltimore MD 21207-4170.
410/944-5452.

Bragunier Masonry Controls Inc.
12107 Boyd Rd, Clear Spring
MD 21722-1605. 301/842-3700.

JMT Inc.
7539 Rickenbacker Dr,

Gaithersburg MD 20879-4700. 301/417-1010.

Leroy E Myers Inc.
14625 National Pike, Clear Spring MD 21722-1736. 301/582-1552.

CARPENTRY AND FLOOR WORK

Harkins Builders Inc.
12301 Old Columbia Pike, Silver Spring MD 20904-1656. 301/622-9000.

Builders Floor Service
7904 Yarnwood Ct, Springfield VA 22153-2826. 703/569-6000.

ROOFING, SIDING, AND SHEET METAL WORK

Cardinal Roofing & Siding Co.
6586 Fleet Dr, Alexandria VA 22310-2427. 703/719-0078.

CONCRETE WORK

Dance Brothers Inc.
825 N Hammonds Ferry Rd Ste C, Linthicum Hts MD 21090-1351. 410/789-8200.

Hi Tec Concrete Co.
8433 Backlick Rd, Lorton VA 22079-1403. 703/550-5300.

Howlin Concrete
1 E Chesapeake Beach Rd, Owings MD 20736-9269. 410/535-3020.

MISC. SPECIAL TRADE CONTRACTORS

Susquehanna Metal Box Company
2102 Albrook Ct, Fallston MD 21047-1529. 410/939-2535.

Genstar Stone Products Company
East South Street, Frederick MD 21701. 301/662-1181.

Gray & Sons Inc.
PO Box 8, Butler MD 21023-0008. 410/771-4311.

Wrecking Corporation America St Louis Inc.
3680 Wheeler Ave, Alexandria VA 22304-6403. 703/823-3850.

Otis Elevator Co. Inc.
4999 Fairview Ave, Linthicum Hts MD 21090-1405. 410/636-5700.

Amtech Reliable Elevator Co.
8055 Penn Randall Pl, Uppr Marlboro MD 20772-2688. 301/735-4391.

Dover Elevator Co.
611-K Hammonds Ferry Rd, Baltimore MD 21225. 410/789-8780.

Asp Construction Inc.
1420 N St NW Ste 102, Washington DC 20005-2843. 202/328-9758.

Mid Atlantic Waterproof Corporation
1040 West St, Laurel MD 20707-3531. 301/206-9500.

MOBILE HOMES

Scotsman Group Inc.
8211 Town Center Dr, Baltimore MD 21236-5904. 410/931-6000.

PREFABRICATED WOOD BUILDINGS AND COMPONENTS

Ryland Building Systems
1000 Tibbetts Ln, New Windsor MD 21776-9097. 410/549-1000.

For more information on career opportunities in architecture, construction and engineering:

Associations

AMERICAN ASSOCIATION OF COST ENGINEERS
209 Prairie Avenue, Suite 100, Morgantown WV 26505-1550. 304/296-8444. 800/858-2678. Toll-free number provides information on scholarships for undergraduates.

AMERICAN CONSULTING ENGINEERS COUNCIL
1015 15th Street NW, Suite 802, Washington DC 20005. 202/347-7474.

AMERICAN INSTITUTE OF ARCHITECTS
1735 New York Avenue NW, Washington DC 20006. 202/626-7300. 800/365-2724. Contact toll-free number for brochures.

AMERICAN SOCIETY FOR ENGINEERING EDUCATION
1818 N Street NW, Suite 600, Washington DC 20036. 202/331-3500. Promotes engineering education. Publishes monthly magazines.

AMERICAN SOCIETY OF CIVIL ENGINEERS
345 East 47th Street, New York NY 10017. 212/705-7496.

AMERICAN SOCIETY OF HEATING, REFRIGERATING AND AIR CONDITIONING ENGINEERS
1791 Tullie Circle NE, Atlanta GA 30329.
404/636-8400. Non-profit. Publishes several books.

AMERICAN SOCIETY OF LANDSCAPE ARCHITECTS
4401 Connecticut Avenue NW, Fifth Floor, Washington DC 20008. 202/686-2752.

AMERICAN SOCIETY OF MECHANICAL ENGINEERS
345 East 47th Street, New York NY 10017. 212/705-7722.

AMERICAN SOCIETY OF NAVAL ENGINEERS
1452 Duke Street, Alexandria VA 22314. 703/836-6727.

AMERICAN SOCIETY OF PLUMBING ENGINEERS
3617 Thousand Oaks Boulevard, Suite 210, Westlake CA 91362-3694. 805/495-7120. Provides technical and educational information.

AMERICAN SOCIETY OF SAFETY ENGINEERS
1800 East Oakton Street, Des Plaines IL 60018-2187. 708/692-4121. Jobline service available at ext. 243.

ASSOCIATED BUILDERS AND CONTRACTORS
1300 North 17th Street, Rosslyn VA 22209. 703/812-2000.

ASSOCIATED GENERAL CONTRACTORS OF AMERICA, INC.
1957 E Street NW, Washington DC 20006. 202/393-2040.

ILLUMINATING ENGINEERING SOCIETY OF NORTH AMERICA
120 Wall Street, 17th Floor, New York NY 10005. 212/248-5000.

JUNIOR ENGINEERING TECHNICAL SOCIETY
1420 King Street, Suite 405, Alexandria VA 22314. 703/548-JETS.

NATIONAL ACTION COUNCIL FOR MINORITIES IN ENGINEERING
3 West 35th Street, New York NY 10001. 212/279-2626. Offers scholarship programs for students.

NATIONAL ASSOCIATION OF HOME BUILDERS
1201 15th Street NW, Washington DC 20005. 202/822-0200.

NATIONAL ASSOCIATION OF MINORITY ENGINEERING
435 North Michigan Avenue, Suite 1115, Chicago IL 60611. 312/670-2095, ext. 744.

NATIONAL SOCIETY OF BLACK ENGINEERS
1454 Duke Street, Alexandria VA 22314. 703/549-2207. A nonprofit organization run by college students. Offers scholarships, editorials, and magazines.

NATIONAL SOCIETY OF PROFESSIONAL ENGINEERS
1420 King Street, Alexandria VA 22314-2794. 703/684-2800. 703/684-2830. This number provides scholarship information for students.

SOCIETY OF FIRE PROTECTION ENGINEERS
1 Liberty Square, Boston MA 02109-4825. 617/482-0686.

UNITED ENGINEERING TRUSTEES
345 East 47th Street, New York NY 10017. 212/705-7000.

Directories

DIRECTORY OF ENGINEERING SOCIETIES
American Association of Engineering Societies, 1111 19th Street NW, Suite 608, Washington DC 20036. 202/296-2237. $185.00. Lists other engineering association members, publications, and convention exhibits.

DIRECTORY OF ENGINEERS IN PRIVATE PRACTICE
National Society of Professional Engineers, 1420 King Street, Alexandria VA 22314. 703/684-2800. $50.00. Lists members and companies.

ENCYCLOPEDIA OF PHYSICAL SCIENCES & ENGINEERING INFORMATION SOURCES
Gale Research Inc., 835 Penobscot Building, Detroit MI 48226. 313/961-2242. $155.00. Offers on-line databases, several topics on physical engineering, and different ways to obtain information on physical engineering.

Magazines

THE CAREER ENGINEER
National Society of Black Engineers, 1454 Duke Street, Alexandria VA 22314. 703/549-2207.

CAREERS AND THE ENGINEER
Adams Media Corporation, 260 Center Street, Holbrook MA 02343. 617/767-8100.

CHEMICAL & ENGINEERING NEWS
American Chemical Society 1155 16th Street NW, Washington DC 20036. 202/872-4600.

COMPUTER-AIDED ENGINEERING
Penton Publishing, 1100 Superior Avenue, Cleveland OH 44114. 216/696-7000.

EDN CAREER NEWS
Cahners Publishing Company, 275 Washington Street, Newton MA 02158. 617/964-3030.

ENGINEERING TIMES
National Society of Professional Engineers, 1420 King Street, Alexandria VA 22314. 703/684-2800.

NAVAL ENGINEERS JOURNAL
American Society of Naval Engineers, 1452 Duke Street, Alexandria VA 22314. 703/836-6727. Subscription: $48.

ARTS AND ENTERTAINMENT/RECREATION

Job opportunities in the entertainment and recreation industries are projected to increase 39 percent to the year 2005, faster than the average for all industries. Higher incomes, growth of leisure time, and increasing awareness of the health benefits of physical fitness will effect employment growth.

The market for leisure activities is changing. In the past, amusement and recreation services catered those in their 20s and 30s who had steadily growing incomes. Now that those baby boomers have grown up, companies are targeting adults between 50 and 75 years old.

The performing arts sector will increase with growing population and rising interest in the arts. Producing, acting, directing, and entertaining jobs will grow much faster than average through 2005. Even so, competition will be as intense as ever.

Amusement and theme parks should experience steady growth and offer many seasonal and part-time job opportunities. Virtually all jobs in the industry should experience job growth, with the exception of communications equipment operators, and typists and word processors. The decline in these jobs will result from new technology that will allow fewer workers to do more work.

AMERICAN SYMPHONY ORCHESTRA LEAGUE
1156 15th Street, Suite 800, Washington DC 20003. 202/628-0099. **Contact:** Sheila Kates, Personnel and Operations Manager. **Description:** A national service organization for America's professional symphony orchestras. **Special Programs:** Internships.

ARENA STAGE
Sixth and Main Avenue Southwest, Washington DC 20024. 202/554-9066. **Fax:** 202/488-4056. **Contact:** Human Resources. **Description:** A resident theater company formed around a core of resident actors, craftspeople, theater technicians, and administrators. **Common positions include:** Customer Service Representative; Public Relations Specialist. **Educational backgrounds include:** Art/Design; Liberal Arts; Theatre. **Benefits:** Disability Coverage; Life Insurance; Medical Insurance; Pension Plan. **Special Programs:** Internships. **Operations at this facility include:** Production. **Number of employees at this location:** 120.

ASSATEAGUE ISLAND NATIONAL SEASHORE
7206 National Seashore Lane, Berlin MD 21811. 410/641-1723. **Contact:** Personnel Specialist. **Description:** Assateabue Island National Seashore is protected by an organization committed to preserving the natural environment.

BOWL AMERICA INC.
6446 Edsall Road, Alexandria VA 22312. 703/941-6300. **Contact:** Human Resources. **Description:** Operates bowling alleys.

FRIENDS OF THE NATIONAL ZOO (FONZ)
National Zoological Park, Washington DC 20008. 202/673-4974. **Fax:** 202/673-4890. **Contact:** Joan Heavey, HR Director, Angela DaNeen and Mark Queener, Recruiters. **Description:** The national zoo. **Common positions include:** Clerical Supervisor; Forester/Conservation Scientist; Human Resources Specialist; Management Trainee; Preschool Worker; Restaurant/Food Service Manager; Transportation/Traffic Specialist. **Educational backgrounds include:** Biology; Liberal Arts; Marketing. **Benefits:** Dental Insurance; Disability Coverage; Employee Discounts; Life Insurance; Medical Insurance; Pension Plan; Profit Sharing; Savings Plan; Tuition Assistance. **Special Programs:** Internships; Training Programs. **Corporate headquarters location:** This Location.

Operations at this facility include: Administration; Research and Development; Sales; Service. **Listed on:** Privately held. **Number of employees at this location:** 500.

NATIONAL AQUARIUM IN BALTIMORE
Pier Three, 501 East Pratt Street, Baltimore MD 21202. 410/576-8236. **Recorded Jobline:** 410/576-3800. **Contact:** Human Resources. **Description:** An aquarium focused on environmental conservation.

NATIONAL ENDOWMENT FOR THE ARTS
1100 Pennsylvania Avenue, Washington DC 20506. 202/682-5400. **Recorded Jobline:** 202/682-5799. **Contact:** Human Resources. **Description:** An organization which fosters artistic excellence in the U.S. through a series of grants.

NATIONAL ENDOWMENT FOR THE HUMANITIES
1100 Pennsylvania Avenue NW, Washington DC 20506. 202/606-8438. **Recorded Jobline:** 202/606-8281. **Contact:** Human Resources. **Description:** Supports programs in the humanities through a series of grants.

NATIONAL MUSEUM OF AFRICAN ART
950 Independence Avenue Southwest, Washington DC 20650. 202/357-4600. **Fax:** 202/357-4879. **Contact:** Human Resources. **Description:** A museum devoted exclusively to the collection, study, and exhibition of African art. An important research and reference center, the museum houses a collection of over 6,000 objects, a library, photographic archives, and a conservation laboratory. **Educational backgrounds include:** Art/Design; Liberal Arts. **Parent company:** Smithsonian Institution.

NATIONAL MUSEUM OF AMERICAN HISTORY
14th Street and Constitution Avenue, Room 1040 MRC 605, Washington DC 20560. 202/357-1606. **Contact:** Human Resources. **Description:** A museum that investigates, interprets, collects, preserves, exhibits, and honors the heritage of the American people.

PLAYTIME
10580 Main Street, Fairfax VA 22030. 703/273-4245. **Contact:** Human Resources. **Description:** An amusement center.

RINGLING BROS.
BARNUM & BAILEY COMBINED SHOWS, INC.
8607 Westwood Center Drive, Vienna VA 22182. 703/448-4000. **Contact:** Gary Baron, Office Manager. **Description:** Operates circuses, television production, and ice shows.

SMITHSONIAN INSTITUTION
OFFICE OF HUMAN RESOURCES
955 L'Enfant Plaza Southwest, Suite 2100, Washington DC 20560. 202/287-3100. **Fax:** 202/287-3088. **Recorded Jobline:** 202/287-3102. **Contact:** Human Resources. **Description:** An independent federal establishment devoted to research, public education, and national service in the arts, sciences and history. Established in 1846. **Common positions include:** Accountant/Auditor; Administrative Services Manager; Advertising Clerk; Aerospace Engineer; Agricultural Engineer; Agricultural Scientist; Architect; Attorney; Biological Scientist/Biochemist; Biomedical Engineer; Blue-Collar Worker Supervisor; Budget Analyst; Chemist; Civil Engineer; Clerical Supervisor; Clinical Lab Technician; Computer Programmer; Computer Systems Analyst; Construction and Building Inspector; Construction Contractor and Manager; Cost Estimator; Counselor; Designer; Draftsperson; Editor; Education Administrator; Electrical/Electronics Engineer; Electrician; Financial Analyst; General Manager; Geographer; Geologist/Geophysicist; Health Services Manager; Human Resources Specialist; Human Service Worker; Industrial Engineer; Landscape Architect; Librarian; Library Technician; Management Analyst/Consultant; Mathematician; Mechanical Engineer; Meteorologist; Paralegal; Physicist/Astronomer; Public Relations Specialist; Reporter; Restaurant/Food Service Manager; Science Technologist; Sociologist; Statistician; Structural Engineer; Teacher; Technical Writer/Editor. **Educational backgrounds include:** Accounting; Art/Design; Biology; Business Administration; Chemistry; Communications; Computer Science; Engineering; Geology; Liberal Arts; Marketing. **Benefits:** Daycare Assistance; Dental Insurance; Disability Coverage; Employee Discounts; Life Insurance; Medical Insurance; Pension Plan; Savings Plan. **Special Programs:** Internships. **Corporate headquarters location:** This Location.

Arts and Entertainment/Recreation/87

Operations at this facility include: Administration; Research and Development; Service.
Number of employees at this location: 6,000.

TILT
4238 Wilson Boulevard, Arlington VA 22203. 703/524-4917. **Contact:** Human Resources. **Description:** An arcade amusement center.

U.S. HEALTH INCORPORATED
BALLY'S HEALTH & TENNIS CORPORATION
300 East Joppa Road, Baltimore MD 20783. 410/296-8800. **Contact:** Human Resources. **Description:** Bally's Health & Tennis Corporation, through the subsidiaries which it controls, is one of the largest (and the only nationwide) commercial operators of fitness centers in the United States in terms of revenues, members, and number and square footage of facilities. Bally's Health & Tennis operates 332 fitness centers located in 27 states with approximately 4.2 million members. The fitness centers operate under the 'Bally's' name in conjuction with various well-recognized names, including Holiday Health, Jack LaLanne, Holiday Spa, Chicago Health Clubs, Scandinavian, President's First Lady, Vic Tanny, and Aerobics Plus, and The Vertical Clubs. Most of the company's fitness centers are located in major metropolitan markets in the United States, including Los Angeles, New York, Chicago, Washington, D.C., Philadelphia, Houston, Dallas, Minneapolis, Detroit, Miami, Atlanta, Cleveland, Seattle, Phoenix and Denver. In addition, the company operates four fitness centers in Canada. Parent company, Bally Entertainment, and its subsidiaries also control the operation of casinos, some with adjacent hotels and fitness centers. **Parent company:** Bally Entertainment Corporation.

THE WALTERS GALLERY
600 North Charles Street, Baltimore MD 21201. 410/547-9000. **Fax:** 410/783-7969. **Contact:** Human Resources. **Description:** An art museum holding the private collections of William and Henry Walters. The Walters Gallery sponsors traveling and special exhibitions to supplement the Walters' original collections. Established in 1931.

Note: Because addresses and telephone numbers of smaller companies change rapidly, we recommend you call each company to verify the information below before inquiring about job opportunities. Mass mailings are not recommended.

Additional employers with under 250 employees:

SPORTING AND RECREATIONAL CAMPS

Kenwood Schools Summer Day Camp
4955 Sunset Ln, Annandale VA 22003-6041. 703/256-4712.

MOTION PICTURE THEATERS

Hagerstown Cinema 10
Leitersburg Pke, Hagerstown MD 21740. 301/797-4747.

Movies 1 Thru 9 At Golden Ring
Golden Ring Mall, Baltimore MD 21237. 410/574-3333.

THEATRICAL PRODUCERS AND SERVICES

John F Kennedy Center For The Arts
New Hampshire Ave, Washington DC 20566. 202/416-8000.

Toby's Dinner Theatre-Columbia
PO Box 1003, Columbia MD 21044-0020. 410/730-8311.

MOTION PICTURE AND VIDEO TAPE PRODUCTION AND DISTRIBUTION

Development Communications Inc.
1800 N Beauregard St, Alexandria VA 22311-1708. 703/379-1200.

Projection Video Services
3922 Vero Rd, Baltimore MD 21227-1518. 410/646-0504.

ENTERTAINERS AND ENTERTAINMENT GROUPS

Baltimore Symphony Orchestra
1212 Cathedral St, Baltimore MD 21201-5545. 410/783-8000.

Bud Forrest Entertainment
4444 Chase Park Ct, Annandale VA 22003-5729. 703/941-4440.

Sound Center Deejays
4918 Van Walbeek Pl, Annandale VA 22003-6025. 703/354-5471.

White House Music & Entertainment
4216 Annandale Rd, Annandale VA 22003-3014. 703/256-8382.

PHYSICAL FITNESS FACILITIES

Brick Bodies Fitness Services Inc.
200 W Padonia Rd, Timonium MD 21093-6925. 410/252-8058.

Diet Center of Annapolis
31 Old Solomons Island Rd, Annapolis MD 21401-3840. 301/261-8011.

PUBLIC GOLF COURSES

Baltimore Municipal Golf Corporation
6131 Hillen Rd, Baltimore MD 21239-2443. 410/444-4933.

River Run Golf Community
11620 Masters Ln, Berlin MD 21811-3217. 410/641-7200.

AMUSEMENT PARKS

Trimpers Windsor Resort Inc.
PO Box 157, Ocean City MD 21842-0157. 410/289-8617.

Discovery Zone
527 Baltimore Pke, Bel Air MD 21014. 410/836-0022.

Michaels Enterprises
3118 Washington Blvd, Arlington VA 22210-9998. 703/527-5800.

MEMBERSHIP SPORTS AND RECREATION CLUBS

Courts Royal Annandale
4317 Ravensworth Rd, Annandale VA 22003-5631. 703/256-6600.

Sport & Health Clubs
1800 Old Meadow Rd, Mc Lean VA 22102-1819. 703/556-6550.

Burke Indoor Raquet Swim Club
6001 Burke Commons Rd, Burke VA 22015-2806. 703/425-7270.

Washington Tennis Center
1524 Spring Hill Rd, Mc Lean VA 22102. 703/356-0335.

AMUSEMENT AND RECREATION SERVICES

DC Lottery & Charitable Games
2101 Martin Luther King Jr Ave, Washington DC 20020-5731. 202/433-8000.

U.S. Wushu Academy
2844 Hartland Rd, Falls Church VA 22043-3526. 703/698-8182.

Baldwin Oaks Pool
12500 Racquet Cir, Manassas VA 22111. 703/361-9382.

M E Associates
2230 George C Marshall Dr, Falls Church VA 22043-2529. 703/876-9545.

MUSEUMS AND ART GALLERIES

Maryland Science Center
601 Light St, Baltimore MD 21230-3812. 410/685-2370.

National Air and Space Museum
Sixth St & Independence Ave Sw, Washington DC 20560. 202/357-2700.

Washington National Cathedral
Wisconsin & Massachusetts Aves, Washington DC 20016. 202/537-6200.

BOTANICAL AND ZOOLOGICAL GARDENS

The Baltimore Zoo
Druid Hill Park, Baltimore MD 21217. 410/366-5466.

United States Botanic Garden
4700 Shepherd Pky Sw, Washington DC 20032-5203. 202/225-6420.

For more information on career opportunities in arts, entertainment and recreation:

Associations

ACTOR'S EQUITY ASSOCIATION
165 West 46th Street, New York NY 10036. 212/869-8530.

AMERICAN ALLIANCE FOR THEATRE AND EDUCATION
Division of Performing Arts, Virginia Tech, Blacksburg VA 24061-0141. 703/231-5335.

AMERICAN ASSOCIATION OF MUSEUMS
1225 I Street NW, Suite 200, Washington DC 20005. 202/289-1818.

AMERICAN COUNCIL FOR THE ARTS
1 East 53rd Street, New York NY 10022. 212/223-2787.

AMERICAN CRAFTS COUNCIL
72 Spring Street, New York NY 10012. 212/274-0630.

AMERICAN DANCE GUILD
31 West 21st Street, New York NY 10010. 212/627-3790.

AMERICAN FEDERATION OF MUSICIANS
1501 Broadway, Suite 600, New York NY 10036. 212/869-1330.

AMERICAN FEDERATION OF TELEVISION AND RADIO ARTISTS
260 Madison Avenue, New York NY 10016. 212/532-0800. Membership required.

AMERICAN FILM INSTITUTE
John F. Kennedy Center for the Performing Arts, Washington DC 20566. 202/828-4000.

AMERICAN GUILD OF MUSICAL ARTISTS
1727 Broadway, New York NY 10019. 212/265-3687.

AMERICAN MUSIC CENTER
30 West 26th Street, Suite 1001, New York NY 10010. 212/366-5260.

AMERICAN SOCIETY OF COMPOSERS, AUTHORS, AND PUBLISHERS (ASCAP)
1 Lincoln Plaza, New York NY 10023. 212/595-3050.

AMERICAN SYMPHONY ORCHESTRA LEAGUE
1156 15th Street NW, Suite 4800,, Washington DC 20005. 202/628-0099.

AMERICAN ZOO AND AQUARIUM ASSOCIATION
Oglebay Park, Wheeling WV 26003. 304/242-2160. Produces a monthly newspaper.

ASSOCIATION OF INDEPENDENT VIDEO AND FILMMAKERS
625 Broadway, 9th Floor, New York NY 10012. 212/473-3400.

NATIONAL ARTISTS' EQUITY ASSOCIATION
P.O. Box 28068, Central Station, Washington DC 20038-8068. 202/628-9633.

NATIONAL DANCE ASSOCIATION
1900 Association Drive, Reston VA 22091. 703/476-3436.

NATIONAL ENDOWMENT FOR THE ARTS
1100 Pennsylvania Avenue NW,
Washington DC 20506. 202/682-5400.

NATIONAL ORGANIZATION FOR HUMAN SERVICE EDUCATION
Brookdale Community College, Newman Springs Road, Lyncroft NJ 07738.
908/842-1900, ext. 546.

NATIONAL RECREATION AND PARK ASSOCIATION
2775 South Quincy Street, Suite 300,
Arlington VA 22206. 703/820-4940.

PRODUCERS GUILD OF AMERICA
400 South Beverly Drive, Suite 211,
Beverly Hills CA 90212. 310/557-0807.

SCREEN ACTORS GUILD
5757 Wilshire Boulevard, Los Angeles CA 90036-3600. 213/954-1600.

THEATRE COMMUNICATIONS GROUP
355 Lexington Avenue, New York NY 10017. 212/697-5230.

WOMEN'S CAUCUS FOR ART
Moore College of Art, 20th & The Parkway,
Philadelphia PA 19103. 215/854-0922.

<u>Directories</u>

ARTIST'S MARKET
Writer's Digest Books, 1507 Dana Avenue,
Cincinnati OH 45207. 513/531-2222.

CREATIVE BLACK BOOK
866 3rd Avenue, 3rd Floor, New York NY 10022. 212/254-1330.

PLAYERS GUIDE
165 West 46th Street, New York NY 10036. 212/869-3570.

ROSS REPORTS TELEVISION
Television Index, Inc., 40-29 27th Street,
Long Island City NY 11101. 718/937-3990.

<u>Magazines</u>

AMERICAN ARTIST
One Astor Place, 1515 Broadway, New York NY 10036. 212/764-7300. 800/346-0085, ext. 477.

AMERICAN CINEMATOGRAPHER
American Society of Cinematographers,
P.O. Box 2230, Hollywood CA 90028.
213/969-4333.

ART BUSINESS NEWS
Myers Publishing Co., 19 Old Kings Highway South, Darien CT 06820.
203/656-3402.

ART DIRECTION
10 East 39th Street, 6th Floor, New York NY 10016. 212/889-6500.

ARTFORUM
65 Bleecker Street, New York NY 10012.
212/475-4000.

ARTWEEK
12 South First Street, Suite 520, San Jose CA 95113. 408/279-2293.

AVISO
American Association of Museums, 1225 I Street NW, Suite 200, Washington DC 20005. 202/289-1818.

BACK STAGE
1515 Broadway, New York NY 10036.
212/764-7300.

BILLBOARD
Billboard Publications, Inc., 1515 Broadway,
New York NY 10036. 212/764-7300.

CASHBOX
157 West 57th Street, Suite 503, New York NY 10019. 212/245-4224.

CRAFTS REPORT
300 Water Street, Wilmington DE 19801.
302/656-2209.

DRAMA-LOGUE
P.O. Box 38771, Los Angeles CA 90038.
213/464-5079.

HOLLYWOOD REPORTER
5055 Wilshire Boulevard, 6th Floor, Los Angeles CA 90036. 213/525-2000.

VARIETY
249 West 17th Street, New York NY 10011. 212/779-1100. 800/323-4345.

WOMEN ARTIST NEWS
300 Riverside Drive, New York NY 10025.
212/666-6990.

AUTOMOTIVE

The automotive industry saw a big turnaround in 1994, with the sales of new cars and trucks reaching a six-year high. The good news is expected to continue through 1995 and 1996 -- Business Week predicted a 4 percent gain in U.S. car sales in 1995. In fact, potential sales seemed to be limited only by the ability of car companies to produce enough to meet market demand. On the downside, increasing interest rates and rising steel prices are putting pressure on the Big Three automakers to cut costs and boost productivity, so that job increases won't be be quite as dramatic as the increases in sales. According to Ronald Glantz, an analyst at Dean Witter, the overall effect on the automotive industry should be a boost in industry profits from $14.6 billion in 1994 to $19.7 billion in 1995 and $26.8 billion in 1996.

AUTOMOTIVE INDUSTRIES, INC.
East Queen Street, Strasburg VA 22657. 703/465-3741. **Contact:** Betty Stelzl, Manager of Personnel. **Description:** Manufactures and distributes automotive trim and accessories. **Common positions include:** Industrial Engineer; Process Engineer; Quality Control Supervisor.

DRESSER INDUSTRIES INC.
P.O. Box 1859, Salisbury MD 21802-1859. **Contact:** Human Resources. **Description:** Develops, manufactures, markets, and services Globe automobile hoists and Wayne gasoline dispensing systems for the domestic and export markets.

ENTERPRISE LEASING COMPANY
9125 Gaither Road, Gaithersburg MD 20877. 301/670-8649. **Fax:** 301/670-9755. **Contact:** Kris Micari, Personnel Supervisor. **Description:** A nationwide automotive leasing and rent-a-car company with over 2,000 offices coast to coast. Number of employees in the metro DC area: 400 with 52 local offices. **Common positions include:** Management Trainee. **Educational backgrounds include:** Business Administration; Communications; Liberal Arts; Marketing. **Benefits:** 401K; Dental Insurance; Disability Coverage; Employee Discounts; Life Insurance; Medical Insurance; Profit Sharing. **Special Programs:** Internships. **Corporate headquarters location:** St. Louis MO. **Other U.S. locations:** Nationwide; Canada; United Kingdom. **Listed on:** Privately held. **Number of employees at this location:** 250. **Number of employees nationwide:** 12,000.

FLEETWOOD TRAVEL TRAILERS
35 South Street, Hancock MD 21750. 301/678-5521. **Contact:** Human Resources. **Description:** Manufactures travel trailers.

GARDEN STATE TANNING
15717 Clear Springs Road, Williamsport MD 21795-1010. 301/223-7500. **Contact:** Human Resources. **Description:** Garden State Tanning, a part of Hanson's Industrial Division, produces high quality leather for the automobile upholstery. The parent company, Hanson, is a diversified industrial management company with major investments in basic industries, including coal, chemicals, propane, building materials, forest products, tobacco, and material handling. Employing 74,000 people worldwide, Hanson's operating subsidiaries are principally located in the UK and the USA. **Corporate headquarters location:** New York NY. **Parent company:** Hanson.

GENERAL MOTORS/TRUCK & BUS GROUP ASSEMBLY PLANT
P.O. Box 17113, Baltimore MD 21203. 410/631-2000. **Contact:** Human Resources Department. **Description:** A truck and bus body manufacturer.

Automotive/91

MACK TRUCKS INC.
13302 Pennsylvania Avenue, Hagerstown MD 21742. 301/790-5400. **Fax:** 301/790-5599. **Contact:** James K. Leigh, Manager of Human Resources. **Description:** Manufacturer of the Mack Truck powertrain consisting of the engine and transmission. **Common positions include:** Accountant/Auditor; Buyer; Ceramics Engineer; Clerical Supervisor; Computer Programmer; Computer Systems Analyst; Cost Estimator; Designer; Draftsperson; Electrical/Electronics Engineer; Electrician; Financial Analyst; General Manager; Human Resources Specialist; Industrial Engineer; Industrial Production Manager; Management Analyst/Consultant; Materials Engineer; Mechanical Engineer; Metallurgical Engineer; Operations/Production Manager; Purchasing Agent and Manager; Quality Control Supervisor; Registered Nurse; Stationary Engineer. **Educational backgrounds include:** Accounting; Business Administration; Computer Science; Engineering. **Benefits:** 401K; Dental Insurance; Disability Coverage; Employee Discounts; Life Insurance; Medical Insurance; Pension Plan; Profit Sharing; Tuition Assistance. **Corporate headquarters location:** Allentown PA. **Other U.S. locations:** Chicago IL; Baltimore MD; Macungie PA; Winnsboro SC. **Parent company:** Renault. **Operations at this facility include:** Administration; Manufacturing; Research and Development. **Number of employees at this location:** 1,300. **Number of employees nationwide:** 5,800.

TRW SYSTEMS
One Federal System Park Drive, Fairfax VA 22033. 703/968-1000. **Contact:** Personnel Director. **Description:** Nationally, TRW Systems operates in three business segments: Car and Truck Components, which produces chassis, engines, and other components for cars, trucks, buses, farm machinery, and off-highway vehicles as well as a variety of products for the replacement parts market; Electronic and Space Systems, which manufactures electronic components for use in the telecommunications, computer, automotive, and home entertainment industries; and an Industrial and Energy segment, which manufactures tools, fasteners, and bearings for industrial users; pumps and valves used by the petroleum industry; and aircraft components for commercial and military aircraft. **Corporate headquarters location:** Cleveland OH. **Listed on:** New York Stock Exchange.

Note: Because addresses and telephone numbers of smaller companies change rapidly, we recommend you call each company to verify the information below before inquiring about job opportunities. Mass mailings are not recommended.

Additional employers with under 250 employees:

AUTOMOTIVE STAMPINGS

Marada Industries Inc.
151 Airport Dr, Westminster MD 21157-3030. 410/876-8000.

Wheaton Pharmatech
618 Beam St, Salisbury MD 21801-7803. 410/546-6441.

MOTOR VEHICLES AND EQUIPMENT

Bowles Fluidics Corporation
6625 Dobbin Rd, Columbia MD 21045-4700. 410/381-0400.

Friction Inc.
1000 Falls Run Dr, Fredericksbrg VA 22406-1107. 703/371-8010.

Johnson Controls Inc.
1207 Belmar Dr, Belcamp MD 21017-1206. 410/575-7171.

MOTOR VEHICLE EQUIPMENT WHOLESALE

Fredericksburg Auto Auction
4907 Jefferson Davis Hwy, Fredericksbrg VA 22408-4261. 703/898-4900.

Jerry's Chevrolet Inc.
1940 E Joppa Rd, Baltimore MD 21234-2798. 410/661-9100.

The Kunkel Service
331 Baltimore Pike, Bel Air MD 21014. 410/838-3344.

Chantilly Spring Works
102 Wade Dr, Chantilly VA 22021-9600. 703/471-1656.

Leer Truck Accessory Center
9826 Washington Blvd N, Laurel MD 20723-1930. 301/470-4440.

AUTOMOTIVE REPAIR SHOPS

Automotive Excellence
10815 Beaver Dam Rd # C, Cockys Ht Vly MD 21030-2208. 410/771-1871.

Jiffy Lube
Cranberry Mall, Westminster MD 21157. 410/857-9999.

Mr. Wash Lube
3825 Dupont Ave, Kensington MD 20895-2002. 301/933-0916.

Windshields America
8031 Belair Rd, Baltimore MD 21236-5734. 410/661-1300.

For more information on career opportunities in the automotive industry:

Associations

ASSOCIATION OF INTERNATIONAL AUTOMOBILE MANUFACTURERS
1001 19th Street North, Suite 1200, Arlington VA 22209. 703/525-7788.

AUTOMOTIVE AFFILIATED REPRESENTATIVES
25 Northwest Point Boulevard, Suite 425, Elk Grove Village IL 60007-1035. 708/228-1310.

AUTOMOTIVE SERVICE ASSOCIATION
1901 Airport Freeway, Suite 100, P.O. Box 929, Bedford TX 76095. 817/283-6205.

MOTOR VEHICLE MANUFACTURERS ASSOCIATION
7430 2nd Avenue, Suite 300, Detroit MI 48202. 313/872-4311.

NATIONAL AUTOMOTIVE PARTS ASSOCIATION
2999 Circle 75 Parkway, Atlanta GA 30339. 404/956-2200.

NATIONAL INSTITUTE FOR AUTOMOTIVE SERVICE EXCELLENCE
13505 Dulles Technology Drive, Herndon VA 22071. 703/713-3800.

Directories

AUTOMOTIVE NEWS MARKET DATA BOOK
Crain Communications, Automotive News, 1400 Woodbridge Avenue, Detroit MI 48207-3187. 313/446-6000.

WARD'S AUTOMOTIVE YEARBOOK
Ward's Communications, 3000 Town Center, Suite 2750, Southville MI 48075. 810/357-0800.

Magazines

AUTOMOTIVE INDUSTRIES
Chilton Book Co., 201 King of Prussia Road, Radnor PA 19089. 800/695-1214.

AUTOMOTIVE NEWS
1400 Woodbridge Avenue, Detroit MI 48207. 313/446-6000.

WARD'S AUTO WORLD
Ward's Communications, Inc., 3000 Town Center, Suite 2750, Southville MI 48075. 810/357-0800.

WARD'S AUTOMOTIVE REPORTS
Ward's Communications, Inc., 3000 Town Center, Suite 2750, Southville MI 48075. 810/357-0800.

BANKING/SAVINGS AND LOANS

The banking industry has fared well for the past three years. Banks reported record earnings from 1992 to 1995, as low interest rates kept the number of bad loans falling and investment profits rising. The early '90s were also a good time for banking professionals, who, despite numerous mergers and consolidations throughout the industry, avoided the large layoffs that hit workers in other industries. As a result of rising interest rates, however, times had changed by 1995. Analysts argue that there are simply too many banks clogging the market. This glut of banks (over 10,000 in the United States as compared to 60 in Canada), an emphasis on multi-branch banking, and a decline in traditional transactions, have forced banks to consolidate and close branches, which in turn is shrinking employment. Dramatic layoffs, involving tellers, bank office workers, and managers, will continue to take place into the next century.

Banks are also facing increasing competition from brokerage houses, mutual fund groups, and other financial service companies, resulting in a drop in commercial lending. Competition will most likely take the form of innovation, with new technology and delivery systems; of securitization, including the conversion of assets into marketable certificates; and of internationalization, with the elimination of geographic barriers.

CARROLLTON BANK
P.O. Box 1391, Baltimore MD 21203. 410/536-4600. **Contact:** Lois Ward, Senior Vice President. **Description:** Operates a full-service commercial bank. **Common positions include:** Bank Officer/Manager; Bank Teller; Branch Manager; Clerical Supervisor; Customer Service Representative. **Educational backgrounds include:** Accounting; Finance. **Benefits:** Dental Insurance; Disability Coverage; Life Insurance; Medical Insurance; Pension Plan; Savings Plan; Tuition Assistance. **Corporate headquarters location:** This Location.

CHASE MANAHATTAN BANK OF MARYLAND
2 North Charles Street, Baltimore MD 21201. 410/347-0900. **Contact:** Human Resources Department. **Description:** The Chase Manhattan Corporation is a global financial services company. Through its global network, Chase services corporations, financial institutions, governments, and private banking clients. Chase serves individuals with a family of financial products in the United States and has a full-service regional banking business in the New York tri-state market.

CITIBANK
7720 York Road, Towson MD 21204. 410/337-2600. **Contact:** Human Resources. **Description:** Citibank operates a global, full-service consumer franchise encompassing branch banking, credit cards, charge cards, and private banking. Citibank is the world's largest charge card issuer, with almost 50 million cards in circulation. Citibank also issues and services approximately 5 million private-label cards for department stores and retail outlets. The Citibank Private Bank is the largest non-Swiss private bank in the world. Private Bank's offices in 31 countries and territories provide a full range of wealth management services. Citicorp, Citibank's parent company, staffs 82,600 people in over 3,400 locations in 94 countries and territories throughout the world.

CITIZENS BANCORP
14401 Sweitzer Lane, Laurel MD 20707-2922. 301/206-6033. **Contact:** Human Resources. **Description:** Citzens Bancorp is a multibank holding company headquartered in Laurel, Maryland, whose principal subsidiaries are Citizens Bank of Maryland, Citizens Bank of Virginia, and Citizens Bank of Washington, N.A. As a full-service financial institution, Citizens Bancorp offers a wide range of services including retail banking, consumer finance, investments, brokerage and trust services, insurance, mortgages, wholesale banking, and real estate finance.

CITIZENS BANK OF MARYLAND
14401 Sweitzer Lane, Laurel MD 20707. 301/206-6000. **Contact:** Manager, Human Resources. **Description:** A full-service commercial bank, offering checking and savings accounts, NOW accounts, Christmas clubs, certificates of deposit, All-Savers certificates, IRA and Keough accounts, safe-deposit boxes, travelers checks, personal money orders, credit cards; commercial, construction, mortgage, consumer and check credit loans; and money market investment services. Citizen's Bank of Maryland also offers trust services, automatic deposit services, and stock and other securities transactions services, and operates 120 branches in Maryland, DC, and northern Virginia. Assets: $3,000,000,000. **Common positions include:** Accountant/Auditor; Bank Officer/Manager; Branch Manager; Credit Manager; Department Manager; Instructor/Trainer; Management Trainee; Marketing Specialist. **Educational backgrounds include:** Accounting; Business Administration; Economics; Finance; Liberal Arts. **Benefits:** Dental Insurance; Disability Coverage; Life Insurance; Medical Insurance; Pension Plan; Savings Plan; Tuition Assistance. **Special Programs:** Training Programs. **Corporate headquarters location:** This Location. **Operations at this facility include:** Administration; Service. **Listed on:** NASDAQ. **Number of employees at this location:** 1,800. **Parent company:** Citizens Bancorp.

CITIZENS NATIONAL BANK
390 Main Street, Laurel MD 20707. 301/725-3100. **Contact:** Personnel. **Description:** Operates a full-service commercial bank with 16 offices.

COLUMBIA FIRST BANK
1560 Wilson Boulevard, Arlington VA 22209. 703/247-5000. **Contact:** Human Resources. **Description:** A large banking and financial services organization. **Other U.S. locations:** Washington DC.

COMMERCIAL CREDIT
300 St. Paul Street, Baltimore MD 21202. 410/332-3606. **Fax:** 410/332-7972. **Contact:** David Emanuel, Human Resources Representative. **Description:** A consumer financial services company with 830 branch offices across the United States. **Common positions include:** Accountant/Auditor; Branch Manager; Budget Analyst; Clerical Supervisor; Computer Programmer; Computer Systems Analyst; Credit Manager; Customer Service Representative; Financial Analyst; Human Resources Specialist; Management Trainee. **Educational backgrounds include:** Accounting; Business Administration; Computer Science; Finance; Liberal Arts; Marketing. **Benefits:** 401K; Dental Insurance; Disability Coverage; Life Insurance; Medical Insurance; Pension Plan; Tuition Assistance. **Special Programs:** Training Programs. **Corporate headquarters location:** This Location. **Parent company:** Travelers, Inc. **Operations at this facility include:** Administration; Divisional Headquarters; Regional Headquarters. **Listed on:** New York Stock Exchange. **Number of employees at this location:** 450. **Number of employees nationwide:** 4,000.

CRESTAR BANK
7500 Wisconsin Avenue, Bethesda MD 20814. 301/718-9200. **Contact:** Manager. **Description:** Operates a full-service commercial bank with 10 area branches. **Corporate headquarters location:** This Location.

CRESTAR BANK N.A.
1445 New York Avenue NW, 5th Floor, Washington DC 20005-2108. 202/879-6000. **Contact:** Human Resources Department. **Description:** A bank.

EXPORT-IMPORT BANK OF THE UNITED STATES
811 Vermont Avenue NW, Room 1005, Washington DC 20571. 202/565-3300. **Fax:** 202/565-3627. **Recorded Jobline:** 202/565-3946. **Contact:** Human Resources Office. **Description:** An agency of the federal government, the bank provides assistance to American exporters through loans, guarantees, and insurance programs. **Common**

Banking/Savings and Loans/95

positions include: Accountant/Auditor; Computer Programmer; Economist/Market Research Analyst; Financial Analyst. **Educational backgrounds include:** Accounting; Economics; Finance. **Benefits:** Life Insurance; Medical Insurance; Pension Plan. **Special Programs:** Internships. **Corporate headquarters location:** This Location.

FARMER AND MECHANICS NATIONAL BANK
P.O. Box 518, 110 Thomas Johnson Drive, Frederick MD 21705. 301/694-4000. **Contact:** Human Resources. **Description:** A commercial bank.

FIRST AMERICAN BANK SHARES
740 15th Street NW, Washington DC 20005. 202/383-1400. **Contact:** Human Resources. **Description:** A financial institution.

FIRST FIDELITY BANK
P.O. Box 896, Baltimore MD 21202-1674. 410/783-6604. **Contact:** Linda Coppidge, Personnel Director. **Description:** A commercial banking and financial services institution.

FIRST MARYLAND BANCORP
25 South Charles Street, Baltimore MD 21201-3330. 410/244-4000. **Contact:** Human Resources. **Description:** First Maryland Bancorp's shares of common stock have been wholly owned by Allied Irish Banks plc (AIB) of Dublin, Ireland since 1983. First Maryland offers customer services such as savings, loans, and investments as well as credit cards and supermarket cards. In 1992, First Maryland was selected by the U.S. Treasury Department to develop a product called Taxlink which allowed businesses to pay Federal taxes electronically.

FIRST NATIONAL BANK OF MARYLAND
25 South Street, Baltimore MD 21201. 410/347-6911. **Contact:** Employment. **Description:** Operates a full-service commercial bank with 11 area branch offices. **Corporate headquarters location:** This location. **Number of employees nationwide:** 4,000.

FIRST NATIONAL BANK OF MARYLAND
110 South Paca Street, Baltimore MD 21201. 410/347-6000. **Recorded Jobline:** 410/347-6562. **Contact:** Stephen J. Tacka, Vice President, Employment. **Description:** A full-service commercial bank. Jobline outside Baltimore area: 800/424-4864. **Corporate headquarters location:** 25 South Street, Baltimore MD 21201. 410/347-6911. **Number of employees nationwide:** 4,000.

FIRST NATIONAL BANK OF MARYLAND
P.O. Box 60, 14700 Main Street, Upper Marlboro MD 20773. 301/952-5600. **Contact:** Carolynn Yotes, Vice President/Personnel Director. **Description:** A full-service commercial bank. **Corporate headquarters location:** Baltimore, MD. **Number of employees nationwide:** 4,000.

FIRST UNION NATIONAL
740 15th Street NW, Washington DC 20005. 202/637-7649. **Contact:** Personnel Department. **Description:** An area savings and loan institution.

FIRST UNION NATIONAL BANK OF VIRGINIA
1970 Chain Bridge Road, McLean VA 22102. 703/821-7777. **Contact:** Human Resources. **Description:** A bank.

FIRST VIRGINIA BANKS INC.
6400 Arlington Boulevard, Falls Church VA 22042. 703/241-3657. **Contact:** Human Resources. **Description:** A multibank holding company with assets of $7.2 billion. Subsidiaries include 20 member banks with 269 offices in Virginia, 37 in Maryland, and 23 in Tennessee, as well as some in Washington DC. **Corporate headquarters location:** This Location. **Listed on:** New York Stock Exchange.

HOUSEHOLD BANK
1352 Charwood Road, Suite A, Hanover MD 27076. **Contact:** Alicia Gutierrez, Human Resources Assistant. **Description:** A full-service savings bank.

HOUSEHOLD BANK
1311 Dolley Madison Boulevard, McLean VA 22101. 703/556-7785. **Contact:** Director of Recruitment. **Description:** A full-service savings bank. **Common positions**

include: Accountant/Auditor; Bank Officer/Manager; Branch Manager; Computer Programmer; Customer Service Representative; Financial Analyst; Insurance Agent/Broker; Loan Officer; Management Trainee; Manufacturer's/Wholesaler's Sales Rep.; Secretary; Underwriter/Assistant Underwriter. **Educational backgrounds include:** Accounting; Business Administration; Communications; Finance; Liberal Arts; Marketing; Mathematics. **Benefits:** Dental Insurance; Life Insurance; Medical Insurance; Paid Vacation; Profit Sharing; Tuition Assistance. **Corporate headquarters location:** This Location.

INTER-AMERICAN DEVELOPMENT BANK
1300 New York Avenue NW, Washington DC 20577. 202/623-1000. **Contact:** Human Resources. **Description:** A development bank corporation.

LOYOLA CAPITAL CORPORATION
1300 North Charles Street, Baltimore MD 21201-5705. 410/332-7000. **Contact:** Human Resources. **Description:** Loyola Capital Corporation is the holding company for Loyola F.S.B., a community banking and financial services enterprise headquartered in Baltimore and serving customers in Maryland, Virginia, Delaware, Pennsylvania, South Carolina, Florida and the District of Columbia. Since its founding in 1879 as a thrift institution, Loyola has become a $2.47 billion diversified financial services institution. Services include small business financing, financial planning, mutual funds, insurance products, consumer checking, and deposit and credit card products.

LOYOLA FEDERAL SAVINGS BANK
1300 North Charles Street, Baltimore MD 21201. 410/332-7000. **Contact:** John Shobert, Human Resources Director. **Description:** A financial services and savings institution headquartered in Baltimore, and serving customers in Maryland, Virginia, Delaware, Pennsylvania, South Carolina, Florida, and the District of Columbia. **Number of employees at this location:** 800.

MARYLAND FEDERAL SAVINGS AND LOAN ASSOCIATION
3505 Hamilton Street, Hyattsville MD 20782. 301/779-1200. **Contact:** Nancy Cohen, Senior Vice President. **Description:** Operates a savings bank with 20 branch offices. **Common positions include:** Accountant/Auditor; Bank Officer/Manager; Bank Teller; Branch Manager; Computer Programmer; Credit Manager; Customer Service Representative; Department Manager; Financial Analyst; Human Resources Specialist; Management Trainee; Systems Analyst. **Educational backgrounds include:** Accounting; Business Administration; Economics; Finance; Liberal Arts; Marketing. **Benefits:** Disability Coverage; Employee Discounts; Life Insurance; Medical Insurance; Pension Plan; Stock Option; Tuition Assistance. **Special Programs:** Training Programs. **Corporate headquarters location:** This Location.

MARYLAND NATIONAL BANK/MNC FINANCIAL
100 South Charles Street, 1st Floor, Baltimore MD 21201. 410/605-5000. **Contact:** Employment Office. **Description:** A diversified full-service regional institution which delivers a broad range of commercial and consumer banking services in Maryland, the District of Columbia, Delaware, Pennsylvania, and Virginia. MNC Financial is the corporate parent of Maryland National Bank, Maryland Bank NA (MBNA), and MNC Affiliates Group. MNC ranks among the largest U.S. bank holding companies.

MARYLAND NATIONAL MORTGAGE COMPANY
111 Market Place, Baltimore MD 21202-4012. 410/244-5500. **Contact:** Human Resources. **Description:** A mortgage company.

MERCANTILE BANCSHARES CORPORATION
MERCANTILE SAFE DEPOSIT & TRUST
750 Old Hammonds Ferry Road, Linthicum MD 21090. 410/347-8260. **Contact:** Kelly Krebs, Human Resources Representative. **Description:** A bank holding company controlling 11 Maryland general commercial banks, including the Mercantile Safe Deposit & Trust, Bank of Southern Maryland, and Potomac Valley Bank, as well as other operations in mortgage, banking, commercial and consumer financing, and insurance. Mercantile Bancshares operates through subsidiaries -- more than eighty branch banking offices throughout Maryland. **Common positions include:** Accountant/Auditor; Administrator; Bank Officer/Manager; Budget Analyst; Buyer; Computer Programmer; Computer Systems Analyst; Customer Service Representative; Financial Analyst; Management Trainee; Operations/Production Manager; Systems Analyst. **Educational backgrounds include:** Accounting; Business Administration; Communications; Computer Science; Economics; Finance; Liberal Arts. **Benefits:**

401K; Dental Insurance; Disability Coverage; Life Insurance; Medical Insurance; Pension Plan; Profit Sharing; Savings Plan; Stock Option; Tuition Assistance. **Corporate headquarters location:** Baltimore MD. **Number of employees at this location:** 400. **Number of employees nationwide:** 5,000.

NATIONS SECURITIES
1801 K Street NW, 2nd Floor, Washington DC 20006. 202/955-8188. **Contact:** Employment. **Description:** Operates a metropolitan bank with seven local branch offices. **Corporate headquarters location:** This Location.

NATIONSBANK
1501 Pennsylvania Avenue NW, Washington DC 20005. 202/624-4000. **Contact:** Personnel Department. **Description:** A large bank with more than 1,800 locations. **NOTE:** Jobseekers, please contact the Human Resources Office in Maryland at 6610 Rock Ledge Drive, 4th Floor, Bethesda, MD, 20817.

NATIONSBANK CORPORATION
6610 Rockledge Drive, Bethesda MD 20817-1876. 301/270-5000. **Recorded Jobline:** 301/897-0547. **Contact:** Employment Manager. **Description:** A large bank with more than 1,800 locations. This location hires for Maryland, Northern Virginia, and the District of Columbia. **Common positions include:** Administrative Worker/Clerk; Bank Officer/Manager; Bank Teller; Credit Manager; Customer Service Representative; Management Trainee. **Educational backgrounds include:** Accounting; Business Administration; Economics. **Benefits:** Dental Insurance; Disability Coverage; Life Insurance; Medical Insurance; Pension Plan; Profit Sharing; Savings Plan; Stock Option; Tuition Assistance. **Other U.S. locations:** FL; GA; SC; TN; TX; VA. **Operations at this facility include:** Administration; Regional Headquarters; Sales; Service. **Number of employees nationwide:** 50,000.

NAVY FEDERAL CREDIT UNION
P.O. Box 3400, Merrifield VA 22119. 703/255-8000. **Recorded Jobline:** 703/255-8800. **Contact:** Human Resources. **Description:** Provides banking and other financial services.

THE PALMER NATIONAL BANK
1667 K Street NW, Washington DC 20006. 202/293-6222. **Contact:** Department of Personnel. **Description:** A small, full-service commercial bank. **Common positions include:** Bank Officer/Manager; Branch Manager; Customer Service Representative; Financial Analyst. **Educational backgrounds include:** Business Administration; Finance. **Benefits:** Dental Insurance; Disability Coverage; Life Insurance; Medical Insurance. **Corporate headquarters location:** This Location. **Parent company:** Palmer National Bancorp. **Number of employees at this location:** 32.

PROVIDENT BANK OF MARYLAND
7210 Ambassador Road, Baltimore MD 21244-7280. 410/281-7280. **Recorded Jobline:** 301/281-7263. **Contact:** Employment. **Description:** Provident Bankshares Corporation is the holding company of Provident Bank of Maryland. A full-service, commercial bank headquartered in Baltimore, Provident has been serving the Baltimore community since 1886 through its branch office system across the region.

RIGGS NATIONAL CORPORATION
P.O. Box 96758, Washington DC 20090. 202/835-6000. **Contact:** Employment Office. **Description:** A bank holding company, Riggs' principal subsidiary is Riggs National Bank, one of the largest banking institution in Washington DC. The bank operates 34 branches in the metropolitan region and has subsidiaries in Miami, FL, London, and Nassau. It also owns Riggs AP Bank, Ltd. in London. Riggs National Bank provides investment advisory services through its subsidiaries in Washington DC, Geneva, and a Bahamian bank and trust company. Riggs National Corporation also operates Riggs National Bank of Virginia with 17 offices in northern Virginia and Riggs National Bank of Maryland with 11 offices. Rigg's Financial Services Group comprises Domestic Private Banking, the Trust Department and Rigg's Investment Management Corporation (RIMCO). The group provides integrated banking, trust and investment management services. For institutions and their workers, Rigg's furnishes investment management, administration and record keeping services for retirement, endowment, capital, operating, and reserve funds. **NOTE:** Resumes should be sent to: Employment Office, 1120 Vermont Avenue NW, Washington, DC 20005.

SIGNET BANK, NA
1850 M Street NW, Washington DC 20036. 202/331-5646. **Contact:** Human Resources Department. **Description:** Signet Banking Corporation, with headquarters in Richmond, Virginia, is a registered multi-bank, multi-state holding company. Signet provides interstate financial services through its four principal subsidiaries: Signet Bank/Virginia, Signet Bank/Maryland, Signet Bank N.A., and Capital One Financial Corporation. Signet is engaged in general commercial and consumer banking businesses, and provides a full range of financial services to individuals, businesses, and organizations through 249 banking offices, 253 automated teller machines and a 24-hour full-service Telephone Banking Center. Signet offers investment services including municipal bond, government, federal agency and money market sales and trading, foreign exchange trading and discount brokerage. In addition, an international operation concentrating on trade finance and specialized services for trust, leasing, asset-based lending, cash management, real estate, insurance and consumer financing are offered. Signet's primary market area is the District of Columbia, Maryland and Virginia. **Corporate headquarters location:** Baltimore, MD.

SIGNET BANK, NA
7799 Leesburg Pike, Falls Church VA 22043. 703/714-5073. **Contact:** Carol Robinette, Assistant Vice President. **Description:** Signet Banking Corporation, with headquarters in Richmond, Virginia, is a registered multi-bank, multi-state holding company. Signet provides interstate financial services through its four principal subsidiaries: Signet Bank/Virginia, Signet Bank/Maryland, Signet Bank N.A., and Capital One Financial Corporation. Signet is engaged in general commercial and consumer banking businesses, and provides a full range of financial services to individuals, businesses, and organizations through 249 banking offices, 253 automated teller machines and a 24-hour full-service Telephone Banking Center. Signet offers investment services including municipal bond, government, federal agency and money market sales and trading, foreign exchange trading and discount brokerage. In addition, an international operation concentrating on trade finance and specialized services for trust, leasing, asset-based lending, cash management, real estate, insurance and consumer financing are offered. Signet's primary market area is the District of Columbia, Maryland and Virginia.**Corporate headquarters location:** Baltimore, MD.

SIGNET BANK/MARYLAND
P.O. Box 1077, Seven St. Paul Street, Baltimore MD 21202-1612. 410/332-5000. **Recorded Jobline:** 410/332-5627. **Contact:** Personnel Administrator. **Description:** Signet Banking Corporation, with headquarters in Richmond, Virginia, is a registered multi-bank, multi-state holding company. Signet provides interstate financial services through its four principal subsidiaries: Signet Bank/Virginia, Signet Bank/Maryland, Signet Bank N.A., and Capital One Financial Corporation. Signet is engaged in general commercial and consumer banking businesses, and provides a full range of financial services to individuals, businesses, and organizations through 249 banking offices, 253 automated teller machines and a 24-hour full-service Telephone Banking Center. Signet offers investment services including municipal bond, government, federal agency and money market sales and trading, foreign exchange trading and discount brokerage. In addition, an international operation concentrating on trade finance and specialized services for trust, leasing, asset-based lending, cash management, real estate, insurance and consumer financing are offered. Signet's primary market area is the District of Columbia, Maryland and Virginia. **Corporate headquarters location:** This Location.

WORLD BANK GROUP
1818 H Street NW, Room 'O' 4146, Washington DC 20433. 202/477-1234. **Contact:** Recruitment Division. **Description:** An international agency responsible for assisting with the development policies of Third World countries.

Note: Because addresses and telephone numbers of smaller companies change rapidly, we recommend you call each company to verify the information below before inquiring about job opportunities. Mass mailings are not recommended.

Additional employers with over 250 employees:

COMMERCIAL BANKS	Farmers National Bancorp Five Church Circle, Annapolis	MD 21401-1926. 410/263-2603.

Banking/Savings and Loans/99

First American Bank Of Md
8401 Colesville Rd, Silver Spring MD 20910-3312. 301/565-7000.

First American Bank Of Va
1751 Pinnacle Dr, Mc Lean VA 22102. 703/821-7777.

SAVINGS INSTITUTIONS

Washington DC Federal Savings Bank
570 Herndon Pky, Herndon VA 22070-5225. 703/478-9100.

CREDIT UNIONS

Agriculture Federal Credit Union
Usda Rm Sm2 South Bldg 14th, Washington DC 20250-0001. 202/479-2270.

Amer. Chem. Society Federal Credit Union
1155 16th St Nw, Washington DC 20036-4800. 202/452-8915.

Bank Fund Staff Federal Credit Union
1818 H St Nw, Washington DC 20433-0001. 202/458-4300.

Budget Federal Credit Union
17th St & Pa Av Nw, Washington DC 20003. 202/638-3562.

Civil Service Federal Credit Union
1919 M St Nw, Washington DC 20036-3505. 202/331-1252.

Coast Guard Federal Credit Union
2100 Second St SW Rm B-814, Washington DC 20593-0001. 202/267-1288.

DC Teachers Federal Credit Union
4250 Connecticut Ave Nw, Washington DC 20008-1173. 202/362-6980.

DC Vamc Federal Credit Union
50 Irving St Nw, Washington DC 20422-0001. 202/745-8266.

Dept. Interior Federal Credit Union
Rm 4043 45 Interior Bldg, Washington DC 20240. 202/208-3936.

Dept. of Justice Federal Credit Union
PO Box 782, Washington DC 20044-0782. 202/842-3200.

Dist. of Columbia Teachers Federal Credit
Ninth & D St Ne, Washington DC 20002. 202/547-4800.

Dist. Govt. Employees Federal Credit
2000 14th St NW 2nd Fl, Washington DC 20009-4473. 202/727-1360.

Geicos Federal Credit Union
5260 Western Ave, Washington DC 20076. 301/986-2082.

Gsa First Federal Credit Union
18th & F Sts NW Rm B101, Washington DC 20405-0002. 202/501-0677.

Gsa Natl. Captl. Federal Credit Union
Seventh & D Sts SW Rm 5021, Washington DC 20407-0002. 202/488-5310.

Hew Federal Credit Union
200 Independence Ave Sw, Washington DC 20201-0004. 202/448-5400.

Ibew 26 Federal Credit Union
6211 N Capitol St Ne, Washington DC 20011-1486. 202/829-5404.

Library Congress Federal Credit Union
PO Box 23766, Washington DC 20026-3766. 202/707-5852.

Locals 25 & 32 Federal Credit Union
1003 K St Nw, Washington DC 20001-4425. 202/638-2152.

NLRB Federal Credit Union
1717 Pennsylvania Ave Nw, Washington DC 20570-0001. 202/254-8776.

PASB World Health Organization Federal Credit Union
525 23rd St Nw, Washington DC 20037-2847. 202/861-3453.

Transit Employees Federal Credit Union
2000 Bladensburg Rd Ne, Washington DC 20018-3603. 202/832-5100.

U.S. Civil Service Federal Credit Union
1900 E St Nw, Washington DC 20006-5100. 202/429-0143.

Veterans Administration
810 Vermont Ave NW Rm C-68, Washington DC 20420. 202/737-6969.

Washington Postal Employees Federal Credit
900 Brentwood Rd NE 2-230, Washington DC 20066-9200. 202/636-4530.

A P A Credit Union
1400 K St Nw, Washington DC 20005-2403. 202/682-6006.

Asbury Credit Union
926 11th St Nw, Washington DC 20001-4408. 202/628-0009.

C W A International Credit Union
501 3rd St Nw, Washington DC 20001-2760. 202/434-1487.

DC Fire Department Credit Union
PO Box 70190, Washington DC 20024-0190. 202/745-2300.

DC Unemployment Credit Union
500 C St Nw, Washington DC 20001-2110. 202/639-1372.

Dhcd Credit Union
1133 N Capitol St Ne, Washington DC 20002-7561. 202/535-1026.

Eastalco Credit Union
5601 Manor Woods Rd, Frederick MD 21701-7947. 301/696-1782.

Education Associations Credit Union
1201 - 16th St NW Rm 104, Washington DC 20036-3207. 202/822-7801.

Hum Credit Union
25 53rd St Ne, Washington DC 20019-6602. 202/398-3411.

Lee Credit Union
PO Box 1741, Washington DC 20013-1741. 202/289-7580.

Maryland General Hospital Credit Union
827 Linden Ave, Baltimore MD 21201-4681. 410/225-8398.

Prince Hall Family Credit Union
PO Box 60695, Washington DC 20039-0695. 202/232-4691.

Queen Of Peace DC Credit Union
3800 Ely Pl Se, Washington DC 20019-3053. 202/581-4986.

Sargent Credit Union
5101 Nannie Helen Burroughs Av, Washington DC 20019-5510. 202/396-1710.

St. Gabriel's Credit Union
26 Grant Cir Nw, Washington DC 20011-4604. 202/726-1965.

Tacomis Credit Union
500 E Street Sw, Washington DC 20436-0003. 202/252-1829.

Washington Typographic Credit Union
4626 Wisconsin Ave Nw, Washington DC 20016-4625. 202/966-5155.

G S Community Hospital Credit Union
1310 Southern Ave Se, Washington DC 20032-4699. 202/574-6810.

G U Credit Union
3700 Reservoir Rd Nw, Washington DC 20007-2100. 202/625-3131.

Georgetown University Credit Union
3700 O Street N W, Washington DC 20057. 202/687-3898.

Napfe Credit Union
1628 11th St Nw, Washington DC 20001-5011. 202/939-6325.

NLRB Credit Union
1099 14th St NW C300, Washington DC 20005-3402. 202/273-4300.

U.S. Customs Service Credit Union
1301 Constitution Ave, Washington DC 20229-0001. 202/927-1650.

Police Credit Union
300 Indiana Ave Nw, Washington DC 20001-2106. 202/727-4262.

Treasury Department Credit Union
PO Box 27301, Washington DC 20038-7301. 202/289-1950.

Agriculture Credit Union
14th and Independence, Washington DC 20250-0002. 202/479-3875.

Transportation Credit Union
400 7th Street S W Pl, Washington DC 20590-0001. 202/366-9400.

Wright Patman Congress Credit Union
PO Box 23267, Washington DC 20026-3267. 202/226-3100.

BRANCHES AND AGENCIES OF FOREIGN BANKS

International Finance
1818 H St N W, Washington DC 20433-0001. 202/477-1234.

OFFICES OF BANK HOLDING COMPANIES

First United Corp.
19 S 2nd St, Oakland MD 21550-1517. 301/334-9471.

Additional employers with under 250 employees:

COMMERCIAL BANKS

Abu Dhabi International Bank
1776 G St Nw, Washington DC 20006-4705. 202/842-8480.

American Security Bank
734 15th St NW # B6 811, Washington DC 20005-1013. 202/624-4179.

American Security Bank
1850 H St NW # 250, Washington DC 20006-3608. 202/624-4950.

American Security Bank
3 Dupont Cir Nw, Washington DC 20036-1162. 202/624-4370.

Banca Commerciale Italiana
1133 21st St Nw, Washington DC 20036-3390. 202/463-7586.

Bank America Business Credit Inc.
400 E Pratt St, Baltimore MD 21202-3116. 410/539-8566.

Dominion Bank of Maryland
7220 Wisconsin Ave Fl 4, Bethesda MD 20814-4812. 301/961-5100.

Fairfax Savings FSB
9038 Liberty Rd, Randallstown MD 21133-3998. 410/521-4300.

Farm Credit Bank of Baltimore
14114 York Rd, Cockys Ht Vly MD 21030. 410/329-5500.

FCNB Bank
PO Box 240, Frederick MD 21705-0240. 301/662-2191.

First Liberty National Bank
1146 19th St Nw, Washington DC 20036-3703. 202/331-7031.

First Union National Bank
1401 New York Ave Nw, Washington DC 20005-2102. 202/537-3595.

First Union National Bank
1325 G St Nw, Washington DC 20005-3104. 202/637-2512.

First Union National Bank
1800 K St Nw, Washington DC 20006-2202. 202/637-2508.

First Union National Bank
1730 Pennsylvania Ave Nw, Washington DC 20006-4706. 202/637-2511.

First Union National Bank
1919 M St Nw, Washington DC 20036-3505. 202/637-2516.

First Union National Bank
1899 L St Nw, Washington DC 20036-3804. 202/624-0488.

First Union National Bank
1300 Connecticut Ave Nw, Washington DC 20036-1703. 202/637-2509.

First United National Bnk & Trst
Thayer Center, Oakland MD 21550. 301/334-8400.

Harford National Bank
8 W Bel Air Ave, Aberdeen MD 21001-3200. 410/272-5000.

John Hanson Savings Bank FSB
16 S Calvert St, Baltimore MD 21202-1305. 410/539-0440.

Mellon Bank
901 Elkridge Landing Rd, Linthicum Hts MD 21090-2920. 410/850-7500.

NCNB Real Estate Lending
201 N Charles St, Baltimore MD 21201-4102. 410/547-9044.

Banking/Savings and Loans/101

Nation Bank
601 13th St Nw,
Washington DC 20005-3807. 202/637-5400.

National Neighbors
1335 P St Nw, Washington DC 20005-3721. 202/986-0240.

Ncnb National Bank
201 N Charles St, Baltimore MD 21201-4102. 410/539-6262.

Perpetual Savings Bank FSB
1901 Pennsylvania Ave Nw, Washington DC 20006-3405. 202/637-4820.

Perpetual Savings Bank FSB
20th & M 1990 St Nw, Washington DC 20036. 202/637-2489.

The Bank of Baltimore
205 W Centre St, Baltimore MD 21201-4562. 410/539-2050.

The First National Bank St. Mary's
PO Box 655, Leonardtown MD 20650-0655. 301/475-8081.

The World Bank
701 18th St Nw, Washington DC 20006-4501. 202/289-9145.

United States First National
1129 20th St Nw, Washington DC 20036-3403. 202/223-4200.

Washington Federal Savings Bank
1680 K St Nw, Washington DC 20006-2801. 202/537-8720.

Washington Federal Savings Bank
1733 I St Nw, Washington DC 20006-2401. 202/537-8300.

Washington Federal Savings Bank
1780 G St Nw, Washington DC 20006-4702. 202/537-8725.

Washington Federal Savings Bank
1901 L St Nw, Washington DC 20036-3506. 202/537-8275.

Abu Dhabi International Bnk Inc.
1020 19th St NW Ste 500, Washington DC 20036-6101. 202/842-7900.

American National Svngs Bnk FSB
211 N Liberty St, Baltimore MD 21201-3978. 410/752-0400.

Atlantic Federal Savings Bank
3005 Solomons Island Rd, Edgewater MD 21037-1413. 410/956-4590.

Baltimore County Svngs Bnk FSB
4208 Ebenezer Rd, Baltimore MD 21236-2198. 410/256-1300.

Banco Do Brasil SA
2020 K St NW Ste 450, Washington DC 20006-1806. 202/857-0320.

Banco Real SA
1800 K St NW Ste 301, Washington DC 20006-2202. 202/452-6870.

Jefferson National Bank
30 Catoctin Cir Se, Leesburg VA 22075-3612. 703/777-5353.

Chevy Chase Savings Bank FSB
14113 Baltimore Ave, Laurel MD 20707-5073. 301/725-7197.

Chevy Chase Savings Bank FSB
2952 Chain Bridge Rd Ste H, Oakton VA 22124-3024. 703/938-7423.

County Banking & Trust
PO Box 100, Elkton MD 21922-0100. 410/398-2600.

Equator Bank Limited
1850 K St NW Ste 390, Washington DC 20006-2213. 202/293-3275.

FCNB Bank
1303 E Patrick St, Frederick MD 21701-3159. 301/662-0660.

Federal Reserve Bank Richmond
502 S Sharp St, Baltimore MD 21201-2498. 410/576-3300.

First American Bank of MD
1st Amr Bk Bldg 200-212 E Lmbd, Baltimore MD 21202. 410/752-7900.

Home Federal Savings Bank
970 15th St Nw, Washington DC 20005-2501. 202/537-8881.

Industrial Bank of Washington
4812 Georgia Ave Nw, Washington DC 20011-4522. 202/722-2000.

International Bank Washington DC
1701 Pennsylvania Ave Nw, Washington DC 20006-5805. 202/452-6500.

Key Federal Savings Bank
7 Gwynns Mill Ct Ste F, Owings Mills MD 21117-3528. 410/363-7050.

Liberty Fed Savings & Loan Association
401 N Howard St, Baltimore MD 21201-3601. 410/752-3070.

Madison & Bradford Fed Svngs
6721 Harford Rd, Baltimore MD 21234-7792. 410/254-3737.

Marshall National Bnk & Trst Co.
8372 W Main St, Marshall VA 22115-3229. 703/364-1555.

Mellon Bank
1901 Research Blvd Fl 5, Rockville MD 20850-3164. 301/217-0600.

Peninsula Bank
11738 Somerset Ave, Princess Anne MD 21853-1239. 410/651-2400.

Peoples Bank of Kent County MD
PO Box 210, Chestertown MD 21620-0210. 410/778-3500.

Peoples Bank of Montross
PO Box 306, Montross VA 22520-0306. 804/493-8031.

Petra International Banking Corporation
Two Lafayette 1133 21st 200, Washington DC 20036. 202/293-2250.

Presidential Savings Bank FSB
1660 K St Nw, Washington DC 20006-2879. 202/223-6500.

Second National Fed Svngs Association
19 S Charles St, Baltimore MD 21201-3327. 410/332-8422.

Southern Financial Fed Svngs Bank
101 W Washington St, Middleburg VA 22117. 703/349-3900.

St. Casimirs Savings Bank
2703 Foster Ave, Baltimore

MD 21224-3814. 410/276-0894.

The Annapolis Banking & Trst Co.
PO Box 311, Annapolis MD 21404-0311. 410/268-3366.

The Bank of Alexandria
PO Box 1727, Alexandria VA 22313-1727. 703/549-8262.

The Columbia Bank
10480 Little Patuxent Pky, Columbia MD 21044-3506. 410/730-5000.

The Forest Hill State Bank
130 S Bond St, Bel Air MD 21014-3836. 410/879-1475.

The Fuji Bank Limited
900 19th St NW Ste 750, Washington DC 20006-2105. 202/467-6660.

The Harbor Bank of Maryland
25 W Fayette St, Baltimore MD 21201-3734. 410/528-1800.

The Industrial Bank Japan Ltd.
1701 Pennsylvania Ave NW

660, Washington DC 20006-5805. 202/835-0455.

The Riggs National Bank of MD
2400 Research Blvd, Rockville MD 20850-3243. 301/417-2000.

Westview Fed Svngs & Loan Association
1000 Ingleside Ave, Baltimore MD 21228-1381. 410/747-6200.

York Federal Savings & Loan Association
2006 Rock Spring Rd, Forest Hill MD 21050. 410/838-5982.

SAVINGS INSTITUTIONS

Piedmont Federal Savings Bank
8700 Centreville Rd, Manassas VA 22110-8411. 703/631-2340.

Vists Federal Savings Bank
1901 K St Nw, Washington DC 20006-1192. 202/223-3042.

Providence Savings and Loan Association
515 Maple Ave E, Vienna VA

22180-4713. 703/938-5900.

CREDIT UNIONS

Municipal Employment Credit Union Baltimore
401 E Fayette St, Baltimore MD 21202-3423. 410/752-8313.

Vista Employees Credit Union
3441 Fairfield Rd, Baltimore MD 21226-1513. 410/355-6200.

OFFICES OF BANK HOLDING COMPANIES

Atlanfed Bancorp Inc.
100 West Rd Ste 201, Baltimore MD 21204-2331. 410/938-8600.

Bank Maryland Corporation
502 Washington Ave, Baltimore MD 21204-4516. 410/494-1000.

George Mason Bankshares
11185 Main St, Fairfax VA 22030-5008. 703/352-1100.

Home Federal Corporation
122-128 W Washington St, Hagerstown MD 21740. 301/733-6300.

For more information on career opportunities in the banking/savings and loans industry:

Associations

AMERICAN BANKERS ASSOCIATION
1120 Connecticut Avenue NW, Washington DC 20036. 202/663-5221. Provides banking education and training services, sponsors industry programs and conventions, and publishes articles, newsletters, and the ABA Service Member Directory.

INDEPENDENT BANKERS ASSOCIATION OF AMERICA
900 19th Street NW, Suite 400, Washington DC 20006. 202/857-3100.

U.S. LEAGUE OF SAVINGS AND LOAN INSTITUTIONS
900 19th Street NW, Suite 400, Washington DC 20006. 202/857-3100.

Directories

AMERICAN BANK DIRECTORY
Thomson Financial Publications, 6195 Crooked Creek Road, Norcross GA 30092. 404/448-1011.

AMERICAN SAVINGS DIRECTORY
McFadden Business Publications, 6195 Crooked Creek Road, Norcross GA 30092. 404/448-1011.

BUSINESS WEEK/TOP 200 BANKING INSTITUTIONS ISSUE
McGraw-Hill, Inc., 1221 Avenue of the Americas, 39th Floor, New York NY 10020. 212/512-4776.

MOODY'S BANK AND FINANCE MANUAL
Moody's Investors Service, Inc., 99 Church Street, First Floor, New York NY 10007. 212/553-0300.

POLK'S BANK DIRECTORY
R.L. Polk & Co., P.O. Box 305100, Nashville TN 37320-5100. 615/889-3350.

RANKING THE BANKS/THE TOP NUMBERS
American Banker, Inc., 1 State Street Plaza, New York NY 10004. 212/943-6700.

Magazines

ABA BANKING JOURNAL
American Bankers Association, 1120 Connecticut Avenue NW, Washington DC 20036. 202/663-5221.

BANK ADMINISTRATION
1 North Franklin, Chicago IL 60606. 800/323-8552.

BANKERS MAGAZINE
Warren, Gorham & Lamont, Park Square Building, 31 St. James Avenue, Boston MA 02116-4112. 617/423-2020.

JOURNAL OF COMMERCIAL BANK LENDING
Robert Morris Associates, P.O. Box 8500 S-1140, Philadelphia PA 19178. 215/851-9100.

BIOTECHNOLOGY, PHARMACEUTICALS, AND SCIENTIFIC R&D

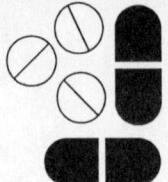

The pharmaceutical industry was characterized by a mass of mergers and acquisitions in 1994, with more of the same expected for 1995 and 1996. Drug companies have also been concentrating on cutting costs, in order to boost profit margins. Many R&D budgets have been slashed as a result. And industry watchers don't expect the arrival of many big-selling new products in the near future. As more patents continue to expire on some of the industry's top-selling drugs, the large pharmaceutical companies that held those patents will see a negative impact on their sales growth. Conversely, the expired patents mean more opportunity for generic drug manufacturers, who should continue to gain market share through 1996.

AMERICAN MEDICAL LABORATORIES, INC.
14225 Newbrook Drive, P.O. Box 10841, Chantilly VA 22021. 703/802-6900. **Recorded Jobline:** 703/802-7282. **Contact:** Human Resources. **Description:** Operated medical laboratories.

ANSER (ANALYTIC SERVICES INC.)
1215 Jefferson Davis Highway, Suite 800, Arlington VA 22202. 703/416-3093. **Contact:** Devette L. Lancon, Senior Employment Administrator. **Description:** An independent, not-for-profit scientific research corporation engaged in program analysis, systems analysis, and operations research for the U.S. Air Force and other government agencies. **Common positions include:** Accountant/Auditor; Aerospace Engineer; Biological Scientist/Biochemist; Budget Analyst; Chemical Engineer; Chemist; Civil Engineer; Computer Programmer; Computer Systems Analyst; Cost Estimator; Economist/Market Research Analyst; Electrical/Electronics Engineer; Environmental Engineer; Financial Analyst; Geologist/Geophysicist; Human Resources Specialist; Industrial Engineer; Mathematician; Mechanical Engineer; Metallurgical Engineer; Physicist/Astronomer; Science Technologist; Software Engineer; Statistician; Systems Analyst; Technical Writer/Editor. **Educational backgrounds include:** Accounting; Computer Science; Economics; Engineering; Mathematics; Physics. **Benefits:** 401K; Dental Insurance; Disability Coverage; Life Insurance; Medical Insurance; Pension Plan; Tuition Assistance. **Special Programs:** Internships; Training Programs. **Corporate headquarters location:** This Location. **Other U.S. locations:** Moscow; Turrance CA; Colorado Springs CO; Tampa FL; Dayton OH; Hampton VA; Newport News VA. **Operations at this facility include:** Research and Development. **Number of employees at this location:** 481.

APPLIED BIOSCIENCE INTERNATIONAL
4350 North Fairfax Drive, Arlington VA 22203-1627. 703/516-2490. **Contact:** Human Resources. **Description:** Applied Bioscience International provides a broad range of services, such as biological safety testing, clinical research and development, management of agrochemical research and development, and the assessment and management of chemical and environmental risks. **Number of employees at this location:** 1,912.

BARRE-NATIONAL INC.
7205 Windsor Boulevard, Baltimore MD 21244. 410/298-1000. **Contact:** Patsy Pasko, Personnel Manager. **Description:** A generic pharmaceutical manufacturer. **Common positions include:** Financial Manager; Quality Control Supervisor; Research/Development Engineer; Supervisor. **Educational backgrounds include:** Biology; Chemistry; Engineering. **Benefits:** Dental Insurance; Disability Coverage; Employee Discounts; Life Insurance; Medical Insurance; Profit Sharing; Savings Plan; Stock Option; Tuition Assistance. **Corporate headquarters location:** Fort Lee NJ. **Parent**

company: A.L. Laboratories. **Operations at this facility include:** Administration; Manufacturing; Research and Development; Sales; Service. **Listed on:** New York Stock Exchange.

BECTON DICKINSON MICROBIOLOGY SYSTEMS
P.O. Box 243, Cockeysville MD 21030. 410/771-0100. **Contact:** L.E. Childress, Human Resources Director. **Description:** Becton Dickson and Company manufactures and sells a broad range of medical supplies and devices and diagnostic systems for use by health care professionals, medical research institutions and the general public. The Diagnostic Division is divided by the Infectious Disease and Cellular Analysis Diagnostics sectors. The Infectious Disease sector provides accurate and timely diagnostic information, which helps target the use of drugs and other therapy. The Cellular Analysis sector provides the products and systems that enable researchers and clinicians to control, regulate and analyze cells and cell functions. The Medical Division is divided into two sectors: Drug Delivery and Technique Products. The Drug Delivery sector provides products that enhance therapy and lower the cost of patient care. The Technique Products sector focuses on products that enhance certain surgical and critical care procedures.

BIOWHITTAKER, INC.
8830 Biggs Ford Road, Walkersville MD 21793. 301/898-7025. **Contact:** Human Resources. **Description:** BioWhittaker, Inc., develops, manufactures, and markets cell cultures, clinical diagnostic tests, and endotoxin detection products. Cell culture products consist of living cell cultures, chemically defined media for the growth of cell culture in the laboratory environment, and cell culture media supplements. The company's clinical diagnostic testing products are used principally by commercial clinical laboratories, hospitals, physician offices, and other testing laboratories to test for infectious diseases, auto-immune diseases, and allergies. The company's entoxin detection products are used by the pharmaceutical industry to test injectable pharmaceuticals and by medical device manufacturers to test implantable medical devices for contamination by entoxins, which are fever-inducing and sometimes fatal substances released by gram negative bacteria.

COLUMBIA RESEARCH CORPORATION
2531 Jefferson Davis Highway, Suite 100, Arlington VA 22202. 703/841-1445. **Contact:** Human Resources. **Description:** A government contractor which is involved in naval and naval logistics research.

CORNING-HAZLETON, INC.
9200 Leesburg Turnpike, Vienna VA 22182. 703/893-5400. **Contact:** Personnel Administrator. **Description:** A life sciences firm, providing biological and chemical research services; also a supplier of laboratory animals and biological products. Clients include research institutes, industrial companies, government agencies, and manufacturers of pharmaceuticals, chemicals, food, and cosmetics. **Common positions include:** Biological Scientist/Biochemist; Chemist. **Educational backgrounds include:** Biology; Chemistry. **Benefits:** 401K; Dental Insurance; Disability Coverage; Employee Discounts; Life Insurance; Medical Insurance; Pension Plan; Profit Sharing; Savings Plan; Tuition Assistance. **Corporate headquarters location:** Heardon VA. **Parent company:** Corning Inc. (Corning, NY). **Operations at this facility include:** Administration; Research and Development. **Listed on:** New York Stock Exchange.

CYTEC ENGINEERED MATERIALS
1300 Revolution Street, Havre de Grace MD 21078. 410/939-1910. **Contact:** Jerry Rath, Personnel Manager. **Description:** A research-based biotechnology and chemical company which develops, manufactures, and markets agricultural, medical, and chemical products throughout the world. The Engineered Materials Department produces adhesive, composite, and structural materials for the aerospace industry. **Common positions include:** Chemical Engineer; Chemist; Mechanical Engineer. **Educational backgrounds include:** Chemistry; Engineering. **Benefits:** 401K; Dental Insurance; Disability Coverage; Life Insurance; Medical Insurance; Pension Plan; Profit Sharing; Savings Plan; Tuition Assistance. **Corporate headquarters location:** West Paterson NJ. **Other U.S. locations:** Anaheim CA. **Parent company:** Cytec Industries Inc. **Operations at this facility include:** Administration; Divisional Headquarters; Manufacturing; Research and Development; Sales; Service. **Listed on:** New York Stock Exchange. **Number of employees at this location:** 225. **Number of employees nationwide:** 5,000.

E.A. LABORATORIES
19 Loveton Circle, Sparks MD 21152. 410/771-4920. **Contact:** Human Resources Department. **Description:** Operates ecological and environmental testing laboratories.

FOGARTY INTERNATIONAL CENTER
NATIONAL INSTITUTES OF HEALTH
900 Rockville Pike, Building 31, Room B2C08, Bethesda MD 20892. **Contact:** Human Resources. **Description:** Encourages the exchange of senior scientists between the U.S. and international countries; coordinates events of the Institutes related to the international health sciences; provides research programs, conferences, and seminars to further international cooperation and collaboration.

GENERAL RESEARCH CORPORATION
1900 Gallows Road, Vienna VA 22182. 703/506-5000. **Contact:** Personnel Administrator. **Description:** Provides applied research and analysis in the following areas: radar and infrared sensors, high-energy lasers, space technology forecasting, space defense systems, management science, operations research, transportation, logistics, strategic studies, economic analysis, cost analysis, management information systems, computer software, database systems, energy, and the environment. GRC's technical staff includes more than 500 degree holding professionals. **Other U.S. locations:** Huntsville AL; Santa Barbara CA. **Parent company:** GRC International.

IIT RESEARCH INSTITUTE
185 Admiral Cochrane Drive, Annapolis MD 21401. 410/573-7223. **Fax:** 410/573-7033. **Contact:** Nate Williams, Administrative Advisor. **Description:** An independent, not-for-profit, contract research and development organization dedicated to solving engineering and scientific problems for government and industry. **Common positions include:** Communications Specialist; Computer Programmer; Computer Systems Analyst; Electrical/Electronics Engineer; Software Engineer. **Educational backgrounds include:** Communications; Computer Science; Engineering; Mathematics; Physics. **Benefits:** 403B; Dental Insurance; Disability Coverage; Life Insurance; Medical Insurance; Pension Plan; Tuition Assistance. **Corporate headquarters location:** Chicago IL. **Operations at this facility include:** Administration; Research and Development. **Number of employees at this location:** 500.

JOHNS HOPKINS UNIVERSITY
THE APPLIED PHYSICS LABORATORY
11100 Johns Hopkins Road, Laurel MD 20723-6099. 301/953-5000. **Contact:** Employment Office. **Description:** A non-profit research and development laboratory, The Applied Physics Laboratory (APL) of The Johns Hopkins University makes contributions in defense, space and biomedicine. APL's primary mission involves national security issues, although the technology developed through defense research is also applied to civil sector problems. **Common positions include:** Communications Engineer; Electrical/Electronics Engineer; Software Engineer; Systems Analyst; Systems Engineer. **Educational backgrounds include:** Physics.

LIFE TECHNOLOGIES, INC.
8400 Helgerman Court, Gaithersburg MD 20884-9980. 301/840-4000. **Fax:** 301/921-2215. **Contact:** Ms. J. Clancy Kress, Human Resources Manager.. **Description:** Life Technologies, Inc., develops, manufactures, and markets more than 4,000 products used principally in life sciences research and the commercial manufacture of genetically engineered products. The company is a supplier of sera and other cell growth media, as well as enzymes and other biological products necessary for recombinant DNA procedures. **Common positions include:** Associate Scientist; Biological Scientist/Biochemist; Chemical Engineer; Chemist; Graphic Artist; Scientist; Technical Writer/Editor. **Educational backgrounds include:** Biology; Engineering; M.I.S. **Benefits:** 401K; Daycare Assistance; Dental Insurance; Disability Coverage; Employee Discounts; Life Insurance; Medical Insurance; Pension Plan; Profit Sharing; Stock Option; Tuition Assistance. **Special Programs:** Internships. **Corporate headquarters location:** This Location. **Other U.S. locations:** Grand Island NY. **Operations at this facility include:** Administration; Divisional Headquarters; Manufacturing; Research and Development; Sales. **Listed on:** NASDAQ. **Number of employees at this location:** 1,400.

MARTIN MARIETTA LABORATORIES
1450 South Rolling Road, Baltimore MD 21227. 410/204-2209. **Fax:** 410/204-2103. **Contact:** Joyce McAleer Robbins, Human Resources Manager. **Description:** Martin

Marietta Laboratories is the central research and development organization for Martin Marietta Corporation, supporting operations in aerospace, defense, communications, information and data management, energy systems, and materials. Research and development activities focus on microelectronics, information processing, and advanced materials. Information and signal processing comprises developments in artificial intelligence, optical signal processing, and neural networks for a variety of applications, including automatic target recognition. These technologies, when combined with sensors and high-speed electronics, offer intelligent electronic subsystems for application to autonomous vehicles, space surveillance, defense, underwater detection, and secure communication. **Common positions include:** Accountant/Auditor; Administrative Services Manager; Aerospace Engineer; Buyer; Ceramics Engineer; Chemical Engineer; Chemist; Computer Programmer; Computer Systems Analyst; Cost Estimator; Editor; Electrical/Electronics Engineer; Electrician; Human Resources Specialist; Library Technician; Materials Engineer; Mechanical Engineer; Metallurgical Engineer; Physicist/Astronomer; Public Relations Specialist; Purchasing Agent and Manager; Science Technologist; Software Engineer; Technical Writer/Editor. **Educational backgrounds include:** Accounting; Business Administration; Chemistry; Communications; Computer Science; Engineering; Finance; Marketing; Physics. **Benefits:** 401K; Dental Insurance; Disability Coverage; Employee Discounts; Life Insurance; Medical Insurance; Pension Plan; Profit Sharing; Savings Plan; Tuition Assistance. **Corporate headquarters location:** Bethesda MD. **Other U.S. locations:** Nationwide. **Parent company:** Lockheed Martin. **Operations at this facility include:** Administration; Research and Development. **Listed on:** NASDAQ; New York Stock Exchange. **Number of employees at this location:** 250. **Number of employees nationwide:** 190,000.

MICROBIOLOGICAL ASSOCIATES INC.
9900 Blackwell Road, Rockville MD 20850. 301/738-1000. **Contact:** Connie Kepner, Director of Personnel. **Description:** Main business operations are biotechnology, molecular virology, toxicology, and genetic toxicology. The toxicology facility is located in Bethesda, MD. **Common positions include:** Animal Handler; Biological Scientist/Biochemist; Maintenance Worker; Secretary; Technical Writer/Editor; Technician. **Educational backgrounds include:** Biology; Immunology; Microbiology; Virology. **Benefits:** 401K; Credit Union; Dental Insurance; Disability Coverage; Life Insurance; Medical Insurance; Savings Plan; Tuition Assistance. **Corporate headquarters location:** This Location. **Operations at this facility include:** Administration; Research and Development.

NATIONAL ACADEMY OF SCIENCES
NATIONAL RESEARCH COUNCIL
2101 Constitution Avenue NW, Washington DC 20418. 202/334-2000. **Contact:** Charlie Starliper, Personnel Department. **Description:** A federally-chartered private corporation of approximately 1,225 members, whose primary aim is to provide an independent source of counsel to the government on matters of science and technology. Academy members are elected. The Academy's research is performed by the National Research Council (NRC). **NOTE:** Maintains a list of professional vacancies which may be viewed at the employment office.

PROGRAM RESOURCES INC.
NCI-FCRDC SAIC, P.O. Box B, Building 371, Frederick MD 21702. 301/846-1146. **Contact:** Robert E. Hardisty, Manager/Human Resources. **Description:** Engaged in biomedical/cancer research. Provides operations and technical support to the National Cancer Institute-Frederick Research and Development Center, including scientific resources; safety, medical and security programs; and business administrative services. **Parent company:** Dyncorp. **Number of employees nationwide:** 1,100.

SCIENCE APPLICATIONS INTERNATIONAL CORPORATION
1710 Goodridge Drive, Room 1408, Mc Lean VA 22102. 703/821-4300. **Contact:** Human Resources. **Description:** A commercial physical and biological research institute.

Note: *Because addresses and telephone numbers of smaller companies change rapidly, we recommend you call each company to verify the information below before inquiring about job opportunities. Mass mailings are not recommended.*

Additional employers with under 250 employees:

MEDICAL AND DENTAL LABORATORIES

Genetics & IVF Institute
3020 Javier Rd, Fairfax VA 22031-4627. 703/698-7355.

Maryland Medical Metpath
5400 Old Court Rd, Randallstown MD 21133-5100. 410/521-3500.

Maryland Medical Metpath
301 Saint Paul Pl, Baltimore MD 21202-2102. 410/576-8380.

Maryland Medical Metpath
1645 Liberty Rd, Sykesville MD 21784-6521. 410/549-1653.

Maryland Medical Metpath
7845 Oakwood Rd Ste 304, Glen Burnie MD 21061-4266. 410/761-0261.

Roche Biomedical Labs
611 Jefferson Davis Hwy, Fredericksbrg VA 22401-4436. 703/373-9673.

Roche Biomedical Labs
4785 Dorsey Hall Dr, Ellicott City MD 21042-7728. 410/964-9530.

Saint Agnes Cardiac Diagnostic Center
724 Maiden Choice Ln, Catonsville MD 21228-5940. 410/455-0200.

RESEARCH AND TESTING

Betac Corporation
2001 N Beauregard St, Alexandria VA 22311-1732. 703/824-3192.

Environmental Protection Systems
3800 Concorde Pky Ste 2100, Chantilly VA 22021-1127. 703/631-2411.

Essex Corporation
1430 Spring Hill Rd, Mc Lean VA 22102-3000. 703/548-4500.

Gillette Capital Corporation
401 Professional Dr, Gaithersburg MD 20879-3432. 301/590-9781.

Mandex Inc.
8003 Forbes Pl, Springfield VA 22151-2215. 703/321-0200.

Planning Systems Inc.
7923 Jones Branch Dr, Mc Lean VA 22102-3304. 703/734-3400.

Prospect Associates Ltd.
1801 Rockville Pike Ste 500, Rockville MD 20852-1683. 301/468-6555.

Radix Systems Inc.
6 Taft Ct, Rockville MD 20850-5331. 301/424-7410.

Rhone Poulenc Research Ctr Inc.
8510 Corridor Rd, Savage MD 20763-9504. 301/498-0812.

Science & Technology Corporation
6410 Dobbin Rd, Columbia MD 21045-4735. 301/621-4433.

Scios Nova Inc.
400 E Pratt St # 300, Baltimore MD 21202-3116. 410/563-6067.

Specialty Brand Inc.
6835 Deer Path Rd, Baltimore MD 21227-6238. 410/796-7644.

Sri International
1611 N Kent St, Arlington VA 22209-2111. 703/524-2053.

Technical Resources
3202 Tower Oaks Blvd Ste 200, Rockville MD 20852-4219. 301/231-5250.

Westvaco Corporation
11101 Johns Hopkins Rd, Laurel MD 20723-6085. 301/497-1300.

Ecoflo Inc.
8520 Corridor Rd # M, Savage MD 20763-9506. 301/498-4550.

McCrone Inc.
Calvert Exec Plaza, Prnc Frederck MD 20678. 410/535-4510.

Professional Service Ind.
806 Barkwood Ct # K, Linthicum Hts MD 21090-1447. 410/789-3548.

R & R International
37 N Philadelphia Blvd, Aberdeen MD 21001-2510. 410/272-1001.

R E Wright Associates
125 Airport Dr Bldg 36, Westminster MD 21157-3021. 410/876-0280.

E-Systems Inc.
141 National Business Pky, Annapolis Jct MD 20701-1026. 301/470-0200.

Pacific-Sierra Research Corporation
1401 Wilson Blvd Ste 1100, Arlington VA 22209-2306. 703/527-4975.

Sky Alland Research
14502 Greenview Dr, Laurel MD 20708-3287. 301/369-2800.

Biotechnology Research Inst.
1330 Piccard Dr Ste A, Rockville MD 20850-4396. 301/258-5200.

Carnegie Instn. of Washington
1530 O St NW Bw, Washington DC 20005-5501. 202/387-6400.

Xsirius Inc.
1110 N Glebe Rd, Arlington VA 22201-4795. 703/522-8600.

Froehling & Robertson
1209 Bernard Dr, Baltimore MD 21223-3373. 410/947-6500.

Pathology Associates
15 Wormans Mill Ct # 1, Frederick MD 21701-8700. 301/663-1644.

Pharmakinetics Labs
302 W Fayette St, Baltimore MD 21201-3451. 410/385-4500.

PHARMACEUTICAL PREPARATIONS

Jason Pharmaceuticals
11445 Cron Hill Dr, Owings Mills MD 21117-2220. 410/581-8042.

Otsuka Amercian Pharmaceuticals Inc. MD
2440 Research Blvd, Rockville MD 20850-3238. 301/990-0030.

BIOLOGICAL PRODUCTS

Medimmune Inc.
35 W Watkins Mill Rd, Gaithersburg MD 20878-4024. 301/417-0770.

North American Vaccine
12103 Indian Creek Ct, Beltsville MD 20705-4223. 301/470-6100.

Univax Biologics Inc.
12280 Wilkins Ave, Rockville MD 20852-1843. 301/770-3099.

For more information on career opportunities in biotechnology, pharmaceuticals, and scientific R&D:

Associations

AMERICAN ASSOCIATION FOR CLINICAL CHEMISTRY
2101 L Street NW, Suite 202, Washington DC 20037-1526. 202/857-0717 or 800/892-1400. International scientific/medical society of individuals involved with clinical chemistry and other clinical labscience-related disciplines.

AMERICAN ASSOCIATION OF COLLEGES OF PHARMACY
1426 Prince Street, Alexandria VA 22314-2841. 703/739-2330. An organization composed of all U.S. pharmacy colleges and over 2,000 school administrators and faculty members. Career publications include: *Shall I Study Pharmacy?*, *Pharmacy A Caring Profession*, and *A Graduate Degree in the Pharmaceutical Sciences: An Option For You?*

AMERICAN COLLEGE OF CLINICAL PHARMACY (ACCP)
3101 Broadway, Suite 380, Kansas City MO 64111. 816/531-2177. Operates ClinNet jobline at 412/648-7893 for both members and non-members, for a fee.

AMERICAN PHARMACEUTICAL ASSOCIATION
2215 Constitution Avenue NW, Washington DC 20037. 202/628-4410. Operates a resume referral service for all members.

AMERICAN SOCIETY FOR BIOCHEMISTRY AND MOLECULAR BIOLOGY
9650 Rockville Pike, Bethesda MD 20814-3996. 301/530-7145. A nonprofit scientific and educational organization whose primary scientific activities are in the publication of the *Journal of Biological Chemistry* and holding an annual scientific meeting. Also publishes a career brochure entitled Unlocking Life's Secrets: Biochemistry and Molecular Biology.

AMERICAN SOCIETY OF HOSPITAL PHARMACISTS
7272 Wisconsin Avenue, Bethesda MD 20814. 301/657-3000.

BIOMEDICAL INDUSTRY COUNCIL
225 Broadway, Suite 1600, San Diego, CA 92101. 619/236-1322.

BIOTECHNOLOGY INDUSTRY ORGANIZATION
1625 K Street NW, Suite 1100, Washington DC 20006-1604. 202/857-0244.

NATIONAL ASSOCIATION OF PHARMACEUTICAL MANUFACTURERS
747 Third Avenue, New York NY 10017. 212/838-3720.

NATIONAL PHARMACEUTICAL COUNCIL
1894 Preston White Drive, Reston VA 22091. 703/620-6390. Organization of leading research-based pharmaceutical companies.

Directories

DRUG TOPICS RED BOOK
Medical Economics Company, 5 Paragon Drive, Montvale, NJ 07645. 201/358-7200.

Magazines

DRUG TOPICS
Medical Economics Company, 5 Paragon Drive, Montvale NJ 07645. 201/358-7200.

PHARMACEUTICAL ENGINEERING
International Society of Pharmaceutical Engineers, 3816 West Linebaugh Avenue, Suite 412, Tampa FL 33624. 813/960-2105.

BUSINESS SERVICES AND NON-SCIENTIFIC RESEARCH

 The business services sector, which includes 16 of the 20 fastest growing industries, covers a broad spectrum of careers, including everything from adjustment and collection services to data processing companies. While the job outlook varies upon which service is being discussed, in general, the business services sector is among the fastest-growing in the nation. Increasingly, American companies are "outsourcing" functions like data processing to outside firms. Often large organizations will go so far as to hand over the management of their entire data center to an outside service provider. This trend is expected to boost opportunities for those who work for data processing services.

Other types of services that benefit from this trend include security, and personnel services firms. Many businesses are using temporary workers instead of hiring new permanent staffers, thus avoiding the much higher overhead costs such as health insurance. Companies that supply these temporary workers, as well as those that place permanent workers, are among the fastest-growing in the nation. While one third of the jobs available are administrative support occupations, there is a growing trend toward specialization which will open up more positions for highly-skilled workers, such as engineers or managers.

ABSTRACT JANITORIAL SERVICES
506 Shaw Road, Sterling VA 20166. 703/709-0773. **Contact:** Human Resources. **Description:** Provides building, cleaning, and maintenance services. **Number of employees at this location:** 250.

ACE-FEDERAL REPORTERS, INC.
1120 G Street NW, Suite 500, Washington DC 20005. 202/347-3700. **Contact:** Mr. Tracy Boylston, Personnel. **Description:** Provides shorthand reporting services.

ALFATECH CORPORATION
6846 Elm Street, McLean VA 22101. 703/442-4552. **Contact:** Human Resources Department. **Description:** Provides professional services contracting and information technology services.

**THE AMERICAN ASSOCIATION
FOR THE ADVANCEMENT OF SCIENCE**
1333 H Street NW, Suite 130, Office of Human Resources, Washington DC 20005. 202/326-6470. **Fax:** 202/682-1630. **Contact:** Dawn Graf, Personnel Coordinator. **Description:** Founded in 1848, the American Association for the Advancement of Science is the world's largest federation of scientific and engineering societies, with nearly 300 affiliate organizations. In addition, AAAS counts more than 142,000 scientists, engineers, science educators, policy makers, and interested citizens among its individual members, making it the largest general scientific organization in the world. Primary operations include the publication of *Science Magazine*. **Common positions include:** Accountant/Auditor; Advertising Clerk; Art Director; Communications Specialist; Computer Graphics Specialist; Editor; Financial Analyst; Financial Manager; Librarian; Marketing/Advertising/PR Manager; Production Manager; Program Manager; Project Manager; Proofreader; Public Relations Specialist; Sales Associate; Services Sales Representative; Technical Illustrator; Writer. **Educational backgrounds include:** Accounting; Art/Design; Biology; Business Administration; Chemistry; Communications; Computer Science; Education; Engineering; English; Finance; International Relations; Liberal Arts; Marketing. **Benefits:** Dental Insurance;

Disability Coverage; Employee Discounts; Life Insurance; Medical Insurance; Retirement Plan; Tuition Assistance. **Corporate headquarters location:** This Location. **Number of employees at this location:** 300.

AMERICAN ASSOCIATION OF UNIVERSITY WOMEN
1111 16th Street NW, Washington DC 20036. 202/785-7700. **Contact:** Personnel Administrator. **Description:** An organization targeting the needs of women in the college community.

AMERICAN BUSING ASSOCIATION
1100 New York Avenue NW, Suite 1050, Washington DC 20005. 202/842-1645. **Contact:** Ken Ryan, Financial Officer. **Description:** An organization representing the inter-city busing industry. **Common positions include:** Administrative Worker/Clerk; Advertising Clerk; Public Relations Specialist. **Educational backgrounds include:** Business Administration; Communications; Liberal Arts. **Benefits:** Dental Insurance; Life Insurance; Medical Insurance; Pension Plan; Tuition Assistance. **Corporate headquarters location:** This Location. **Operations at this facility include:** Administration.

AMERICAN COUNCIL OF LIFE INSURANCE
1001 Pennsylvania Avenue NW, Suite 500, Washington DC 20004-2599. 202/624-2361. **Contact:** Manager of Human Resources. **Description:** A non-profit trade association representing the life insurance industry. **Common positions include:** Actuary; Attorney; Financial Analyst; Legal Writer/Editor; Public Relations Specialist. **Educational backgrounds include:** Accounting; Business Administration; Communications; Computer Science; Economics; Finance; Journalism; Law/Pre-Law; Mathematics. **Benefits:** 401K; Adoption Assistance; Dental Insurance; Disability Coverage; Flextime Plan; Life Insurance; Medical Insurance; Pension Plan; Reimbursement Accts.; Tuition Assistance. **Special Programs:** Internships. **Corporate headquarters location:** This Location. **Operations at this facility include:** Administration; Public Affairs. **Number of employees at this location:** 250.

AMERICAN FEDERATION OF STATE, COUNTY AND MUNICIPAL EMPLOYEES (AFSCME)
1625 L Street NW, Washington DC 20036. 202/452-4800. **Contact:** Marianne Brown, Employment Specialist. **Description:** A million-plus member trade union, representing a wide range of professions at the state, county and municipal government level. Affiliated with the AFL-CIO. **Common positions include:** Accountant/Auditor; Budget Analyst; Computer Programmer; Computer Systems Analyst; Economist/Market Research Analyst. **Educational backgrounds include:** Law/Pre-Law. **Benefits:** 401K; Daycare Assistance; Dental Insurance; Disability Coverage; Employee Discounts; Life Insurance; Medical Insurance; Pension Plan; Savings Plan; Tuition Assistance. **Special Programs:** Internships. **Corporate headquarters location:** This Location. **Operations at this facility include:** Administration. **Number of employees at this location:** 270. **Number of employees nationwide:** 460.

AMERICAN HEALTHCARE ASSOCIATION
1201 L Street NW, Washington DC 20005. 202/842-4444. **Contact:** Kimberly Drabik, Director of Personnel. **Description:** A national association of nursing homes and related long-term care facilities.

AMERICAN PETROLEUM INSTITUTE (API)
1220 L Street NW, Washington DC 20005. 202/682-8000. **Contact:** Bob Cunningham, Human Resources Manager. **Description:** An independent trade association representing all sectors of the domestic petroleum industry; membership includes some 300 companies and approximately 8,000 people engaged in or associated with petroleum operations in the United States, Mexico, and Canada. Membership represents a cross-section of industry operations in the areas of exploration, production, transportation, refining, synthetic fuels, finance, and marketing; also suppliers of equipment and services. Operates through the following offices: Industry Affairs; Public Affairs; Federal Government Affairs; State Relations; Health, Environment, Finance, and Statistics; Policy Analysis; External Liaison; Land Use; Legal Counsel; and two API staff offices primarily concerned with internal operations. **Corporate headquarters location:** This Location.

AMERICAN POSTAL WORKERS UNION
1300 L Street, Washington DC 20005. 202/842-4200. **Contact:** Gary Parrish, Personnel. **Description:** A labor union.

AMERICAN PSYCHOLOGICAL ASSOCIATION
750 First Street Northeast, Washington DC 20002. 202/336-5627. **Contact:** Human Resources. **Description:** APA is a large association of psychologists. Membership includes more than 124,000 researchers, educators, clinicians, and students. APA works to advance psychology as a science, as a profession, and as a means of promoting human welfare. There are divisions in 49 subfields of psychology and affiliations with 57 state and Canadian provincial associations. **Common positions include:** Accountant/Auditor; Administrative Worker/Clerk; Computer Programmer; Customer Service Representative; Lobbyist; Marketing/Advertising/PR Manager; Receptionist; Secretary; Typist/Word Processor. **Educational backgrounds include:** Accounting; Business Administration; Communications; Computer Science; Finance; Liberal Arts; Marketing; Psychology. **Benefits:** Dental Insurance; Disability Coverage; Life Insurance; Medical Insurance; Reimbursement Accts.; Retirement Plan. **Corporate headquarters location:** This Location. **Number of employees at this location:** 450.

AMERICAN TRUCKING ASSOCIATIONS
2200 Mill Road, Alexandria VA 22314. 703/838-1726. **Fax:** 703/836-5880. **Recorded Jobline:** 703/838-1726. **Contact:** Human Resources. **Description:** This national federation of the trucking industry represents all types of trucking companies. It is affiliated with 51 independent state trucking associations and 10 national conferences, which represent particular segments of the trucking industry. The American Trucking Associations (ATA) consist of the Executive Office, the Foundation, and five divisions: Communications, Federation Relations, Law and Finance, Government Affairs, and Membership and Marketing. Included in this structure are seven councils allowing experts in particular aspects of trucking operations to join and interact with their peers. ATA publishes a weekly trade newspaper, *Transport Topics*. **Common positions include:** Customer Service Representative; Marketing Specialist; Transportation/Traffic Specialist; Writer. **Educational backgrounds include:** Accounting; Business Administration; Communications; Economics; Finance; Marketing; Public Policy; Transportation/Logistics. **Benefits:** Dental Insurance; Disability Coverage; Employee Discounts; Life Insurance; Medical Insurance; Pension Plan; Tuition Assistance. **Corporate headquarters location:** This Location. **Operations at this facility include:** Administration; Communications; Legal/Legal Research; Marketing; Publishing; Sales; Service. **Number of employees nationwide:** 302.

ARMS CONTROL ASSOCIATION
1726 M Street NW, Suite 201, Washington DC 20036. 202/463-8270. **Fax:** 202/463-8273. **Contact:** Personnel Department. **Description:** An organization providing information on arms control issues.

ASPEN CORPORATION
APPLIED MANAGEMENT SCIENCES DIVISION
962 Wayne Avenue, Suite 701, Silver Spring MD 20910. 301/585-8181. **Contact:** Kevin Attanaiso, Personnel Director. **Description:** A private, professional services research firm. Established in 1970. Provides a broad range of analytical, technical, and information support services in the energy and environment, defense, health, information and management systems, and human resources fields. These support services reach both the private and public sectors at the national, regional, state, and local levels. **Common positions include:** Accountant/Auditor; Civil Engineer; Computer Programmer; Department Manager; Economist/Market Research Analyst; Electrical/Electronics Engineer; Geological Engineer; Human Resources Specialist; Mechanical Engineer; Petroleum Engineer; Statistician; Systems Analyst; Technical Writer/Editor. **Educational backgrounds include:** Computer Science; Engineering; Mathematics. **Benefits:** Dental Insurance; Disability Coverage; Life Insurance; Medical Insurance; Paid Vacation; Pension Plan; Profit Sharing; Tuition Assistance. **Corporate headquarters location:** This Location. **Operations at this facility include:** Regional Headquarters.

ASPEN SYSTEMS CORPORATION
1600 Research Boulevard, Rockville MD 20850. 301/251-5000. **Contact:** Human Resources. **Description:** Provides information management services. Primary customer is the Federal Government.

BOAT AMERICA CORPORATION
880 South Pickett Street, Alexandria VA 22304. 703/823-9550. **Fax:** 703/461-4395. **Contact:** Employment Manager. **Description:** Provides boating services, including

marine insurance, and representation in Congress to members of Boat/US, the national association of recreational boat owners. **Common positions include:** Adjuster; Management Trainee; Technical Writer/Editor; Underwriter/Assistant Underwriter. **Educational backgrounds include:** Business Administration; Liberal Arts; Marketing. **Benefits:** 401K; Dental Insurance; Employee Discounts; ESOP; Life Insurance; Medical Insurance; Tuition Assistance. **Corporate headquarters location:** This Location. **Other U.S. locations:** 33 locations. **Operations at this facility include:** Administration; Sales; Service. **Number of employees at this location:** 500. **Number of employees nationwide:** 1,000.

THE BROOKINGS INSTITUTION
1775 Massachusetts Avenue NW, Washington DC 20036. 202/797-6210. **Contact:** Cathleen Burke, Personnel Coordinator. **Description:** A private, nonprofit organization devoted to research, education, and publication in economics, government, foreign policy, and the social sciences. Its activities are carried out through three research programs (Economic Studies, Governmental Studies, Foreign Policy Studies); the Center for Public Policy Education; the Social Science Computation Center; and the Publications Program.

CENTER FOR STRATEGIC & INTERNATIONAL STUDIES
1800 K Street NW, Suite 400, Washington DC 20006. 202/887-0200. **Contact:** Human Resources Department. **Description:** An institute for commercial research and strategic and international studies.

COMMUNICATIONS WORKERS OF AMERICA
501 3rd Street NW, Washington DC 20001. 202/434-1444. **Contact:** Brenda Stuart, Human Resources Administrator. **Description:** Administrative offices for the nationwide trade union, representing a wide range of professions.

CORT FURNITURE RENTAL
3137 Pennsy Drive, Landover MD 20785. 301/336-7600. **Contact:** Kimberly Martin, Human Resources Manager. **Description:** A furniture leasing firm, offering products for both residential and commercial use. **Common positions include:** Management Trainee; Sales Associate. **Educational backgrounds include:** Business Administration; Economics; Marketing. **Benefits:** Disability Coverage; Employee Discounts; Life Insurance; Medical Insurance; Pension Plan; Profit Sharing; Savings Plan; Tuition Assistance. **Corporate headquarters location:** Atlanta GA. **Parent company:** Amev. **Operations at this facility include:** Regional Headquarters; Sales.

DISCLOSURE INC.
5161 River Rd., Bethesda MD 20816. 301/951-1439. **Contact:** Dan Banner, Director, Human Resources. **Description:** Receives, organizes, and converts to microfiche and compact disc more than 110,000 reports filed each year by more than 11,000 public companies whose stock is traded on the New York Stock Exchange, American Stock Exchange, NASDAQ, and Over-The-Counter. **Number of employees at this location:** 420.

ECHELON SERVICE COMPANY
7400 York Road, Towson MD 21204. 410/321-8254. **Fax:** 410/321-8385. **Contact:** Gordon J. Barclay, Personnel Manager. **Description:** Echelon Service Company provides engineers and support staff on a contract basis to the government and other industries. **Common positions include:** Aerospace Engineer; Biological Scientist/Biochemist; Biomedical Engineer; Buyer; Ceramics Engineer; Chemical Engineer; Computer Programmer; Computer Systems Analyst; Cost Estimator; Designer; Draftsperson; Electrical/Electronics Engineer; Environmental Engineer; General Manager; Human Resources Specialist; Industrial Engineer; Industrial Production Manager; Materials Engineer; Metallurgical Engineer; Purchasing Agent and Manager; Quality Control Supervisor; Science Technologist; Structural Engineer; Technical Writer/Editor. **Educational backgrounds include:** Computer Science; Engineering; Manufacturing Management; Mathematics; Physics. **Benefits:** 401K; Dental Insurance; Disability Coverage; Employee Discounts; Life Insurance; Medical Insurance; Pension Plan; Profit Sharing; Savings Plan. **Corporate headquarters location:** Phoenix AZ. **Other U.S. locations:** Tempe AZ. **Parent company:** Amtech Systems, Inc. **Operations at this facility include:** Administration; Divisional Headquarters; Manufacturing; Regional Headquarters; Research and Development; Sales; Service. **Listed on:** NASDAQ. **Number of employees at this location:** 156. **Number of employees nationwide:** 350.

EDISON ELECTRIC INSTITUTE
701 Pennsylvania Avenue NW, Washington DC 20004-2696. 202/508-5492. **Contact:** Human Resources Coordinator. **Description:** An association whose membership includes all investor-owned electric utility companies in the United States. **Common positions include:** Accountant/Auditor; Administrator; Advertising Clerk; Attorney; Computer Programmer; Department Manager; Economist/Market Research Analyst; Electrical/Electronics Engineer; Financial Analyst; Librarian; Lobbyist; Marketing Specialist; Mechanical Engineer; Policy Analyst; Public Relations Specialist; Statistician; Systems Analyst; Technical Writer/Editor. **Corporate headquarters location:** This Location.

FERTILIZER INSTITUTE
501 2nd Street Northeast, Washington DC 20002. 202/675-8250. **Contact:** Linda McAbee, Director of Conventions. **Description:** An association that represents the agricultural industry and supports legislation to aid them. **Benefits:** Dental Insurance; Disability Coverage; Life Insurance; Medical Insurance; Pension Plan; Savings Plan; Tuition Assistance. **Special Programs:** Internships. **Corporate headquarters location:** This Location. **Number of employees at this location:** 22.

GENERAL ELECTRIC INFORMATION SERVICES
401 North Washington Street, Rockville MD 20850. 301/340-4000. **Contact:** Manager/College Relations. **Description:** A diversified information services company. General Electric is comprised of independently operated businesses competing in a wide variety of industries. Manufactures 65-cent light bulbs, 400,000-pound locomotives, and billion-dollar power plants. GE's engines power over 18,000 commercial and military aircraft worldwide. Also manufactures medical diagnostic imaging equipment. Other businesses include GE Aircraft Engines, GE Appliances, GE Capital Services, GE Electrical Distribution and Control, GE Industrial and Power Systems, GE Lighting, GE Medical Systems, GE Motors, GE Plastics, GE Transportation, and NBC. Projected hires are for entry level positions. An equal opportunity employer. **Common positions include:** Computer Programmer; Electrical/Electronics Engineer; Financial Analyst; Instructor/Trainer; Management Trainee; Marketing Specialist; Services Sales Representative; Systems Analyst; Teacher; Technical Writer/Editor. **Educational backgrounds include:** Business Administration; Computer Science; Engineering; Finance; Marketing. **Benefits:** Dental Insurance; Disability Coverage; Employee Discounts; Eye Care; Life Insurance; Medical Insurance; Pension Plan; Savings Plan; Tuition Assistance. **Special Programs:** Internships; Training Programs. **Corporate headquarters location:** This Location. **Other U.S. locations:** Los Angeles CA; San Francisco CA; Atlanta GA; Chicago IL; Boston MA; Detroit MI; New York NY; Dallas TX; Houston TX. **Parent company:** General Electric Company. **Listed on:** New York Stock Exchange. **Number of employees worldwide:** 230,000.

GENERAL MAINTENANCE SERVICE COMPANY, INC.
2800 Shirlington Road, Arlington MD 22206. 703/578-6440. **Contact:** Director of Personnel. **Description:** Provides maintenance services for area offices. **Common positions include:** Blue-Collar Worker Supervisor; Management Trainee. **Benefits:** Disability Coverage; Life Insurance; Medical Insurance; Tuition Assistance. **Special Programs:** Training Programs. **Corporate headquarters location:** This Location. **Operations at this facility include:** Service.

GENERAL PHYSICS CORPORATION
6700 Alexander Bell Drive, Columbia MD 21046. 410/290-2300. **Fax:** 410/290-2573. **Contact:** Human Resources Department. **Description:** Provides training, engineering, and technical services to hundreds of clients in the aerospace, automotive, defense, government, manufacturing, utility, independent power, pharmaceutical, and process industries. **Subsidiaries include:** GP Environmental and GP Technologies. **Common positions include:** Ceramics Engineer; Chemical Engineer; Chemist; Civil Engineer; Electrical/Electronics Engineer; Environmental Engineer; Food Scientist/Technologist; Geologist/Geophysicist; Industrial Engineer; Materials Engineer; Mechanical Engineer; Metallurgical Engineer; Nuclear Engineer; Petroleum Engineer; Structural Engineer. **Educational backgrounds include:** Chemistry; Engineering; Geology. **Benefits:** 401K; Dental Insurance; Disability Coverage; Life Insurance; Medical Insurance; Tuition Assistance. **Corporate headquarters location:** This Location. **Other U.S. locations:** Nationwide. **Parent company:** National Patent Development Corporation. **Operations at this facility include:** Administration. **Listed on:** New York Stock Exchange. **Number of employees at this location:** 100. **Number of employees nationwide:** 1,300.

HEALTHCARE AUTOMATION
11447 Cron Hill Drive, Suite D, Owings Mills MD 21117. 410/581-3900. **Contact:** Human Resources Department. **Description:** Provides billing services for medical centers and doctors.

INTERNATIONAL ASSOCIATION OF CHIEFS OF POLICE
515 North Washington Street, Alexandra VA 22314. 703/836-6767. **Contact:** Personnel Manager. **Description:** National headquarters for the trade association representing police chiefs and other ranking law enforcement officials. **Common positions include:** Accountant/Auditor; Administrator; Computer Programmer; Technical Writer/Editor. **Educational backgrounds include:** Accounting; Business Administration; Communications; Computer Science. **Benefits:** Medical Insurance.

INTERNATIONAL BROTHERHOOD OF ELECTRICAL WORKERS
1125 15th Street NW, Washington DC 20005. 202/833-7000. **Contact:** Peter Keenan, Director of Personnel. **Description:** International headquarters for the trade union organization.

INTERNATIONAL BROTHERHOOD OF TEAMSTERS
25 Louisiana Avenue NW, Washington DC 20001. 202/624-8773. **Contact:** Sarah Pruett, Human Resources Administrator. **Description:** International headquarters for the trade union. **Common positions include:** Accountant/Auditor; Attorney; Budget Analyst; Clerical Supervisor; Computer Programmer; Computer Systems Analyst; Economist/Market Research Analyst; Editor; Financial Analyst; General Manager; Human Resources Specialist; Librarian. **Educational backgrounds include:** Accounting; Business Administration; Communications; Computer Science; Economics; Finance; Liberal Arts. **Benefits:** Dental Insurance; Disability Coverage; Life Insurance; Medical Insurance; Pension Plan. **Special Programs:** Internships. **Corporate headquarters location:** This Location. **Operations at this facility include:** Administration; Divisional Headquarters; Research and Development; Service. **Number of employees at this location:** 400. **Number of employees nationwide:** 500.

INTERNATIONAL BUSINESS AND ECONOMIC RESEARCH CORPORATION
2121 K Street NW, Suite 700, Washington DC 20037. 202/955-6155. **Contact:** Angela Kraft, Secretary. **Description:** An economic research corporation.

INTERNATIONAL UNION OF ELECTRIC ROAD MACHINERY WORKERS
1126 16th Street NW, Washington DC 20036. 202/296-1200. **Contact:** Walter Phillips, Director of Personnel. **Description:** The national office for an American labor union.

MAINSTREAM, INC.
#3 Bethesda Metro Center, Suite 830, Bethesda MD 20814. 301/654-2400. **Contact:** Patricia Jackson, Executive Director. **Description:** An employment service for persons with physical or mental disabilities. Also provides training and publications for employers.

NATIONAL ALLIANCE OF BUSINESS
1201 New York Avenue NW, Suite 700, Washington DC 20005. 202/289-2888. **Contact:** Patricia Thomas, Personnel. **Description:** A non-profit corporation whose purpose is to increase private-sector training and job opportunities for the economically disadvantaged.

NATIONAL ASSOCIATION OF BLACK ACCOUNTANTS
7249-A Hanover Parkway, Greenbelt MD 20770. 301/474-6222. **Fax:** 301/474-3114. **Contact:** Vivian Jenkins, Manager of Administrative Services. **Description:** A membership organization for accounting and business professionals and students, with nationwide chapters. **Common positions include:** Accountant/Auditor; Administrative Services Manager; Budget Analyst; Financial Manager; Payroll Clerk. **Educational backgrounds include:** Accounting; Business Administration; Finance; Marketing. **Benefits:** Dental Insurance; Disability Coverage; Life Insurance; Medical Insurance; Pension Plan; Tuition Assistance. **Special Programs:** Internships. **Corporate headquarters location:** This Location. **Operations at this facility include:** Administration. **Listed on:** Privately held. **Number of employees at this location:** 10.

NATIONAL ASSOCIATION OF LIFE UNDERWRITERS
1922 F Street NW, Washington DC 20006. 202/331-6007. **Fax:** 202/835-9616. **Contact:** Patricia Rutherford, Assistant Vice President/Human Resources. **Description:** The NALU is a trade organization representing life underwriters throughout the United States. **Common positions include:** Accountant/Auditor; Advertising Clerk; Computer Operator; Computer Programmer; Computer Systems Analyst; Payroll Clerk; Secretary. **Educational backgrounds include:** Accounting; Art/Design; Business Administration; Communications; Finance. **Benefits:** Dental Insurance; Disability Coverage; Employee Discounts; Life Insurance; Medical Insurance; Pension Plan; Profit Sharing; Savings Plan; Tuition Assistance. **Corporate headquarters location:** This Location.

NATIONAL ASSOCIATION OF MANUFACTURERS
1331 Pennsylvania Avenue NW, Suite 1500 North, Washington DC 20004-1790. 202/637-3016. **Contact:** Nellcine Ford, Assistant Vice President of Personnel. **Description:** An association involved in lobbying for the interests of manufacturers. **Common positions include:** Attorney; Editor; Lobbyist; Reporter; Services Sales Representative. **Educational backgrounds include:** Communications; Liberal Arts; Political Science. **Benefits:** Dental Insurance; Disability Coverage; Life Insurance; Medical Insurance; Pension Plan; Savings Plan; Tuition Assistance. **Corporate headquarters location:** This Location. **Operations at this facility include:** Administration; Service.

NATIONAL CENTER FOR PUBLIC POLICY RESEARCH
300 I Street Northeast, Suite 3, Washington DC 20002. 202/543-1286. **Contact:** Human Resources Department. **Description:** A non-profit foundation that publishes briefing papers and conducts special projects on policy issues from the conservative perspective.

NATIONAL EDUCATION ASSOCIATION (NEA)
1201 16th Street NW, Washington DC 20036-3290. 202/822-7642. **Contact:** Employment Manager. **Description:** A national, non-profit membership organization that represents teachers, the teaching profession, and education support personnel. The goals and objectives are carried out through various activities conducted by the following administrative and program areas: Centers for Administration and Finance; Membership and Affiliates; Policy and Strategic Planning; Public Affairs; Advocacy; and Teaching and Learning. Major programs and functions include: organizing and membership; education policy; government relations; communications; publishing; research; human and civil rights; negotiations; and administration. **Common positions include:** Accountant/Auditor; Computer Programmer; Editor; Electrical/Electronics Engineer; Human Resources Specialist; Information Specialist; Lobbyist; Mechanical Engineer; Reporter; Systems Analyst; Technical Writer/Editor. **Educational backgrounds include:** Accounting; Business Administration; Communications; Computer Science; Education; Liberal Arts; Political Science. **Benefits:** 401K; Dental Insurance; Disability Coverage; Life Insurance; Medical Insurance; Pension Plan; Tuition Assistance. **Corporate headquarters location:** This Location. **Number of employees at this location:** 500.

NATIONAL RIFLE ASSOCIATION OF AMERICA
11250 Waples Mill Road, Fairfax VA 22030. 703/267-1260. **Fax:** 703/267-3938. **Contact:** Stephanie Cheeman, Recruitment Specialist. **Description:** Founded in 1871, the NRA promotes marksmanship skills, firearm safety, and firearm educational programs. Sponsors yearly seminars, clinics, training courses, and competitions designed to promote safe and responsible firearms ownership and to improve marksmanship skills. **Common positions include:** Accountant/Auditor; Chef/Cook/Kitchen Worker; Computer Operator; Computer Programmer; Marketing Research Analyst; Public Relations Specialist; Receptionist; Secretary; Telephone Service Representative. **Educational backgrounds include:** Business Administration; English; Marketing; Political Science; Public Administration. **Benefits:** Cafeteria; Dental Insurance; Disability Coverage; Employee Discounts; Fitness Program; Life Insurance; Medical Insurance; Pension Plan; Tuition Assistance. **Special Programs:** Internships. **Corporate headquarters location:** This Location. **Number of employees nationwide:** 530.

NATIONAL RURAL ELECTRIC COOPERATIVE ASSOCIATION
1800 Massachusetts Avenue NW, Washington DC 20036. 202/857-9610. **Contact:** George Simpson, Manager of Employment. **Description:** A national service organization of nearly 1,000 rural electric systems (more than 950 cooperatively owned), which

Business Services/Non-Scientific Research/117

provide power to more than 25 million people in 46 states. Operates through four departments: Government Relations/Energy and Environmental Policy, Public and Association Affairs, Management Services, and Retirement/Safety/Insurance, with 20 divisions within these departments handling such matters as legislation; technical information and training; an overseas assistance program; insurance and employee benefits; publications; and public relations. **Common positions include:** Accountant/Auditor; Actuary; Claim Representative; Computer Programmer; Customer Service Representative; Editor; Insurance Agent/Broker; Public Relations Specialist; Reporter; Underwriter/Assistant Underwriter. **Benefits:** 401K; Dental Insurance; Disability Coverage; Life Insurance; Medical Insurance; Savings Plan; Tuition Assistance; Vision Insurance. **Corporate headquarters location:** This Location.

NATIONAL TRUST FOR HISTORIC PRESERVATION
1785 Massachusetts Avenue NW, Washington DC 20036. 202/673-4120. **Contact:** Human Resources. **Description:** Non-profit organization that encourages public participation in the preservation of buildings, objects, sites, and districts significant in the history and culture of the nation. Established in 1949.

NEWSPAPER ASSOCIATION OF AMERICA
Newspaper Center, 11600 Sunrise Valley Drive, Reston VA 22091-1412. 703/648-1000. **Contact:** Sandy Weatley, Personnel Director. **Description:** A professional association dedicated to servicing the needs and interests of the newspaper publishing industry.

OGDEN PROFESSIONAL SERVICES
3211 Jermantown Road, Fairfax VA 22030. 703/246-0200. **Contact:** Ruth Campbell, Manager of Human Resources. **Description:** A research and development corporation specializing in defense contracting. **Common positions include:** Accountant/Auditor; Computer Programmer; Electrical/Electronics Engineer; Mechanical Engineer; Systems Analyst; Technical Writer/Editor. **Educational backgrounds include:** Accounting; Business Administration; Computer Science; Engineering; Finance; Mathematics; Physics. **Benefits:** Dental Insurance; Disability Coverage; Life Insurance; Medical Insurance; Pension Plan; Savings Plan; Tuition Assistance. **Corporate headquarters location:** This Location. **Operations at this facility include:** Research and Development. **Listed on:** New York Stock Exchange.

OMNI SERVICES, INC.
14115 Lovers Lane, Culpeper VA 22701. 703/825-6800. **Fax:** 703/825-2365. **Contact:** Human Resources Generalist. **Description:** Provides uniform rental services, industrial laundering, and restroom services. Omni Services, Inc. has locations nationwide. **Subsidiaries include:** Rus, Sanis. **Common positions include:** Accountant/Auditor; Blue-Collar Worker Supervisor; Computer Programmer; Computer Systems Analyst; General Manager; Human Resources Specialist; Industrial Engineer; Industrial Production Manager; Management Trainee; Manufacturer's/Wholesaler's Sales Rep.; Mechanical Engineer; Quality Control Supervisor; Services Sales Representative. **Educational backgrounds include:** Accounting; Business Administration; Computer Science; Economics; Engineering; Finance; Liberal Arts; Marketing; Mathematics; Physics. **Benefits:** Dental Insurance; Disability Coverage; Employee Discounts; Life Insurance; Medical Insurance; Pension Plan; Savings Plan; Tuition Assistance. **Corporate headquarters location:** This Location. **Operations at this facility include:** Administration; Divisional Headquarters; Manufacturing; Regional Headquarters; Sales; Service. **Listed on:** Privately held. **Number of employees at this location:** 140. **Number of employees nationwide:** 2,600.

PHH CORPORATION
11333 McCormick Road, Hunt Valley MD 21031-1001. 410/771-3600. **Contact:** Human Resources. **Description:** Founded in 1946, PHH offers diverse business services to private and public sector organizations across North America, the United Kingdom and Europe. The corporation specializes in three key areas: vehicle management services, relocation and real estate services and mortgage banking services. Vehicle management services primarily consist of the management, purchase, leasing and resale of vehicle for corporate clients and governmental agencies, including fuel and expense management programs and other fee-based services for clients' vehicle fleets. Relocation services primarily consist of the purchase, management and resale of homes for transferred employees of corporate clients, governmental agencies and affinity groups. Mortgage banking services primarily include the origination, sale and servicing of residential first mortgage loans as well as related insurance products.

PAN AMERICAN HEALTH ORGANIZATION
525 23rd Street NW, Personnel Department, Washington DC 20037. 202/861-3376. **Fax:** 202/861-3379. **Contact:** Dr. Diana Serrano LaVertu, Chief of Personnel. **Description:** An international agency responsible for assisting Latin and Caribbean governments in instituting national health programs. **Common positions include:** Biological Scientist/Biochemist; Biomedical Engineer; Food Scientist/Technologist; Health Services Manager; Medical Doctor; Registered Nurse; Veterinarian. **Educational backgrounds include:** M.D./Medicine. **Benefits:** Dental Insurance; Disability Coverage; Life Insurance; Medical Insurance; Pension Plan; Tuition Assistance.

UNITED MINE WORKERS OF AMERICA INTERNATIONAL UNION
900 15th Street NW, Washington DC 20005. 202/842-7220. **Fax:** 202/842-7307. **Contact:** Timothy J. Baker, Administrative Assistant to the President. **Description:** The national headquarters for the major trade union organization. **Benefits:** Daycare Assistance; Dental Insurance; Life Insurance; Medical Insurance; Pension Plan. **Special Programs:** Internships. **Corporate headquarters location:** This Location. **Operations at this facility include:** Administration. **Number of employees at this location:** 145. **Number of employees nationwide:** 603.

Note: Because addresses and telephone numbers of smaller companies change rapidly, we recommend you call each company to verify the information below before inquiring about job opportunities. Mass mailings are not recommended.

Additional employers with over 250 employees:

BUSINESS ASSOCIATIONS

American Academy of Ophthalmology
1101 Vermont Ave Nw, Suite 700, Washington DC 20005-3521. 202/737-6662.

National Auto Dealers Assn.
8400 Westpark Dr, Mc Lean VA 22102-3522. 703/821-7000.

CLEANING AND MAINTENANCE SERVICES

Institutional & Environ. Mgmt.
1313 Dolley Madison Blvd, Suite 333, Mc Lean VA 22101-3926. 703/821-2574.

United States Service Ind.
1424 K St Nw, 4th Floor, Washington DC 20005-2410. 202/783-2030.

DETECTIVE, GUARD, AND ARMORED CAR SERVICES

Master Security Inc.
200 E Joppa Rd, Suite 300, Baltimore MD 21286-3150. 410/828-6008.

Additional employers with under 250 employees:

LINEN SUPPLY

Domestic Linen & Unfrm Supl. Co.
3921 Vero Rd, Baltimore MD 21227-1564. 410/242-4400.

National Linen Service
725 S Pickett St, Alexandria VA 22304-4603. 703/751-5783.

ADJUSTMENT AND COLLECTION SERVICES

National Credit Management
10155 York Rd, Cockeysville MD 21030-3336. 410/628-5300.

American Resource Mgmt. Inc.
207 Old Padonia Rd, Timonium MD 21093. 410/252-1144.

National Credit Service
444 N Frederick Ave Ste 4, Gaithersburg MD 20877-2432. 301/258-2888.

Tri State Credit Corporation
6 Village Grn # A, Crofton MD 21114-2014. 301/261-3661.

SECRETARIAL AND COURT REPORTING SERVICES

Interoffice Inc.
3 Bethesda Metro Ctr Ste 700, Bethesda MD 20814-6300. 301/564-4949.

Kelly Temporary Services
412 Malcolm Dr, Westminster MD 21157-6129. 410/857-1588.

DISINFECTING AND PEST CONTROL SERVICES

Connors Pest Control
7219 Poplar St, Annandale VA 22003-3011. 703/658-8824.

Orkin Exterminating Co.
Harford County, Bel Air MD 21014. 410/838-8250.

Orkin Exterminating Co.
Dorchester, Queen Anne MD 21657. 410/376-3455.

Paramount Pest Control
406 Hudgins Rd, Fredericksbrg VA 22408-4143. 703/373-1234.

Pied Piper Pest Control
9322 Liberty Rd, Randallstown MD 21133-3526. 410/655-5888.

CLEANING AND MAINTENANCE SERVICES

American Building Maintenance
301 N High St, Baltimore MD 21202-4807. 410/576-1010.

Arrow General Inc.
331 S Patrick St, Alexandria

VA 22314-3575. 703/683-9773.

Capital Building Services
4300 Evergreen Loan Ste 102, Annandale VA 22003-3214. 703/941-3900.

M & G Services Inc.
PO Box 512, Springfield VA 22150-0512. 703/550-8030.

Multivac Inc.
10903 Indian Head Hwy Ste 301, Ft Washington MD 20744-4000. 301/292-8030.

Scrupples Janitorial Service
3255 K St Nw, Washington DC 20007-4412. 202/625-0222.

United States Service Industries
1424 K St Nw, Washington DC 20005-2410. 202/783-2030.

Centurion National Corporation
851 Brightseat Rd, Hyattsville MD 20785-4740. 301/808-1440.

Continental Building Maintenance Inc.
4265 Brookfield Corporate Dr, Chantilly VA 22021-1696. 703/631-7300.

Eastern Facilities Maintenance
9596 Deereco Rd, Timonium MD 21093-2119. 410/561-8892.

Stevens and Son Inc.
15742 Crabbs Branch Way, Rockville MD 20855-2620. 301/670-4160.

COMPUTER PROCESSING AND DATA PREPARATION SERVICES

Authorization Systems
1801 Rockville Pike Ste 216, Rockville MD 20852-1633. 301/770-1625.

Columbia Services Group
901 N Stuart St Ste 800, Arlington VA 22203-1854. 703/528-8100.

Data Transformation Corporation
8121 Georgia Ave Ste 300, Silver Spring MD 20910-4933. 301/587-4580.

Diversified International Sciences
9901 Business Pky Ste R, Lanham MD 20706-1840. 301/731-9070.

Institute of Modern Procedures
1025 Vermont Ave NW Ste 1130, Washington DC 20005-3516. 202/393-6210.

Sita Corporation
6858 Old Dominion Dr, Mc Lean VA 22101-3832. 703/821-8178.

Advanced Techlgy & Research Corporation
15210 Dino Dr, Burtonsville MD 20866-1172. 301/989-8049.

Intergraph Corporation
802 Stonehaven Dr, Jarrettsville MD 21084-1704. 410/638-0570.

Data Systems Analysts Inc.
10400 Eaton Pl Ste 500, Fairfax VA 22030-2208. 703/591-3704.

Maintech
3800 Concorde Pky Ste 500, Chantilly VA 22021-1127. 703/818-1280.

Management Data Services
5301 Harford Rd, Baltimore MD 21214-2214. 410/426-2129.

DETECTIVE, GUARD, AND ARMORED CAR SERVICES

Blue Ridge Security Guard Service Inc.
PO Box 57, Marshall VA 22115-0057. 703/364-1617.

Loughlin Security Agency
7926 E Baltimore St, Baltimore MD 21224-2010. 410/285-8400.

Special Response Corporation
521 W Joppa Rd, Baltimore MD 21204-3819. 410/494-1900.

Stop Private Invstgtn Agency
2509 St Paul St # 6, Baltimore MD 21218-4610. 410/366-3313.

Federal Armored Express
9603 Deereco Rd, Timonium MD 21093-2173. 410/560-1100.

Burns International Sec. Service
8300 Old Courthouse Rd, Vienna VA 22182-3822. 703/448-3306.

Central Security Invstg
770 W North Ave, Baltimore MD 21217-4431. 410/728-1802.

Colorado Security Agency Inc.
5521 Colorado Ave Nw, Washington DC 20011-7845. 202/829-9233.

Columbia Canine Security Service
4811 Georgia Ave Nw, Washington DC 20011-4533. 202/829-6445.

Dennis Detective Agency
515 Benfield Rd, Severna Park MD 21146-2519. 410/647-4202.

Elite Service Inc.
2411 Blueridge Ave, Wheaton MD 20902-4513. 301/949-9716.

Guarsmark Inc.
101 W Read St, Baltimore MD 21201-4915. 410/528-1324.

Security Personnel Services
1916 Eastern Ave, Baltimore MD 21231-2594. 410/276-0010.

The Wackenhut Corporation
6930 Carroll Ave, Takoma Park MD 20912-4414. 301/891-1210.

Watkins Security Agency
8055 Cryden Way, Forestville MD 20747-4509. 301/967-0522.

Worldwide Protective Services
324 Rittenhouse St Nw, Washington DC 20011-1310. 202/829-0594.

SECURITY SYSTEMS SERVICES

Securiguard Inc.
6849 Old Dominion Dr Ste 420, Mc Lean VA 22101-3705. 703/821-6777.

Adt Security Systems
6855 Deerpath Road, Baltimore MD 21227. 410/379-5050.

Adt Security Systems
7399 Boston Blvd, Springfield VA 22153-2805. 703/644-0112.

Battery Warehouse
208 N Tollgate Rd, Bel Air MD 21014-4206. 410/879-4323.

MISC. BUSINESS SERVICES

Ardmore Enterprises
3010 Lottsford Vista Rd, Mitchellville MD 20721-4001. 301/577-5496.

B&B Information & Image Mgmt.
300 Prince Georges Blvd, Uppr Marlboro MD 20772-7409. 410/792-3760.

Spotsylvania Vol. Fire Dept.
4234 Mine Rd, Fredericksbrg VA 22408-2588. 703/898-0052.

Washington Convention Center
900 9th St Nw, Washington DC 20001-4496. 202/789-1600.

Corderman Interior Design
5317 Leavells Crossing Dr, Fredericksbrg VA 22407-7709. 703/898-8480.

Ellstreet Corporation
1445 New York Ave Nw, Washington DC 20005-2158. 202/737-1020.

Gardiners Furniture
6415 Baltimore National Pike, Catonsville MD 21228-3904. 410/719-6900.

Darome Conference Calling Service
2000 14th St N, Arlington VA 22201-2500. 703/276-4300.

American Phone Mktng Grp Inc.
2070 Chain Bridge Rd Ste 400, Vienna VA 22182-2536. 703/790-3635.

Outreach Affiliates
1717 Massachusetts Ave Nw, Washington DC 20036-2001. 202/797-5200.

Sturner & Klein
11900 Parklawn Dr Ste 412, Rockville MD 20852-2670. 301/881-2720.

Henderson Bonding Co.
Hc 3 Box 235A, Rochelle VA 22738-9801. 703/672-0841.

Justus Serves
PO Box 90375, Washington DC 20090-0375. 202/396-5050.

Barwood Delivery Service
4925 Nicholson Ct, Kensington MD 20895-1004. 301/984-1888.

Cohee Design Co.
Seward Rd, Ridgely MD 21660. 410/758-3037.

Rgis Inventory Specialists
1323 Mount Hermon Rd # 4-A, Salisbury MD 21801-5258. 410/543-0707.

Wilkins Systems
6940 Carroll Ave, Takoma Park MD 20912-4446. 301/270-4501.

BUSINESS ASSOCIATIONS

Air Transport Association America
1301 Pennsylvania Ave Ste 1100, Washington DC 20004-1701. 202/626-4000.

Aircraft Owners & Pilots Association
421 Aviation Way, Frederick MD 21701-4756. 301/695-2000.

American Automobile Mfrs Association
1401 H St Nw, Washington DC 20005-2110. 202/408-8310.

American Heart Assn. VA
8735 Plantation Ln, Manassas VA 22110-4506. 703/361-2707.

American Insurance Association
1130 Connecticut Ave Nw, Washington DC 20036-3904. 202/828-7100.

American Society of Assn. Execs
1575 I St NW Ste 11, Washington DC 20005-1105. 202/626-2723.

Carroll Cnty Assn. for the Retarded
180 Kriders Church Rd, Westminster MD 21158-4307. 410/876-2422.

Central Maryland Farm Credit
P.O. Box 607, Frederick MD 21705. 301/663-4192.

Harford Mall Merchants Association
Harford Mall, Bel Air MD 21014. 410/838-3322.

Health Insurance Assn. of America
1025 Connecticut Avenw, Washington DC 20036. 202/223-7780.

Howard Cnty Assn. for the Retarded
10705 Charter Dr, Columbia MD 21044-2870. 410/730-0638.

Nat'l Alliance of Business
1201 New York Ave Nw, Washington DC 20005-3917. 202/289-2888.

Nat'l Assn. of Broadcasters
1771 N St Nw, Washington DC 20036-2805. 202/429-5300.

Nat'l Electrical Manufacturers
2101 L St Nw, Washington DC 20037-1526. 202/457-8400.

Nat'l Food Processors Association
1401 New York Ave Nw, Washington DC 20005-2154. 202/639-5900.

Nat'l League of Postmasters
1023 N Royal St, Alexandria VA 22314-1569. 703/548-5922.

Nat'l Restaurant Association
1200 17th St Nw, Washington DC 20036-3006. 202/331-5900.

Nat'l Solid Wastes Mgmt. Association
1730 Rhode Island Ave Nw, Washington DC 20036-3101. 202/659-4613.

Society Of The Plastics Industry
1275 K St Nw, Washington DC 20005-4006. 202/371-5200.

Washington Airports Task Force
PO Box 17349, Washington DC 20041-0349. 703/661-8040.

Graduate School USDA
600 Maryland Ave Sw, Washington DC 20024-2520. 202/447-4419.

Methyl Chloride Industry Association
1001 Pennsylvania Ave Nw, Washington DC 20004-2505. 202/637-2200.

The American Film Institute
The Jfk Ctr For Performing Art, Washington DC 20566. 202/828-4000.

Association of Maryland Pilots
3720 Dillon St, Baltimore MD 21224-5202. 410/276-1337.

PROFESSIONAL MEMBERSHIP ORGANIZATIONS

American Occuptnl Thrpy Association
PO Box 1725, Rockville MD 20849-1725. 301/948-9626.

Eye Care
1412 28th St Nw,
Washington DC 20007-3145. 202/628-3816.

Human Resources Research Organization
66 Canal Center Plz Ste 400, Alexandria VA 22314-1591. 703/549-3611.

LABOR ORGANIZATIONS

Air Line Pilots Assn. International
1625 Massachusetts Ave Nw, Washington DC 20036-2212. 703/689-2270.

National Treasury Employees Union
901 E St NW Ste 600, Washington DC 20004-2001. 202/783-4444.

MISC. MEMBERSHIP ORGANIZATIONS

Women In Community Service
1900 N Beauregard St Ste 103, Alexandria VA 22311-1716. 703/671-0500.

For more information on career opportunities in miscellaneous business services and non-scientific research:

Associations

AMERICAN SOCIETY OF APPRAISERS
P.O. Box 17265, Washington DC 20041. 703/478-2228.

EQUIPMENT LEASING ASSOCIATION OF AMERICA
1300 17th Street, Suite 1010, North Arlington VA 22209. 703/527-8655.

NATIONAL ASSOCIATION OF PERSONNEL SERVICES
3133 Mt. Vernon Avenue, Alexandria VA 22305. 703/684-0180.

CHARITIES AND SOCIAL SERVICES

The outlook for social service workers is better than average. In fact, opportunities for qualified applicants are expected to be excellent, partly due to the rapid turnover in the industry due as a result of lower wages offered.

Note: Because of the high turnover rate and the continuous need for social services, the outlook for this industry has remained constant over the past few years.

ACTION
1100 Vermont Avenue NW, Washington DC 20525. 202/606-5263. **Recorded Jobline:** 202/606-5039. **Contact:** Human Resources. **Description:** Mobilizes volunteers for various human service programs.

AMERICAN COUNCIL OF THE BLIND
1155 15th Street NW, Suite 720, Washington DC 20005. **Contact:** Human Resources. **Description:** The Amercian Council of the Blind (ACB) is a national membership organization established to promote the independence, dignity, and well-being of blind and visually impaired people. Members are blind, visually impaired, or fully sighted people. ACB was formed in 1961 and is one of the largest organizations of blind people in the U.S. with over 70 state and special interest affiliates and a national network of chapters and members. This office serves as the organization's headquarters where all Council programs and services are administered. By providing numerous programs and services, ACB enables blind people to live and work independently, contribute to their communities, and learn to advocate for themselves. **Corporate headquarters location:** This Location.

B'NAI B'RITH INTERNATIONAL
1640 Rhode Island Avenue NW, Washington DC 20036. 202/857-6600. **Fax:** 202/857-1099. **Contact:** Ms. Rita Greenfield, Director of Human Resources. **Description:** Headquarters for the broadly-diversified Jewish social services and political action organization. B'Nai B'Rith has seven districts located across the United States. **Common positions include:** Fundraising Specialist; Social Worker. **Benefits:** Life Insurance; Medical Insurance; Pension Plan; Savings Plan. **Special Programs:** Internships. **Corporate headquarters location:** This Location. **Operations at this facility include:** Administration; Public Affairs.

CHESAPEAKE AND OHIO CANAL NATIONAL HISTORIC PARK
P.O. Box 4, Sharpsburg MD 21782. 301/739-4200. **Contact:** Human Resources. **Description:** Preserves the cultural and national history of the Chesapeake and Ohio Canal.

CHILD WELFARE LEAGUE OF AMERICA
440 First Street NW, Suite 310, Washington DC 20001-2085. 202/942-0280. **Contact:** Human Resources. **Description:** The Child Welfare League of America (CWLA) is a national non-profit organization that unites almost 800 public and private agencies, which together serve more than two million children and their families every year. CWLA and its agencies are experts in the many areas of child welfare, including adoption, child day care, child protection, family foster care, chemical dependency prevention and treatment, and housing and homelessness. CWLA was ranked the fourth most efficient charity in the country by *Worth* magazine.

THE CHIMES, INC.
1700 Reistertown Road, Suite 226, Baltimore MD 21208. 410/602-4025. **Fax:** 410/602-4001. **Recorded Jobline:** 410/521-4417. **Contact:** Paul Dutton, Personnel Specialist. **Description:** The Chimes, a Baltimore-based, non-sectarian, not-for-profit agency was established in 1947 as The School of The Chimes. Today, with a staff of nearly 600 professionals and support staff, The Chimes offers a broad array of vocational, rehabilitative, residential, educational, and support services for nearly 1,100 individuals in Central Maryland, Northern Virginia, and Washington, DC. The Chimes is dedicated to helping children, adults, and senior citizens with mental

retardation and related disabilities move from dependence to independence. **Common positions include:** Counselor; Human Service Worker. **Educational backgrounds include:** Human Services; Psychology; Sociology. **Benefits:** 403B; Credit Union; Dental Insurance; Disability Coverage; Employee Discounts; Life Insurance; Medical Insurance; Pension Plan; Tuition Assistance. **Corporate headquarters location:** This Location. **Other U.S. locations:** DC; DE; VA. **Number of employees nationwide:** 500.

COUNTY COMMISSION ON AGING
520 North Market Street, Frederick MD 21701. 301/694-1605. **Contact:** Human Resources. **Description:** A commission studying and advocating the rights of the elderly.

FAMILY AND CHILD SERVICES OF WASHINGTON, DC, INC.
929 L Street NW, Washington DC 20001. 202/289-1510. **Contact:** Rhoda L. Veney, Executive Director. **Description:** A private, nonprofit social services organization, which offers a broad range of services, including counseling, adoption, family daycare, foster care, summer and winter camping, and services to older Americans. **Common positions include:** Administrative Worker/Clerk; Counselor; Social Worker. **Benefits:** Disability Coverage; Life Insurance; Medical Insurance; Pension Plan. **Special Programs:** Internships; Training Programs. **Corporate headquarters location:** This Location. **Operations at this facility include:** Service.

INTERNATIONAL BRAILLE AND TECHNOLOGY CENTER FOR THE BLIND
1800 Johnson Street, Baltimore MD 21230. 410/659-9314. **Contact:** Human Resources. **Description:** The International Braille and Technology Center is located at the National Center for the Blind. The IBTC was opened in 1990 and is the only facility of its kind in the world. It houses at least one of each type of Braille-producing, computer-driven Braille printer currently on the market, as well as computers with refreshable Braille displays, raised-line drawing equipment of various sorts, optical character recognition equipment used to transform printed characters into electronically produced speech or Braille, and an array of voice output computer screen reading systems. **Parent company:** National Center for the Blind.

INTERNATIONAL VOLUNTARY SERVICES, INC.
1424 16th Street NW, Suite 603, Washington DC 20036. 202/387-5533. **Contact:** Recruitment. **Description:** A private, independent, non-profit agency that supplies volunteer technical assistance for development projects in developing countries. IVS has nine Washington staff members and 10 international staff members. **NOTE:** This organization reports it will not be actively recruiting until 1997. **Common positions include:** Economist/Market Research Analyst; Forester/Conservation Scientist; Health Services Worker; Marketing Specialist; Systems Analyst; Veterinarian. **Benefits:** Dental Insurance; Medical Insurance. **Special Programs:** Internships.

MONTGOMERY COUNTY COMMUNITY CORRECTIONS
11651 Nebel Street, Rockville MD 20852. 301/468-4200. **Contact:** Human Resources. **Description:** Provides effective community correctional alternatives between probation/parole supervision and security confinement for male and female offenders.

NATIONAL ALLIANCE FOR THE MENTALLY ILL
200 North Glebe Road, Suite 1015, Arlington VA 22203-3754. 703/524-7600. **Contact:** Human Resources. **Description:** NAMI provides a wide range of services to families living with mental illness: Support, which offers support groups and special interest networks; Education, which provides up-to-date, scientific information through publications, a toll-free Helpline, and annual Mental Illness Awareness Week campaigns; Advocacy for Services; and Support for Research.

NATIONAL FEDERATION OF THE BLIND
1800 Johnson Street, Baltimore MD 21230. 410/659-9314. **Contact:** Human Resources. **Description:** The National Federation of the Blind is one of the largest organizations of the blind in America. Founded in 1940, the Federation has grown to include more than fifty thousand of the nation's blind. The Federation is organized in every state and has local chapters in almost every community of any size in the nation. The headquarters of the Federation is located at the National Center for the Blind, as is the International Braille and Technology Center for the Blind and Job Opportunities for the Blind. **Corporate headquarters location:** This Location.

124/The Metropolitan Washington JobBank

NATIONAL 4-H COUNCIL
7100 Connecticut Avenue, Chevy Chase MD 20815. 301/961-2965. **Contact:** Human Resources. **Description:** Provides on-site educational programs for youth groups.

ROCK CREEK FOUNDATION
700 Roeder Road, 4th Floor, Silver Spring MD 20910. 301/589-6675. **Contact:** Human Resources. **Description:** A national training site engaged in creating opportunities for disabled adults. Individuals get involved in various areas of community integration, preparing for educational, volunteer, and employment opportunities.

UNITED WAY OF AMERICA
701 North Fairfax Street, Alexandria VA 22314-2045. 703/836-7100. **Contact:** Human Resources. **Description:** Through a vast network of volunteers and local charities, local United Way organizations throughout America help meet the health and human-care needs of millions of people. United Way's 107-year history is built on local organizations helping people in their own communities. The United Way system includes approximately 1,900 community-based organizations. United Way of America is the national service and training center, supporting its members with national services that include advertising, training, corporate relations, research, networks, and government relations. **Corporate headquarters location:** This Location.

Note: Because addresses and telephone numbers of smaller companies change rapidly, we recommend you call each company to verify the information below before inquiring about job opportunities. Mass mailings are not recommended.

Additional employers with under 250 employees:

JOB TRAINING AND VOCATIONAL REHABILITATION SERVICES

B A R C Subcontract
7200 Rutherford Rd, Baltimore MD 21244-2704. 410/323-8000.

Change Inc.
420 S Bishop St, Westminster MD 21157-5443. 410/848-1824.

Prologue Inc.
37 Walker Ave, Baltimore MD 21208-4000. 410/653-6190.

RESIDENTIAL CARE

Carroll Lutheran Village
205 Saint Mark Way, Westminster MD 21158-4103. 410/876-8113.

Brooke Grove Nursing Home
18100 Marden Ln, Olney MD 20832. 301/924-2811.

Goodwin House West
3440 S Jefferson St, Falls Church VA 22041-3120. 703/820-1488.

Sunrise of Towson
7925 York Rd, Baltimore MD 21204-7009. 410/296-8900.

MISC. SOCIAL SERVICES

United Negro College Fund Inc.
34 Market Pl, Baltimore MD 21202-6704. 410/752-8623.

Goodwill Ind. Baltimore
152 Chartley Dr, Reisterstown MD 21136-2331. 410/526-7618.

Blind Industries and Service MD
1510 Caton Center Dr, Baltimore MD 21227-1540. 410/247-3737.

Juvenile Diabetes Foundation
5 Gwynns Mill Ct, Owings Mills MD 21117-3529. 410/356-4555.

World Relief Refugee Services
6940 Carroll Ave, Takoma Park MD 20912-4446. 301/270-0881.

YMCA of Metropolitan Washington
3422 13th St N, Arlington VA 22201-4906. 703/525-5420.

For more information on career opportunities in charities and social services:

Associations

AMERICAN COUNCIL OF THE BLIND
1155 15th Street NW, Suite 720, Washington DC 20005. 202/467-5081. Membership. Offers an annual conference, a monthly magazine, and scholarships.

CATHOLIC CHARITIES USA
1731 King Street, Suite 200, Alexandria VA 22314. 703/549-1390. Membership.

FAMILY SERVICE ASSOCIATION OF AMERICA
11700 West Lake Park Drive, Park Place, Milwaukee WI 53224. 414/359-1040. Membership.

NATIONAL COUNCIL ON FAMILY RELATIONS
3989 Central Avenue NE, Suite 550, Minneapolis MN 55421. 612/781-9331. Fax: 612/781-9348. Membership. Publishes two quarterly journals. Offers an annual conference and newsletters.

NATIONAL FEDERATION OF THE BLIND
1800 Johnson Street, Baltimore MD 21230. 410/659-9314. Membership of 50,000 in 600 local chapters. Monthly magazine.

NATIONAL FEDERATION OF SOCIETIES FOR CLINICAL SOCIAL WORK, INC.
P.O. Box 3740, Arlington VA 22203. 703/522-3866. A lobbying organization. Offers newsletters and a conference every two years to membership organizations.

NATIONAL MULTIPLE SCLEROSIS SOCIETY
733 Third Avenue, New York NY 10017. 212/986-3240. Toll-free: 800/344-4867. Offers a quarterly magazine.

CHEMICALS/RUBBER AND PLASTICS

First the good news: overall growth in the chemical industry is on the upswing. Sales were expected to rise as much as eight percent in 1995. Chemical products and services are currently in high demand, thus creating a demand for more workers, and recent price increases are holding steady. During 1994, the U.S. chemical trade surplus grew four percent.

Now the bad news: costs for pollution reduction are rising. Factories are running at 85 percent capacity, and if companies increase spending on plant and equipment, an oversupply could result if economic growth slows too quickly.

Growth prospects for the domestic synthetic rubber industry remain mixed, reflecting the industry's dependence on tire manufacturing. The tire industry shows signs of stabilizing after undergoing a period characterized by massive restructuring, the effects of recession in the domestic market, and consistently high levels of imports.

In the plastics industry, greater reliance on computer-aided design and manufacturing is expected in the last half of the 1990s, as production is streamlined. These measures will be aimed at strengthening the industry's competitiveness in the areas of quality control and improved client relations.

THE BELKO CORPORATION
11931 Jericho Road, Kingsville MD 21087. 410/592-9191. **Contact:** Tom Janda, Executive Vice President/Administration. **Description:** Produces a variety of molded and extruded rubber products and rubber-coated rollers. The Belko Corporation is a subsidiary of Alco-Standard Corporation (Valley Forge, PA), a diversified corporation engaged in distribution, manufacturing, and resources. **Corporate headquarters location:** Valley Forge PA. **Parent company:** Alco-Standard Corporation.

THE CELLO CHEMICAL COMPANY
1354 Old Post Road, Havre de Grace MD 21078. 410/939-1234. **Contact:** Danies Brown, Personnel Director. **Description:** Produces a wide range of sanitary and cleaning products, including sanitary chemicals, acrylic resins, floor finishes and waxes, deodorants, aerosols, washroom maintenance products, soaps, detergents, liquid and aerosol household cleaners and polishes, floor machines, and insecticides. **Corporate headquarters location:** This Location. **Parent company:** Grow Group, Inc.

CHEMETALS, INC.
610 Pittman Road, Baltimore MD 21226. 410/636-7101. **Fax:** 410/636-4317. **Contact:** John Tenerowicz, Manager of Human Resources. **Description:** A producer of fine manganese products. **Common positions include:** Accountant/Auditor; Buyer; Chemical Engineer; Chemist; Customer Service Representative; Electrical/Electronics Engineer; Electrician; Environmental Engineer; Human Resources Specialist; Industrial Engineer; Industrial Production Manager; Mechanical Engineer; Operations/Production Manager; Quality Control Supervisor; Stationary Engineer. **Educational backgrounds include:** Accounting; Business Administration; Chemistry; Computer Science; Economics; Engineering; Finance; Liberal Arts; Marketing. **Benefits:** 401K; Dental Insurance; Disability Coverage; Life Insurance; Medical Insurance; Pension Plan; Savings Plan; Tuition Assistance. **Special Programs:** Internships. **Corporate headquarters location:** This Location. **Other U.S. locations:** TN. **Parent company:**

Comilog. **Operations at this facility include:** Administration; Divisional Headquarters; Manufacturing; Research and Development; Sales; Service. **Listed on:** Privately held. **Number of employees at this location:** 160. **Number of employees nationwide:** 275.

CONSTAR INTERNATIONAL
350 Old Bay Lane, Havre de Grace MD 21078. 410/939-1500. **Contact:** Ms. Pat McPartland, Personnel Officer. **Description:** Constar International is a producer of a variety of plastic containers, including plastic beverage bottles. **Corporate headquarters location:** Atlanta GA.

DURON PAINTS & WALL COVERINGS
10406 Tucker Street, Beltsville MD 20705. 301/937-8323. **Fax:** 301/595-0435. **Recorded Jobline:** 800/723-8766x5627. **Contact:** Human Resources. **Description:** Duron Paints & Wall Coverings is one of the East Coast's largest manufacturers and wholesalers of a variety of paint and paint-related products for the professional painter. **Common positions include:** Accountant/Auditor; Adjuster; Administrative Services Manager; Budget Analyst; Buyer; Chemist; Clerical Supervisor; Clinical Lab Technician; Collector; Computer Programmer; Computer Systems Analyst; Construction Contractor and Manager; Credit Manager; Customer Service Representative; Draftsperson; Editor; Financial Analyst; Human Resources Specialist; Investigator; Operations/Production Manager; Property and Real Estate Manager; Purchasing Agent and Manager; Quality Control Supervisor; Services Sales Representative; Transportation/Traffic Specialist. **Educational backgrounds include:** Business Administration; Communications; High School Diploma; Liberal Arts. **Benefits:** 401K; Dental Insurance; Disability Coverage; Employee Discounts; Life Insurance; Medical Insurance; Pension Plan; Profit Sharing; Tuition Assistance. **Corporate headquarters location:** This Location. **Operations at this facility include:** Administration; Manufacturing; Regional Headquarters; Research and Development; Sales; Service. **Listed on:** Privately held. **Number of employees at this location:** 350. **Number of employees nationwide:** 1,500.

FMC CORPORATION
AGRICULTURAL CHEMICALS GROUP
1701 East Patapsco Avenue, Baltimore MD 21223-1523. 410/355-6400x2413. **Fax:** 410/354-5019. **Contact:** Mr. Michael Albright, Human Resources Representative. **Description:** As one of FMC Corporation's Performance Chemicals businesses, the Agricultural Products Group produces a variety of crop protection and pest control chemicals for worldwide markets. More than fifty percent of the group's sales are international. The Agricultural Products Group serves a variety of markets, including food growers and pest control markets. FMC Corporation boasts a strong global position in both developed and developing countries. The company also has a strong insecticide portfolio, and has been successful in a number of attempts to develop a new class of herbicides. The Agricultural Products Group expects rapid expansion of many of its new and existing products in several foreign countries, primarily in Latin America and Asia. Recent developments include new joint ventures in areas of Indonesia and China, and the building of a new manufacturing plant to produce a new family of herbicidal products. The parent company, FMC Corporation, is one of the world's leading producers of chemicals and machinery for the industrial, agricultural, and governmental markets. FMC Corporation participates on a worldwide basis in selected segments of five broad markets: Performance Chemicals; Industrial Chemicals; Machinery and Equipment; Defense Systems; and Precious Metals. **Common positions include:** Accountant/Auditor; Agricultural Engineer; Agricultural Scientist; Blue-Collar Worker Supervisor; Clinical Lab Technician; Computer Programmer; Computer Systems Analyst; Environmental Engineer; Financial Analyst; Human Resources Specialist; Mechanical Engineer; Operations/Production Manager; Registered Nurse. **Educational backgrounds include:** Engineering. **Benefits:** 401K; Dental Insurance; Disability Coverage; Life Insurance; Medical Insurance; Pension Plan; Tuition Assistance. **Special Programs:** Internships. **Corporate headquarters location:** Chicago IL. **Other U.S. locations:** Nationwide. **Operations at this facility include:** Administration; Manufacturing; Research and Development. **Listed on:** New York Stock Exchange. **Number of employees at this location:** 310. **Number of employees nationwide:** 21,000. **Parent company:** FMC Corporation.

FARBOIL COMPANY
8200 Fischer Road, Baltimore MD 21222. 410/477-8200. **Contact:** Purchasing Agent. **Description:** Produces a variety of marine, industrial, and architectural paints; specialty coatings; and powder coatings. **Parent company:** Beatrice (Chicago, IL).

FAWN PLASTICS COMPANY, INC.
311 International Circle, Suite 140, Hunt Valley MD 21030. 410/584-1300. **Contact:** Hugh Martin, Vice President of Sales. **Description:** Produces a range of molded plastic products, including electronic assembly products.

W.R. GRACE & COMPANY
DAVISON CHEMICAL DIVISION
P.O. Box 2117, Baltimore MD 21203-2117. 410/659-9000. **Contact:** John Willin, Employee Relations Manager. **Description:** Produces a broad range of specialty chemicals, including industrial catalysts, silicas, petroleum catalysts, and many others. Nationally, the company is a diversified, multi-national products and services firm with significant activities in chemicals, natural resources, and consumer products and services. **Common positions include:** Accountant/Auditor; Chemical Engineer; Chemist; Human Resources Specialist; Secretary. **Educational backgrounds include:** Accounting; Chemistry; Engineering. **Benefits:** Dental Insurance; Disability Coverage; Life Insurance; Medical Insurance; Pension Plan; Savings Plan; Tuition Assistance. **Corporate headquarters location:** Boca Raton FL. **Operations at this facility include:** Divisional Headquarters. **Listed on:** New York Stock Exchange. **Number of employees at this location:** 325. **Number of employees nationwide:** 1,600.

HEDWIN CORPORATION
1600 Roland Heights Avenue, Baltimore MD 21211. 410/467-8209. **Contact:** Thomas Trlica, Director of Human Resources. **Description:** Produces industrial plastic containers. **Common positions include:** Accountant/Auditor; Chemical Engineer; Industrial Engineer; Mechanical Engineer. **Educational backgrounds include:** Engineering. **Benefits:** Dental Insurance; Disability Coverage; Life Insurance; Medical Insurance; Pension Plan; Tuition Assistance. **Corporate headquarters location:** This Location. **Other U.S. locations:** Laporte IN. **Parent company:** Spivaz America. **Operations at this facility include:** Administration; Manufacturing; Research and Development; Sales; Service.

J.M. HUBER CORPORATION
CHEMICALS DIVISION
907 Revolution Street, P.O. Box 310, Havre de Grace MD 21078. 410/939-3500. **Contact:** David C. Tanner, VP, Human Resources & Safety. **Description:** A inorganic chemical manufacturer. **Common positions include:** Accountant/Auditor; Buyer; Chemist; Draftsperson; Purchasing Agent and Manager. **Educational backgrounds include:** Chemistry. **Benefits:** 401K; Dental Insurance; Disability Coverage; Life Insurance; Medical Insurance; Pension Plan; Profit Sharing; Tuition Assistance. **Corporate headquarters location:** Edison NJ. **Other U.S. locations:** Nationwide. **Operations at this facility include:** Administration; Divisional Headquarters; Manufacturing; Research and Development; Sales. **Listed on:** Privately held. **Number of employees at this location:** 160. **Number of employees nationwide:** 5,000.

INTERNATIONAL PAPER
NEVAMAR CORPORATION
8339 Telegraph Road, Odenton MD 21113. 410/551-5000. **Contact:** Human Resources. **Description:** A manufacturer of laminated plastics.

KELLY-SPRINGFIELD TIRE COMPANY
12501 Willowbrook Road SE, Cumberland MD 21502-2599. 301/777-6000. **Contact:** Human Resources Department. **Description:** Manufacturer of tires and inner tubes. Parent company, Goodyear, has principal business in the development, manufacture, distribution, marketing and sale of tires for most applications worldwide. Goodyear also manufactures and sells a broad spectrum of rubber products and rubber-related chemicals for various industrial and consumer markets and provides auto repair services. Goodyear operates 32 plants in the United States and 42 plants in 29 other countries and more than 1,800 retail tire and service centers and other distribution facilities around the globe. **Parent company:** Goodyear.

KETEMA INC.
8335 Telegraph Road, Odenton MD 21113. 410/551-4500. **Contact:** Billie Clark, Personnel Administrator. **Description:** Produces a wide variety of synthetic filaments

including polypropylene, polyethylene, polyester, nylon, PEEK and other engineering thermoplastics. Nationally, the company designs, develops, manufactures and markets in the following business segments: Industrial Products and Engineered Products and Services. **Common positions include:** Accountant/Auditor; Chemist; Customer Service Representative; Draftsperson; Electrical/Electronics Engineer; Electrician; General Manager; Human Resources Specialist; Industrial Production Manager; Manufacturer's/Wholesaler's Sales Rep.; Mechanical Engineer; Operations/Production Manager; Purchasing Agent and Manager; Quality Control Supervisor; Registered Nurse; Services Sales Representative. **Educational backgrounds include:** Accounting; Business Administration; Chemistry; Engineering; Marketing. **Benefits:** 401K; Dental Insurance; Disability Coverage; Life Insurance; Medical Insurance; Pension Plan; Tuition Assistance. **Special Programs:** Training Programs. **Corporate headquarters location:** Denver CO. **Other U.S. locations:** CA; PA; TX. **Operations at this facility include:** Administration; Divisional Headquarters; Manufacturing; Research and Development; Sales. **Listed on:** Privately held. **Number of employees at this location:** 96.

LEVER BROTHERS COMPANY
5300 Holabird Avenue, Baltimore MD 21224. 410/631-5000. **Contact:** Personnel Manager. **Description:** Produces a variety of soap and detergent products as a division of the international manufacturer and distributor of soaps and cleaning products, specialty foods, toothpastes, and detergents. **Common positions include:** Accountant/Auditor; Blue-Collar Worker Supervisor; Buyer; Chemical Engineer; Chemist; Computer Programmer; Department Manager; Draftsperson; Electrical/Electronics Engineer; Human Resources Specialist; Industrial Engineer; Mechanical Engineer; Purchasing Agent and Manager. **Educational backgrounds include:** Accounting; Business Administration; Chemistry; Engineering. **Benefits:** Dental Insurance; Disability Coverage; Life Insurance; Medical Insurance; Profit Sharing; Savings Plan; Tuition Assistance.

McCORMICK & COMPANY INC.
18 Loveton Circle, Sparks MD 21152-6000. 410/771-7301. **Recorded Jobline:** 410/527-6969. **Contact:** Human Resources. **Description:** Produces spices, seasonings, gravy and sauce mixes, and other food products which are sold to food services, institutional clients, retail companies, and industrial markets worldwide. Trademarks include McCormick and Schilling. The company also manufactures plastic bottles and tubes used in the pharmaceutical, cosmetic, and food packaging and preparation industries. McCormick owns a cogeneration facility which supplies energy to a subsidiary and is sold to utility companies. **Listed on:** NASDAQ.

McCORMICK & COMPANY INC.
10950 Beaver Dam Rd., Hunt Valley MD 21031. 410/771-7595. **Contact:** Janis M. Leftridge, Human Relations Manager. **Description:** Produces spices, seasonings, gravy and sauce mixes, and other food products which are sold to food services, institutional clients, retail companies, and industrial markets worldwide. Trademarks include McCormick and Schilling. The company also manufactures plastic bottles and tubes used in the pharmaceutical, cosmetic, and food packaging and preparation industries. McCormick owns a cogeneration facility which supplies energy to a subsidiary and is sold to utility companies. **Listed on:** NASDAQ. **Number of employees nationwide:** 7,500.

O'SULLIVAN CORPORATION
P.O. Box 3510, Winchester VA 22604. 703/667-6666. **Contact:** Human Resources. **Description:** A plastic, vinyl sheeting, and molded plastics manufacturer.

POLY-SEAL CORPORATION
8303 Pulaski Highway, Baltimore MD 21237. 410/682-3000. **Contact:** Maria Hayward, Personnel Manager. **Description:** Manufactures plastic closures, bottle caps, and jars. **Common positions include:** Accountant/Auditor; Administrator; Chemical Engineer; Computer Programmer; Customer Service Representative; Department Manager; Draftsperson; Human Resources Specialist; Manufacturer's/Wholesaler's Sales Rep.; Mechanical Engineer; Operations/Production Manager; Purchasing Agent and Manager; Quality Control Supervisor; Systems Analyst. **Educational backgrounds include:** Accounting; Business Administration; Computer Science; Engineering; Marketing. **Benefits:** Dental Insurance; Disability Coverage; Life Insurance; Medical Insurance; Pension Plan; Tuition Assistance. **Corporate headquarters location:** This Location. **Operations at this facility include:** Administration; Manufacturing.

RUBBERMAID COMMERCIAL PRODUCTS, INC.
3124 Valley Avenue, Winchester VA 22601. 703/667-8700. **Fax:** 703/542-8770. **Contact:** Salaried Associate Relations Manager. **Description:** Manufactures plastic products for maintenance, refuse, food service, and agriculture markets. **Common positions include:** Accountant/Auditor; Designer; Financial Analyst; General Manager; Industrial Engineer; Manufacturer's/Wholesaler's Sales Rep.; Materials Engineer; Mechanical Engineer; Operations/Production Manager; Purchasing Agent and Manager; Quality Control Supervisor. **Educational backgrounds include:** Business Administration; Economics; Engineering; Finance; Marketing. **Benefits:** 401K; Dental Insurance; Disability Coverage; Employee Discounts; Life Insurance; Medical Insurance; Pension Plan; Profit Sharing; Tuition Assistance. **Corporate headquarters location:** Wooster OH. **Parent company:** Rubbermaid, Inc. **Operations at this facility include:** Administration; Divisional Headquarters; Manufacturing; Research and Development; Sales. **Listed on:** New York Stock Exchange. **Number of employees at this location:** 900.

SCM CHEMICALS INC.
7 St. Paul Street, Suite 1010, Baltimore MD 21202. 410/783-1120. **Contact:** Human Resources. **Description:** A chemicals company.

SCM CHEMICALS, INC.
3901 Fort Armistead Road, Baltimore MD 21226. 410/355-3600. **Fax:** 410/354-7343. **Contact:** J.H. Martin, Supervisor-Professional Employment. **Description:** Produces specialized titanium dioxide pigments for industrial and related uses as a division of the manufacturer of paints, coatings, resins, and lacquers. A subsidiary of SCM Corporation (New York, NY), a diversified corporation with interests in paper, consumer goods, chemicals, metals, foods, and other areas. **Common positions include:** Accountant/Auditor; Budget Analyst; Chemical Engineer; Chemist; Computer Programmer; Computer Systems Analyst; Customer Service Representative; Draftsperson; Electrical/Electronics Engineer; Environmental Engineer; Financial Analyst; Human Resources Specialist; Mechanical Engineer; Transportation/Traffic Specialist. **Educational backgrounds include:** Accounting; Chemistry; Engineering. **Benefits:** 401K; Dental Insurance; Disability Coverage; Employee Discounts; Life Insurance; Medical Insurance; Pension Plan; Tuition Assistance. **Corporate headquarters location:** Baltimore MD. **Other U.S. locations:** White Marsh MD; Ashtabula OH. **Parent company:** Hanson Industries. **Operations at this facility include:** Administration; Manufacturing. **Number of employees at this location:** 800. **Number of employees nationwide:** 1,500.

SCHLUMBERGER MALCO, INC
9800 Reisterstown Road, Owings Mills MD 21117. 410/363-1600. **Fax:** 410/581-3054. **Contact:** Gaye Saller, Employment Coordinator. **Description:** A plastics products manufacturer, producing such diverse items as credit cards and advertising specialties, as well as providing screen process printing, lithography, and embossing services. **Common positions include:** Blue-Collar Worker Supervisor; Buyer; Chemist; Computer Systems Analyst; Mechanical Engineer. **Benefits:** Dental Insurance; Disability Coverage; Life Insurance; Medical Insurance; Pension Plan; Profit Sharing; Tuition Assistance. **Corporate headquarters location:** This Location. **Parent company:** Schlumberger. **Operations at this facility include:** Manufacturing. **Listed on:** New York Stock Exchange. **Number of employees at this location:** 310.

SHERWIN WILLIAMS COMPANY
2325 Hollins Ferry Road, Baltimore MD 21230. **Contact:** Personnel. **Description:** Produces a line of paints, varnishes, lacquers, and spray paints. **Corporate headquarters location:** Cleveland OH.

THE VALSPAR CORPORATION
1401 Severn Street, Baltimore MD 21230. 410/625-7200. **Contact:** Personnel Department. **Description:** Nationally, the company is engaged in the manufacture and distribution of paint and coatings through Consumer Coatings, Industrial Coatings, and Special Products divisions. Consumer Coatings division manufactures and distributes a full line of latex and oil-based paints, stains, and varnishes for consumer and industrial use. Industrial Coatings division manufactures and distributes decorative and protective finishes for OEMs, as well as other specialized industrial coatings. Special Products division produces and markets resins, emulsions, colorants, and paint specialty colors. This facility produces consumer paints, industrial coatings, and synthetic resins. **Corporate headquarters location:** Minneapolis MN. **Listed on:** American Stock Exchange.

Chemicals/Rubber and Plastics/131

VISTA CHEMICALS COMPANY
3441 Fairfield Road, Baltimore MD 21226. 410/355-6200. **Contact:** David Mahler, Director of Human Resources. **Description:** Produces petroleum detergent intermediates and plasticizers. **Common positions include:** Accountant/Auditor; Administrative Services Manager; Blue-Collar Worker Supervisor; Chemical Engineer; Chemist; Clerical Supervisor; Construction and Building Inspector; Construction Contractor and Manager; Designer; Draftsperson; Electrician; Employment Interviewer; Financial Services Sales Rep.; Human Resources Specialist; Industrial Production Manager; Mechanical Engineer; Millwright; Payroll Clerk; Purchasing Agent and Manager; Receptionist; Securities Sales Rep.; Stationary Engineer; Water Transportation Worker; Welder. **Educational backgrounds include:** Accounting; Business Administration; Chemistry; Engineering. **Benefits:** Daycare Assistance; Dental Insurance; Disability Coverage; Employee Discounts; Life Insurance; Medical Insurance; Pension Plan; Savings Plan. **Special Programs:** Apprenticeships; Internships; Training Programs. **Corporate headquarters location:** Houston TX. **Operations at this facility include:** Manufacturing. **Number of employees at this location:** 170. **Number of employees nationwide:** 1,600.

Note: Because addresses and telephone numbers of smaller companies change rapidly, we recommend you call each company to verify the information below before inquiring about job opportunities. Mass mailings are not recommended.

Additional employers with over 250 employees:

PLASTICS MATERIALS, SYNTHETICS, AND ELASTOMERS

Gts Duratek Inc.
8955 Guilford Rd, Columbia MD 21046-2623. 410/312-5100.

ADHESIVES AND SEALANTS

American Cyanimid Co.
1300 Revolution St, Hvre De Grace MD 21078-3800. 410/939-1910.

PLASTICS PRODUCTS

Nevamar Corp.
8339 Telegraph Rd, Odenton MD 21113-1397. 410/551-5000.

Burnett & Co. Inc.
2112 Montevideo Rd, Jessup MD 20794-9728. 410/799-1788.

Cambridge Incorporated
P O Box 399, Cambridge MD 21613-0399. 410/228-3000.

Certain-Teed Corp.
PO Box 290, Williamsport MD 21795-0290. 301/223-7900.

Maryland Plastics Division
251 E Central Ave, Federalsburg MD 21632-1313. 410/754-5566.

Moldcraft Plastic & Poly Seal
4211 Shannon Dr, Baltimore MD 21213-2152. 410/325-4090.

Additional employers with under 250 employees:

INDUSTRIAL INORGANIC CHEMICALS

Miles Inc.
5601 Eastern Ave, Baltimore MD 21224-2726. 410/633-9550.

PLASTICS MATERIALS, SYNTHETICS, AND ELASTOMERS

William T Burnett & Co.
2112 Montevideo Rd, Jessup MD 20794-9728. 410/799-1788.

PAINTS, VARNISHES, AND RELATED PRODUCTS

Bruning Paint Company
601 S Haven St, Baltimore MD 21224-4347. 410/342-3636.

Lenmar Inc.
150 S Calverton Rd,
Baltimore MD 21223-2151. 410/947-7020.

Mc Cormick Paint Works Co.
2355 Lewis Ave, Rockville MD 20851-2391. 301/770-3235.

INDUSTRIAL ORGANIC CHEMICALS

Medo Manufacturing Corporation
1900 Johnson St, Baltimore MD 21230-4915. 410/547-0131.

ADHESIVES AND SEALANTS

W L Gore & Associates
2401 Singerly Rd, Elkton MD 21921-2733. 410/398-6400.

PRINTING INK

Sicpa Securink Corporation
8000 Research Way,
Springfield VA 22153-3131. 703/455-8050.

CHEMICALS AND CHEMICAL PREPARATIONS

American Type Culture Collect
12301 Parklawn Dr, Rockville MD 20852-1749. 301/881-2600.

Himont USA Inc.
912 Appleton Rd, Elkton MD 21921-3920. 410/398-0319.

MISC. RUBBER AND PLASTICS PRODUCTS

Monarch Rubber Co.
3500 Pulaski Hwy, Baltimore MD 21224-1532. 410/342-8510.

UNSUPPORTED PLASTICS PRODUCTS

F&CG American Mirrex
601 Marvel Rd, Salisbury MD 21801. 410/548-7759.

Occidental Chemical Corporation
Northwood Industrial Pk, Salisbury MD 21801. 410/749-0344.

PLASTICS PRODUCTS

Russell-William Ltd.
1710 Midway Rd, Odenton MD 21113-1186. 410/551-3600.

Briggs & Company
3921 Vero Rd, Baltimore MD 21227-1564. 410/536-2070.

Continental Plastic Containers
7100 E Baltimore St, Baltimore MD 21224-1830. 410/288-4500.

Owens-Illinois Inc.
201 Kane St, Baltimore MD 21224-1729. 410/633-8282.

Southeastern Container
265 Brooke Rd, Fredericksbrg VA 22405-1868. 703/722-2600.

Adell Plastics Inc.
4530 Annapolis Rd, Baltimore MD 21227-4899. 410/789-7780.

Maryland Lava Co.
PO Box 527, Bel Air MD 21014-0527. 410/838-4114.

Old Line Plastics Inc.
1515 Melrose Loan # D, Forest Hill MD 21050-3048. 410/879-6010.

P T P Industries Inc.
2 Wells St, Baltimore MD 21230-4834. 410/727-1828.

Rehau Inc.
PO Box 1706, Leesburg VA 22075-1706. 703/777-5255.

Superfos Packaging
11301 Superfos Dr, Cumberland MD 21502. 301/759-3145.

CHEMICALS AND ALLIED PRODUCTS WHOLESALE

Airco Industrial Gas
3901 Glidden Rd, Baltimore MD 21226-1803. 410/354-1613.

Laroche Industries
8143 Beachwood Rd, Baltimore MD 21222-3633. 410/477-1870.

Master Builders Inc.
7216 Patton Dr, Ellicott City MD 21043. 410/781-7336.

PAINTS, VARNISHES, AND SUPPLIES WHOLESALE

Felmor Corporation
2020 Hollins Ferry Rd, Baltimore MD 21230-1694. 410/669-6000.

Duron Paints and Wallcoverings
6301 Coventry Way, Clinton MD 20735-2257. 301/856-4940.

Duron Paints and Wallcoverings
7 Carroll Plaza Shopping Ctr, Westminster MD 21157-4601. 410/876-8383.

For more information on career opportunities in the chemicals/rubber and plastics industries:

Associations

AMERICAN ASSOCIATION FOR CLINICAL CHEMISTRY
2101 L Street NW, Suite 202, Washington DC 20037-1526. 202/857-0717 or 800/892-1400. International scientific/medical society of individuals involved with clinical chemistry and other clinical labscience-related disciplines.

AMERICAN CHEMICAL SOCIETY
Career Services, 1155 16th Street NW, Washington DC 20036. 202/872-4600.

AMERICAN INSTITUTE OF CHEMICAL ENGINEERS
345 East 47th Street, New York NY 10017. 212/705-7338 or 800/242-4363. Provides leadership in advancing the chemical engineering profession as it meets the needs of society.

AMERICAN INSTITUTE OF CHEMISTS, INC.
7315 Wisconsin Avenue, Suite 502 E, Bethesda MD 20814. 301/652-2447. A professional organization supporting the social, economic, and career objectives of the individual scientist.

CHEMICAL MANUFACTURERS ASSOCIATION
2501 M Street NW, Washington DC 20037. 202/887-1100. A trade association that develops and implements programs and services and advocates public policy that benefits the industry and society.

CHEMICAL MANAGEMENT RESEARCH ASSOCIATION
60 Bay Street, Suite 702, Staten Island NY 10301. 718/876-8800.

SOCIETY OF PLASTICS ENGINEERS
14 Fairfield Drive, P.O. Box 403, Brookfield CT 06804-0403. 203/775-0471. Dedicated to helping members attain higher professional status through increased scientific, engineering, and technical knowledge.

THE SOCIETY OF THE PLASTICS INDUSTRY, INC.
1275 K Street NW, Suite 400, Washington DC 20005. 202/371-5200. Promotes the development of the plastics industry and enhances public understanding of its contributions while meeting the needs of society.

Directories

CHEMICAL INDUSTRY DIRECTORY
State Mutual Book and Periodical Service, Order Department, 17th Floor, 521 5th Avenue, New York NY 10175. 516/537-1104.

CHEMICALS DIRECTORY
Cahners Publishing, 275 Washington Street, Newton MA 02158. 617/964-3030.

DIRECTORY OF CHEMICAL ENGINEERING CONSULTANTS
American Institute of Chemical Engineering, 345 East 47th Street, New York NY 10017. 212/705-7338.

DIRECTORY OF CHEMICAL PRODUCERS
SRI International, 333 Ravenswood Avenue, Menlo Park CA 94025. 415/326-6200.

Magazines

CHEMICAL & ENGINEERING NEWS
American Chemical Society 1155 16th Street NW, Washington DC 20036. 202/872-4600.

CHEMICAL MARKETING REPORTER
Schnell Publishing Co., 80 Brot Street, 23rd Floor, New York NY 10004. 212/248-4177.

CHEMICAL PROCESSING
Putnam Publishing Co., 301 East Erie Street, Chicago IL 60611. 312/644-2020.

CHEMICAL WEEK
888 7th Avenue, 26th Floor, New York NY 10106. 212/621-4900.

COMMUNICATIONS: TELECOMMUNICATIONS & BROADCASTING

Telecommunications: Business is booming with the dramatic acceleration in telecommunications to reach new ground and more customers, especially in wireless phone service. Regulations are changing, causing doors to open and companies to come together in the cable and local and long distance phone business. Nearly all of the top-rated companies in the industry have experienced an increase in sales and revenues in the past year.

Broadcasting: Competition is high in this industry, especially for high-profile positions such as newscasters and dee-jays. In television, the hottest industry is cable. Cable companies are rapidly expanding requiring a need for people in the industry, more so in technical fields. In radio, syndicated radio shows are tearing up the air waves. Larger stations with more money, experience, and bigger names are producing shows which smaller stations are picking up to save money. This increase in syndication will result in even higher competition in the radio industry.

AT&T (AMERICAN TELEPHONE & TELEGRAPH)
3033 Chain Bridge Road, Oakton VA 22185. 703/691-5000. **Contact:** Personnel Coordinator. **Description:** Provides a wide range of long-distance telecommunications services throughout the United States and internationally as part of AT&T Communications, Inc. **Corporate headquarters location:** New York NY.

AT&T (AMERICAN TELEPHONE & TELEGRAPH)
8403 Colesville Road, Silver Spring MD 20910. 301/608-4000. **Contact:** Human Resources. **Description:** Provides a wide range of long-distance telecommunications services throughout the United States and internationally as part of AT&T Communications, Inc. **Corporate headquarters location:** New York NY.

ALLIEDSIGNAL AEROSPACE
GOVERNMENT ELECTRONIC SYSTEMS
1300 East Joppa Road, Baltimore MD 21286. 410/583-4469. **Fax:** 410/832-2203. **Contact:** Recruiter. **Description:** Develops and manufactures airborne communications systems, such as CID, microwave landing systems, and airborne radar applications. A division of AlliedSignal Aerospace, which is a business sector of AlliedSignal Corporation. AlliedSignal Corporation is one of the nation's largest industrial organizations, serving a broad spectrum of industries through more than 40 strategic businesses. **Common positions include:** Accountant/Auditor; Blue-Collar Worker Supervisor; Commercial Artist; Computer Programmer; Computer Systems Analyst; Cost Estimator; Electrical/Electronics Engineer; Mechanical Engineer; Metallurgical Engineer; Precision Assembler; Purchasing Agent and Manager; Quality Control Supervisor; Secretary; Software Engineer; Typist/Word Processor. **Educational backgrounds include:** Accounting; Business Administration; Computer Science; Engineering. **Benefits:** 401K; Dental Insurance; Disability Coverage; Employee Discounts; Life Insurance; Medical Insurance; Paid Vacation; Pension Plan; Savings Plan; Tuition Assistance. **Special Programs:** Training Programs. **Corporate headquarters location:** Morristown NJ. **Parent company:** AlliedSignal Corporation. **Listed on:** New York Stock Exchange. **Number of employees at this location:** 1,100. **Number of employees nationwide:** 86,000.

AMERICA ONLINE INC.
8619 Westwood Center Drive, Vienna VA 22182-2285. 703/448-8700. **Contact:** Human Resources. **Description:** America Online provides on-line services to

consumers, including electronic mail, conferencing, stock quotes, software, computing support and on-line classes. **Number of employees at this location:** 527.

ARBITRON COMPANY
9705 Patuxent Woods Drive, Columbia MD 21046. 410/312-8000. **Contact:** Wanda Kemp, Professional Recruiter. **Description:** Engaged in the field of broadcast audience measurement. The field staff of more than 3,000 interviewers contact more than 2 million households, representing a cross-section of Americans in every country, to obtain television viewing and radio listening information. The company produces the Arbitron Television and Radio Reports, which describes television viewing or radio listening patterns in more than 200 marketing areas in the United States. Advertisers and their agencies use these reports when planning, buying, or evaluating their advertising schedules to determine the cost-efficiency of their campaigns. More than 2,000 radio stations, 580 television stations, and 3,500 advertisers and their agencies and buying services use the reports. **Other U.S. locations:** Los Angeles CA; San Francisco CA; Washington DC; Atlanta GA; Chicago IL.

BELL ATLANTIC
1710 H Street NW, Washington DC 20006. **Contact:** Corporate Personnel Office. **Description:** Bell Atlantic Corporation is a diversified telecommunications company founded in 1984, providing advanced voice and data services in the mid-Atlantic region, and wireless communications throughout East Coast markets and parts of the Southeast and Southwest. Bell Atlantic continues to pursue growth opportunities in wireless and video and entertainment markets, both domestically and internationally. **Common positions include:** Accountant/Auditor; Computer Programmer; Marketing Specialist. **Educational backgrounds include:** Accounting; Computer Science; Marketing. **Benefits:** Dental Insurance; Disability Coverage; Employee Discounts; Life Insurance; Medical Insurance; Pension Plan; Profit Sharing; Savings Plan; Tuition Assistance. **Corporate headquarters location:** Philadelphia PA.

BELL ATLANTIC
1320 North Court House Road, 6th Floor, Arlington VA 22201. 703/974-3000. **Contact:** Mr. Gene Weidemoyer, Human Resources. **Description:** Bell Atlantic Corporation is a diversified telecommunications company founded in 1984, providing advanced voice and data services in the mid-Atlantic region, and wireless communications throughout East Coast markets and parts of the Southeast and Southwest. Bell Atlantic continues to pursue growth opportunities in wireless and video and entertainment markets, both domestically and internationally. **Corporate headquarters location:** Philadelphia PA.

BELL ATLANTIC MARYLAND
1 East Pratt Street, Baltimore MD 21202. 410/539-9900. **Contact:** Edie Worrell, Director of Human Resources. **Description:** Bell Atlantic Corporation is a diversified telecommunications company founded in 1984, providing advanced voice and data services in the mid-Atlantic region, and wireless communications throughout East Coast markets and parts of the Southeast and Southwest. Bell Atlantic continues to pursue growth opportunities in wireless and video and entertainment markets, both domestically and internationally. **Corporate headquarters location:** Philadelphia PA.

BLACK ENTERTAINMENT TELEVISION
1900 W Place NW, Washington DC 20018. 202/608-2000. **Fax:** 202/608-2589. **Recorded Jobline:** 202/608-2800. **Contact:** Lynne D. Carter, Vice President, Human Resources. **Description:** The Black Entertainment Television Network (BET Network) is an advertiser-supported basic cable television network. It is the only television network whose programming specifically targets the interests and concerns of black Americans. Parent company, BET Holdings, is also the publisher of *YSB* and *Emerge*, two magazines that also serve black Americans. **Common positions include:** Accountant/Auditor; Attorney; Broadcast Technician; Computer Systems Analyst; Editor; Electrical/Electronics Engineer; Human Resources Specialist; Operations/Production Manager. **Educational backgrounds include:** Accounting; Communications; Computer Science; Liberal Arts. **Benefits:** 401K; Dental Insurance; Disability Coverage; Life Insurance; Medical Insurance; Profit Sharing. **Special Programs:** Internships. **Corporate headquarters location:** This Location. **Other U.S. locations:** Santa Monica CA; Chicago IL; New York NY. **Parent company:** BET Holdings. **Operations at this facility include:** Administration; Sales. **Listed on:** New York Stock Exchange. **Number of employees nationwide:** 475.

BUREAU OF BROADCASTING
330 Independence Avenue Southwest, Room 1543, Washington DC 20547. 202/619-3117. **Recorded Jobline:** 202/619-0909. **Contact:** Personnel Office. **Description:** Produces and broadcasts Voice of America and other radio programs for international transmission.

CBS NEWS/WASHINGTON OFFICE
2020 M Street NW, Washington DC 20036. 202/457-4321. **Contact:** Personnel Administrator. **Description:** An office for CBS News, one of six divisions in CBS Inc.'s Broadcast Group. **Corporate headquarters location:** New York NY.

CNN AMERICA INC.
820 First Street, Washington DC 20002. 202/515-2913. **Recorded Jobline:** 404/827-5144. **Contact:** Human Resources. **Description:** Well-known cable news network offering 24 hours of news and information. **Common positions include:** Broadcast Technician; Editor; Library Technician; Reporter; Technical Writer/Editor. **Educational backgrounds include:** Communications; Liberal Arts; Political Science. **Benefits:** 401K; Dental Insurance; Disability Coverage; Employee Discounts; Life Insurance; Medical Insurance; Pension Plan; Tuition Assistance. **Corporate headquarters location:** Atlanta GA. **Parent company:** Turner Broadcasting System, Inc.

CABLE AND WIRELESS, INC.
8219 Leesburg Pike, Vienna VA 22182. 703/790-5300. **Fax:** 703/760-1758. **Contact:** Human Resources. **Description:** Offers domestic and international voice and data services to businesses. Locations in 40 major cities around the U.S. **Common positions include:** Accountant/Auditor; Adjuster; Attorney; Budget Analyst; Buyer; Computer Operator; Computer Programmer; Computer Systems Analyst; Credit Clerk and Authorizer; Customer Service Representative; Draftsperson; Electrical/Electronics Engineer; Employment Interviewer; Financial Analyst; Manufacturer's/Wholesaler's Sales Rep.; Marketing Research Analyst; Paralegal; Payroll Clerk; Receptionist; Secretary; Software Engineer; Systems Analyst; Technical Writer/Editor; Typist/Word Processor. **Educational backgrounds include:** Accounting; Business Administration; Communications; Computer Science; Engineering; Finance; Liberal Arts; Marketing; Mathematics. **Benefits:** Dental Insurance; Disability Coverage; Employee Discounts; Life Insurance; Medical Insurance; Pension Plan; Savings Plan; Stock Option; Tuition Assistance. **Parent company:** Cable & Wireless PLC. **Operations at this facility include:** Administration; Manufacturing; Research and Development; Sales; Service. **Listed on:** New York Stock Exchange. **Number of employees at this location:** 800. **Number of employees nationwide:** 2,000.

CABLE TELEVISION OF MONTGOMERY
20 West Gude Drive, Rockville MD 20850-1151. 301/294-7600. **Contact:** Grace Killelea, Director of Human Resources. **Description:** A provider of cable television services. **Common positions include:** Accountant/Auditor; Communications Engineer; Customer Service Representative; Data Processor; Electrical/Electronics Engineer; Financial Analyst.

CAPITAL CITIES/ABC
1717 DeSales Street NW, Washington DC 20036. 202/222-7777. **Contact:** Human Resources. **Description:** A national broadcasting company.

COMMUNICATIONS SATELLITE CORPORATION
5560 Rock Spring Drive, Bethesda MD 20817. 301/214-3000. **Contact:** Bruce Crockett, CEO/President. **Description:** A telecommunications company.

COMSAT CORPORATION
6560 Rock Spring Drive, Bethesda MD 20817-1146. 301/214-3000. **Contact:** Human Resources. **Description:** COMSAT Corporation is engaged in two businesses; international telecommunications and entertainment. Using the global INTELSAT and Inmarsat satellite communications networks, COMSAT transmits voice, fax, data and video services to a growing global market. Through an increasing number of telecommunications ventures that serve overseas markets, COMSAT provides its customers with a wide array of private-line and public-switched digital communications services. COMSAT also manufactures telecommunications components and offers turnkey systems for wireless networks. COMSAT Laboratories is a leading distributor of on-demand entertainment programming and information services to the domestic hospitality industry. COMSAT also owns the NBA Denver

Communications: Telecommunications/Broadcasting/137

Nuggets and Beacon Communications Corporation, a Los Angeles-based film and television production company. **Number of employees nationwide:** 1,644.

DENRO INC.
9318 Gaither Road, Gaithersburg MD 20877. 301/840-1597. **Contact:** Jody Friend, Human Resources Manager. **Description:** Designs, manufactures, and services electronic communications equipment primarily for the air traffic control industry. Denro is co-owned by five of its executives, and a Canadian company, Firan Corporation. **Common positions include:** Accountant/Auditor; Buyer; Computer Operator; Customer Service Representative; Draftsperson; Electrical/Electronics Engineer; Marketing/Advertising/PR Manager; Purchasing Agent and Manager; Software Engineer. **Educational backgrounds include:** Accounting; Business Administration; Communications; Computer Science; Engineering; Finance; Marketing. **Benefits:** Dental Insurance; Disability Coverage; Life Insurance; Medical Insurance; Savings Plan; Tuition Assistance. **Special Programs:** Internships. **Corporate headquarters location:** This Location. **Parent company:** Firan Corporation. **Operations at this facility include:** Manufacturing; Research and Development; Sales; Service. **Listed on:** Canadian Stock Exchange. **Annual Revenues:** $33,000,000. **Number of employees at this location:** 238. **Number of employees nationwide:** 250.

GM HUGHES NETWORK SYSTEMS
11717 Exploration Lane, Germantown MD 20876-2700. 301/428-5500. **Contact:** Mark Balzer, Personnel. **Description:** GM Hughes Electronics Corporation markets and serves high technology electronic systems and products for global defense, telecommunications and space and automotive industries. In the Defense Division, there are four product groups including Radar and Communication Systems, Electro-Optical Systems, Weapons Systems and Information Systems. Products in the Defense Division include airborne, land- and ship-based radar, laser rangefinders, cruise and tactical guided missiles and command and control systems. The Telemarketing and Space Division produces satellites and satellite-based telecommunication systems and services. The corporation's Automotive Electronics Division develops, manufactures and markets electronics for vehicles worldwide. Their products include airbag electronics, antilock brake modules, remote keyless entry, engine and transmission controls and pressure sensors. The Commercial Technologies Division utilizes core defense and space technologies for commercial and non-defense government applications. Major products include large-scale database management systems, air traffic control systems and large-screen projector systems. **Parent company:** Hughes Aircraft Company. **Number of employees at this location:** 340. **Number of employees nationwide:** 1,050.

GTE GOVERNMENT SYSTEMS
15000 Conference Center Drive, P.O. Box 10814, Chantilly VA 22021. 703/818-4000. **Contact:** Staffing. **Description:** A telephone communications firm. **Common positions include:** Accountant/Auditor; Administrator; Electrical/Electronics Engineer; Technician. **Educational backgrounds include:** Computer Science; Engineering; Finance; Mathematics. **Benefits:** Dental Insurance; Disability Coverage; Life Insurance; Medical Insurance; Pension Plan; Savings Plan; Tuition Assistance. **Corporate headquarters location:** Stamford CT. **Operations at this facility include:** Administration; Regional Headquarters. **Listed on:** New York Stock Exchange.

INTELSAT
3400 International Drive NW, Washington DC 20008. 202/944-6800. **Contact:** Dan Davis, Senior Recruitment Officer. **Description:** Office of an international communications satellite organization. **Common positions include:** Aerospace Engineer; Computer Programmer; Electrical/Electronics Engineer; Financial Analyst; Human Resources Specialist; Purchasing Agent and Manager; Systems Analyst. **Educational backgrounds include:** Business Administration; Communications; Computer Science; Engineering; French; Liberal Arts; Mathematics; Physics; Spanish. **Benefits:** Dental Insurance; Disability Coverage; Employee Discounts; Extensive Vacation; Life Insurance; Medical Insurance; Pension Plan; Savings Plan; Tuition Assistance. **Corporate headquarters location:** This Location. **Operations at this facility include:** Administration.

MCI COMMUNICATIONS CORPORATION
1801 Pennsylvania Avenue NW, Washington DC 20006. 202/872-1600. **Recorded Jobline:** 800/777-6063. **Contact:** Corporate Human Resources. **Description:** MCI is one of the nation's largest long-distance companies and the fifth largest international carrier, providing a full array of sophisticated domestic and international

telecommunications services to millions of residential and business customers, state and federal government agencies, and other organizations. MCI has divisional offices in Atlanta, GA, Rye Brook, NY, and Arlington, VA, and more than 65 overseas offices in 60 countries. The company has over 40,000 employees worldwide. **NOTE:** Systems Engineering job hotline: 800/695-2380. **Educational backgrounds include:** Accounting; Business Administration; Communications; Computer Science; Engineering; Finance; Liberal Arts; Marketing; Mathematics; Physics. **Benefits:** Dental Insurance; Disability Coverage; Life Insurance; Medical Insurance; Pension Plan; Tuition Assistance. **Special Programs:** Internships. **Corporate headquarters location:** This Location. **Listed on:** NASDAQ. **Other U.S. locations:** Atlanta, GA; Rye Brook, NY; Arlington, VA.

MONTGOMERY COMMUNITY TELEVISION
7548 Standish Place, Rockville MD 20855. 301/424-1730. **Contact:** Human Resources. **Description:** Operates two cable channels, produces original programming, and provides production training and facilities for residents of Montgomery County, Maryland. **Corporate headquarters location:** This Location. **Number of employees at this location:** 80.

NATIONAL PUBLIC RADIO
635 Massachusetts Avenue NW, Washington DC 20001-3753. 202/414-2000. **Fax:** 202/414-3329. **Contact:** Director of Personnel. **Description:** A non-profit membership organization and production center. **Common positions include:** Computer Programmer; Customer Service Representative; Editor; Electrical/Electronics Engineer; Financial Analyst; Marketing Specialist; Public Relations Specialist; Radio/TV Producer; Reporter. **Benefits:** Cafeteria; Dental Insurance; Disability Coverage; Employee Discounts; Life Insurance; Medical Insurance; Pension Plan. **Special Programs:** Internships; Training Programs. **Corporate headquarters location:** This Location. **Operations at this facility include:** Regional Headquarters.

PENRIL DATACOMM NETWORKS
1300 Quince Orchard Boulevard, Gaithersburg MD 20878. 301/417-0552. **Contact:** Human Resources. **Description:** Designs, develops, manufactures, and markets, through its divisions and subsidiaries, data communications networking systems and specialized electronic instrumentation equipment. The company's operating entities are its data communications division and wholly-owned subsidiaries, Electro-Metrics, Inc., and Technipower, Inc.

POST-NEWSWEEK STATIONS, INC.
1150 15th Street NW, Washington DC 20071. 202/334-6656. **Contact:** Barbara Reising, Human Resource Director. **Description:** A television production and advertising firm. Company affiliates: WDIV (Detroit, MI); WPLG (Miami, FL); WJXT (Jacksonville, FL); WFSB (Hartford, CT); and the Washington DC News Bureau. **Benefits:** Adoption Assistance; Daycare Assistance; Dental Insurance; Disability Coverage; Legal Services; Life Insurance; Medical Insurance; Pension Plan; Savings Plan; Tuition Assistance. **Corporate headquarters location:** This Location. **Parent company:** The Washington Post Company.

PULSECOM/A SUBSIDIARY OF HUBBELL, INC.
2900 Towerview Road, Herndon VA 22071. 703/471-2900. **Contact:** DeeDee Mendez, Human Resources. **Description:** Produces telecommunications products, and remote-control supervisory systems for industrial processes. **Common positions include:** Electrical/Electronics Engineer. **Educational backgrounds include:** Engineering. **Benefits:** Dental Insurance; Disability Coverage; Life Insurance; Medical Insurance; Pension Plan; Savings Plan; Tuition Assistance. **Corporate headquarters location:** Orange CT. **Operations at this facility include:** Administration; Divisional Headquarters; Manufacturing; Research and Development; Sales; Service.

RACAL AVIONICS INC.
8851 Monard Drive, Silver Spring MD 20910. 301/495-6695. **Fax:** 301/585-7578. **Contact:** Human Resources. **Description:** A supplier of flight and navigation management systems; and satellite communication systems. The company's principal clients include the U.S. government and major U.S. and international airlines. **NOTE:** This company does not accept unsolicited resumes. Jobseekers should only apply for advertised openings. **Parent company:** The Racal Corporation.

Communications: Telecommunications/Broadcasting/139

RACAL COMMUNICATIONS, INC.
5 Research Place, Rockville MD 20850. 301/948-4420. **Fax:** 301/948-6015. **Contact:** Human Resources. **Description:** Manufactures military tactical and strategic radio and communications equipment with clients in over 140 countries. Products include communication systems for electronic warfare, security, simulation, and training; electro-acoustic and ground-sensor systems; and satellite communications equipment. Other services include design automation, instrumentation, and health and safety. **Corporate headquarters location:** Sunrise FL. **Parent company:** The Racal Corporation.

RACAL-GUARDATA, INC.
480 Spring Park Place, Herndon VA 22070. 703/471-0892. **Fax:** 703/437-9333. **Contact:** Human Resources. **Description:** Manufactures data communications equipment including WANs, LANs, and access products. The company also offers related services including project management, installation, consultation, network integration, maintenance, disaster recovery, and training. Foreign locations in Asia, Europe, Canada, Australia, and France. **Parent company:** The Racal Corporation.

RADIO FREE EUROPE/RADIO LIBERTY, INC.
1201 Connecticut Avenue NW, Suite 1100, Washington DC 20036. 202/457-6900. **Contact:** Human Resources. **Description:** A radio station.

SFA DATACOMM, INC.
7450 New Technology Way, P.O. Box 502, Frederick MD 21705-0502. 301/662-5901. **Contact:** Vivian Smith-Thompson, Director of Human Resources. **Description:** Designs and markets data communications (packet switching and radio frequency) equipment on a worldwide basis. **Common positions include:** Accountant/Auditor; Administrator; Buyer; Computer Programmer; Department Manager; Draftsperson; Electrical/Electronics Engineer; Financial Analyst; General Manager; Mechanical Engineer; Purchasing Agent and Manager; Quality Control Supervisor; Sales Associate; Systems Analyst; Technical Writer/Editor. **Educational backgrounds include:** Business Administration; Computer Science; Engineering; Marketing. **Benefits:** Dental Insurance; Disability Coverage; Life Insurance; Medical Insurance; Savings Plan; Stock Option; Tuition Assistance. **Corporate headquarters location:** Landover MD. **Parent company:** SFA, Inc. **Operations at this facility include:** Administration; Research and Development; Sales. **Number of employees at this location:** 52.

SALISBURY TECHNOLOGIES, LLC
600 Glen Avenue, Salisbury MD 21801. 410/548-7800. **Fax:** 410/548-7839. **Contact:** Director of Human Resources. **Description:** Provides electronic assembly cables and harnesses for military and commercial telecommunications. **Common positions include:** Aerospace Engineer; Industrial Engineer; Mechanical Engineer. **Educational backgrounds include:** Accounting; Business Administration; Communications; Computer Science; Engineering; Finance; Marketing. **Benefits:** Dental Insurance; Life Insurance; Medical Insurance; Profit Sharing. **Corporate headquarters location:** This Location. **Operations at this facility include:** Administration; Manufacturing. **Listed on:** Privately held. **Number of employees at this location:** 57.

SPRINT INTERNATIONAL
12490 Sunrise Valley Drive, Reston VA 22096. 703/689-6000. **Contact:** Human Resources. **Description:** A long-distance telecommunications company.

TECHNICAL AND MANAGEMENT SERVICES CORPORATION
TAMSCO
4041 Powder Mill Road, Suite 500, Calverton MD 20705. 301/595-0710. **Contact:** Tracy Kerns, Human Resources Administrator. **Description:** Engaged in products and services oriented to ADP and telecommunications system development, manufacturing, and integration. These include requirements definition, system engineering, systems design, telecommunications network design, software development, electronics and telecommunications equipment, hardware development and manufacturing, systems integration, and implementation. **Common positions include:** Aerospace Engineer; Aircraft Mechanic/Engine Specialist; Budget Analyst; Computer Programmer; Computer Systems Analyst; Designer; Draftsperson; Electrical/Electronics Engineer; Financial Analyst; Management Analyst/Consultant; Mechanical Engineer; Software Engineer; Technical Writer/Editor. **Educational backgrounds include:** Business Administration; Computer Science; Engineering. **Benefits:** 401K; Dental Insurance; Disability Coverage; Life Insurance; Medical Insurance; Tuition Assistance. **Corporate headquarters location:** This Location.

Operations at this facility include: Administration. Listed on: Privately held. Number of employees at this location: 40. Number of employees nationwide: 500.

TELECOMMUNICATIONS TECHNIQUES CORPORATION
20400 Observation Drive, Germantown MD 20876-4023. 301/353-1550. **Fax:** 301/353-9380. **Contact:** Recruiter. **Description:** Telecommunications Techniques, a division of Dynatech, provides equipment and services that support and build worldwide information infrastructures. Dynatech's business is separated into two businesses. One segment, Information Support Products, consists of the businesses which support voice, video and data communications. The other, smaller segment, Diversified Instrumentation, represents a group of electronics and software businesses. The infrastructure consists of three elements: Generation, Transmission and Presentation. Generation involves supplying broadcasters, cable-TV operators and video production companies with products they use to generate, manipulate, edit, store and recall video information. Transmission is addressed by Dynatech's communications test and network products businesses. In Presentation, Dynatech is involved in hardware and software that facilitate video-related applications such as video conferencing through a workstation network. **Common positions include:** Accountant/Auditor; Buyer; Customer Service Representative; Electrical/Electronics Engineer; Industrial Production Manager; Software Engineer; Technical Writer/Editor. **Educational backgrounds include:** Accounting; Business Administration; Computer Science; Engineering. **Benefits:** 401K; Dental Insurance; Disability Coverage; Employee Discounts; Life Insurance; Medical Insurance; Profit Sharing; Tuition Assistance. **Corporate headquarters location:** This Location. **Other U.S. locations:** Nationwide. **Parent company:** Dynatech Corporation. **Operations at this facility include:** Administration; Divisional Headquarters; Manufacturing; Regional Headquarters; Research and Development; Sales; Service. **Listed on:** NASDAQ. **Number of employees at this location:** 600. **Number of employees nationwide:** 800.

WBAL-TV
3800 Hooper Avenue, Baltimore MD 21211. 410/467-3000. **Contact:** Human Resources. **Description:** Previously a CBS-affiliated television station WBAL-TV became an NBC affiliate on January 2, 1995. **Common positions include:** Broadcast Technician; Reporter. **Educational backgrounds include:** Communications; Marketing. **Benefits:** 401K; Dental Insurance; Disability Coverage; Life Insurance; Medical Insurance; Pension Plan; Profit Sharing. **Special Programs:** Internships. **Corporate headquarters location:** New York NY. **Other U.S. locations:** Pittsburg KS; Charlotte NC; Dayton OH; Milwaukee WI. **Parent company:** Hearst Broadcasting. **Operations at this facility include:** Sales. **Listed on:** Privately held. **Number of employees at this location:** 300. **Number of employees nationwide:** 7,000.

WDCA-TV
UPN/CHANNEL 20
5202 River Road, Bethesda MD 20816. 301/986-9322. **Fax:** 301/654-3517. **Recorded Jobline:** 301/961-3327. **Contact:** Human Resources. **Description:** A television station. **Common positions include:** Administrative Worker/Clerk; Administrator; Sales/Marketing Director; Technician; Writer/Producer/Director. **Educational backgrounds include:** Accounting; Communications; Liberal Arts; Marketing. **Benefits:** Dental Insurance; Disability Coverage; Life Insurance; Medical Insurance; Tuition Assistance. **Special Programs:** Internships. **Corporate headquarters location:** Hollywood CA. **Parent company:** Paramount. **Operations at this facility include:** Administration; Production; Sales. **Listed on:** New York Stock Exchange. **Number of employees at this location:** 62.

WJLA-TV
3007 Tilden Street NW, Washington DC 20008. 202/364-7777. **Contact:** Human Resources. **Description:** A television station.

W.R.C. NBC NEWS
4001 Nebraska Avenue NW, Washington DC 20016. 202/885-4000. **Contact:** Human Resources. **Description:** A national broadcasting company.

WTTG FOX TELEVISION STATIONS
5151 Wisconsin Avenue NW, Washington DC 20016. 202/895-3232. **Contact:** Human Resources. **Description:** A broadcast television station.

Communications: Telecommunications/Broadcasting/141

Note: Because addresses and telephone numbers of smaller companies change rapidly, we recommend you call each company to verify the information below before inquiring about job opportunities. Mass mailings are not recommended.

Additional employers with over 250 employees:

COMMUNICATIONS EQUIPMENT

Microdyne Corp.
207 S Peyton St, Alexandria VA 22314-2812. 703/739-0500.

Ensco Inc.
5400 Port Royal Rd, Springfield VA 22151-2301. 703/321-9000.

Watkins-Johnson Co.
700 Quince Orchard Rd, Gaithersburg MD 20878-1794. 301/948-7550.

CABLE/PAY TELEVISION SERVICES

Bet Holdings Inc.
1232 31st St Nw, Washington DC 20007-3402. 202/337-5260.

Media General Cable Of Fairfax
14650 Lee Rd, Chantilly VA 22021-1707. 703/378-8411.

MISC. COMMUNICATION SERVICES

Aeronautical Radio Inc.
2551 Riva Rd, Annapolis MD 21401-7435. 410/266-4000.

GTE Contel Federal Systems
15000 Conference Center Dr, Chantilly VA 22021. 703/818-4000.

Additional employers with under 250 employees:

COMMUNICATIONS EQUIPMENT

International Telesystems Corporation
555 Herndon Pky, Herndon VA 22070-5226. 703/478-9808.

Cici Inc.
15200 Omega Dr, Rockville MD 20850-3240. 301/590-7079.

Comsearch
2002 Edmund Halley Dr, Reston VA 22091-3436. 703/620-6300.

Defense Systems Inc.
1521 Westbranch Dr, Mc Lean VA 22102-3201. 703/883-1000.

Earth Observation Satellite Co.
4300 Forbes Blvd, Lanham MD 20706-4383. 301/552-0500.

Superior Engineering & Electric Co.
2361 Jefferson Davis Hwy #600, Arlington VA 22202-3876. 703/920-4446.

Wordpro Inc.
250 Hungerford Dr # 109, Rockville MD 20850-4100. 301/738-3232.

Airbus Industries of North America
593 Herndon Parkview Exec Ctr, Herndon VA 22070. 703/834-3400.

Coherent Communications System
44084 Riverside Pky Ste 200, Leesburg VA 22075-5102. 703/934-1690.

Phelps Protection Systems
1908 Forest Dr Ste L, Annapolis MD 21401-4340. 410/263-7220.

TELEPHONE COMMUNICATIONS

Celutel Inc.
900 Bestgate Rd Ste 400, Annapolis MD 21401-3066. 410/573-5200.

Crowley Cellular Telecom
1 Wisconsin Cir, Chevy Chase MD 20815-7001. 301/913-0409.

Cleartel Communications
1232 22nd St NW Ste 100, Washington DC 20037-1201. 202/463-8500.

Kobe Fiber Optics
1633 Carriage House Ter Apt A, Silver Spring MD 20904-2272. 410/623-9155.

Microlog Corporation
20270 Goldenrod Ln, Germantown MD 20876-4065. 301/428-9100.

Agency Services
12510 Prosperity Dr, Silver Spring MD 20904-1663. 301/622-0453.

Atlantic Phone Systems
8019 Belair Rd, Baltimore MD 21236-3711. 410/882-5210.

Brothers On The Move
18 N High St, Baltimore MD 21202-4718. 410/332-8064.

C&P Telephone Co.
14 Bloomsbury Ave, Catonsville MD 21228-4642. 410/747-4825.

Capital Telecom MD
521 E Joppa Rd, Baltimore MD 21286-5484. 410/337-3808.

Executive Telecard
6015 Montrose Rd, Rockville MD 20852-4801. 301/770-2029.

Inter/Tel/Telcom
10219 Southard Dr, Beltsville MD 20705-2126. 301/595-3207.

Kahar Telecommunication Corporation
801 N Fillmore St, Arlington VA 22201-2030. 703/525-6845.

U.S. Digital Network
8575D Sudley Rd, Manassas VA 22110-3811. 703/361-1520.

United States Spirit
1875 I St Nw, Washington DC 20006-5409. 202/416-6200.

Capitol Communication Corporation
8575 Sudley Rd # D, Manassas VA 22110-3811. 703/330-7777.

GTE Telemessenger
2021 K St Nw, Washington DC 20006-1003. 202/223-7900.

Acacia Communications Corporation
1220 L St Nw, Washington

DC 20005-4018. 202/789-2929.

Applied Quality Commctns Inc.
2875 Towerview Dr, Herndon VA 22071-3205. 703/318-9481.

Applied Quality Commctns Inc.
8230 Old Courthouse Rd, Vienna VA 22182-3853. 703/903-9790.

Atlantic & Pac Telecom Corporation
14221 Willard Rd # B, Chantilly VA 22021-2957. 703/968-9701.

Baxter Technologies
1323 N Calvert St, Baltimore MD 21202-3966. 410/332-4444.

C E C Communications Mgt.
8602 Inwood Rd, Baltimore MD 21244-1101. 410/655-4801.

C S Technology Inc.
12050 Baltimore Ave, Beltsville MD 20705-4219. 301/419-0094.

Curtain Call Communications Co.
15523 Langside St, Silver Spring MD 20905-4133. 301/989-2255.

Esprit Telecom Ltd.
2021 L St Nw, Washington DC 20036-4909. 202/467-1992.

Fairchild Communications
8075 Leesburg Pike, Vienna VA 22182-2739. 703/506-3500.

Fargorya Enterprises
111 W Centre St, Baltimore MD 21201-4570. 410/385-1651.

Faxguard Systems Corporation
8230 Old Courthouse Rd, Vienna VA 22182-3853. 703/448-6100.

Global Long Distance Mid Atl
2709 Quarry Heights Way, Baltimore MD 21209-1068. 410/486-6873.

Icomnet
2021 L St Nw, Washington DC 20036-4909. 202/223-0615.

Its Gateway USA
11201 Raehn Ct, Sterling VA 22170. 703/450-5719.

Jaycomm Inc.
15120 Bauer Dr, Rockville MD 20853-1537. 301/871-6050.

Keystone Corporation
1850 Centennial Park Dr, Reston VA 22091-1517. 703/715-7900.

National Operator Service
6701 Democracy Blvd Ste 109, Bethesda MD 20817-1572. 301/493-5353.

Order By Phone Inc.
1 E Chase St, Baltimore MD 21202-2526. 410/539-2200.

Realcom Office Communications
1300 I St Nw, Washington DC 20005-3314. 202/962-3898.

Realistic Techl Systems & Service
1015 H St Ne, Washington DC 20002-3743. 202/396-8332.

Samuels Telecommunications
820 7th St Ne, Washington DC 20002-3610. 202/543-7509.

Startec
6000 Executive Blvd, Rockville MD 20852-3803. 301/816-3101.

Telco Communications
1045 Taylor Ave, Baltimore MD 21286-8331. 410/321-7690.

Telcom Technologies
2211 Pinneberg Ave, Rockville MD 20851-1561. 301/309-9530.

Teledebit
1600 Anderson Rd, Mc Lean VA 22102-1609. 703/734-9889.

Virtual Network Services Corporation
12 N Claverty Sr, Baltimore MD 21202. 410/837-2112.

World Communications
1828 L St Nw, Washington DC 20036-5118. 202/223-3022.

RADIO BROADCASTING STATIONS

Mutual Broadcasting System Inc.
1755 Jefferson Davis Hwy, Arlington VA 22202-3509. 703/413-8300.

Nhk Japan Broadcasting Corporation
2030 M St NW Ste 706, Washington DC 20036-3306. 202/828-5180.

Sconnix Broadcasting
1921 Gallows Rd Ste 850, Vienna VA 22182-3900. 703/356-6000.

Stoner Broadcasting System Inc.
410 Severn Ave Ste 309-10, Annapolis MD 21403-2524. 410/263-1030.

Swiss Broadcasting Corporation
2030 M St Nw, Washington DC 20036-3304. 202/293-7477.

Swiss Television
2030 M St Nw, Washington DC 20036-3304. 202/293-7202.

WWRC Am
8121 Georgia Ave, Silver Spring MD 20910-4933. 301/587-4900.

TELEVISION BROADCASTING STATIONS

AP Broadcast Services
1825 K St Nw, Washington DC 20006-1202. 202/955-7200.

C Span
400 N Capitol St NW Ste 650, Washington DC 20001-1511. 202/737-3220.

Katz National Television
1233 20th St NW Ste 203, Washington DC 20036-2304. 202/872-5880.

Multivision Cable Tv
9609 Annapolis Rd, Lanham MD 20706-2026. 301/731-5560.

WBFF
2000 W 41st St, Baltimore MD 21211-1420. 410/467-4545.

WBOC TV
PO Box 2057, Salisbury MD 21802-2057. 410/749-1111.

WJZ TV
Tv Hill, Baltimore MD 21211. 410/466-0013.

WMAR TV
6400 York Rd, Baltimore MD 21212-2111. 410/377-2222.

WNUV TV
3001 Druid Park Dr, Baltimore MD 21215-7861. 410/462-5400.

WUSA
4100 Wisconsin Ave Nw, Washington DC 20016-2810. 202/895-5999.

Communications: Telecommunications/Broadcasting

WVSA TV
4001 Brandywine St Nw, Washington DC 20016-1800. 202/364-3900.

Ebony Broadcasting
1129 20th St Nw, Washington DC 20036-3403. 202/857-0912.

Global News & Commctns Inc.
2030 M St Nw, Washington DC 20036-3304. 202/833-5060.

Prestige Channel 3
10843 Houser Dr, Fredericksbrg VA 22408-2451. 703/891-0176.

RIAS TV Washington
601 D St, Andrews Afb MD 20331-6101. 202/393-7427.

Vox Film & Television
1705 Desales St Nw, Washington DC 20036-4405. 202/457-0990.

Wken Radio
4601 Hillen Rd, Baltimore MD 21239-4005. 410/426-2618.

Worldviews
4806 York Rd, Baltimore MD 21212-4423. 410/323-3884.

CABLE/PAY TELEVISION SERVICES

Jones Intercable Inc.
PO Box 267, Gambrills MD 21054-0267. 410/987-7054.

Jones Intercable
336 Post Office Rd, Waldorf MD 20602-2717. 301/843-3520.

MISC. COMMUNICATION SERVICES

Allnewsco Inc.
7600D Boston Blvd, Springfield VA 22153-3136. 703/912-5300.

American Mobile Satellite Corporation
10802 Parkridge Blvd, Reston VA 22091-5416. 703/758-6000.

Source Telecomputing Corporation
1616 Anderson Rd, Mc Lean VA 22102-1602. 703/734-7500.

For more information on career opportunities in the communications industries:

Associations

ACADEMY OF TELEVISION ARTS & SCIENCES
5220 Lankershim Boulevard, North Hollywood CA 91601. 818/754-2800.

AMERICAN WOMEN IN RADIO AND TV, INC.
1650 Tysons Boulevard, Suite 200, McLean VA 22102. 703/506-3290.

BROADCAST PROMOTION AND MARKETING EXECUTIVES
2029 Century Park East, Suite 555, Los Angeles CA 90028. 310/788-7600. Fax 310/788-7616.

INTERACTIVE SERVICES ASSOCIATION
Suite 865, 8403 Colesville Road, Siver Springs MD 20910. 301/495-4955.

INTERNATIONAL TELEVISION ASSOCIATION
6311 North O'Connor Road, Suite 230, Irving TX 75309. 214/869-1112. Membership required.

NATIONAL ASSOCIATION OF BROADCASTERS
1771 N Street NW, Washington DC 20036. 202/429-5300, ext. 5490. 202/429-5359. Provides employment information.

NATIONAL CABLE TELEVISION ASSOCIATION
1724 Massachusetts Avenue NW, Washington DC 20036. 202/775-3550.

UNITED STATES TELEPHONE ASSOCIATION
900 19th Street NW, Suite 800, Washington DC 20006. 202/326-7300.

Magazines

BROADCASTING AND CABLE
Broadcasting Publications Inc., 1705 DeSales Street NW, Washington DC 20036. 202/659-2340.

ELECTRONIC MEDIA
Crain Communications, 220 East 42nd Street, New York NY 10017. 212/210-0100.

COMPUTER HARDWARE, SOFTWARE AND SERVICES

Hardware and Software: Companies are starting to invest more in corporate technology after several years of lean spending. Network servers have been the hot business product recently -- anticipate spending to jump nearly 30 percent in 1995. Expect a revival in big machines -- parallel computers, mainframes, and minicomputers -- to support a growing interest in online databases, accessing the Internet, and e-mail. PCs will remain the strongest part of the hardware market. Employment numbers were expected to level off during 1995 after tumbling 90,000 since 1990. The composition of the software industry is shrinking with many firms merging or acquiring others. Expect to see cable television and telephone companies move to acquire a greater foothold in the software market. Despite consolidation in the industry, the overall number of software jobs is still rising.

What's hot on the market? Strong PC sales has fueled demand for multimedia CD-ROM titles. Sales of CD-ROMs were expected to grow 25 percent in 1995. Also, the commercial online services and the Internet are creating new opportunities for software companies.

Services: Computer services professionals perform three activities: systems integration, custom programming, and consulting/training. Consulting and integration servers will be among the fastest-growing segments in computing, due to the demand for networking. And with more computer power made available, more computer support will be needed.

AMERICAN MANAGEMENT SYSTEMS INC.
1777 North Kent Street, Arlington VA 22209. 703/841-6000. **Contact:** Personnel Officer. **Description:** American Management Systems is engaged in helping large organizations solve complex management problems by applying information technology and systems engineering. Its marketing and development resources are targeted at large organizations that have a crucial need for these services. The company combines specific industry experience, business function expertise, proven systems development practices and technical competence to help clients achieve their business goals. Industries and markets served include: financial service institutions, insurance companies, federal agencies, defense, state and local government, colleges and universities, telecommunications firms, health care providers, and energy companies. **Common positions include:** Computer Engineer; Computer Programmer; Computer Scientist; Manager of Information Systems; Software Engineer. **Number of employees at this location:** 3,200.

AMERIDATA
220 Girard Street, Caller 6004, Gaithersburg MD 20884. 301/258-2965. **Contact:** Human Resources. **Description:** Provides computer systems integration services and consulting services. Ameridata specializes in integrating desktop publishing and networking systems.

ANSTEC, INCORPORATED
10530 Rosehaven Street, Suite 600, Fairfax VA 22030-2840. 703/591-4000. **Contact:** Curt White, Staffing Manager. **Description:** Provides computer systems integration and design services. **Common positions include:** Computer Engineer; Computer Programmer; Customer Service Representative; Production Coordinator.

BDM INTERNATIONAL, INC.
1501 BDM Way, McLean VA 22102. 703/848-5000. **Fax:** 703/848-5006. **Contact:** Employment Center. **Description:** BDM International, Inc. is a global provider of information technology and other technology solutions, systems, and support for governmental and commercial clients. The largest BDM company, BDM Federal, Inc., provides advanced information technology and other technology services and systems to the federal government. BDM Technologies, Inc. brings highly focused information technology expertise and solutions to industry, commercial enterprises, and state and local governments. The companies of BDM operate in the U.S., Europe, the Middle East, and elsewhere; employ 7,000 people in over 60 locations worldwide. **NOTE:** The company's e-mail address is collrela@lan.mcl.bdm.com. **Common positions include:** Computer Programmer; Computer Systems Analyst; Electrical/Electronics Engineer; Environmental Engineer; Financial Analyst; Industrial Engineer; Management Analyst/Consultant; Science Technologist; Software Engineer; Statistician. **Educational backgrounds include:** Computer Science; Engineering; Mathematics; Technology. **Benefits:** 401K; Daycare Assistance; Dental Insurance; Disability Coverage; Employee Discounts; Life Insurance; Medical Insurance; Savings Plan; Stock Option; Tuition Assistance. **Special Programs:** Internships. **Corporate headquarters location:** This Location. **Other U.S. locations:** Huntsville AL; Boulder CO; Denver CO; Albuquerque NM; Dayton OH. **Operations at this facility include:** Administration; Divisional Headquarters; Regional Headquarters; Research and Development; Service. **Listed on:** NASDAQ. **Number of employees nationwide:** 7,000.

BTG, INC.
1945 Old Gallows Road, Vienna VA 22182. 703/556-6518. **Contact:** Mr. Winder Heller, Director of Human Resources. **Description:** Providers of computer engineering services. **Common positions include:** Software Engineer.

BANCTEC SYSTEMS
2120 Industrial Parkway, Silver Spring MD 20904. 301/622-3500. **Contact:** Ms. Pat Sellers, Manager, Human Resources. **Description:** Designs, develops, and manufactures microprocessor-based, electro-mechanical optical character-reading equipment. Company markets this equipment for incorporation into computerized document processing systems. Principal purchasers of these systems include major commercial banks, utilities, insurance firms, retail companies, and other businesses handling a high volume of machine-readable documents.

CACI, INC.
1100 North Glebe Road, Arlington VA 22201. 703/841-7800. **Contact:** Personnel Manager. **Description:** An international high-technology and professional services corporation. CACI is a leader in advanced information systems, systems engineering, logistics sciences, proprietary analytical software products, market analysis consulting services, and information products and systems. **Common positions include:** Accountant/Auditor; Computer Programmer; Department Manager; Electrical/Electronics Engineer; Financial Analyst; Marketing Specialist; Purchasing Agent and Manager; Quality Control Supervisor; Systems Analyst; Technical Writer/Editor. **Educational backgrounds include:** Accounting; Business Administration; Computer Science; Engineering; Finance; Marketing; Mathematics. **Benefits:** Dental Insurance; Disability Coverage; Life Insurance; Medical Insurance; Pension Plan; Tuition Assistance. **Corporate headquarters location:** This Location. **Operations at this facility include:** Administration.

CERNER CORPORATION
2201 Cooperative Way, Suite 301, Herndon VA 22071-3024. 703/904-1871. **Contact:** Human Resources. **Description:** Cerner designs, installs, and supports information systems for the health care industry worldwide, including hospitals, HMOs, clinics, physicians' offices, and integrated health organizations. All Cerner applications are structured around a single architectural design, called Health Network Architecture (HNA), which allows information to be shared among clinical disciplines and across multiple facilities. Health professionals using Cerner systems are able to make more effective decisions, deliver care more effectively, and ultimately streamline their processes. Cerner's information systems are focused in four areas: Clinical Management, Care Management, Repositories, and Knowledge. Clinical management systems include: PathNet, which automates the processes of the clinical laboratory; MedNet, which supports pulmonary medicine, respiratory care, and other internal medicine departments; RadNet, which focuses on automating radiology department operations; PharmNet, which automates the processes of the pharmacy; SurgiNet,

which addresses the information management needs of the operating room team; and MSMEDS, which provides information management for the pharmacy. Care management systems include ProNet, which automates the processes of patient management and registration, order communication, scheduling, and tracking. Repositories include the Open Clinical Foundation, an enterprise-wide, relational database that contains information captured by various clinical systems to form the computer-based patient record; Open Management Foundation, a repository of process-related information to support management analysis and decision making; MRNet, which automates the chart management process for the medical records department; and Open Engine, an interface engine that collates interfaces, linking systems at a single point. Cerner's knowledge system is Discern, a family of applications that provides support for improving the quality and effectiveness of care.

COMNET CORPORATION
4200 Parliament Place, Suite 600, Lanham MD 20706-1852. 301/918-0400. **Contact:** Trent Lutz, Human Resources Manager. **Description:** Provides a broad range of computer services. Principal services are facilities management (systems tailored for use by a single customer with specific needs), and remote data processing services (variety of customers). **Common positions include:** Accountant/Auditor; Administrative Worker/Clerk; Attorney; Credit Manager; Human Resources Specialist. **Educational backgrounds include:** Accounting; Business Administration; Economics; Finance; Liberal Arts. **Benefits:** 401K; Dental Insurance; Disability Coverage; Life Insurance; Medical Insurance; Tuition Assistance. **Corporate headquarters location:** This Location. **Operations at this facility include:** Administration. **Listed on:** NASDAQ. **Annual Revenues:** $33,669,000. **Number of employees at this location:** 208.

COMPUCARE COMPANY
12110 Sunset Hills Road, Suite 500, Reston VA 22090. 703/709-2300. **Fax:** 703/709-2490. **Contact:** Human Resources Specialist. **Description:** A developer of both hardware and software information systems for hospitals and other health care facilities. **Common positions include:** Computer Programmer; Computer Systems Analyst; Software Engineer. **Educational backgrounds include:** Business Administration; Computer Science. **Benefits:** 401K; Dental Insurance; Disability Coverage; Life Insurance; Medical Insurance; Tuition Assistance. **Corporate headquarters location:** This Location. **Other U.S. locations:** Fountain Valley CA. **Operations at this facility include:** Administration; Research and Development; Sales; Service. **Listed on:** Privately held. **Number of employees at this location:** 150. **Number of employees nationwide:** 250.

COMPUTER DATA SYSTEMS, INC.
One Curie Court, Rockville MD 20850. 301/921-7000. **Contact:** Susan King, Recruiter. **Description:** Professional services firm which provides consulting and data processing for both federal and commercial clients at sites throughout the United States. **Common positions include:** Accountant/Auditor; Computer Programmer; Financial Analyst; Quality Control Supervisor; Systems Analyst. **Educational backgrounds include:** Accounting; Business Administration; Computer Science. **Benefits:** Dental Insurance; Employee Discounts; Life Insurance; Medical Insurance; Pension Plan; Tuition Assistance. **Corporate headquarters location:** This Location.

COMPUTER SCIENCES CORPORATION
3160 Fairview Park Drive, Falls Church VA 22042. 703/876-1000. **Fax:** 703/573-9311. **Contact:** Director. **Description:** Applies and evaluates the applications of advanced technology to practical problems in the military systems sciences, from concept and analysis through test and delivery to operations support.

COMPUTER SCIENCES CORPORATION
1301 Piccard Drive, Rockville MD 20850-4305. 301/670-2000. **Contact:** Human Resources. **Description:** The Computer Sciences Corporation primarily services the U.S. Government. The four sectors of the company include the Systems Group division, the Consulting division, the Industry Services Group and the CSC divisions. The Systems Group Division designs, engineers and integrates computer based systems and communications systems, providing all the hardware, software, training and related elements necessary to operate a system. The Consulting division includes consulting and technical services in the development of computer and communication systems to non-federal organizations. The Industry Services Group provides service to health care, insurance and financial services, as well as providing large-scale claim processing and other insurance-related services. CSC Health Care markets business systems and services to the managed health care industry, clinics and physicians. CSC

Enterprises provides consumer credit reports and account management services to credit grantors.

COMPUTER SCIENCES CORPORATION
7471 Candlewood Road, Hanover MD 21076. 410/684-3500. **Fax:** 410/684-3593. **Contact:** Human Resources. **Description:** Computer Sciences Corporation primarily services the U.S. government. Another company sector, the Systems Group division, designs, engineers, and integrates computer-based systems and communications systems, providing all the hardware, software, training, and related elements necessary to operate a system. The consulting division includes consulting and technical services in the development of computer and communication systems to non-federal organizations in the U.S. and Europe. The Industry Services Group provides services to health care, insurance, and financial services, as well as providing large-scale claim processing and other insurance-related services. CSC Health Care markets business systems and services to the managed health care industry, clinics, and physicians. CSC Enterprise provides consumer credit reports and account management services to credit grantors.

COMSYS TECHNICAL SERVICES INC.
4 Research Place, Suite 300, Rockville MD 20850. 301/921-3600. **Contact:** Human Resources. **Description:** Provider of contract programming and computer and software consulting services.

CRAY COMMUNICATIONS
9020 Junction Drive, Annapolis Junction MD 20701. 301/317-7710. **Contact:** Corrine Rawlins, Manager of Personnel. **Description:** A manufacturer of data communications products including modems, multiplexors, network management systems and message switching systems. **Common positions include:** Accountant/Auditor; Administrator; Advertising Clerk; Blue-Collar Worker Supervisor; Buyer; Claim Representative; Commercial Artist; Computer Programmer; Credit Manager; Customer Service Representative; Draftsperson; Editor; Electrical/Electronics Engineer; Human Resources Specialist; Industrial Engineer; Management Trainee; Manufacturer's/Wholesaler's Sales Rep.; Marketing Specialist; Mechanical Engineer; Operations/Production Manager; Purchasing Agent and Manager; Quality Control Supervisor; Reporter; Systems Analyst; Technical Writer/Editor; Transportation/Traffic Specialist. **Educational backgrounds include:** Accounting; Art/Design; Business Administration; Communications; Computer Science; Engineering; Finance; Marketing; Mathematics. **Benefits:** Dental Insurance; Disability Coverage; Life Insurance; Medical Insurance; Tuition Assistance. **Corporate headquarters location:** This Location. **Parent company:** Dowty PLC. **Operations at this facility include:** Administration; Manufacturing; Research and Development; Sales; Service.

DELEX SYSTEMS INC.
1953 Gallows Road, Suite 700, Vienna VA 22182. 703/734-8300. **Fax:** 703/893-5338. **Contact:** Director of Human Resources. **Description:** Provides operationally oriented systems engineering and analyses. Provides computer-based training systems and intelligence analysis to the defense community. **Common positions include:** Accountant/Auditor; Aerospace Engineer; Computer Programmer; Computer Systems Analyst; Economist/Market Research Analyst; Electrical/Electronics Engineer; Financial Analyst; Human Resources Specialist; Purchasing Agent and Manager; Software Engineer; Technical Writer/Editor. **Educational backgrounds include:** Computer Science; Engineering; Mathematics; Physics. **Benefits:** 401K; Dental Insurance; Disability Coverage; Life Insurance; Medical Insurance; Tuition Assistance. **Corporate headquarters location:** This Location. **Other U.S. locations:** CA; OH. **Operations at this facility include:** Administration; Sales. **Listed on:** Privately held. **Number of employees at this location:** 140. **Number of employees nationwide:** 250.

DIGITAL EQUIPMENT CORPORATION
8301 Professional Place, Landover MD 20785. 301/459-7900. **Contact:** Human Resources Department. **Description:** Maryland office of the computer equipment and peripherals manufacturer.

DIGITAL SYSTEMS CORPORATION
3 North Main Street, P.O. Box 158, Walkersville MD 21793-0158. 301/845-4141. **Fax:** 301/898-3331. **Contact:** Personnel Administrator. **Description:** Manufactures the proprietary Galaxy Access Control System, special purpose computers for commercial

and government markets. **Common positions include:** Computer Programmer; Computer Systems Analyst; Electrical/Electronics Engineer; Manufacturer's/Wholesaler's Sales Rep.; Quality Control Supervisor; Software Engineer. **Educational backgrounds include:** Engineering; Marketing. **Benefits:** Life Insurance; Medical Insurance. **Corporate headquarters location:** This Location. **Operations at this facility include:** Administration; Manufacturing; Regional Headquarters; Research and Development; Sales; Service. **Listed on:** Privately held. **Number of employees at this location:** 30.

FEDERAL DATA CORPORATION
4800 Hampden Lane, Suite 1100, Bethesda MD 20814. 301/986-0800. **Contact:** Vicki Pearson, EEO/Affirmative Action Administrator. **Description:** A computer wholesale resaler. Primary customers are government contractors. **Common positions include:** Computer Programmer; Computer Systems Analyst; Software Engineer. **Educational backgrounds include:** Business Administration; Computer Science. **Benefits:** Medical Insurance; Savings Plan. **Corporate headquarters location:** This Location. **Number of employees at this location:** 145.

GTSI
4100 Lafayette Center Drive, Chantilly VA 22021. 703/631-3333. **Fax:** 703/222-5240. **Contact:** Cathy Skahan, Manager, Human Resource Services. **Description:** Resells microcomputer hardware, software, work stations, allied software, peripherals, and networking products to all departments and agencies of the federal and state governments. **Common positions include:** Accountant/Auditor; Budget Analyst; Computer Systems Analyst; Customer Service Representative; Financial Analyst; Software Engineer. **Educational backgrounds include:** Business Administration; Marketing. **Benefits:** 401K; Dental Insurance; Disability Coverage; Life Insurance; Medical Insurance. **Corporate headquarters location:** This Location. **Operations at this facility include:** Administration; Sales; Service. **Listed on:** NASDAQ. **Number of employees at this location:** 433.

GENERAL SCIENCES CORPORATION
6100 Chevy Chase Drive, Laurel MD 20707. 301/953-2700. **Contact:** Mrs. Pat Robinson, Personnel Manager. **Description:** Provides computer software and programming services.

GENICOM CORPORATION
One Genicom Drive, Waynesboro VA 22980. 703/949-1000. **Contact:** Human Resources. **Description:** Firm develops, manufactures and markets electronic printers for data processing/word processing applications. Also manufactures and markets high-reliability relays for aerospace and other applications. **Common positions include:** Accountant/Auditor; Buyer; Computer Programmer; Electrical/Electronics Engineer; Financial Analyst; Industrial Engineer; Marketing Specialist; Mechanical Engineer; Software Engineer. **Educational backgrounds include:** Accounting; Business Administration; Computer Science; Engineering; Finance; Physics. **Benefits:** 401K; Dental Insurance; Disability Coverage; Life Insurance; Medical Insurance; Savings Plan; Tuition Assistance. **Corporate headquarters location:** Chantilly VA. **Other U.S. locations:** Nationwide. **Operations at this facility include:** Administration; Manufacturing; Research and Development. **Number of employees nationwide:** 2,000.

GENICOM CORPORATION
14800 Conference Center Drive, Suite 400, Chantilly VA 22021. 703/802-9200. **Fax:** 703/802-9039. **Contact:** Claudia M. Bassett, Senior Human Resource Representative. **Description:** Develops, manufactures and markets electronic printers for data processing/word processing applications. Also manufactures high-reliability relays for aerospace and other applications. **Common positions include:** Accountant/Auditor; Services Sales Representative. **Educational backgrounds include:** Business Administration; Computer Science; Marketing. **Benefits:** 401K; Dental Insurance; Disability Coverage; Life Insurance; Medical Insurance. **Corporate headquarters location:** This Location. **Other U.S. locations:** Nationwide. **Operations at this facility include:** Administration; Divisional Headquarters; Sales. **Number of employees at this location:** 30. **Number of employees nationwide:** 2,000.

GNOSSOS SOFTWARE INC.
1625 K Street NW, Washington DC 20006-1604. 202/463-1200. **Contact:** President. **Description:** A small, entrepreneurial company engaged in software consulting and development. Focuses on database applications for client businesses using Paradox for Windows and Delphi. Products include Keep in Touch: Government Relations for

managing corporate affairs departments, and Keep in Touch: Contact Marketing System for sales and marketing departments. **Common positions include:** Computer Programmer; Computer Systems Analyst; Marketing Specialist; Technical Support Representative. **Educational backgrounds include:** Art/Design; Biology; Business Administration; Computer Science; Liberal Arts; Marketing; Mathematics. **Benefits:** Life Insurance; Medical Insurance; Profit Sharing; Savings Plan; Tuition Assistance. **Special Programs:** Training Programs. **Corporate headquarters location:** This Location. **Listed on:** Privately held. **Number of employees at this location:** 14.

GOVERNMENT TECHNOLOGY SERVICES INC.
4100 Lafayette Center Drive, Chantilly VA 22021-0808. 703/502-2000. **Fax:** 703/502-5240. **Contact:** Cathy Skahan, Manager of Human Resources. **Description:** Government Technology Services, Inc. specializes in providing government customers with the broadest selection of brand name computer hardware, software, and peripheral products. GTSI sells directly to all departments and agencies of the federal government, many state and local governments, and indirectly to the government market through hundreds of system integrators and prime contractors. GTSI's selection of desktop, mobile, and engineering workstation computing products continues to expand along with its ability to provide technical expertise in systems integration and network configuration to an ever-expanding Government market. Recent acquisitions include Falcon Microsystems, Inc. **Common positions include:** Accountant/Auditor; Buyer; Manufacturer's/Wholesaler's Sales Rep.; Marketing Specialist; Services Sales Representative. **Benefits:** 401K; Credit Union; Daycare Assistance; Dental Insurance; Disability Coverage; Life Insurance; Medical Insurance; Tuition Assistance. **Special Programs:** Internships. **Corporate headquarters location:** This Location. **Listed on:** NASDAQ. **Number of employees at this location:** 440.

GROUP 1 SOFTWARE, INC.
4200 Parliament Place, Suite 600, Lanham MD 20706-1844. 301/731-2300. **Contact:** Trent Lutz, Human Resources Manager. **Description:** Develops, acquires, markets, and supports specialized, integrated list management, mail management, and marketing support software systems. Publisher of list and mail management software products. **Common positions include:** Administrator; Computer Programmer; Customer Service Representative; Instructor/Trainer; Marketing Specialist; Sales Associate; Software Developer; Systems Analyst; Technical Writer/Editor. **Educational backgrounds include:** Accounting; Business Administration; Communications; Computer Science; Engineering; Marketing. **Benefits:** 401K; Dental Insurance; Disability Coverage; Life Insurance; Medical Insurance; Tuition Assistance. **Corporate headquarters location:** This Location. **Parent company:** Comnet Corporation. **Operations at this facility include:** Administration; Research and Development; Sales; Service. **Listed on:** NASDAQ. **Number of employees at this location:** 185.

HFSI
7900 Westpark Drive, Suite 100, McLean VA 22102. 703/827-3061. **Fax:** 703/827-3390. **Contact:** Dennis Brandon, Contract Recruiter. **Description:** Systems integrator and provider of computer services to the federal government and prime contractors worldwide. **Common positions include:** Accountant/Auditor; Attorney; Computer Operator; Computer Programmer; Computer Systems Analyst; Customer Service Representative; Department Manager; Electrical/Electronics Engineer; Employment Interviewer; Financial Manager; General Manager; Graphic Artist; Human Resources Specialist; Marketing/Advertising/PR Manager; Payroll Clerk; Purchasing Agent and Manager; Receptionist; Software Engineer. **Educational backgrounds include:** Mathematics. **Benefits:** 401K; Disability Coverage; Life Insurance; Medical Insurance; Tuition Assistance. **Special Programs:** Internships. **Corporate headquarters location:** This Location. **Operations at this facility include:** Administration; Research and Development; Sales; Service. **Number of employees at this location:** 960.

HEKIMIAN LABORATORIES INC.
15200 Omega Drive, Rockville MD 20850-3240. 301/590-3600. **Contact:** Thomas D. Kruzic, Director of Human Resources. **Description:** HEKIMIAN designs, manufactures, and markets systems for test, access, and performance monitoring of telecommunications networks. **Common positions include:** Accountant/Auditor; Buyer; Customer Service Representative; Draftsperson; Electrical/Electronics Engineer; Operations/Production Manager; Sales Associate; Software Engineer; Technical Writer/Editor. **Educational backgrounds include:** Business Administration; Communications; Computer Science; Engineering; Mathematics. **Benefits:** 401K; Dental Insurance; Disability Coverage; Life Insurance; Medical Insurance; Pension Plan; Tuition Assistance. **Corporate headquarters location:** This Location. **Parent company:**

Axel Johnson, Inc. **Operations at this facility include:** Administration; Manufacturing; Research and Development; Sales; Service. **Listed on:** Privately held.

IBM CORPORATION
1301 K Street NW, Washington DC 20005. 202/515-4000. **Contact:** Human Resources. **Description:** International Business Machines (IBM) is a developer, manufacturer, and marketer of advanced information processing products, including computers and microelectronic technology, software, networking systems and information technology-related services. The company strives to offer value worldwide, through its United States, Canada, Europe/Middle East/Africa, Latin America and Asia Pacific business units, by providing comprehensive and complete product choices.

IBM CORPORATION
WORKFORCE SOLUTIONS COMPANY
16710 Rockledge Drive, Bethesda MD 20817. 301/803-6000. **Contact:** Central Employment. **Description:** International Business Machines (IBM) is a developer, manufacturer, and marketer of advanced information processing products, including computers and microelectronic technology, software, networking systems and information technology-related services. The company strives to offer value worldwide, through its United States, Canada, Europe/Middle East/Africa, Latin America and Asia Pacific business units, by providing comprehensive and complete product choices. **NOTE:** For personnel, contact the National Information Center at Bo1/Building 101, 10001 W.T. Harris Boulevard, Charlotte NC, 28262-8563. **Common positions include:** Chemical Engineer; Computer Operator; Computer Programmer; Data Entry Clerk; Electrical/Electronics Engineer; Manufacturing Engineer; Mechanical Engineer; Sales Representative; Secretary; Software Engineer; Systems Analyst; Technical Writer/Editor; Technician.

INTERNATIONAL RESEARCH INSTITUTE
12200 Sunrise Valley Drive, Suite 300, Reston VA 22091. 703/715-9605. **Contact:** Human Resources Department. **Description:** A software research company.

INTERSOLV
3200 Tower Oaks Boulevard, Rockville MD 20852. 301/230-3200. **Contact:** Personnel Director. **Description:** Provides computer programming and software services.

LEGENT CORPORATION
575 Herndon Parkway, Herndon VA 22070. 703/708-3000. **Contact:** Cathy C. Peters, Human Resources Representative. **Description:** A software development and consulting firm. Note: Programmers should have experience in Object Oriented Development. **Common positions include:** Administrative Services Manager; Buyer; Clerical Supervisor; Customer Service Representative; Editor; Financial Analyst; Human Resources Specialist; Public Relations Specialist; Quality Control Supervisor; Software Developer; Software Engineer; Teacher; Technical Writer/Editor. **Educational backgrounds include:** Business Administration; Communications; Computer Science; Marketing. **Benefits:** Daycare Assistance; Dental Insurance; Disability Coverage; Employee Discounts; Life Insurance; Medical Insurance; Tuition Assistance. **Special Programs:** Internships. **Corporate headquarters location:** This Location. **Other U.S. locations:** Marlboro MA; NY; Columbus OH; Pittsburgh PA. **Operations at this facility include:** Administration; Divisional Headquarters; Research and Development; Sales; Service. **Listed on:** NASDAQ. **Number of employees at this location:** 400. **Number of employees nationwide:** 2,400.

LIGICON SYSTEM CORPORATION
8110 Gatehouse Road, Falls Church VA 22042-1212. 202/342-4000. **Contact:** Jean Cox, Technical Recruiter. **Description:** A computer programming service.

MANUGISTICS, INC.
2115 East Jefferson Street, Rockville MD 20852. 301/984-5000. **Contact:** Human Resources. **Description:** Provides decision support software and services for *Fortune* 500 manufacturing, transportation, and distribution companies. **Common positions include:** Computer Programmer; Industrial Engineer; Instructor/Trainer; Mechanical Engineer; Operations/Production Manager; Statistician; Systems Analyst; Technical Writer/Editor; Transportation/Traffic Specialist. **Educational backgrounds include:** Business Administration; Computer Science; Engineering; Marketing. **Benefits:** Dental Insurance; Disability Coverage; Life Insurance; Medical Insurance; Savings Plan; Stock

Option; Tuition Assistance. **Special Programs:** Internships; Training Programs. **Corporate headquarters location:** This Location. **Operations at this facility include:** Administration; Research and Development; Sales; Service. **Number of employees at this location:** 300.

MAXIMA CORPORATION
4200 Parliament Place, Lanham MD 20706-1849. 301/459-2000. **Contact:** Human Resources. **Description:** A manufacturer of high technological equipment.

MICROS SYSTEMS, INC.
12000 Baltimore Avenue, Beltsville MD 20705. 301/210-8041. **Fax:** 301/210-3727. **Contact:** Lisa Goldman, Employment Specialist. **Description:** Micros Systems, Inc. develops point of sale systems and property management systems for the hospitality industry. **Common positions include:** Accountant/Auditor; Blue-Collar Worker Supervisor; Buyer; Clerical Supervisor; Computer Programmer; Computer Systems Analyst; Customer Service Representative; Draftsperson; Software Engineer; Technical Writer/Editor. **Educational backgrounds include:** Computer Science; Engineering. **Benefits:** 401K; Dental Insurance; Disability Coverage; Life Insurance; Medical Insurance; Tuition Assistance. **Other U.S. locations:** Nationwide. **Operations at this facility include:** Administration; Divisional Headquarters; Manufacturing; Research and Development; Sales; Service. **Listed on:** NASDAQ. **Number of employees at this location:** 450. **Number of employees nationwide:** 650.

NYMA, INC.
7501 Greenway Center Drive, Suite 1200, Greenbelt MD 20770. 301/345-0832. **Contact:** Human Resources. **Description:** A computer services company specializing in custom software development and systems integration. The company operates in four business areas: Air Traffic Systems, Aerospace Systems, Information Systems, and Computer Products.

ORACLE COMPLEX SYSTEMS CORPORATION
196 Van Buren Street, Herndon VA 22070. 703/904-8200. **Contact:** Human Resources Department. **Description:** A computer systems integration company providing solutions and services to federal and commercial clients.

PRC, INC.
1500 PRC Drive, McLean VA 22102. 703/556-1000. **Fax:** 703/556-2269. **Contact:** Margaret R. Caine, Human Resources Representative. **Description:** PRC is a global provider of scientific and technology-based systems and services to government and commercial clients. Founded in 1954, PRC, Inc. provides computer systems integration, systems engineering, software development, environmental engineering, and consulting services to government and commercial clients worldwide. **Common positions include:** Accountant/Auditor; Aerospace Engineer; Attorney; Budget Analyst; Chemical Engineer; Computer Operator; Computer Programmer; Computer Systems Analyst; Editor; Electrical/Electronics Engineer; Employment Interviewer; Financial Analyst; Graphic Artist; Industrial Engineer; Mechanical Engineer; Meteorologist; Nuclear Engineer; Receptionist; Secretary; Software Engineer; Technical Support Representative; Typist/Word Processor. **Educational backgrounds include:** Accounting; Computer Science; Economics; Engineering; Finance; Geology; Liberal Arts. **Benefits:** 401K; Dental Insurance; Disability Coverage; Employee Discounts; Life Insurance; Medical Insurance; Pension Plan; Savings Plan; Tuition Assistance. **Special Programs:** Training Programs. **Corporate headquarters location:** This Location. **Parent company:** Black & Decker. **Operations at this facility include:** Administration; Regional Headquarters. **Listed on:** New York Stock Exchange. **Number of employees at this location:** 3,500. **Number of employees nationwide:** 7,000.

QUES TECH, INC.
7600W Leesburg Pike, Falls Church VA 22043. 703/760-1000. **Fax:** 703/760-1062. **Contact:** Mark Hartung, Manager of Personnel. **Description:** A diversified high-technology company that provides scientific, engineering, and management services in electronics, computer science, and other advanced technologies to government and industry. These services encompass the entire life cycle of fielded hardware. This process includes research and development, system design, engineering, technical and program management support, test and evaluation, and system installation and maintenance. **Common positions include:** Accountant/Auditor; Aerospace Engineer; Buyer; Draftsperson; Electrical/Electronics Engineer; Physicist/Astronomer; Software Engineer; Statistician; Systems Analyst; Technical Writer/Editor. **Educational backgrounds include:** Accounting; Communications; Computer Science; Engineering;

Mathematics; Physics. **Benefits:** Dental Insurance; Disability Coverage; Life Insurance; Medical Insurance; Pension Plan; Profit Sharing; Savings Plan; Tuition Assistance; Vision Insurance. **Operations at this facility include:** Administration; Divisional Headquarters; Research and Development. **Listed on:** NASDAQ.

REYNOLDS & REYNOLDS
Executive Plaza IV, Hunt Valley MD 21031. 410/771-9211. **Contact:** Personnel Department. **Description:** Engaged in the sales and service of turnkey minicomputer systems, specifically in the vehicle industry. **Operations at this facility include:** Manufacturing; Sales; Service.

SFA, INC.
1401 McCormick Drive, Landover MD 20785. 301/925-9400. **Fax:** 301/925-8568. **Contact:** Vivian Smith-Thompson, Director, Human Resources. **Description:** SFA, Inc., is a diversified international supplier of products and services aimed at helping clients capitalize on leading edge systems and technologies. SFA conducts advanced research studies, designs, and develops state-of-the-art prototypes, and produces custom hardware and software systems for defense, communications, and other commercial applications. **Subsidiaries include:** SFA DataComm, Inc. and SFA SACOM. **Common positions include:** Accountant/Auditor; Aerospace Engineer; Biological Scientist/Biochemist; Biomedical Engineer; Buyer; Chemist; Computer Systems Analyst; Electrical/Electronics Engineer; Financial Analyst; Materials Engineer; Mechanical Engineer; Metallurgical Engineer; Physicist/Astronomer; Purchasing Agent and Manager; Software Engineer; Technical Writer/Editor. **Educational backgrounds include:** Accounting; Biology; Communications; Computer Science; Engineering; Marketing; Mathematics; Physics. **Benefits:** 401K; Dental Insurance; Disability Coverage; Life Insurance; Medical Insurance; Tuition Assistance. **Corporate headquarters location:** This Location. **Other U.S. locations:** Washington DC; Columbia MD; Frederick MD; Landover MD; Lexington Park MD. **Operations at this facility include:** Administration; Manufacturing; Research and Development; Sales; Service. **Listed on:** Privately held. **Number of employees at this location:** 300.

SOFTWARE AG OF NORTH AMERICA
11190 Sunrise Valley Drive, Reston VA 22091. 703/860-5050. **Contact:** Human Resources Representative. **Description:** A supplier of advanced information system development software. Products include: ADABAS, COM-PLETE, and NATURAL. **NOTE:** This company does not accept unsolicited resumes. Jobseekers should only apply for advertised openings.

STATISTICA
30 West Gude Drive, Suite 300, Rockville MD 20850. 301/424-1911. **Contact:** Human Resources. **Description:** Provides professional and computer systems engineering consulting services.

TELOS CORPORATION
460 Herndon Parkway, Herndon VA 22070. 703/471-6000. **Fax:** 703/318-1895. **Contact:** Human Resources. **Description:** Telos corporation is a leader in providing complete computer information management solutions. The company offers hardware production and creation, extensive software and system engineering and software support, as well as hardware and system maintenance and training. **Common positions include:** Accountant/Auditor; Buyer; Draftsperson; Electrical/Electronics Engineer; Financial Analyst; Industrial Engineer; Mechanical Engineer; Operations/Production Manager; Quality Control Supervisor; Receptionist; Secretary; Software Engineer; Stock Clerk; Systems Analyst; Technical Writer/Editor. **Educational backgrounds include:** Accounting; Business Administration; Economics; Finance; Marketing. **Benefits:** Daycare Assistance; Dental Insurance; Disability Coverage; Life Insurance; Medical Insurance; Pension Plan; Tuition Assistance. **Corporate headquarters location:** This Location. **Operations at this facility include:** Administration; Manufacturing; Research and Development; Sales; Service. **Listed on:** NASDAQ. **Number of employees at this location:** 280. **Number of employees nationwide:** 2,100.

TRESP ASSOCIATES, INCORPORATED
4900 Seminary Road, Suite 700, Alexandria VA 22311. 703/845-9400. **Contact:** Human Resources. **Description:** TRESP Associates, Incorporated is a diversified, high technology company specializing in the applications of information systems technologies in solving complex technical problems for government and commercial clients. Areas of specialization include 1) Network engineering and LAN technology, including support and network administration; 2) Applied information technology,

including research and analysis, information engineering, maintenance, and administration, and program support; 3) Logistics, including inventory and distribution, logistic systems management, and maintenance operations; and 4) Training. TRESP Associates' major projects include research, MIS and Administrative Support for the U.S. Department of Transportation Federal Highway Administration; Integrated Management and Technical Support for the Defense Information Systems Agency, The Center for Information Management's Office of Technical Integration; Facilities Management for the Office of the Secretary of Defense; Logistics Support for the U.S. Army Strategic Logistics Agency; Conference and Meeting Planning for the U.S. Department of Transportation Urban Mass Transit Administration; LAN/Office Automation for the U.S. Army; Network Engineering/LAN Technology for the U.S. Department of Justice National Institute of Corrections; and Program Coordination and Evaluation for the NASA Office of Education.

VITRO CORPORATION
45 West Gude Drive, Rockville MD 20850. 301/738-4000. **Contact:** Staffing Supervisor. **Description:** A company providing computer integrated systems design.

Note: Because addresses and telephone numbers of smaller companies change rapidly, we recommend you call each company to verify the information below before inquiring about job opportunities. Mass mailings are not recommended.

Additional employers with over 250 employees:

COMPUTER SOFTWARE, PROGRAMMING, AND SYSTEMS DESIGN

Microprose Software Inc.
180 Lakefront Dr, Ht Vly MD 21030-2215. 410/771-0440.

James Martin & Co. Inc.
2100 Reston Pky Ste 300, Reston VA 22091-1218. 703/620-9504.

MRJ Inc.
10560 Arrowhead Drive, Fairfax VA 22030. 703/385-0700.

Additional employers with under 250 employees:

COMPUTERS AND COMPUTER EQUIPMENT WHOLESALE

Cray Research Inc.
4041 Powder Mill Rd Ste 600, Beltsville MD 20705-3106. 301/595-5100.

Datawatch Corporation
14310 Sullyfield Cir, Chantilly VA 22021-1629. 703/802-0034.

Telco
4219 Lafayette Center Dr, Chantilly VA 22021-1209. 703/803-0330.

Thomas-Conrad Corporation
6103 Winnepeg Dr, Burke VA 22015-3846. 703/321-8053.

COMPUTER SOFTWARE, PROGRAMMING, AND SYSTEMS DESIGN

Anadac Inc.
2011 Crystal Dr Ste 401, Arlington VA 22202-3709. 703/685-0021.

Datatel Inc.
4375 Fair Lakes Ct, Fairfax VA 22033-4234. 703/968-9000.

Information Mgmt. Cnslnts
7915 Westpark Dr, Mc Lean VA 22102-4201. 703/893-3100.

Mpr Associates Inc.
320 King St, Alexandria VA 22314-3230. 703/519-0250.

National Data Corporation
1300 Piccard Dr, Rockville MD 20850-4303. 301/590-7700.

Psi International Inc.
10306 Eaton Pl Ste 400, Fairfax VA 22030-2201. 703/352-8700.

Railinc Corporation
50 F St Nw, Washington DC 20001-1530. 202/639-5580.

The Centech Group
4200 Wilson Blvd Ste 700, Arlington VA 22203-1800. 703/525-6852.

Viable Info Prcsg Systems
1 W Pennsylvania Ave Ste 700, Baltimore MD 21204-5025. 410/832-8300.

Comeau & Associates
8260 Greensboro Dr Ste 320, Mc Lean VA 22102-3806. 703/760-7650.

Zyga Corporation
4600 E West Hwy, Bethesda MD 20814-3415. 301/913-9000.

Cap Gemini America
10055 Red Run Blvd, Owings Mills MD 21117-4892. 410/581-5022.

Claritas Corporation
201 N Union St, Alexandria VA 22314-2642. 703/683-8300.

Computer Associates
12120 Sunset Hills Rd, Reston VA 22090-3231. 703/709-4500.

Computer Resource Mgmt.
950 Herndon Pky Ste 360, Herndon VA 22070-5531. 703/435-7613.

Deltek Systems Inc.
8280 Greensboro Dr Ste 30, Mc Lean VA 22102-3807. 703/734-8606.

Edunetics Corporation
1600 Wilson Blvd Ste 710, Arlington VA 22209-2505. 703/243-2602.

Envirotest Technologies
10240 Old Columbia Rd,
Columbia MD 21046-1716.
410/995-6096.

Genasys Corporation
11820 Parklawn Dr,
Rockville MD 20852-2529.
301/770-4600.

Infodata Systems Inc.
5205 Leesburg Pike, Falls
Church VA 22041-3802.
703/578-3430.

Landmark Systems Corporation
8000 Towers Cres Dr 150,
Vienna VA 22182-2700.
703/902-8000.

Logicon Operating Systems
2100 Washington Blvd,
Arlington VA 22204-5703.
703/486-3500.

McDonnell Douglas Electronic
8201 Greensboro Dr Ste
500, Mc Lean VA 22102-3810. 703/883-3900.

National Con-Serv Inc.
451 Hungerford Dr Ste 408,
Rockville MD 20850-4151.
301/251-1880.

Nci Information Systems
8260 Greensboro Dr Ste
400, Mc Lean VA 22102-3806. 703/903-0325.

S M Systems & Research Corporation
8401 Corporate Dr, Landover
MD 20785-2224. 301/459-3322.

Social & Scientific Systems
7101 Wisconsin Ave,
Bethesda MD 20814-4805.
301/986-4870.

Software Productivity Consortm
2214 Rock Hill Rd, Herndon
VA 22070-4214. 703/742-8877.

User Technology Associates
4301 Fairfax Dr, Arlington
VA 22203-1628. 703/522-5132.

Van Dyke J B & Associates
6701 Rockledge Dr,
Bethesda MD 20817-1813.
301/897-8970.

Verdix Corporation
205 Van Buren St Fl 4,
Herndon VA 22070-5336.
703/318-5800.

Potomac Systems Engrg
7611 Little River Tpke,
Annandale VA 22003-2602.
703/642-1000.

Scientific & Commercial Systems
4651 King St, Alexandria VA
22302-1214. 703/824-8240.

Sema Inc.
5111 Leesburg Pike, Falls
Church VA 22041-3206.
703/845-1200.

Universal Systems Incorporated
4350 Fair Lakes Ct, Fairfax
VA 22033-4233. 703/222-2840.

COMPUTER RENTAL AND LEASING

Pcr-Personal Computer Rentals
7405 Alban Station Ct,
Springfield VA 22150-2318.
703/866-5503.

COMPUTER MAINTENANCE AND REPAIR

General Analytics Corporation
7918 Jones Branch Dr Ste
34, Mc Lean VA 22102-3307. 703/847-4660.

Internat Computers&Telecommuni
18310 Montgomery Village
610, Gaithersburg MD
20879-3553. 301/949-0200.

Tab Products Company
50 Painters Mill Rd, Owings
Mills MD 21117-3621.
410/356-4646.

Storage Technology
12200 Tech Rd, Silver
Spring MD 20904-1983.
301/622-7866.

MISC. COMPUTER RELATED SERVICES

Computer Management Services
3905 National Dr Ste 290,
Burtonsville MD 20866-1100. 301/236-4900.

Ght Limited
4301 Fairfax Dr, Arlington
VA 22203-1627. 703/243-1200.

Optimum Services & Systems Inc.
4351 Nicole Dr, Lanham MD
20706-4372. 301/459-9100.

Rgi Inc.
5203 Leesburg Pike Ste
1300, Falls Church VA
22041-3401. 703/820-4900.

Stephens Engineering Co.
4601 Forbes Blvd Ste 300,
Lanham MD 20706-4807.
301/306-9355.

Keane Inc.
36 SW Charles St, Baltimore
MD 21201. 410/659-5390.

COMPUTERS AND RELATED EQUIPMENT

McSi Technologies
8401 Colesville Rd Ste 305,
Silver Spring MD 20910-3363. 301/495-4444.

Galcom Inc.
211 Perry Pky Ste 4,
Gaithersburg MD 20877-2144. 301/990-7100.

General Kinetics Inc.
13505 Dallas Tech Dr,
Herndon VA 22071.
703/713-1400.

Netrix Corporation
13595 Dulles Technology Dr,
Herndon VA 22071-3413.
703/742-6000.

For more information on career opportunities in the computer industry:

Associations

ASSOCIATION FOR COMPUTING MACHINERY
1515 Broadway, 17th Floor, New York NY
10036. 212/869-7440. Membership required.

INFORMATION AND TECHNOLOGY ASSOCIATION OF AMERICA
1616 North Fort Myer Drive, Suite 1300,
Arlington VA 22209. 703/522-5055.

Directories

INFORMATION INDUSTRY DIRECTORY
Gale Research Inc., 835 Penobscot Building,
Detroit MI 48226. 313/961-2242.

Magazines

COMPUTER-AIDED ENGINEERING
Penton Publishing, 1100 Superior Avenue,
Cleveland OH 44114. 216/696-7000.

COMPUTERWORLD
IDG, 375 Cochituate Road, P.O. Box 9171, Framingham MA 01701-9171. 508/879-0700.

DATA COMMUNICATIONS
McGraw-Hill, 1221 Avenue of the Americas, New York NY 10020. 212/512-2000.

DATAMATION
Cahners Publishing, 275 Washington Street, Newton MA 02158. 617/964-3030.

IDC REPORT
International Data Corporation, Five Speen Street, Framingham MA 01701. 508/872-8200.

EDUCATIONAL SERVICES

Job prospects for college and university faculty, elementary school teachers, counselors, and education administrators should show moderate improvement throughout the '90s, although most of the openings will result from retirements. Among kindergarten and elementary school teachers, the best opportunities await those with training in special education. The employment outlook is also good for teacher aides, as many assist special education teachers, as school reforms call for more individual attention to students, and as the number of students who speak English as a second language rises. Adult education and secondary school teachers, and sports and physical fitness instructors and coaches are other occupations expected to grow faster than average.

THE AMERICAN UNIVERSITY
4400 Massachusetts Avenue NW, Washington DC 22206. 202/885-2591. **Fax:** 202/885-2558. **Recorded Jobline:** 202/885-2639. **Contact:** Nicolas L. Relacion, Human Resource Development. **Description:** An independent, co-educational university. Faculty vacancies/appointments are handled by academic discipline. Program offerings within School of Public Affairs, School of Communications, College of Arts & Sciences, Washington College of Law, Kogod College of Business Administration, and School of International Services, as well as return-to-school programs. **Common positions include:** Accountant/Auditor; Administrator; Architect; Blue-Collar Worker Supervisor; Broadcast Technician; Buyer; Clerical Supervisor; Computer Operator; Computer Programmer; Computer Systems Analyst; Counselor; Customer Service Representative; Draftsperson; Editor; Education Administrator; Electrician; Employment Interviewer; Heating/AC/Refrigeration Technician; Human Resources Specialist; Payroll Clerk; Physician Assistant; Psychologist; Public Relations Specialist; Reporter; Secretary; Systems Analyst; Teacher; Technical Writer/Editor. **Educational backgrounds include:** Accounting; Business Administration; Communications; Computer Science; Finance; Liberal Arts; Marketing. **Benefits:** Dental Insurance; Disability Coverage; Employee Discounts; Life Insurance; Medical Insurance; Retirement Plan; Savings Plan; Tuition Assistance. **Special Programs:** Apprenticeships. **Corporate headquarters location:** This Location. **Operations at this facility include:** Administration; Service. **Number of employees at this location:** 1,100. **Number of employees nationwide:** 2,000.

BALTIMORE COUNTY PUBLIC SCHOOLS
6901 North Charles Street, Towson MD 21204. 410/887-4191. **Recorded Jobline:** 410/887-4080. **Contact:** Human Resources. **Description:** A 148-school district.

BOWIE STATE UNIVERSITY
14000 Jericho Park Road, Bowie MD 20715. 301/464-3000. **Contact:** Human Resources. **Description:** A state college.

DALE CARNEGIE LEADERSHIP INSTITUTE
6000 Executive Boulevard, Suite 603, Rockville MD 20852. 301/770-2444. **Contact:** Human Resources. **Description:** An professional services institute offering a wide variety of training classes for sales people in the following areas: motivation, time management, and leadership.

THE CATHOLIC UNIVERSITY OF AMERICA
620 Michigan Avenue Northeast, Washington DC 20064. 202/319-5050. **Recorded Jobline:** 202/319-5263. **Contact:** Monica E. Hensel, Employment Administrator. **Description:** A Catholic university. **Common positions include:** Accountant/Auditor; Administrator; Architect; Biological Scientist/Biochemist; Biomedical Engineer; Blue-Collar Worker Supervisor; Chemical Engineer; Civil Engineer; Claim Representative; Computer Programmer; Counselor; Customer Service Representative; Draftsperson;

Editor; Electrical/Electronics Engineer; General Manager; Human Resources Specialist; Marketing Specialist; Mechanical Engineer; Metallurgical Engineer; Public Relations Specialist; Purchasing Agent and Manager; Quality Control Supervisor; Reporter; Secretary; Systems Analyst; Technical Writer/Editor. **Benefits:** Daycare Assistance; Dental Insurance; Disability Coverage; Employee Discounts; Life Insurance; Medical Insurance; Pension Plan; Tuition Assistance. **Special Programs:** Training Programs. **Corporate headquarters location:** This Location.

COMMUNITY COLLEGE OF BALTIMORE
2901 Liberty Heights Avenue, Baltimore MD 21215. 410/333-5444. **Contact:** Human Resources Department. **Description:** A junior college.

COPPIN STATE COLLEGE
2500 West North Avenue, Baltimore MD 21216. 410/383-5757. **Contact:** Valerie A. Bell, Director of Human Resources. **Description:** A four-year liberal arts school, offering both undergraduate and graduate programs. **Common positions include:** Accountant/Auditor; Budget Analyst; Buyer; Counselor; Electrician; Human Resources Specialist; Librarian; Library Technician; Licensed Practical Nurse; Mechanical Engineer; Purchasing Agent and Manager; Stationary Engineer. **Educational backgrounds include:** Accounting; Art/Design; Biology; Business Administration; Chemistry; Communications; Computer Science; Economics; Engineering; Finance; Health Care; Liberal Arts; Marketing; Mathematics; Physics. **Benefits:** 401K; Dental Insurance; Life Insurance; Medical Insurance; Pension Plan; Savings Plan; Tuition Assistance. **Special Programs:** Internships. **Corporate headquarters location:** This Location. **Operations at this facility include:** Administration; Service. **Number of employees at this location:** 532.

ESSEX COMMUNITY COLLEGE
7201 Rossville Boulevard, Baltimore MD 21237-3855. 410/682-6000. **Contact:** Human Resources. **Description:** Essex Community College serves over 11,000 day and evening students enrolled in 60 different certificate and degree programs and options. In addition, the college serves more than 12,000 community members through its noncredit course offerings designed for personal enrichment, skill improvement and intellectual development and more than 200,000 community members through other community programs and use of its facilities. The College is accredited by the Middle States Association of Colleges and Schools and the Maryland Higher Education Commission. The College offers associate degrees in Arts, including English, Music, and Theatre; Science, including Accounting, Criminal Justice, and Sports Management; and Applied Science, including Early Childhood Development, Human Resource Management, and Veterinary Technology.

GEORGE MASON UNIVERSITY
4087 University Drive, Fairfax VA 22030-4000. 703/993-2600. **Recorded Jobline:** 703/993-8799. **Contact:** Personnel Department. **Description:** A university.

GEORGE WASHINGTON UNIVERSITY
2125 G Street NW, Washington DC 20052. 202/994-4470. **Contact:** Campus Recruitment. **Description:** A four-year liberal arts college.

GEORGETOWN UNIVERSITY
37th and O Street, Washington DC 20057-1021. 202/687-2500. **Recorded Jobline:** 202/687-2900. **Contact:** Personnel Department. **Description:** A private four-year liberal arts school, offering both undergraduate and graduate programs.

HOWARD UNIVERSITY
2400 6th Street NW, Washington DC 20059. 202/806-6100. **Recorded Jobline:** 202/806-7711. **Contact:** Human Resources. **Description:** A private, medium-sized research university, with law, dental, and medical schools.

JAMES MADISON UNIVERSITY
Employee Relations and Training, Harrisonburg VA 22807. 703/568-6144. **Fax:** 703/568-7916. **Recorded Jobline:** 703/568-3561. **Contact:** Kathy Shuler, Employment Representative. **Description:** A university. **Common positions include:** Accountant/Auditor; Administrator; Blue-Collar Worker Supervisor; Buyer; Computer Programmer; Editor; Human Resources Specialist; Public Relations Specialist; Purchasing Agent and Manager; Reporter; Systems Analyst; Teacher. **Benefits:** Dental Insurance; Disability Coverage; Employee Discounts; Life Insurance; Medical Insurance; Pension Plan; Tuition Assistance. **Corporate headquarters location:** This Location.

MONTGOMERY COLLEGE
900 Hungerford Drive, Rockville MD 20850. 301/279-5353. **Recorded Jobline:** 301/279-5374. **Contact:** Human Resources. **Description:** A two-year state college.

MORGAN STATE UNIVERSITY
Cold Spring Lane & Hillen Road, Baltimore MD 21239. 410/319-3333. **Contact:** Human Resources. **Description:** Morgan State University is an historically Black Institution with the designation as Maryland's public urban research, doctoral granting university. The research program of the University involves both basic and applied research. A substantial amount of research is focused on urban life and phenomena with a bent toward education, service and public policy development. The research is oftentimes oriented toward specific urban problems and issues, such as human resource development, economic development and competitiveness, health care, environment, transportation, aging, and substance abuse. The University has three divisions in which to obtain Bachelor Degrees in Arts and Sciences: The College of Arts and Sciences, The School of Education and Urban Studies, and The School of Engineering.

THE NATIONAL LEARNING CENTER
CAPITOL CHILDREN'S MUSEUM
800 Third Street, Washington DC 20002. 202/675-4180. **Fax:** 202/675-4140. **Contact:** Sodartha V. Guion, Personnel Director. **Description:** Research and development institution involved with innovative educational methods for children. There are five main departments: Capitol Children's Museum (hands-on, interactive museum), Model Early Learning Center (preschool for inner city children), Options School (alternative 7th grade), Community Access Computer Center (neighborhood computer center), and Media Arts Center (film and animation). Established in 1979. **Common positions include:** Blue-Collar Worker Supervisor; Counselor; Management Trainee; Preschool Worker; Teacher. **Educational backgrounds include:** Art/Design; Business Administration; Finance; Liberal Arts; Marketing. **Benefits:** Dental Insurance; Medical Insurance. **Special Programs:** Internships. **Corporate headquarters location:** This Location. **Operations at this facility include:** Administration; Research and Development; Service. **Number of employees at this location:** 80.

NORTHERN VIRGINIA COMMUNITY COLLEGE
4001 Wakefield Chapel Road, Annandale VA 22003. 703/323-3000. **Recorded Jobline:** 703/323-3444. **Contact:** Human Resources. **Description:** A community college.

TOWSON STATE UNIVERSITY
8000 York Road, Towson MD 21204. 410/830-2000. **Recorded Jobline:** 410/830-2161. **Contact:** Personnel Department. **Description:** The institution known today as Towson State University opened its door in 1866 in downtown Baltimore as the Maryland State Normal School - the only institution devoted exclusively to the preparation of teachers for the public schools of Maryland. Students choose their programs of study from the university's academic colleges and school: The College of Allied Health Sciences and Physical Education, The College of Education, The College of Fine Arts and Communication, The College of Liberal Arts, The College of Natural and Mathematical Sciences and The School of Business and Economics. Nearly 80 percent of the 471 full-time faculty have earned the highest degree of academic preparation in their field.

UNIVERSITY OF MARYLAND
COOPERATIVE EXTENSION SERVICE
Room 1105, Symons Hall, College Park MD 20742. 301/405-1177. **Contact:** Gene A. Johnson, Director of Personnel. **Description:** A branch of the large university.

UNIVERSITY OF MARYLAND
UNIVERSITY COLLEGE
University Boulevard at Adelphi Road, College Park MD 20742. 301/985-7058. **Recorded Jobline:** 301/738-6055. **Contact:** William F. Fiedler, Director of Personnel. **Description:** A branch of the large university providing adult and continuing education. **Common positions include:** Accountant/Auditor; Buyer; Clerical Supervisor; Education Administrator. **Educational backgrounds include:** Accounting; Art/Design; Business Administration. **Benefits:** 401K; Dental Insurance; Disability Coverage; Employee Discounts; Life Insurance; Medical Insurance; Pension Plan; Savings Plan; Tuition Assistance. **Corporate headquarters location:** Hyallsville MD. **Parent company:**

University of Maryland. **Operations at this facility include:** Administration; Divisional Headquarters. **Number of employees at this location:** 650.

UNIVERSITY OF MARYLAND AT BALTIMORE
737 West Lombard Street, Baltimore MD 21201. 410/706-7171. **Fax:** 410/706-8178. **Recorded Jobline:** 410/706-5JOB. **Contact:** Human Resources, Employment Division. **Description:** The University of Maryland at Baltimore is the public institution in Maryland responsible for educating health and human service professionals. **Common positions include:** Accountant/Auditor; Biological Scientist/Biochemist; Biomedical Engineer; Blue-Collar Worker Supervisor; Budget Analyst; Buyer; Chemist; Civil Engineer; Clerical Supervisor; Clinical Lab Technician; Computer Programmer; Computer Systems Analyst; Construction Contractor and Manager; Cost Estimator; Dental Assistant/Dental Hygienist; Dental Lab Technician; Education Administrator; Emergency Medical Technician; Financial Analyst; Human Resources Specialist; Human Service Worker; Librarian; Mechanical Engineer; Pharmacist; Psychologist; Registered Nurse; Social Worker; Statistician; Structural Engineer; Technical Writer/Editor. **Educational backgrounds include:** Basic Sciences; Biology; Business Administration; Chemistry; Computer Science. **Benefits:** 401K; Dental Insurance; Disability Coverage; Employee Discounts; Life Insurance; Medical Insurance; Pension Plan; Tuition Assistance. **Corporate headquarters location:** This Location. **Operations at this facility include:** Administration; Research and Development. **Number of employees at this location:** 4,500.

UNIVERSITY OF MARYLAND AT COLLEGE PARK
Chesapeake Building, Room 1326, College Park MD 20742. 301/405-1000. **Recorded Jobline:** 301/405-5677. **Contact:** Deborah Glenn, Coordinator/Employment Services. **Description:** A university. **Common positions include:** Accountant/Auditor; Administrator; Architect; Assistant Manager; Blue-Collar Worker Supervisor; Buyer; Computer Programmer; Counselor; Customer Service Representative; Department Manager; Dietician/Nutritionist; Financial Analyst; Food Scientist/Technologist; General Manager; Human Resources Specialist; Marketing Specialist; Operations/Production Manager; Systems Analyst; Teacher. **Educational backgrounds include:** Accounting; Business Administration; Communications; Computer Science; Engineering; Finance; Liberal Arts; Marketing; Mathematics. **Benefits:** Daycare Assistance; Dental Insurance; Disability Coverage; Employee Discounts; Life Insurance; Medical Insurance; Pension Plan; Savings Plan; Stock Option; Tuition Assistance. **Special Programs:** Internships; Training Programs. **Corporate headquarters location:** This Location. **Operations at this facility include:** Administration; Education; Research and Development; Service. **Number of employees nationwide:** 7,000.

UNIVERSITY OF MARYLAND BALTIMORE COUNTY
5401 Wilkens Avenue, Baltimore MD 21228-5398. 410/455-2337. **Fax:** 410/455-1064. **Recorded Jobline:** 410/455-1100. **Contact:** Elmer Falconer, Employment Manager. **Description:** A research university serving the Baltimore metropolitan region, UMBC places special emphasis on its undergraduate programs, offering 27 majors ranging from the sciences and engineering to the arts and humanities. The facility's graduate and research emphasis is on sciences, engineering, and public policy. Founded in 1966, the university is home to more than 10,500 students and is staffed by a full-time faculty of nearly 400. **Common positions include:** Computer Programmer; Education Administrator; Human Service Worker. **Benefits:** Medical Insurance; Tuition Assistance. **Corporate headquarters location:** This Location. **Parent company:** University of Maryland System. **Operations at this facility include:** Administration; Divisional Headquarters; Research and Development; Service. **Number of employees at this location:** 1,800.

UNIVERSITY OF THE DISTRICT OF COLUMBIA
4200 Connecticut Avenue NW, Building 48, Room 3002, Washington DC 20008. 202/274-5020. **Contact:** Office of Personnel. **Description:** The University of the District of Columbia was created in 1976 through the merger of three of Washington's institutions: District of Columbia Teachers College, Federal City College, and Washington Technical Institute. Academic programs are offered through two colleges: the College of Professional Studies, which includes the School of Business and Public Administration and the School of Engineering and Applied Science; and the College of Arts and Sciences, encompassing the School of Arts and Education and the School of Science and Mathematics. Each year at the University's commencement, 800 to 900 graduates receive one-year certificates, two-year Associate in Applied Science and Associate of Arts degrees, four-year Bachelor of Arts and Bachelor of Science degrees,

and master's degrees. Of the 433 full-time faculty members, 44 percent have earned the highest degree in their field.

Note: Because addresses and telephone numbers of smaller companies change rapidly, we recommend you call each company to verify the information below before inquiring about job opportunities. Mass mailings are not recommended.

Additional employers with over 250 employees:

ELEMENTARY AND SECONDARY SCHOOLS

Lodge School
500 W Montgomery Ave, Rockville MD 20850-3892. 301/424-8300.

COLLEGES, UNIVERSITIES, AND PROFESSIONAL SCHOOLS

College Of Notre Dame Maryland
4701 N Charles St, Baltimore MD 21210-2404. 410/435-0100.

Gallaudet University
800 Florida Ave Ne, Washington DC 20002-3600. 202/651-5000.

Hood College
401 Rosemont Ave, Frederick MD 21701-8524. 301/663-3131.

Mary Washington College
1301 College Ave, Fredericksbrg VA 22401-5300. 703/899-4100.

Maryland Inst. College Of Art
1300 W Mount Royal Ave, Baltimore MD 21217-4134. 410/669-9200.

Marymount University
2807 N Glebe Rd, Arlington VA 22207-4299. 703/522-5600.

University Of Baltimore
1420 N Charles St, Baltimore MD 21201-5720. 410/625-3000.

Western Maryland College
2 College Hl, Westminster MD 21157. 410/848-7000.

JUNIOR COLLEGES AND TECHNICAL INSTITUTES

Prince Georges Comm. College
301 Largo Rd, Uppr Marlboro MD 20772-2199. 301/336-6000.

Additional employers with under 250 employees:

ELEMENTARY AND SECONDARY SCHOOLS

Paul Vi High School
10675 Lee Hwy, Fairfax VA 22030-4314. 703/352-0925.

Bais Yaakov School For Girls
11111 Park Heights Ave, Owings Mills MD 21117-3042. 410/363-3300.

Bryn Mawr School
109 W Melrose Ave, Baltimore MD 21210-1326. 410/323-8800.

Charles E Smith Jewish Day School
1901 E Jefferson St, Rockville MD 20852-4029. 301/881-1400.

French International School
9600 Forest Rd, Bethesda MD 20814-1792. 301/530-8260.

Friends School of Baltimore
5114 N Charles St, Baltimore MD 21210-2021. 410/435-2800.

Georgetown Day School
4200 Davenport St Nw, Washington DC 20016-4560. 202/966-2666.

Gilman School
5407 Roland Ave, Baltimore MD 21210-1991. 410/323-3800.

Hebrew Academy of Gtr Washington
2010 Linden Ln, Silver Spring MD 20910-1799. 301/587-4100.

McDonogh School
8600 McDonogh Rd Box 380, Owings Mills MD 21117. 410/363-0600.

Sidwell Friends School
3825 Wisconsin Ave Nw, Washington DC 20016-2999. 202/537-8100.

The Potomac School
PO Box 430, Mc Lean VA 22101-0430. 703/356-4101.

Washington Int'l Upper School
3100 Macomb St Nw, Washington DC 20008-3324. 202/364-1800.

Developmental School
14901 Broschart Rd, Rockville MD 20850-3318. 301/279-8625.

Model Sec. School For The Deaf
800 Florida Ave Ne, Washington DC 20002-3660. 202/651-5466.

The Ivymount School
11614 Seven Locks Rd, Rockville MD 20854-3261. 301/469-0223.

Lake Clifton-East Sr High School
2801 Saint Lo Dr, Baltimore MD 21213-1325. 410/396-6637.

Harford Heights Elem School
1919 N Broadway, Baltimore MD 21213-1497. 410/396-9342.

Grace Metz Junior High School
9700 Fairview Ave, Manassas VA 22111-5106. 703/368-5580.

Hammond Junior High School
4646 Seminary Rd, Alexandria VA 22304-1424. 703/461-4100.

Perry Hall Middle School
4300 Ebenezer Rd, Baltimore MD 21236-2197. 410/887-5100.

Annandale High School
4700 Medford Dr, Annandale VA 22003-5497. 703/256-4600.

Annapolis Senior High School
2700 Riva Rd, Annapolis MD 21401-7205. 410/266-5240.

Arundel Senior High School
1001 Annapolis Rd, Gambrills MD 21054-1033. 410/674-6500.

Blair Senior High School
313 Wayne Ave, Silver
Spring MD 20910-5500.
301/650-6600.

Chantilly High School
4201 Stringfellow Rd,
Chantilly VA 22021-2600.
703/222-3090.

Eastern Senior High School
17th and E Capitol Sts Se,
Washington DC 20003.
202/724-4805.

Edison High School
5801 Franconia Rd,
Alexandria VA 22310-2799.
703/971-6850.

Fairfax High School
3500 Old Lee Hwy, Fairfax
VA 22030-1888. 703/591-
8350.

Fauquier High School
705 Waterloo Rd, Warrenton
VA 22186-3093. 703/347-
6100.

Frederick Sr High School
650 Carroll Pky, Frederick
MD 21701-4973. 301/694-
1367.

Gaithersburg Sr High School
314 S Frederick Ave,
Gaithersburg MD 20877-
2392. 301/840-4700.

Gar-Field High School
14000 Smoketown Rd,
Woodbridge VA 22192-
4704. 703/670-2131.

Glen Burnie Senior High School
7550 Baltimore Annapolis
Blvd, Glen Burnie MD 21060-
7357. 410/761-8950.

Hayfield Secondary School
7630 Telegraph Rd,
Alexandria VA 22315-3898.
703/922-5020.

Herndon High School
700 Bennett St, Herndon VA
22070-3199. 703/437-
6800.

High Point High School
3601 Powder Mill Rd,
Beltsville MD 20705-3599.
301/937-1000.

Jefferson Sci-Tech High School
6560 Braddock Rd,
Alexandria VA 22312-2206.
703/750-8300.

Lake Braddock High School
9200 Burke Lake Rd, Burke
VA 22015-1682. 703/323-
9000.

Largo High School
505 Largo Rd, Uppr Marlboro

MD 20772-2197. 301/336-
8280.

Laurel High School
8000 Cherry Ln, Laurel MD
20707-9264. 301/725-
8300.

Lee High School
6540 Franconia Rd,
Springfield VA 22150-1499.
703/971-6000.

Madison High School
2500 James Madison Dr,
Vienna VA 22181-5536.
703/938-2225.

McLean High School
1633 Davidson Rd, Mc Lean
VA 22101-4399. 703/356-
0700.

Montgomery High School
250 Richard Montgomery Dr,
Rockville MD 20852-1147.
301/279-8400.

Mount Vernon High School
8515 Old Mount Vernon Rd,
Alexandria VA 22309-2015.
703/360-5900.

North Stafford High School
839 Garrisonville Rd,
Stafford VA 22554-3900.
703/659-4176.

Northwestern High School
7000 Adelphi Rd, Hyattsville
MD 20782-1497. 301/779-
5400.

Oakton High School
2900 Sutton Rd, Vienna VA
22181-6199. 703/281-
4900.

Osbourn Park High School
8909 Euclid Ave, Manassas
VA 22111-2498. 703/361-
1101.

Oxon Hill High School
6701 Leyte Dr, Oxon Hill MD
20745-2199. 301/839-
1100.

Perry Hall High School
4601 Ebenezer Rd, Baltimore
MD 21236-1999. 410/887-
5108.

Potomac High School
16706 Jefferson Davis Hwy,
Dumfries VA 22026-2115.
703/221-1134.

Quince Orchard High School
15800 Quince Orchard Rd,
Gaithersburg MD 20878-
3442. 301/840-4686.

Robinson Secondary School
5035 Sideburn Rd, Fairfax
VA 22032-2637. 703/323-
7500.

Roosevelt High School
7601 Hanover Pky,
Greenbelt MD 20770-2099.
301/513-5400.

South Lakes High School
11400 S Lakes Dr, Reston
VA 22091-4199. 703/476-
5270.

Springbrook Senior High School
201 Valley Brook Dr, Silver
Spring MD 20904-2946.
301/989-5700.

Stafford Senior High School
33 Stafford Indians Ln,
Fredericksbrg VA 22405-
5803. 703/371-7200.

Stonewall Jackson High School
8820 Rixlew Ln, Manassas
VA 22110-3799. 703/368-
2106.

Stuart High School
3301 Peace Valley Ln, Falls
Church VA 22044-1508.
703/820-1114.

Suitland High School
5200 Silver Hill Rd, District
Hts MD 20747-2045.
301/568-7770.

West Potomac High School
6500 Quander Rd,
Alexandria VA 22307-1099.
703/768-2121.

Westminster High School
1225 Washington Rd,
Westminster MD 21157-
5899. 410/848-5050.

Williams Senior High School
3330 King St, Alexandria VA
22302-3001. 703/842-
6800.

Woodbridge High School
3001 Old Bridge Rd,
Woodbridge VA 22192-
3221. 703/494-7135.

Woodlawn High School
1801 Woodlawn Dr,
Baltimore MD 21207-4075.
410/887-1309.

Woodson High School
9525 Main St, Fairfax VA
22031-4099. 703/323-
1911.

Eastern Voc-Tech School
1100 Mace Ave, Baltimore
MD 21221-3315. 410/887-
0190.

Mergenthaler Voc-Tech School
3500 Hillen Rd, Baltimore
MD 21218-2299. 410/396-
6496.

Fredericksburg City School Dist
817 Princess Anne St,
Fredericksbrg VA 22401-5819. 703/372-1130.

Somerset County School Dist
30500 Prince William St,
Princess Anne MD 21853-1229. 410/651-1616.

VOCATIONAL SCHOOLS

Rets Technical Training Center
1520 S Caton Ave, Baltimore MD 21227-1013. 410/644-6400.

COLLEGES, UNIVERSITIES, AND PROFESSIONAL SCHOOLS

Capitol College
11301 Springfield Rd, Laurel MD 20708-9759. 301/953-0060.

Columbia Union College
7600 Flower Ave, Takoma Park MD 20912-7794. 301/270-9200.

Goucher College
1021 Dulaney Valley Rd, Baltimore MD 21204-2753. 410/337-6000.

Washington College
300 Washington Ave, Chestertown MD 21620-1197. 410/778-2800.

JUNIOR COLLEGES AND TECHNICAL INSTITUTES

Allegany Community College
Willowbrook Road, Cumberland MD 21502. 301/724-7700.

Chesapeake College
PO Box 8, Wye Mills MD 21679-0008. 410/822-5400.

Dundalk Community College
7200 Sollers Point Rd, Baltimore MD 21222-4649. 410/282-6700.

Frederick Community College
7932 Opossumtown Pike, Frederick MD 21702-2097. 301/846-2400.

Germanna Community College
PO Box 339, Locust Grove VA 22508-0339. 703/423-1333.

Hagerstown Jr College
11400 Robinwood Dr, Hagerstown MD 21742-6514. 301/790-2800.

Howard Community College
Little Patuxent Parkway, Columbia MD 21044. 410/992-4800.

Montgomery College of Germantown
20200 Observation Dr, Germantown MD 20876-4098. 301/353-7700.

BUSINESS, SECRETARIAL, AND DATA PROCESSING SCHOOLS

Strayer College
3045 Columbia Pike, Arlington VA 22204-4338. 703/892-5100.

CHILD DAYCARE SERVICES

Fair Lakes Children's Center
4750 Rippling Pond Dr, Fairfax VA 22033-5077. 703/818-9002.

Kiddie Academy/Merritt
1623 Merritt Blvd, Baltimore MD 21222-2116. 410/285-8563.

Kindercare #1301
4880 Forbes Blvd, Lanham MD 20706-4304. 301/577-3790.

Kindercare Learning Centers
11919 Rutherford Dr, Fredericksbrg VA 22407-6764. 703/786-5437.

La Petite Academy
20110 Ashburn Village Blvd, Ashburn VA 22011-3346. 703/729-0500.

People Karch International
14800 Conference Center Dr, Chantilly VA 22021-3810. 703/631-7859.

Rocking Horse Child Care Center
13501 Braddock Rd, Clifton VA 22024-1016. 703/968-3696.

St. Andrews Play School
PO Box 600, California MD 20619-0600. 301/862-3325.

Tysons Corner Play & Learn
7711 Old Springhouse Rd, Mc Lean VA 22102-3404. 703/761-1151.

For more information on career opportunities in educational services:

Associations

AMERICAN ASSOCIATION OF SCHOOL ADMINISTRATORS
1801 North Moore Street, Arlington VA 22209. 703/528-0700.

AMERICAN FEDERATION OF TEACHERS
555 New Jersey Avenue NW, Washington DC 20001. 202/879-4400.

COLLEGE AND UNIVERSITY PERSONNEL ASSOCIATION
1233 20th Street NW, Suite 301, Washington DC 20036. 202/429-0311. Membership required.

NATIONAL ASSOCIATION OF BIOLOGY TEACHERS
11250 Roger Bacon Drive, #19, Reston VA 22090. 703/471-1134.

NATIONAL ASSOCIATION OF COLLEGE ADMISSION COUNSELORS
1631 Prince Street, Alexandria VA 22314. 703/836-2222. An education association of secondary school counselors, college and university admission officers, and related individuals who work with students as they make the transition from high school to post-secondary education.

NATIONAL ASSOCIATION OF COLLEGE AND UNIVERSITY BUSINESS OFFICERS
1 DuPont Circle, Suite 500, Washington DC 20036. 202/861-2500. Association for those involved in the financial administration and management of higher education. Membership required.

NATIONAL SCIENCE TEACHERS ASSOCIATION
1840 Wilson Boulevard, Arlington VA 22201-3000. 703/243-7100. Organization committed to the improvement of science education at all levels, preschool through college. Publishes five journals, a newspaper, and a number of special publications. Also conducts national and regional conventions.

Books

ACADEMIC LABOR MARKETS
Falmer Press, Taylor & Francis, Inc., 1900 Frost Road, Suite 101, Bristol PA 19007. 800/821-8312.

HOW TO GET A JOB IN EDUCATION
Adams Media Corporation, 260 Center Street, Holbrook MA 02343. 617/767-8100.

Directories

WASHINGTON HIGHER EDUCATION ASSOCIATION DIRECTORY
Council for Advancement and Support of Education, 11 DuPont Circle NW, Suite 400, Washington DC 20036 202/328-5900.

ELECTRONIC/INDUSTRIAL ELECTRICAL EQUIPMENT

Heading into 1995, industry analysts expected productivity in the fast-paced electronics industry to spiral, even as the number of production workers in the industry declined. Intense competition from overseas has companies cutting costs by sending labor-intensive operations to low-wage regions like the Far East and Mexico. On the other hand, the increased computerization of the industry is increasing the demand for highly-trained knowledge workers.

Semiconductor manufacturers, in particular, are on a roll. This sector far exceeded growth projections in 1993 and 1994 with a robust growth rate of 29 percent. Many chipmakers predicted that 1995 growth would surpass the 15 percent growth rate forecast by the Semiconductor Industry Association. Factors spawning a high demand for semiconductors: a surging PC market; new Information Highway markets; and a stronger telecommunications and consumer electronics market -- bolstered by a recovering Japanese economy. All told, the number of jobs in the semiconductor industry in 1995 was expected to hit 240,000 for the first time since 1990.

AAI CORPORATION
P.O. Box 126, Hunt Valley MD 21030-0126. 410/666-1400. **Contact:** Suzanne Seilz, Manager of Employment. **Description:** AAI is engaged in the fields of electronic warfare simulation, automatic test systems, combat vehicle ordnance, remotely piloted vehicles (RPV's), and materials handling equipment. **Common positions include:** Accountant/Auditor; Buyer; Draftsperson; Electrical/Electronics Engineer; Mechanical Engineer; Systems Analyst; Technical Writer/Editor. **Educational backgrounds include:** Business Administration; Engineering.

ALLIANT TECHSYSTEMS INC.
SIGNAL ANALYSIS CENTER
401 Defense Highway, Annapolis MD 21401. 410/266-1860. **Fax:** 410/224-0887. **Contact:** Pat Catterton, Human Resources Manager. **Description:** An electronics testing center and manufacturing facility. **Common positions include:** Computer Systems Analyst; Draftsperson; Electrical/Electronics Engineer; General Manager; Hardware Engineer; Mechanical Engineer; Software Engineer; Technical Writer/Editor. **Educational backgrounds include:** Business Administration; Engineering; Finance; Mathematics; Physics. **Benefits:** Dental Insurance; Disability Coverage; Life Insurance; Medical Insurance; Pension Plan; Savings Plan; Tuition Assistance. **Corporate headquarters location:** Minneapolis MN. **Other U.S. locations:** Annapolis MD; Patuxent River MD; Eatontown NJ; San Antonio TX. **Operations at this facility include:** Administration; Manufacturing; Research and Development; Sales; Testing. **Listed on:** American Stock Exchange; New York Stock Exchange. **Number of employees at this location:** 100.

AMECOM
5115 Calvert Road, College Park MD 20740-3898. 301/864-5600. **Contact:** Human Resources Department. **Description:** Amecon is a subsidiary of Litton Industries. Litton, founded in 1953 as a small electronics firm, has evolved into a $3.4 billion aerospace/defense company. Litton is one of the leaders in the high-technology markets for navigation, guidance and control, electronic warfare and command, control and communications systems. Litton is a primary builder of large multimission surface combatant ships for the U.S. Navy and a provider of overhaul, repair, modernization, ship design and engineering services. Principal operations are located throughout the United States, Germany, Canada and Italy. At the end of 1994, the

workforce consisted of approximately 29,000 employees. **Common positions include:** Computer Programmer; Electrical/Electronics Engineer; Industrial Engineer; Mechanical Engineer; Software Engineer. **Educational backgrounds include:** Engineering. **Benefits:** 401K; Dental Insurance; Disability Coverage; Employee Discounts; Life Insurance; Medical Insurance; Pension Plan; Tuition Assistance. **Corporate headquarters location:** Beverly Hills CA. **Parent company:** Litton Systems, Inc. **Operations at this facility include:** Administration; Manufacturing; Regional Headquarters; Research and Development; Sales; Service. **Number of employees at this location:** 400. **Number of employees nationwide:** 32,000.

AMTOTE INTERNATIONAL, INC.
11311 McCormick Road, Hunt Valley MD 21030. 410/771-8700. **Contact:** Human Resources. **Description:** Manufactures totalisator machines for the pari-mutuel wagering industry. **Corporate headquarters location:** This Location.

AUTOMATA, INC.
1200 Severn Way, Sterling VA 20166. 703/450-2600. **Contact:** Personnel Director. **Description:** Manufactures printed circuit boards. **Common positions include:** Accountant/Auditor; Blue-Collar Worker Supervisor; Buyer; Chemist; Computer Programmer; Customer Service Representative; Designer; Human Resources Specialist; Industrial Engineer; Manufacturer's/Wholesaler's Sales Rep.; Mechanical Engineer; Operations/Production Manager; Purchasing Agent and Manager; Quality Control Supervisor. **Educational backgrounds include:** Accounting; Chemistry; Engineering; Marketing. **Benefits:** Dental Insurance; Disability Coverage; Life Insurance; Medical Insurance; Profit Sharing; Tuition Assistance. **Corporate headquarters location:** This Location. **Operations at this facility include:** Administration; Manufacturing; Research and Development; Sales.

DCS CORPORATION
1330 Braddock Place, Alexandria VA 22314. **Contact:** Rhonda O'Bannon, Human Resources Administrator. **Description:** Research and development firm providing services and products for the government and private industry in areas such as electro-optics, virtual reality, fiber optics, and defense weapons and tactics. **Common positions include:** Computer Systems Analyst; Electrical/Electronics Engineer; Software Engineer. **Educational backgrounds include:** Computer Science; Engineering; Physics. **Benefits:** 401K; Dental Insurance; Disability Coverage; Life Insurance; Medical Insurance; Pension Plan; Profit Sharing; Tuition Assistance. **Corporate headquarters location:** This Location. **Other U.S. locations:** nationwide; CA; MD; MO. **Operations at this facility include:** Administration; Research and Development. **Listed on:** Privately held. **Number of employees at this location:** 150. **Number of employees nationwide:** 320.

DYNALECTRIC COMPANY
1420 Spring Hill Road, Suite 500, McLean VA 22102. 703/556-8000. **Contact:** Human Resources. **Description:** An electronics company.

DYNCORP
2000 Edmund Halley Drive, Reston VA 22091. **Contact:** Manager of Personnel. **Description:** An electronics company.

E-SYSTEMS/MELPAR DIVISION
7700 Arlington Boulevard, Falls Church VA 22046. 703/560-5000. **Fax:** 703/280-4267. **Contact:** Human Resources/Staffing Department. **Description:** A systems contractor in the areas of remotely controlled reconnaissance, information processing and display, electronic combat operations, digitally controlled communications, and intrusion detection. **Common positions include:** Computer Programmer; Draftsperson; Electrical/Electronics Engineer; Industrial Engineer; Mechanical Engineer; Physicist/Astronomer; Systems Analyst; Technical Writer/Editor. **Educational backgrounds include:** Computer Science; Engineering; Mathematics; Physics. **Benefits:** Credit Union; Dental Insurance; Disability Coverage; Employee Discounts; Life Insurance; Medical Insurance; Pension Plan; Savings Plan; Stock Option; Tuition Assistance. **Corporate headquarters location:** Dallas TX. **Parent company:** E-Systems, Inc. **Operations at this facility include:** Divisional Headquarters; Manufacturing; Research and Development.

E.I.L. INSTRUMENTS, INC.
10946A Golden West Drive, Hunt Valley MD 21031. 410/584-7400. **Contact:** Kathryn Marr, Human Resources Manager. **Description:** Distributes a variety of test

measurement and control electrical and electronic equipment. **Common positions include:** Customer Service Representative; Electrical/Electronics Engineer; Electronics Technician; Manufacturer's/Wholesaler's Sales Rep.; Sales Manager; Technician. **Educational backgrounds include:** Accounting; Business Administration; Electronics; Engineering; Marketing. **Benefits:** 401K; Dental Insurance; Disability Coverage; Life Insurance; Medical Insurance; Paid Vacation; Prescription Drugs; Tuition Assistance.

ENSCO INC.
5400 Port Royal Road, Springfield VA 22151. 703/321-9000. **Contact:** Bill Moore, Technical Recruiter. **Description:** A research, development, applied systems engineering, and professional services firm providing computer and sensor-based systems in the areas of defense, transportation, and business applications. **Common positions include:** Computer Programmer; Computer Systems Analyst; Department Manager; Electrical/Electronics Engineer; Mechanical Engineer; Systems Analyst; Technical Writer/Editor. **Educational backgrounds include:** Computer Science; Engineering; Mathematics; Physics. **Benefits:** Dental Insurance; Disability Coverage; Employee Discounts; Life Insurance; Medical Insurance; Pension Plan; Tuition Assistance. **Corporate headquarters location:** This Location. **Other U.S. locations:** CA; FL; IN; NY. **Operations at this facility include:** Administration; Divisional Headquarters; Research and Development. **Listed on:** Privately held. **Number of employees at this location:** 140. **Number of employees nationwide:** 400.

HALIFAX CORPORATION
5250 Cherokee Avenue, P.O. Box 11904, Alexandria VA 22312. 703/750-2202. **Fax:** 703/658-2999. **Contact:** Claudette Wassell, Personnel Administration. **Description:** Halifax is an electronics and facilities support services company, serving U.S. government agencies, systems integrators, financial institutions and the educational community worldwide since 1967. Engaged in the installation, operation, maintenance, and logistics support of equipment, systems and facilities, ranging from common hardware to technically sophisticated equipment, such as local area networks, computers, and communications systems. **Common positions include:** Accountant/Auditor; Aerospace Engineer; Buyer; Clerical Supervisor; Computer Programmer; Computer Systems Analyst; Customer Service Representative; Electrical/Electronics Engineer; Electrician; Payroll Clerk; Purchasing Agent and Manager; Quality Control Supervisor; Receptionist; Secretary; Services Sales Representative; Software Engineer; Stationary Engineer. **Educational backgrounds include:** Accounting; Business Administration; Computer Science; Marketing. **Benefits:** 401K; Dental Insurance; Disability Coverage; Employee Discounts; Life Insurance; Medical Insurance; Profit Sharing; Tuition Assistance. **Corporate headquarters location:** This Location. **Operations at this facility include:** Administration; Regional Headquarters; Sales; Service. **Listed on:** American Stock Exchange. **Number of employees at this location:** 70. **Number of employees nationwide:** 490. **Other U.S. locations:** Nationwide.

HEINEMANN PRODUCTS
EATON CORPORATION
2300 Northwood Drive, Salisbury MD 21801. 410/546-9778. **Contact:** Roger Weseman, Human Resources Manager. **Description:** The Eaton Corporation is a global manufacturer of highly engineered products which serve the automotive, industrial, construction, commercial, aerospace and marine markets. Principal products include truck transmissions and axles, engine components, hydraulic products, electrical power distribution and control equipment, ion implanters and a wide variety of controls. Headquartered in Eaton Center in Cleveland, the company has 51,000 employees and 150 manufacturing sites in 18 countries around the world. Heinemann Products is a division which manufacturers circuit breakers and control systems. **Common positions include:** Accountant/Auditor; Administrator; Blue-Collar Worker Supervisor; Buyer; Computer Operator; Customer Service Representative; Department Manager; Designer; Draftsperson; Electrical/Electronics Engineer; Industrial Engineer; Manufacturer's/Wholesaler's Sales Rep.; Manufacturing Engineer; Quality Control Supervisor. **Educational backgrounds include:** Business Administration; Computer Science; Engineering; Marketing. **Benefits:** Dental Insurance; Disability Coverage; Life Insurance; Medical Insurance; Pension Plan; Profit Sharing; Tuition Assistance. **Corporate headquarters location:** Cleveland OH. **Parent company:** Eaton Corporation. **Operations at this facility include:** Administration; Manufacturing; Sales. **Listed on:** New York Stock Exchange.

Electronic/Industrial Electrical Equipment/167

HEWLETT-PACKARD COMPANY
2101 Gaither Road, Rockville MD 20850. 301/258-2000. **Contact:** Personnel. **Description:** Local facility of a worldwide firm engaged in the design, manufacture, marketing, and servicing of a broad array of precision electronics instruments and systems for measurement, analysis, and computation.

KAYDON RING & SEAL INC.
P.O. Box 626, Baltimore MD 21203. 410/547-7700. **Contact:** Industrial Relations Supervisor. **Description:** Produces power transmission equipment (couplings) and adjustable-speed transmission drives. Nationally, Kaydon Ring & Seal Inc. is a diversified manufacturer offering specialized engineering and construction capabilities to various industries. Other operations serve the iron and steel industries in the design and construction of basic steel-making facilities. The company also manufactures road paving, roofing, railroad ties, and lumber products; as well as machinery for the mining, paper, packaging, and agriculture industries. Two facilities located in Baltimore. **Corporate headquarters location:** Pittsburgh PA. **Listed on:** New York Stock Exchange.

LORAL ADVANCED PROJECTS
P.O. Box 1339, Manassas VA 22110. 703/367-2371. **Contact:** Human Resources. **Description:** Loral develops advanced concepts for aircraft, maritime and land combat vehicle self-protection systems, precision guided weapons, reconnaissance and surveillance systems, and navigation law applications. Performs operations research in support of Loral Corporation product development and concentrates on applications which cut across multiple Loral divisions. The parent company, Loral Corporation, manufactures a wide array of defense electronics technologies which are concentrated on six growth businesses. Those are electronic combat, reconnaissance, training, tactical weapons, C3I, and space systems. The defense divisions serve all four branches of the U.S. military, while space systems support NASA, the National Oceanic and Atmospheric Administration, the U.S. Defense Department, and international telecommunication and broadcast companies. **Common positions include:** Electrical/Electronics Engineer; Physicist/Astronomer. **Educational backgrounds include:** Engineering; Physics. **Benefits:** 401K; Daycare Assistance; Dental Insurance; Disability Coverage; Employee Discounts; Life Insurance; Medical Insurance; Pension Plan; Savings Plan; Tuition Assistance. **Corporate headquarters location:** New York NY. **Other U.S. locations:** Nationwide. **Parent company:** Loral Corporation. **Operations at this facility include:** Research and Development. **Listed on:** New York Stock Exchange. **Number of employees at this location:** 10. **Number of employees nationwide:** 40,000.

LORAL WESTERN DEVELOPMENT LABS EAST COAST OPERATIONS
7100 Standard Drive, Hanover MD 21076. 410/796-4800. **Fax:** 410/796-7888. **Contact:** Human Resources. **Description:** A major field office for one of the nation's largest defense electronics manufacturers. The parent company, Loral Corporation, manufactures a wide array of defense electronics technologies which are concentrated on six growth businesses. Those businesses are electronic combat, reconnaissance, training, tactical weapons, C3I, and space systems. The defense divisions serve all four branches of the U.S. military, while space systems support NASA, the National Oceanic and Atmospheric Administration, the U.S. Defense Department, and international telecommunication and broadcast companies. **Corporate headquarters location:** New York NY. **Parent company:** Loral Corporation.

LUCAS INDUSTRIES INC.
11180 Sunrise Valley Drive, Reston VA 22091. 703/620-8901. **Contact:** Human Resources Department. **Description:** Manufactures automotive and aerospace electronics products.

MINITECH MECHANICAL PRODUCTS, INC.
51 Airport View Drive, St. Mary's Industrial Park, Hollywood MD 20636. 301/373-8601. **Contact:** Personnel Director. **Description:** Manufactures circuit breakers and circuit protection equipment and systems.

MOTOROLA COMMUNICATIONS & ELECTRONICS INC.
7230 Parkway Drive, Hanover MD 21076. 410/712-6200. **Contact:** Personnel. **Description:** This location is the regional sales office. Motorola Communications & Electronics, Inc., manufactures electronic equipment and components.

PHILIPS TECHNOLOGY/AIRPAX CORP.
807 Woods Road, Cambridge MD 21613-9468. 410/228-4600. **Contact:** Human Resources. **Description:** An electronic components manufacturer.

RJO ENTERPRISES
4640 Forbes Boulevard, Lanham MD 20706. 301/731-3600. **Fax:** 301/731-8413. **Contact:** Kimberly P. Fields, Manager, Human Resources. **Description:** RJO designs, integrates and manages complex programs built around computers, telecommunications, electronics and acquisition systems. RJO is a provider of innovative technology solutions. **Common positions include:** Accountant/Auditor; Aerospace Engineer; Budget Analyst; Buyer; Computer Programmer; Computer Systems Analyst; Electrical/Electronics Engineer; Electronics Technician; Financial Analyst; Mechanical Engineer; Software Engineer. **Educational backgrounds include:** Accounting; Business Administration; Computer Science; Engineering; Marketing. **Benefits:** 401K; Dental Insurance; Disability Coverage; Life Insurance; Medical Insurance; Profit Sharing; Tuition Assistance. **Corporate headquarters location:** This Location. **Other U.S. locations:** Hunt Valley MD; Dayton OH; Middletown RI. **Operations at this facility include:** Administration; Divisional Headquarters. **Number of employees at this location:** 65. **Number of employees nationwide:** 306.

TEKTRONIX INC.
700 Professional Drive, P.O. Box 6026, Gaithersburg MD 20884. 301/948-7151. **Contact:** Personnel Director. **Description:** Manufactures and markets electronic test and measurement equipment and a highly specialized line of computer graphics terminals and peripherals for the engineering and scientific market. **Common positions include:** Application Engineer; Computer Programmer; Electrical/Electronics Engineer; Manufacturer's/Wholesaler's Sales Rep.; Sales Engineer; Systems Analyst. **Educational backgrounds include:** Business Administration; Computer Science; Engineering; Physics. **Benefits:** Daycare Assistance; Dental Insurance; Disability Coverage; Employee Discounts; Life Insurance; Medical Insurance; Pension Plan; Profit Sharing; Tuition Assistance. **Corporate headquarters location:** Beaverton OR. **Operations at this facility include:** Sales; Service. **Listed on:** New York Stock Exchange. **Number of employees nationwide:** 10,000.

TRACOR APPLIED SCIENCES INC.
1601 Research Boulevard, Rockville MD 20850. 301/279-4624. **Fax:** 301/279-4460. **Contact:** Jack Hix, Manager, Employment. **Description:** Engaged in the testing and evaluation of U.S. Navy electronics, communications, radar, sonar, and combat systems; and in surface ship and submarine maintenance. **Common positions include:** Biological Scientist/Biochemist; Chemical Engineer; Computer Programmer; Draftsperson; Electrical/Electronics Engineer; Electronics Technician; Financial Analyst; Industrial Engineer; Industrial Hygienist; Management Trainee; Mechanical Engineer; Quality Control Supervisor; Secretary; Systems Analyst; Technical Writer/Editor; Typist/Word Processor. **Educational backgrounds include:** Accounting; Business Administration; Communications; Computer Science; Engineering; Finance. **Benefits:** 401K; Dental Insurance; Disability Coverage; Employee Discounts; Life Insurance; Medical Insurance; Pension Plan; Savings Plan; Tuition Assistance. **Corporate headquarters location:** Austin TX. **Other U.S. locations:** CA; CT; SC. **Parent company:** Tracor, Inc. **Operations at this facility include:** Administration; Regional Headquarters; Service. **Number of employees at this location:** 400. **Number of employees nationwide:** 2,000.

TRANS-TECH INC./ALPHA INDUSTRIES INC.
5520 Adamstown Road, Adamstown MD 21710. 301/695-9400. **Fax:** 301/695-7065. **Contact:** Judy Baisey, Human Resources Manager. **Description:** Manufactures a number of electronic-grade ceramic materials used in microwave electronic components such as link telephones. **Common positions include:** Accountant/Auditor; Buyer; Ceramics Engineer; Chemical Engineer; Chemist; Department Manager; Electrical/Electronics Engineer; General Manager; Mechanical Engineer; Purchasing Agent and Manager; Quality Control Supervisor. **Educational backgrounds include:** Accounting; Chemistry; Engineering; Physics. **Benefits:** 401K; Dental Insurance; Disability Coverage; Life Insurance; Medical Insurance; Stock Option; Tuition Assistance. **Parent company:** Alpha Industries (Woburn, MA). **Operations at this facility include:** Administration; Manufacturing; Research and Development; Sales. **Listed on:** American Stock Exchange.

Electronic/Industrial Electrical Equipment/169

WESTINGHOUSE ELECTRIC CORPORATION
7323 Aviation Boulevard, Linthicum Heights MD 21090. 410/765-1000. **Contact:** Human Resources. **Description:** Engaged in research and development, design, integration, and manufacture of advanced electronic systems for use in radar and electronic countermeasures, command and control systems, communications systems, space systems, air traffic control systems, and other applications for both governmental and commercial customers.

WESTINGHOUSE ELECTRIC CORPORATION
895 Oceanic Drive, Annapolis MD 21401-6104. 410/260-5000. **Contact:** Human Resources. **Description:** Engaged in research and development, design, integration, and manufacture of advanced electronic systems for use in radar and electronic countermeasures, command and control systems, communications systems, space systems, air traffic control systems, and other applications for both governmental and commercial customers.

WESTINGHOUSE ELECTRIC CORPORATION
ELECTRONIC SYSTEMS
P.O. Box 1693, Mail Stop 1162, Baltimore MD 21203. 410/765-4489. **Fax:** 410/993-7800. **Contact:** Earl S. King, Manager of Human Resource Business Operations. **Description:** Engaged in research and development, design, integration, and manufacture of advanced electronic systems for use in radar and electronic countermeasures, command and control systems, communications systems, space systems, air traffic control systems, and other applications for both governmental and commercial customers. **Common positions include:** Accountant/Auditor; Aerospace Engineer; Aircraft Mechanic/Engine Specialist; Attorney; Buyer; Ceramics Engineer; Chemical Engineer; Computer Programmer; Computer Systems Analyst; Electrical/Electronics Engineer; Financial Analyst; Industrial Engineer; Licensed Practical Nurse; Materials Engineer; Mathematician; Mechanical Engineer; Metallurgical Engineer; Physicist/Astronomer; Registered Nurse; Software Engineer; Technical Writer/Editor. **Educational backgrounds include:** Accounting; Computer Science; Engineering; Mathematics; Sales. **Benefits:** 401K; Dental Insurance; Disability Coverage; Life Insurance; Medical Insurance; Pension Plan; Savings Plan; Tuition Assistance. **Special Programs:** Training Programs. **Corporate headquarters location:** Pittsburgh PA. **Other U.S. locations:** Nationwide. **Parent company:** Westinghouse Electric Corp. **Operations at this facility include:** Administration; Manufacturing; Research and Development; Sales. **Listed on:** New York Stock Exchange. **Number of employees at this location:** 8,000.

Note: Because addresses and telephone numbers of smaller companies change rapidly, we recommend you call each company to verify the information below before inquiring about job opportunities. Mass mailings are not recommended.

Additional employers with over 250 employees:

ELECTRIC LIGHTING AND WIRING EQUIPMENT

The Rochester Corporation
751 Old Brandy Rd, Culpeper VA 22701-2866. 703/825-2111.

ELECTRONIC COMPONENTS AND ACCESSORIES

Automated Design Service
13 Firstfield Rd, Gaithersburg MD 20878-1700. 301/840-2220.

K & L Microwave Inc.
408 Coles Cir, Salisbury MD 21801-3214. 410/749-2424.

Melpar
7700 Arlington Blvd, Falls Church VA 22042-2902. 703/560-5000.

Paramax Systs Corp.
12010 Sunrise Valley Dr, Reston VA 22091-3499. 703/620-7000.

ELECTRICAL ENGINE EQUIPMENT

Blue Chip Products Inc.
301 Singerly Ave, Elkton MD 21921-5528. 410/398-5900.

SWITCHGEAR AND SWITCHBOARD APPARATUS

Powercon Corp.
PO Box 477, Severn MD 21144-0477. 410/551-6500.

ELECTRICAL EQUIPMENT, MACHINERY, AND SUPPLIES

Cae-Link Corp.
11800 Tech Rd, Silver Spring MD 20904-1987. 301/622-4400.

System Planning Corporation
1500 Wilson Blvd, Arlington VA 22209-2454. 703/351-8200.

Additional employers with under 250 employees:

ELECTRONIC COMPONENTS AND ACCESSORIES

Eurotherm Circuits
4230 Lafayette Center Dr,
Chantilly VA 22021-1208.
703/968-4533.

Spectra Inc.
22250 Comsat Dr,
Clarksburg MD 20871-9487.
301/428-7222.

AlliedSignal Micro Electronic
9140 Route 108, Columbia
MD 21045. 410/964-4000.

Pace Inc.
9893 Brewers Ct, Laurel MD
20723-1990. 301/490-9860.

ELECTRICAL EQUIPMENT, MACHINERY, AND SUPPLIES

Arrow Hart
8955 Early April Way,
Columbia MD 21046-2422.
410/381-5665.

General Electric Supply Co.
3701 Commerce Dr,
Baltimore MD 21227-1633.
410/247-6100.

Lasercon Corporation
6303 Ivy Ln, Greenbelt MD
20770-1479. 301/345-0350.

ELECTRICAL EQUIPMENT WHOLESALE

Dominion Electric Supply
5053 Lee Hwy, Arlington VA
22207-2582. 703/536-4400.

Interstate Electric Supply Co.
14110 Sullyfield Cir,
Chantilly VA 22021-1615.
703/631-2500.

Maurice Electrical Supl. Co. Inc.
500 Penn St Ne, Washington
DC 20002-7024. 202/675-9400.

Tristate Electrical Supl. Co. Inc.
209-D E Jarrettsville Rd,
Forest Hill MD 21050.
410/836-9222.

Abb Industrial Systems
1818 Queen Anne Sq, Bel
Air MD 21015-2556.
410/893-9605.

ELECTRONIC PARTS AND EQUIPMENT WHOLESALE

Bell Industries
8945 Guilford Rd, Suite 130,
Columbia MD 21046-2620.
410/290-5100.

Cellular One
7855 Walker Drive,
Greenbelt MD 20770-3212.
301/220-3600.

Metromedia Paging
9030 Route 108, Columbia
MD 21045. 410/995-0509.

Mx4 Electronics Inc.
2203 Greenspring Dr,
Timonium MD 21093-3115.
410/941-0743.

National Instruments
15807 Crabbs Branch Way #
A, Rockville MD 20855-2635. 301/258-0125.

Newark Electronics
7272 Park Dr, Baltimore MD
21234-7023. 410/712-6922.

Pioneer/Technologies Group Inc.
15810 Gaither Dr,
Gaithersburg MD 20877-1434. 301/921-3800.

Teleglobe Communications Prod.
360 Herndon Pky, Herndon
VA 22070-4820. 703/904-0550.

Metrocall
14012 Sullyfield Cir,
Chantilly VA 22021-1617.
703/378-9200.

Peirce-Phelps Inc.
7 Metropolitan Ct,
Gaithersburg MD 20878-4016. 301/948-5266.

Motorola Arlington Service Center
4064 S Four Mile Run Dr,
Arlington VA 22206-2307.
703/671-9300.

Motorola Chantilly Service Center
14301 Sullyfield Cir Ste F,
Chantilly VA 22021-1630.
703/378-1166.

Motorola Rappahanock Regional Service
52 Le Way Dr, Fredericksbrg
VA 22406-1030. 703/373-0778.

For more information on career opportunities in the electronic/industrial electrical equipment industry:

Associations

AMERICAN CERAMIC SOCIETY
735 Ceramic Place, Westerville OH 43081.
614/890-4700. 800/837-1804. Provides
ceramics futures information. Membership
required.

ELECTROCHEMICAL SOCIETY
10 South Main Street, Pennington NJ 08534-2896. 609/737-1902.

ELECTRONIC INDUSTRIES ASSOCIATION
25000 Wilshire Boulevard, Arlington VA
22201. 202/457-4900.

ELECTRONICS TECHNICIANS ASSOCIATION
602 North Jackson Street, Greencastle IN
46135. 317/653-8262. Offers published job-hunting advice from the organization's officers and members. Also offers educational material and certification programs.

INSTITUTE OF ELECTRICAL AND ELECTRONICS ENGINEERS (IEEE)
345 East 47th Street, New York NY 10017.
212/705-7900. Toll-free customer service line:
800/678-4333.

INSTITUTE OF ELECTRICAL AND ELECTRONICS ENGINEERS (IEEE)
1828 Elm Street NW, Suite 1202, Washington
DC 20036-5104. Professional activities line:
202/785-0017. National information line:
202/785-2180.

INTERNATIONAL BROTHERHOOD OF ELECTRICAL WORKERS
1125 15th Street NW, Washington DC
20005. 202/833-7000. Has over 1,000
apprenticeship programs.

INTERNATIONAL SOCIETY OF CERTIFIED ELECTRONICS TECHNICIANS
2708 West Berry Street, Ft. Worth TX 76109.
817/921-9101.

NATIONAL ELECTRONICS SALES AND SERVICES ASSOCIATION
2708 West Berry, Ft. Worth TX 76109.
817/921-9061. Provides newsletters and directories to members.

ROBOTICS INTERNATIONAL OF THE SOCIETY OF MANUFACTURING ENGINEERS (SME)
P.O. Box 930, One SME Drive, Dearborn MI 48121. 313/271-1500.

ENVIRONMENTAL SERVICES

According to the Environmental Protection Agency, the increase in environmental awareness over recent decades is more than just a trend. State and national legislation, such as the 1990 amendments to the Clean Air Act, have generated a new range of opportunities in skilled administrative, professional, and technical areas. However, the most critical positions needing to be filled are for scientists and engineers. These two groups develop new solutions to old problems, and therefore are instrumental in the research and development stages.

On the other hand, the current climate in the Congress is significantly cooler towards environmental regulation than in years past. Many members of Congress argue that American business is already overburdened by the Federal government, and some propose that the Environmental Protection Agency itself be disbanded.

ANALYSAS CORPORATION
1615 L Street NW, Suite 1250, Washington DC 20036-5610. 202/429-5653. **Fax:** 202/331-8578. **Contact:** Nikki Binford, Personnel Administrator. **Description:** Provides technical and administrative support in areas such as program management, environmental regulatory analysis, waste management technology development, technical writing and editing, graphic arts, and word processing. **Common positions include:** Computer Programmer; Computer Systems Analyst; Environmental Engineer; Geologist/Geophysicist; Software Engineer. **Educational backgrounds include:** Computer Science; Engineering; Geology. **Benefits:** 401K; Dental Insurance; Disability Coverage; Employee Discounts; Life Insurance; Medical Insurance; Profit Sharing; Tuition Assistance. **Corporate headquarters location:** This Location. **Other U.S. locations:** Oak Ridge TN.

AUTOMATED SCIENCES GROUP, INC.
1010 Wayne Avenue, Silver Spring MD 20910-5600. 301/587-8750. **Contact:** Human Resources. **Description:** An energy and environmental technology and systems integration consulting firm. The environmental consulting group is organized according to the following functional disciplines: environmental technology and engineering, regulatory compliance and analysis, health and safety programs, quality assurance and control, environmental information management systems, privatization, and energy. Programs include economic, safety, and environmental assessments of waste management alternatives; hazardous/radioactive and mixed waste management strategy development; facility design; operations; decontamination/decommissioning optimization, environmental regulation and policy analysis, environmental compliance strategy development, quality assurance and quality control program development and implementation; environmental systems; and environmental site assessments. **Corporate headquarters location:** This Location.

BIOSPHERICS INC.
12051 Indian Creek Court, Beltsville MD 20705. 301/419-3900. **Fax:** 301/210-4908. **Contact:** Mary Jo Lavorata, Employee Relations Manager. **Description:** Biospherics is a health information and environmental services company. The company employs professionals with health care backgrounds and liberal arts backgrounds to respond to public and professional inquiries on a range of subjects from pharmaceutical products to government information hotlines. Biospherics also provides a range of environmental services: asbestos abatement training/monitoring, lead-in-paint testing, and environmental hazard assessments. **Common positions include:** Biological Scientist/Biochemist; Computer Programmer; Computer Systems Analyst; Counselor; Customer Service Representative; Editor; Environmental Engineer; Geologist/Geophysicist; Industrial Hygienist; Licensed Practical Nurse; Pharmacist;

Registered Nurse; Reporter; Teacher; Technical Writer/Editor. **Educational backgrounds include:** Biology; Chemistry; Computer Science; Environmental Science; Geology; Health Care; Nursing. **Benefits:** 401K; Dental Insurance; Disability Coverage; Life Insurance; Medical Insurance. **Special Programs:** Training Programs. **Corporate headquarters location:** This Location. **Other U.S. locations:** Cumberland MD; Cleveland OH. **Operations at this facility include:** Administration; Research and Development. **Listed on:** NASDAQ. **Number of employees at this location:** 300. **Number of employees nationwide:** 480.

ENVIRONMENTAL ELEMENTS CORPORATION
3700 Koppers St., Baltimore MD 21227. 410/368-7080. **Contact:** Linda J. Young, Manager/Employee Relations. **Description:** An air-pollution-control equipment supply company. **Number of employees at this location:** 250.

ENVIRONMENTAL TECHNOLOGIES GROUP, INC.
1400 Taylor Avenue, P.O. Box 9840, Baltimore MD 21284-9840. 410/321-5200. **Fax:** 410/321-5255. **Contact:** Roger Morin, Manager of Human Resources. **Description:** A manufacturing, research, and development company. **Common positions include:** Biomedical Engineer; Chemical Engineer; Human Resources Specialist; Mechanical Engineer. **Educational backgrounds include:** Engineering. **Benefits:** 401K; Dental Insurance; Disability Coverage; Employee Discounts; Life Insurance; Medical Insurance; Pension Plan; Profit Sharing; Savings Plan; Tuition Assistance. **Special Programs:** Training Programs. **Listed on:** Privately held. **Number of employees at this location:** 400.

ICF INTERNATIONAL, INC.
9300 Lee Highway, Fairfax VA 22031-1207. 703/934-3000. **Contact:** Employment Manager. **Description:** An environmental and professional services firm. **Common positions include:** Biological Scientist/Biochemist; Chemist; Civil Engineer; Computer Programmer; Economist/Market Research Analyst; Electrical/Electronics Engineer; Financial Analyst; Geologist/Geophysicist; Industrial Engineer; Mechanical Engineer; Petroleum Engineer; Physicist/Astronomer; Statistician; Systems Analyst. **Educational backgrounds include:** Biology; Business Administration; Chemistry; Computer Science; Economics; Engineering; Geology; Liberal Arts; Mathematics; Physics. **Benefits:** Dental Insurance; Disability Coverage; Life Insurance; Medical Insurance; Pension Plan; Tuition Assistance. **Corporate headquarters location:** This Location. **Listed on:** NASDAQ.

NATIONAL WILDLIFE FEDERATION
1400 16th Street NW, Washington DC 20036-2266. 202/797-6800. **Contact:** Robert Ertter, Director of Personnel. **Description:** A conservation society dedicated to preserving the nation's wildlife.

SMITHSONIAN ENVIRONMENTAL RESEARCH CENTER
P.O. Box 28, Edgewater MD 21037. 301/261-4190. **Contact:** Helen M. Dalask, Administrative Officer. **Description:** The environmental research branch of the Smithsonian Institution. **Common positions include:** Biological Scientist/Biochemist; Chemist; Environmental Engineer; Environmental Scientist. **Educational backgrounds include:** Biology; Chemistry. **Benefits:** Life Insurance; Medical Insurance; Pension Plan. **Special Programs:** Internships. **Operations at this facility include:** Administration; Research and Development. **Number of employees at this location:** 85.

For more information on career opportunities in environmental services:

Associations

AIR AND WASTE MANAGEMENT ASSOCIATION
One Gateway Center, Third Floor, Pittsburgh PA 15222. 412/232-3444. A nonprofit, technical and educational organization providing a neutral forum where all points of view of an environmental management issue can be addressed.

ASSOCIATION OF STATE & INTERSTATE WATER POLLUTION CONTROL ADMINISTRATORS
750 First Street NE, Suite 910, Washington DC 20002. 202/898-0905.

ENVIRONMENTAL INDUSTRY ASSOCIATION
4301 Connecticut Avenue N, Suite 300, Washington DC 20008. 202/659-4613. Fax 202/966-4818.

INSTITUTE OF CLEAN AIR COMPANIES
1707 L Street NW, Suite 570, Washington DC 20036. 202/457-0911-4201. National association of companies involved in stationary source air pollution control.

U.S. ENVIRONMENTAL PROTECTION AGENCY
401 M Street SW, Washington DC 20460. 202/260-2090. Provides EPA background career information.

WATER ENVIRONMENT FEDERATION
601 Wythe Street, Alexandria VA 22314. 703/684-2400. Subscription to jobs newsletter required for career information.

Magazines

CAREERS AND THE ENGINEER
Adams Media Corporation, 260 Center Street, Holbrook MA 02343. 617/767-8100.

JOURNAL OF AIR AND WASTE MANAGEMENT ASSOCIATION
One Gateway Center, Third Floor, Pittsburgh PA 15222. 412/232-3444.

FABRICATED/PRIMARY METALS AND PRODUCTS

Nineteen Ninety-Four brought a surge in demand for steel, with U.S. steel consumption growing 8 percent. The biggest push came from U.S. automakers, particularly from the increased sales of minivans and other light trucks, which use more steel than cars. Residential and road and bridge construction also contributed to the higher steel sales. The U.S. steel industry even began to expand its exports to satisfy a growing foreign market. In fact, industry demand was so high that, despite steel mills operating at near full capacity, orders still exceeded deliveries by at least 5 percent. This caused a jump in steel prices (an average hike of about 5 percent in 1994, with a similar increase expected in 1995), which in turn led to increased profits for integrated steel companies. However, while higher prices are good news for the big companies, they have the opposite effect on minimills. Higher steel prices cause parallel rises in the price of scrap, the main raw material for minimills. In addition to the increases in scrap prices, minimills will also have to deal with rapidly rising competition, with about 10 new minimills scheduled to open between 1995 and 1998.

ATLAS MACHINE & IRON WORKS INC.
13951 Lee Highway, Gainesville VA 22065. 703/754-4171. **Contact:** Personnel Director. **Description:** Produces a wide range of fabricated steel plates.

CLENDENIN BROTHERS, INC.
4309 Erdman Avenue, Baltimore MD 21213. 410/327-4500. **Contact:** Lisa Ditillo, Personnel Director. **Description:** Manufactures brass, copper, aluminum, and stainless steel products.

COLUMBIA SPECIALTY COMPANY, INC.
6301 Eastern Avenue, Baltimore MD 21224. 410/633-6900. **Contact:** Jack Doherty, Manager. **Description:** Manufactures metal closures and stampings.

INDEPENDENT CAN COMPANY
1300 Brass Mill Road, Belcamp MD 21017. 410/272-0090. **Contact:** Personnel Office. **Description:** Manufactures decorative metal tins. **Corporate headquarters location:** This Location. **Other U.S. locations:** City of Industry CA; Ft. Madison IA. **Operations at this facility include:** Manufacturing; Sales.

MARYLAND SPECIALTY WIRE COMPANY
100 Cockeysville Road, Cockeysville MD 21030. 410/785-2500. **Contact:** Gail Murphy, Personnel Administrator. **Description:** Produces stainless steel and alloy wire used for springs, reinforced hose, wire rope, ball bearings, and other products. **Common positions include:** Accountant/Auditor; Computer Programmer; Human Resources Specialist; Industrial Production Manager; Management Trainee; Manufacturer's/Wholesaler's Sales Rep.; Mechanical Engineer; Operations/Production Manager. **Educational backgrounds include:** Accounting; Business Administration; Computer Science; Engineering; Marketing. **Benefits:** Dental Insurance; Disability Coverage; Life Insurance; Medical Insurance; Pension Plan; Savings Plan; Tuition Assistance. **Corporate headquarters location:** This Location. **Parent company:** Handy & Harmon. **Operations at this facility include:** Divisional Headquarters.

REPUBLIC ENGINEERED STEELS
3501 East Biddle Street, Baltimore MD 21213. 410/563-5624. **Contact:** Employment. **Description:** Produces stainless steel, alloy steel, billets, bar, rod, wire, special shapes, and nickel-based alloys.

STROMBERG SHEET METAL WORKS
1235 West Street Northeast, Washington DC 20018. 202/526-8350. **Contact:** Lou Curtain, Production Manager. **Description:** A sheet metal manufacturing corporation.

THOMPSON STEEL COMPANY INC.
4515 North Point Boulevard, P.O. Box 6610, Sparrows Point MD 21219. 410/477-0400. **Contact:** Industrial Relations Manager. **Description:** Produces cold-rolled strip steel. **Common positions include:** Accountant/Auditor; Administrator; Buyer; Customer Service Representative; Department Manager; Industrial Engineer; Metallurgical Engineer; Quality Control Supervisor. **Educational backgrounds include:** Accounting; Business Administration; Chemistry; Communications; Engineering; Marketing; Physics. **Benefits:** Dental Insurance; Disability Coverage; Life Insurance; Medical Insurance; Pension Plan; Tuition Assistance. **Corporate headquarters location:** Canton MA. **Operations at this facility include:** Administration; Manufacturing; Sales; Service.

UNC INCORPORATED
175 Admiral Cochrane Drive, Annapolis MD 21401-7367. 410/266-7333. **Contact:** Human Resources Department. **Description:** Engaged in fabricated plate work.

U.S. CAN COMPANY
1101 Todds Lane, Baltimore MD 21237. 410/686-6363. **Contact:** Patty Russell, Human Resources. **Description:** Manufactures a variety of metal and composite cans.

U.S. CAN COMPANY
2010 Reservoir Road, Sparrows Point MD 21219. 410/477-3131. **Contact:** Personnel. **Description:** Produces metal cans, sanitary containers, and beverage containers. Also an international manufacturer of packaging products.

WELLS ALUMINUM CORPORATION
809 Glen Eagles Court, Baltimore MD 21286-2201. 410/494-4500. **Contact:** Human Resources. **Description:** A manufacturer of aluminum products.

Note: Because addresses and telephone numbers of smaller companies change rapidly, we recommend you call each company to verify the information below before inquiring about job opportunities. Mass mailings are not recommended.

Additional employers with over 250 employees:

FABRICATED METAL PRODUCTS

Avasta Shefield East
P.O. Box 1975, Baltimore MD 21203. 410/522-6200.

FABRICATED STRUCTURAL METAL PRODUCTS

Canan Steel Corporation
PO Box C-285, Pt Of Rocks MD 21777-0285. 301/874-5141.

FABRICATED WIRE PRODUCTS

Sibaco/National Wire Products Ind. Inc.
8203 Fischer Rd, Baltimore MD 21222-3696. 410/477-1700.

Additional employers with under 250 employees:

FABRICATED METAL PRODUCTS

Dietrich Industries Inc.
8911 Bethlehem Blvd, Baltimore MD 21219-2526. 410/477-8700.

IRON AND STEEL FOUNDRIES

Bingham & Taylor Corporation
601 Nalle Pl, Culpeper VA 22701-2862. 703/825-8334.

NONFERROUS ROLLING AND DRAWING OF METALS

Halethorpe Extrusions
2000 Halethorpe Ave, Halethorpe MD 21227-4596. 410/242-2800.

DIE-CASTINGS

North American Die Casting
1104 Summit St, Fredericksbrg VA 22401-7033. 703/371-9220.

METAL CONTAINERS

Crown Cork & Seal Co.
U S Rt 13, Fruitland MD 21826. 410/742-8761.

Easterna Division Fruitland Plant
PO Box 338, Fruitland MD 21826-0338. 410/742-8761.

Fabricated/Primary Metals and Products/177

Steeltin Can Corporation
1101 Todds Ln, Baltimore MD 21237-2905. 410/686-6363.

WHOLESALE METALS SERVICE CENTERS AND OFFICES

Durrett-Sheppard Steel Co.
6800 E Baltimore St, Baltimore MD 21224-1892. 410/633-6800.

Lyon Conklin & Co.
2101 Race St, Baltimore MD 21230-4848. 410/752-6800.

Worthington Steel Co.
8911 Kelso Dr, Baltimore MD 21221-3167. 410/574-7904.

Benhill Steel Inc.
2001 Benhill Ave, Baltimore MD 21226-1435. 410/355-6700.

Infra-Metals Co.
4501 Curtis Ave, Baltimore MD 21226-1360. 410/355-2550.

FABRICATED STRUCTURAL METAL PRODUCTS

General Products Co.
PO Box 7387, Fredericksbrg VA 22404-7387. 703/898-5700.

Jamison Door Co.
PO Box 70, Hagerstown MD 21741-0070. 301/733-3100.

Evapco Inc.
5151 Allendale Ln, Taneytown MD 21787-2155. 410/756-2600.

Rockwell International
1745 Jefferson Davis Hwy, Arlington VA 22202-3402. 703/553-6600.

Danzer Metal Works
17500 York Rd, Hagerstown MD 21740-7599. 301/582-2000.

Sagamore Heating & Air Conditioning
2901 Dede Rd, Finksburg MD 21048-2300. 410/833-2300.

Warren-Ehret Co. of MD
610 W West St, Baltimore MD 21230-2608. 410/752-4922.

Miscellaneous Metals
5719 Industry Ln, Frederick MD 21701-5182. 301/695-8820.

For more information on career opportunities in the fabricated/primary metals and products industries:

Associations

AMERICAN FOUNDRYMEN'S SOCIETY
505 State Street, Des Plaines IL 60016-708/824-0181.

ASM INTERNATIONAL: THE MATERIALS INFORMATION SOCIETY
Materials Park OH 44073. 800/336-5152. Gathers, processes, and disseminates technical information to foster the understanding and application of engineered materials.

AMERICAN WELDING SOCIETY
550 LeJeune Road NW, Miami FL 33126. 305/443-9353.

Directories

DIRECTORY OF STEEL FOUNDRIES IN THE UNITED STATES, CANADA, AND MEXICO
Steel Founder's Society of America, 455 State Street, Des Plaines IL 60016. 708/299-9160.

Magazines

AMERICAN METAL MARKET
25 7th Avenue, New York NY 10019. 212/887-8580.

IRON AGE NEW STEEL
191 South Gary, Carol Stream IL 60188. 708/462-2285.

IRON & STEEL ENGINEER
Association of Iron and Steel Engineers, Three Gateway Center, Suite 2350, Pittsburgh PA 15222. 412/281-6323.

MODERN METALS
625 North Michigan Avenue, Suite 2500, Chicago IL 60611. 312/654-2300.

FINANCIAL SERVICES

During 1994, the financial services sector has seen higher interest rates, increased regulation, and corporate consolidation. Rising rates in 1994 and 1995 have led to large trading losses for securities firms. Analysts expected that consolidations due to mergers, coupled with globalization, would mean 10,000 layoffs industry-wide in 1995. Other financial instruments have also been slumping, including bonds and the once-hot mutual funds. New investment in mutual funds dropped better than 50 percent in 1994. Because of losses in bond funds, many investors sought out safer money-market funds and bank certificates of deposit.

On the bright side: Some dominant U.S investment banks have successfully gone global, and those professionals specializing in consulting and underwriting are in great demand. Naturally, those with expertise in mergers and acquisitions consulting will also benefit.

THE ACACIA GROUP
51 Louisiana Avenue NW, Washington DC 20001. 202/628-4506x512. **Fax:** 202/638-5383. **Contact:** Pat Franklin, CCP, Senior Human Resources Generalist. **Description:** Engaged in diversified financial services. **Common positions include:** Accountant/Auditor; Actuary; Attorney; Bank Officer/Manager; Branch Manager; Brokerage Clerk; Claim Representative; Computer Systems Analyst; Customer Service Representative; Financial Analyst; Human Resources Specialist; Insurance Agent/Broker; Paralegal; Securities Sales Rep. **Educational backgrounds include:** Accounting; Business Administration; Finance; Liberal Arts; Marketing. **Benefits:** 401K; Daycare Assistance; Dental Insurance; Disability Coverage; Employee Discounts; Life Insurance; Medical Insurance; Profit Sharing; Tuition Assistance. **Corporate headquarters location:** This Location. **Operations at this facility include:** Administration; Service. **Number of employees at this location:** 300. **Number of employees nationwide:** 1,000.

THE ADAMS EXPRESS COMPANY
Seven St. Paul Street, Baltimore MD 21202. 410/752-5900. **Contact:** R.F. Koloski, Vice President/Human Resources. **Description:** A financial services and investment advisory firm.

BOLLING FEDERAL CREDIT UNION
P.O. Box 6973, Washington DC 20032. 202/562-5385. **Fax:** 202/562-8210. **Contact:** Michael Beylo, Vice President of Operations. **Description:** Provides financial products and services to its membership, primarily Air Force personnel. **Common positions include:** Accountant/Auditor; Bank Teller; Services Sales Representative. **Benefits:** Disability Coverage; Medical Insurance; Pension Plan; Tuition Assistance. **Corporate headquarters location:** This Location. **Operations at this facility include:** Administration; Service. **Number of employees at this location:** 22.

ALEX BROWN & SONS INCORPORATED
135 East Baltimore Street, Baltimore MD 21202. 410/727-1700. **Recorded Jobline:** 410/783-5350. **Contact:** Amy Vankirk, Coordinator of Employment. **Description:** A financial services, investment advisory, and investment banking firm.

CALVERT GROUP
4550 Montgomery Avenue, Suite 1000 North, Bethesda MD 20814. 301/951-4800. **Contact:** Judy Shober, Employment Coordinator. **Description:** A financial services, investment advisory, and investment banking firm.

Financial Services/179

COMMODITY FUTURES TRADING COMMISSION
2033 K Street NW, Washington DC 20581. 202/254-6387. **Recorded Jobline:** 202/254-3346. **Contact:** Human Resources. **Description:** Regulates futures trading.

DERWOOD INVESTMENT CORPORATION
8401 Connecticut Avenue, Chevy Chase MD 20815. 301/986-6100. **Contact:** Human Resources. **Description:** Derwood Investment Corporation is an investment company of Saul Centers, Inc. Saul Centers is a self-managed, self-administered equity real estate investment trust. Saul Centers currently operates and manages a real estate portfolio of 32 properties totaling approximately 5.6 million square feet of gross leasable area with over 75 percent of the cash flow generated from properties in the Washington, D.C./Baltimore metropolitan area. The portfolio initially included 26 neighborhood and community shopping centers, one office property, one office/retail property and one research park. During 1994, the company acquired two additional neighborhood shopping centers and developed one center, all located in the northern Virginia suburbs of Washington, D.C. Shares of Saul Centers are traded under the symbol 'BFS.'. **Listed on:** New York Stock Exchange.

FANNIE MAE
3900 Wisconsin Avenue NW, Washington DC 20016. 202/752-7000. **Contact:** Frances Jordan, Director of Operations. **Description:** A stockholder-owned corporation, chartered by Congress, whose purpose is to help finance housing by supplementing the supply of mortgage funds. Purchases a variety of mortgage plans, including adjustable rate mortgages, conventional fixed rate home mortgages, and second mortgages. Also participates in pools of conventional first and second mortgages, and guarantees conventional mortgage-based securities. Regional offices are located in Philadelphia, Atlanta, Chicago, and Dallas. **Common positions include:** Attorney; Computer Programmer; Computer Systems Analyst; Economist/Market Research Analyst; Financial Analyst. **Educational backgrounds include:** Accounting; Business Administration; Computer Science; Economics; Finance; Mathematics. **Benefits:** 401K; Daycare Assistance; Dental Insurance; Disability Coverage; Employee Discounts; Life Insurance; Medical Insurance; Pension Plan; Profit Sharing; Savings Plan; Tuition Assistance. **Special Programs:** Internships; Training Programs. **Corporate headquarters location:** This Location. **Other U.S. locations:** Nationwide. **Operations at this facility include:** Administration; Divisional Headquarters; Regional Headquarters; Sales; Service. **Listed on:** New York Stock Exchange. **Number of employees at this location:** 3,000.

FEDERAL HOME LOAN MORTGAGE CORPORATION
8200 Jones Branch Drive, McLean VA 22102. 703/903-2000. **Contact:** Human Resources. **Description:** In 1970, the U.S. government established the Federal Home Loan Mortgage Corporation -- nicknamed "Freddie Mac" -- to increase mortgage credit for housing. Freddie Mac is now a provider of secondary mortgages. **Listed on:** New York Stock Exchange.

FIDELITY & DEPOSIT COMPANY OF MARYLAND
P.O. Box 1227, Baltimore MD 21203. **Contact:** Human Resources Representative. **Description:** Deals in surety bonds and insurance. An affiliate of Swiss Reinsurance Company and Zurich Insurance Company. **Common positions include:** Actuary; Underwriter/Assistant Underwriter. **Educational backgrounds include:** Business Administration; Computer Science; Law/Pre-Law; Mathematics. **Benefits:** Dental Insurance; Disability Coverage; Life Insurance; Medical Insurance; Pension Plan; Thrift Plan; Tuition Assistance. **Special Programs:** Internships.

JOHNSTON, LEMON & COMPANY INC.
1101 Vermont Avenue NW, Suite 800, Washington DC 20005. 202/842-5500. **Contact:** Patty Maddox, Personnel Director. **Description:** Underwrites, distributes, and deals in corporate and municipal securities, revenue bonds, and mutual funds; and provides related and unrelated business management services. **Corporate headquarters location:** This Location.

LEGG MASON
111 South Calvert Street, Baltimore MD 21202. 410/539-3400. **Contact:** Human Resources. **Description:** Legg Mason is a holding company with subsidiaries engaged in securities brokerage and trading; investment management of mutual funds and individual and institutional accounts; underwriting of corporate and municipal securities and other investment banking activities; sales of annuity and banking; and the provision of other financial services. Principal units are Baltimore-based Legg Mason,

Wood Walker, and New Orleans-based Howard, Weil, Labouisse, Friedrichs, Inc. The company serves its brokerage clients through 86 offices. As investment advisors, they manage more than $16 billion in assets for individual and institutional accounts and mutual funds. The company's mortgage banking subsidiaries have direct and master servicing responsibilities for $12 billion of commercial mortgages. **Number of employees nationwide:** 2,440.

LEHMAN BROTHERS
800 Connecticut Avenue NW, Suite 1200, Washington DC 20006. 202/452-4700. **Contact:** Human Resources. **Description:** Provides financial services.

MERRILL LYNCH
1850 K Street NW, Suite 700, Washington DC 20006. 202/659-7333. **Contact:** Office Manager. **Description:** Provides financial services in the following areas: securities, extensive insurance, and real estate and related services. One of the largest securities brokerage firms in the United States. Also brokers commodity futures and options; corporate and municipal securities; and is engaged in investment banking activities. **Common positions include:** Branch Manager; Customer Service Representative; Management Trainee; Operations/Production Manager; Services Sales Representative. **Benefits:** Disability Coverage; Employee Discounts; Medical Insurance; Pension Plan; Profit Sharing; Savings Plan; Tuition Assistance. **Corporate headquarters location:** New York NY. **Operations at this facility include:** Sales. **Listed on:** New York Stock Exchange.

NATIONAL ASSOCIATION OF SECURITIES DEALERS, INC.
1735 K Street NW, Washington DC 20006. 202/728-8470. **Contact:** John Buergenthal, Human Resource Manager. **Description:** A self-regulatory organization of the securities industry responsible for the regulation of NASDAQ and the over-the-counter securities markets. **Common positions include:** Attorney; Customer Service Representative; Human Resources Specialist; Marketing Specialist; Statistician; Systems Analyst. **Educational backgrounds include:** Accounting; Business Administration; Finance; Marketing. **Benefits:** Dental Insurance; Disability Coverage; Life Insurance; Medical Insurance; Pension Plan; Savings Plan; Tuition Assistance. **Special Programs:** Internships; Training Programs. **Corporate headquarters location:** This Location.

OXFORD DEVELOPMENT CORPORATION
7200 Wisconsin Avenue, 11th Floor, Bethesda MD 20814. 301/654-3100. **Contact:** Lisa Brookhart, Human Resources Director. **Description:** A financial services firm.

SECURITY PACIFIC FINANCE
P.O. Box 1370, Olmey MD 20830-1370. 301/924-0904. **Contact:** Frank Cortina, Regional Manager. **Description:** A money-lending firm, primarily serving individual lenders in a wide range of income levels. Offers home improvement, college expenses, vacation and other general-purpose loans.

STUDENT LOAN MARKETING ASSOCIATION
1050 Thomas Jefferson Street NW, Washington DC 20007. 202/298-2590. **Contact:** Janet Mahaney, Employment Manager. **Description:** Nicknamed 'Sallie Mae,' the Student Loan Marketing Association was established by Congress in 1972. It is the major financial intermediary to the educational financing market in the U.S. and provides student loan services as well as other financial and management services to loan originators. Sallie Mae also provides financing for academic equipment. **Common positions include:** Accountant/Auditor; Computer Programmer; Financial Analyst; Marketing Specialist; Systems Analyst. **Number of employees nationwide:** 3,275.

THE TRAVELERS, INC.
300 St. Paul Place, Baltimore MD 21202. 410/332-3281. **Contact:** Ms. D.A. Wade, Vice President/Human Resources. **Description:** A diversified financial organization engaged in insurance, investment, mortgage banking, and consumer financial services companies. Subsidiaries recruit each year for jobs at various levels of responsibility throughout the United States. **Common positions include:** Accountant/Auditor; Branch Manager; Claim Representative; Computer Programmer; Credit Manager; Customer Service Representative; Financial Analyst; Systems Analyst. **Educational backgrounds include:** Accounting; Business Administration; Communications; Computer Science; Finance. **Benefits:** Dental Insurance; Disability Coverage; Life Insurance; Medical Insurance; Pension Plan; Savings Plan; Tuition Assistance. **Corporate headquarters**

location: New York NY. **Operations at this facility include:** Administration; Divisional Headquarters. **Listed on:** New York Stock Exchange.

Note: Because addresses and telephone numbers of smaller companies change rapidly, we recommend you call each company to verify the information below before inquiring about job opportunities. Mass mailings are not recommended.

Additional employers with under 250 employees:

MISC. FINANCIAL SERVICES

Farmers National Bank of MD
Heritage Harbour, Annapolis MD 21401. 410/224-4006.

Fleet Financenter
8480 Baltimore National Pike, Ellicott City MD 21043-3369. 410/465-9004.

Nationscredit Financial Service Corporation
1010 Beards Hill Rd, Aberdeen MD 21001-2230. 410/273-6886.

Associates Financial Services
4300 Plank Rd Apt 210, Fredericksbrg VA 22407-0102. 703/786-0085.

MORTGAGE BANKERS

Signet Mortgage Corporation
5 Bel Air South Pky, Bel Air MD 21015-6043. 410/515-1238.

Weyerhaeuser Mortgage Co.
806 W Diamond Ave, Gaithersburg MD 20878-1415. 301/417-1438.

American Home Funding
3516 Plank Rd, Fredericksbrg VA 22407-9901. 703/371-4711.

Guild Mortgage Company
605 Jefferson Davis Hwy, Fredericksbrg VA 22401-4436. 703/373-7273.

Household Finance Corporation
Plaza At Landmark, Annandale VA 22003. 703/658-4604.

Household Finance Corporation
Fairfax Court Shopping Center, Fairfax VA 22031. 703/352-1500.

Ameribanc Mortgage
3114 Golansky Blvd, Woodbridge VA 22192-4231. 703/680-3000.

Equity One Mortgage
1300 York Rd, Lutherville MD 21093-6016. 410/823-1072.

First Washington Mortgage Corporation
7700 Little River Tpke, Annandale VA 22003-2406. 703/642-2400.

American Heritage Financial Corporation
1511 K St Nw, Washington DC 20005-1401. 202/783-4870.

American Residential Mortgage Corporation
116 Defense Hwy Ste 102, Annapolis MD 21401-7040. 301/970-2541.

Atlantic Coast Mortgage Co.
12700 Fair Lakes Cir, Fairfax VA 22033-4905. 703/631-0098.

Atlantic Residential Mortgage
120 E Baltimore St Ste 23, Baltimore MD 21202-1674. 410/832-1900.

Brannum Mortgage Company Inc.
1011 Wahler Pl Se, Washington DC 20032-4332. 202/561-4699.

Capital Mortgage Banker
100 West Rd, Baltimore MD 21204-2329. 410/296-5660.

Crestar Mortgage Corporation
7617 Little River Tpke, Annandale VA 22003-2603. 703/813-4000.

Ctx Mortgage Company
11200 Waples Mill Rd, Fairfax VA 22030-7407. 703/385-6100.

Equity One
4411 Plank Rd, Fredericksbrg VA 22407-4809. 703/785-0074.

Fairfax Mortgage
7133 Rutherford Rd, Baltimore MD 21244-2703. 410/298-1300.

First Advantage Mortgage Corporation
8910 Rte 108, Columbia MD 21045. 410/964-4800.

First Advantage Mortgage Corporation
805 15th St NW Ste 810, Washington DC 20005-2207. 202/637-4612.

First National Mortgage Corporation
2 Cardinal Park Dr Se, Leesburg VA 22075-4458. 703/771-8383.

First Savings Mortgage Corporation
804 W Diamond Ave, Gaithersburg MD 20878-1414. 301/948-2585.

Icm Mortgage Corporation
10600 Arrowhead Dr Ste 250, Fairfax VA 22030-7306. 703/934-9350.

Investors Home Mortgage Corporation
3516 Plank Rd, Fredericksbrg VA 22407-6861. 703/786-2134.

Market Street Mortgage Corporation
7700 Little River Tpke, Annandale VA 22003-2406. 703/941-6600.

National City Mortgage Co.
1355 Back Creek Ct, Solomons MD 20688. 410/326-9258.

Ncnb Mortgage
7920 McDonogh Rd, Owings Mills MD 21117-5273. 410/363-4416.

North American Mortgage Co
7833 Walker Dr, Greenbelt MD 20770-3211. 301/474-4717.

Prosperity Mortgage Corporation
Calvert Village Shopping Cente, Prnc Frederck MD 20678. 410/535-6552.

Radcliffe Mortgage & Inv. Service
1200 G St Nw, Washington DC 20005-3814. 202/434-8728.

Rapid Mortgage
5100 14th St Nw, Washington DC 20011-6928. 202/785-3893.

Ryland Mortgage
3102 Golansky Blvd,
Woodbridge VA 22192-
4200. 703/730-0388.

Unity Mortgage Corporation
1700 Rockville Pike,
Rockville MD 20852-1631.
301/816-9171.

Washington Mortgage Association
5528 4th St Nw,
Washington DC 20011-
6510. 202/265-8939.

Washington Suburban Mortgage Co.
5225 Wisconsin Ave Nw,
Washington DC 20015-
2014. 202/362-2300.

SECURITY BROKERS AND DEALERS

Ferris Baker Watts Inc.
1720 I St Nw, Washington
DC 20006-3704. 202/429-
3500.

Derand Corporation of America
2201 Wilson Blvd Ste 300,
Arlington VA 22201-3323.
703/247-2900.

Git Investment Fund
1655 Fort Myer Dr, Arlington
VA 22209-3108. 703/528-
3600.

Hannon Armstrong
112 S Alfred St Ste 400,
Alexandria VA 22314-3061.
703/684-7776.

Alex Brown & Sons
375 Padonia Rd, Timonium
MD 21093. 410/561-9550.

Dean Witter Reynolds
1850 K St Nw, Washington
DC 20006-2213.
202/8629000.

Ferris Baker Watts
600 E Jefferson St Ste 210,
Rockville MD 20852-1150.
301/309-2600.

Ferris Baker Watts
112 S Main St, Bel Air MD
21014-3853. 410/879-
7331.

Legg Mason
P.O. Box 9700, Mc Lean VA
22102-3809. 703/821-
9100.

Marcie Finnell
107 Loudoun St Se,
Leesburg VA 22075-3106.
703/771-1931.

Olde Discount Stockbrokers
1438 Davis Ford Rd,
Woodbridge VA 22192-
2708. 703/491-7200.

Quick & Reilly Inc.
4520 E West Hwy, Bethesda
MD 20814-3319. 301/913-
0313.

INVESTMENT ADVISORS

T Rowe Price Associates
100 E Pratt St, Baltimore MD
21202-1009. 410/547-
2000.

Moore Manzo & Co.
1122 Kenilworth Dr Ste 501-
E, Baltimore MD 21204-
2139. 410/889-0900.

Apex Capital
14160 Newbrook Dr,
Chantilly VA 22021-2223.
703/631-0788.

TRUSTS

Manville Trust
1825 I St Nw, Washington
DC 20006-5403. 202/872-
9044.

For more information on career opportunities in financial services:

Associations

FINANCIAL EXECUTIVES INSTITUTE
P.O. Box 1938, Morristown NJ 07962-
1938. 201/898-4600. Fee and membership
required. Publishes biennial member
directory. Provides member referral service.

INSTITUTE OF FINANCIAL EDUCATION
111 East Wacker Drive, Chicago IL 60601.
312/946-8800. Offers career development
program.

NATIONAL ASSOCIATION OF BUSINESS ECONOMISTS
1233 20th Street NW, Suite 505,
Washington DC 20036. 202/463-6223.
Bulletin board number: 216/241-6254.
Newsletter and electronic bulletin board list
job openings. Members can upload resumes
and listed positions wanted to bulletin
board.

NATIONAL ASSOCIATION OF CREDIT MANAGEMENT
8815 Centre Park Drive, Suite 200,
Columbia MD 21045-2158. 410/740-5560.
Contact: Delores Richman. Publishes a
business credit magazine.

NATIONAL ASSOCIATION OF REAL ESTATE INVESTMENT TRUSTS
1129 20th Street NW, Suite 305,
Washington DC 20036. 202/785-8717.
Contact: Donna Smith/ Membership.

PUBLIC SECURITIES ASSOCIATION
40 Broad Street, 12th Floor, New York NY
10004. 212/809-7000. Contact: Caroline
Binn x427. Has an annual report and several
newsletters.

SECURITIES INDUSTRY ASSOCIATION
120 Broadway, 35th Floor New York NY
10271. 212/608-1500. Contact: Phil
Williams/Membership. Publishes a security
industry yearbook.

TREASURY MANAGEMENT ASSOCIATION
7315 Wisconsin Avenue, Suite 1250-W,
Bethesda MD 20814. 301/907-2862.

Directories

DIRECTORY OF AMERICAN FINANCIAL INSTITUTIONS
Thomson Business Publications, 6195
Crooked Creek Road, Norcross GA 30092.
404/448-1011. Sales 800/321-3373.

MOODY'S BANK AND FINANCE MANUAL
Moody's Investor Service, 99 Church
Street, New York NY 10007. 212/553-
0300.

Magazines

BARRON'S: NATIONAL BUSINESS AND FINANCIAL WEEKLY
Dow Jones & Co., 200 Liberty Street, New
York NY 10281. 212/416-2700.

FINANCIAL PLANNING
40 West 57th Street, 11th Floor, New York
NY 10019. 212/765-5311.

FINANCIAL WORLD
Financial World Partners, 1328 Broadway,

3rd Floor, New York NY 10001. 212/594-5030.

FUTURES: THE MAGAZINE OF COMMODITIES AND OPTIONS
250 South Wacker Drive, Suite 1150, Chicago IL 60606. 312/977-0999.

INSTITUTIONAL INVESTOR
488 Madison Avenue, 12th Floor, New York NY 10022. 212/303-3300.

FOOD AND BEVERAGES/AGRICULTURE

Employment in food processing is expected to fall slightly through 2005. Although the industry's output should grow, increasing automation and productivity will mean food can be produced with fewer workers. However, some food processing industries are likely to remain fairly labor intensive. For example, meat packing and poultry processing are difficult to fully automate because each animal processed is different. Professional specialty occupations, although small in number, are also expected to grow. The growth of these occupations -- including engineers, systems analysts, and food scientists -- reflects the industry's emphasis on scientific research to improve food products and production processes. Demand for food scientists will also grow in response to expanding government inspection and regulation of food production.

Several factors may slow the decline in food processing employment. As consumers increasingly seek 'ready-to-heat' foods, the food processing industry has introduced many new products. Many of these new goods, which require more processing than the items they are replacing, will help maintain the demand for food processors in the future. In addition, the food processing industry is taking advantage of new technology to perform much of the processing formerly done by retailers. One other factor that may help stem employment decline is growing international trade in food products. Food processing firms expect growing trade to provide new markets for their products. The emerging field of biotechnology and other new food science technologies may also provide new jobs.

ALLEN FAMILY FOODS INCORPORATED
P.O. Box 168, Cordova MD 21625-0168. 410/820-2100. **Contact:** Human Resources. **Description:** A manufacturer of food products.

AMSPICE INC./BALTIMORE SPICE COMPANY
9740 Reisterstown Road, Owings Mills MD 21117. 410/363-1700. **Description:** Produces a wide variety of spices and seasonings. **Common positions include:** Accountant/Auditor; Biological Scientist/Biochemist; Blue-Collar Worker Supervisor; Buyer; Computer Programmer; Credit Manager; Customer Service Representative; Department Manager; Electrical/Electronics Engineer; Food Scientist/Technologist; Industrial Engineer; Operations/Production Manager; Purchasing Agent and Manager; Quality Control Supervisor; Sales Associate; Transportation/Traffic Specialist. **Educational backgrounds include:** Accounting; Business Administration; Finance; Food Science. **Benefits:** Disability Coverage; Employee Discounts; Life Insurance; Medical Insurance; Pension Plan; Savings Plan; Tuition Assistance. **Special Programs:** Internships. **Corporate headquarters location:** Baltimore MD. **Other U.S. locations:** Grand Forks ND; Sparks NV. **Parent company:** Fuchs Spice. **Operations at this facility include:** Manufacturing. **Number of employees at this location:** 230.

BAGEL MASTER, INC.
RUBY FOODS
12036 Old Baltimore Pike, Beltsville MD 20705. 301/937-2100. **Fax:** 301/937-3068. **Contact:** Personnel Department. **Description:** A bagel wholesaler. **Benefits:** Dental Insurance; Disability Coverage; Life Insurance; Medical Insurance. **Corporate headquarters location:** This Location. **Operations at this facility include:**

Administration; Manufacturing; Sales; Service. **Number of employees at this location:** 90.

CATER AIR INTERNATIONAL CORPORATION
776 Elkridge Landing Road, Baltimore MD 21240. 310/262-2172. **Contact:** Human Resources. **Description:** Caters food and beverages to airlines.

CLOVERLAND FARMS DAIRY, INC.
2200 North Monroe Street, Baltimore MD 21217. 410/669-2222. **Contact:** Frank Gargiulo, Personnel Manager. **Description:** Produces fluid milk, frozen dessert mixes, and other dairy products.

CONAGRA, INC.
37 Delaware Avenue, Hurlock MD 21643-0340. 410/943-1400. **Contact:** Human Resources. **Description:** ConAgra is a diversified, international food company. ConAgra developed in 1919 when four Nebraska flour mills consolidated and incorporated as Nebraska Consolidated Mills. In 1971, Nebraska Consolidated Mills changed its name to ConAgra, Inc. In September, 1994, ConAgra celebrated its 75th anniversary with 87,000 employees in all 50 states and 27 countries. The company's products range from convenient prepared foods to supplies farmers need to grow crops. ConAgra has major businesses in branded grocery products -- shelf-stable and frozen foods, processed meats, chicken and turkey products and cheese -- as well as major businesses in potato products, private label grocery products, beef, pork, seafood, grain and pulse merchandising, grain processing, specialty retailing, crop protection chemicals, fertilizers and animal feed.

DOMINO SUGAR CORPORATION
P.O. Box 838, Baltimore MD 21203. 410/752-6150. **Contact:** Ron Frey, Employee Relations Manager. **Description:** Operates a sugar cane refinery.

EMBASSY DAIRY
SUBSIDIARY OF MORNINGSTAR FOODS, INC.
P.O. Box 114, Mattawoman Drive, Waldorf MD 20604. 301/843-1212. **Contact:** Personnel. **Description:** A dairy engaged in the processing and distribution of milk and ice cream. **Corporate headquarters location:** This Location.

GREEN SPRING DAIRY
2701 Lock Raven Road, Baltimore MD 21218. 410/235-4477. **Contact:** Personnel Manager. **Description:** Produces and distributes milk, ice cream, bakery products, and citrus juices. **Corporate headquarters location:** This Location.

HIGH'S OF BALTIMORE
1340-L Charwood Road, Hanover MD 21076. 410/859-3636. **Contact:** Office Manager. **Description:** Produces and distributes a wide range of dairy products.

JP FOODSERVICE
9830 Patuxent Wood Drive, Columbia MD 21046. 410/712-7111. **Contact:** Pam Harris, Human Resources Director. **Description:** A food wholesaler.

THE KRONHEIM COMPANY
99 Ray Road, Baltimore MD 21227. 410/242-8000. **Contact:** Personnel Department. **Description:** A liquor wholesaler. **Common positions include:** Administrator; Manufacturer's/Wholesaler's Sales Rep.; Purchasing Agent and Manager; Sales Manager. **Benefits:** Dental Insurance; Disability Coverage; Life Insurance; Medical Insurance; Tuition Assistance. **Special Programs:** Training Programs.

MARS, INC.
6885 Elm Street, McLean VA 22101. 703/821-4900. **Contact:** Human Resources. **Description:** A food processing company.

McCORMICK & COMPANY INC.
18 Loveton Circle, Sparks MD 21152-6000. 410/771-7301. **Recorded Jobline:** 410/527-6969. **Contact:** Human Resources. **Description:** Produces spices, seasonings, gravy and sauce mixes, and other food products which are sold to food services, institutional clients, retail companies, and industrial markets worldwide. Trademarks include McCormick and Schilling. The company also manufactures plastic bottles and tubes used in the pharmaceutical, cosmetic, and food packaging and preparation

industries. McCormick owns a cogeneration facility which supplies energy to a subsidiary and is sold to utility companies. **Listed on:** NASDAQ.

McCORMICK & COMPANY INC.
10950 Beaver Dam Rd., Hunt Valley MD 21031. 410/771-7595. **Contact:** Janis M. Leftridge, Human Relations Manager. **Description:** Produces spices, seasonings, gravy and sauce mixes, and other food products which are sold to food services, institutional clients, retail companies, and industrial markets worldwide. Trademarks include McCormick and Schilling. The company also manufactures plastic bottles and tubes used in the pharmaceutical, cosmetic, and food packaging and preparation industries. McCormick owns a cogeneration facility which supplies energy to a subsidiary and is sold to utility companies. **Listed on:** NASDAQ.

MURRY'S INC.
8300 Pennsylvania Avenue, Upper Marlboro MD 20772-2673. 301/420-6400. **Contact:** Gary Sanders, Director of Personnel. **Description:** Engaged in the manufacturing, distribution, and retail and wholesale of frozen meats and specialty food items. **Corporate headquarters location:** This Location. **Other U.S. locations:** Washington DC; Baltimore MD.

NATIONAL FRUIT PRODUCT CO., INC.
P.O. Box 2040, Winchester VA 22604-1240. 703/662-3401. **Fax:** 703/665-4686. **Contact:** Herb Glass, Corporate Human Resources Manager. **Description:** A food processor. Main products are apple juice, apple sauce, vinegar, apple butter, apple slices, and pie fillings. **Common positions include:** Accountant/Auditor; Blue-Collar Worker Supervisor; Buyer; Computer Programmer; Computer Systems Analyst; Electrical/Electronics Engineer; Food Scientist/Technologist; General Manager; Human Resources Specialist; Industrial Production Manager; Mechanical Engineer; Operations/Production Manager; Purchasing Agent and Manager. **Educational backgrounds include:** Accounting; Business Administration; Chemistry; Computer Science; Engineering. **Benefits:** Disability Coverage; Employee Discounts; Life Insurance; Medical Insurance; Pension Plan; Profit Sharing; Tuition Assistance. **Corporate headquarters location:** This Location. **Operations at this facility include:** Administration; Manufacturing; Research and Development; Sales. **Listed on:** Privately held. **Number of employees at this location:** 500. **Number of employees nationwide:** 1,000.

PERDUE FARMS, INC.
P.O. Box 1537, Salisbury MD 21802. 410/543-3175. **Fax:** 410/543-3292. **Contact:** Rob Heflin, Director of Human Resources. **Description:** Perdue Farms is the largest supplier of fresh poultry products in the Northeast and is the fourth largest in the United States. The company's birds are sold in supermarkets, small groceries and quality butcher shops from Maine to Georgia and as far west as Chicago, IL. It is a fully integrated operation, from breeding and hatching to delivering packaged goods to market. The company was originally a supplier of table eggs, later selling chickens to large companies like Swift and Armour. In 1968 the company began to sell its own brand of chickens. The company operated under the name A.W. Perdue & Son until 1971. **Common positions include:** Accountant/Auditor; Agricultural Engineer; Blue-Collar Worker Supervisor; Buyer; Clerical Supervisor; Computer Programmer; Credit Manager; Customer Service Representative; Department Manager; Field Service Engineer; Financial Analyst; Food Scientist/Technologist; Human Resources Specialist; Industrial Engineer; Management Trainee; Manufacturer's/Wholesaler's Sales Rep.; Marketing Specialist; Operations/Production Manager; Purchasing Agent and Manager; Quality Control Supervisor; Registered Nurse; Systems Analyst; Transportation/Traffic Specialist. **Educational backgrounds include:** Biology; Business Administration; Chemistry; Computer Science; Engineering; Finance; Food Services; Marketing; Mathematics. **Benefits:** 401K; Disability Coverage; Employee Discounts; Life Insurance; Medical Insurance; Pension Plan; Savings Plan; Tuition Assistance. **Special Programs:** Internships. **Corporate headquarters location:** This Location. **Operations at this facility include:** Administration; Divisional Headquarters; Regional Headquarters; Research and Development; Sales. **Number of employees at this location:** 550. **Number of employees nationwide:** 18,000.

QUEST INTERNATIONAL FLAVORING AND FOOD INGREDIENTS, INC.
10 Painters Mill Road, Owings Mills MD 21117. 410/363-2550. **Contact:** Anna Hankey, Personnel Secretary. **Description:** A producer of flavorings and food ingredients.

ROCCO INC.
P.O. Box 549, One Kratzer Road, Harrisonburg VA 22801. 703/568-1400. **Contact:** William Christian, Vice President of Human Resources. **Description:** A producer and marketer of poultry food products. **Common positions include:** Accountant/Auditor; Computer Programmer; Customer Service Representative; Department Manager; General Manager; Manufacturer's/Wholesaler's Sales Rep.; Quality Control Supervisor. **Educational backgrounds include:** Accounting; Marketing. **Special Programs:** Training Programs. **Corporate headquarters location:** This Location.

SHOWELL FARMS, INC.
P.O. Box 158, Showell MD 21862. 410/352-5411. **Contact:** Personnel. **Description:** A poultry processor. **Parent company:** Perdue Farms (A large supplier of poultry products).

SMELKINSON SYSCO
8000 Dorsey Run Road, P.O. Box 1009, Jessup MD 20794. 410/799-7000. **Contact:** Human Resources. **Description:** A grocery wholesaler.

SMITHFIELD PACKAGING COMPANY
5801 Columbia Park Road, Landover MD 20785. 301/773-3322. **Contact:** Personnel Director. **Description:** A meat processor.

VIE DE FRANCE CORPORATION
85 South Bragg Street, Suite 600, Alexandria VA 22312. 703/750-9600. **Contact:** Betsy Powell, Accounting Manager. **Description:** A frozen specialties foods producer. **Common positions include:** Accountant/Auditor; Administrative Services Manager; Chef/Cook/Kitchen Worker; Computer Programmer; Electrical/Electronics Engineer; Food Scientist/Technologist; Industrial Production Manager; Manufacturer's/Wholesaler's Sales Rep.; Operations/Production Manager. **Educational backgrounds include:** Accounting; Computer Science; Cooking; Marketing. **Benefits:** 401K; Dental Insurance; Disability Coverage; Employee Discounts; Life Insurance; Medical Insurance. **Corporate headquarters location:** This Location. **Operations at this facility include:** Administration; Divisional Headquarters; Manufacturing; Sales. **Number of employees at this location:** 100.

WLR FOODS
P.O. Box 7000, Broadway VA 22815. 703/896-7001. **Contact:** Human Resources. **Description:** A fully-integrated poultry and meat processor, marketer, and distributor. The company offers over 250 brand name and private label poultry and related products, and operates seven processing plants and packaging facilities, and three further processing plants. Non-food subsidiary, May Supply Company, Inc., is a wholesale distributor of plumbing supplies and equipment. Another subsidiary, Cassco Corp., makes and distributes ice and offers refrigerated warehouse storage services. **Corporate headquarters location:** This Location. **Listed on:** NASDAQ.

Note: Because addresses and telephone numbers of smaller companies change rapidly, we recommend you call each company to verify the information below before inquiring about job opportunities. Mass mailings are not recommended.

Additional employers with over 250 employees:

MEAT AND POULTRY PROCESSING

Campbell Soup Co.
PO Box 29, Chestertown MD 21620-0029. 410/778-3131.

Hudson Foods Inc.
Rte 346 PO Box 7, Berlin MD 21811. 410/641-0900.

DAIRY PRODUCTS

East Coast Ice Cream
9090 Whiskey Bottom Rd, Laurel MD 20723-1397. 301/776-7727.

Gold Bond Ice Cream
1100 Frederick St, Hagerstown MD 21740-6867. 301/797-9603.

PRESERVED FRUITS AND VEGETABLES

Van Den Bergh Foods Co.
3701 Southwestern Blvd, Baltimore MD 21229-5030. 410/644-4900.

BAKERY PRODUCTS

Giant Food Bakery
930 King St, Silver Spring MD 20910-4840. 301/495-3225.

BEVERAGES

G Heileman Brewing Co.
4501 Hollins Ferry Rd, Baltimore MD 21227-4660. 410/247-1600.

House Of Seagram
5001 Washington Blvd, Baltimore MD 21227-5000. 410/247-1000.

Pepsi-Cola Bottling Co.
Pepsi Pl, Hyattsville MD 20781. 301/322-7000.

FOOD WHOLESALE

Case Farms Inc.
1325 Beaglin Park Plaza, Salisbury MD 21801. 410/749-3202.

Mazo Lerch Co. Inc.
4720 Eisenhower Ave, Alexandria VA 22304-4892. 703/370-5900.

Stantoni's Market
1304 Stockton Rd, Joppa MD 21085-1410. 410/671-0001.

Additional employers with under 250 employees:

FLORICULTURE AND NURSERY PRODUCTS

Paris Florists & Greenhouses
401 Thompson Creek Rd, Stevensville MD 21666-2507. 410/643-4836.

POULTRY AND EGGS

Allen's Hatchery Inc.
39 Delaware Ave, Hurlock MD 21643-3601. 410/943-0045.

MEAT AND POULTRY PROCESSING

Kolker Brothers Inc.
1301 W St Ne, Washington DC 20018-3502. 202/832-7050.

Royal Quality Foods
510 West Rd, Salisbury MD 21801. 410/219-3900.

Yoder's Inc.
Rt 669, Grantsville MD 21536. 301/895-5121.

Parks Sausage Company
PO Box 854, Baltimore MD 21203-0854. 410/664-5050.

Purity Bacon Co.
925 Eastern Shore Dr, Salisbury MD 21801-6461. 410/749-6324.

GRAIN MILL PRODUCTS

Culpeper Farmers Cooperative Inc.
819 James Madison Hwy, Culpeper VA 22701-2405. 703/825-2200.

Wilkins-Rogers Inc.
27 Frederick Rd, Ellicott City MD 21043-4709. 410/465-5800.

DAIRY PRODUCTS

Shenandoah's Pride Dairy
5325 Port Royal Rd, Springfield VA 22151-2159. 703/321-9500.

Maryland & Virgina Milk Producers
1985 Isaac Newton Sq S, Reston VA 22090-5008. 703/742-6800.

Safeway Stores Inc.
6200 Columbia Pike Road, Landover MD 20785. 301/386-6700.

PRESERVED FRUITS AND VEGETABLES

Bloch & Guggenheimer
Rt 392 Delaware Ave, Hurlock MD 21643. 410/943-4933.

Martin Gillet Co. Inc.
6801 Eastern Ave, Baltimore MD 21224-3002. 410/633-6000.

Saulsbury Brothers
Railroad Ave, Ridgely MD 21660. 410/634-2141.

BAKERY PRODUCTS

A & P Bakery
3301 Annapolis Rd, Baltimore MD 21230-3404. 410/566-2433.

Best Foods Baking Group
7110 English Muffin Way, Frederick MD 21701-8314. 301/694-8100.

Heller's Bakery Inc.
3221 My Pleasant St Nw, Washington DC 20010. 202/382-7455.

MI Dessert Corporation
8210 Colonial Ln, Silver Spring MD 20910-3350. 301/589-2818.

Montgomery Doughnut Co. Inc.
241 Derwood Cir, Rockville MD 20850-1267. 301/424-7700.

Ms Desserts Inc.
2275 Rolling Run Dr, Baltimore MD 21244-1847. 410/281-2000.

Ottenberg's Bakers
655 Taylor St Ne, Washington DC 20017-2097. 202/529-5800.

Candy Kitchen Shoppes
5301 Coastal Hwy, Ocean City MD 21842-3140. 410/524-6002.

SUGAR AND CONFECTIONERY PRODUCTS

Goetze's Candy Co.
3900 E Monument St, Baltimore MD 21205-2928. 410/342-2010.

BEVERAGES

Alexander Distilling Co. Ltd.
10451 Mill Run Cir, Owings Mills MD 21117-5577. 410/581-2839.

Beverage Capital Corporation
1620 Whitehead Ct, Baltimore MD 21207-4099. 410/944-9340.

Canada Dry Potomac Corporation
1201 E West Hwy, Silver Spring MD 20910-3214. 301/589-2030.

Mid-Atlantic Coca Cola Bottling Inc.
2012 Hammonds Ferry Rd, Baltimore MD 21227-1719. 410/247-8000.

Pepsi Cola of Washington DC
PO Box 10520, Washington DC 20020-0820. 202/337-3774.

Pepsi-Cola Bottling
330 Snow Hill Rd, Salisbury MD 21801-5623. 410/546-1136.

R C/Seven Up Bottling
5330 Port Royal Rd,

Springfield VA 22151-2105.
703/321-7900.

FLAVORING EXTRACTS/SYRUPS

Coca-Cola USA
1215 E Fort Ave, Baltimore MD 21230-5133. 410/752-4150.

SEAFOOD

Bevans Oyster Co.
RR 1 Box 315, Kinsale VA 22488-9738. 804/472-2331.

John T Handy Co. Inc.
101 N 7th St, Crisfield MD 21817-1022. 410/968-1772.

Warren Denton Seafood
3946 Oyster House Rd, Broomes Is MD 20615-3038. 410/586-0300.

CHIPS AND SNACKS

Ihrie & Sons Inc.
2 N Smallwood St, Baltimore MD 21223-1518. 410/947-5200.

FOOD PREPARATIONS

Chun King Corporation
902 Woods Rd, Cambridge MD 21613-9470. 410/228-2713.

Mc Cormick & Co.
350 Clubhouse Rd, Cockys Ht Vly MD 21031-1305. 410/771-7077.

Red Star Yeast
2100 Van Deman St, Baltimore MD 21224-6608. 410/633-8000.

Tortilla Maya
7608 Fullerton Rd # F, Springfield VA 22153-2814. 703/455-0155.

FOOD WHOLESALE

A&E Foods Inc.
8869 Greenwood Pl # C, Savage MD 20763-9719. 410/792-0691.

Baer Foods Inc.
300 W Franklin St, Hagerstown MD 21740-4751. 301/739-5111.

Continental Foods Inc.
2730 Wilmarco Ave, Baltimore MD 21223-3306. 410/233-5500.

Doskocil Companies
9515 Deereco Rd, Timonium MD 21093-2108. 410/561-2033.

Herbert Halperin Distributing Co. Inc.
4801 Forbes Blvd, Lanham MD 20706-4357. 301/731-5600.

I Feldman & Co. Inc.
8730 Bollman Pl, Savage MD 20763-9747. 301/725-1122.

McLane Distribution Center
PO Box 5339, Falmouth VA 22403-0339. 703/374-2000.

Rmi & Associates Inc.
9198 Red Branch Rd, Columbia MD 21045-2017. 410/964-1600.

Rykoff-Sexton Inc.
3411 Pennsy Dr, Landover MD 20785-1608. 301/772-3005.

Santoni's Market Inc.
3800 E Lombard St, Baltimore MD 21224-2400. 410/276-2990.

Supervalu Inc. Maryland Division
PO Box 109, Williamsport MD 21795-0109. 301/582-4990.

Quaker Oats Frozen Foods Division
4 N Park Dr, Cockys Ht Vly MD 21030-1800. 410/683-1711.

Utz Quality Foods
8561 Virginia Meadows Dr, Manassas VA 22110-7824. 703/330-5232.

Maryland Hotel Supply Co. Inc.
701 W Hamburg St, Baltimore MD 21230-2597. 410/539-7055.

P J's Inc.
3212 Washington Blvd, Baltimore MD 21230-1030. 410/525-0903.

C D Beggs Co. Inc.
Maryland Wholesale Produce Mkt, Jessup MD 20794. 410/799-7766.

Gilbert Foods Inc.
7251 Standard Dr, Hanover MD 21076-1345. 410/712-6000.

Frank A Serio and Sons
PO Box 247, Jessup MD 20794-0247. 410/792-4122.

Athens Automatic Rolls
7111 Commercial Ave, Baltimore MD 21237-1003. 410/488-2550.

Wonder Bread Depot
52nd Av & Addison Rd, Capital Hts MD 20743. 301/773-6565.

Pacific Molasses Co.
Dundalk Marine Terminal, Baltimore MD 21222. 410/288-3860.

ALCOHOL WHOLESALE

Bob Hall Inc.
5600 Crain Hwy, Uppr Marlboro MD 20772-3126. 301/627-1900.

Bond Distributing Co.
1220 Bernard Dr, Baltimore MD 21223-3396. 410/945-5600.

Forman Brothers Corporation
4235 Sheriff Rd Ne, Washington DC 20019-3736. 202/388-8400.

Quality Brands Inc.
226 Dover Rd, Glen Burnie MD 21060-6414. 410/787-5656.

House of Seagram
1430 Joh Ave, Baltimore MD 21227-1046. 410/247-4721.

FARM SUPPLIES WHOLESALE

Commerce Distributors
700 Evelyn Ave, Linthicum Hts MD 21090-1325. 410/636-1100.

Lesco Inc.
1304 Governor Ct, Fork MD 21051. 410/679-0701.

FLOWERS AND FLORAL PRODUCTS WHOLESALE

The Pennock Co.
7399 Ward Park Ln, Springfield VA 22153-2825. 703/644-6600.

For more information on career opportunities in the food and beverage, and agriculture industries:

Associations

AMERICAN ASSOCIATION OF CEREAL CHEMISTS (AACC)
3340 Pilot Knob Road, St. Paul MN 55121. 612/454-7250. Contact: Marla Meyers. Dedicated to the dissemination of technical information and continuing education in cereal science.

AMERICAN FROZEN FOOD INSTITUTE
1764 Old Meadow Lane, Suite 350. McLean VA 22102. 703/821-0770. National trade association representing the interests of the frozen food industry.

AMERICAN SOCIETY OF AGRICULTURAL ENGINEERS
2950 Niles Road, St. Joseph MI 49085. 616/429-0300. Contact: Julie Swim.

AMERICAN SOCIETY OF BREWING CHEMISTS ASSOCIATION
3340 Pilot Knob Road, St. Paul MN 55121. 612/454-7250. Founded in 1934 to improve and bring uniformity to the brewing industry on a technical level.

CIES - THE FOOD BUSINESS FORUM
3800 Moore Plaza, Alexandria VA 22305. 703/549-4525. A global food business network. Membership is on a company basis. Members learn how to manage their businesses more effectively and gain access to information and contacts.

DAIRY AND FOOD INDUSTRIES SUPPLY ASSOCIATION (DFISA)
1451 Dolley Madison Boulevard, McLean VA 22101-3850. 703/761-2600. Contact: Dorothy Brady. A trade association whose members are suppliers to the food, dairy, liquid processing, and related industries.

MASTER BREWERS ASSOCIATION OF THE AMERICAS (MBAA)
2421 North Mayfair Road, Suite 310, Wauwatosa, WI 53226. 414/774-8558. Promotes, advances, improves, and protects the professional interests of brew and malt house production and technical personnel. Disseminates technical and practical information.

NATIONAL AGRICULTURAL CHEMICALS ASSOCIATION
1156 15th Street NW, Suite 900, Washington DC 20005. 202/296-1585.

NATIONAL BEER WHOLESALERS' ASSOCIATION
1100 South Washington Street, Alexandria VA 22314-4494. 703/683-4300. Fax: 703/683-8965. Contact: Karen Craig.

NATIONAL FOOD PROCESSORS ASSOCIATION
1401 New York Avenue NW, Suite 400, Washington DC 20005. 202/639-5900. Contact: Ned Endler.

NATIONAL SOFT DRINK ASSOCIATION
1101 16th Street NW, Washington DC 20036. 202/463-6732.

UNITED DAIRY INDUSTRY ASSOCIATION (UDIA)
10255 West Higgins Road, Suite 900, Rosemont IL 60018. 708/803-2000. A federation of state and regional dairy promotion organizations that develop and execute effective programs to increase consumer demand for U.S.-produced milk and dairy products.

Directories

FOOD ENGINEERING'S DIRECTORY OF U.S. FOOD PLANTS
Chilton Book Co., Chilton Way, Radnor PA 19089. 800/695-1214.

THOMAS FOOD INDUSTRY REGISTER
Thomas Publishing Co., Five Penn Plaza, New York NY 10001. 212/695-0500.

Magazines

BEVERAGE WORLD
Keller International Publishing Corporation. 150 Great Neck Road, Great Neck NY 11021. 516/829-9210.

FOOD PROCESSING
301 East Erie Street, Chicago IL 60611. 312/644-2020.

FROZEN FOOD AGE
Maclean Hunter Media, #4 Stamford Forum, Stamford CT 06901. 203/325-3500.

PREPARED FOODS
Gorman Publishing Co., 8750 West Bryn Mawr, Chicago IL 60631. 312/693-3200.

GOVERNMENT

While the Federal government is still the nation's largest employer, the number of federal jobs is on the decline. Department of Defense employment is dropping because of the collapse of the Soviet Union and increasing concern over federal deficits. The Defense Department will gradually reduce its workforce through attrition over the next decade.

Employment in other executive agencies is expected to fall slightly or remain stable due to reorganization. Many workers in the Department of Defense and other executive agencies are being offered buyouts, early retirement, and other incentives to leave the Federal government. Demand remains strong, however, for nurses and engineers. For information on application procedures for federal employment, see Section Four of this book, **Working for the Federal Government**.

Nationwide, the outlook for state and local government workers is somewhat better. While opportunities vary from one state to the next, the BLS forecasts a 16 percent job rise through 2005. Adding to the demand is the rising demand for services. Since the early '80s, government has decentralized and states have assumed more responsibility for providing services. Many policy decisions have been shifted to states, who increasingly are dealing with transportation problems, health care issues, energy policies, and poverty.

Even so, future job growth may be slowed by budgetary constraints. In fact, the local government of the District of Columbia is virtually bankrupt. Mayor Marion Barry has been forced to cede budgetary control to Congressional overseers. That means the city will be going on a strict spending diet, including strong doses of layoffs.

ABERDEEN PROVING GROUNDS
Cdr, USAAPGSA, Attn: STEAP-CP-R, Aberdeen Prvg Grnds MD 21005-5795. 410/278-5678. **Contact:** Quinette M. Henderson, College Recruitment Coordinator. **Description:** APG is a military installation that employs civilians in the research, development, testing, and evaluation of military materials for use by soldiers on the battlefield. **Common positions include:** Aerospace Engineer; Chemical Engineer; Chemist; Electrical/Electronics Engineer; Industrial Engineer; Industrial Hygienist; Mechanical Engineer; Physicist/Astronomer; Psychologist. **Educational backgrounds include:** Engineering. **Benefits:** Disability Coverage; Life Insurance; Tuition Assistance.

ALEXANDRIA, CITY OF
301 King Street, Alexandria VA 22314. 703/838-4745. **Recorded Jobline:** 703/838-4422. **Contact:** Human Resources. **Description:** Provides municipal services.

ARLINGTON COUNTY
2100 Clarendon Boulevard, Suite 511, Arlington VA 22201. 703/358-3500. **Recorded Jobline:** 703/358-3363. **Contact:** Human Resources. **Description:** Provides county government services.

BALTIMORE, CITY OF
111 North Calvert Street, Baltimore MD 21202. 410/396-3856. **Recorded Jobline:** 410/887-5627. **Contact:** Human Resources. **Description:** Provides municipal services.

BALTIMORE COUNTY
308 Allegheny Avenue, Towson MD 21204. 410/887-5627. **Recorded Jobline:** 410/887-5627. **Contact:** Personnel Office. **Description:** Provides county government services.

BALTIMORE HOUSING AUTHORITY
417 East Fayette Street, Baltimore MD 21202. 410/396-3250. **Contact:** Human Resources Department. **Description:** A government agency.

BALTIMORE PUBLIC WORKS BUREAU
200 North Holliday, Room 4, Baltimore MD 21202. 410/396-5187. **Contact:** Personnel Department. **Description:** Engaged in public works functions.

BOARD OF GOVERNORS OF THE FEDERAL RESERVE SYSTEM
21st and C Streets NW, Mail Stop 129, Washington DC 20551. 202/452-3850. **Recorded Jobline:** 202/452-3038. **Contact:** Anthony DiGioia, Manager of Human Resources. **Description:** The primary function of the Board of Governors of the Federal Reserve System is the setting of monetary policy to foster stable economic conditions and long-term economic growth. The Board makes policy through the Federal Open Market Committee, which consists of the seven members of the Board, the president of the New York Federal Reserve Bank, and four of the presidents of the other 11 District banks, who serve in rotation. In addition, the Board has broad supervisory and regulatory responsibilities over the activities of the Federal Reserve Banks, its member banks, bank holding companies, and other financial institutions. It sets margin requirements on credit purchases in the stock market and oversees certain international banking activities. Through its Division of Consumer and Community Affairs, the Board carries out its responsibilities for protecting consumers' rights in borrowing transactions and implements laws to help communities meet their credit needs. The Board's commitment to its mission can be measured in part by its ability to attract and retain scholars and other highly professional staff from across the country. **Common positions include:** Bank Officer/Manager; Computer Programmer; Economist/Market Research Analyst; Financial Analyst; Systems Analyst. **Educational backgrounds include:** Business Administration; Economics; MBA; Ph.D. **Benefits:** Dental Insurance; Disability Coverage; Life Insurance; Medical Insurance; Pension Plan; Savings Plan; Tuition Assistance. **Special Programs:** Internships. **Corporate headquarters location:** This Location. **Number of employees nationwide:** 1,600.

CENTRAL INTELLIGENCE AGENCY
Office of Personnel, P.O. Box 12727, Arlington VA 22209-8727. 703/482-1100. **Recorded Jobline:** 703/482-0677. **Contact:** Human Resources. **Description:** Collects, analyzes and disseminates information needed to protect national security.

DEFENSE LOGISTICS AGENCY ADMINISTRATIVE SUPPORT CENTER
Cameron Station, Alexandria VA 22304-6130. 703/274-6043. **Contact:** Office of Civilian Personnel. **Description:** An administrative support center for the Defense Logistics Agency.

DEMOCRATIC NATIONAL COMMITTEE
430 South Capitol Street Southeast, Washington DC 20003. 202/863-8000. **Contact:** Director of Human Resources. **Description:** National headquarters for the Democratic Party. Looking for individuals with campaign experience for referrals to campaigns across the country. Also looking for individuals with grass roots organizing, fundraising, or communications experience. **Common positions include:** Accountant/Auditor; Administrator; Attorney; Computer Programmer; Customer Service Representative; Editor; Marketing Specialist; Operations/Production Manager; Reporter. **Benefits:** Disability Coverage; Medical Insurance. **Special Programs:** Internships; Training Programs. **Corporate headquarters location:** This Location. **Operations at this facility include:** Administration; Research and Development. **Number of employees at this location:** 125.

DRUG ENFORCEMENT ADMINISTRATION (DEA)
Office of Forensic Sciences, Laboratory Operations Section, 7th Floor, Washington DC 20537. 202/307-8880. **Fax:** 202/307-8851. **Contact:** Robert P. Bianchi, Section Chief. **Description:** The Drug Enforcement Administration (DEA) is the federal law enforcement agency which has the responsibility of combating drug abuse. DEA was established to control narcotic and dangerous drug abuse through enforcement and prevention. The DEA is responsible for the laws and statues relating to narcotic drugs, marijuana, depressants, stimulants, anabolic steroids and hallucinogenic drugs. The

DEA has 19 domestic field divisions and 49 foreign country offices. Additionally, it has numerous resident offices throughout the United States and overseas. DEA also regulates the legal trade in narcotics and dangerous drugs. This includes establishing import, export and manufacturing quotas for some controlled drugs. DEA also provides federal, state, local and foreign law enforcement officers with specialized training in narcotic and dangerous drug control. Special training is offered in forensic drug chemistry to chemists employed by state, local and foreign law enforcement agencies. The Office of Forensics is the laboratory testing division of the DEA. In forensics, chemists scientifically identify new and bizarre compounds as well as analyze evidence, provide expert testimony in courts, and develop intelligence data used to determine trends. **Common positions include:** Biological Scientist/Biochemist; Chemist; Pharmacist. **Educational backgrounds include:** Biology; Chemistry; Mathematics; Physics. **Benefits:** Dental Insurance; Disability Coverage; Life Insurance; Medical Insurance; Pension Plan; Savings Plan; Tuition Assistance. **Corporate headquarters location:** This Location. **Number of employees at this location:** 15. **Number of employees nationwide:** 150.

ENVIRONMENTAL PROTECTION AGENCY (EPA)
401 M Street Southwest, Washington DC 20460. 202/260-3266. **Contact:** Human Resources. **Description:** The headquarters location and center of operations for the Environmental Protection Agency. In addition there are over 10,000 employees in 30 locations across the country. EPA headquarters is divided into twelve offices; Office of Administrator; Office of Water; Office of Solid Waste and Emergency Response; Office of Air and Radiation; Office of Prevention, Pesticides and Toxic Substances; Office of Research and Development; Office of Administration and Resources Management; Office of Enforcement; Office of Communications, Education, and Public Affairs; Office of International Activities; Office of Inspector General. There are also 10 regional offices that provide technical assistance to state, local and tribal governments. The EPA's field offices specialize in three primary categories: research and development, investigations and administration and compliance. EPA research and development programs are conducted and managed from 20 different locations around the country in 12 scientific laboratories located from Narragansett, Rhode Island to Corvallis, Oregon. **Corporate headquarters:** This location.

EXECUTIVE OFFICE OF THE PRESIDENT
The White House, 1600 Pennsylvania Avenue NW, Washington DC 20500. 202/456-1414. **Recorded Jobline:** 202/395-5982. **Contact:** Human Resources. **Description:** The policy-making staff of the White House. **NOTE:** All positions are filled through the Office of Personnel Management.

FAIRFAX, CITY OF
10455 Armstrong Street, Fairfax VA 22030. 703/385-7850. **Recorded Jobline:** 703/385-7861. **Contact:** Human Resources. **Description:** Provides municipal services.

FAIRFAX COUNTY
12000 Government Center Parkway, Room 166, Fairfax VA 22035. 703/222-5872. **Recorded Jobline:** 703/324-5627. **Contact:** Charles Hargrove, Supervisor/Employment Division. **Description:** Provides county government services. **Common positions include:** Accountant/Auditor; Attorney; Automotive Mechanic/Body Repairer; Budget Analyst; Civil Engineer; Computer Programmer; Computer Systems Analyst; Counselor; Emergency Medical Technician; Human Service Worker; Librarian; Management Analyst/Consultant; Psychologist; Registered Nurse; Social Worker; Software Engineer. **Educational backgrounds include:** Accounting; Business Administration; Computer Science; Engineering; Finance. **Benefits:** Dental Insurance; Life Insurance; Medical Insurance; Pension Plan; Savings Plan. **Corporate headquarters location:** This Location. **Operations at this facility include:** Administration. **Number of employees at this location:** 10,000.

FALLS CHURCH, CITY OF
300 Park Avenue, Falls Church VA 22046. 703/241-5025. **Recorded Jobline:** 703/241-5163. **Contact:** Human Resources. **Description:** Provides municipal services.

FARM CREDIT ADMINISTRATION
1501 Farm Credit Drive, McLean VA 22102-5090. 703/883-4135. **Contact:** Human Resources. **Description:** A government agency which regulates and examines the Farm Credit System. Eight field locations. Provides benefits due to federal government employees. Applicants must submit appropriate form (Government Form SF-171) following specific vacancy announcements; unsolicited resumes are disregarded.

Common positions include: Accountant/Auditor; Attorney; Computer Engineer; Economist/Market Research Analyst; Financial Analyst. **Educational backgrounds include:** Accounting; Business Administration; Economics; Finance. **Corporate headquarters location:** This Location. **Operations at this facility include:** Administration.

FEDERAL BUREAU OF INVESTIGATION (FBI)
10th Street and Pennsylvania NW, J. Edgar Hoover Building, Washington DC 20535. 202/324-3000. **Contact:** Thomas Coyle, Personnel Officer. **Description:** Central headquarters of the national law enforcement agency.

FEDERAL COMMUNICATIONS COMMISSION (FCC)
1919 M Street NW, Room 212, Washington DC 20554. 202/418-0130. **Recorded Jobline:** 202/632-0101. **Contact:** Office of Personnel. **Description:** Regulates interstate and international communications by radio, television, wire, satellite, and cable.

FEDERAL DEPOSIT INSURANCE CORPORATION (FDIC)
550 17th Street NW, ATTN: PA-1700-5124, Washington DC 20429-9990. 202/393-8400. **Recorded Jobline:** 800/695-8052. **Contact:** Norman J. Cox, Chief of Recruitment/Placement. **Description:** A federal bank regulatory agency. **Common positions include:** Accountant/Auditor; Administrator; Attorney; Computer Programmer; Economist/Market Research Analyst; Financial Analyst; Human Resources Specialist; Instructor/Trainer; Marketing Specialist; Paralegal; Public Relations Specialist. **Educational backgrounds include:** Accounting; Business Administration; Communications; Computer Science; Economics; Finance; Marketing. **Benefits:** Dental Insurance; Life Insurance; Medical Insurance; Pension Plan; Savings Plan. **Corporate headquarters location:** This Location. **Number of employees nationwide:** 12,000.

FEDERAL EMERGENCY MANAGEMENT AGENCY
500 C Street Southwest, Washington DC 20472. 202/646-4040. **Fax:** 202/646-3350. **Recorded Jobline:** 202/646-3244. **Contact:** Headquarters Personnel Operations Division. **Description:** Responsible for preparing for and responding to natural and man-made disasters nationwide.

FEDERAL TRADE COMMISSION (FTC)
6th and Pennsylvania Avenue NW, Room 148, Washington DC 20580. 202/326-2020. **Contact:** Division of Personnel. **Description:** A federal government regulatory agency which includes the Bureau of Consumer Protection, the Bureau of Competition, and the Bureau of Economics. The Federal Trade Commission was created in 1914 to protect the general public (consumers and businesses) against anticompetitive behavior and deceptive and unfair practices. **Common positions include:** Attorney; Economist/Market Research Analyst. **Educational backgrounds include:** Economics; Law/Pre-Law; Ph.D. **Benefits:** Disability Coverage; Life Insurance; Medical Insurance; Pension Plan. **Special Programs:** Internships. **Corporate headquarters location:** This Location.

HARTFORD COURTS
220 South Main Street, Bel Air MD 21014. 410/638-3201. **Recorded Jobline:** 410/638-4473. **Contact:** Human Resources. **Description:** Provides county government services.

HERNDON, CITY OF
200 Spring Street, Suite 132, P.O. Box 427, Herndon VA 22070. 703/435-6817. **Recorded Jobline:** 703/481-3892. **Contact:** Human Resources. **Description:** Provides municipal services.

HOWARD COUNTY
3430 Court House Drive, Ellicott City MD 21043. 410/313-2033. **Recorded Jobline:** 410/313-4460. **Contact:** Human Resources. **Description:** Provides county government services.

INTERNATIONAL MONETARY FUND
700 19th Street NW, Washington DC 20431. 202/623-7000. **Contact:** Division Chief, Recruitment Division. **Description:** The Washington office of the international lending agency, primarily responsible for lending to Third World nations. **Common positions**

include: Economist/Market Research Analyst. **Number of employees nationwide:** 2,000.

LIBRARY OF CONGRESS
101 Independence Avenue Southeast, Room LM 107, Washington DC 20540-4315. 202/707-5000. **Recorded Jobline:** 202/707-4315. **Contact:** Human Resources. **Description:** National library of the United States, with many extensive collections for research purposes.

LOUDOUN COUNTY
748 Miller Drive SW, Suite F-1, Leesburg VA 22075. 703/478-8410. **Recorded Jobline:** 703/777-0536. **Contact:** Human Resources. **Description:** Provides county government services.

MARYLAND, STATE OF
Saratoga State Center, 311 West Saratoga Street, Baltimore MD 21201. 410/767-7000. **Recorded Jobline:** 410/333-7510. **Contact:** Human Resources. **Description:** Provides state government services.

MARYLAND STATE DEPARTMENT OF HEALTH AND MENTAL HYGIENE
201 West Preston Street, Baltimore MD 21201. 410/225-6403. **Fax:** 410/333-5998. **Contact:** Joseph Elliot, Personnel Officer. **Description:** A state government organization which provides laboratory and other services involving regulatory, public, mental, environmental, and medico-public health on a statewide basis. The department also offers services for citizens with addictions. **Common positions include:** Biological Scientist/Biochemist; Chemist; Counselor; Dietician/Nutritionist; Financial Analyst; Health Services Worker; Medical Record Technician; Mental Health Worker; Occupational Therapist; Pharmacist; Physical Therapist; Physician; Psychologist; Recreational Therapist; Registered Nurse; Social Worker; Speech-Language Pathologist; Statistician; Systems Analyst. **Educational backgrounds include:** Biology; Chemistry; Computer Science; Economics; Finance; Health Care; Mathematics. **Benefits:** 401K; Dental Insurance; Disability Coverage; Life Insurance; Medical Insurance; Pension Plan; Savings Plan; Tuition Assistance. **Corporate headquarters location:** This Location. **Operations at this facility include:** Administration; Divisional Headquarters; Regional Headquarters; Service. **Number of employees nationwide:** 13,000.

METROPOLITAN WASHINGTON COUNCIL OF GOVERNMENTS
777 North Capitol Street Northeast, Suite 300, Washington DC 20002. 202/962-3200. **Recorded Jobline:** 202/962-3397. **Contact:** Robin G. Wilson, Director, Office of Personnel Services. **Description:** The only area-wide governmental organization concerned with all aspects of metropolitan development. Works toward solutions of regional problems such as energy, traffic congestion, inadequate housing, air and water pollution, water supply, and land use. Also serves as the regional planning agency, including transportation planning, for metro Washington. **Common positions include:** Accountant/Auditor; Budget Analyst; Chemical Engineer; Civil Engineer; Computer Systems Analyst; Environmental Engineer; Geologist/Geophysicist; Human Resources Specialist; Human Service Worker; Planner; Public Relations Specialist; Purchasing Agent and Manager; Receptionist; Secretary; Social Worker; Systems Analyst; Transportation/Traffic Specialist; Urban/Regional Planner. **Educational backgrounds include:** Biology; Business Administration; Chemistry; Engineering; Geology; Meteorology; Public Administration; Transportation/Logistics; Urban Planning. **Benefits:** Dental Insurance; Disability Coverage; Life Insurance; Medical Insurance; Pension Plan; Tuition Assistance. **Special Programs:** Internships. **Corporate headquarters location:** This Location. **Operations at this facility include:** Administration. **Number of employees at this location:** 125.

NATIONAL SCIENCE FOUNDATION
4201 Wilson Boulevard, Arlington VA 22230. 703/306-1640. **Recorded Jobline:** 202/357-7735. **Contact:** Human Resources. **Description:** Promotes science and engineering through research and educational programs.

NAVAL RESEARCH LABORATORIES
4555 Overlook Avenue Southwest, Washington DC 20375. **Contact:** Human Resources. **Description:** Provides in-house research for the physical, engineering, space, and environmental sciences; broadly-based exploratory and advanced development programs in response to identified and anticipated Navy needs; multi-

disciplinary support to the Naval Warfare Centers; and space and space systems technology development and support.

OFFICE OF THE COMPTROLLER OF THE CURRENCY (OCC)
250 E Street Southwest, MS 4-15, Washington DC 20219. 202/874-4590. **Fax:** 202/874-5447. **Contact:** DeeDee Tostanoski, National Recruitment Coordinator. **Description:** The Office of the Comptroller of the Currency is a federal regulatory agency with supervisory responsibility for the country's national banks. The key figure in fulfilling the OCC's regulatory mission is the national bank examiner. **Common positions include:** National Bank Examiner. **Educational backgrounds include:** Accounting; Business Administration; Economics; Finance. **Benefits:** 4-Day Work Week; 401K; Dental Insurance; Disability Coverage; Eye Care; Leave Time; Life Insurance; Medical Insurance; Pension Plan; Savings Plan. **Corporate headquarters location:** This Location. **Number of employees at this location:** 600. **Number of employees nationwide:** 4,000.

OVERSEAS PRIVATE INVESTMENT CORP.
1100 New York Avenue NW, Washington DC 20527. 202/336-8400. **Recorded Jobline:** 202/336-8682. **Contact:** Human Resources. **Description:** Assists U.S. investors in making profitable investments in developing countries.

POSTAL RATE COMMISSION
1333 H Street NW, Suite 300, Washington DC 20268. 202/789-6840. **Contact:** Cyril J. Pittack, Personnel Officer. **Description:** Central office of the federal government agency responsible for overseeing U.S. postal rates. **Common positions include:** Accountant/Auditor; Attorney; Computer Programmer; Economist/Market Research Analyst; Industrial Engineer; Statistician. **Educational backgrounds include:** Accounting; Business Administration; Computer Science; Economics; Engineering; Law/Pre-Law; Marketing. **Benefits:** Dental Insurance; Disability Coverage; Life Insurance; Medical Insurance; Pension Plan; Savings Plan; Tuition Assistance. **Corporate headquarters location:** This Location.

REPUBLICAN NATIONAL COMMITTEE
310 First Street Southeast, Washington DC 20003. 202/863-8500. **Contact:** Jeff Nulf, Personnel Director. **Description:** National headquarters for the Republican Party; engaged in a wide range of political and legislative support functions.

U.S. CHAMBER OF COMMERCE
1615 H Street NW, Washington DC 20062-2000. 202/463-5731. **Contact:** Michelle Pizzo, Employment Manager. **Description:** Headquarters for a large and diverse business organization, encompassing 220,000 business members, 3,000 state and local chambers of commerce, 1,200 trade and professional associations, and 69 American chambers of commerce overseas. Provides information, analysis, and opinion on federal legislation, policies, and programs affecting business and the overall economic climate of the nation. Promotes the development of business ideas and conveys them to Congress, government agencies, and the public. Conducts a wide variety of public outreach and information activities. Houses diverse affiliated operations, including the National Chamber Litigation Center, which represents business interests and concerns in court; and the Center for International Private Enterprise, which promotes free enterprise values throughout the world; the Center for Workforce Preparation which promotes innovative educational programs and alliances among business, educators, and government to support and encourage excellence in education. Also operates a separate communications area which provides a morning television business news program (First Business), a weekly half-hour TV debate program (It's Your Business); and two national magazines, *Nations Business* and *The Business Advocate*. Via satellite television, citizens can receive the U.S. Chamber of Commerce's Quality Learning Services, which provide consulting and training in Total Quality Management, and other practical business skills. **Common positions include:** Accountant/Auditor; Administrative Assistant; Administrator; Attorney; Broadcast Technician; Computer Programmer; Customer Service Representative; Economist/Market Research Analyst; Lobbyist; Systems Analyst. **Educational backgrounds include:** Accounting; Art/Design; Business Administration; Communications; Computer Science; Finance; Law/Pre-Law; Liberal Arts; Marketing; Political Science. **Benefits:** Disability Coverage; Life Insurance; Medical Insurance; Pension Plan; Savings Plan; Tuition Assistance. **Corporate headquarters location:** This Location. **Operations at this facility include:** Administration; Communications; Policy Development. **Number of employees at this location:** 350. **Number of employees nationwide:** 1,100.

Government/197

U.S. MERIT SYSTEMS PROTECTION BOARD
1120 Vermont Avenue, Washington DC 20419. 202/653-5916. **Fax:** 202/653-7821. **Recorded Jobline:** 202/254-8013. **Contact:** Shelya White, Supervisor/Personnel Management Specialist. **Description:** Protects the integrity of federal merit systems and the rights of federal employees working in them. **NOTE:** There is currently a hiring freeze in effect at this organization. **Common positions include:** Attorney. **Educational backgrounds include:** Law/Pre-Law. **Benefits:** Life Insurance; Medical Insurance; Thrift Plan. **Operations at this facility include:** Administration; Divisional Headquarters. **Number of employees at this location:** 280.

U.S. NAVY CIVIL ENGINEER CORPS (CEC)
Naval Facilities Engineering Command, Code 12A1, 200 Stovall Street, Alexandria VA 22332-2300. 703/614-3635. **Contact:** LCDR David Stewart, Accessions Officer. **Description:** CEC officers are U.S. Naval officers who are responsible for the design, construction, maintenance, repair, and operation of the Navy's shore facilities. Worldwide assignment possibilities. **NOTE:** If preferred, contact one of the regional Accessions Officers: Western U.S. - Lt. Gary Wick at 415/244-2005; Eastern U.S. - Lt. Paul Webb at 202/433-7285. **Common positions include:** Architect; Chemical Engineer; Civil Engineer; Construction Contractor and Manager; Department Manager; Electrical/Electronics Engineer; Financial Manager; General Manager; Industrial Engineer; Landscape Architect; Mechanical Engineer; Petroleum Engineer; Structural Engineer; Surveyor. **Educational backgrounds include:** Architecture; Engineering. **Benefits:** Daycare Assistance; Dental Insurance; Disability Coverage; Life Insurance; Medical Insurance; Pension Plan; Tuition Assistance. **Special Programs:** Training Programs. **Number of employees nationwide:** 1,400.

U.S. PATENT AND TRADEMARK OFFICE
Office of Human Resources, 2011 Crystal Drive Suite 200, Arlington VA 22202. 703/305-8231. **Fax:** 703/305-8501. **Recorded Jobline:** 703/305-4221. **Contact:** Dawn Dowell, Recruitment Coordinator. **Description:** Reviews applications for patents and makes legal determinations concerning the granting of patents. Employs more than 1,000 people, primarily scientists and engineers. **NOTE:** Send resumes to the chosen department: Recruitment/Patent, Kim Minnigh; Recruitment, Kim Clark; or Recruitment/Patent, Nancy Strother. **Common positions include:** Aerospace Engineer; Architect; Architectural Engineer; Biological Scientist/Biochemist; Biomedical Engineer; Chemical Engineer; Chemist; Civil Engineer; Computer Engineer; Electrical/Electronics Engineer; Food Scientist/Technologist; Industrial Designer; Industrial Engineer; Mechanical Engineer; Metallurgical Engineer; Mining Engineer; Petroleum Engineer; Physicist/Astronomer. **Educational backgrounds include:** Architecture; Art/Design; Chemistry; Communications; Computer Science; Engineering; Physics. **Benefits:** Dental Insurance; Disability Coverage; Life Insurance; Medical Insurance; Pension Plan; Profit Sharing; Sick Days; Tuition Assistance. **Corporate headquarters location:** This Location. **Parent company:** Department of Commerce.

U.S. POSTAL SERVICE
475 L'Enfant Plaza Southwest, Room 1813, Washington DC 20260-4261. 202/268-3638. **Fax:** 202/268-3488. **Contact:** Corporate Personnel Operations. **Description:** Field offices provide a complete range of mail pick-up and delivery services throughout the country and internationally. They also act as centers for passport acceptance, government program applications, government registration activities, and other activities. **Common positions include:** Accountant/Auditor; Administrator; Advertising Clerk; Architect; Attorney; Biological Scientist/Biochemist; Blue-Collar Worker Supervisor; Branch Manager; Buyer; Chemist; Claim Representative; Commercial Artist; Computer Programmer; Customer Service Representative; Department Manager; Draftsperson; Economist/Market Research Analyst; Editor; Electrical/Electronics Engineer; Financial Analyst; General Manager; Industrial Designer; Industrial Engineer; Marketing Specialist; Mechanical Engineer; Metallurgical Engineer; Operations/Production Manager; Public Relations Specialist; Purchasing Agent and Manager; Quality Control Supervisor; Reporter; Services Sales Representative; Statistician; Systems Analyst; Technical Writer/Editor; Transportation/Traffic Specialist. **Educational backgrounds include:** Business Administration; Computer Science; Economics; Engineering. **Benefits:** Dental Insurance; Disability Coverage; Life Insurance; Medical Insurance; Pension Plan; Savings Plan; Tuition Assistance. **Corporate headquarters location:** This Location. **Operations at this facility include:** Administration; Policy Development. **Number of employees nationwide:** 700,000.

UNITED STATES COURTS, THE ADMINISTRATIVE OFFICE OF
One Columbus Circle Northeast, Washington DC 20544. 202/273-2777. **Recorded Jobline:** 202/273-2760. **Contact:** Human Resources. **Description:** Handles the nonjudicial, administrative business of the United States Courts.

UNITED STATES DEPARTMENT OF AGRICULTURE
Agricultural Research Service, 6305 Ivy Lane, Beltsville MD 20705. 301/344-0106. **Recorded Jobline:** 301/344-2288. **Contact:** Human Resources. **Description:** Solves agricultural problems through applied research.

UNITED STATES DEPARTMENT OF AGRICULTURE
FOREST SERVICE
14th Street and Independence Avenue Southwest, P.O. Box 96060, Washington DC 20090-6090. **Recorded Jobline:** 202/235-5627. **Contact:** Human Resources. **Description:** Manages the National Forest System's natural resources for their continued use and protection.

UNITED STATES DEPARTMENT OF COMMERCE
14th and Constitution Avenue, The Herbert Hoover Building, Washington DC 20230. 202/482-2000. **Recorded Jobline:** 202/482-5138. **Contact:** Human Resources. **Description:** Serves and supports national economic growth, international trade, and technological advancement.

UNITED STATES DEPARTMENT OF COMMERCE
National Institute of Standards and Technology, Gaithersburg MD 20899. 301/975-2000. **Recorded Jobline:** 301/926-4851. **Contact:** Human Resources. **Description:** The science and engineering laboratory for measurement technology and standards research.

UNITED STATES DEPARTMENT OF DEFENSE
DEFENSE CONTRACT AUDIT AGENCY
Building 4, Room 4A395, Cameron Station, Alexandria VA 22304-6178. 703/274-7328. **Recorded Jobline:** 703/274-4068. **Contact:** Human Resources, CPO. **Description:** Provides all necessary contract audit functions for the Department of Defense.

UNITED STATES DEPARTMENT OF DEFENSE
DEFENSE INTELLIGENCE AGENCY (DIA)
3100 Clarendon Boulevard, Attention: DPH-2, Arlington VA 22201-5322. 703/907-1724. **Contact:** Julie E. Lee, Human Resources Manager. **Description:** An intelligence organization within the Department of Defense. Mission is to collect, analyze, interpret, and disseminate foreign military intelligence. DIA products are used by executive, legislative, and military leaders in the formulation and execution of national security policies. **Common positions include:** Computer Graphics Specialist; Computer Systems Analyst; Geographer. **Educational backgrounds include:** Computer Science; Industrial Relations.

UNITED STATES DEPARTMENT OF DEFENSE
DEFENSE INTELLIGENCE AGENCY (DIA)
The Pentagon, Washington DC 20340-0001. 703/907-1724. **Recorded Jobline:** 703/284-1110. **Contact:** Human Resources. **Description:** An intelligence organization within the Department of Defense. Mission is to collect, analyze, interpret, and disseminate foreign military intelligence. DIA products are used by executive, legislative, and military leaders in the formulation and execution of national security policies.

UNITED STATES DEPARTMENT OF ENERGY
1000 Independence Avenue Southwest, Washington DC 20585. 202/586-5000. **Recorded Jobline:** 202/586-4333. **Contact:** Human Resources. **Description:** Coordinates and administers the energy functions of the federal government.

UNITED STATES DEPARTMENT OF HEALTH AND HUMAN SERVICES
FOOD AND DRUG ADMINISTRATION (FDA)
759 Parklawn Building, 5600 Fisher Lane, Rockville MD 20857. 301/443-2234. **Recorded Jobline:** 301/443-1969. **Contact:** Human Resources. **Description:** Protects U.S. citizens from unsafe foods, drugs, and cosmetics.

UNITED STATES DEPARTMENT OF HEALTH AND HUMAN SERVICES
200 Independence Avenue Southwest, Washington DC 20201. 202/619-0257. **Recorded Jobline:** 202/619-2560. **Contact:** Human Resources. **Description:** Provides and services and programs to maintain the health and welfare of the national population.

UNITED STATES DEPARTMENT OF HEALTH AND HUMAN SERVICES
NATIONAL INSTITUTES OF HEALTH
9000 Rockville Pike, Bldg. 31-B3C15, Bethesda MD 20892. 301/496-4197. **Recorded Jobline:** 301/496-2403x1. **Contact:** Human Resources. **Description:** Organizations seeking to improve the health of U.S. citizens.

UNITED STATES DEPARTMENT OF HEALTH AND HUMAN SERVICES
OFFICE OF THE ASSISTANT SECRETARY OF HEALTH
5600 Fishers Lane, Room 1748, Rockville MD 20857. 301/443-6900. **Recorded Jobline:** 301/443-1986. **Contact:** Human Resources. **Description:** Assists in the planning and direction of the Public Health Service.

UNITED STATES DEPARTMENT OF HEALTH AND HUMAN SERVICES
SUBSTANCE ABUSE AND MENTAL HEALTH SERVICES ADMINISTRATION
5600 Fishers Lane, Rockwall II Room 90-10, Rockville MD 20857. 301/443-0365. **Recorded Jobline:** 301/443-2282. **Contact:** Human Resources. **Description:** Develops and executes strategies on dealing with alcohol and drug problems.

UNITED STATES DEPARTMENT OF HOUSING AND URBAN DEVELOPMENT
451 7th Street Southwest, Room 2258, Washington DC 20410. 202/708-0408. **Recorded Jobline:** 202/708-3203. **Contact:** Human Resources. **Description:** Concerned with the United States' housing needs, fair housing opportunities, and community development.

UNITED STATES DEPARTMENT OF JUSTICE
BUREAU OF PRISONS
320 1st Street NW, Room 161, Washington DC 20534. 202/307-1304. **Recorded Jobline:** 800/347-7744. **Contact:** Human Resources. **Description:** Provides confinement services for offenders committed by the federal court system.

UNITED STATES DEPARTMENT OF JUSTICE
IMMIGRATION AND NATURALIZATION SERVICE
425 I Street NW, Room 2011, Washington DC 20536. 202/514-2531. **Recorded Jobline:** 202/514-4301. **Contact:** Human Resources. **Description:** Regulates and enforces immigration laws.

UNITED STATES DEPARTMENT OF JUSTICE
UNITED STATES MARSHALS SERVICE
600 Army Navy Drive, Arlington VA 22202-4210. 202/307-9000. **Recorded Jobline:** 202/307-9400. **Contact:** Human Resources. **Description:** Secures federal courts, arrests and transports suspects, and operates a witness protection program.

UNITED STATES DEPARTMENT OF LABOR
OFFICE OF PERSONNEL MANAGEMENT SERVICES
200 Constitution Avenue NW, RM C-5516, Washington DC 20210. 202/219-6677. **Fax:** 202/219-5820. **Recorded Jobline:** 202/219-6646. **Contact:** Gary Saturn, Acting Personnel Director. **Description:** Promotes and reports on work force conditions. **Common positions include:** Accountant/Auditor; Attorney; Budget Analyst; Computer Programmer; Computer Systems Analyst; Cost Estimator; Economist/Market Research Analyst; Financial Analyst; Human Resources Specialist; Management Analyst/Consultant; Paralegal. **Benefits:** Dental Insurance; Life Insurance; Medical Insurance; Pension Plan; Savings Plan. **Special Programs:** Internships. **Corporate headquarters location:** This Location. **Operations at this facility include:** Administration; Divisional Headquarters; Service.

UNITED STATES DEPARTMENT OF THE NAVY
Naval Air Warfare Center/Aircraft Division, Human Resources Office, Building 2189, MS-53, Patuxent River MD 20670-5304. 301/826-4801. **Contact:** Human Resources. **Description:** The naval branch of the United States Armed Forces.

UNITED STATES DEPARTMENT OF THE NAVY
HUMAN RESOURCES OFFICE
Washington Navy Yard, Building 2009, 901 M Street Southeast, Washington DC 20374-5050. 202/433-5370. **Recorded Jobline:** 202/433-4930. **Contact:** Human Resources. **Description:** Naval branch of the U.S. Armed Forces.

UNITED STATES DEPARTMENT OF STATE
2201 C Street NW, Washington DC 20520. 202/647-4000. **Recorded Jobline:** 202/647-7284. **Contact:** Human Resources. **Description:** Government organization responsible for advising the President on foreign policy.

UNITED STATES DEPARTMENT OF THE AIR FORCE
1460 Air Force Pentagon, Room 5E871, Washington DC 20330-1000. 703/697-0580. **Recorded Jobline:** 703/693-6550x1,1. **Contact:** Human Resources. **Description:** Provides aerial protection to retain national security.

UNITED STATES DEPARTMENT OF THE ARMY
Civilian Personnel Advisory Center, Fort Myers Building 203, Fort Myers VA 22211-5050. 703/696-3134. **Recorded Jobline:** 202/695-2589. **Contact:** Human Resources. **Description:** Organizes, trains, and equips forces to defend the security of the United States.

UNITED STATES DEPARTMENT OF THE INTERIOR
GEOLOGICAL SURVEY
601 National Center, 12201 Sunrise Valley Drive, Renton VA 22092. 703/648-6131. **Recorded Jobline:** 703/648-7676. **Contact:** Human Resources. **Description:** Analyzes national natural resources, and investigates global change and natural hazards.

UNITED STATES DEPARTMENT OF THE INTERIOR
OFFICE OF THE SECRETARY
1849 C Street NW, Washington DC 20240. **Recorded Jobline:** 800/336-4562. **Contact:** Human Resources. **Description:** Manages most of the nation's public lands and natural resources.

UNITED STATES DEPARTMENT OF THE TREASURY
BUREAU OF ALCOHOL, TOBACCO AND FIREARMS
650 Massachusetts Avenue NW, Room 4170, Washington DC 20226. 202/927-8610. **Fax:** 202/927-8649. **Recorded Jobline:** 202/927-8423. **Contact:** Personnel Division, Employment Branch. **Description:** Administers laws covering the production, use, and distribution of alcohol, tobacco, and firearms. **Common positions include:** Accountant/Auditor; Budget Analyst; Computer Programmer; Human Resources Specialist; Special Agent. **Corporate headquarters location:** This Location. **Number of employees at this location:** 600. **Number of employees nationwide:** 4,000.

UNITED STATES DEPARTMENT OF TRANSPORTATION
D.O.T. CONNECTION CUSTOMER SERVICE CENTER
400 7th Street Southwest, Room Plaza Level 402, Washington DC 20590. 202/366-9397. **Fax:** 202/493-2244. **Recorded Jobline:** 202/366-9397. **Contact:** Human Resources. **Description:** Establishes the nation's transportation policies. **Common positions include:** Accountant/Auditor; Administrative Services Manager; Aerospace Engineer; Aircraft Mechanic/Engine Specialist; Attorney; Budget Analyst; Buyer; Clerical Supervisor; Computer Programmer; Computer Systems Analyst; Customer Service Representative; Economist/Market Research Analyst; Editor; Electrical/Electronics Engineer; Environmental Engineer; Financial Analyst; Human Resources Specialist; Industrial Engineer; Librarian; Library Technician; Management Analyst/Consultant; Management Trainee; Materials Engineer; Mathematician; Mechanical Engineer; Offers a wide range of positions; Operations/Production Manager; Paralegal; Public Relations Specialist; Purchasing Agent and Manager; Quality Control Supervisor; Software Engineer; Statistician; Structural Engineer; Technical Writer/Editor; Transportation/Traffic Specialist. **Benefits:** Credit Union; Daycare Assistance; Fitness Program; Life Insurance; Medical Insurance; Retirement Plan; Savings Plan. **Special Programs:** Internships. **Corporate headquarters location:** This Location. **Other U.S. locations:** Nationwide. **Operations at this facility include:** Administration; Research and Development; Service. **Number of employees nationwide:** 65,000.

UNITED STATES INFORMATION AGENCY
301 4th Street Southwest, Washington DC 20547. 202/619-4656. **Recorded Jobline:** 202/619-4539. **Contact:** Human Resources. **Description:** Manages the U.S. government's international information and cultural programs.

UNITED STATES SENATE
142 Hart Senate Office Building, Washington DC 20510. 202/224-9167. **Recorded Jobline:** 202/228-5627. **Contact:** Placement Office. **Description:** Makes legislation under the U.S. constitution. The placement office accepts applications for administrative positions.

Note: Because addresses and telephone numbers of smaller companies change rapidly, we recommend you call each company to verify the information below before inquiring about job opportunities. Mass mailings are not recommended.

Additional employers with under 250 employees:

FINANCE, TAXATION, AND MONETARY POLICY BODIES

Maryland State Lottery
6776 Reisterstown Rd,
Baltimore MD 21215-2345.
410/764-5700.

NATIONAL SECURITY AND INTERNATIONAL AFFAIRS

Germany Embassy
4645 Reservoir Rd Nw,
Washington DC 20007-1918. 202/298-4000.

China Embassy/The Peoples Republic
2300 Connecticut Ave Nw,
Washington DC 20008-1724. 202/328-2500.

Japan Embassy
2520 Massachusetts Ave Nw, Washington DC 20008-2822. 202/939-6700.

Embassy of Russian Federation
2650 Wisconsin Ave Nw,
Washington DC 20007-4601. 202/628-7551.

UNITED STATES POSTAL SERVICE

West Springfield Branch P.O.
6200 Rolling Rd, Springfield VA 22152-9998. 703/451-6131.

For information on application procedures for federal employment, see Section Four of this book, **Working for the Federal Government.**

For more information about career opportunities in the government:

Directories

ACCESS...FCO ON-LINE
Federal Research Service, Inc., P.O. Box 1059, 243 Church Street, Vienna VA 22183-1059.
703/281-0200. This is the on-line service of the *Federal Career Opportunities* publication. To join on-line, the cost is $25 for the set-up and $45 for one hour, payable by credit card over the phone.

HEALTH CARE: SERVICES, EQUIPMENT AND PRODUCTS

With no time to worry about the failure of government-proposed health care reforms, the health care industry is surging ahead with its own solutions, pressured by a competitive marketplace to cut costs. HMOs and insurance providers are looking to nursing homes and home care companies as an alternative to long-term hospital stays, and shifting from inpatient to less expensive outpatient care. Hospitals are streamlining operations and consolidating, with cutback efforts targeting staff, as well as unnecessary tests and laboratory fees. Hospital cost-cutting has also hurt medical equipment suppliers, as many hospitals form networks to share expensive equipment.

Even so, from 1990 to 1995, the number of health care workers in the United States grew from 8.86 million 10.5 million. Despite pressure to cut back, the health care industry remains a growth area. As the elderly population continues to grow faster than the population as a whole and the survival rate of the severely ill continues to improve, the need for new workers will continue to increase, and the large employment base will create replacement needs.

ALEXANDRIA HOSPITAL
4320 Seminary Road, Alexandria VA 22304. 703/504-3000. **Contact:** Human Resources. **Description:** A general medical and surgical hospital.

ANNE ARUNDEL MEDICAL CENTER
Franklin and Cathedral Streets, Annapolis MD 21401. 410/267-1000. **Contact:** Human Resources. **Description:** Since opening in 1902 as an 11-bed emergency hospital in downtown Annapolis, Anne Arundel Medical Center has now grown into a 291-bed acute care hospital serving more than 64,000 people. Its staff of more than 300 physicians and 515 nurses is specialized in all areas of medicine. Its family practice and internal medicine physicians provide comprehensive care for family members, including diagnosis, treatment and prevention of illnesses. And its specialists - from orthopedists to oncologists to anesthesiologists and surgeons - stay abreast of new therapies and high-tech procedures. Other affiliates of the Medical Center include Anne Arundel Diagnostics, a complete out-patient radiology service which offers general and specialized radiology services, Anne Arundel Magnetic Resonance Imaging, which incorporates talents of physicians, computer experts and radiologists to diagnose previously hidden disorders, and Pathways, a 40-bed treatment facility for adolescents and young adults 12 to 25 who suffer from some form of substance abuse or dependency.

BAUSCH & LOMB
265 Bausch & Lomb Drive, Oakland MD 21550. 301/334-9933. **Contact:** Human Resources. **Description:** Bausch & Lomb competes in selected segments of global health care and optical markets. The Healthcare Segment consists of three sectors: Personal Health, Medical, and Biomedical. The Personal Health Sector is comprised of branded products purchased directly by consumers in health and beauty aid sections of pharmacies, food stores and mass merchandise outlets. Products include lens care solutions; oral care, eye care, and skin care products; and non-prescription medications. The Medical Sector consists of contact lenses, ophthalmic pharmaceuticals, hearing aids, dental implants and other products sold to health care professionals, or which are obtained by consumers only through a prescription. The Biomedical Sector includes products and services supplied to customers engaged in

the research and development of pharmaceuticals and the production of genetically engineered materials. These include purpose-bred research animals, bioprocessing services and products derived from specific pathogen-free eggs. The Optics Segment consists primarily of premium-priced sunglasses sold under such internationally recognized brand names as Ray-Ban and Revo. Manufacturing or marketing organizations have been established in 34 countries, and the company's products are distributed in more than 70 other nations. The company employs 14,400 worldwide. **Corporate headquarters location:** Rochester NY.

BECTON DICKINSON DIAGNOSTIC INSTRUMENT SYST.
7 Loveton Circle, P.O. Box 999, Sparks Glenco MD 21152. 410/316-4000. **Contact:** Manager/Human Resources. **Description:** Becton Dickinson Diagnostic Instrument Systems is a division of Becton Dickinson and Company, an international medical technology firm. Manufactures and sells a broad range of medical supplies, devices, and diagnostic systems for use by health care professionals, medical research institutions, and the general public. Becton Dickinson, with corporate headquarters in Franklin Lakes, New Jersey, maintains offices and facilities in over 70 locations worldwide. **Common positions include:** Accountant/Auditor; Biological Scientist/Biochemist; Biomedical Engineer; Blue-Collar Worker Supervisor; Buyer; Chemical Engineer; Chemist; Computer Programmer; Credit Manager; Customer Service Representative; Department Manager; Draftsperson; Electrical/Electronics Engineer; Financial Analyst; General Manager; Human Resources Specialist; Industrial Designer; Industrial Engineer; Mechanical Engineer; Operations/Production Manager; Purchasing Agent and Manager; Quality Control Supervisor; Sales Associate; Systems Analyst; Technical Writer/Editor. **Educational backgrounds include:** Biology; Business Administration; Chemistry; Computer Science; Liberal Arts. **Benefits:** Dental Insurance; Disability Coverage; Employee Discounts; Life Insurance; Medical Insurance; Pension Plan; Profit Sharing; Savings Plan; Tuition Assistance. **Parent company:** Becton Dickinson & Company. **Operations at this facility include:** Divisional Headquarters; Manufacturing; Research and Development; Sales; Service. **Listed on:** New York Stock Exchange.

BON SECOURS HOSPITAL
2000 West Baltimore Street, Baltimore MD 21223. 410/362-3030. **Fax:** 410/947-3210. **Contact:** Connie Vagrin, Recruitment Coordinator. **Description:** An acute care hospital. **Common positions include:** Offers a wide range of positions. **Benefits:** Dental Insurance; Life Insurance; Medical Insurance; Pension Plan; Tuition Assistance. **Corporate headquarters location:** Marriottsville MD.

CARROLL COUNTY GENERAL HOSPITAL (CCGH)
200 Memorial Avenue, Westminster MD 21157. 410/848-3000. **Contact:** Human Resources. **Description:** Carroll County General Hospital is a private, not-for-profit hospital governed by a community-based board. With 158 beds, CCGH is the only acute care hospital located in Carroll County and is fully accredited by the Joint Commission on the Accreditation of Healthcare Organizations. The hospital has 280-plus physicians on its medical staff, representing some 31 medical specialties. More than 85 percent of CCGH physicians are board certified in their specialty fields. Approximately 1,100 associates work at the hospital, making CCGH the county's fourth largest employer. CCGH's full range of services includes comprehensive laboratory and radiology services, an ambulatory surgery center, a cardiac catheterization lab and angiography service, an inpatient psychiatric unit, and state-of-the-art surgical technology utilizing lasers and laparascopes, as well as computerized pain pumps.

CHARTER MEDICAL CORPORATION
730 Maryland Route 3, Gambrills MD 21054-1304. 410/923-6022. **Contact:** Human Resources. **Description:** Charter Medical Corporation is one of the largest investor-owned providers of behavioral health care in the United States. At calendar year-end 1994, Charter had 111 facility-based systems and 150 outpatient centers in 31 states and two foreign countries. With approximately $1 billion in revenues and more than 20,000 employees worldwide, Charter is transforming itself from a large hospital management company into a health care system provider and manager of care capable of offering an extensive array of services. Charter Medical trades under the symbol 'CMD.'. **Corporate headquarters location:** Atlanta GA. **Listed on:** American Stock Exchange.

CHILDREN'S NATIONAL MEDICAL CENTER
111 Michigan Avenue NW, Washington DC 20010-2970. 202/884-5000. **Contact:** Human Resources. **Description:** The Children's National Medical Center was established 125 years ago for the sole purpose of benefiting children. Over the years, the center has pioneered studies of antibiotic resistance and the causes of severe respiratory tract infection, developed a special form of Vitamin D to treat kidney failure, accomplished the first bone marrow and heart transplants, and identified three viruses that cause infant pneumonia, infant diarrhea and croup. The center offers comprehensive home care programs and is the regional pediatric trauma center. A non-profit health center, the Children's National Medical Center relies on donations and fundraising from corporations, foundations, clubs, and individuals to help support building projects, establish new programs, and provide care to children whose families cannot afford their services.

COLUMBIA HOSPITAL FOR WOMEN MEDICAL CENTER
2425 L Street NW, Washington DC 20037-1485. 202/293-6500. **Contact:** Human Resources. **Description:** A women's medical center.

FALLSTON GENERAL HOSPITAL
200 Milton Avenue, Fallston MD 21047-2777. 410/877-3700. **Contact:** Human Resources. **Description:** The Upper Chesapeake Health System is a locally owned and managed not-for-profit health system developed in 1984. Fallston General and Harford Memorial are member hospitals offering medical, diagnostic and emergency services. **Parent company:** Upper Chesapeake Health System.

FRANKLIN SQUARE HOSPITAL CENTER
9000 Franklin Square Drive, Baltimore MD 21237-3901. 410/682-7000. **Contact:** Human Resources. **Description:** Franklin Square Hospital Center is a 405-bed, full-service, general acute care community hospital in Baltimore County. The sixth largest hospital in the greater Baltimore area, Franklin Square is one the state's busiest in many areas, including emergency medicine, oncology, cardiology, labor and delivery and general medicine. Other major programs are family health, neonatology, psychiatry and pediatrics. The Helix Health System, in which Franklin Square was a founding member, offers three member hospitals, two nursing homes, teaching programs, Ask-A-Nurse health information and physician referral, home health care, rehabilitation services, mental health services, and physical, occupational and speech therapy. Franklin Square is also a teaching hospital. Some 90 resident physicians provide care while they complete their medical training in Family practice, Obstetrics/Gynecology and Medicine.

GARLOCK MEMORIAL CONVALESCENT HOME
241 South Prospect Street, Hagerstown MD 21740. 301/733-3310. **Contact:** Human Resources. **Description:** A nursing and personal care facility.

GARRETT COUNTY MEMORIAL HOSPITAL
251 North 4th Street, Oakland MD 21550. 301/334-2155. **Fax:** 301/334-5298. **Contact:** Human Resources. **Description:** A county hospital. **Common positions include:** Accountant/Auditor; Buyer; Claim Representative; Clinical Lab Technician; Computer Programmer; Computer Systems Analyst; Counselor; Credit Manager; Customer Service Representative; Dietician/Nutritionist; Education Administrator; Human Resources Specialist; Licensed Practical Nurse; Medical Record Technician; Nuclear Medicine Technologist; Pharmacist; Public Relations Specialist; Purchasing Agent and Manager; Quality Control Supervisor; Radiologic Technologist; Registered Nurse; Respiratory Therapist; Restaurant/Food Service Manager; Surgical Technician. **Educational backgrounds include:** Accounting; Business Administration; Finance; Health Care. **Benefits:** Disability Coverage; Employee Discounts; Life Insurance; Medical Insurance; Pension Plan; Savings Plan; Tuition Assistance. **Corporate headquarters location:** This Location. **Number of employees at this location:** 350.

GENESIS HEALTH VENTURES
515 Fairmount Avenue, Suite 800, Towson MD 21286. 410/296-1000. **Contact:** Jim Tabak, Director of Human Resources. **Description:** A health care management firm.

GEORGE WASHINGTON UNIVERSITY HOSPITAL
901 23rd Street NW, Washington DC 20037-2377. 202/994-1000. **Contact:** Human Resources. **Description:** The George Washington University Medical Center (GWUMC) is a nationally recognized, interdisciplinary health care facility which includes the University Hospital, a top-ranked School of Medicine and Health Sciences, a

comprehensive basic and clinical research program and a 22-year-old health maintenance organization -- the George Washington University Health Plan. Clinical Services are provided through the University Hospital and the Medical Faculty Associates, a group of specialists who practice and teach at George Washington. The University Hospital is center-city facility which is also the health care provider for the President of the United States. The Emergency Department sees approximately 48,000 patients annually and more than 17,000 are admitted to the hospital every year. More than 1,000 physicians are affiliated with the hospital. The University Hospital is also a certified Level-1 Trauma Center, having met the American College of Surgeon's requirements for medical staff training and clinical research on trauma care.

GREATER LAUREL REGIONAL HOSPITAL
7300 Van Dusen Road, Laurel MD 20707. 301/725-4300. **Contact:** Human Resources Department. **Description:** A regional hospital.

GREATER SOUTHEAST COMMUNITY HOSPITAL
1310 Southern Avenue Southeast, Washington DC 20032-4699. 202/574-6000. **Contact:** Human Resources. **Description:** Since 1966, the 450-bed Greater Southeast Community Hospital has offered comprehensive care, including medical and surgical care, obstetrics and gynecology services, psychiatry, pediatrics, 24-hour emergency care, rehabilitation services and home health care. Greater Southeast addresses the needs of seniors through programs and services offered at the Center for the Aging, which provides long-term care for frail elderly. The 183-bed Health Care Institute and the 150-bed Livingston Health Care Center offer intermediate and skilled nursing home care for residents. Greater Southeast recently acquired the Fort Washington Medical Center, a 33-bed hospital in southern Prince George's County, Maryland that provides in and outpatient services, including medical and surgical care, 24-hour emergency services and diagnostic testing.

HARFORD MEMORIAL HOSPITAL
501 South Union Avenue, Havre De Grace MD 21078-3493. 410/939-2400. **Contact:** Human Resources. **Description:** The Upper Chesapeake Health System is a locally owned and managed not-for-profit health system developed in 1984. Harford Memorial and Fallston General are member hospitals offering medical, diagnostic and emergency services. **Parent company:** Upper Chesapeake Health System.

HEALTH CARE MANAGEMENT CORPORATION
1314 Chester Boulevard, Baltimore MD 21286-2028. 410/296-3282. **Description:** Management office of the BelAir and North Arundel nursing homes.

HELIX HEALTH SYSTEM
2330 West Joppa Road, Suite 301, Lutherville MD 21903-4635. 410/296-6050. **Contact:** Human Resources. **Description:** Helix Health System includes Franklin Square Hospital, Union Memorial and Good Samaritan Hospital, two nursing centers, Ask-A-Nurse health information and physician referral, home health care services, rehabilitation services, mental health services, and physical, occupational and speech therapy. The System also offers teaching programs in Internal Medicine, Family Practice, Obstetrics/Gynecology, Orthopedics, Physical Medicine and Rehabilitation and Surgery.

HOLY CROSS HOSPITAL
1500 Forest Glen Road, Silver Spring MD 20910-1460. 301/905-0100. **Contact:** Human Resources. **Description:** Holy Cross Hospital is a 442-bed community teaching hospital located in the residential suburb of Silver Spring. It is also one of the largest providers of complex primary and secondary health care in both Montgomery and Prince George's counties, serving almost 200,000 patients each year. Holy Cross has teaching affiliations with George Washington University School of Medicine in obstetrics and gynecology, general medicine and surgery, and with Children's National Medical Center in pediatrics. Holy Cross Hospital also offers Healthy Side, a program of health seminars, classes, support groups and special events.

HOMECALL, INC.
92 Thomas Johnson Drive, Frederick MD 21702-4383. 301/663-8818. **Contact:** Human Resources. **Description:** HomeCall, Inc., along with its subsidiary, FirstCall, Inc., are two new subsidiaries to Mid-Atlantic Medical Services, Inc. (MAMSI). HomeCall provides in-house nursing and care to patients who are confined to their homes. MAMSI, a holding company with subsidiaries active in managed health care, is one of the largest managed care companies in its market, which currently includes

Maryland, Virginia, Washington, D.C. and West Virginia. In 1994, MAMSI's health care products totaled 1,206,000, including 508,000 enrollees in managed care and indemnity health products and 698,000 enrollees in the Alliance/MAPSI network.

HOWARD COUNTY GENERAL HOSPITAL
5755 Cedar Lane, Columbia MD 21044. 410/740-7815. **Fax:** 410/740-7542. **Contact:** Denise Smith, Employee Relations/Employment Manager. **Description:** A hospital. **Common positions include:** Biomedical Engineer; Buyer; Computer Systems Analyst; Dietician/Nutritionist; EEG Technologist; EKG Technician; Electrician; Emergency Medical Technician; Financial Analyst; Food Scientist/Technologist; Human Resources Specialist; Licensed Practical Nurse; Medical Record Technician; Nuclear Medicine Technologist; Occupational Therapist; Pharmacist; Physical Therapist; Physician; Psychologist; Public Relations Specialist; Radiologic Technologist; Registered Nurse; Respiratory Therapist; Social Worker; Speech-Language Pathologist; Surgical Technician. **Educational backgrounds include:** Biology; Business Administration; Chemistry; Health Care; Mathematics; Nursing; Psychology. **Benefits:** 401K; Dental Insurance; Disability Coverage; Employee Discounts; Free Parking; Life Insurance; Medical Insurance; Profit Sharing; Savings Plan; Tuition Assistance. **Special Programs:** Internships. **Operations at this facility include:** Administration. **Listed on:** Privately held. **Number of employees at this location:** 1,600.

HUMANA GROUP HEALTH PLAN
GROUP HEALTH ASSOCIATION
4301 Connecticut Avenue NW, Washington DC 20008. 202/364-2080. **Contact:** Human Resources. **Description:** A health maintenance organization delivering health and wellness programs throughout metropolitan Washington. **Common positions include:** Accountant/Auditor; Administrator; Attorney; Buyer; Claim Representative; Computer Programmer; Department Manager; Human Resources Specialist; Marketing Specialist; Public Relations Specialist; Purchasing Agent and Manager; Systems Analyst. **Educational backgrounds include:** Accounting; Computer Science; Finance; Marketing. **Benefits:** Dental Insurance; Life Insurance; Medical Insurance; Pension Plan.

INOVA HEALTH SYSTEMS, INC.
8001 Braddock Road, Springfield VA 22151. 703/321-4200. **Recorded Jobline:** 800/854-6682. **Contact:** Human Resources. **Description:** Operates three non-profit hospitals.

INSTITUTE OF MEDICINE
National Academy of Sciences, 2101 Constitution Avenue NW, Washington DC 20418. 202/334-3300. **Contact:** Human Resources. **Description:** An organization of public health workers who are elected based upon their achievements in the healthcare industry. The Institute of Medicine also works on public policy, advising the government on issues regarding health.

INTEGRATED HEALTH SERVICES, INC.
10065 Red Run Boulevard, Owings Mills MD 21117. 410/998-8400. **Contact:** Human Resources. **Description:** Integrated Health Services, Inc., provides medical services, primarily sub-acute care, for geriatric patients, and manages assisted living facilities and retirement communities.

JOHNS HOPKINS HOSPITAL
600 North Wolfe Street, Baltimore MD 21287-0002. 410/955-5000. **Contact:** Human Resources. **Description:** For four consecutive years, the John Hopkins Hospital has been named the Best of the Best in the *U.S. News & World Report*'s annual ranking. Hopkins' programs in AIDS and cancer treatment, cardiology, endocrinology, gastroenterology, geriatrics, neurology, orthopedics, otolaryngology, rheumatology, urology, ophthalmology, pediatrics and psychiatry were all rated in the nation's top ten. The program in gynecology was named number one. Since 1986, the 1,036-bed hospital has been a part of the John Hopkins Health System, which includes the John Hopkins Bayview Medical Center, an outpatient center, a geriatrics center and the John Hopkins Home Care Group. Overall, the John Hopkins Health System accounts for more than one of every 10 inpatient admissions in Maryland.

KENNEDY KRIEGER INSTITUTE
707 North Broadway, Baltimore MD 21205. 410/550-9000. **Contact:** Human Resources. **Description:** The Kennedy Krieger Institute began as the Children's Rehabilitation Center in 1937 to serve children with cerebral palsy. Today, Kennedy Krieger has grown to become one of the nation's foremost centers for treatment and

research in children's brain diseases. From the diagnosis and assessment stages through treatment and into adulthood, the Phelps Cerebral Palsy Treatment Center is a resource for children with cerebral palsy and their families. The Institute's Spina Bifida Center mirrors the Phelps Center by providing medical and mental health services provided to help children meet the challenges that will arise in their lives. The Kennedy Krieger School for children with physical, emotional, and learning disabilities offers extended day programs for adolescents with severe emotional disabilities. In 1994, over 9,000 children from around the world went to Kennedy Kreiger for treatment. Over 400 children needed the Institute's in-patient and rehabilitative services required to treat severe head or spinal cord injuries. The remaining children went for diagnosis and treatment for metabolic and degenerative brain diseases, birth defects such as Down Syndrome and spina bifida, and other disorders such as cerebral palsy, feeding difficulties, lead poisoning, and behavioral problems.

MD-INDIVIDUAL PRACTICE ASSOCIATION
4 Taft Court, Rockville MD 20850-5310. 301/762-8205. **Contact:** Human Resources. **Description:** MD-Individual Practice Association, Inc. (M.D. IPA) is a federally qualified HMO. Parent company, Mid Atlantic Medical Services, Inc. (MAMSI), is a holding company whose subsidiaries are active in managed health care. Other subsidiaries include: Optimum Choice, Inc. (OCI), a non-federally qualified HMO that serves commercial and other specialized markets such as Medicare and Medicaid; Alliance PPO, Inc., a Preferred Provider Organization marketing its provider network product to self-insured employers, indemnity carriers, and other health care purchasing groups; Mid Atlantic Psychiatric Services, Inc. (MAPSI), which provides specialized non-risk mental health services; and HomeCall and FirstCall, both of which provide in-house nursing and care to patients who are confined to their homes. MAMSI's market currently includes Maryland, Virginia, Washington, D.C., Delaware and West Virginia. In 1994, MAMSI's various health care products covered a total of 1,206,000 lives. **Parent company:** Mid Atlantic Medical Services, Incorporated.

MANOR HEALTHCARE CORPORATION
10770 Columbia Pike, Silver Spring MD 20901. 301/681-9400. **Recorded Jobline:** 800/348-2041. **Contact:** Employment Department. **Description:** Manor HealthCare Corporation is a provider of long-term care services operating nursing centers nationwide, an acute care hospital, retirement living units, and pharmacy outlets. The brandnames used by Manor HealthCare in the operation of over 166 long-term care facilities in 28 states are Manor Care, Americana, Leader Nursing and Rehabilitation, MedBridge, Vitalink Pharmacy and Four Seasons. **Common positions include:** Dietician/Nutritionist; Management Trainee; Marketing Research Analyst; Marketing/Advertising/PR Manager; Occupational Therapist; Operations Research Analyst; Physical Therapist; Public Relations Specialist; Purchasing Agent and Manager; Quality Control Supervisor; Recreational Therapist; Registered Nurse; Social Worker. **Educational backgrounds include:** Health Care; Marketing. **Benefits:** Dental Insurance; Disability Coverage; Employee Discounts; Life Insurance; Medical Insurance; Pension Plan; Savings Plan; Tuition Assistance. **Special Programs:** Training Programs. **Corporate headquarters location:** This Location. **Parent company:** Manor Care, Inc. **Operations at this facility include:** Divisional Headquarters; Regional Headquarters; Research and Development; Service. **Listed on:** New York Stock Exchange. **Number of employees at this location:** 503. **Number of employees nationwide:** 25,000.

MEDLANTIC HEALTHCARE GROUP
100 Irving Street NW, Washington DC 20010-2911. 202/877-6006. **Contact:** Human Resources. **Description:** Medlantic Healthcare is a not-for-profit group. Medlantic is the holder of the Washington Hospital Center, which offers services in cancer, ophthalmology, renal transplants, heart care, OB/GYN, critical care, and asthma and allergies.

MERCY MEDICAL CENTER
301 St. Paul Place, Baltimore MD 21202. 410/332-9742. **Fax:** 410/783-5863. **Recorded Jobline:** 410/332-9414. **Contact:** Wendy S. Kelly, Recruiter. **Description:** An acute general care hospital. Specialties include: eating disorders, women's services, detox facilities, and a sexual assault and crisis center. **Common positions include:** Dietician/Nutritionist; EEG Technologist; Emergency Medical Technician; Occupational Therapist; Pharmacist; Physical Therapist; Registered Nurse; Respiratory Therapist;

Surgical Technician. **Benefits:** Dental Insurance; Disability Coverage; Life Insurance; Medical Insurance; Pension Plan; Tuition Assistance. **Corporate headquarters location:** This Location. **Number of employees at this location:** 1,800.

MID-ATLANTIC MEDICAL SERVICES, INC.
4 Taft Court, Rockville MD 20850. 301/294-5140. **Contact:** Human Resources Department. **Description:** A holding company whose subsidiaries are active in managed health care. Subsidiaries include: MD-Individual Practice Association, Inc. (M.D. IPA), a federally qualified HMO; Optimum Choice, Inc. (OCI), a non-federally qualified HMO that serves commercial and other specialized markets such as Medicare and Medicaid; Alliance PPO, Inc., a Preferred Provider Organization marketing its provider network product to self-insured employers, indemnity carriers, and other health care purchasing groups; Mid Atlantic Psychiatric Services, Inc. (MAPSI), which provides specialized non-risk mental health services; and HomeCall and FirstCall, both of which provide in-house nursing and care to patients who are confined to their homes. MAMSI's market currently includes Maryland, Virginia, Washington, D.C., Delaware and West Virginia. In 1994, MAMSI's various health care products covered a total of 1,206,000 lives.

MONTGOMERY GENERAL HOSPITAL
18101 Prince Philip Drive, Olney MD 20832. 301/774-8666. **Fax:** 301/774-7389. **Recorded Jobline:** 301/774-8787. **Contact:** Vivian Hisia, Human Resources Consultant. **Description:** A 229-bed non-profit, general acute care community hospital. **Common positions include:** Buyer; Clerical Supervisor; Clinical Lab Technician; Computer Programmer; Computer Systems Analyst; Dietician/Nutritionist; EKG Technician; Electrician; Emergency Medical Technician; Medical Record Technician; Nuclear Medicine Technologist; Occupational Therapist; Pharmacist; Physical Therapist; Registered Nurse; Respiratory Therapist; Social Worker; Stationary Engineer; Surgical Technician. **Benefits:** 401K; Dental Insurance; Disability Coverage; Employee Discounts; Life Insurance; Medical Insurance; Pension Plan; Tuition Assistance. **Corporate headquarters location:** This Location. **Operations at this facility include:** Administration. **Listed on:** Privately held. **Number of employees at this location:** 850.

NATIONAL CANCER INSTITUTE
OFFICE OF CANCER COMMUNICATIONS
9000 Rockville Pike, Building 31 Room 3A19, Bethesda MD 20892-4000. 301/496-6756. **Contact:** Human Resources. **Description:** Develops and manages communications activities for the institute.

NATIONAL REHABILITATION HOSPITAL
102 Irving Street NW, Washington DC 20010-2921. 202/877-1000. **Contact:** Human Resources. **Description:** National Rehabilitation Hospital provides rehabilitation with patient care, assistive technology, research, education and training, and advocacy. Patient care services include the outpatient center at Bethesda, providing musculosketetal rehabilitation; the Performance Diagnostic Laboratory, offering sophisticated video and computer technology to analyze individual's movements; the Brain Injury Rehabilitation and the Stroke Recovery Program, offering day-treatment programs for those who are re-entering the community; the Department of Obstetrics and Gynecology, offering OB/GYN Services for women with disabilities; and Multiple Sclerosis services. In 1994, inpatient admissions reached over 1,500 and outpatient visits reached 55,000.

NORTH ARUNDEL HOSPITAL
301 Hospital Drive, Glen Burnie MD 21061. 410/787-4790. **Contact:** Human Resources. **Description:** North Arundel offers services in Ambulatory Surgery, Cariology, Community Health and Wellness Programs, Comprehensive Rehabilitation Care, Emergency, Endoscopy, Home Care, Laboratory, Nursing, Oncology, Orthopedic, Primary Care, Pediatrics, Psychiatry, Radiology, and Respiratory and Pulmonary Services.

NORTHERN VIRGINIA DOCTORS HOSPITAL
601 South Carlin Springs Road, Arlington VA 22204. 703/578-2045. **Contact:** Robert Muir, SPHR, Director, Human Resources. **Description:** An adult medicine, surgery, and psychiatric acute health care facility. **Common positions include:** Licensed Practical Nurse; Pharmacist; Physical Therapist; Radiologic Technologist; Registered Nurse; Respiratory Therapist. **Educational backgrounds include:** Nursing. **Benefits:** 401K; Daycare Assistance; Dental Insurance; Disability Coverage; Employee Discounts; Life

Insurance; Medical Insurance; Profit Sharing; Tuition Assistance. **Corporate headquarters location:** Nashville TN. **Operations at this facility include:** Service. **Listed on:** New York Stock Exchange. **Number of employees at this location:** 500. **Number of employees nationwide:** 30,000.

NORTHWEST HOSPITAL CENTER
5401 Old Court Road, Randallstown MD 21133-5103. 410/521-2200. **Contact:** Human Resources. **Description:** Northwest Hospital Center is a 240-bed private, not-for-profit hospital with more than 500 doctors in a range of specialties. The hospital serves the health care needs of the northwest Baltimore metropolitan area. Northwest Hospital Center is accredited by the Joint Commission on Accreditation of Healthcare Organizations, the American Association of Blood Banks, and the College of American Pathologists. The hospital is affiliated with Cherrywood Manor Extended Care Centre, a 161-bed, medically directed nursing home. Northwest Hospital Center is also a member of the SunHealth Network, the Preferred Health Network of Maryland and the Maryland Hospital Association.

PHYSICIANS MEMORIAL HOSPITAL
701 East Charles Street, LaPlata MD 20646. 301/609-4444. **Fax:** 301/609-4417. **Recorded Jobline:** 301/934-5385. **Contact:** Karen Savoy, Employment/Recruitment Coordinator. **Description:** A 131-bed full-service community hospital located in Southern Maryland. **Common positions include:** Accountant/Auditor; Adjuster; Administrative Services Manager; Clerical Supervisor; Clinical Lab Technician; Collector; Computer Programmer; Dietician/Nutritionist; EEG Technologist; EKG Technician; Electrician; Emergency Medical Technician; Health Services Manager; Human Service Worker; Investigator; Mechanical Engineer; Medical Record Technician; Nuclear Medicine Technologist; Occupational Therapist; Pharmacist; Physical Therapist; Physician; Psychologist; Public Relations Specialist; Radiologic Technologist; Recreational Therapist; Registered Nurse; Respiratory Therapist; Social Worker; Speech-Language Pathologist; Surgical Technician. **Educational backgrounds include:** Accounting; Biology; Business Administration; Chemistry; Commercial Art; Computer Science; Engineering; Finance; Marketing. **Benefits:** 403B; Dental Insurance; Disability Coverage; Employee Discounts; Life Insurance; Medical Insurance; Pension Plan; Savings Plan; Tuition Assistance. **Operations at this facility include:** Administration; Service. **Number of employees at this location:** 650.

PROVIDENCE HOSPITAL
1150 Varnum Street Northeast, Washington DC 20017-2180. 202/269-7000. **Contact:** Human Resources. **Description:** Providence Hospital offers a variety of programs, treatments, and counseling. The Wellness Institute and Women's Center provides cancer assessments, exercise programs, and classes in nutrition, weight management, hyperextension, stress management, and smoking cessation. The Senior Connection Program, Telecare, is a service that phones seniors who, due to age, illness or immobility, spend most of their time home alone. The Fort Lincoln Family Medicine Center provides continuous health care and serves as the outpatient training site for 21 family practice residents. Center for Life helps pregnant women in urban areas who have difficulties in language, money, and transportation. Seton Home provides in- and outpatient treatment, inpatient psychiatric care and a special program for patients with both psychiatric and substance abuse problems. Umoja Treatment Service is a full-service, hospital-based alcohol and drug abuse center.

ROCKINGHAM MEMORIAL HOSPITAL
235 Cantrell Avenue, Harrisonburg VA 22801. 703/433-4106. **Fax:** 703/564-5446. **Contact:** Diane R. Mullins, Recruitment/Employment Manager. **Description:** A 330-bed, non-profit community hospital located in the Shenandoah Valley. **Common positions include:** Accountant/Auditor; Clerical Supervisor; Computer Programmer; Computer Systems Analyst; Customer Service Representative; Dentist; EEG Technologist; EKG Technician; Electrician; Financial Analyst; Human Resources Specialist; Librarian; Licensed Practical Nurse; Mechanical Engineer; Medical Record Technician; Nuclear Medicine Technologist; Occupational Therapist; Pharmacist; Physical Therapist; Physician; Purchasing Agent and Manager; Recreational Therapist; Registered Nurse; Respiratory Therapist; Restaurant/Food Service Manager; Social Worker; Surgical Technician. **Educational backgrounds include:** Accounting; Business Administration; Engineering; Finance; Marketing. **Benefits:** Dental Insurance; Disability Coverage;

Employee Discounts; Life Insurance; Medical Insurance; Pension Plan; Savings Plan; Tuition Assistance. **Corporate headquarters location:** This Location. **Operations at this facility include:** Service. **Number of employees at this location:** 1,500.

ST. JOSEPH MEDICAL CENTER
7620 York Road, Baltimore MD 21204. 410/337-1000. **Contact:** Human Resources. **Description:** St. Joseph Medical Center, a member of the Franciscan Health System, is a regional medical center providing comprehensive acute care with diversified specialty services, and is sponsored by the Sisters of St. Francis of Philadelphia.

SHEPPARD PRATT HEALTH SYSTEM
6501 North Charles Street, P.O. Box 6815, Baltimore MD 21204. 410/938-3000. **Contact:** Human Resources. **Description:** A not-for-profit health system, Sheppard Pratt is a provider of managed behavioral health care services. They offer integrated EAP/managed mental health programs, case management, claims processing and at-risk or fee-for-service contracting.

SIBLEY MEMORIAL HOSPITAL
5255 Loughboro Road NW, Washington DC 20016. 202/537-4750. **Fax:** 202/363-6267. **Recorded Jobline:** 202/364-8665. **Contact:** Karen Robertson Keck, Employment Manager. **Description:** A 362-bed community hospital. **Common positions include:** Accountant/Auditor; EEG Technologist; EKG Technician; Financial Analyst; Licensed Practical Nurse; Medical Record Technician; Nuclear Medicine Technologist; Occupational Therapist; Pharmacist; Physical Therapist; Physician; Radiologic Technologist; Recreational Therapist; Registered Nurse; Respiratory Therapist; Social Worker; Stationary Engineer; Surgical Technician. **Benefits:** Dental Insurance; Disability Coverage; Employee Discounts; Life Insurance; Medical Insurance; Pension Plan; Tuition Assistance. **Corporate headquarters location:** This Location. **Number of employees at this location:** 1,400.

SURVIVAL TECHNOLOGY, INC.
CORPORATE OFFICES
2275 Research Boulevard, Rockville MD 20850. 301/216-2915. **Fax:** 301/926-1800. **Contact:** Doris L. Geier, Corporate Director of Human Resources. **Description:** STI is a worldwide leader in auto-injector technology. The auto-injector contains a concealed needle and automatically injects a controlled dose of medication at the required depth. STI supplies a number of products to the U.S. Department of Defense and allied governments. More than three million auto-injectors were shipped during Operation Desert Storm. Since Desert Storm, there continues to be a heightened awareness of the worldwide nerve gas threat. The requirements of battlefield medicine present a variety of applications for auto-injector technology. STI offers a wide array of research and development services, including formulation and analytical methods development, device and drug clinical materials, stability batch production, process validation and pilot plant/manufacturing scale-up. STI can also design a device to fit the unique requirements of a customer's drug. With a 110,000 square foot FDA-licensed manufacturing facility in St. Louis, STI is equipped to aseptically fill auto-injectors, syringes and vials with a customer's product. STI can then inspect, label, package and ship the finished units to U.S. or international destinations. STI's facility is fully validated in accordance with Good Manufacturing Practices and is licensed to produce Schedules II, IV and V Controlled Substances.

UNITED STATES DEPARTMENT OF VETERANS AFFAIRS MEDICAL CENTER
50 Irving Street NW, 05-A, Washington DC 20422. 202/745-8204. **Recorded Jobline:** 202/745-8000x1. **Contact:** Human Resources. **Description:** The Department of Veterans Affairs (VA) was established March 15, 1989 to resume responsibility for providing federal benefits to veterans and their dependents. Headed by the Secretary of Veterans Affairs, VA is the second largest of the 14 cabinet departments and operates nationwide programs of health care, assistance services and national cemeteries. The most visible of all VA benefits and services is its health care system, the largest in the nation. From 54 hospitals in 1930, the VA health care system has grown to include 171 medical centers; more than 364 outpatient, community and outreach clinics; 130 nursing home care units and 37 domiciliaries. VA operates at least one medical center in each of the 48 contiguous states, Puerto Rico and the District of Columbia. With approximately 76,000 medical center beds, VA treats nearly a million patients in VA hospitals, 75,000 in nursing home care units and 25,000 in domiciliaries. VA's outpatient clinics register approximately 24 million visits a year.

Health Care: Services, Equipment and Products/211

UNITED STATES DEPARTMENT OF VETERANS AFFAIRS MEDICAL CENTER
10 North Greene Street, Baltimore MD 21201-1524. 410/605-7001. **Contact:** Human Resources. **Description:** The Department of Veterans Affairs (VA) was established March 15, 1989 to resume responsibility for providing federal benefits to veterans and their dependents. Headed by the Secretary of Veterans Affairs, VA is the second largest of the 14 cabinet departments and operates nationwide programs of health care, assistance services and national cemeteries. The most visible of all VA benefits and services is VA's health care system, the largest in the nation. From 54 hospitals in 1930, the VA health care system has grown to include 171 medical centers; more than 364 outpatient, community and outreach clinics; 130 nursing home care units and 37 domicilaries. VA operates at least one medical center in each of the 48 contiguous states, Puerto Rico and the District of Columbia. With approximately 76,000 medical center beds, VA treats nearly a million patients in VA hospitals, 75,000 in nursing home care units and 25,000 in domiciliaries. VA's outpatient clinics register approximately 24 million visits a year.

UNIVERSITY OF MARYLAND MEDICAL CENTER
22 South Greene Street, Baltimore MD 21201. **Contact:** Employment Manager. **Description:** An academic medical center. Clinical care is enhanced by on-going research. State-of-the-art facilities offer patients access to the most advanced diagnostic equipment. **Number of employees nationwide:** 4,000.

VISITING NURSE ASSOCIATION OF WASHINGTON DC
5151 Wisconsin Avenue NW, Suite 400, Washington DC 20016. 202/686-8723. **Contact:** Human Resources Specialist. **Description:** A home health care organization providing skilled nursing care to patients in their homes. Serves the District of Columbia, and Montgomery and Prince George's Counties in Maryland. Several area locations. **Common positions include:** Account Executive; Accountant/Auditor; Administrative Worker/Clerk; Health Services Worker; Occupational Therapist; Physical Therapist; Registered Nurse; Social Worker. **Educational backgrounds include:** M.D./Medicine. **Benefits:** Dental Insurance; Disability Coverage; Life Insurance; Medical Insurance; Pension Plan; Savings Plan; Tuition Assistance. **Corporate headquarters location:** This Location.

WASHINGTON COUNTY HOSPITAL ASSOCIATION
251 East Antietam Street, Hagerstown MD 21740-5771. 301/790-8000. **Contact:** Human Resources. **Description:** An acute care, non-profit, regional medical center, Washington County Hospital serves a tri-state region, including western Maryland, southern Pennsylvania, and northern West Virginia. Designated the Region II Trauma Center by the State of Maryland, it is served by nearly 200 physicians who represent more than 30 sub-specialties and more than 1,500 employees, making it one of the largest health care providers in western Maryland. The Washington County Hospital association includes: 371-bed facilities; Region II Trauma Center; Intensive Care, Coronary Care, and Progressive Care Units; a Cardiac Catheterization Lab; a Family Birthing Center; a full range of Radiologic/diagnostic services; a Pediatric Unit; In- and Out- Patient Mental health Units/Services; a certified Oncology Program; extended care facilities; Alzheimer's Disease & related disorders programs; Cardiac Rehabilitation; community education programs; physician practices; and home health care.

WASHINGTON HOSPITAL CENTER
110 Irving Street NW, Washington DC 20010-2975. 202/877-7000. **Contact:** Human Resources. **Description:** Washington Hospital Center, a not-for-profit member of Medlantic, employs 5,100 employees and 1,402-member medical and dental staff as well as over 230 physicians in 36 residents. Washington Heart at Washington Hospital annually performs almost 1,700 heart operations and more than 10,000 cardiac catheterization procedures. The Washington Cancer Institute provides cancer care including surgical, radiation and chemotherapy treatments, counseling, education and community outreach. Washington Hospital Center is the home of the MedSTAR trauma unit whose two helicopters transport more than 3,000 critically ill and injured patients each year. The Center also consists of The Institute for Asthma & Allergy, a burn center, women's services, and the Washington National Eye Center. **Parent company:** Medlantic.

212/The Metropolitan Washington JobBank

Note: Because addresses and telephone numbers of smaller companies change rapidly, we recommend you call each company to verify the information below before inquiring about job opportunities. Mass mailings are not recommended.

Additional employers with over 250 employees:

DOCTORS' OFFICES AND CLINICS

Georgetown University Medical Center
3800 Reservoir Rd Nw, Washington DC 20007-2196. 202/687-4952.

NURSING AND PERSONAL CARE FACILITIES

Meridian Healthcare Inc.
515 Fairmount Ave, Baltimore MD 21286-5466. 410/296-1000.

Union Memorial Hospital
201 E University Pky, Baltimore MD 21218. 410/554-2000.

HOSPITALS AND MEDICAL CENTERS

Calvert Memorial Hospital
100 Hospital Rd, Prnc Frederck MD 20678-4017. 410/535-4000.

Dimensions Health Corporation
9200 Basil Ct Ste 500, Hyattsville MD 20785-5309. 301/925-7000.

Eastern Shore Hospital Center
POB 800, Cambridge MD 21613. 410/228-0800.

HCA Reston Hospital Center
1850 Town Center Pkwy, Reston VA 22090. 703/689-9023.

Potomac Hospital
2300 Opitz Blvd, Woodbridge VA 22191-3398. 703/670-1313.

Union Hospital Of Cecil County
106 Singerly Ave, Elkton MD 21921-5596. 410/398-4000.

Upper Chesapeake Hlth. Systems
1916 Bel Air Rd, Fallston MD 21047-2742. 410/893-0322.

Hospice Of Northern Virginia
4715 15th St N, Arlington VA 22205-2699. 703/525-7070.

Saint Luke Institute
2420 Brooks Dr, Suitland MD 20746-1100. 301/967-3700.

Hospital For Sick Children
1731 Bunker Hill Rd Ne, Washington DC 20017-3096. 202/635-6125.

Deer's Head Center
PO Box 2018, Salisbury MD 21802-2018. 410/543-4000.

Psychiatric Institute Of Washington
4228 Wisconsin Ave Nw, Washington DC 20016-2138. 202/965-8550.

Deaton Hospital & Medical Center
611 S Charles St, Baltimore MD 21230-3801. 410/547-8500.

Sinai Hospital Of Baltimore
2401 W Belvedere Ave, Baltimore MD 21215-5271. 410/578-5678.

Gundry-Glass Hospital
2 N Wickham Rd, Baltimore MD 21229-3399. 410/347-3200.

Child Natl. Medical Ctr. At Fairfax
3022 Williams Dr, Fairfax VA 22031-4600. 703/573-9383.

District Of Columbia General Hospital
19th St & Massachusetts Ave Se, Washington DC 20003. 202/675-5000.

Howard University Hospital
2041 Georgia Ave Nw, Washington DC 20060-0001. 202/865-6100.

Rappahannock General Hospital
PO Box 1449, Kilmarnock VA 22482-1449. 804/435-8000.

Sacred Heart Hospital
900 Seton Dr, Cumberland MD 21502-1850. 301/759-4200.

Shady Grove Adventist Hospital
9901 Medical Center Dr, Rockville MD 20850-3395. 301/279-6000.

SPECIALTY OUTPATIENT FACILITIES

Church Hospital Corporation
100 N Broadway, Baltimore MD 21231. 410/522-8000.

Clinical Center National Institute of Health
9000 Rockville Pike, Bethesda MD 20892-0001. 301/496-3227.

Hadley Memorial Hospital
4601 Martin Luther King Jr Ave, Washington DC 20032-1199. 202/574-5700.

Loudoun Hospital Center
224 Cornwall St Nw, Leesburg VA 22075-2799. 703/777-3300.

Montebello Rehabilitation Hospital
2201 Argonne Dr, Baltimore MD 21218-1627. 410/554-5200.

Liberty Medical Center
2600 Liberty Heights Ave, Baltimore MD 21215-7892. 410/383-4000.

Washington Adventist Hospital
7600 Carroll Ave, Takoma Park MD 20912-6392. 301/891-7600.

Arlington Hospital
1701 N George Mason Dr, Arlington VA 22205-3698. 703/558-5000.

Culpeper Memorial Hospital
PO Box 592, Culpeper VA 22701-0592. 703/829-4100.

Fairfax Hospital
3300 Gallows Rd, Falls Church VA 22042-3352. 703/698-1110.

Mary Washington Hospital
2300 Fall Hill Ave, Fredericksbrg VA 22401-3354. 703/899-1100.

HEALTH AND ALLIED SERVICES

PHP Healthcare Corp.
4900 Seminary Rd 12th Floor, Alexandria VA 22311-1811. 703/998-7808.

Health Care: Services, Equipment and Products

SOCIAL SERVICES AT HOSPITALS

Prince William Hospital
PO Box 2610, Manassas VA 22110-0867. 703/369-8000.

Fauquier Hospital
500 Hospital Dr, Warrenton VA 22186-3099. 703/347-2550.

MEDICAL EQUIPMENT

Kirschner Medical Corp.
9690 Deereco Rd Ste 600, Luthvle Timon MD 21093-6902. 410/560-3333.

Additional employers with under 250 employees:

MEDICAL EQUIPMENT AND SUPPLIES WHOLESALE

Asco Healthcare Inc.
9515 Gerwig Ln, Columbia MD 21046-1576. 410/381-7600.

Asco Retail Columbia
9515 Gerwig Ln, Columbia MD 21046-1576. 410/381-3663.

Hologic Inc.
5905 Sir Cambridge Way, Alexandria VA 22315-4722. 703/922-8234.

Roberts Home Medical
13309 Baltimore Ave, Laurel MD 20707-9234. 301/470-4822.

Technicare Corporation
2000 Century Plaza, Columbia MD 21044. 410/997-4155.

Recovery Room
Easton Plaza, Easton MD 21601. 410/822-4323.

Toshiba America Medical Systems
9030 Red Branch Rd, Columbia MD 21045-2116. 410/992-3435.

DOCTORS' OFFICES AND CLINICS

American Psych. Management Inc.
1560 Wilson Blvd Ste 1000, Arlington VA 22209-2409. 703/528-2255.

DENTISTS' OFFICES AND CLINICS

Periodontal Associates
180 Admiral Cochrane Dr, Annapolis MD 21401-7366. 410/224-8606.

OFFICES AND CLINICS OF HEALTH PRACTITIONERS

Allegany Optical
19336 Leitersburg Pike, Hagerstown MD 21742-1495. 301/733-4944.

United Optical
Twilley Centre, Delmar MD 21875. 410/742-6148.

Burch Rhoads & Loomis
22 Truck House Rd, Severna Park MD 21146-2728. 410/544-5883.

Freestate Rehabilitation Agency
22 Truck House Rd, Severna Park MD 21146-2728. 410/544-0170.

Henning & Cole Therapy Associates
1922 Greenspring Dr Ste 7, Timonium MD 21093-7603. 410/560-2700.

Rehabilitation Associates MD Inc.
7505 Greenway Center Dr # 301, Greenbelt MD 20770-3507. 301/474-2425.

Norrell Health Care
692 Ritchie Hwy, Severna Park MD 21146-3938. 410/544-9602.

NURSING AND PERSONAL CARE FACILITIES

Althea Woodland Nursing Home
1000 Daleview Dr, Silver Spring MD 20901-3698. 301/434-2646.

Armacost Nursing Home
812 Regester Ave, Baltimore MD 21239-1398. 410/377-5225.

Ashburton Nursing Home
3520 Hilton Rd, Baltimore MD 21215-7495. 410/466-2400.

Bedford Court/A Marriott Senior Living
3701 International Dr, Silver Spring MD 20906-1556. 301/598-2900.

Belvoir Woods Assisted Living
9160 Belvoir Woods Pky, Fort Belvoir VA 22060-2703. 703/799-1333.

Berlin Nursing Home
US 50 & Rt 113, Berlin MD 21811. 410/641-4400.

Brevin Nursing Home
421 S Union Ave, Hvre De Grace MD 21078-3394. 410/939-1740.

Brighton Manor Nurse & Geriatric Center
1501 N Dukeland St, Baltimore MD 21216-4098. 410/945-7433.

Brooke Grove Nursing Home
18430 Brooke Grove Rd, Olney MD 20832. 301/924-5176.

Caroline Nursing Home
Rt 404, Denton MD 21629. 410/479-2130.

Chapel Hill Convalescent Home
Liberty & Robosson Rds, Randallstown MD 21133. 410/922-2443.

Chestertown Nursing and Rehabilitation
415 Morgnec Rd, Chestertown MD 21620-1046. 410/778-1900.

Church Home Corporation
101 N Bond St, Baltimore MD 21231-1535. 410/732-0456.

Circle Manor Nursing Home
10231 Carroll Pl, Kensington MD 20895-3399. 301/949-0230.

Clearview Nursing Home
9946 Downsville Pike, Hagerstown MD 21740-1727. 301/582-1654.

Coffman Nursing Home
1304 Pennsylvania Ave, Hagerstown MD 21742-3108. 301/733-2914.

Collington Episcopal Life Care
10450 Lottsford Rd, Mitchellville MD 20721-2734. 301/731-6040.

Colonial Villa
12325 New Hampshire Ave, Silver Spring MD 20904-2997. 301/622-4600.

Desting Rest Home
735 E Church St, Salisbury MD 21801-4354. 410/546-8197.

Devine Haven Nursing Home
224 E Main St, Elkton MD 21921-5716. 410/575-7136.

Edenwald
800 Southerly Rd, Baltimore MD 21286-8403. 410/339-6000.

Eagle Nursing Home
57 Jackson St, Lonaconing MD 21539-1397. 301/463-5451.

Fairland Nursing Center
2101 Fairland Rd, Silver Spring MD 20904-5498. 301/384-6161.

Gladys Spellman Nursing Center
2900 Mercy Ln, Cheverly MD 20785-1157. 301/618-2010.

Glasgow Nursing Home
311 Glenburn Ave, Cambridge MD 21613-1599. 410/228-3780.

Golden Age Guest Home
1442 Buckhorn Rd, Sykesville MD 21784-9303. 410/795-2737.

Golden Touch Care Center Inc.
740 W Lafayette Ave, Baltimore MD 21217-2920. 410/342-6644.

Hillhaven Nursing Center
3210 Powder Mill Rd, Adelphi MD 20783-1098. 301/937-3939.

Holly Hill Manor
531 Stevenson Ln, Baltimore MD 21286-7699. 410/823-5310.

Jefferson/A Marriott Senior Living
900 N Taylor St, Arlington VA 22203-1858. 703/351-0011.

Kensington Gardens Nurse & Rehabilitation
3000 McComas Ave, Kensington MD 20895-2399. 301/933-0060.

Key Circle Hospice
4915 Holder Ave, Baltimore MD 21214-3012. 410/319-9557.

Knollwood Manor Nursing Home
899 Cecil Ave, Millersville MD 21108-2111. 410/987-1644.

Little Sisters of The Poor
4200 Harewood Rd Ne, Washington DC 20017-1550. 202/269-1831.

Lorein Frankford Nurse & Rehabilitation
5009 Frankford Ave, Baltimore MD 21206-5353. 410/325-4000.

Louise Lisner Dickson Home
5425 Western Ave Nw, Washington DC 20015-2931. 202/966-6667.

Magnolia Hall Nurse & Convalescence
200 Morgnec Rd, Chestertown MD 21620-1026. 410/778-4550.

Manokin Manor
11974 Edgehill Terrace Rd, Princess Anne MD 21853-2100. 410/543-4697.

Maryland Baptist Aged Home Inc.
2801 Rayner Ave, Baltimore MD 21216-4696. 410/945-7650.

Maryland Manor Glen Burnie Inc.
7575 E Howard Rd, Glen Burnie MD 21060-8399. 410/768-8200.

Medical Facilities of America
763 Madison Rd, Culpeper VA 22701-3342. 703/825-4261.

Melchor Nursing Home
2327 N Charles St, Baltimore MD 21218-5172. 410/235-8997.

Meridian Healthcare Center
3227 Bel Pre Rd, Silver Spring MD 20906-2423. 301/871-2000.

Meridian Healthcare Center
35 Milkshake Ln, Annapolis MD 21403-1507. 410/269-5100.

Meridian Nurse Center
16 Fusting Ave, Baltimore MD 21228-4413. 410/747-1800.

Meridian Nursing Center
9109 Liberty Rd, Randallstown MD 21133-3521. 410/655-7373.

Milford Manor Nursing Home
4204 Old Milford Mill Rd, Baltimore MD 21208-6075. 410/486-1500.

North Oaks
725 Mount Wilson Ln, Baltimore MD 21208-1105. 410/484-7300.

Oak Meadow Inc.
1510 Collingwood Rd, Alexandria VA 22308-1698. 703/765-6107.

Park Manor Nursing Home
1802 Eutaw Pl, Baltimore MD 21217-3899. 410/523-4370.

Queen Annes Hospice
206 N Commerce St, Centreville MD 21617-1015. 410/758-3043.

Ravenwood Lutheran Village
1183 Luther Dr, Hagerstown MD 21740-7490. 301/790-1000.

Saint Joseph's Nursing Home
1222 Tugwell Dr, Baltimore MD 21228-5897. 410/747-0026.

Sharon Nursing Home
18201 Marden Lane, Olney MD 20832. 301/924-4020.

Solomons Nursing Center
30 Church St, Prnc Frederck MD 20678-4115. 410/535-0984.

Tappahannock Manor
Marsh St, Tappahannock VA 22560. 804/746-1491.

The Harrison House
430 W Market St, Snow Hill MD 21863-1197. 410/632-3755.

The Kenesaw Nursing Home Inc.
2601 Roslyn Ave, Baltimore MD 21216-2299. 410/466-3900.

The Wesley Home Inc.
2211 W Rogers Ave, Baltimore MD 21209-4424. 410/664-4006.

Trinity Geriatric Center
7600 Clays Ln, Baltimore MD 21244-2050. 410/298-1400.

Vantage House
5400 Vantage Point Rd, Columbia MD 21044-2681. 410/964-5454.

Mount Vernon Nursing Center
8111 Tis Well Dr, Alexandria VA 22306-3297. 703/360-4000.

Walls' In Home Care
9901 Councell Rd, Cordova MD 21625-2517. 410/822-5389.

William Hill Health Care Center
525 Glenburn Ave, Cambridge MD 21613-1414. 410/476-5204.

Williamsport Nursing Home
154 N Artizan St, Williamsport MD 21795-1104. 301/223-7971.

Health Care: Services, Equipment and Products/215

Annapolis Nursing & Conval Center
900 Van Buren Dr, Annapolis MD 21403-2124. 410/267-8653.

Bayview Nursing Facility
5200 Eastern Ave, Baltimore MD 21224-2736. 410/550-2933.

Bowling Green Health Care Center
120 Anderson Ave, Bowling Green VA 22427-9401. 804/633-4839.

Brookwood Nursing Home
140 Andrew Chapel Rd, Stafford VA 22554-5520. 703/659-4670.

Cherrywood Extended Care Center
12020 Reisterstown Rd, Reisterstown MD 21136-3089. 410/833-3974.

Friends Nursing Home
17340 Quaker Ln, Sandy Spring MD 20860-1247. 301/924-4900.

Goodwill Mennonite Home
Dorsey Hotel Rd, Grantsville MD 21536. 301/895-5194.

Harbor Hospital Center
3001 S Hanover St, Baltimore MD 21225-1290. 410/347-3089.

Kent County Hospice Home Health
125 Lynchburg St, Chestertown MD 21620. 410/778-1050.

Mountain View Nursing Home
HC 5 Box 186, Aroda VA 22709-9709. 703/948-6831.

Rappahannock Westminster
10 Lancaster Dr, Irvington VA 22480-9740. 804/438-4000.

Roland Park Place
830 W 40th St, Baltimore MD 21211-2115. 410/243-5800.

Thomas House
1330 Massachusetts Ave Nw, Washington DC 20005-4155. 202/628-3844.

Vindobona Nursing Home
PO Box 318, Braddock Hts MD 21714-0318. 301/371-7160.

Wicomico Nursing Home
PO Box 2378, Salisbury MD 21802-2378. 410/742-8896.

Carr Hill Nursing Home
5040 Plank Rd, Fredericksbrg VA 22407-6647. 703/786-4549.

Northern VA Healthcare Center
8605 Centreville Rd, Manassas VA 22110-5265. 703/257-6200.

HOSPITALS AND MEDICAL CENTERS

Baltimore Industrial Medical Center
1419 Knecht Ave, Baltimore MD 21227-1442. 410/247-9595.

Edward W. McCready Memorial Hospital
201 Hall Hwy, Crisfield MD 21817-1237. 410/968-1200.

Gundry-Glass Hospital
PO Box 1777, Baltimore MD 21203-1777. 410/484-2700.

Hospice of Northern Virginia
4715 15th St N, Arlington VA 22205-2699. 703/525-7070.

New Beginnings At Warwick Manor
3680 Warwick Rd, E New Market MD 21631-1420. 410/943-8108.

HOME HEALTH CARE SERVICES

Supportive Lifeline
2512 N Charles St, Baltimore MD 21218-4601. 410/235-7346.

Central VA Home Theraputics Inc.
312 Progress St, Fredericksbrg VA 22401-3356. 703/372-1493.

Kimberly Home Health Care Inc.
8630 Fenton St, Silver Spring MD 20910-3803. 301/587-7788.

Prince William Hosp Home Health
8650 Sudley Rd, Manassas VA 22110-4416. 703/369-8448.

SPECIALTY OUTPATIENT FACILITIES

Alternatives
920 Market St, Denton MD 21629-1149. 410/479-2798.

Center for Psychc. & Addiction
8700 Sudley Rd, Manassas VA 22110-4405. 703/369-8464.

HEALTH AND ALLIED SERVICES

American International Health Care
30 W Gude Dr, Rockville MD 20850-1161. 301/251-8600.

Baltimore Medical System Inc.
1101 Edison Hwy, Baltimore MD 21213-4020. 410/732-8800.

Birch & Davis Associates
8905 Fairview Rd Ste 300, Silver Spring MD 20910-4147. 301/589-6760.

MEDICAL EQUIPMENT

Cryomedical Sciences
1300 Piccard Dr Ste 102, Rockville MD 20850-4303. 301/417-7070.

Ohmeda
9065 Guilford Rd Ste A, Columbia MD 21046-1836. 410/381-2555.

For more information on career opportunities in the health care industry:

Associations

AMERICAN ACADEMY OF FAMILY PHYSICIANS
8880 Ward Parkway, Kansas City MO 64114. 816/333-9700. Promotes continuing education for family physicians.

AMERICAN ACADEMY OF PHYSICIAN ASSISTANTS
950 North Washington Street, Alexandria VA 22314. 703/836-2272. Promotes the use of physician assistants.

AMERICAN ASSOCIATION FOR CLINICAL CHEMISTRY
2101 Lovely Street NW, Suite 202, Washington, DC 20037-1526. 202/857-0717. A non-profit association for clinical, chemical, medical, and technical doctors.

AMERICAN ASSOCIATION OF COLLEGES OF OSTEOPATHIC MEDICINE
6110 Executive Boulevard, Suite 405, Rockville MD 20852. 301/468-2037. Provides applications processing services for colleges of osteopathic medicine.

AMERICAN ASSOCIATION OF COLLEGES OF PODIATRIC MEDICINE
1350 Piccard Drive, Suite 322, Rockville MD 20850. 301/990-7400. Provides applications processing services for colleges of podiatric medicine.

AMERICAN ASSOCIATION OF DENTAL SCHOOLS
1625 Massachusetts Avenue NW, Washington DC 20036. 202/667-9433.

AMERICAN ASSOCIATION OF MEDICAL ASSISTANTS
20 North Wacker Drive, Suite 1575, Chicago IL 60606. 312/899-1500.

AMERICAN ASSOCIATION OF NURSE ANESTHETISTS
222 South Prospect Avenue, Park Ridge IL 60068-4001. 708/692-7050.

AMERICAN ASSOCIATION FOR RESPIRATORY CARE
11030 Ables Lane, Dallas TX 75229-4593. 214/243-2272. Promotes the art and science of respiratory care, while focusing on the needs of the patients.

AMERICAN CHIROPRACTIC ASSOCIATION
1701 Clarendon Boulevard, Arlington VA 22209. 703/276-8800.

AMERICAN COLLEGE OF HEALTHCARE ADMINISTRATORS
325 South Patrick Street, Alexandria VA 22314. 703/549-5822.

AMERICAN COLLEGE OF HEALTHCARE EXECUTIVES
One North Franklin, Suite 1700, Chicago IL 60606. 312/424-2800.

AMERICAN DENTAL ASSOCIATION
211 East Chicago Avenue, Chicago IL 60611. 312/440-2500.

AMERICAN DENTAL HYGIENISTS ASSOCIATION
Division of Professional Development, 444 North Michigan Avenue, Suite 3400, Chicago IL 60611. 312/440-8900.

AMERICAN DIETETIC ASSOCIATION
216 West Jackson Boulevard, Chicago IL 60606-6995. 312/899-0040 or 800/877-1600. Promotes optimal nutrition to improve public health and well-being.

AMERICAN MEDICAL ASSOCIATION
515 North State Street, Chicago IL 60610. 312/464-5000. An organization for medical doctors.

AMERICAN HEALTH INFORMATION MANAGEMENT ASSOCIATION
919 North Michigan Avenue, Suite 1400, Chicago IL 60611. 312/787-2672.

AMERICAN MEDICAL TECHNOLOGISTS
710 Higgins Road, Park Ridge IL 60068. 708/823-5169.

AMERICAN NURSES ASSOCIATION
600 Maryland Avenue SW, Suite 100W, Washington DC 20024-2571. 202/554-4444.

AMERICAN OCCUPATIONAL THERAPY ASSOCIATION
4720 Montgomery Lane, Bethesda MD 20824-1220. 301/652-2682. 800/377-8555. Fax: 301/652-7711.

AMERICAN OPTOMETRIC ASSOCIATION
243 North Lindbergh Boulevard, St. Louis MO 63141. 314/991-4100. Offers publications, discounts, and insurance programs for members.

AMERICAN PHYSICAL THERAPY ASSOCIATION
1111 North Fairfax Street, Alexandria VA 22314. 703/684-2782. Small fee required for information.

AMERICAN VETERINARY MEDICAL ASSOCIATION
1931 North Meacham Road, Suite 100, Schaumburg IL 60173-4360. 708/925-8070. Provides a forum for the discussion of issues of importance to the veterinary profession, and for the development of official positions.

NATIONAL MEDICAL ASSOCIATION
1012 Tenth Street NW, Washington DC 20001. 202/347-1895.

NATIONAL PHARMACEUTICAL COUNCIL
1894 Preston White Drive, Reston VA 22091. 202/620-6390. Fax: 703/476-0904. Fax requests to the attention of Pat Adams, Vice President of Finance and Administration.

Directories

ENCYCLOPEDIA OF MEDICAL ORGANIZATIONS AND AGENCIES
Gale Research Inc., 835 Penobscot Building, Detroit MI 48226. 313/961-2242.

HEALTH ORGANIZATIONS OF THE UNITED STATES, CANADA, AND THE WORLD
Gale Research Inc., 835 Penobscot Building, Detroit MI 48226. 313/961-2242.

MEDICAL AND HEALTH INFORMATION DIRECTORY
Gale Research Inc., 835 Penobscot Building, Detroit MI 48226. 313/961-2242.

NATIONAL DIRECTORY OF HEALTH MAINTENANCE ORGANIZATIONS
Group Health Association of America, 1129 20th Street NW, Suite 600, Washington DC 20036. 202/778-3200.

Magazines

AMERICAN MEDICAL NEWS
American Medical Association, 515 North State Street, Chicago IL 60605. 312/464-5000.

CHANGING MEDICAL MARKETS
Theta Corporation, Theta Building, Middlefield CT 06455. 203/349-1054.

HEALTH CARE EXECUTIVE
American College of Health Care
Executives, One North Franklin, Suite 1700,
Chicago IL 60606. 312/424-2800.

MODERN HEALTHCARE
Crain Communications, 740 North Rush
Street, Chicago IL 60611. 312/649-5374.

NURSEFAX
Springhouse Corporation, 1111 Bethlehem
Pike, P.O. Box 908, Springhouse PA
19477. This is a jobline service designed to
be used in conjunction with *Nursing*
magazine.

HOTELS AND RESTAURANTS

Job opportunities in the restaurant industry are plentiful. A number of trends will boost job growth, including population growth, rising incomes, and more dual-income families. Some demand will be met through labor saving innovations like salad bars, untended meal stations, automated beverage stations, and central kitchens that serve a number of establishments in the same restaurant chain. In the fast-food sector, use of labor-saving technology is essential to remain competitive. Since most time consuming transaction at drive-in windows is making change, some restaurants are experimenting with debit and credit cards to reduce transaction time. However, despite labor-saving innovations, the increased demand for services will increase the need for workers.

Jobs in hotels, motels and other lodging places will be plentiful throughout the next decade. Driving the growth will be many of the same trends affecting the restaurant industry, as well as low-cost airfares and foreign tourism in the U.S. Another hot trend: legalized gambling. The hotel and motel industry invests heavily in the gaming industry, and that has further fueled job growth. This growth will continue as hotels increasingly attract families by offering relatively inexpensive casino vacation packages.

The greatest growth is in all-suite properties and budget motels. Since they don't have restaurants, dining rooms, lounges, or kitchens, these properties offer few jobs for food and beverage workers, but jobs should be available for managers and assistant managers. The trend toward chain affiliated lodging places should provide managers with opportunities for advancement into general manager positions and corporate administrative jobs.

THE AMERICAN CAFE
4095 Powder Mill Pond, Beltsville MD 20705. 301/937-0653. **Fax:** 301/937-0654. **Contact:** Yogi Kumar, Director of Operations. **Description:** A cafe. **Common positions include:** Restaurant/Food Service Manager. **Educational backgrounds include:** Business Administration; Cooking. **Benefits:** Dental Insurance; Disability Coverage; Employee Discounts; Life Insurance; Medical Insurance; Profit Sharing. **Corporate headquarters location:** This Location. **Parent company:** Magic Restaurants, Inc. **Operations at this facility include:** Regional Headquarters. **Listed on:** NASDAQ. **Number of employees at this location:** 75. **Number of employees nationwide:** 800.

THE AMERICAN CAFE
227 Massachusetts Avenue Northeast, Washington DC 20002. 202/547-8500. **Contact:** Human Resources. **Description:** A cafe. **Common positions include:** Restaurant/Food Service Manager. **Educational backgrounds include:** Business Administration; Cooking. **Benefits:** Dental Insurance; Disability Coverage; Employee Discounts; Life Insurance; Medical Insurance; Profit Sharing. **Corporate headquarters location:** Beltsville MD. **Parent company:** Magie Restaurants, Inc. **Number of employees nationwide:** 800. **Listed on:** NASDAQ.

ARLTEC INC.
5530 Wisconsin Avenue, Suite 1230, Chevy Chase MD 20815. 301/656-1047. **Contact:** Human Resources Department. **Description:** A hotel management firm.

BETHESDA MARRIOTT HOTELS
5151 Pooks Hill Road, Bethesda MD 20814-5499. 301/897-9400. **Contact:** Human Resources Department. **Description:** Operates a chain of hotels and resorts.

CANTEEN CORPORATION
7650 Preston Drive, Landover MD 20785. 301/772-2424. **Contact:** Human Resources. **Description:** Operates a food and vending service, as well as several cafeterias.

CAPITOL HILTON
16th & K Streets NW, Washington DC 20036. 202/639-5769. **Fax:** 202/942-1393. **Recorded Jobline:** 202/639-5745. **Contact:** Melissa G. Storino, Employment Relations Coordinator. **Description:** A 543-room hotel. **Common positions include:** Accountant/Auditor; Hotel Manager/Assistant Manager; Mechanical Engineer. **Educational backgrounds include:** Accounting; Business Administration; Computer Science; Engineering; Finance; Hospitality/Restaurant; Marketing. **Benefits:** Dental Insurance; Disability Coverage; Employee Discounts; Life Insurance; Medical Insurance; Profit Sharing. **Corporate headquarters location:** Los Angeles CA. **Parent company:** Hilton Hotels Corporation. **Operations at this facility include:** Administration; Sales; Service. **Number of employees at this location:** 475.

CHESAPEAKE BAY SEAFOOD HOUSE
8027 Leesburg Pike, Suite 506, Vienna VA 22182. 703/827-0320. **Contact:** Becky Wedemeyer, Director of Human Resources. **Description:** Corporate offices for a restaurant chain. Currently operates 20 restaurants and will continue to expand in the Washington, DC market. **Common positions include:** Assistant Manager; Management Trainee. **Educational backgrounds include:** Business Administration; Hotel Administration. **Benefits:** Dental Insurance; Disability Coverage; Employee Discounts; Life Insurance; Medical Insurance; Pension Plan. **Special Programs:** Internships; Training Programs. **Corporate headquarters location:** This Location. **Operations at this facility include:** Administration; Research and Development.

CHOICE HOTELS INTERNATIONAL
10750 Columbia Pike, Silver Spring MD 20901. 800/348-2041. **Fax:** 301/681-8740. **Contact:** Employment Department. **Description:** An internationally franchised hotel company. **Common positions include:** Administrative Services Manager; Advertising Clerk; Buyer; Computer Operator; Computer Programmer; Computer Systems Analyst; Customer Service Representative; Financial Manager; Graphic Artist; Hotel Manager/Assistant Manager; Hotel/Motel Clerk; Marketing/Advertising/PR Manager; Property and Real Estate Manager; Public Relations Specialist; Purchasing Agent and Manager; Quality Control Supervisor; Receptionist; Secretary; Services Sales Representative; Travel Agent; Typist/Word Processor. **Educational backgrounds include:** Hospitality/Restaurant; Marketing. **Benefits:** Dental Insurance; Disability Coverage; Employee Discounts; Life Insurance; Medical Insurance; Pension Plan; Profit Sharing; Savings Plan; Tuition Assistance. **Corporate headquarters location:** This Location. **Parent company:** Manor Care, Inc. **Operations at this facility include:** Sales. **Listed on:** New York Stock Exchange. **Number of employees at this location:** 200. **Number of employees nationwide:** 350.

DAKA FOOD SERVICE MANAGEMENT, INC.
14th Street and Constitution Avenue NW, Washington DC 20560. 202/371-0726. **Contact:** Human Resources. **Description:** A food service company involved in servicing cafeterias. This restaurant is located in the Smithsonian Museum of Art History.

DOMINO'S TEAM WASHINGTON, INC.
817B Slatlers Lane, Alexandria VA 22314. 703/684-5000. **Contact:** Human Resources. **Description:** Owns a number of Domino's Pizza franchises.

DUPONT PLAZA HOTEL
1500 New Hampshire Avenue NW, Washington DC 20036. 202/483-6000. **Contact:** Elaine Lee, Human Resources. **Description:** A downtown hotel facility, with 314 rooms, banquet facilities, and a restaurant.

ENDEAVOR FOODS, INC.
P.O. Box 7680, Baltimore MD 21207. 410/298-3120. **Contact:** Jennifer Hughes, Manager of Administration. **Description:** Operates the franchise of Rax Restaurants, a chain of fast-food restaurants featuring roast beef and specialty sandwiches. **Common positions include:** Management Trainee; Restaurant/Food Service Manager. **Educational

backgrounds include: Accounting; Business Administration; Economics; Marketing. Benefits: Life Insurance; Medical Insurance. Corporate headquarters location: This Location. Other U.S. locations: Belle Vernon PA; Uniontown PA. Listed on: Privately held. Number of employees nationwide: 50.

THE ENGLISH COMPANY
1123 South Division Street, Salisbury MD 21801. 410/742-9511. Contact: Human Resources. Description: A restaurant chain.

GUEST SERVICES
3055 Prosperity Avenue, Fairfax VA 22031. 703/849-9300. Contact: Personnel. Description: Manages a variety of contract food and hospitality services. Common positions include: Accountant/Auditor; Administrator; Claim Representative; Computer Programmer; Customer Service Representative; Dietician/Nutritionist; Electrical/Electronics Engineer; Hotel Manager/Assistant Manager; Human Resources Specialist; Industrial Engineer; Management Trainee; Manufacturer's/Wholesaler's Sales Rep.; Marketing Specialist; Mechanical Engineer; Operations/Production Manager; Public Relations Specialist. Benefits: Dental Insurance; Disability Coverage; Employee Discounts; Life Insurance; Medical Insurance; Pension Plan; Savings Plan; Tuition Assistance. Special Programs: Training Programs. Corporate headquarters location: This Location. Operations at this facility include: Regional Headquarters. Number of employees at this location: 80. Number of employees nationwide: 3,500.

HOLIDAY INN CROWNE PLAZA
1750 Rockville Pike, Rockville MD 20852. 301/468-1100. Recorded Jobline: 301/230-6770. Contact: Human Resources. Description: A 315-room hotel.

HOTEL HARRINGTON
436 11th Street NW, Washington DC 20004. 202/628-8140. Contact: Ann Terry, Personnel Manager. Description: A 300-room hotel, with dining and cocktail facilities; meeting rooms; and other facilities.

HOTEL WASHINGTON
515 15th Street NW, Washington DC 20004. 202/638-5900. Contact: Peggy Link, Director of Sales. Description: Operates a 350-room hotel, with three dining rooms. Common positions include: Accountant/Auditor; Credit Manager; General Manager; Hotel Manager/Assistant Manager; Public Relations Specialist; Services Sales Representative. Corporate headquarters location: Galveston TX.

HYATT REGENCY BALTIMORE INNER HARBOR
300 Light Street, Baltimore MD 21202. 410/528-1234. Contact: Human Resources. Description: A 487-room hotel. NOTE: Ask for job hotline extension.

HYATT REGENCY BETHESDA
1 Bethesda Metro Center, Bethesda MD 20814. 301/657-1234. Recorded Jobline: 301/657-6434. Contact: Human Resources. Description: A 380-room hotel. Ask for the job hotline extension.

HYATT REGENCY CRYSTAL CITY-NATIONAL AIRPORT
2799 Jefferson Davis Highway, Arlington VA 22202. 703/418-1234. Recorded Jobline: 703/418-7222. Contact: Human Resources. Description: A 685-room hotel.

HYATT REGENCY WASHINGTON ON CAPITOL HILL
400 New Jersey Avenue NW, Washington DC 20001. 202/737-1234. Fax: 202/942-1552. Recorded Jobline: 202/942-1586. Contact: Jason Salamon, Employment Manager. Description: An 834-room hotel. Common positions include: Accountant/Auditor; Credit Manager; Electrician; Human Resources Specialist; Mechanical Engineer; Restaurant/Food Service Manager. Educational backgrounds include: Accounting; Business Administration; Communications; Engineering; Hotel Administration. Benefits: 401K; Dental Insurance; Disability Coverage; Employee Discounts; Housing Allowance; Life Insurance; Medical Insurance; Tuition Assistance. Special Programs: Internships. Corporate headquarters location: Chicago IL. Other U.S. locations: Nationwide. Parent company: Hyatt Hotels Corporation. Operations at this facility include: Administration; Sales; Service. Number of employees at this location: 550. Number of employees nationwide: 40,000.

MARRIOTT INTERNATIONAL
One Marriott Drive, Department 93551, Washington DC 20058. **Recorded Jobline:** 301/380-1202. **Contact:** Staffing and Placement. **Description:** Operates and manages retail restaurants, hotels, and institutional food services. Also offers food and beverage concessions in airports; merchandise gift and specialty shops in airports, hotels, and resorts; brand food and retail concessions on turnpikes; food and beverage concessions in stadiums and arenas.

MARRIOTT METRO CENTER
775 12th Street NW, Washington DC 20005. 202/737-2200. **Recorded Jobline:** 202/737-2200x2031. **Contact:** Human Resources. **Description:** A 456-room hotel.

MARTIN'S INC.
6821 Dogwood Rd, Baltimore MD 21244-2608. 410/265-1300. **Description:** A catering company, primarily serving the Baltimore area. **Corporate headquarters location:** This Location.

McDONALD'S CORPORATION
3015 Williams Drive, Fairfax VA 22031. 703/698-4000. **Contact:** Paul Van Sickle, Personnel Director. **Description:** Regional offices for the worldwide developer, operator, franchiser, and servicer of a system of restaurants which process, package, and sell a limited menu of fast foods. Overall, the company is one of the largest restaurant chains, and the largest food service organization in the world, operating 6,000 McDonald's restaurants in all 50 states and in 26 foreign countries. **Corporate headquarters location:** Oak Brook IL. **Listed on:** New York Stock Exchange.

McLEAN HILTON AT TYSON'S CORNER
7920 Jones Branch Boulevard, McLean VA 22102. 703/847-5000. **Recorded Jobline:** 703/761-5155. **Contact:** Human Resources. **Description:** A 457-room hotel.

OMNI INNER HARBOR HOTEL
101 West Fayette Street, Baltimore MD 21201. 410/752-1100. **Recorded Jobline:** 410/385-6442. **Contact:** Human Resources. **Description:** A 702-room hotel.

OMNI SHOREHAM HOTEL
2500 Calvert Street, Washington DC 20008. 202/234-0700. **Fax:** 202/986-3468. **Recorded Jobline:** 202/483-1119. **Contact:** Deanne Johnson, Human Resources Manager. **Description:** A historic landmark in the nation's capital consisting of 770 rooms and 100,000 square feet of meeting space. **Common positions include:** Accountant/Auditor; Hotel Manager/Assistant Manager; Restaurant/Food Service Manager. **Benefits:** 401K; Dental Insurance; Employee Discounts; Life Insurance; Medical Insurance. **Special Programs:** Internships. **Number of employees at this location:** 538.

PHILLIPS FLAGSHIP RESTAURANT
900 Water Street Southwest, Washington DC 20024. 202/488-8515. **Contact:** Human Resources. **Description:** A restaurant.

RADISSON PLAZA HOTEL AT MARK CENTER
5000 Seminary Road, Alexandria VA 22311. 703/845-1010. **Recorded Jobline:** 703/845-7654. **Contact:** Human Resources. **Description:** A 500-room hotel.

RAMADA HOTEL TYSON'S
7801 Leesburg Pike, Falls Church VA 22043. 703/893-1340. **Recorded Jobline:** 703/821-3161. **Contact:** Human Resources. **Description:** A 404-room hotel.

RAMADA PLAZA HOTEL
10 Thomas Circle NW, Washington DC 20005. 202/842-1300. **Contact:** Personnel. **Description:** Operates a full-service hotel facility, with 300 rooms and complete dining facilities.

ROY ROGERS RESTAURANTS
A DIVISION OF HARDEE'S FOOD SYSTEMS
1099 Winterson Road, Linthicum Heights MD 21090-2215. 410/859-8822. **Fax:** 410/859-8665. **Contact:** Douglas Kramer, Regional Human Resource Manager. **Description:** A fast food restaurant chain. **Common positions include:** Restaurant/Food Service Manager. **Corporate headquarters location:** Rocky Mount NC. **Other U.S. locations:** Nationwide. **Parent company:** Imasco.

SERVICE AMERICA CORPORATION
Allegheny Circle, Cheverly MD 20781. 301/341-6200. **Contact:** Human Resources. **Description:** A food service company operating cafeterias and vending machines.

SERVICE AMERICA/NBSE
900 9th Street NW, Washington Convention Center, Washington DC 20001. 202/371-3135. **Contact:** Human Resources. **Description:** A food service company operating cafeterias and vending machines.

SHERATON/CARLTON HOTEL
923 16th Street NW, Washington DC 20006. 202/638-2626. **Contact:** Vivian Taylor, Director of Human Resources. **Description:** A downtown luxury hotel, with 197 rooms, 15 suites, and complete dining facilities. **Common positions include:** Accountant/Auditor; Administrative Worker/Clerk; Credit Manager; Customer Service Representative; Department Manager; Food Service Manager; General Manager; Hotel Manager/Assistant Manager; Human Resources Specialist; Management Trainee; Public Relations Specialist; Purchasing Agent and Manager; Restaurant/Food Service Manager; Sales Manager; Sales/Marketing Director; Systems Analyst; Training Director. **Educational backgrounds include:** Hospitality/Restaurant. **Benefits:** Dental Insurance; Disability Coverage; Employee Discounts; Life Insurance; Medical Insurance; Pension Plan; Profit Sharing; Savings Plan; Tuition Assistance. **Corporate headquarters location:** Boston MA.

SHERATON INNER HARBOR HOTEL
300 South Charles Street, Baltimore MD 21201. 410/962-8300. **Recorded Jobline:** 410/347-1808. **Contact:** Human Resources. **Description:** A 339-room hotel.

SHERATON PREMIERE AT TYSON'S CORNER
8661 Leesburg Pike, Vienna VA 22182. 703/448-1234. **Recorded Jobline:** 703/506-2518. **Contact:** Human Resources. **Description:** A 455-room hotel.

SHERATON WASHINGTON HOTEL
2660 Woodley Road NW, Washington DC 20008. 202/328-2909. **Fax:** 202/387-6658. **Recorded Jobline:** 202/328-5617. **Contact:** Debi Noerper, Employment Manager. **Description:** A 1,505-room hotel. **Common positions include:** Caterer; Guest Services Agent; Reservationist; Sales Representative. **Benefits:** Dental Insurance; Disability Coverage; Employee Discounts; Life Insurance; Medical Insurance; Savings Plan; Tuition Assistance. **Special Programs:** Internships. **Corporate headquarters location:** Boston MA. **Parent company:** ITT. **Operations at this facility include:** Administration; Sales; Service. **Number of employees at this location:** 900.

STOUFFER HARBORPLACE HOTEL
202 East Pratt Street, Baltimore MD 21202. 410/547-1200. **Recorded Jobline:** 410/752-1920. **Contact:** Human Resources. **Description:** A 662-room hotel.

WASHINGTON DC RENAISSANCE HOTEL
999 9th Street NW, Washington DC 20001. 202/898-9000. **Recorded Jobline:** 202/682-3456. **Contact:** Human Resources. **Description:** An 801-room hotel.

WASHINGTON HILTON AND TOWERS
1919 Connecticut Avenue NW, Washington DC 20009. 202/483-3000. **Recorded Jobline:** 202/797-5818. **Contact:** Frank Toncic, Director of Human Resources. **Description:** Operates a convention hotel with over 1,000 rooms and extensive meeting and function space. Hotel features complete dining and lounge facilities. Parent company is engaged in the operations and management of hotels and inns throughout the United States and the world, including more than 200 franchised hotels operating in the United States. **Common positions include:** Accountant/Auditor; Hotel Manager/Assistant Manager; Management Trainee. **Educational backgrounds include:** Hospitality/Restaurant; Restaurant Management. **Benefits:** Dental Insurance; Disability Coverage; Employee Discounts; Life Insurance; Medical Insurance; Pension Plan; Savings Plan. **Corporate headquarters location:** Beverly Hills CA. **Parent company:** Hilton Hotels Corporation. **Listed on:** New York Stock Exchange.

WILLARD INTER-CONTINENTAL
1401 Pennsylvania Avenue NW, Washington DC 20004. 202/628-9100. **Recorded Jobline:** 202/637-7445. **Contact:** Human Resources. **Description:** A 365-room hotel.

Note: Because addresses and telephone numbers of smaller companies change rapidly, we recommend you call each company to verify the information below before inquiring about job opportunities. Mass mailings are not recommended.

Additional employers with under 250 employees:

EATING PLACES

Adam's/The Place For Ribs
Rt 261 & Mears Av,
Chesapeak Bch MD 20732.
410/257-2427.

Applebee's Neighborhood Grill & Bar
14441 Brookfield Tower Dr,
Chantilly VA 22021-3718.
703/263-2667.

Boston Market
Southdale Shopping Ctr, Glen Burnie MD 21061. 410/760-2800.

Broadway-Payne Inc.
11 W North Ave, Baltimore MD 21201-5903. 410/752-0272.

Burger King
3 Metro Center, Bethesda MD 20814. 301/652-1229.

Burger King
9011 Snowden River Pky,
Columbia MD 21046-1657.
410/312-4988.

Carlos O'Kelly's Mexican Cafe
2306 Plank Rd, Fredericksbrg VA 22401-4902. 703/373-5436.

Chili's Grill & Bar
502 Bel Air Rd, Bel Air MD 21014-4305. 410/638-2992.

Chili's Grill & Bar
2936 Annandale Rd, Falls Church VA 22042-2147.
703/237-8532.

Crystal Dinery
1664 Crystal Square Arc,
Arlington VA 22202-3322.
703/920-3930.

Domino's Pizza
7502 Connelley Dr, Hanover MD 21076-1705. 410/553-0030.

Fritter's Restaurant
5745 Burke Centre Pky,
Burke VA 22015-2204.
703/239-9324.

Fritzbe's
7050 Columbia Pike,
Annandale VA 22003-3104.
703/354-4560.

Good Food Services
2209 Varnum St, Mount Rainier MD 20712-1457.
301/864-1780.

Great Occasions
1 Chesley Ave, Baltimore MD 21206-1002. 410/668-6283.

Harbor Cruises Ltd.
301 Light St, Baltimore MD 21202-1037. 410/727-3113.

Hard Time Cafe
1117 Nelson St, Rockville MD 20850-2030. 301/294-9720.

Hard Times Cafe
3028 Wilson Blvd, Arlington VA 22201-3810. 703/528-2233.

Kentucky Fried Chicken
2838 Jefferson Davis Hwy,
Stafford VA 22554-1784.
703/659-6106.

LFB Enterprises
7514 Ritchie Hwy, Glen Burnie MD 21061-3752.
410/760-0100.

Lone Star Steakhouse & Saloon
14220 Centreville Sq,
Centreville VA 22020-2398.
703/803-2974.

Long John Silver
11937 Lee Jackson Memorial Hwy, Fairfax VA 22033. 703/359-6098.

Olive Garden Italian Restaurant
14650 Baltimore Ave, Laurel MD 20707-4954. 301/498-0881.

Olive Garden Italian Restaurant
7501 Broken Branch Ln,
Manassas VA 22110-2657.
703/369-3635.

Philly Steaks & Burgers
Eastpoint Mall, Baltimore MD 21219. 410/288-2539.

Pizza Hut
5700 Pickwick Rd,
Centreville VA 22020-4730.
703/830-0801.

Pizza Hut
14215-K Centreville Sq,
Centreville VA 22020.
703/803-3333.

Roy Rogers Family Restaurants
530 Dundalk Ave, Baltimore MD 21224-2902. 410/633-7399.

Ruby Tuesday Restaurant
1003 Edwards Ferry Rd Ne,
Leesburg VA 22075-3347.
703/771-4008.

Sbarro The Italian Eatery
St Charles Town Center,
Waldorf MD 20603.
301/705-8115.

Soupmasters Restaurant
Towson Town Center,
Baltimore MD 21204.
410/337-8242.

Subway Sandwiches
9275 Baltimore National Pike, Ellicott City MD 21042-3943. 410/461-4710.

Taco Bell
6430 Freetown Rd, Columbia MD 21044-4051. 410/531-5611.

Taco Bell
543 Jefferson Davis Hwy,
Fredericksbrg VA 22401-4420. 703/371-2577.

TGI Friday's
13071 Worldgate Dr,
Herndon VA 22070-4374.
703/787-9630.

Wendy's Old Fashioned Hamburgers
2301 Plank Rd # A,
Fredericksbrg VA 22401-4901. 703/373-8886.

Wendys Old Fashioned Hamburgers
Pidgeon Hill Dr, Sterling VA 22170. 703/450-6976.

Baskin Robbins 31 Flavors
11700 Reisterstown Rd Ste A, Reisterstown MD 21136-3353. 410/833-3611.

Checkers Drive-Thru
1410 Crain Hwy N, Glen Burnie MD 21061-9303.
410/761-3830.

Domino's Pizza
6111 Franconia Rd,
Alexandria VA 22310-2508.
703/971-3033.

Little Caesars Pizza Arlington
5705 Lee Hwy, Arlington VA

22207-1424. 703/534-1100.

Nasha Inc.
1900 Fairfax Rd, Annapolis MD 21401-4341. 410/269-4258.

Key Largo Seafood & Steak House
20th & Coastal Hwy, Ocean City MD 21842. 410/723-4200.

HOTELS AND MOTELS

Barcelo Washington Hotel
2121 P St Nw, Washington DC 20037-1093. 202/293-3100.

Brookshire Inner Harbor Suite Hotel
120 E Lombard St, Baltimore MD 21202-5541. 410/625-1300.

Days Inn Baltimore Inner Harbor
100 Hopkins Pl, Baltimore MD 21201-2602. 410/576-1000.

Embassy Suites Hotel-Hunt Valley
213 International Cir, Cockys Ht Vly MD 21030-1388. 410/584-1400.

Guest Quarters Alexandria
100 S Reynolds St, Alexandria VA 22304-3199. 703/370-9600.

Historic Inns of Annapolis
16 Church Cir, Annapolis MD 21401-1993. 410/263-2641.

Hyatt Arlington
1325 Wilson Blvd, Arlington VA 22209-2301. 703/525-1234.

Ramada Renaissance Hotel
950 N Stafford St, Arlington VA 22203-1813. 703/528-6000.

Savoy Suites Hotel
2505 Wisconsin Ave Nw, Washington DC 20007-4575. 202/337-9700.

The Grand Hotel
2350 M St Nw, Washington DC 20037-1490. 202/429-0100.

The Hay-Adams Hotel
800 16th St Nw, Washington DC 20006-4168. 202/638-2260.

The Rosslyn Westpark Hotel
1900 Fort Myer Dr, Arlington VA 22209-1602. 703/527-4814.

Tremont Hotel
8 E Pleasant St, Baltimore MD 21202-2160. 410/576-1200.

Wyndham Bristol
2430 Pennsylvania Ave Nw, Washington DC 20037-1791. 202/955-6400.

Budget Beach Motel
Coastal Hwy & 32nd St, Ocean City MD 21842. 410/289-1808.

Comfort Inn of Tysons Corners
1587 Spring Hill Rd, Vienna VA 22182-2200. 703/448-8020.

Econo Lodge
I 95 Springfield Exit, Springfield VA 22150. 703/644-5311.

Embassy Suites Hotel
4300 Military Rd Nw, Washington DC 20015-2020. 202/362-9300.

Hampton Inn
10860 Lee Hwy, Fairfax VA 22030-4318. 703/385-2600.

Howard Johnson
5327 Jefferson Davis Hwy, Fredericksbrg VA 22408-2607. 703/898-1800.

Quality Inn Executive
6111 Arlington Blvd, Falls Church VA 22044-2708. 703/534-9100.

Red Roof Inn
827 Elkridge Landing Rd, Linthicum Hts MD 21090-2990. 410/850-7600.

Super 8 Motel
9150 Baltimore Ave, College Park MD 20740-1348. 301/474-0894.

Super 8 Motel
929 Pulaski Hwy, Hvre De Grace MD 21078-2601. 410/939-1880.

Annapolis Ramada Hotel
173 Jennifer Rd, Annapolis MD 21401-3043. 410/841-6385.

The Coconut Malorie Hotel
60th St In The Bay, Ocean City MD 21842. 410/723-6100.

The Tidewater Inn
101 E Dover St, Easton MD 21601-3001. 410/822-1300.

For more information on career opportunities in hotels and restaurants:

Associations

AMERICAN HOTEL AND MOTEL ASSOCIATION
1201 New York Avenue NW, Suite 600, Washington DC 20005-3931. 202/289-3100. Provides lobbying services and educational programs, maintains and disseminates industry data, and produces a variety of publications.

THE EDUCATIONAL FOUNDATION OF THE NATIONAL RESTAURANT ASSOCIATION
250 South Wacker Drive, 14th Floor, Chicago IL 60606. 312/715-1010. Offers educational products, including textbooks, manuals, instruction guides, manager and employee training programs, videos, and certification programs.

NATIONAL RESTAURANT ASSOCIATION
1200 17th Street NW, Washington DC 20036. 202/331-5900. Provides a number of services, including government lobbying, communications, research and information, and the Educational Foundation (see separate address).

Directories

DIRECTORY OF CHAIN RESTAURANT OPERATORS
Business Guides, Inc., Lebhar-Friedman, Inc., 3922 Coconut Palm Drive, Tampa FL 33619-8321. 813/664-6700.

DIRECTORY OF HIGH-VOLUME INDEPENDENT RESTAURANTS
Lebhar-Friedman, Inc., 3922 Coconut Palm Drive, Tampa FL 33619-8321. 813/664-6700.

Magazines

CORNELL HOTEL AND RESTAURANT ADMINISTRATION QUARTERLY
Cornell University School of Hotel Administration, Statler Hall, Ithaca NY 14853-6902. 607/255-9393.

HOTEL AND MOTEL MANAGEMENT
120 West 2nd Street, Duluth MN 55802. 218.

INNKEEPING WORLD
Box 84108, Seattle WA 98124. 206/362-7125.

NATION'S RESTAURANT NEWS
Lebhar-Friedman, Inc., 3922 Coconut Palm Drive, Tampa, FL 33619. 813/664-6700.

INSURANCE

What's the job picture in insurance? That depends upon which industry segment you're looking at. Health insurers, who avoided any Washington-based reforms in 1994, are reaping record profits, while property and casualty insurers are still trying to climb out from under the rocks that Mother Nature tossed their way. The California earthquake, snowstorms in the Northeast, floods in both the South and the West -- and especially a growing number of environmental claims made 1994 the property-casualty industry's second worst year in history. While property insurers still have huge cash reserves, many are now paying for cleanups of environmental sites, thanks to liability policies sold back in the '60s and '70s. Analysts expect that some of the burden on the property-casualty industry will be eased by higher premiums.

The life insurance segment is also under a dark cloud. The reputation of the entire industry suffered when Metropolitan Life Insurance agents illegally sold policies as retirement plans. According to Business Week, *the scandal was partly responsible for a four percent industry-wide decline in life insurance sales in 1994.*

The picture in health insurance is much brighter. By moving more and more consumers into managed care, insurers are benefitting from the economies of scale. Many of the biggest players in the insurance industry have moved into managed care ---- Metropolitan Life and Travelers Corporation, for example, combined health insurance operations into Metra Health in order to compete with leaders like CIGNA, Aetna, and Prudential.

AEGON USA, INC.
1111 North Charles Street, Baltimore MD 21201-5544. 410/576-4571. **Contact:** Patricia H. Wlodarczyk, Senior Administrator/Personnel. **Description:** AEGON USA operates through four groups encompassing 11 insurance divisions. The four groups are Agency, Asset Accumulation, Health, and Home Services. The Individual, Western Reserve Life, and Monumental Life Divisions sell life and health insurance products, mutual funds, and annuities. The Insurance Center administers group hospital expense insurance programs that are sold exclusively to the 300,000-plus members of the National Association for the Self-Employed. The NOL Division markets traditional and interest-sensitive life insurance and disability income products. Servicing the financial planning need of high income, high net worth clients, the Advanced Products Division offers products including estate planning, deferred compensation, capital transfer, and key-man programs. Offering plan design, participant communication programs, record-keeping services and technical guidance, the Diversified Investment Advisors service the retirement plan markets. The Financial Markets Division provides fixed and variable annuity products through national and state banks, savings and loans, and regional brokerage firms. Monumental General has seven business units, each with district objectives, including credit, Medicare Supplement, and accidental death insurance. The Long Term Care Division markets long-term care/nursing home products, including nursing home, home health, assisted living, and adult day-care services, while the Supplemental Insurance Division markets cancer, intensive care, long term care, and accident insurance products. **Corporate headquarters location:** The Netherlands. **Parent company:** AEGON Insurance Group.

ALLSTATE INSURANCE COMPANY
12150 East Monument Drive, Suite 600, Fairfax VA 22033. **Fax:** 703/218-0097. **Recorded Jobline:** 800/999-6693. **Contact:** Adrienne Snider, Human Resources. **Description:** One of the nation's largest insurance companies. **Common positions include:** Claim Representative; Education Administrator; Human Resources Specialist; Insurance Agent/Broker; Underwriter/Assistant Underwriter. **Benefits:** 401K; Dental Insurance; Disability Coverage; Life Insurance; Medical Insurance; Pension Plan; Profit Sharing; Tuition Assistance. **Corporate headquarters location:** Chicago IL. **Other U.S. locations:** Nationwide. **Operations at this facility include:** Regional Headquarters. **Number of employees at this location:** 2,000. **Number of employees nationwide:** 3,000.

AMERICAN CREDIT INDEMNITY COMPANY
100 East Pratt Street, Baltimore MD 21202. 410/554-0700. **Fax:** 410/554-0606. **Contact:** Stephen D. Sass, VP, Human Resources & Administration. **Description:** North America's largest provider of business credit insurance. **Educational backgrounds include:** Accounting; Finance; Marketing. **Parent company:** Dun & Bradstreet. **Operations at this facility include:** Administration. **Number of employees at this location:** 165. **Number of employees nationwide:** 285.

AVEMCO CORPORATION
411 Aviation Way, Frederick MD 21701. 301/694-5700. **Contact:** Shirley Shank, Personnel Director. **Description:** An aviation insurance company.

BALTIMORE LIFE INSURANCE COMPANY
10075 Red Run Boulevard, Owings Mills MD 21117. 410/581-6629. **Contact:** Rosalind McElrath, Assistant Vice President of Human Resources. **Description:** A mutual life insurance company. Product line includes individual life insurance products and annuities. **Common positions include:** Accountant/Auditor; Actuary; Administrator; Attorney; Claim Representative; Computer Programmer; Customer Service Representative; Human Resources Specialist; Insurance Agent/Broker; Systems Analyst; Underwriter/Assistant Underwriter. **Educational backgrounds include:** Accounting; Computer Science; Mathematics. **Benefits:** Dental Insurance; Disability Coverage; Life Insurance; Medical Insurance; Pension Plan; Tuition Assistance. **Special Programs:** Internships. **Corporate headquarters location:** This Location. **Operations at this facility include:** Service. **Number of employees at this location:** 193.

BANNER LIFE INSURANCE COMPANY
1701 Research Boulevard, Rockville MD 20850. 301/279-4128. **Contact:** Melissa MacMillan, Manager of Human Resources. **Description:** A life insurance company that specializes in individual life insurance products and annuities. **Common positions include:** Accountant/Auditor; Actuary; Attorney; Budget Analyst; Buyer; Claim Representative; Computer Programmer; Computer Systems Analyst; Customer Service Representative; Department Manager; General Manager; Human Resources Specialist; Marketing Specialist; Operations/Production Manager; Paralegal; Payroll Clerk; Public Relations Specialist; Purchasing Agent and Manager; Receptionist; Typist/Word Processor; Underwriter/Assistant Underwriter. **Educational backgrounds include:** Accounting; Business Administration; Communications; Computer Science; Finance; Liberal Arts; Marketing; Mathematics. **Benefits:** Dental Insurance; Disability Coverage; Life Insurance; Medical Insurance; Pension Plan; Profit Sharing; Savings Plan; Tuition Assistance. **Special Programs:** Internships. **Corporate headquarters location:** This Location. **Parent company:** Legal and General America. **Operations at this facility include:** Administration; Service. **Number of employees at this location:** 150.

BLUE CROSS & BLUE SHIELD OF MARYLAND
11447 Cronhill Drive, Owings Mills MD 21117-2270. 410/581-3500. **Contact:** Susan T. Slaysman, Employment and EEO Manager. **Description:** A comprehensive managed health care insurance company. **Common positions include:** Accountant/Auditor; Actuary; Attorney; Budget Analyst; Cashier; Claim Representative; Clerical Supervisor; Computer Operator; Computer Programmer; Customer Service Representative; Department Manager; Dietician/Nutritionist; Editor; EEG Technologist; EKG Technician; Emergency Medical Technician; Employment Interviewer; Financial Manager; Health Services Manager; Human Resources Specialist; Licensed Practical Nurse; Marketing Research Analyst; Marketing/Advertising/PR Manager; Medical Record Technician; Nuclear Medicine Technologist; Nursing Psychiatric Aide; Occupational Therapist; Optician; Paralegal; Payroll Clerk; Physical Therapist; Physician; Physician Assistant; Public Relations Specialist; Purchasing Agent and Manager; Radiologic Technologist; Receptionist; Registered Nurse; Respiratory Therapist; Sales Associate; Secretary;

Statistician; Systems Analyst; Technical Writer/Editor; Typist/Word Processor; Underwriter/Assistant Underwriter. **Educational backgrounds include:** Accounting; Business Administration; Computer Science; Economics; Finance; Marketing; Mathematics. **Corporate headquarters location:** This Location. **Operations at this facility include:** Administration; Sales; Service. **Number of employees at this location:** 3,000.

BLUE CROSS & BLUE SHIELD OF THE NATIONAL CAPITAL AREA
550 12th Street Southwest, Washington DC 20065. 202/479-7470. **Contact:** Recruiting. **Description:** An insurance organization administering health care coverage for private industry, government, and non-group subscribers. **Common positions include:** Accountant/Auditor; Actuary; Claim Representative; Computer Programmer; Marketing Specialist; Public Relations Specialist; Services Sales Representative; Systems Analyst. **Benefits:** Dental Insurance; Disability Coverage; Employee Discounts; Life Insurance; Medical Insurance. **Operations at this facility include:** Administration; Sales; Service. **Number of employees nationwide:** 2,400.

CAPITALCARE INC.
550 12th Street SW, Washington DC 20065. 703/761-5400. **Description:** Providers of health insurance.

CHESAPEAKE HEALTH PLAN
814 Light Street, Baltimore MD 21230-3945. 410/539-8622. **Description:** Providers of HMOs.

COLUMBIA MEDICAL PLAN
2 Knoll North Drive, Columbia MD 21045-2298. 410/997-8500. **Description:** A staff-modeled HMO.

DC CHARTERED HEALTH PLAN
820 1st Street NE, Suite LL100, Washington DC 20002-4205. 202/408-4710. **Contact:** Human Resources Department. **Description:** A health insurance company.

HARFORD MUTUAL INSURANCE COMPANY
200 North Main Street, Bel Air MD 21014-3544. 410/838-4000. **Contact:** Human Resources. **Description:** A fire and casualty insurance company.

LOUDOUN MUTUAL INSURANCE COMPANY
P.O. Box 58, Waterford VA 22190. 703/882-3232. **Contact:** Human Resources. **Description:** A property and casualty insurance company operating exclusively in the state of Virginia. **Number of employees at this location:** 15.

MARKEL CORPORATION
4551 Cox Road, Glen Allen VA 23060. **Contact:** Human Resources. **Description:** Markel is an insurance company which markets and underwrites specialty insurance products. **Common positions include:** Accountant/Auditor; Actuary; Computer Programmer; Computer Systems Analyst; Insurance Agent/Broker. **Educational backgrounds include:** Accounting; Business Administration; Finance; Liberal Arts. **Benefits:** 401K; Daycare Assistance; Dental Insurance; Disability Coverage; Life Insurance; Medical Insurance; Profit Sharing; Tuition Assistance. **Special Programs:** Internships. **Corporate headquarters location:** This Location. **Other U.S. locations:** Evanston IL; Pewaukee WI. **Listed on:** NASDAQ. **Number of employees at this location:** 470.

MARYLAND INSURANCE GROUP
3910 Keswick Road, Baltimore MD 21211. 410/338-9001. **Contact:** Employment Assistant. **Description:** Provides personal and commercial insurance products. **Corporate headquarters location:** Baltimore MD.

MONUMENTAL LIFE INSURANCE COMPANY
2 East Chase Street, Baltimore MD 21202. 410/685-2900. **Contact:** Personnel. **Description:** A life insurance company.

PEOPLE SECURITY
817 Maiden Choice Lane, Suite 100, Baltimore MD 21228. 410/944-4004. **Contact:** Office Manager. **Description:** A life insurance company.

UNITED STATES FIDELITY & GUARANTY CORPORATION

P.O. Box 1138, Baltimore MD 21203. 410/547-3000. **Contact:** Personnel Department. **Description:** USF&G Corporation is composed of property/casualty and life insurance subsidiaries. The principal subsidiary is United States Fidelity and Guaranty Company, a property and casualty insurer founded in 1896. Life insurance products and annuities are written through Fidelity and Guaranty Life Insurance Company, founded in 1959. USF&G provides commercial, personal, fidelity/surety, life, and reinsurance products. Commercial lines offer general, umbrella and professional liability, workers' compensation, business owners' policies, and commercial auto insurance. Personal lines of insurance include auto, property, personal excess, and watercraft, and are marketed to individuals and families. Fidelity/Surety offers surety, financial, judicial, and public official bonds as well as commercial crime and kidnap and ransom. F&G Reinsurance products are treaty reinsurances including traditional and finite risk. The Life Insurance line offers annuities, structured settlements, and term and universal life insurance to structured settlement candidates, senior citizens, teachers, and rural markets.

Note: Because addresses and telephone numbers of smaller companies change rapidly, we recommend you call each company to verify the information below before inquiring about job opportunities. Mass mailings are not recommended.

Additional employers with over 250 employees:

INSURANCE COMPANIES

Primark Corporation
8251 Greensboro Dr Suite 700, McLean VA 22102-3809. 703/790-7600.

Maryland Casualty Company
3910 Keswick Rd, Baltimore MD 21211-2296. 410/366-1000.

United Services Life Insurance Co.
4601 N Fairfax Dr, Arlington VA 22203-1500. 703/875-3400.

Unity Mutual Life Insurance Co.
3230 PA Ave SE, PO Box 31239, Washington DC 20030. 202/584-1000.

Baltimore Equitable Society
21 N Eutaw St, Baltimore MD 21201-1794. 410/727-1794.

Potomac Surety Insurance Co.
1133 15th St NW Ste 1100, Washington DC 20005-2710. 202/457-0290.

Additional employers with under 250 employees:

INSURANCE AGENTS, BROKERS, AND SERVICES

Riggs Counselman Michaels & Downes
555 Fairmount Ave, Baltimore MD 21286-5491. 410/339-7263.

AAA Insurance Agency
1401 W Mount Royal Ave, Baltimore MD 21217-4245. 410/462-4000.

Aetna Casualty & Surety
7467 New Ridge Rd, Hanover MD 21076-3105. 410/691-1400.

Cigna-Property & Casualty
10440 Little Patuxent Pky, Columbia MD 21044-3561. 410/740-3800.

Transamerica Ins Fin Corporation
110 West Rd Ste 230, Baltimore MD 21204-2316. 410/296-8432.

Fireman's Fund Insurance
9680 Deereco Rd, Luthvle Timon MD 21093-2120. 410/560-4700.

The Hartford Insurance Group
200 International Cir, Cockys Ht Vly MD 21030-1331. 410/584-9000.

United Insurance Co. of America
3102 Timanus Ln, Baltimore MD 21244-2876. 410/944-8411.

Victor O. Schinnerer & Company Ltd.
2 Wisconsin Cir, Chevy Chase MD 20815-7022. 301/961-1800.

Hudig Rollins Hall
1120 20th St Nw, Washington DC 20036-3406. 202/223-0673.

INSURANCE COMPANIES

Healthplus Inc.-MD
7601 Ora Glen Dr, Greenbelt MD 20770-3641. 301/441-1600.

Montgomery Mutual Insurance Co.
17810 Meeting House Rd, Sandy Spring MD 20860-1003. 301/924-4700.

Legal Mutual Liability Insurance Society of MD
17810 Meeting House Rd, Sandy Spring MD 20860-1003. 301/924-6099.

Selective Insurance Group
201 International Cir, Cockys Ht Vly MD 21030-1304. 410/771-6500.

For more information on career opportunities in insurance:

Associations

ALLIANCE OF AMERICAN INSURERS
1501 Woodfield Road, Suite 400 West, Schaumburg IL 60173-4980. 708/330-8500.

HEALTH INSURANCE ASSOCIATION OF AMERICA
555 13th Street North, Suite 600E, Washington DC 20004. 202/824-1600.

INSURANCE INFORMATION INSTITUTE
110 William Street, 24th Floor, New York NY 10038. 212/669-9200. Provides informational products on property/casualty insurance.

SOCIETY OF ACTUARIES
475 North Martingale Road, Suite 800, Schaumburg IL 60173-2226. 708/706-3500.

Directories

INSURANCE ALMANAC
Underwriter Printing and Publishing Co., 50 East Palisade Avenue, Englewood NJ 07631. 201/569-8808. Hardcover annual, 639 pages, $115. Available at libraries.

INSURANCE MARKET PLACE
Rough Notes Company, Inc., P.O. Box 564, Indianapolis IN 46206. 317/634-1541.

INSURANCE PHONE BOOK AND DIRECTORY
Reed Reference Publishing, 121 Chanlon Road, New Providence NJ 07974. 800/521-8110. $89.95, new editions available every other year. Might also be available at libraries.

Magazines

BEST'S REVIEW
A.M. Best Co., A.M. Best Road, Oldwick NJ 08858-9988. 908/439-2200. Monthly.

INSURANCE JOURNAL
Wells Publishing, 9191 Towne Centre Drive, Suite 550, San Diego, CA 92122-1231 619/455-7717. A biweekly magazine covering the insurance industry. Subscription: $78 per year, $3 for a single issue.

INSURANCE TIMES
M & S Communications, 20 Park Plaza, Suite 1101, Boston MA 02116. 617/292-7117. A regional biweekly insurance newspaper for insurance professionals.

LEGAL SERVICES

The number of people working in the legal services field has exploded since the early '70s. According to a 1969 survey by the Bureau of Labor Statistics (BLS) there were 387,000 workers in legal services. By 1994, that number had risen to 1.2 million. The glut of lawyers has led to tremendous competition in the legal profession. Law firms are laying off associates and firing unproductive partners. Graduates of prestigious law schools face tough competition for jobs, although for the top graduates, the offers will be there. According to Jon Sargent, an economist for the Office of Economic Growth at the BLS, some jobseekers looking to break in to this industry may need to look outside the mainstream legal services industry: non-profit companies, government positions, or law firms in smaller communities.

Paralegals have carved out a niche for themselves and continue to be the fastest growing profession in legal services. "Paralegals have become a cost-effective way to provide legal services in many cases," says Sargent, referring to the realization by many employers that paralegals can do many of the same jobs as associates at a much lower cost.

ARNOLD & PORTER
555 12th Street NW, Washington DC 20004. 202/872-6700. **Contact:** Elizabeth Respess, Recruiter. **Description:** A law firm.

COVINGTON & BURLINGTON
1201 Pennsylvania Avenue NW, P.O. Box 7566, Washington DC 20044-7566. 202/662-6000. **Contact:** Lorraine Brown, Legal Recruitment Coordinator. **Description:** A law firm.

HOGAN & HARTSON
555 13th Street NW, Columbia Square Building, Washington DC 20004-1109. 202/637-5600. **Contact:** Ellen Swank, Legal Recruitment Coordinator. **Description:** A law firm.

HOWRY & SIMON
1299 Pennsylvania Avenue NW, Warner Theatre Building, Washington DC 20004. 202/783-0800. **Contact:** Ralph Savarese, Managing Partner. **Description:** A law firm.

JONES, DAY, REAVIS & POGUE
1450 G Street NW, 7th Floor, Washington DC 20005-2088. 202/879-3939. **Fax:** 202/737-2832. **Contact:** Meg Meserole, Human Resources Coordinator. **Description:** A law firm. **Common positions include:** Paralegal. **Educational backgrounds include:** Liberal Arts. **Benefits:** Dental Insurance; Life Insurance; Medical Insurance; Savings Plan. **Corporate headquarters location:** Cleveland OH.

NILES BARTON & WILMER
111 South Calvert Street, Suite 1400, Baltimore MD 21202-6174. 410/783-6300. **Contact:** Human Resources Department. **Description:** A law firm.

STEPTOE & JOHNSON
1330 Connecticut Avenue NW, Washington DC 20036. 202/429-8036. **Contact:** Rosemary Kelly Morgan, Director of Recruiting. **Description:** A law firm. **Common positions include:** Attorney. **Special Programs:** Training Programs.

Note: Because addresses and telephone numbers of smaller companies change rapidly, we recommend you call each company to verify the information below before inquiring about job opportunities. Mass mailings are not recommended.

Additional employers with under 250 employees:

LEGAL SERVICES

Alagia Day Marshall Mintmire
1000 Thomas Jefferson St Nw, Washington DC 20007-3835. 202/342-0342.

Baker & McKenzie
815 Connecticut Ave Nw, Washington DC 20006-4004. 202/452-7000.

Beveridge & Diamond
1350 I St NW Ste 700, Washington DC 20005-3305. 202/789-6000.

Caplin & Drysdale
1 Thomas Cir NW Ste 1100, Washington DC 20005-5802. 202/862-5000.

Collier Shannon & Scott
1055 Thomas Jefferson St Nw, Washington DC 20007-5202. 202/342-8400.

Dechert Price & Rhoads
1500 K St Nw, Washington DC 20005-1209. 202/783-0200.

Dunnells Duvall
2110 Pennsylvania Ave Nw, Washington DC 20037-3201. 202/861-1400.

Epstein Becker & Green
1140 19th St Nw, Washington DC 20036-6601. 202/861-0900.

Fragomen Del Rey & Bernsen
1212 New York Ave NW Ste 850, Washington DC 20005-3987. 202/223-5515.

Fulbright and Jaworski
801 Pennsylvania Ave Nw, Washington DC 20004-2615. 202/662-0200.

Ginsburg Feldman & Bress
1250 Connecticut Ave NW Ste 80, Washington DC 20036-2603. 202/637-9020.

Horowitz & Bonard
1818 N St Nw, Washington DC 20036-2406. 202/828-8200.

Kirkland & Ellis
655 15th St NW Ste 1200, Washington DC 20005-5701. 202/879-5000.

Kirkpatrick & Lockhart
1800 M St Nw, Washington DC 20036-5891. 202/778-9000.

Kutak Rock & Campbell
1101 Connecticut Ave Nw, Washington DC 20036-4303. 202/828-2400.

Leboeuf Lamb Leiby & MacRae
1875 Connecticut Ave NW # 1200, Washington DC 20009-5728. 202/986-8000.

Linowes & Blocher
800 K St Nw, Washington DC 20001-8000. 202/872-9080.

Linowes & Blocher
1010 Wayne Ave Ste 1000, Silver Spring MD 20910-5600. 301/588-8580.

Littler Mendelson Fostif Tichy
World Trade Ctr, Baltimore MD 21202. 410/528-9545.

McDermott Will & Emery
1850 K St Nw, Washington DC 20006-2213. 202/887-8000.

Melrod Redman & Gartlan
1801 K St NW Ste 1100, Washington DC 20006-1301. 202/822-5300.

Morgan Lewis & Bockius
1800 M St Nw, Washington DC 20036-5869. 202/467-7000.

Morrison & Foerster
2000 Pennsylvania Ave NW 5500, Washington DC 20006-1812. 202/887-1500.

Nixon Hargrave Devans Doyle
1 Thomas Cir Nw, Washington DC 20005-5802. 202/223-7200.

O'Melveny & Myers
555 13th St NW Ste 500, Washington DC 20004-1109. 202/383-5300.

Pepper Hamilton & Scheetz
1300 19th St Nw, Washington DC 20036-1609. 202/828-1200.

Pierson Ball & Dowd
1200 18th St Nw, Washington DC 20036-2506. 202/437-6100.

Piper & Marbury
1200 19th St NW Fl 7, Washington DC 20036-2430. 202/861-3900.

Reid & Priest
701 Pennsylvania Ave Nw, Washington DC 20004-2608. 202/508-4000.

Seyforth Shaw Fairweather
815 Connecticut Ave Nw, Washington DC 20006-4004. 202/463-2400.

Shea & Gardner
1800 Massachusetts Ave Nw, Washington DC 20036-1806. 202/828-2000.

Sidley & Austin
1722 I St NW Lowr 8, Washington DC 20006-3705. 202/736-8000.

Swidler & Berlin Chartered
3000 K St Nw, Washington DC 20007-5109. 202/944-4300.

Venable Baetjer & Howard
1800 Mercantile Bnk & Tr Bldg, Baltimore MD 21201. 410/244-7771.

Verner Lipfert Bernhard McPherson Hand 901 15th St Nw, Washington DC 20005. 202/452-8744.

Vinson & Elkins
1455 Pennsylvania Ave NW 700 T, Washington DC 20004-1008. 202/639-6500.

Weinberg & Green
100 S Charles St, Baltimore MD 21201-2725. 410/332-8600.

Wilkes Artis Hedrick & Lane
1666 K St Nw, Washington DC 20006-2803. 202/457-7800.

Wilkie Farr & Gallagher
1155 21st St Nw, Washington DC 20036-3302. 202/328-8000.

Banner Birch McKie & Beckett
1001 G St NW Fl 11, Washington DC 20001-4545. 202/508-9100.

Keller and Heckman
1101 G St NW Ste 500

West, Washington DC 20005-3805. 202/434-4100.

Chadbourne & Parke
1101 Vermont Ave NW # 900, Washington DC 20005-3521. 202/289-3000.

Foley & Lardner
3000 K St NW Ste 500, Washington DC 20007-5109. 202/672-5300.

Cohn and Marks
1333 New Hampshire Ave Nw, Washington DC 20036-1511. 202/293-3860.

Anderson Kill Olick & Oshinsky
2000 Pennsylvania Ave Nw, Washington DC 20006-1812. 202/728-3100.

Cushman Darby & Cushman
1100 New York Ave NW # 900, Washington DC 20005-3934. 202/861-3000.

Carr Morris & Graeff
1120 G St NW Ste 930, Washington DC 20005-3801. 202/789-1000.

Ross Dixon & Masback
601 Pennsylvania Ave Nw, Washington DC 20004-2601. 202/662-2000.

Newman & Holtzinger
1615 L St NW Ste 925, Washington DC 20036-5610. 202/955-6600.

Hunton & Williams
PO Box 19230, Washington DC 20036-9230. 202/955-1500.

Interdonato Reilly & Comstock
5225 Wisconsin Ave NW Ste 300, Washington DC 20015-2014. 202/966-5788.

Nolan Plumhoff & Williams
210 W Pennsylvania Ave, Baltimore MD 21204-5325. 410/823-7800.

Squire Sanders & Dempsey
PO Box 407, Washington DC 20044-0407. 202/626-6600.

For more information on career opportunities in legal services:

<u>Associations</u>

AMERICAN BAR ASSOCIATION
750 North Lake Shore Drive, Chicago IL 60611. 312/988-5000. A non-profit organization.

FEDERAL BAR ASSOCIATION
1815 H. Street NW, Suite 408, Washington DC 20006-3697. 202/638-0252.

NATIONAL ASSOCIATION OF LEGAL ASSISTANTS
1516 South Boston, Suite 200, Tulsa OK 74119-4013. 918/587-6828. An educational association. Offers the National Voluntary Association Exam. Memberships are available.

NATIONAL FEDERATION OF PARALEGAL ASSOCIATIONS
P.O. Box 33108, Kansas City MO 64114-0108. 816/941-4000. Offers magazines, seminars, and internet job listings.

NATIONAL PARALEGAL ASSOCIATION
P.O. Box 629, 6186 Honey Hollow Road, Doylestown PA 18901. 215/297-8333.

MANUFACTURING AND WHOLESALING: MISCELLANEOUS CONSUMER

The consumer goods manufacturing industry is more than just one industry. To forecast generally about the entire range of companies that make products for consumers is risky, since so much can differ from one segment to the next. In fact, many consumer manufacturers are listed under more specific categories in this book.

With that said, some general statements can be made about the outlook for this gigantic field. Over the long term, many analysts are optimistic. An improved economy, as well as an aging baby boom generation with growing disposable income, should provide stimulus for increases in personal durables. Continued growth in international trade should also point to a favorable long-term outlook for household consumer durables.

U.S. exports of household durables should also expand as trade barriers drop. The North American Free Trade Agreement (NAFTA), passed in early 1994, will give U.S. manufacturers even greater access to what is already the second-largest export market for U.S. household durables. Other trade agreements may follow with several Latin American countries. Potential markets in Eastern Europe and independent states of the former Soviet Union may also open.

AW INDUSTRIES
8415 Ardmore Road, Landover MD 20785. 301/322-1000. **Contact:** Director of Personnel. **Description:** Company manufactures Serta mattresses and box springs, sleeper sofas, and stationary furniture; also distributes carpeting, tile furniture, and electrical appliances. **Corporate headquarters location:** This Location.

AMERICAN WOODMARK CORPORATION
3102 Shawnee Drive, Winchester VA 22601. 703/665-9100. **Contact:** Human Resources. **Description:** American Woodmark manufactures and distributes modular kitchen cabinets and vanities to remodeling and new home construction markets. **Number of employees at this location:** 2,170.

BLACK & DECKER CORPORATION
701 East Joppa Road, Towson MD 21286. 410/716-3900. **Contact:** Human Resources Department. **Description:** With products and services marketed in more than 100 countries, Black & Decker is a global marketer and manufacturer of quality products used in and around the home and for commercial applications. It is also a major supplier of information technology and services to governmental and commercial clients worldwide. The company is one of the world's largest producers of power tools, power tool accessories, security hardware, and electric lawn and garden tools, and it is one of the largest global suppliers of engineered fastening systems to the markets it serves. **Common positions include:** Computer-Aided Designer; Electrical/Electronics Engineer; Mechanical Engineer.

BLACK & DECKER CORPORATION
626 Hanover Pike, Hampstead MD 21074-2049. 410/239-5000. **Contact:** Human Resources. **Description:** With products and services marketed in more than 100

countries, Black & Decker is a global marketer and manufacturer of quality products used in and around the home and for commercial applications. It is also a major supplier of information technology and services to governmental and commercial clients worldwide. The company is one of the world's largest producers of power tools, power tool accessories, security hardware, and electric lawn and garden tools, and it is the largest global supplier of engineered fastening systems to the markets they serve.

DAVID-EDWARD LTD.
1407 Parker Road, Baltimore MD 21227. 410/242-2222. **Contact:** Jim Herold, Plant Manager. **Description:** Manufactures custom-made upholstered chairs and sofas. **Corporate headquarters location:** This Location.

KENFAIR MANUFACTURING COMPANY
840 South Pickett Street, Alexandria VA 22304. 703/751-5900. **Contact:** Human Resources. **Description:** A drapery hardware and window blinds manufacturer.

MARYLAND RIBBON COMPANY
857 Willow Circle, Hagerstown MD 21740. 301/739-6314. **Contact:** Human Resources. **Description:** A carbon paper and inked ribbon manufacturer.

PROCTER AND GAMBLE
COSMETIC AND FRAGRANCE PRODUCTS
11050 York Road, Hunt Valley MD 21030-2098. 410/785-5580. **Contact:** Human Resources. **Description:** Develops, manufactures, and distributes cosmetics, toiletries, and fragrances. **Number of employees nationwide:** 2,500.

THOMAS SOMERVILLE CO.
4912 6th Street Northeast, Washington DC 20017. 202/635-4100. **Contact:** Personnel Department. **Description:** A distributor of plumbing, heating, and air-conditioning supplies.

KIRK STIEFF COMPANY
800 Wyman Park Drive, Baltimore MD 21211. 410/338-6000. **Contact:** Personnel Office. **Description:** Produces sterling silver, pewter, and plated dinnerware decorative items. **Common positions include:** Accountant/Auditor; Administrator; Advertising Clerk; Blue-Collar Worker Supervisor; Commercial Artist; Computer Programmer; Credit Manager; Customer Service Representative; Department Manager; Financial Analyst; Human Resources Specialist; Manufacturer's/Wholesaler's Sales Rep.; Operations/Production Manager; Purchasing Agent and Manager; Quality Control Supervisor; Systems Analyst. **Educational backgrounds include:** Accounting; Architecture; Business Administration; Finance; Liberal Arts; Marketing; Mathematics. **Corporate headquarters location:** This Location. **Operations at this facility include:** Administration; Manufacturing; Research and Development; Sales; Service.

SWEETHEART CUP CORPORATION
10100 Reisterstown Road, Owings Mills MD 21117. 410/363-1111. **Contact:** Employment Manager. **Description:** Manufactures and distributes paper and plastic cups, containers, bowls, plates, lids, cutlery, and drinking straws. Sweetheart Cup Corporation also produces ice-cream cones. Two divisions manufacture packaging and production machinery. **Common positions include:** Accountant/Auditor; Computer Programmer; Customer Service Representative; Draftsperson; Electrical/Electronics Engineer; Human Resources Specialist; Mechanical Engineer; Systems Analyst. **Educational backgrounds include:** Accounting; Business Administration; Computer Science; Engineering; Liberal Arts. **Operations at this facility include:** Administration; Manufacturing; Research and Development.

Note: Because addresses and telephone numbers of smaller companies change rapidly, we recommend you call each company to verify the information below before inquiring about job opportunities. Mass mailings are not recommended.

Additional employers with over 250 employees:

HOUSEHOLD FURNITURE

Sealy Furniture Of MD
510 Naylor Mill Rd, Salisbury MD 21801-9626. 410/742-1566.

Mohasco Corp.
4401 Fair Lakes Ct, Fairfax VA 22033-3898. 703/968-8000.

Classic Corp.
8214 Wellmoor Ct, Jessup MD 20794-9624. 301/953-1133.

SMALL ARMS

Beretta USA Corp.
17601 Beretta Dr, Accokeek MD 20607-9566. 301/283-2191.

Additional employers with under 250 employees:

HOUSEHOLD FURNITURE

Keller Manufacturing Co.
RR 3, Culpeper VA 22701-9803. 703/825-1201.

Statton Furniture Manufacturing Co.
E First St, Hagerstown MD 21740. 301/739-0360.

MISC. FURNITURE AND FIXTURES

Eastern Standard Corporation
1601 Wicomico St, Baltimore MD 21230-1705. 410/332-4540.

HOUSEHOLD AUDIO AND VIDEO EQUIPMENT

Polk Audio Inc.
5601 Metro Dr, Baltimore MD 21215-3208. 410/358-3600.

JEWELRY, SILVERWARE, AND PLATED WARE

M H Ruben Ltd.
1220 E West Hwy, Silver Spring MD 20910-3244. 301/585-8565.

BROOMS AND BRUSHES

Maryland Brush Co.
3221 Frederick Ave, Baltimore MD 21229-3807. 410/945-3300.

Rubberset Co.
26466 Silver Lane, Crisfield MD 21817. 410/968-1050.

HARDWARE WHOLESALE

Blaine Window Hardware
17319 Blaine Dr, Hagerstown MD 21740-9442. 301/797-6500.

Reico Inc.
6790 Commercial Dr, Springfield VA 22151-4209. 703/256-6400.

PAPER AND OFFICE SUPPLIES WHOLESALE

Frank Parsons Paper
2270 Beaver Rd, Landover MD 20785-3277. 301/386-4700.

Ris Paper Company Mid-Atlantic Region
9101 Easthampton Dr, Capitol Hts MD 20743. 301/336-8833.

Stanford Paper Co.
1901 Stanford Ct, Landover MD 20785-3220. 301/772-1900.

Tab Products
1749 Old Meadow Rd Ste 210, McLean VA 22102-4310. 703/506-0099.

Moore Business Forms
6695 Business Pky, Elkridge MD 21227-6349. 410/379-0095.

Standard Register Mideastern Region
901 Dulaney Valley Rd, Baltimore MD 21204-2600. 410/337-0616.

Boise Cascade Office Products
7125 Thomas Edison Dr, Columbia MD 21046-2113. 410/995-6888.

For more information on career opportunities in consumer manufacturing and wholesaling:

Associations

ASSOCIATION FOR MANUFACTURING TECHNOLOGY
7901 Westpark Drive, McLean VA 22102. 703/893-2900. Offers research services.

ASSOCIATION OF HOME APPLIANCE MANUFACTURERS
20 North Wacker Drive, Chicago IL 60606. 312/984-5800.

NATIONAL ASSOCIATION OF MANUFACTURERS
1331 Pennsylvania Avenue, NW, Suite 1500, Washington DC 20004. 202/637-3000. A lobbying association for manufacturers.

NATIONAL HOUSEWARES MANUFACTURERS ASSOCIATION
6400 Schafer Court, Suite 650, Rosemont IL 60018. 708/292-4200. Offers shipping discounts and other services.

SOCIETY OF MANUFACTURING ENGINEERS
P.O. Box 930, One SME Drive, Dearborn MI 48121. 313/271-1500. Offers educational events and educational materials on manufacturing.

SOAP AND DETERGENT ASSOCIATION
475 Park Avenue South, 27th Floor, New York NY 10016. 212/725-1262. A trade association and research center.

Directories

APPLIANCE MANUFACTURER ANNUAL DIRECTORY
Appliance Manufacturer, 5900 Harper Road, Suite 105, Solon OH 44139. 216/349-3060. $25.00.

HOUSEHOLD AND PERSONAL PRODUCTS INDUSTRY BUYERS GUIDE
Rodman Publishing Group, 17 South Franklin Turnpike, Ramsey NJ 07446. 201/825-2552. $12.00.

Magazines

APPLIANCE
1110 Jorie Boulevard, Oak Brook IL 60522-9019. 708/990-3484. Monthly. $70.00 for a one-year subscription.

COSMETICS INSIDERS REPORT
Advanstar Communications, 7500 Old Oak Boulevard, Cleveland OH 44130. 216/243-8100. $189.00. Monthly. Features timely articles on cosmetics marketing and research.

MANUFACTURING AND WHOLESALING: MISCELLANEOUS INDUSTRIAL

Factories have been operating at their highest rate of capacity in more than five years. After an unparalleled year for growth, machine manufacturers expect another good year. With money to spend, manufacturers should be adding more equipment to increase production and efficiency. Export markets are expected to pick up the demand where the domestic market leaves off. With increased product demand, the demand for engineers should also increase.

The employment of the wholesale trade is closely tied to the growth of the economy. However, industry trends will change the composition and nature of much of the wholesale trade employment. Consolidation of the industry into fewer firms and the spread of new technology should slow growth in some occupations, but many new jobs will be created in others as firms provide a growing array of support services. In addition, these trends will change the role of many other workers.

Heightened competition and pressure to lower operating costs should continue to force distributors to merge with or acquire other firms. The resulting consolidation of wholesale trade among fewer, larger firms will reduce the demands for some workers as merged companies eliminate duplicated staff. Consolidation and greater competition among wholesale trade firms, however, will lead more firms to expand customer service, increasing demands for related workers. Clerks or sales workers will advance to many of these new customer service or marketing jobs, and new workers may be needed for financial, logistical, technical, or advertising positions.

AIRFLOW COMPANY
295 Bailes Lane, Frederick MD 21701. 301/695-6500. **Contact:** Personnel Manager. **Description:** Produces a line of specialized air conditioners and dehumidifying equipment and systems.

ALLEGANY TECHNOLOGY
P.O. Box 1744, Cumberland MD 21502-1744. 301/722-7330. **Contact:** Human Resources. **Description:** Manufacturer of technological weighing equipment and industrial-sized scales.

ALLIED RESEARCH CORPORATION
Suite 750, 8000 Towers Crescent Drive, Vienna VA 22182. 703/847-5268. **Contact:** Human Resources. **Description:** Allied Research develops, designs, manufactures and sells ammunitions and weapons systems, and designs, produces, tests, and inspects documentation for government and industries. **Number of employees at this location:** 475.

AMERICAN TRADING & PRODUCTION CORP.
Blaustein Building, P.O. Box 238, Baltimore MD 21203. 410/347-7000. **Contact:** Human Resources. **Description:** A diversified conglomerate with operations in oil and gas exploration and production, electronics, office products, and real estate.

ATLANTIC RESEARCH CORPORATION
5945 Wellington Road, Gainsville VA 22065. 703/754-5300. **Contact:** Human Resources. **Description:** Designs, develops, and manufactures solid propellant rocket motors for missile systems and other uses. Also manufactures electromagnetic security systems and offers professional services. **Common positions include:** Accountant/Auditor; Aerospace Engineer; Chemical Engineer; Chemist; Computer Programmer; Department Engineer; Electrical/Electronics Engineer; General Manager; Industrial Engineer; Mechanical Engineer; Metallurgical Engineer; Operations/Production Manager; Purchasing Agent and Manager; Quality Control Supervisor; Systems Analyst; Technical Writer/Editor. **Educational backgrounds include:** Accounting; Business Administration; Chemistry; Computer Science; Engineering. **Benefits:** Dental Insurance; Disability Coverage; Life Insurance; Medical Insurance; Pension Plan; Savings Plan; Tuition Assistance. **Corporate headquarters location:** This Location. **Operations at this facility include:** Administration; Divisional Headquarters; Manufacturing; Research and Development; Sales; Service.

J.L. CLARK MANUFACTURING COMPANY, INC.
STONE INDUSTRIAL
9207 51st Avenue, College Park MD 20740. 301/474-3100. **Contact:** Steven Lieb, Director of Personnel. **Description:** Produces paper tubing and tubes, high-temperature plastic tubing, and heat-shrinkable plastic tubing. Nationally, the company operates in three industry segments: packaging items (metal and plastic containers, metal tubes, composite containers, and various specialty chemicals); filters (oil, air, fuel, coolant, hydraulic fluid, and chemical solution filters used in a variety of products and industries); and paper and plastic tubes. A second facility in Havre de Grace, Maryland produces decorated metal ends, battery sleeves, and metal signs, and is engaged in flat sheet decorating. **Corporate headquarters location:** Rockford IL.

DANAHER CORPORATION
1250 24th Street NW, Suite 800, Washington DC 20037. 202/828-0850. **Contact:** Personnel. **Description:** Danaher is a producer of hand tools, automotive and transportation products, and process and environmental controls. The Danaher Tools segment manufactures tools, holders, and fasteners for industrial, professional, and consumer markets under brand names including Allen, Sears Craftsman, K-D, and NAPA. The transportation operations of the company include air conditioning equipment through subsidiary Fayette Tubular and wheel aligners and balancers, brake parts, and other automotive components through Hennessy Industries. Danaher also builds control and detection systems, sensors, monitors, and measuring systems. **Listed on:** New York Stock Exchange.

DAVIS & HEMPHILL, INC.
5710 Furnace Avenue, Elkridge MD 21227. 410/796-2290. **Contact:** Mr. Francis Duncan, President. **Description:** Manufactures a variety of screw machine products.

EG&G PRESSURE SCIENCE, INC.
11642 Old Baltimore Pike, Beltsville MD 20705-1294. 301/937-3141. **Contact:** Human Resources. **Description:** A manufacturer of mechanical components and subsystems for aerospace and industrial applications.

ELLICOTT MACHINE CORPORATION
1611 Bush Street, Baltimore MD 21230. 410/837-7900. **Contact:** Sandra Crawford, Vice President of Human Resources. **Description:** Produces dredges, dredging machinery, and related equipment. **Common positions include:** Accountant/Auditor; Blue-Collar Worker Supervisor; Buyer; Computer Programmer; Customer Service Representative; Draftsperson; Human Resources Specialist; Manufacturer's/Wholesaler's Sales Rep.; Mechanical Engineer; Operations/Production Manager; Purchasing Agent and Manager; Quality Control Supervisor; Systems Analyst; Transportation/Traffic Specialist. **Educational backgrounds include:** Accounting; Business Administration; Computer Science; Engineering; Finance. **Benefits:** 401K; Dental Insurance; Disability Coverage; Life Insurance; Medical Insurance; Tuition Assistance. **Corporate headquarters location:** This Location. **Operations at this facility include:** Administration; Manufacturing. **Number of employees at this location:** 110.

EVAPO, INC.
P.O. Box 1300, Westminster MD 21158. 410/756-2600. **Contact:** Office Manager. **Description:** Produces evaporative condensers and closed-circuit coolers.

FAIRCHILD INDUSTRIES INC.
P.O. Box 10803, 300 West Service Road, Chantilly VA 22021. 703/478-5800. **Fax:** 703/478-5767. **Contact:** Personnel. **Description:** Operates nationwide in the following business segments: Aerospace Fasteners, Industrial Products, and Communication Services. **Common positions include:** Accountant/Auditor; Administrator; Attorney. **Educational backgrounds include:** Accounting; Business Administration; Liberal Arts. **Benefits:** Dental Insurance; Disability Coverage; Medical Insurance; Pension Plan; Savings Plan; Tuition Assistance.

FREDERICK TRADING COMPANY
P.O. Box 400, Frederick MD 21705. 301/662-2161. **Contact:** Human Resources Department. **Description:** A wholesale distributor of hardware, automotive, and lumber commodities.

FUSION SYSTEMS CORPORATION
7600 Standish Place, Rockville MD 20855. **Contact:** Human Resources. **Description:** Fusion Systems Corporation is a leading worldwide supplier of ultraviolet curing equipment and a leading supplier of photostabilizers and ashers to the semiconductor industry. Fusion UV Curing Systems' (a subsidiary) equipment is used in a wide range of graphic arts and industrial applications, including the curing or drying of inks, coatings, and adhesives on paper, metal, and plastic substrates. Fusion Semiconductor Systems, another subsidiary, makes photostabilizers and ashers used at critical steps in producing advanced semiconductor devices. Fusion's semiconductor tools are used by most large chipmakers around the world to increase productivity and yields in producing devices. **Common positions include:** Accountant/Auditor; Blue-Collar Worker Supervisor; Budget Analyst; Buyer; Computer Programmer; Computer Systems Analyst; Customer Service Representative; Economist/Market Research Analyst; Electrical/Electronics Engineer; Electrician; Financial Analyst; Human Resources Specialist; Industrial Engineer; Industrial Production Manager; Manufacturer's/Wholesaler's Sales Rep.; Materials Engineer; Mechanical Engineer; Operations/Production Manager; Purchasing Agent and Manager; Quality Control Supervisor; Services Sales Representative; Software Engineer. **Educational backgrounds include:** Accounting; Business Administration; Computer Science; Engineering; Finance; Marketing. **Benefits:** 401K; Dental Insurance; Disability Coverage; Life Insurance; Medical Insurance; Profit Sharing; Tuition Assistance. **Corporate headquarters location:** This Location. **Operations at this facility include:** Administration; Divisional Headquarters; Manufacturing; Regional Headquarters; Research and Development; Sales; Service. **Listed on:** NASDAQ. **Number of employees at this location:** 500.

GAF BUILDING MATERIALS CORPORATION
1500 South Ponca Street, Baltimore MD 21224. 410/633-7200. **Contact:** Human Resources Manager. **Description:** Produces roofing products, shingles, and other construction materials.

HARMAN INTERNATIONAL INDUSTRIES, INC.
1101 Pennsylvania Avenue NW, Suite 1010, Washington DC 20004. 202/393-1101. **Contact:** Vice President of Human Resources. **Description:** Harman International Industries produces and distributes audio merchandise for consumers, original equipment manufacturers (OEMs), and the professional market. The company's products include home and automobile equipment, loud speakers, professional electronics, and home theater products. Brand names include Pyle, Infinity, JBL, EPI, Rivera, Soundcraft, and Audax. Segments of Harman International Industries include Harman Marketing Units; Automotive OEM; Manufacturing, which is performed in California, Denmark, and France; and International Distributing, with subsidiaries in France, Germany, U.K., and Japan. **Listed on:** New York Stock Exchange. **NOTE:** All employment inquiries must be sent to Vice President of Human Resources, 8500 Balboa Boulevard, Northridge CA 91329.

HOPPMANN CORPORATION
P.O. Box 601, 14560 Lee Road, Chantilly VA 22021. 703/631-2700. **Contact:** Barbara O. Egnor, Director of Human Resources. **Description:** Produces automated parts-handling systems. **Common positions include:** Administrator; Customer Service Representative; Designer; Draftsperson; Electrical/Electronics Engineer; Electrician; Mechanic; Mechanical Engineer; Purchasing Agent and Manager; Technical Writer/Editor. **Educational backgrounds include:** Business Administration; Drafting; Engineering; Liberal Arts. **Benefits:** 401K; Daycare Assistance; Dental Insurance; Disability Coverage; Leave Time; Life Insurance; Medical Insurance; Profit Sharing; Tuition Assistance. **Corporate headquarters location:** This Location. **Other U.S.**

locations: Madison Heights VA. **Operations at this facility include:** Administration; Divisional Headquarters; Manufacturing; Research and Development; Sales; Service. **Number of employees at this location:** 150.

HYDRO THERM INC.
10 Maryland Avenue, Baltimore MD 21222. 410/285-2300. **Contact:** Personnel Supervisor. **Description:** Manufactures baseboard heaters and boiler systems. **Corporate headquarters location:** This Location.

IDEAS, INC.
7120 Columbia Gateway Drive, Columbia MD 21046. 410/312-2004. **Contact:** Tim Daley, Manager, Human Resources. **Description:** A privately owned, high-technology engineering and manufacturing firm with expertise in the application of state-of-the-art technology to individual product design and custom-engineered systems. **NOTE:** Most of the technical positions require current SBI with polygraph. **Common positions include:** Accountant/Auditor; Administrator; Buyer; Computer Scientist; Draftsperson; Electrical/Electronics Engineer; Hardware Engineer; Human Resources Specialist; Purchasing Agent and Manager; Quality Control Supervisor; Radio Frequency Engineer; Software Engineer; Systems Engineer; Technical Writer/Editor. **Educational backgrounds include:** Accounting; Computer Science; Engineering; Finance; Liberal Arts. **Benefits:** Dental Insurance; Disability Coverage; Investment Plan; Life Insurance; Medical Insurance; Savings Plan; Stock Option; Tuition Assistance. **Operations at this facility include:** Administration; Research and Development; Service. **Number of employees at this location:** 260. **Number of employees nationwide:** 450.

C.M. KEMP MANUFACTURING COMPANY
7280 Baltimore-Annapolis Boulevard, Glen Burnie MD 21061. 410/582-0629. **Fax:** 410/766-9105. **Contact:** Robin Walker, Human Resources Supervisor. **Description:** Produces a range of heating equipment, gas generators, and desiccant dryers.

KOP-FLEX, INC.
7565 Harmonies, Hanover MD 21076. 410/768-2000. **Fax:** 410/787-8424. **Contact:** Colleen Rigatti, Employee Relations Representative. **Description:** A manufacturer of power transmission couplings and components for use in steel mills, paper mills and navy ships. **Common positions include:** Ceramics Engineer; Designer; Draftsperson; Human Resources Specialist; Industrial Engineer; Materials Engineer; Mechanical Engineer; Metallurgical Engineer; Services Sales Representative. **Educational backgrounds include:** Business Administration; Engineering; Liberal Arts. **Benefits:** 401K; Dental Insurance; Disability Coverage; Life Insurance; Medical Insurance; Pension Plan; Profit Sharing; Tuition Assistance. **Special Programs:** Internships. **Corporate headquarters location:** This Location. **Operations at this facility include:** Administration; Research and Development; Sales; Service. **Listed on:** Privately held. **Number of employees at this location:** 323.

MEMTEC AMERICA CORPORATION
2033 Green Spring Drive, Timonium MD 21093. 410/252-0800. **Fax:** 410/252-6027. **Contact:** Ms. Karmen Lodgen, Human Resources Manager. **Description:** Produces filters, filtration equipment, strainers, and related items. Also operates related research facilities. **Common positions include:** Accountant/Auditor; Chemist; Customer Service Representative; Draftsperson; Industrial Engineer; Manufacturer's/Wholesaler's Sales Rep.; Mechanical Engineer; Technical Writer/Editor. **Educational backgrounds include:** Economics; Engineering. **Benefits:** 401K; Dental Insurance; Disability Coverage; Life Insurance; Medical Insurance; Tuition Assistance. **Corporate headquarters location:** This Location. **Other U.S. locations:** San Diego CA. **Parent company:** Memtec Limited. **Operations at this facility include:** Administration; Manufacturing; Regional Headquarters; Research and Development; Sales; Service. **Listed on:** American Stock Exchange; New York Stock Exchange. **Number of employees at this location:** 400.

R.E. MICHEL COMPANY INC.
One R.E. Michel Drive, Glen Burnie MD 21061. 410/760-4000. **Contact:** Human Resources Department. **Description:** A wholesale distributor of parts and supplies for air conditioners and refrigerators.

MINE SAFETY APPLIANCES COMPANY (MSA)
38 Loveton Circle, Sparks MD 21152. 410/628-5440. **Contact:** Gina Resch, Administrative Manager. **Description:** MSA manufactures a variety of gas masks and respiratory protection, protective headgear, and gas and vapor sensors. The company's products are generally supplied to the fire service, mining, construction,

and industrial subcontracting industries. The company is divided into two major operating groups. MSA's Safety Products Division designs and manufactures full face pieces for self-contained breathing apparatuses, respirators, communication equipment for breathing apparatuses, cooling vests designed to combat heat stress, and a hand-held infrared heat detector. The company's Instrument Division makes a variety of monitors and sensors. MSA's International Affiliates manufacture a wide array of equipment, ranging from thermal imaging cameras to air supply units. The company's products are sold worldwide. **Common positions include:** Chemical Engineer; Chemist; Draftsperson; Industrial Engineer; Mechanical Engineer. **Educational backgrounds include:** Chemistry; Engineering; Mathematics. **Benefits:** Dental Insurance; Disability Coverage; Life Insurance; Medical Insurance; Pension Plan; Savings Plan; Tuition Assistance; Vision Plan. **Special Programs:** Training Programs. **Corporate headquarters location:** Pittsburgh PA. **Number of employees at this location:** 30.

PACIFIC SCIENTIFIC COMPANY
HAIC/ROYCO DIVISION
11801 Tech Road, Silver Spring MD 20904. 301/680-7000. **Contact:** Human Resources Manager. **Description:** A manufacturer of particle-monitoring instruments used to size and count particles in air, liquids, and gases. The company's primary markets (both domestic and international) are the pharmaceutical, semiconductor, fluid power, and aerospace industries. **Common positions include:** Accountant/Auditor; Administrator; Application Engineer; Buyer; Customer Service Representative; Manufacturing Engineer; Marketing Specialist; Operations/Production Manager; Sales Engineer; Software Engineer; Technical Writer/Editor. **Educational backgrounds include:** Accounting; Business Administration; Chemistry; Computer Science; Engineering; Finance; Marketing; Mathematics; Physics. **Benefits:** Dental Insurance; Disability Coverage; Life Insurance; Medical Insurance; Pension Plan; Savings Plan; Tuition Assistance. **Corporate headquarters location:** Newport CA. **Operations at this facility include:** Administration; Divisional Headquarters; Manufacturing; Research and Development; Sales; Service. **Listed on:** New York Stock Exchange.

PULSE, INC.
12101 Indian Creek Court, Beltsville MD 20705. 301/470-6000. **Contact:** Russ Walker, Personnel Manager. **Description:** Engaged in the design, development, and manufacturing of machine tools, special machinery, and aerospace prototypes, as well as the production of related technical publications.

RACAL HEALTH & SAFETY, INC.
7305 Executive Way, Frederick MD 21701. 301/695-8200. **Fax:** 301/695-4413. **Contact:** Linda Freeman, Human Resources Manager. **Description:** Specializes in OSHA-approved powdered-air and supplied-air systems and self-contained breathing apparatus (SCBA). Racal's products include gas mask filters, industrial air filters, respiratory protection filters, Airstream helmets, the Powerflow full-facepiece respirator with motor and filter, and the Delta line of disposable particulate respirators. The company also produces fully overwrapped composite pressure vessels used in firefighting. **Corporate headquarters location:** Sunrise FL. **Parent company:** The Racal Corporation. **Number of employees at this location:** 107.

RESOURCE CONSULTANTS, INC. (RCI)
1960 Gallows Road, Vienna VA 22182. 703/893-6120. **Fax:** 703/893-0917. **Contact:** Robert J. Duarte, Employment Director. **Description:** A diversified defense contractor supporting many U.S. Navy life cycle management and communications equipment contracts. Also provides job placement counseling to the U.S. Army at over 50 locations worldwide. **Common positions include:** Counselor; Electrical/Electronics Engineer; Management Analyst/Consultant; Software Engineer; Technical Writer/Editor; Technician. **Educational backgrounds include:** Computer Science; Economics; Engineering. **Corporate headquarters location:** This Location. **Other U.S. locations:** Vallejo CA; Panama City FL; Charleston SC. **Parent company:** Gilbert Associates. **Listed on:** NASDAQ. **Number of employees at this location:** 100. **Number of employees nationwide:** 1,200.

TATE ACCESS FLOORS, INC.
7510 Montevideo Road, Jessup MD 20794. 410/799-4200. **Contact:** Victoria Ramina, Director of Human Resources. **Description:** Manufactures access flooring and accessories. **Common positions include:** Accountant/Auditor; Blue-Collar Worker Supervisor; Computer Programmer; Customer Service Representative; Department Manager; Draftsperson; Electrical/Electronics Engineer; Human Resources Specialist; Industrial Engineer; Marketing Specialist; Mechanical Engineer; Operations/Production

Manager; Quality Control Supervisor. **Educational backgrounds include:** Accounting; Business Administration; Engineering; Finance. **Benefits:** Dental Insurance; Disability Coverage; Life Insurance; Medical Insurance; Pension Plan; Profit Sharing; Savings Plan; Tuition Assistance. **Corporate headquarters location:** This Location. **Operations at this facility include:** Manufacturing.

THIOKOL CORPORATION
55 Thiokol Road, Elkton MD 21921. 410/392-1000. **Contact:** Human Resources. **Description:** Develops and produces high-technology solid rocket motors for aerospace, defense and commercial launch applications. Also manufactures precision fastening systems for aerospace and industrial markets worldwide. Thiokol has annual sales of one billion dollars and a work force of 8,000 at locations throughout the world. For the space market, Thiokol produces solid rocket motors for most of the nation's satellite systems, the world's only human-related solid rocket motors for the Space Shuttle and the Castor 120 motor for commercial launch vehicles. For the defense market, the company produces components of the first and second stages of the Navy's Trident II missile system and propulsion systems for tactical missiles. The commercial side of the business is focused on the transportation industry. The precision fastening systems produced by Huck International, Inc. are used on planes, trucks, trains - supporting almost every facet of the aerospace and industrial fastening markets. In the 68 years since its founding, Thiokol Corporation has supplied solid rocket propulsion for every manned space program and every land-based U.S. intercontinental solid rock ballistic missile program.

TRIANGLE PACIFIC BUILDING PRODUCTS
10500 Ewing Road, Beltsville MD 20705. 301/937-5000. **Contact:** Mrs. Caine, Personnel. **Description:** Produces lumber, doors, windows, and a wide range of other building products.

VULCAN HART PMI
3600 North Point Boulevard, Baltimore MD 21222. 410/284-0660. **Contact:** General Manager. **Description:** A manufacturer of commercial cooking equipment, including gas and electric ovens, ranges, broilers, and fryers. **Corporate headquarters location:** Louisville KY. **Other U.S. locations:** Compton CA; St. Louis MO.

M.S. WILLETT, INC.
220 Cockeysville Road, P.O. Box 266, Cockeysville MD 21030. 410/771-0460. **Contact:** Barbara A. Conroy, Personnel. **Description:** A world-class tool and die manufacturer, engaged in metal stamping and punch press automation services. **Common positions include:** Accountant/Auditor; Computer Programmer; Draftsperson; Electrical/Electronics Engineer; Manufacturer's/Wholesaler's Sales Rep.; Marketing Specialist; Mechanical Engineer; Purchasing Agent and Manager; Quality Control Supervisor. **Educational backgrounds include:** Accounting; Business Administration; Engineering; Marketing. **Benefits:** Dental Insurance; Disability Coverage; Life Insurance; Medical Insurance; Tuition Assistance. **Special Programs:** Training Programs. **Corporate headquarters location:** This Location. **Operations at this facility include:** Administration; Manufacturing; Research and Development; Sales; Service. **Number of employees at this location:** 110.

XEROX CORPORATION
1616 Fort Myer Drive, Arlington VA 22209. 703/527-6400. **Contact:** Human Resources. **Description:** An office machine manufacturing company. **NOTE:** Send resumes to: Human Resources, P.O. Box 660512, Dallas, TX 75266. The phone number for that office is 800/428-2203.

Note: Because addresses and telephone numbers of smaller companies change rapidly, we recommend you call each company to verify the information below before inquiring about job opportunities. Mass mailings are not recommended.

Additional employers with over 250 employees:

ELEVATORS AND MOVING STAIRWAYS

General Elevator Co.
PO Box 1702, Baltimore MD 21203-1702. 410/789-0200.

SPECIAL INDUSTRIAL MACHINERY

Hughes Training Inc.
13775 McLearen Rd,
Herndon VA 22071-3212.
703/481-4500.

COMMERCIAL FURNITURE AND FIXTURES

Douglas & Lomason Co.
PO Box 308, Hvre De Grace MD 21078-0308. 410/939-0781.

AIR-CONDITIONING, HEATING, AND REFRIGERATION EQUIPMENT

Rotorex Co.
8301 Retreat Rd Ste B, Walkersville MD 21793-8410. 301/898-7011.

MEASURING AND CONTROLLING EQUIPMENT

Terumo Medical Corp.
950 Elkton Blvd, Elkton MD 21921-5322. 410/398-8500.

GRC International Inc.
1900 Gallows Rd, Vienna VA 22182-3865. 703/506-5000.

INDUSTRIAL AND COMMERCIAL MACHINERY AND EQUIPMENT

Crown Cork & Seal Co.
PO Box 5129, Baltimore MD 21224-0129. 410/563-6700.

Additional employers with under 250 employees:

WHOLESALE FURNITURE AND EQUIPMENT

Andy Stern Office Furniture Inc.
9107 Gaither Rd, Gaithersburg MD 20877-1455. 301/921-2700.

Price-Modern Inc.
9700 Martin Luther King Jr Hwy, Lanham MD 20706-1837. 301/459-8111.

Prince Office Furniture
5402 Reisterstown Rd, Baltimore MD 21215-4405. 410/358-5402.

Restaurant Equipment International
210 The Strand, Alexandria VA 22314-3320. 703/370-1301.

Contessa Design Inc.
3501 7th St, Baltimore MD 21225-1959. 410/355-8844.

OFFICE EQUIPMENT WHOLESALE

T Talbott Bond Co.
7138 Windsor Blvd, Baltimore MD 21244-2705. 410/265-8600.

Eastman Kodak Company
1100 N Glebe Rd Fl 13, Arlington VA 22201-4798. 703/908-5200.

COMMERCIAL EQUIPMENT WHOLESALE

Shelby Williams Industries Inc.
11400 Rockville Pike, Rockville MD 20852-3004. 301/231-9441.

Ebbit Green Electronics
4905 40th Pl, Hyattsville MD 20781-2104. 301/779-4484.

METAL HARDWARE

Caldwell Manufacturing
Rt 68 & Prosperity Ln, Williamsport MD 21795. 301/223-6500.

CONVEYORS AND CONVEYING EQUIPMENT

American Bottlers Equipment
10330 S Dolfield Rd, Owings Mills MD 21117-3597. 410/363-4400.

Novatec Corporation
222 Thomas Ave, Baltimore MD 21225-3327. 410/789-4811.

MISC. INDUSTRIAL MACHINE TOOLS

Langston Staley Machinery Corporation
11110 Pepper Rd, Cockys Ht Vly MD 21031-1203. 410/785-1550.

FOOD PRODUCTS MACHINERY

DCA Food Industries
8106 Stayton Dr, Jessup MD 20794-9622. 410/792-4300.

PUMPS AND PUMPING EQUIPMENT

Frederick Foundry & Machine Inc.
701 East St, Frederick MD 21701-5238. 301/663-1020.

FANS, BLOWERS, AND AIR PURIFICATION EQUIPMENT

Air-Cure Environmental
275 West St Ste 204, Annapolis MD 21401-3400. 410/268-2450.

PACKAGING MACHINERY

National Instrument
4119 Fordleigh Rd, Baltimore MD 21215-2292. 410/764-0900.

MISC. INDUSTRIAL MACHINERY AND EQUIPMENT

Manufacturing Systems & Tech Center
9200 Berger Rd, Columbia MD 21046-1602. 410/993-5700.

W L Gore & Associates
100 Airport Rd # 3, Elkton MD 21921-4125. 410/392-4440.

ENGINE PARTS

Precision Alternator Starter
4260 Entre Ct, Chantilly VA 22021-2105. 703/573-4600.

AEROSPACE AND/OR NAUTICAL SYSTEMS AND INSTRUMENTS

Quintron Corporation
3901 Centreville Rd # L, Chantilly VA 22021-3203. 703/478-2830.

TAS
200 Professional Dr, Gaithersburg MD 20879-3417. 301/921-8100.

MEASURING AND CONTROLLING EQUIPMENT

Data Measurement Corporation
15884 Gaither Dr, Gaithersburg MD 20877-1404. 301/948-2450.

Telenex Corp./A R Test Systems
7401 Boston Blvd, Springfield VA 22153-3195. 703/644-9190.

Commonwealth Scientific Corporation
500 Pendleton St, Alexandria VA 22314-1999. 703/548-0800.

Lucas Weinschel
1 Weinschel Loan # 6001, Gaithersburg MD 20878-4094. 301/948-3434.

Hunter Associates Lab
11491 Sunset Hills Rd, Reston VA 22090-5207. 703/471-6870.

Leica Inc.
14600 York Rd, Sparks MD

Manufacturing and Wholesaling: Misc. Industrial/245

21152-9306. 410/666-2100.

MISC. DURABLE GOODS WHOLESALE

Al Harring Assoc. Inc.
4409 Holter Ct, Jefferson MD 21755-8633. 301/371-7711.

Duxbak Inc.
903 Woods Rd, Cambridge MD 21613-9469. 410/228-2990.

Forman Distributors
7550 Accotink Park Rd, Springfield VA 22150-3644. 703/644-2425.

Frederick P. Winner Ltd.
1101 Desoto Rd, Baltimore MD 21223-3297. 410/646-5500.

Ikea
8352 Honeygo Blvd, Baltimore MD 21236-5906. 410/931-5400.

KD Tools
7200 Standard Dr, Hanover MD 21076-1351. 410/796-0410.

Latin Imports
14500 Lee Rd, Chantilly VA 22021. 703/631-8825.

Republic Electronics Corporation
5801 Lee Hwy, Arlington VA 22207-1495. 703/533-8555.

Russell Associates
260 Gateway Dr, Bel Air MD 21014-4274. 410/879-9180.

Ruth Wider
9319 Gaither Rd, Gaithersburg MD 20877-1438. 301/921-0100.

Tessco Inc.
34 Loveton Cir, Sparks MD 21152-9269. 410/472-7300.

SCRAP AND WASTE MATERIALS WHOLESALE

Keywell Co.
7600 Rolling Mill Rd, Baltimore MD 21224-2034. 410/282-9500.

Samuel Meisel & Company
6691 Baymeadow Dr, Glen Burnie MD 21060-6424. 410/787-1414.

United Iron & Metal Co.
2545 Wilkens Ave, Baltimore MD 21223-3333. 410/342-5454.

INDUSTRIAL MACHINERY AND EQUIPMENT WHOLESALE

Baltimore Forklift Recyclers I
11408 Pulaski Hwy, White Marsh MD 21162-1512. 410/335-0131.

Meter Box Covers Inc.
11548 Pulaski Hwy, White Marsh MD 21162-1215. 410/335-7545.

Johnson & Tower Baltimore Inc. MD
500 Wilson Point Rd, Baltimore MD 21220-4209. 410/687-0500.

Summit Precision Machining Inc.
2300 Sulphur Spring Rd, Baltimore MD 21227-2934. 410/247-8500.

McCall Handling Co.
3321 75th Ave, Landover MD 20785-1519. 301/341-1500.

Ambec
10330 S Dolfield Rd, Baltimore MD 21215. 410/363-4400.

Frenzelit North America
43990 Maiden Creek Ct, Ashburn VA 22011-3923. 703/318-9444.

Grinnell Fire Protect Systems
9640 Gerwig Ln, Columbia MD 21046-1519. 410/381-1400.

Chesapeake Sprinkler Co. VA
44642 Guilford Dr Ste 108, Ashburn VA 22011-6005. 703/478-8811.

For more information on career opportunities in industrial manufacturing and wholesaling:

Associations

APPLIANCE PARTS DISTRIBUTORS ASSOCIATION
228 East Baltimore Street, Detroit MI 48202. 313/875-8455. A wholesale distributor of parts.

ASSOCIATION FOR MANUFACTURING TECHNOLOGY
7901 Westpark Drive, McLean VA 22102. 703/893-2900. A trade association.

INSTITUTE OF INDUSTRIAL ENGINEERS
25 Technology Park, Norcross GA 30092. 404/449-0460. A non-profit organization with 27,000 members. Conducts seminars and offers reduced rates on their books and publications.

NATIONAL ASSOCIATION OF MANUFACTURERS
1331 Pennsylvania Avenue, NW, Suite 1500, Washington DC 20004. 202/637-3000. A lobbying association.

NATIONAL SCREW MACHINE PRODUCTS ASSOCIATION
6700 West Snowville Road, Brecksville OH 44141. 216/526-0300. Provides resource information.

NATIONAL TOOLING AND MACHINING ASSOCIATION
9300 Livingston Road, Fort Washington MD 20744. 301/248-1250. Reports on wages and operating expenses. Produces monthly newsletters. Offers legal advice.

SOCIETY OF MANUFACTURING ENGINEERS
P.O. Box 930, One SME Drive, Dearborn MI 48121. 313/271-1500. Offers educational events and educational materials on manufacturing.

Directories

DIRECTORY OF TEXAS MANUFACTURERS
University of Texas at Austin, Bureau of Business Research, Box 7459, Austin TX 78713. 512/471-1616.

TEXAS MANUFACTURERS REGISTER
Manufacturer's News, Inc., 1633 Central Street, Evanston IL 60201. 708/864-7000.

246/The Metropolitan Washington JobBank

Special Programs

BUREAU OF APPRENTICESHIP AND TRAINING
U.S. Department of Labor, 200 Constitution Avenue, NW, Washington, DC 20210. 202/219-6540.

MINING/GAS/PETROLEUM/ENERGY RELATED

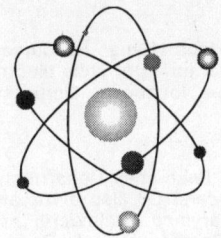

The energy industry is poised for a potentially huge growth cycle. While 10 years of layoffs and restructuring have tempered this optimism, a huge demand abroad is causing U.S. oil companies to turn their attention overseas. However, if the Iraqi oil embargo is lifted, foreign demand will be softer.

Even so, jobseekers can't expect increased production to lead to much employment growth. Layoffs are expected to continue, but advanced technologies used by the energy industry continue to crop up, and jobseekers with engineering backgrounds should watch for energy-related high-tech jobs.

In mining, earnings are much higher than average, but technological innovations, international competition, and environmental regulation will reduce employment. Best bets in the mining industry right now are for scientific technicians, professional specialty workers (such as geologists), and truck drivers.

CROWN CENTRAL PETROLEUM
One North Charles Street, P.O. Box 1168, Baltimore MD 21203. 410/539-7400. **Contact:** Human Resources. **Description:** Crown Central Petroleum refines and markets petroleum products and petrochemicals and has subsidiaries in the convenience store market. The company owns two refineries in Texas and operates 17 terminals across the southeastern and midwestern U.S. Petroleum products are marketed through 18 states and Washington DC. The company also operates 376 convenience stores and gas outlets under the Fast Fare and Zippy Mart names in Alabama, Florida, North and South Carolina, and Georgia. **Listed on:** American Stock Exchange.

DRYDEN OIL COMPANY
9300 Pulaski Highway, Baltimore MD 21220. 410/574-5000. **Fax:** 410/682-9486. **Contact:** Human Resources. **Description:** A manufacturer of oils and greases. **Common positions include:** Accountant/Auditor; Administrator; Blue-Collar Worker Supervisor; Branch Manager; Chemist; Computer Programmer; Credit Manager; Customer Service Representative; Department Manager; Financial Analyst; Human Resources Specialist; Industrial Engineer; Manufacturer's/Wholesaler's Sales Rep.; Mechanical Engineer; Operations/Production Manager; Quality Control Supervisor. **Educational backgrounds include:** Accounting; Business Administration; Chemistry; Computer Science; Engineering; Finance. **Benefits:** Dental Insurance; Disability Coverage; Employee Discounts; Life Insurance; Medical Insurance; Savings Plan; Tuition Assistance. **Corporate headquarters location:** This Location. **Other U.S. locations:** Orlando FL; Atlanta GA; Worcester MA; Charlotte NC; Lewisberry PA; Warminster PA; Richmond VA. **Operations at this facility include:** Administration; Manufacturing; Research and Development; Sales; Service.

METTIKI COAL CORPORATION
293 Table Rock Road, Oakland MD 21550. 301/334-3952. **Contact:** Human Resources. **Description:** A coal mining company.

MOBIL CORPORATION
3225 Gallows Road, Fairfax VA 22037. 703/846-3000. **Recorded Jobline:** 703/846-2777. **Contact:** Recruitment. **Description:** An integrated oil company engaged in petroleum and chemical products marketing, refining, manufacturing, exploration, production, transportation, and research and development in more than 100 countries. Exploration is conducted in 34 countries. The company has interests in 21 refineries in 12 countries, owns 28 oil tankers, and has interests in over 36,000 miles of pipeline

worldwide. Mobil markets its products through more than 19,000 company-owned retail outlets in over 90 countries. Other products include fabricated plastics, films, food bags, houseware, garbage bags, and building materials. The company also has subsidiaries involved in real estate development and mining operations. **Listed on:** New York Stock Exchange.

SOLAREX CORPORATION
630 Solarex Court, Frederick MD 21701. 301/698-4512. **Contact:** Human Resources. **Description:** Engaged in the research, development, and manufacturing of solar electric systems, primarily photovoltaic cells and panels. Three area locations. **Corporate headquarters location:** This Location.

SOUTHERN MARYLAND OIL
Box E, La Plata MD 20646. 301/934-8101. **Contact:** Human Resources Department. **Description:** Distributor of petroleum products. Southern Maryland Oil also owns and operates a chain of 50 convenience stores throughout Maryland, Delaware, and Virginia. **Common positions include:** Customer Service Representative; General Manager; Management Trainee. **Benefits:** Dental Insurance; Disability Coverage; Employee Discounts; Life Insurance; Medical Insurance; Pension Plan; Profit Sharing; Savings Plan; Tuition Assistance. **Special Programs:** Internships; Training Programs. **Corporate headquarters location:** This Location. **Operations at this facility include:** Administration.

For more information on career opportunities in the mining, gas, petroleum and energy industries:

Associations

AMERICAN ASSOCIATION OF PETROLEUM GEOLOGISTS
P.O. Box 979, Tulsa OK 7410-0979. 918/584-2555. International headquarters for petroleum geologists.

AMERICAN GEOLOGICAL INSTITUTE
4220 King Street, Alexandria VA 22302-1507. 703/379-2480. Scholarships available. Publishes monthly *Geotimes*. Offers job listings.

AMERICAN NUCLEAR SOCIETY
555 North Kensington Avenue, La Grange Park IL 60525. 708/352-6611. Offers educational services.

AMERICAN PETROLEUM INSTITUTE
1220 L Street NW, Suite 900, Washington DC 20005. 202/682-8000. A trade association.

GEOLOGICAL SOCIETY OF AMERICA
3300 Penrose Place, P.O. Box 9140, Boulder CO 80301. 303/447-2020. Membership of over 17,000. Offers sales items and publications. Also conducts society meetings.

SOCIETY OF EXPLORATION GEOPHYSICISTS
P.O. Box 702740, Tulsa OK 74170-2740. 918/493-3516. A membership association. Offers publications.

Directories

BROWN'S DIRECTORY OF NORTH AMERICAN AND INTERNATIONAL GAS COMPANIES
Advanstar Communications, 7500 Old Oak Boulevard, Cleveland OH 44130. 800/225-4569.

NATIONAL PETROLEUM NEWS FACT BOOK
Hunter Publishing Co., 25 NW Point Boulevard, Suite 800, Elk Grove Village, IL 60007. 708/427-9512.

OIL AND GAS DIRECTORY
Geophysical Directory, Inc., P.O. Box 130508, Houston TX 77219. 713/529-8789.

Magazines

AMERICAN GAS MONTHLY
1515 Wilson Boulevard, Arlington VA 22209. 703/841-8686.

GAS INDUSTRIES
Gas Industries News, Inc., 6300 North River Road, Suite 505, Rosemont IL 60018. 312/693-3682.

NATIONAL PETROLEUM NEWS
Hunter Publishing Co., 25 NW Point Boulevard, Elk Grove IL 60007. 708/296-0770.

OIL AND GAS JOURNAL
PennWell Publishing Co., 1421 South Sheridan Road, P.O. Box 1260. Tulsa OK 74101. 918/835-3161.

PAPER AND WOOD PRODUCTS

Midway through the year, 1995 was shaping up to be a great year for the paper industry. As of April 1995, paper prices were up 63 percent from the previous August. And continuing price increases and growing demand should allow paper companies to prosper in the next few years. Expansion and new facilities for many companies are expected, but only after debt from the last five years is payed off and restructuring occurs. In the next several years, mergers and the sale of family-owned companies (which are prevalent in this industry) may occur as some of the largest firms have already sold portions of their companies in order to focus on fewer markets. Environmental concerns voiced by the public should give the paper packaging segment an advantage over plastics, as companies move to become "green." The industry hopes to recycle at least half of the paper they make by the turn of the century.

Although the forestry sector is struggling with increasing costs and a decreasing supply of timber and wood adhesives, the outlook for college students enrolled in forest products programs is promising -- available positions exceed the number of jobseekers entering this industry. Especially promising for these students: jobs with the U.S. Forestry Service.

BELL'S PAPER RECYCLING COMPANY
310 Chapel Alley, Frederick MD 21701. 301/695-4081. **Contact:** Human Resources Department. **Description:** A paper mill.

CHESAPEAKE FIBER PACKAGING CORPORATION
P.O. Box 97, Hunt Valley MD 21031. 410/785-2233. **Contact:** Marilyn Weitzenkorn, Office Manager. **Description:** Produces folding and corrugated boxes. **Common positions include:** Manufacturer's/Wholesaler's Sales Rep. **Educational backgrounds include:** Marketing. **Benefits:** Disability Coverage; Life Insurance; Medical Insurance; Pension Plan. **Parent company:** Chesapeake Paperboard.

CHESAPEAKE PAPERBOARD COMPANY
Fort Avenue and Woodall Street, Baltimore MD 21230. 410/752-1842. **Contact:** Nancy Todd, Office Manager. **Description:** Produces a variety of paperboard products. **Corporate headquarters location:** This Location.

MERILLAT INDUSTRIES, INC.
1325 Industrial Park, P.O. Box 719, Mt. Jackson VA 22842. 703/477-2961. **Fax:** 703/477-2838. **Contact:** Glenn E. Wood, Personnel Manager. **Description:** A kitchen and bath cabinet manufacturer. **Common positions include:** Accountant/Auditor; Computer Programmer; Human Resources Specialist; Industrial Engineer; Industrial Production Manager; Mechanical Engineer; Quality Control Supervisor. **Educational backgrounds include:** Accounting; Business Administration. **Benefits:** 401K; Dental Insurance; Disability Coverage; Employee Discounts; Life Insurance; Medical Insurance; Pension Plan; Tuition Assistance. **Corporate headquarters location:** Adrian MI. **Parent company:** MASCO. **Operations at this facility include:** Administration; Manufacturing. **Listed on:** New York Stock Exchange. **Number of employees at this location:** 320. **Number of employees nationwide:** 2,200.

THE NELSON COMPANY
2116 Sparrows Point Road, Baltimore MD 21219. 410/477-3000. **Contact:** Mr. Pete Caltrider, President. **Description:** Produces wooden boxes, pallets, crates, and corrugated boxes. **Corporate headquarters location:** This Location.

SOLO CUP COMPANY
P.O. Box 129, Federalsburg MD 21632. 410/479-4800. **Contact:** Human Resources. **Description:** A paper products manufacturer.

WESTVACO CORPORATION
3400 East Biddle Street, Baltimore MD 21213. 410/327-7376. **Contact:** Warren Chamber, Administrative Manager. **Description:** Westvaco is a manufacturer of papers for high-quality graphic reproduction, consumer and industrial packaging and specialty chemicals for industrial and environmental applications. The company is also one of the largest envelope manufacturers in the world. Westvaco manages 1.5 million acres of timberlands in the United States and Brazil.

WESTVACO CORPORATION
300 Pratt Street, Luke MD 21540. 301/359-3311. **Contact:** Human Resources. **Description:** Westvaco is a manufacturer of papers for high-quality graphic reproduction, consumer and industrial packaging and specialty chemicals for industrial and environmental applications. The company is also one of the largest envelope manufacturers in the world. Westvaco manages 1.5 million acres of timberlands in the United States and Brazil.

Note: Because addresses and telephone numbers of smaller companies change rapidly, we recommend you call each company to verify the information below before inquiring about job opportunities. Mass mailings are not recommended.

Additional employers with under 250 employees:

LUMBER AND WOOD WHOLESALE

J Gibson McIlvain Co.
10701 Philadelphia Rd # 222, White Marsh MD 21162-1715. 410/335-9600.

Saco Supply
21 W Timonium Rd, Timonium MD 21093-3172. 410/252-3030.

WOOD MILLS

Century Stair Co. Inc.
15175 Washington St, Haymarket VA 22069-2951. 703/385-0078.

Conestoga Wood Specialties
3502 Hughes Rd, Darlington MD 21034-1371. 410/457-5123.

Foreign & Domestic Woods Inc.
U S Hwy 301 S, Bowling Green VA 22427. 804/633-5001.

MILLWORK, PLYWOOD, AND STRUCTURAL MEMBERS

Annandale Millwork Corporation
PO Box 387, Haymarket VA 22069-0387. 703/754-7177.

KC Company Inc.
12100 Baltimore Ave, Beltsville MD 20705-1363. 301/419-2200.

The Taney Corporation
5130 Allendale Ln, Taneytown MD 21787-2104. 410/756-6671.

Chesapeake Building Components
29469 Reagan Dr, Easton MD 21601-7039. 410/822-6406.

Chopp & Company
7 Pika Dr, Waldorf MD 20602-2722. 301/843-2467.

NVR Building Products
210 N Carroll St, Thurmont MD 21788-1746. 301/271-4659.

Shelter Systems Ltd.
633 Stone Chapel Rd, Westminster MD 21157-6731. 410/876-3900.

WOOD PRESERVING

Potomac Supply Corporation
U S Hwy 203 N, Kinsale VA 22488. 804/472-2527.

PAPER MILLS

Interstate Resources
1800 N Kent St Ste 1200, Arlington VA 22209-2145. 703/243-3355.

Simkins Maryland Board
PO Box 3249, Baltimore MD 21228-0249. 410/747-5100.

INDUSTRIAL PAPER AND RELATED PRODUCTS WHOLESALE

Nationwide Papers
7190 Parkway Dr, Hanover MD 21076-1386. 410/712-6805.

Wilcox-Walter Furlong Paper Co.
8750 Larkin Rd, Savage MD 20763-9725. 410/792-8666.

PAPERBOARD CONTAINERS AND BOXES

J.E. Smith Co./Rigid Box Division
8313 Grover Rd, Millersville MD 21108. 410/987-4006.

L. Gordon & Son Inc.
1050 S Paca St, Baltimore MD 21230-2590. 410/539-6537.

Container Corporation of America
6541 Eastern Ave, Baltimore MD 21224-2985. 410/633-8700.

St. Joe Container Co.
2200 Hollins Ferry Rd, Baltimore MD 21230-1692. 410/837-1200.

Clarcor
51st Ave & Cree Ln, College Park MD 20740. 301/474-3100.

Eastfield Corporation
1501 Russell St, Baltimore MD 21230-2017. 410/727-3838.

PAPER PRODUCTS

Oles Envelope Corporation
532 E 25th St, Baltimore MD 21218-5403. 410/243-1520.

PAPER BAGS

Maryland Paper Box Company
4545 Annapolis Rd, Baltimore MD 21227-4898. 410/789-1700.

DIE-CUT PAPER AND PAPER PRODUCTS

C & J Graphics Inc.
8906 Yellow Brick Rd, Baltimore MD 21237-2304. 410/682-6440.

For more information on career opportunities in the paper and wood products industries:

Associations

AMERICAN FOREST AND PAPER ASSOCIATION
1111 19th Street NW, Suite 700, Washington DC 20036. 202/463-2700. A lobbying group that conducts informational gatherings.

AMERICAN FOREST AND PAPER ASSOCIATION
260 Madison Avenue, New York NY 10016. 212/340-0600. Headquartered in Washington DC. A lobbying group that conducts informational gatherings.

FOREST PRODUCTS SOCIETY
2801 Marshall Court, Madison WI 53705-2295. 608/231-1361. An international, nonprofit, educational association that provides an information network for all segments of the forest products industry. Offers employment referral service.

NATIONAL PAPER TRADE ASSOCIATION
111 Great Neck Road, Great Neck NY 11021. 516/829-3070. Offers management services to wholesalers. Offers books and seminars; and research services.

PAPERBOARD PACKAGING COUNCIL
888 17th Street NW, Suite 900, Washington DC 20006. 202/289-4100. Offers statistical and lobbying services.

TECHNICAL ASSOCIATION OF THE PULP AND PAPER INDUSTRY
P.O. Box 105113, Atlanta GA 30348.
404/446-1400. Non-profit. Offers conferences and education.

Directories

DIRECTORY OF THE FOREST PRODUCTS INDUSTRY
Miller Freeman Publications, Inc., 600 Harrison Street, San Francisco CA 94107. 415/905-2200.

LOCKWOOD-POST'S DIRECTORY OF THE PAPER AND ALLIED TRADES
Miller Freeman Publications, Inc., 600 Harrison Street, San Francisco CA 94107. 415/905-2200.

POST'S PULP AND PAPER DIRECTORY
Miller Freeman Publications, Inc., 600 Harrison Street, San Francisco CA 94107. 415/905-2200.

Magazines

PAPERBOARD PACKAGING
Advanstar Communications, 131 West First Street, Duluth MN 55802. 218/723-9200.

PULP AND PAPER WEEK
Miller Freeman Publications, Inc., 600 Harrison Street, San Francisco CA 94107. 415/905-2200.

WOOD TECHNOLOGIES
Miller Freeman Publications, Inc., 600 Harrison Street, San Francisco CA 94107. 415/905-2200.

PRINTING AND PUBLISHING

The big news in publishing is the paper shortage. As of April 1995, paper prices were up 63 percent from the previous August. The cost of paper accounts for 30 to 40 percent of the manufacturing costs of a book, which in turn represent about one-third of the total book cost. Fortunately, rising costs are not expected to result in job losses, but instead will be compensated for through tighter design, lower paper grades, and increased book prices. The paper pinch is also affecting the magazine and newspaper industries. Newsprint prices rose more than 30 percent from early 1994 to early 1995, and magazines are growing noticeably shorter. One good sign for newspapers and magazines: as the economy improves, companies will increase their print advertising budgets.

Another way some publishers are balancing their books against the paper crunch is by looking to electronic media, a competitive and rapidly expanding medium. Many book publishers are offering CD-ROM versions of popular books, especially educational, reference, and children's books. Also, books on tape are growing in popularity. Magazines and newspapers also are jumping on the electronic bandwagon -- many periodicals and newspapers are now available online.

Book printing and distribution is also evolving. Traditionally, long print runs were necessary to keep costs down. But thanks to new digital presses that don't use plates, books can now be printed and distributed in small batches according to demand. Instead of printing and then distributing, publishers can now distribute and then print. Publishers will be able to use many small presses across the country, instead of one or two strategically placed large presses. The result: increased demand for computer-savvy printing professionals and dramatic cuts in shipping and warehousing.

AFRO-AMERICAN NEWSPAPERS INC.
2519 North Charles Street, Baltimore MD 21218. 410/554-8200. **Fax:** 410/554-8218. **Contact:** Mr. Verdel Elliot, Director of Human Resources. **Description:** A newspaper marketed to the Afro-American community. **Common positions include:** Accountant/Auditor; Advertising Clerk; Clerical Supervisor; Computer Systems Analyst; Editor; Human Resources Specialist; Librarian; Library Technician; Reporter. **Educational backgrounds include:** Accounting; Communications; Computer Science. **Benefits:** Life Insurance; Medical Insurance; Pension Plan; Tuition Assistance. **Special Programs:** Internships. **Corporate headquarters location:** This Location. **Other U.S. locations:** Washington DC; Richmond VA. **Number of employees at this location:** 55. **Number of employees nationwide:** 87.

AGORA, INC.
824 East Baltimore Street, Baltimore MD 21202. 410/234-0515. **Contact:** Human Resources. **Description:** A publisher of financial and travel newsletters, books, and special reports.

Printing and Publishing/253

AMERICAN PRESS, INC.
One American Place, Gordonsville VA 22942. 703/832-2253. **Fax:** 703/832-7253. **Contact:** Jerry Bortner, Human Resources Manager. **Description:** Printer of high-quality magazines and catalogues, utilizing web offset processes. **Common positions include:** Accountant/Auditor; Advertising Clerk; Blue-Collar Worker Supervisor; Buyer; Computer Programmer; Computer Systems Analyst; Cost Estimator; Credit Manager; Customer Service Representative; Electrical/Electronics Engineer; Electrician; Financial Analyst; General Manager; Human Resources Specialist; Industrial Engineer; Industrial Production Manager; Mechanical Engineer; Operations/Production Manager; Purchasing Agent and Manager; Quality Control Supervisor. **Educational backgrounds include:** Accounting; Art/Design; Business Administration; Communications; Computer Science; Engineering; Finance; Liberal Arts; Marketing. **Benefits:** Disability Coverage; Life Insurance; Medical Insurance; Pension Plan; Savings Plan; Tuition Assistance. **Operations at this facility include:** Administration; Divisional Headquarters; Manufacturing; Sales. **Listed on:** Privately held. **Number of employees at this location:** 250.

APPLIED GRAPHICS TECHNOLOGIES
2400 N Street NW, Washington DC 20037. 202/955-2518. **Fax:** 202/659-4831. **Contact:** Human Resources. **Description:** This location offers publication services, four-color facsimile or digital transmittal, and a desktop service bureau. Applied Graphics Technologies (AGT) is one of the largest providers of integrated graphic communications services to advertising agencies, magazine and catalog publishers, and corporate clients in various industries. For more than 30 years the company has helped apply new developments in the graphic arts to the specific requirements of clients. The company's services include commercial printing, color separation and retouching, facilities management, photo CD and digital image archiving, electronic imaging services, flexo/packaging services, publication and catalog services, satellite transmission services, creative design services, technical support and training services, and black and white ad production. International. **Corporate headquarters location:** New York NY.

AUTO TRADER
3920B Vero Road, Baltimore MD 21227. 410/242-4604. **Contact:** Human Resources Department. **Description:** A magazine publishing company.

BALMAR PRINTING AND GRAPHICS, INC.
5130 Wilson Boulevard, Arlington VA 22205. 703/528-9000. **Contact:** Human Resources. **Description:** A commercial lithographic printer. **Number of employees at this location:** 100.

THE BALTIMORE SUN
501 North Calvert Street, Baltimore MD 21278. 410/332-6268. **Contact:** Manager of Employment. **Description:** A publishing company operating various news bureaus around the world. *The Sun* and *The Evening Sun* both cover the Baltimore area. **Common positions include:** Advertising Clerk; Computer Systems Analyst; Customer Service Representative; Editor; Librarian; Reporter; Technical Writer/Editor. **Educational backgrounds include:** Accounting; Advertising; Art/Design; Business Administration; Cartography; Commercial Art; Communications; Computer Science; English; Finance; Journalism; Liberal Arts; Marketing. **Benefits:** 401K; Dental Insurance; Life Insurance; Medical Insurance; Pension Plan; Tuition Assistance. **Special Programs:** Internships. **Corporate headquarters location:** Los Angeles CA. **Parent company:** Times Mirror. **Operations at this facility include:** Administration; Manufacturing; Sales; Service. **Number of employees at this location:** 2,300.

BARTON-COTTON INC.
1405 Parker Road, Baltimore MD 21227. **Contact:** Manager. **Description:** A printer and publisher of greeting cards, stationery, and a number of other types of literature.

BRUBACH CORPORATION
P.O. Box 15629, Chevy Chase MD 20825. 301/986-5545. **Fax:** 301/986-0658. **Contact:** Human Resources. **Description:** A producer of the following publications: *Opportunities in Public Affairs*, *Environmental Career Opportunities*, and *Entertainment Jobs*.

BUREAU OF ENGRAVING AND PRINTING
14th and C Streets Southwest, Washington DC 20228. 202/874-3019. **Contact:** Human Resources. **Description:** The Bureau produces all U.S. paper currency, a

majority of U.S. postage stamps, and many other security documents issued by the federal government. Research and development programs for strengthening counterfeit deterrence, improving the quality of products and reducing manufacturing costs are integral facets of its operations. Other activities at the Bureau include engraving plates and dies; manufacturing certain inks used in security products; purchasing materials, supplies and equipment; and storing and delivering products in accordance with requirements of customers. The Bureau occupies three government-owned facilities. The Main Facility and Annex Building, located in Washington, produce Federal Reserve Notes, postage stamps, and other security products. The Western Currency Facility, located in Fort Worth, Texas, is dedicated to the production of Federal Reserve Notes. **Parent company:** Department of Treasury.

THE BUREAU OF NATIONAL AFFAIRS, INC.
1231 25th Street NW, Room SC-100, Washington DC 20037. 202/452-4335. **Contact:** Employment Services. **Description:** Prepares, publishes, and sells legal and economic periodicals and publications, books, pamphlets, films, and other materials. Also publishes other material, including labor, environmental, and safety services training and communications films. Equal Opportunity Employer, M/F. **Common positions include:** Accountant/Auditor; Attorney; Commercial Artist; Computer Programmer; Customer Service Representative; Editor; Human Resources Specialist; Manufacturer's/Wholesaler's Sales Rep.; Marketing Specialist; Operations/Production Manager; Reporter; Systems Analyst; Technical Writer/Editor. **Educational backgrounds include:** Accounting; Art/Design; Business Administration; Communications; Computer Science; Finance; Journalism. **Benefits:** Daycare Assistance; Dental Insurance; Disability Coverage; Life Insurance; Medical Insurance; Pension Plan; Profit Sharing; Stock Option; Tuition Assistance. **Corporate headquarters location:** This Location. **Operations at this facility include:** Administration; Research and Development.

CADMUS JOURNAL SERVICES, INC.
500 Cadmus Lane, Easton MD 21601-0969. **Fax:** 410/822-0438. **Contact:** Mel Rappleyea, Sr. Human Resource Director. **Description:** Cadmus Communications Corporation partners with its customers to advance science, medicine, technology, and education by integrating, packaging, and distributing breakthrough information to the world. Formed by the combination of the Byrd Press Journal Division and the acquisition of Waverly Press, Cadmus Journal Services is an international leader in the production of research journals. This product line serves four distinct markets: medical and biomedical; technical and scientific; learned and scholarly; and mathematics. Parent company, Cadmus Communications Corporation, is a graphic communications company offering specialized products and services in three broad areas: printing, marketing, and publishing. Cadmus is the 26th largest graphic communications company in North America. Product lines include annual reports, catalogs, direct marketing financial printing, point-of-sale marketing, promotional printing, publishing, research journals, specialty magazines, and specialty packaging. **Other subsidiaries include:** American Graphics, Inc. (Atlanta, GA); Cadmus Color Center, Inc. (Richmond, VA); Cadmus Direct Marketing, Inc. (Charlotte, VA); Cadmus Interactive (Tucker, GA); Central Florida Press, L.C. (Orlando, FL); Expert Brown (Richmond, VA); Garamond, Inc. (Baltimore, MD); Graphtech Corporation (Charlotte, NC); Marblehead Communications, Inc. (Boston, MA); Three Score, Inc. (Tucker, GA); Tuff Stuff Publications, Inc. (Washburn Graphics, Inc. (Charlotte, NC); The William Byrd Press (Richmond, VA). **NOTE:** The number of employees grew from 1,780 to 2,400 between 1993 and 1994. **Common positions include:** Accountant/Auditor; Blue-Collar Worker Supervisor; Budget Analyst; Customer Service Representative; Desktop Publishing Specialist; Electrical/Electronics Engineer; Electrician; Financial Analyst; Industrial Engineer; Industrial Production Manager; Mechanical Engineer; Printing Press Operator; Quality Control Supervisor; Software Engineer. **Educational backgrounds include:** Accounting; Art/Design; Business Administration; Computer Science; Engineering; Finance; Printing. **Benefits:** 401K; Computer Loans; Dental Insurance; Disability Coverage; Employee Discounts; Life Insurance; Medical Insurance; Pension Plan; Profit Sharing; Savings Plan; Tuition Assistance. **Special Programs:** Internships. **Corporate headquarters location:** Richmond VA. **Other U.S. locations:** Linthicum MD. **Parent company:** Cadmus Communications Corporation. **Operations at this facility include:** Administration; Manufacturing; Research and Development; Sales; Service. **Listed on:** NASDAQ. **Number of employees at this location:** 700. **Number of employees nationwide:** 2,500.

CADMUS JOURNAL SERVICES, INC.
Airport Square 7, 940 Elkridge Landing Road, Linthicum MD 21090-2908. 410/850-0500. **Contact:** Human Resources. **Description:** Formed by the combination of the

Byrd Press Journal Division and the acquisition of Waverly Press, Cadmus Journal Services is an international leader in the production of research journals. This product line serves four distinct markets: medical and biomedical; technical and scientific; learned and scholarly; and mathematics. Parent company, Cadmus Communications Corporation, is a graphic communications company offering specialized products and services in three broad areas: printing, marketing, and publishing. Cadmus is the 26th largest graphic communications company in North America. Product lines include annual reports, catalogs, direct marketing financial printing, point-of-sale marketing, promotional printing, publishing, research journals, specialty magazines, and specialty packaging. **Other subsidiaries include:** American Graphics, Inc. (Atlanta, GA); Cadmus Color Center, Inc. (Richmond, VA); Cadmus Direct Marketing, Inc. (Charlotte, VA); Cadmus Interactive (Tucker, GA); Central Florida Press, L.C. (Orlando, FL); Expert Brown (Richmond, VA); Garamond, Inc. (Baltimore, MD); Graphtech Corporation (Charlotte, NC); Marblehead Communications, Inc. (Boston, MA); Three Score, Inc. (Tucker, GA); Tuff Stuff Publications, Inc. (Washburn Graphics, Inc. (Charlotte, NC); The William Byrd Press (Richmond, VA). **NOTE:** The number of employees grew from 1,780 to 2,400 between 1993 and 1994. **Corporate headquarters location:** Richmond VA. **Other U.S. locations:** Easton MD. **Parent company:** Cadmus Communications Corporation.

CAPITAL GAZETTE NEWSPAPERS INC.
(ANNAPOLIS EVENING CAPITAL)
P.O. Box 911, Annapolis MD 21404. 410/268-5000. **Contact:** Tom Marquardt, Managing Editor. **Description:** Publishes the *Annapolis Evening Capital*, a daily newspaper. **Corporate headquarters location:** This Location.

CARROLL COUNTY TIMES
201 Railroad Avenue, Westminster MD 21157-4823. 410/848-4400. **Fax:** 410/857-1176. **Contact:** Bob Campitelli, Business Office Manager. **Description:** An area newspaper. **Common positions include:** Advertising Clerk; Bindery Worker; Commercial Artist; Computer Programmer; Credit Clerk and Authorizer; Credit Manager; Customer Service Representative; Department Manager; Designer; Editor; Financial Manager; General Manager; Graphic Artist; Manufacturer's/Wholesaler's Sales Rep.; Marketing/Advertising/PR Manager; Photographer/Camera Operator; Printing Press Operator; Typist/Word Processor. **Educational backgrounds include:** Accounting; Business Administration; Communications; Computer Science; Finance; Marketing. **Benefits:** Disability Coverage; Life Insurance; Medical Insurance; Pension Plan; Savings Plan; Tuition Assistance. **Corporate headquarters location:** Shelbyville KY.

CONGRESSIONAL QUARTERLY
1414 22nd Street NW, Washington DC 20037. 202/887-8500. **Contact:** John Coyle, Business Manager. **Description:** Publishes the *Congressional Quarterly*, and the daily *Congressional Monitor*, as well as a wide range of government-related publications.

CRAFTSMAN PRESS, INC.
P.O. Box 467, Bladensburg MD 20710. 301/277-9400. **Contact:** Sharon Hall, Office Manager. **Description:** Provides a wide range of commercial printing services.

DIAMOND PRESS
1819 East Preston Street, Baltimore MD 21213. 410/327-5600. **Contact:** Personnel Manager. **Description:** A commercial printer, primarily engaged in the printing of circulars.

DOW JONES & COMPANY
11501 Columbia Pike, Silver Spring MD 20904. 301/680-2900. **Contact:** Business Office Representative. **Description:** The company publishes *The Wall Street Journal* as part of the national financial news service and publishing company.

EDITORS PRESS, INC.
6200 Editors Park Drive, Hyattsville MD 20782. 301/853-4900. **Contact:** Personnel Manager. **Description:** Provides a variety of commercial printing and direct mail services, including the printing of advertising literature, brochures, folders, booklets, pamphlets, maps, catalogs, and periodicals. **Corporate headquarters location:** This Location. **Parent company:** Kiplinger Washington Editors (Washington, DC).

FOREIGN POLICY MAGAZINE
2400 N Street NW, Washington DC 20037. 202/862-7940. **Fax:** 202/862-2610. **Contact:** Human Resources. **Description:** Quarterly journal that publishes scholarly articles on international affairs. Established in 1970.

GANNETT COMPANY, INC.
1100 Wilson Boulevard, Arlington VA 22234. 703/284-6226. **Recorded Jobline:** 703/284-6054. **Contact:** Cyndi Makowski, Recruiter. **Description:** Gannett, a nationwide news and information company, publishes 81 newspapers including *USA Today* and *Gannett News Service*, and is the largest outdoor advertising company in North America. Gannett is also involved in marketing, television news and program production, research satellite information systems, and owns a national group of commercial printing facilities. Gannett has operations in 41 states, the District of Columbia, Guam, the Virgin Islands, Canada, Great Britain, Hong Kong, Singapore, and Switzerland. **Common positions include:** Accountant/Auditor; Attorney; Buyer; Computer Programmer; Financial Analyst; Human Resources Specialist; Operations/Production Manager; Paralegal; Purchasing Agent and Manager; Secretary. **Benefits:** 401K; Adoption Assistance; Dental Insurance; Disability Coverage; Employee Discounts; Life Insurance; Medical Insurance; Pension Plan; Profit Sharing; Stock Option; Tuition Assistance. **Special Programs:** Internships; Training Programs. **Corporate headquarters location:** This Location. **Number of employees nationwide:** 37,000.

GARAMOND, INC.
2717 Wilmarco Avenue, Baltimore MD 21223-3372. 410/624-4400. **Contact:** Human Resources. **Description:** Garamond, Inc. produces annual reports, promotional printing, and financial printing products. Parent company, Cadmus Communications Corporation, is a graphic communications company offering specialized products and services in three broad areas: printing, marketing, and publishing. Cadmus is the 26th largest graphic communications company in North America. Product lines include annual reports, catalogs, direct marketing financial printing, point-of-sale marketing, promotional printing, publishing, research journals, specialty magazines, and specialty packaging. **Other subsidiaries include:** American Graphics, Inc. (Atlanta, GA); Cadmus Color Center, Inc. (Richmond, VA); Cadmus Direct Marketing, Inc. (Charlotte, VA); Cadmus Interactive (Tucker, GA); Cadmus Journal Services (Linthicum, MD, Eaton, MD, and Richmond, VA); Central Florida Press, L.C. (Orlando, FL); Expert Brown (Richmond, VA); Graphtech Corporation (Charlotte, NC); Marblehead Communications, Inc. (Boston, MA); Three Score, Inc. (Tucker, GA); Tuff Stuff Publications, Inc. (Washburn Graphics, Inc. (Charlotte, NC); The William Byrd Press (Richmond, VA). **NOTE:** The number of employees grew from 1,780 to 2,400 between 1993 and 1994. **Parent company:** Cadmus Communications Corporation.

INTERNATIONAL MEDICAL NEWS GROUP
12230 Wilkins Avenue, Rockville MD 20852-1834. 301/770-6170. **Contact:** Human Resources. **Description:** A periodicals publisher.

THE JOHNS HOPKINS UNIVERSITY PRESS
2715 North Charles Street, Baltimore MD 21218. 410/516-6975. **Recorded Jobline:** 410/516-8022. **Contact:** Personnel Department. **Description:** A division of the Johns Hopkins University which publishes books, journals, and other material for education. **NOTE:** All hiring is administered through the Johns Hopkins University Personnel Department at Garland Hall, Baltimore MD 21218.

JUDD'S INCORPORATED
1500 Eckington Place Northeast, Washington DC 20002. 202/635-1200. **Contact:** Tom Michaels, Personnel Director. **Description:** Provides commercial printing services, primarily of magazines and catalogs. **Common positions include:** Customer Service Representative; Human Resources Specialist; Industrial Engineer; Mechanical Engineer. **Educational backgrounds include:** Accounting; Business Administration; Engineering. **Benefits:** 401K; Dental Insurance; Disability Coverage; Life Insurance; Medical Insurance; Pension Plan; Profit Sharing; Tuition Assistance. **Corporate headquarters location:** This Location. **Other U.S. locations:** Pikesville MD; New York NY; Strasburg VA. **Number of employees at this location:** 17. **Number of employees nationwide:** 1,000.

JUDD'S INCORPORATED
294 Front Royal Road, Strasburg VA 22657. 703/465-6606. **Fax:** 703/465-6610. **Contact:** Carl Dysart, Personnel Manager. **Description:** Provides commercial printing

services, primarily of magazines and catalogs. **Common positions include:** Accountant/Auditor; Administrative Services Manager; Buyer; Computer Programmer; Computer Systems Analyst; Cost Estimator; Customer Service Representative; Electrical/Electronics Engineer; Electrician; Mechanical Engineer; Purchasing Agent and Manager. **Educational backgrounds include:** Business Administration. **Benefits:** 401K; Dental Insurance; Disability Coverage; Life Insurance; Medical Insurance; Pension Plan; Profit Sharing; Savings Plan; Tuition Assistance. **Corporate headquarters location:** Washington DC. **Other U.S. locations:** Baltimore MD. **Operations at this facility include:** Administration; Manufacturing. **Listed on:** Privately held. **Number of employees at this location:** 735. **Number of employees nationwide:** 1,200.

THE KIPLINGER WASHINGTON EDITOR INC.
1729 H Street NW, Washington DC 20006. 202/887-6400. **Contact:** Nancy Fisher, Director of Personnel. **Description:** Produces a nationally-distributed newsletter and *Changing Times* magazine. **Corporate headquarters location:** This Location.

LANDMARK COMMUNITY NEWSPAPERS OF MARYLAND INC.
201 Railroad Avenue, Westminster MD 21157. 410/875-5400. **Contact:** Business Manager. **Description:** Provides newspaper publishing, specialty publications, and commercial printing. **Common positions include:** Accountant/Auditor; Blue-Collar Worker Supervisor; Commercial Artist; Department Manager; Editor; General Manager; Layout Specialist; Manufacturer's/Wholesaler's Sales Rep.; Reporter. **Educational backgrounds include:** Accounting; Art/Design; Business Administration; Communications; Liberal Arts; Marketing. **Benefits:** Disability Coverage; Employee Discounts; Life Insurance; Medical Insurance; Pension Plan; Savings Plan; Tuition Assistance. **Corporate headquarters location:** Norfolk VA. **Operations at this facility include:** Sales; Service.

LERNER PROCESSING LABS
1 Choke Cherry Road, Rockville MD 20850. 301/948-2800. **Fax:** 301/921-0242. **Contact:** Deborah Stevenson, Human Resources Manager. **Description:** Offers complete amateur photofinishing and processing services. **Common positions include:** Blue-Collar Worker Supervisor; Customer Service Representative; Electronics Technician; Operations/Production Manager; Production Worker; Quality Control Supervisor; Secretary. **Educational backgrounds include:** High School Diploma; Management/Planning. **Benefits:** Dental Insurance; Disability Coverage; Employee Discounts; Life Insurance; Medical Insurance; Pension Plan; Profit Sharing; Savings Plan. **Corporate headquarters location:** Santa Ana CA. **Operations at this facility include:** Manufacturing. **Number of employees at this location:** 150.

JOHN D. LUCAS PRINTING COMPANY
1820 Portal Street, Baltimore MD 21224. 410/633-4200. **Contact:** Personnel Director. **Description:** Involved in all aspects of printing and book-making, including books and job printing, composition and binding services, typesetting, and lithography. **Common positions include:** Customer Service Representative; Manufacturer's/Wholesaler's Sales Rep. **Educational backgrounds include:** Accounting; Business Administration; Liberal Arts. **Benefits:** Dental Insurance; Disability Coverage; Life Insurance; Medical Insurance; Profit Sharing; Tuition Assistance. **Corporate headquarters location:** This Location. **Operations at this facility include:** Administration; Manufacturing; Sales; Service.

MARYLAND INDEPENDENT NEWSPAPERS
CHESAPEAKE PUBLISHING CORPORATION
7 Industrial Park Circle, Waldorf MD 20602. 301/645-9480. **Contact:** Human Resources. **Description:** Publishes five area newspapers: *Enterprise* (circulation: 14,000); *Maryland Independent* (circulation 12,500); *South County Current* (circulation 33,000); *Calvert County Recorder* (circulation 5,500); and *Flightline* (circulation 9,000). The company also provides commercial printing services. **Common positions include:** Accountant/Auditor; Administrator; Advertising Clerk; Credit Manager; Customer Service Representative; Department Manager; Editor; General Manager; Manufacturer's/Wholesaler's Sales Rep.; Operations/Production Manager; Reporter. **Educational backgrounds include:** Accounting; Art/Design; Business Administration; Journalism; Marketing. **Benefits:** Disability Coverage; Life Insurance; Medical Insurance; Pension Plan; Tuition Assistance. **Corporate headquarters location:** Easton MD. **Operations at this facility include:** Administration; Divisional Headquarters; Manufacturing; Sales; Service.

McARDLE PRINTING COMPANY, INC.
800 Commerce Drive, Upper Marlboro MD 20772. 301/390-8500. **Contact:** Virgil W. Wright, Senior Vice President. **Description:** A commercial printing firm. **Common positions include:** Accountant/Auditor; Blue-Collar Worker Supervisor; Cost Estimator; Customer Service Representative; Human Resources Specialist; Manufacturer's/Wholesaler's Sales Rep.; Operations/Production Manager; Purchasing Agent and Manager. **Educational backgrounds include:** Accounting; Business Administration. **Benefits:** 401K; Disability Coverage; Life Insurance; Medical Insurance; Profit Sharing. **Corporate headquarters location:** This Location. **Parent company:** Bureau of National Affairs. **Operations at this facility include:** Administration; Manufacturing; Sales. **Listed on:** Privately held. **Number of employees at this location:** 200.

McGRAW-HILL INC.
1200 G Street NW, Suite 1100, Washington DC 20005. 202/383-2100. **Contact:** Gloria Kassabian, Office Manager. **Description:** A publishing company. **Corporate headquarters location:** New York NY.

McGREGOR PRINTING CORPORATION
2121 K Street NW, Suite 810, Washington DC 20037. 202/333-4411. **Contact:** Fred Fearing, Vice President. **Description:** A printer of business forms.

MONARCH AVALON
4517 Hartford Road, Baltimore MD 21214. 410/254-9200. **Contact:** Steve Szekely, Vice President. **Description:** A commercial printing firm, also manufactures envelopes. **Corporate headquarters location:** This Location.

NATIONAL GEOGRAPHIC SOCIETY
11555 Darnestown Road, Gaithersburg MD 20878. 301/921-1253. **Contact:** Human Resources. **Description:** The world's largest non-profit organization, the National Geographic Society offers various products and services. The society offers four major publications, including *National Geographic*, which reaches 10 million members and an estimated 40 million readers; *National Geographic Traveler*, providing travel information; *National Geographic World*, for children eight-years-old and over; and *National Geographic Research and Exploration*, a scientific journal. The society also offers maps and globes, as well as books and games for young adults. "The National Geographic Explorer" is a two-hour cable series with a magazine format, airing weekly on TBS. The National Geographic Education Program offers geography education programs to schools through films, computer software, videos, and other high-tech multimedia classroom materials. Since 1890, the society's Committee for Research and Exploration has supported more than 4,000 projects that research and explore various geographic locations. The society also offers public services with annual series of lectures and events and the JASON Project, which involves students with interactive television links.

NATIONAL JOURNAL
1501 M Street NW, 3rd Floor, Washington DC 20005. 202/739-8400. **Contact:** Executive Editor. **Description:** A weekly magazine devoted to covering national politics and federal policy. Established in 1968.

THE OIL DAILY COMPANY
1401 New York Avenue NW, Suite 500, Washington DC 20005. 202/662-0700. **Fax:** 202/662-0751. **Contact:** Kathleen Mahoney, Accountant and Personnel Coordinator. **Description:** Publishes oil and gas industry newsletters and magazines. **Common positions include:** Accountant/Auditor; Advertising Clerk; Computer Systems Analyst; Customer Service Representative; Editor; Graphic Artist; Human Resources Specialist; Marketing/Advertising/PR Manager; Payroll Clerk; Receptionist; Reporter; Technical Writer/Editor. **Educational backgrounds include:** Accounting; Art/Design; Business Administration; Communications; Computer Science; Economics; Finance; Journalism; Marketing. **Benefits:** 401K; Dental Insurance; Disability Coverage; Life Insurance; Medical Insurance. **Corporate headquarters location:** This Location. **Other U.S. locations:** Houston TX. **Parent company:** EEOP. **Operations at this facility include:** Administration; Divisional Headquarters; Research and Development; Sales; Service. **Number of employees at this location:** 41.

OPTIC GRAPHICS, INC.
101 Dover Road, Glen Burnie MD 21060. 410/768-3000. **Contact:** Patricia Pirog, Human Resources Director. **Description:** A book manufacturer, utilizing both web and sheet-fed offset equipment. Provides a variety of finishing, including saddle-stitch,

perfect-binding, wire-o and plastic binding, loose-leaf binder manufacturing, index tabs printing, and foil stamping. **Corporate headquarters location:** This Location.

QUEBECOR PRINTING INC.
7364 Baltimore-Annapolis Boulevard, Glen Burnie MD 21061. 410/761-0440. **Contact:** Industrial Relations Manager. **Description:** Quebecor Printing Inc. is one of the world's largest commercial printers with 84 printing and related services facilities in Canada, the United States, France, the United Kingdom, Mexico and India. The company's major product categories include inserts and circulars, magazines, books, catalogues, directories, cheques, bonds and banknotes, specialty printing and newspapers. Quebecor Printing also offers web offset, gravure and sheetfed printing capacity, plus related services that include advanced electronic prepress and imaging, database and list management, shipping and distribution and CD-ROM mastering and replicating. Quebecor Printing Inc. has 36 plants and 13,000 employees in 21 states. Quebecor Printing Inc. became the one of the largest book manufacturers in North America with the formation of its new group, Quebecor Printing Book Group. The Group serves more than 1,000 publishing firms, including Random House, Simon & Schuster, McGraw-Hill, and Penguin USA.

QUEBECOR PRINTING INC.
201 North Charles Street, Baltimore MD 21201-4102. 410/783-5200. **Contact:** Human Resources. **Description:** Quebecor Printing Inc. is one of the world's largest commercial printers with 84 printing and related services facilities in Canada, the United States, France, the United Kingdom, Mexico and India. The company's major product categories include inserts and circulars, magazines, books, catalogues, directories, cheques, bonds and banknotes, specialty printing and newspapers. Quebecor Printing also offers web offset, gravure and sheetfed printing capacity, plus related services that include advanced electronic prepress and imaging, database and list management, shipping and distribution and CD-ROM mastering and replicating. Quebecor Printing Inc. has 36 plants and 13,000 employees in 21 states. Quebecor Printing Inc. became the one of the largest book manufacturers in North America with the formation of its new group, Quebecor Printing Book Group. The Group serves more than 1,000 publishing firms, including Random House, Simon & Schuster, McGraw-Hill and Penguin USA.

RANDOM HOUSE INC.
400 Hahn Road, Westminster MD 21157. 410/876-2280. **Contact:** Personnel Department. **Description:** A publishing company.

SAUL'S LITHOGRAPH COMPANY INC.
2424 Evarts Street Northeast, Washington DC 20018. 202/529-9100. **Contact:** Edward Bozzella, President. **Description:** Offers a complete range of commercial printing services, including offset and lithography services.

THE SENTINEL NEWSPAPERS
P.O. Box 1272, Rockville MD 20849. 301/948-4630. **Contact:** General Manager. **Description:** Publishes two weekly newspapers, the *Prince George Sentinel* and the *Montgomery Sentinel*, with a circulation of more than 200,000. **Common positions include:** Editor; Public Relations Specialist; Reporter; Sales Associate. **Benefits:** Dental Insurance; Life Insurance; Medical Insurance. **Special Programs:** Internships; Training Programs. **Corporate headquarters location:** This Location. **Operations at this facility include:** Sales; Service.

SMITHSONIAN INSTITUTION PRESS
470 L'Enfant Plaza, Suite 7100, Washington DC 20560. 202/287-3738. **Contact:** Human Resources. **Description:** Publishing division of the Smithsonian Institution. The Smithsonian Institution Press produces 300 publications a year, as well as several recordings and videos, all relating to Smithsonian collections and research interest.

TIME-LIFE INC.
777 Duke Street, Alexandria VA 22314. 703/838-7000. **Contact:** Human Resources. **Description:** A publishing company.

U.S. NEWS & WORLD REPORT
2400 N Street NW, Washington DC 20037. 202/955-2039. **Fax:** 202/955-2035. **Contact:** Page Bentzel, Personnel Services Representative. **Description:** An American news magazine, with more than 20 million readers. **Common positions include:** Accountant/Auditor; Administrative Services Manager; Computer Operator; Computer

Programmer; Computer Systems Analyst; Marketing Research Analyst; Reporter; Services Sales Representative; Systems Analyst. **Educational backgrounds include:** Accounting; Business Administration; Computer Science; Finance; Liberal Arts; Marketing; Mathematics. **Benefits:** 401K; Dental Insurance; Disability Coverage; Employee Discounts; Life Insurance; Medical Insurance; Savings Plan; Spending Account; Tuition Assistance. **Special Programs:** Internships. **Corporate headquarters location:** This Location. **Other U.S. locations:** New York NY. **Operations at this facility include:** Administration.

USA TODAY
1000 Wilson Boulevard, Arlington VA 22229. 703/276-3400. **Contact:** Human Resources. **Description:** A national newspaper. **Parent company:** Gannett Co., Inc.

UNITED PRESS INTERNATIONAL
1400 Eye Street, Washington DC 20005. 202/898-8200. **Contact:** Personnel Officer. **Description:** One of the largest independent news gathering organizations in the world, with news bureaus located throughout the world. **Common positions include:** Editor; Radio/TV Announcer/Newscaster; Reporter. **Educational backgrounds include:** Journalism. **Benefits:** 401K; Dental Insurance; Medical Insurance. **Special Programs:** Internships. **Corporate headquarters location:** This Location. **Other U.S. locations:** Miami FL; Chicago IL; New York NY; Dallas TX. **Operations at this facility include:** Administration; Research and Development; Sales. **Listed on:** Privately held.

WASHINGTON BUSINESS JOURNAL
2000 14th Street North, Suite 500, Arlington VA 22201. 703/875-2200. **Fax:** 703/875-2231. **Contact:** Ellen Duhamel, Business Manager. **Description:** Publishers of a weekly business newspaper. **Common positions include:** Advertising Account Executive; Advertising Clerk; Credit Manager; Customer Service Representative; Department Manager; Editor; General Manager; Marketing Specialist; Operations/Production Manager; Radio/TV Announcer/Newscaster; Reporter; Services Sales Representative; Technical Writer/Editor. **Educational backgrounds include:** Accounting; Art History; Communications; Liberal Arts; Marketing. **Benefits:** 401K; Dental Insurance; Disability Coverage; Life Insurance; Medical Insurance; Savings Plan; Stock Option. **Special Programs:** Internships. **Corporate headquarters location:** Charlotte NC. **Parent company:** American City Business Journals. **Operations at this facility include:** Administration; Publishing; Sales; Service. **Listed on:** NASDAQ. **Number of employees at this location:** 45.

THE WASHINGTON POST CO.
1150-15th Street NW, Washington DC 20071. 202/334-6630. **Recorded Jobline:** 202/334-5350. **Contact:** Wanda Morrison, Manager of Human Resources. **Description:** The principal business activities of The Washington Post Company consist of newspaper publishing (*The Washington Post*; *The Herald* in Everett WA; and the *Gazette* weekly papers in Maryland); television broadcasting (network affiliated stations in Detroit MI, Hartford CT, Houston TX, Jacksonville FL, Miami FL, and San Antonio TX); the ownership and operation of cable television systems; and magazine publishing (*Newsweek* magazine). The company also owns Stanley H. Kaplan Educational Centers and Legi-Slate Inc. (a legislative and regulatory computerized database). **Benefits:** Adoption Assistance; Daycare Assistance; Dental Insurance; Disability Coverage; Employee Discounts; Legal Services; Life Insurance; Medical Insurance; Pension Plan; Savings Plan; Tuition Assistance. **Corporate headquarters location:** This Location. **Listed on:** New York Stock Exchange. **Number of employees nationwide:** 6,800.

THE WASHINGTON TIMES
3600 New York Avenue Northeast, Washington DC 20002. 202/636-4949. **Contact:** Sherrie Palmer, Employment Specialist. **Description:** A metropolitan daily newspaper. **Common positions include:** Accountant/Auditor; Administrative Services Manager; Advertising Clerk; Computer Programmer; Customer Service Representative; Editor; Electrician; Employment Interviewer; Graphic Artist; Librarian; Library Technician; Mechanical Engineer; Paralegal; Payroll Clerk; Postal Clerk/Mail Carrier; Printing Press Operator; Receptionist; Reporter; Secretary; Services Sales Representative; Typist/Word Processor. **Educational backgrounds include:** Accounting; Art/Design; Business Administration; Communications; Computer Science; Economics; Engineering; Finance; Liberal Arts; Marketing. **Benefits:** 401K; Dental Insurance; Free Parking; Life Insurance; Medical Insurance; Vision Insurance. **Special Programs:** Apprenticeships; Internships. **Corporate headquarters location:** This Location. **Other U.S. locations:** Newington VA. **Operations at this facility include:** Administration;

Manufacturing; Regional Headquarters; Research and Development; Sales; Service. **Number of employees at this location:** 700. **Number of employees nationwide:** 800.

WASHINGTONIAN MAGAZINE
1828 L Street NW, Suite 200, Washington DC 20036. 202/296-3600. **Contact:** Human Resources. **Description:** A general interest magazine about Washington, D.C.

WAVERLY, INC.
1310 Guilford Avenue, Baltimore MD 21202. 410/528-4065. **Contact:** Human Resources Department. **Description:** Publishers and printers of medical and scientific books, journals, and periodicals that are marketed and sold worldwide. Primary customers are medical and scientific practitioners, libraries, and universities. **Common positions include:** Accountant/Auditor; Computer Programmer; Computer Systems Analyst; Customer Service Representative; Editor; Financial Analyst; Manufacturer's/Wholesaler's Sales Rep.; Marketing Specialist; Operations/Production Manager; Purchasing Agent and Manager; Technical Writer/Editor. **Educational backgrounds include:** Accounting; Finance. **Benefits:** 401K; Dental Insurance; Disability Coverage; Employee Discounts; Life Insurance; Medical Insurance; Pension Plan; Savings Plan; Tuition Assistance. **Corporate headquarters location:** This Location. **Other U.S. locations:** Easton MD; Malvern PA. **Operations at this facility include:** Administration; Sales; Service. **Number of employees at this location:** 400. **Number of employees nationwide:** 1,100.

Note: Because addresses and telephone numbers of smaller companies change rapidly, we recommend you call each company to verify the information below before inquiring about job opportunities. Mass mailings are not recommended.

Additional employers with over 250 employees:

COMMERCIAL PRINTING

Forms Direct Inc.
4845 Govermors Way, Frederick MD 21701-8383. 301/698-0404.

John D. Lucas Printing
1820 Portal St, Baltimore MD 21224-6596. 410/633-4200.

PERIODICALS: PUBLISHING AND/OR PRINTING

Western Publishing Co.
PO Box 802, Cambridge MD 21613-0802. 410/228-4000.

Phillips Publishing International
7811 Montrose Rd, Potomac MD 20854. 301/340-2100.

BUSINESS FORMS

Moore Business Communication Services
1 Poplar Ave, Thurmont MD 21788-1714. 301/271-7171.

PRINTING TRADE SERVICES

American Chemical Society
1155 16th St Nw, Washington DC 20036. 202/872-4600.

Additional employers with under 250 employees:

NEWSPAPERS: PUBLISHING AND/OR PRINTING

Al-Riyadh Newspaper
1155 15th St Nw, Washington DC 20005-2706. 202/822-0814.

Alternative Print
2935 Frederick Ave, Baltimore MD 21223-2750. 410/233-7600.

Anacostia Grape Vine
3510 Brothers Pl Se, Washington DC 20032-1520. 202/575-8423.

Audio Video News
2201 C St Nw, Washington DC 20520-0001. 202/861-0398.

Chesapeake Publishing Corporation
PO Box 600, Easton MD 21601-7000. 410/822-1500.

Chesapeake Publishing Corporation
PO Box 429, Elkton MD 21921-5307. 410/398-3311.

Comprint Inc.
9030 Comprint Ct, Gaithersburg MD 20877-1303. 301/948-1520.

Daily News
US Capitol, Washington DC 20515. 202/488-4742.

Daily News
2201 C St Nw, Washington DC 20520-0001. 202/861-0581.

Electronic News
1333 H St Nw, Washington DC 20005-4707. 202/789-8166.

Fairchild Publications
601 13th St NW Ste 520S, Washington DC 20005-3807. 202/639-6900.

Fairchild Publications
1333 H St Nw, Washington DC 20005-4707. 202/682-3200.

Great Southern Printing & Manufacturing
200 E Patrick St, Frederick MD 21701-5666. 301/662-2753.

Herald Mail Co.
100 Summit Ave,
Hagerstown MD 21740-5563. 301/733-5131.

Homestead Publishing
10 S Hays St, Bel Air MD 21014-3643. 410/838-4400.

Jack Anderson Enterprises
1531 P St Nw, Washington DC 20005-1991. 202/483-1442.

London Daily News
1110 Vermont Ave Nw, Washington DC 20005-3522. 202/331-7898.

London Times Mirror
9 E Market St, Leesburg VA 22075-3013. 703/777-1111.

Louisville Courier Journal
1000 Wilson Blvd, Arlington VA 22209-3901. 703/276-5423.

Moore's Weekly
1530 P St Nw, Washington DC 20005-1910. 202/232-5175.

Mount Airy Courier Gazette
218 S Main St, Mount Airy MD 21771. 410/549-0079.

National Hispanic Reporter
810 1st St Ne, Washington DC 20002-4227. 202/898-4153.

Our Sunday Visitor
605 14th St Nw, Washington DC 20005-2008. 202/628-9380.

Portland Press Herald
2716 N Wyoming St, Arlington VA 22213-1722. 703/237-0560.

Potomac Newspaper
14010 Smoketown Rd, Woodbridge VA 22192-4704. 703/878-8000.

Record Publishing Co.
7676 Fenton St, Silver Spring MD 20910-4903. 301/589-6400.

Schlein News Bureau
308 E Capitol St Ne, Washington DC 20003-3809. 202/544-5893.

Seattle Times
245 2nd St Ne, Washington DC 20002-5719. 202/546-4700.

Southern Maryland Classifieds
St Marys Line, Waldorf MD 20602. 301/373-8000.

St. Petersburg Times
607 14th St Nw, Washington DC 20005-2007. 202/393-4553.

Sueddeutsche Zeitung
1099 22nd St Nw, Washington DC 20037-1802. 202/296-4183.

Sundial
501 N Calvert St, Baltimore MD 21202-3604. 410/783-1800.

The Bay Times
102 E Main St, Stevensville MD 21666-4000. 410/643-7770.

The Chronicle of Philanthropy
1255 23rd St Nw, Washington DC 20037-1125. 202/466-1200.

The Final Call Newspaper
236 Massachusetts Ave NE 204, Washington DC 20002-4980. 202/543-7796.

The Free Lance-Star
616 Amelia St, Fredericksbrg VA 22401. 703/373-5000.

The New York Times
1st & Constitutn Av Ne, Washington DC 20002. 202/863-0414.

The News Journal Co.
400 W Lee St, Baltimore MD 21230-2439. 410/625-5770.

Thomson Newspaper
US Capitol Senate Press Galler, Washington DC 20515. 202/488-0188.

Thomson Newspapers
115 E Carroll St, Salisbury MD 21801-5421. 410/749-7171.

Times & Alleganian
19 Baltimore St, Cumberland MD 21502-3023. 301/722-4600.

PERIODICALS: PUBLISHING AND/OR PRINTING

Hanley-Wood Inc.
655 15th St NW Ste 475, Washington DC 20005-5701. 202/737-0717.

Patuxent Publishing Corporation
10750 Little Patuxent Pky, Columbia MD 21044-3103. 410/730-3620.

Phillips Publishing Inc.
7811 Montrose Rd, Potomac MD 20854-3363. 301/340-2100.

BOOKS: PUBLISHING AND/OR PRINTING

Aspen Publishers Inc.
200 Orchard Ridge Dr Ste 200, Gaithersburg MD 20878-5440. 301/417-7500.

Custom Printing Co.
200 Monroe Ave, Frederick MD 21701-3196. 301/663-1494.

EPM Publications
1003 Turkey Run Rd, Mc Lean VA 22101-1707. 703/442-7810.

Janes Information Group
1340 Braddock Pl Ste 300, Alexandria VA 22314-1657. 703/683-3700.

The Taft Group
12300 Twinbrook Pky Ste 520, Rockville MD 20852-1606. 301/816-0210.

University Publications of America
4520 E West Hwy, Bethesda MD 20814-3319. 301/657-3200.

Science Press
1730 N Lynn St Ste 403, Arlington VA 22209-2004. 703/276-7660.

Webcraft Technologies
2015 Indl Pkwy, Salisbury MD 21801. 410/546-4474.

MISC. PUBLISHING

Editorial Experts Inc.
85 S Bragg St Ste 400, Alexandria VA 22312-2731. 703/642-3040.

Datanational
3800 Concorde Pky Ste 500, Chantilly VA 22021-1119. 703/818-0120.

COMMERCIAL PRINTING

Business Form Service East Inc.
211 Stockholm St, Baltimore MD 21230-2627. 410/752-3400.

Byrd Press Inc.
1800 Diagonal Rd, Alexandria VA 22314-2840. 703/519-8300.

Corporate Press Inc.
403 Brightseat Rd, Landover MD 20785-4737. 301/499-9200.

Deluxe Check Printers
7480 Candlewood Rd, Hanover MD 21076-3121. 410/850-7575.

Printing and Publishing/263

EU Services
649 N Horners Ln, Rockville MD 20850-1299. 301/424-3300.

FDI Services
4845 Governors Way, Frederick MD 21701-8383. 301/698-0404.

Gamse Lithographing
7413 Pulaski Hwy, Baltimore MD 21237-2580. 410/866-4700.

Goodway Graphics
6628 Electronic Dr, Springfield VA 22151-4301. 703/941-1160.

Graphtec of MD Inc.
1724 Whitehead Rd, Baltimore MD 21207-4028. 410/298-6100.

Kelly Press Inc.
1701 Cabin Branch Rd, Cheverly MD 20785-3820. 301/386-2800.

Lawson Martin Group
6901 Rolling Mill Rd, Baltimore MD 21224-2030. 410/282-4500.

NCR Corporation
301 International Cir, Cockys Ht Vly MD 21030-1360. 410/329-1600.

Peake Printers Inc.
2500 Schuster Dr, Hyattsville MD 20781-1123. 301/341-4600.

Presstar Printing Corporation
12201 Old Columbia Pike, Silver Spring MD 20904-1968. 301/622-5000.

Printing Corporation of America
15 W Aylesbury Rd, Timonium MD 21093-4142. 410/561-5533.

Reproductions Inc.
7621 Rickenbacker Dr, Gaithersburg MD 20879-4785. 301/840-5400.

Review & Herald Publishers Association
55 W Oak Ridge Dr, Hagerstown MD 21740-7390. 301/791-7000.

S & S Graphics Inc.
14880 Sweitzer Ln, Laurel MD 20707-2913. 301/206-7777.

Sinclair Grey Enterprises
3311 Toledo Ter, Hyattsville MD 20782-4135. 301/559-9626.

Smith Lithograph Corporation
1029 E Gude Dr, Rockville MD 20850-1333. 301/424-1400.

Stephenson Printing
5731 General Washington Dr, Alexandria VA 22312-2418. 703/642-9000.

The Art Litho Co.
1500 W Patapsco Ave, Baltimore MD 21230-3420. 410/355-3200.

Tidewater Publishing Corporation
Rts 301 & 304, Centreville MD 21617. 410/758-1500.

United Lithographic Services Inc.
2818 Fallfax Dr, Falls Church VA 22042-2804. 703/560-5700.

Xerox Reproduction Center
1530 Wilson Blvd, Arlington VA 22209-2447. 703/841-0900.

Interchecks Inc.
9006 Yellow Brick Rd, Baltimore MD 21237-4773. 410/780-0502.

Printpack Inc.
3551 Lee Hill Dr, Fredericksbrg VA 22408-7323. 703/373-7251.

Stationery House Inc.
1000 Florida Ave, Hagerstown MD 21740-3695. 301/739-4487.

Sullivan Graphics Inc.
1211 Belmar Dr, Belcamp MD 21017-1206. 410/273-7200.

BUSINESS FORMS

Standard Register Co.
600 Marvel Rd, Salisbury MD 21801-7818. 410/546-2211.

BLANK BOOKS AND BOOKBINDING

American Stand Graphic Arts Group
Friendship International Airpo, Glen Burnie MD 21061. 410/761-7131.

Bindagraphics Inc.
2701 Wilmarco Ave, Baltimore MD 21223-3339. 410/362-7200.

Specialties Bindery
4815 Lawrence St, Hyattsville MD 20781-1084. 301/699-8800.

PRINTING TRADE SERVICES

Byrd Data Imaging
5408 Port Royal Rd # D, Springfield VA 22151-2301. 703/321-8610.

Chronicle of Higher Education
1255 23rd St NW Ste 700, Washington DC 20037-1125. 202/466-1000.

Goldsmith-Nagan Inc.
1545 New York Ave Ne, Washington DC 20002-1765. 202/628-1600.

COMMERCIAL ART AND GRAPHIC DESIGN

Litigations Sciences
2200 Clarendon Blvd, Arlington VA 22201-3331. 703/841-1225.

PHOTO FINISHING LABORATORIES

Ritz Camera Centers
3737 Branch Ave, Temple Hills MD 20748-1405. 301/423-1990.

Snap Shops Photo
1615 Rockville Pike, Rockville MD 20852-1619. 301/881-8919.

For more information on career opportunities in printing and publishing:

Associations

AMERICAN BOOKSELLERS ASSOCIATION
828 South Broadway, Tarrytown NY 10591. 914/591-2665.

NEWSPAPER ASSOCIATION OF AMERICA
Newspaper Center, 11600 Sunrise Valley Drive, Reston VA 22091. 703/648-1000.

The technology department publishes marketing research.

AMERICAN INSTITUTE OF GRAPHIC ARTS
919 3rd Avenue, 22nd Floor, New York NY 10003-3004. 212/807-1990. A 36-chapter, nationwide organization sponsoring programs and events for graphic designers and related professionals.

AMERICAN SOCIETY OF NEWSPAPER EDITORS
P.O. Box 4090, Reston VA 22090-1700. 703/648-1144.

ASSOCIATION OF GRAPHIC ARTS
330 7th Avenue, 9th Floor, New York NY 10001-5010. 212/279-2100. Offers educational classes and seminars.

BINDING INDUSTRIES OF AMERICA
70 East Lake Street, Suite 300, Chicago IL 60601. 312/372-7606. Offers credit collection, government affairs, and educational services.

THE DOW JONES NEWSPAPER FUND
P.O. Box 300, Princeton NJ 08543-0300. 609/520-4000. Publishes *The Wall Street Journal*.

GRAPHIC ARTISTS GUILD
11 West 20th Street, 8th Floor, New York NY 10011. 212/463-7730. A union for artists.

INTERNATIONAL GRAPHIC ARTS EDUCATION ASSOCIATION
4615 Forbes Avenue, Pittsburgh PA 15213. 412/682-5170.

MAGAZINE PUBLISHERS ASSOCIATION
919 Third Avenue, 22nd Floor, New York NY 10022. 212/752-0055. A membership association.

NATIONAL ASSOCIATION OF PRINTERS AND LITHOGRAPHERS
780 Pallisade Avenue, Teaneck NJ 07666. 201/342-0700. Membership. Offers consulting services and a publication.

NATIONAL NEWSPAPER ASSOCIATION
1525 Wilson Boulevard, Arlington VA 22209. 703/907-7900.

NATIONAL PRESS CLUB
529 14th St. NW, 13th Floor, Washington DC 20045. 202/662-7500. Offers a private club/meeting hall, private restaurants, and private health clubs.

THE NEWSPAPER GUILD
Research and Information Department, 8611 2nd Avenue, Silver Spring MD 20910. 301/585-2990. A trade union.

PRINTING INDUSTRIES OF AMERICA
100 Dangerfield Road, Alexandria VA 22314. 703/519-8100. Members are offered publications, insurance, and political action.

TECHNICAL ASSOCIATION OF THE GRAPHIC ARTS
68 Lomb memorial Drive, Rochester NY 14623. 716/475-7470. Conducts an annual conference and offers newsletters.

WRITERS GUILD OF AMERICA WEST
8955 Beverly Boulevard, West Hollywood CA 90048. 310/550-1000. A membership association which registers scripts.

Directories

EDITOR & PUBLISHER INTERNATIONAL YEARBOOK
Editor & Publisher Co. Inc., 11 West 19th Street, New York NY 10011. 212/675-4380. $100.00. Offers newspapers to editors in both the United States and foreign countries.

GRAPHIC ARTS BLUE BOOK
A.F. Lewis & Co., 245 Fifth Avenue, New York NY 10016. 212/679-0770. $80.00. Manufacturers and dealers.

JOURNALISM CAREER AND SCHOLARSHIP GUIDE
The Dow Jones Newspaper Fund, P.O. Box 300, Princeton NJ 08543-0300. 609/520-4000.

Magazines

AIGA JOURNAL
American Institute of Graphic Arts, 164 Third Avenue, New York NY 10010. 212/752-0813. $21.50. A 56-page quarterly magazine dealing with contemporary issues.

EDITOR AND PUBLISHER
Editor & Publisher Co. Inc., 164 Third Avenue, New York NY 10010. 212/807-1990.

GRAPHIC ARTS MONTHLY
249 West 49th Street, New York NY 10011. 212/463-6836.

GRAPHIS
141 Lexington Avenue, New York NY 10016. 212/532-9387. $89.00. Magazine covers portfolios, articles, designers, advertising, and photos.

PRINT
104 Fifth Avenue, 19th Floor New York NY 10011. 212/463-0600. Offers a graphic design magazine. $55.00 for subscription.

PUBLISHER'S WEEKLY
249 West 17th Street, New York NY 10011. Weekly publication for book publishers and sellers.

Special Book and Magazine Programs

THE NEW YORK UNIVERSITY SUMMER PUBLISHING PROGRAM
48 Cooper Square, Room 108, New York NY 10003. 212/998-7219.

THE RADCLIFFE PUBLISHING COURSE
77 Brattle Street, Cambridge MA 02138. 617/495-8678.

RICE UNIVERSITY PUBLISHING PROGRAM
Office of Continuing Studies, P.O. Box 1892, Houston TX 77251-1892. 713/520-6022.

UNIVERSITY OF DENVER PUBLISHING INSTITUTE
2075 South University Boulevard, #D-114, Denver CO 80208. 303/871-4868.

REAL ESTATE

Rising interest rates have already begun causing housing starts to drop and sales of existing single-family homes to moderately decline. However, solid opportunities for jobseekers are available for those looking to enter the real estate field. Occupancy will go up in the office sector as little new office properties are being built. Apartment construction, on the other hand, is on the rise. Commercial property sales will help keep up employment opportunities for real estate agents, brokers, and appraisers. The number of job openings in these occupations is expected to match the number of openings for most other careers nationwide. Most of these openings, however, will be replacement positions, as agents return or leave the field, rather than new positions being created.

Property and real estate managers will have even greater luck finding employment, as more openings appear for these positions than other occupations. The people with the most qualified backgrounds for these positions will be those with college degrees in business administration and other related studies.

BRESLER & REINER INC.
401 M Street Southwest, Waterside Mall, Washington DC 20024. 202/488-8800. **Contact:** Burton Reiner, President. **Description:** Engaged in two primary business segments: Home and Condominium Construction (with completed or planned developments in six Maryland and Virginia communities), and Rental Property Ownership and Management (owns and operates apartment buildings and commercial property for rent). **Corporate headquarters location:** This Location.

CARR REAL ESTATE SERVICES
1700 Pennsylvania Avenue NW, Suite 700, Washington DC 20006. 202/624-1700. **Contact:** Personnel Director. **Description:** A real estate/architectural/construction management firm, with significant operations in the metropolitan District of Columbia area. Operates in four divisions: Acquisitions, which locates, evaluates, and purchases land and buildings that are candidates for improvement; Development, which defines the market, creates the initial design concept, determines economic feasibility, and arranges financing; Construction, which supervises the final design and actualizes the plan from girders to doorknobs; and Operations, which markets and manages the finished product. Specializes in the construction and/or renovation of mixed-use developments. **Corporate headquarters location:** This Location.

COOPERATIVE HOUSING FOUNDATION
8300 Colesville Road, Suite 420, Silver Springs MD 20910. 301/587-4700. **Contact:** Administrative Support Officer. **Description:** A foundation serving the needs of the cooperative housing industry both domestically and internationally. **Common positions include:** Accountant/Auditor; Architect; Economist/Market Research Analyst; Real Estate Agent. **Educational backgrounds include:** Accounting; Business Administration; Communications; Economics; Engineering; Liberal Arts. **Benefits:** Credit Union; Dental Insurance; Disability Coverage; Life Insurance; Medical Insurance. **Corporate headquarters location:** This Location. **Operations at this facility include:** Regional Headquarters.

FEDERAL REALTY INVESTMENT TRUST
4800 Hampden Lane, Suite 500, Bethesda MD 20814. 301/652-3360. **Contact:** Peggy Fowler, Director of Personnel. **Description:** An equity real estate investment firm that acquires and improves strip shopping centers along heavily developed highways. **Common positions include:** Accountant/Auditor; Attorney; Blue-Collar Worker Supervisor; Computer Programmer. **Benefits:** Dental Insurance; Flexible Benefits; Life Insurance; Medical Insurance; Pension Plan. **Corporate headquarters location:** This

Location. **Operations at this facility include:** Administration; Sales; Service. **Listed on:** New York Stock Exchange.

C. WILLIAM HETZER, INC.
P.O. Box 506, Hagerstown MD 21741. 301/733-7300. **Contact:** Mrs. Cheryl Grove, Office Manager. **Description:** Managers and rentors of apartment buildings.

HOLLADAY CORPORATION
3400 Idaho Avenue NW, Suite 500, Washington DC 20016. 202/362-2400. **Contact:** Vice President. **Description:** A real estate development corporation.

INTERSTATE GENERAL COMPANY, L.P.
222 Smallwood Village Center, Waldorf MD 20602. 301/645-6833. **Contact:** Nancy M. Davis, Director of Personnel. **Description:** A real estate investment company that operates through four major divisions: community development; home building; investment property; and property management. **Common positions include:** Accountant/Auditor; Branch Manager; Civil Engineer; Collections Agent; Customer Service Representative; Draftsperson; Leasing Specialist/Consultant; Maintenance Worker; Property and Real Estate Manager; Public Relations Specialist; Secretary; Systems Analyst. **Educational backgrounds include:** Accounting; Business Administration; Computer Science; Engineering; Marketing. **Benefits:** Dental Insurance; Disability Coverage; Employee Discounts; Life Insurance; Medical Insurance; Pension Plan; Profit Sharing; Tuition Assistance. **Corporate headquarters location:** This Location. **Operations at this facility include:** Administration; Regional Headquarters. **Listed on:** New York Stock Exchange; Pacific Exchange.

NATIONAL CORPORATION FOR HOUSING PARTNERSHIPS
1225 Eye Street NW, Suite 601, Washington DC 20005-3914. 202/269-7000. **Contact:** Human Resources. **Description:** NHP, Incorporated is a real estate investment and management company focused primarily on multifamily rental housing. Two of NHP's affiliated units, the National Housing Partnership and National Corporation for Housing Partnerships, were authorized by Congress in 1968 to provide low and moderate income housing. NHP, through its operating units, is a general partner of approximately 84,000 units of multifamily rental housing; while many of the newer units are market rate, approximately 64,000 units were produced and are still operated under a variety of federal and state housing assistance programs. NHP is also one of the largest property managers of multifamily housing with more than 65,000 units under direct management. NHP has property locations in 39 states, Washington DC and Puerto Rico.

PREMIER MANAGEMENT GROUP, INC.
1505 Bloomfield Avenue, Baltimore MD 21227. 410/525-1800. **Contact:** Human Resources. **Description:** A real estate management company.

THE ROUSE COMPANY
10275 Little Patuxent Parkway, Columbia MD 21044. 410/992-6000. **Contact:** Personnel Office. **Description:** The Rouse Company develops, acquires, owns and/or manages commercial real estate projects, primarily large regional retail centers. The company currently manages approximately 200 projects across the United States, including Fanueil Hall Marketplace in Boston, South Street Seaport in New York, Harborplace in Baltimore, Bayside Marketplace in Miami, Arizona Center in Phoenix, Pioneer Place in Portland and Westlake Center in Seattle. The company is also the developer of Columbia, Maryland, a new city located midway between Washington and Baltimore. Columbia, which began in 1962, currently has 79,000 residents, 30,000 dwelling units, 2,400 businesses and 54,000 jobs, and is the home of the company's corporate headquarters.

SMITHY BRAEDON COMPANY
3040 Williams Drive, Suite 300, Fairfax VA 22031. 703/641-8000. **Contact:** Human Resources Department. **Description:** A full-service commercial real estate firm covering Maryland, Virginia, and the District of Columbia.

VIRGINIA BAPTIST HOMES
P.O. Box 191, Culpepper VA 22701. 703/825-1569. 703/825-1569. **Contact:** Human Resources. **Description:** A retirement community.

Note: Because addresses and telephone numbers of smaller companies change rapidly, we recommend you call each company to verify the information below before inquiring about job opportunities. Mass mailings are not recommended.

Additional employers with under 250 employees:

REAL ESTATE OPERATORS

3900 Corporation
5518 Baltimore National Pike, Baltimore MD 21228-1531. 410/744-6142.

Landmark Development
5 Light St, Baltimore MD 21202-1230. 410/752-6565.

North Plaza Mall
8966 Waltham Woods Rd, Parkville MD 21234-2404. 410/882-4444.

Regional Management
11 E Fayette St, Baltimore MD 21202-1679. 410/539-2370.

Security Management Corporation
9901 Langs Rd, Baltimore MD 21220-2602. 410/682-4040.

Arborview At Riverside
1300 Liriope Ct, Belcamp MD 21017-1386. 410/273-6100.

Burton Manor Apts
601 Cornell St, Aberdeen MD 21001-3150. 410/272-7250.

Camden At Kendall Ridge
8399 Tamar Dr, Columbia MD 21045-5701. 410/740-9074.

Charter Oak Apartments
11637 Charter Oak Ct, Reston VA 22090-4522. 703/471-5335.

Chase Gables
5115 Woodmere Dr, Centreville VA 22020-4301. 703/631-9535.

Chelsea Square
5734 Backlick Rd, Springfield VA 22150-3205. 703/451-8550.

Condominium Mgmt.
1903 Key Blvd, Arlington VA 22201-3227. 703/525-5557.

Crescent Apartments
1527 Cameron Crescent Dr, Reston VA 22090-3614. 703/471-4663.

Crystal House II Apts
2000 S Eads St, Arlington VA 22202-3136. 703/521-4200.

Ferry Harrison Apartments
43 Delaware Ave, Hurlock MD 21643-3630. 410/943-8535.

Glenmont Garden & Tower Apts
6902 Lachlan Cir, Baltimore MD 21239-1001. 410/821-8819.

Great Oaks Apartments
3008 Autumn Branch Ln, Ellicott City MD 21043-3510. 410/465-6500.

Hamilton Manor Apartments
3340 Lancer Dr, Hyattsville MD 20782-3219. 301/559-6702.

Hendersen-Webb Inc.
1025 Cranbrook Rd, Cockeysville MD 21030-4899. 410/628-7400.

Hunters Crossing Apartments
36-13 Fort Evans Rd Ne, Leesburg VA 22075-4411. 703/777-3863.

Liberty Gardens Apts
7005 Rudisill Ct, Randallstown MD 21133. 410/655-7000.

Manor At England Run
101 Knights Ct, Fredericksbrg VA 22406-6413. 703/372-3793.

Red Run Apartments
4300 Flint Hill Dr, Owings Mills MD 21117-5800. 410/363-2105.

Taylor Park East and West Apts
35 Mopec Cir, Baltimore MD 21236-4519. 410/882-0915.

The Brittany
4500 S Four Mile Run Dr, Arlington VA 22204-3558. 703/671-2646.

The Lincoln At Tysons
1526 Lincoln Cir, Mc Lean VA 22102-5829. 703/734-3030.

Tor Apartments
5764 Stevens Forest Rd, Columbia MD 21045-3673. 410/730-3000.

University Heights Apts
20300 River Ridge Ter, Ashburn VA 22011-2655. 703/478-8388.

Vernon Mount Properties
11902 Tarragon Rd, Reisterstown MD 21136-3163. 410/526-6611.

Village of Pine Run Apts
103 Village of Pine Ct, Randallstown MD 21133. 410/655-8300.

Woodstream Apartments
700 Stoney Mill Ct, Cockys Ht Vly MD 21030-3852. 410/667-1234.

REAL ESTATE AGENTS AND MANAGERS

Barnes Morris Pardoe & Foster
601 13th St NW Ste 800-N, Washington DC 20005-3807. 202/783-8200.

CFM Management Services Inc.
4900 Seminary Rd Ste 101, Alexandria VA 22311-1811. 703/820-3800.

Champion Realty Inc.
541-B Baltimore-Annapolis Blvd, Severna Park MD 21146-3809. 410/544-6004.

Gates Hudson & Associates Inc.
3020 Hamaker Ct Ste 301, Fairfax VA 22031-2220. 703/876-9590.

Gelman Management Corporation
2120 L St NW Ste 800, Washington DC 20037-1527. 202/872-9070.

Legum & Norman Inc.
1430 Spring Hill Rd Ste 300, Mc Lean VA 22102-3000. 703/848-4321.

Tristar Management
40 York Rd, Baltimore MD 21204-5243. 410/321-9729.

WC Pinkard & Co.
7 E Redwood St # 1200, Baltimore MD 21202-1115. 410/752-4285.

Baldus Real Estate
21 Industrial Park Dr,

Waldorf MD 20602-2751. 301/843-9306.

CB Commercial
8260 Greensboro Dr, Mc Lean VA 22102-3808. 703/790-3333.

CB Commercial
1650 Tysons Blvd, Mc Lean VA 22102-3915. 703/734-4700.

Coldwell Banker Grempler Realty
8525 Baltimore National Pike, Ellicott City MD 21043-4290. 410/465-7700.

Hylton Realty Inc.
13301 Orangewood Dr, Woodbridge VA 22193-3961. 703/690-3459.

Long & Foster Realtors
Rt 219 US 301 South, La Plata MD 20646. 301/870-2350.

Long & Foster Realtors
6619 March Dr, Oxon Hill MD 20745-2213. 301/839-8000.

Long & Foster Realtors
702 Russell Ave, Gaithersburg MD 20877-2606. 301/840-1545.

Long & Foster Realtors
Uptown 4200 Wisconsin Av Nw, Silver Spring MD 20901. 202/363-9700.

Long & Foster Realtors
Crossroads Square Shopping Ctr, Westminster MD 21157. 410/857-5020.

Long & Foster Realtors
11701-2nd Coastal Hwy, Ocean City MD 21842. 410/524-1700.

Long & Foster Realtors
7010 Little River Tpke, Annandale VA 22003-3241. 703/750-2800.

Long & Foster Realtors
5739 Burke Centre Pky, Burke VA 22015-2296. 703/425-9042.

Long & Foster Realtors
4421 Dale Blvd, Dale City VA 22193-2550. 703/680-5001.

O'Conor Piper & Flynn
1631 N Main St, Hampstead MD 21074-2132. 410/239-8110.

O'Conor Piper & Flynn
22 W Padonia St Ste 348C, Timonium MD 21093-2226. 410/561-8800.

O'Conor Piper & Flynn
639 Main St, Reisterstown MD 21136-1931. 410/833-2080.

O'Conor Piper & Flynn Realtors
2037 Liberty Rd, Sykesville MD 21784-6624. 410/795-5300.

O'Conor Piper & Flynn Realtors
52nd St, Ocean City MD 21842. 410/723-1000.

O'Conor Piper & Flynn Realtors
North Region, Timonium MD 21093. 410/252-8501.

Prentiss Properties Ltd.
3112 Fairview Park Dr, Falls Church VA 22042-4501. 703/560-4700.

Pulte Homes Corporation
703 Catoctin Cir Ne, Leesburg VA 22075-4949. 703/689-1316.

Residential Sales Offices
206 Three Notch Rd N, Lexingtn Park MD 20653-1520. 301/862-3000.

Sumner Village Condominiums
4910 Sentinel Dr, Bethesda MD 20816-3503. 301/229-2278.

Town & Country Escrow & Title
3018 Javier Rd, Fairfax VA 22031-4609. 703/641-0411.

Town & Country Properties Inc.
4701 Old Dominion Dr, Arlington VA 22207-3596. 703/522-7474.

Washington Homes At Bowl Brook
9200 Brewington Ln, Laurel MD 20723-5839. 410/880-4326.

Weichert Realtors
7821 Tuckerman Ln, Potomac MD 20854-3240. 301/718-4100.

Compass Management and Leasing
4601 Fairfax Dr, Arlington VA 22203-1500. 703/908-0300.

Gilbane Properties Inc.
7901 Sandy Spring Rd, Laurel MD 20707-3589. 410/792-0533.

Lincoln Property Co.
2661 Riva Rd, Annapolis MD 21401-7315. 410/224-4296.

The Galbreath Company
2111 Wilson Blvd, Arlington VA 22201-3001. 703/527-9444.

Whetstone Co.
17 Meem Ave, Gaithersburg MD 20877-2117. 301/948-2929.

Mt Vernon Realty Inc.
2 Cardinal Park Dr Se, Leesburg VA 22075-4458. 703/777-3977.

Walker and Dunlop Multif
2100 Pennsylvania Ave NW 280, Washington DC 20037-3202. 202/872-7788.

LAND SUBDIVIDERS AND DEVELOPERS

Banyan Management
Rt 5 & St Charles Pkwy, Waldorf MD 20602-9805. 301/870-9211.

Cafritz Group Inc.
1735 I St Nw, Washington DC 20006-2400. 202/331-3800.

Carl M. Freeman Associates Inc.
11325 Seven Locks Rd, Potomac MD 20854-3205. 301/983-0400.

Miller & Smith Inc.
1568 Spring Hill Rd Ste 401, Mc Lean VA 22102-3016. 703/821-2500.

Phoenix Development Corporation
PO Box 220598, Chantilly VA 22022-0598. 703/385-8333.

Quadrangle Development Corporation
1001 G St NW Ste 700W, Washington DC 20001-4545. 202/393-1999.

US Home At Bay Hills
706 Pine Valley Ct, Arnold MD 21012-3103. 410/974-4511.

Weaver Brothers Insurance
5530 Wisconsin Ave, Bethesda MD 20815-4404. 301/986-4400.

West Group
1600 Anderson Rd, Mc Lean VA 22102-1609. 703/356-2400.

William A Hazell Co.
4305 Hazel Park Ct,
Chantilly VA 22021-2925.
703/378-8300.

For more information on career opportunities in real estate:

Associations

INSTITUTE OF REAL ESTATE MANAGEMENT
430 North Michigan Avenue, P.O. Box 109025, Chicago IL 60610-9025. 312/661-1930. Dedicated to educating and identifying real estate managers who are committed to meeting the needs of real estate owners and investors.

INTERNATIONAL ASSOCIATION OF CORPORATE REAL ESTATE EXECUTIVES
440 Columbia Drive, Suite 100, West Palm Beach FL 33409. 407/683-8111. An international association of real estate brokers.

Magazines

JOURNAL OF PROPERTY MANAGEMENT
Institute of Real Estate Management, 430 North Michigan Avenue, Chicago IL 60610. 312/661-1930.

NATIONAL REAL ESTATE INVESTOR
6151 Powers Ferry Road, Atlanta GA 30339. 404/955-2500.

RETAIL

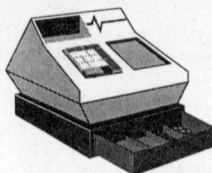

The '90s have been turbulent times for the retail industry. During the early years of the decade, the industry struggled as the national economy remained mired in recession. Even as late as 1994, the troubled department store sector was still straggling. During that year alone, two of retail's giants, Federated Department Stores and R.H. Macy's merged, while Kmart continued to struggle, and even once-booming companies like The Limited and The Gap hit bumps in the road.

On the other hand, 1994 was actually a great year for retailers. Especially hot: the sale of men's suits and personal computers. While rising interest rates have cut into consumer spending, at press time the industry appeared to be in for a relatively solid 1996. Clothing prices have fallen, partly due to increased imports and efforts by Sears, Wal-Mart, Kmart and JCPenney to strengthen their apparel businesses. The reason behind this focus on apparel is simple: clothes generate much higher profit margins than hard goods.

Even so, jobseekers can expect the retail industry to be as volatile as ever. New stores will continually open and others will close. Alternative retail outlets, such as mail order companies or home shopping have carved a niche for themselves in the market and have taken away customers who usually shop at the traditional retail stores. And look for mergers, acquisitions and even bankruptcies among the large department stores to continue.

ALBAN TRACTOR COMPANY, INC.
8531 Pulaski Highway, P.O. Box 9595, Baltimore MD 21237. 410/686-7777. **Contact:** Human Resources. **Description:** Sells and services Caterpillar equipment in a four-state territory. **Common positions include:** Mechanic. **Educational backgrounds include:** Technology. **Benefits:** 401K; Dental Insurance; Disability Coverage; Life Insurance; Medical Insurance; Profit Sharing; Tuition Assistance. **Corporate headquarters location:** This Location. **Operations at this facility include:** Administration. **Listed on:** Privately held.

ANGELS FOOD MARKET, INC.
4681 Mountain Road, Pasadena MD 21122. 410/255-6800. **Contact:** Joyce Clocker, Personnel Director. **Description:** An area supermarket.

BASICS & METRO FOOD MARKETS
5483 Baltimore National Pike, Baltimore MD 21229. 410/455-5400. **Description:** Corporate offices of the Basics and Metro Foods grocery stores.

BEST PRODUCTS COMPANY
2800 South Randolph Street, Arlington VA 22206. 703/578-4600. **Contact:** Personnel Department. **Description:** A retailer of jewelry, electronics, sporting goods, and other hard-line brand name merchandise. **Common positions include:** Department Manager; Retail Sales Worker; Warehouse/Distribution Worker. **Educational backgrounds include:** Accounting; Business Administration. **Benefits:** Dental Insurance; Disability Coverage; Employee Discounts; Life Insurance; Medical Insurance; Pension Plan; Savings Plan; Tuition Assistance. **Corporate headquarters location:** Richmond VA.

CASUAL CORNER
1017 Connecticut Avenue NW, Washington DC 20036. 202/659-8344. **Contact:** Roxanne Reid, District Manager. **Description:** Area management offices for a chain of specialized retail clothing stores. **Common positions include:** Management Trainee.

Educational backgrounds include: Business Administration; Liberal Arts; Marketing. Benefits: 401K; Dental Insurance; Disability Coverage; Employee Discounts; Life Insurance; Medical Insurance; Pension Plan. Corporate headquarters location: Enfield CT. Parent company: U.S. Shoe. Operations at this facility include: Sales. Listed on: New York Stock Exchange.

THE COSMETIC CENTER
8839 Greenwood Place, Savage MD 20763. 301/497-6800. Contact: Bruce Strohl, Vice President of Finance. Description: The company operates 38 cosmetics stores: 16 in Washington, two in Richmond, five in Baltimore, and 15 in Chicago. Common positions include: Accountant/Auditor; Computer Programmer; Retail Manager; Retail Sales Worker. Benefits: Dental Insurance; Employee Discounts; Medical Insurance; Pension Plan. Corporate headquarters location: This Location. Listed on: NASDAQ. Number of employees at this location: 880.

CROWN BOOKS
3300 75th Avenue, Landover MD 20785. 301/731-1200. Contact: Anne Lezinton, Personnel Director. Description: One of the largest discount bookstore chains coast-to-coast, offering a full range of titles at discount prices with over 260 stores. Crown Books has a significant retail presence in the metropolitan Washington DC area; Chicago; San Diego; Los Angeles; San Francisco Bay Area; Seattle/Tacoma; and Houston. Common positions include: Retail Sales Worker; Store Manager. Benefits: Dental Insurance; Employee Discounts; Life Insurance; Long-Term Care; Medical Insurance; Paid Vacation; Profit Sharing; Tuition Assistance. Parent company: The Dart Group. Other U.S. locations: Nationwide.

DEVLIN LUMBER & SUPPLY CORPORATION
P.O. Box 1306, Rockville MD 20849-1306. 301/881-1000. Contact: James Quinn, President. Description: A retailer of building products to both consumers and the commercial construction trade. Products include lumber, millwork, pressure-treated lumber, wood building trusses, and many others. Corporate headquarters location: This Location.

DISTRICT PHOTO, INC.
10619 Baltimore Avenue, Beltsville MD 20705. 301/937-5300. Contact: Timothy Bieber, Personnel Administrator. Description: Engaged in the retail sale of photographic equipment and supplies. Also provides amateur photofinishing services.

GENESYS CORPORATION
4 North Park Drive, Suite 400, Hunt valley MD 21030-1838. 410/785-0000. Contact: Human Resources. Description: A computer and computer software retail store.

GRIFFITH CONSUMERS COMPANY
2510 Schuster Drive, Cheverly MD 20781. 301/322-3111. Contact: Kathy Aponte, Director of Personnel. Description: Griffith is a full-service, independent retail distributor of petroleum products, principally heating oil and gasoline, operating in Washington, DC; Maryland; Delaware; Virginia; West Virginia; and portions of New Jersey and Pennsylvania. Griffith also sells diesel fuel, heavy oils, kerosene, and products and services related to its energy business. The company has been in the fuel distribution business since 1898. Common positions include: Accountant/Auditor; Credit Manager; Customer Service Representative; Human Resources Specialist; Sales Associate. Educational backgrounds include: Accounting; Finance; Marketing. Benefits: Dental Insurance; Employee Discounts; Life Insurance; Medical Insurance; Pension Plan. Corporate headquarters location: This Location. Operations at this facility include: Administration; Divisional Headquarters; Regional Headquarters; Research and Development; Sales; Service.

HEAD SKI & SPORTSWEAR, INC.
9189 Red Branch Road, Columbia MD 21045. 410/730-8300. Contact: Cynthia Pillars, Personnel Manager. Description: A sportswear retailer.

HECHINGER STORES COMPANY
1801 McCormick Drive, Landover MD 20785. 301/925-3726. Recorded Jobline: 301/341-0526. Contact: Arletta Nidell, Recruiting Manager. Description: Hechinger Company is a specialty retailer, currently operating 128 home center stores: 72 Hechinger stores and 56 Home Quarters Warehouse stores in 23 states and the District of Columbia. The company serves the growing home improvement industry through two operating subsidiaries: Hechinger Stores Company and Home Quarters

Warehouse, Inc. **Common positions include:** Accountant/Auditor; Buyer; Computer Programmer; Economist/Market Research Analyst; General Manager; Human Resources Specialist; Management Trainee; Marketing/Advertising/PR Manager. **Number of employees at this location:** 10,000.

THE HECHT COMPANY
685 North Glebe Road, Arlington VA 22203-2199. 703/558-1200. **Contact:** Human Resources. **Description:** A general merchandise retailer.

HIT OR MISS, INC.
6600 Baltimore National Pike, Cantonsville MD 21228. 410/719-0643. **Fax:** 410/747-8812. **Contact:** Human Resources Manager. **Description:** A chain of women's fashion stores with over 500 locations in 32 states across the country. Hit or Miss plans to open several new stores and expects to hire hundreds of new employees nationwide. **Common positions include:** Assistant Manager; Buyer; General Manager; Management Trainee; Wholesale and Retail Buyer. **Educational backgrounds include:** Business Administration; Fashion; Liberal Arts; Merchandising. **Benefits:** 401K; Dental Insurance; Disability Coverage; Employee Discounts; Life Insurance; Medical Insurance; Pension Plan; Savings Plan; Tuition Assistance. **Special Programs:** Internships; Training Programs. **Corporate headquarters location:** Stoughton MA. **Parent company:** TJX, Inc. **Operations at this facility include:** Regional Headquarters. **Listed on:** New York Stock Exchange. **Number of employees at this location:** 1,000. **Number of employees nationwide:** 5,000.

HUB FURNITURE
9701 Fort Meade Road, Laurel MD 20708. 301/498-1600. **Contact:** Manager. **Description:** A furniture retailer with 12 area locations.

JOSEPH A. BANK CLOTHIERS INC.
113 West North Avenue, Baltimore MD 21201. 410/727-8700. **Contact:** Human Resources. **Description:** Retails men's clothing.

LORD & TAYLOR
5255 Western Avenue NW, Washington DC 20015. 202/362-9600. **Contact:** Human Resources. **Description:** A full-line department store carrying high-quality clothing, accessories, home furnishings, and many other retail items. Stores in many major United States metropolitan areas. **Corporate headquarters location:** New York NY. **Parent company:** May Department Stores Co.

LORD & TAYLOR
Tyson Corner, 7950 Tyson Corner Center, McLean VA 22102. 703/506-1156. **Contact:** Personnel Director. **Description:** A full-line department store carrying high-quality clothing, accessories, home furnishings, and many other retail items. Stores in many major United States metropolitan areas. **Corporate headquarters location:** New York NY. **Parent company:** May Department Stores Co.

LUSKIN INC.
7125 Columbia Gateway Dr, Columbia MD 21046-2140. 410/290-1111. **Description:** A retailer and audio and video products.

MARS SUPERMARKETS, INC.
7183 Holabird Avenue, Baltimore MD 21222. 410/282-2100. **Contact:** Personnel Director. **Description:** Operates retail grocery stores. **Common positions include:** Accountant/Auditor; Advertising Clerk; Credit Manager; Human Resources Specialist; Management Trainee; Purchasing Agent and Manager. **Educational backgrounds include:** Accounting; Business Administration; Computer Science. **Benefits:** Dental Insurance; Disability Coverage; Life Insurance; Medical Insurance; Pension Plan; Tuition Assistance. **Corporate headquarters location:** This Location.

MERRY-GO-ROUND ENTERPRISES
3300 Fashion Way, Joppa MD 21085. 410/538-1000. **Contact:** Jeff Austin, Vice President of Human Resources. **Description:** Merry-Go-Round Enterprises operates 1,991 specialty apparel stores in 44 states and in Washington, D.C. In May 1993, Merry-Go-Round acquired the Chess King chain from the Melville Corporation. **Common positions include:** Accountant/Auditor; Adjuster; Administrative Services Manager; Architect; Blue-Collar Worker Supervisor; Budget Analyst; Buyer; Claim Representative; Clerical Supervisor; Computer Programmer; Computer Systems Analyst; Construction and Building Inspector; Designer; Electrical/Electronics Engineer;

Financial Analyst; General Manager; Human Resources Specialist; Industrial Engineer; Industrial Production Manager; Management Trainee; Restaurant/Food Service Manager; Software Engineer. **Educational backgrounds include:** Accounting; Business Administration; Computer Graphics; Engineering; Finance; Marketing. **Benefits:** 401K; Dental Insurance; Disability Coverage; Employee Discounts; Life Insurance; Medical Insurance; Pension Plan; Tuition Assistance. **Special Programs:** Internships. **Corporate headquarters location:** This Location. **Other U.S. locations:** nationwide. **Operations at this facility include:** Administration; Divisional Headquarters; Regional Headquarters. **Listed on:** New York Stock Exchange. **Number of employees at this location:** 700. **Number of employees nationwide:** 20,000.

MONTGOMERY WARD & CO., INC.
11160 Viers Mill Road, Wheaton MD 20902. 301/468-5216. **Fax:** 301/468-5230. **Contact:** Angie Mason, Assistant Human Resources Manager. **Description:** Montgomery Ward & Co., Inc., is a multi-billion dollar retailer, one of the oldest and largest in the nation. The company operates specialty stores, distribution centers, and product service centers from coast to coast. Its primary business is specialty retailing with focus in apparel, fine jewelry, appliances, electronics, home, and automotive. **Common positions include:** Department Manager; General Manager; Human Resources Specialist; Management Trainee; Retail Sales Worker; Services Sales Representative. **Benefits:** Disability Coverage; Employee Discounts; Life Insurance; Medical Insurance; Profit Sharing; Savings Plan. **Corporate headquarters location:** Chicago IL. **Operations at this facility include:** Regional Headquarters. **Number of employees at this location:** 200. **Number of employees nationwide:** 40,000.

RELIABLE STORES INC.
6301 Stevens Forest Road, Columbia MD 21046. 410/381-9650. **Fax:** 410/381-5190. **Contact:** Gina Kuhn, Personnel Manager. **Description:** A retailer. **Common positions include:** Accountant/Auditor; Adjuster; Advertising Clerk; Branch Manager; Buyer; Collector; Computer Programmer; Credit Manager; Customer Service Representative; Designer; General Manager; Investigator. **Educational backgrounds include:** Accounting; Art/Design; Business Administration; Communications; Computer Science; Mathematics. **Benefits:** 401K; Dental Insurance; Disability Coverage; Employee Discounts; Life Insurance; Medical Insurance. **Corporate headquarters location:** This Location. **Operations at this facility include:** Administration; Regional Headquarters; Service. **Listed on:** Privately held. **Number of employees at this location:** 210. **Number of employees nationwide:** 1,050.

**RODMAN DISCOUNT FOOD & DRUG
dba RODMAN DRUGS**
4945 Wyaconda Road, Rockville MD 20852. 301/230-8930. **Contact:** Yale Rodman, Vice President. **Description:** A retailer of drugs, appliances, cameras, health and beauty aids, beer, and wine.

SAFEWAY, INC.
4551 Forbes Boulevard, Lanham MD 20706. 301/918-7102. **Contact:** Vickie Ferchak, Employment Supervisor. **Description:** A regional food store. **Common positions include:** Adjuster; Buyer; Computer Programmer; Management Trainee; Payroll Clerk; Retail Sales Worker. **Educational backgrounds include:** Accounting; Business Administration; Marketing. **Benefits:** Dental Insurance; Disability Coverage; Life Insurance; Medical Insurance; Pension Plan; Savings Plan; Tuition Assistance. **Special Programs:** Training Programs. **Corporate headquarters location:** Oakland CA. **Operations at this facility include:** Regional Headquarters. **Listed on:** New York Stock Exchange.

SAKS FIFTH AVENUE
5555 Wisconsin Avenue, Chevy Chase MD 20815. 301/657-9000. **Contact:** Rita Smithfield, Assistant Personnel Director. **Description:** A fashion-forward department store chain with branches in 30 United States cities. Stores specialize in soft-good products, particularly apparel for men, women, and children. The company's stores emphasize high-quality fashion items, with subsidiary companies operating a catalogue operation and a corporate gift service. Nationally, the company is a subsidiary of Gimbel Brothers, Inc., but is operated autonomously with respect to operations, personnel, merchandising, purchasing, and other areas. **Corporate headquarters location:** New York NY.

SEARS, ROEBUCK & COMPANY
7103 Democracy Boulevard, Bethesda MD 20817. 301/469-4000. **Contact:** Personnel Manager. **Description:** One of the world's largest retailers.

SOUTHLAND CORPORATION
7-ELEVEN FOOD STORES
5300 Shawnee Road, Alexandria VA 22312. 703/642-0711. **Fax:** 703/354-0492. **Recorded Jobline:** 800/JOB-0711. **Contact:** Janine Mohl, Division Recruiter. **Description:** The Southland Corporation, 7-Eleven Convenience Stores, is one of the largest store chains in the world. Founded in 1927 in Dallas, Southland operates and franchises more than 6,000 7-Eleven and other convenience units in the United States and Canada. **Common positions include:** Assistant Manager; Field Consultant Trainee; Management Trainee; Store Manager. **Educational backgrounds include:** Business Administration; Liberal Arts; Marketing. **Benefits:** 401K; Credit Union; Dental Insurance; Disability Coverage; Life Insurance; Medical Insurance; Profit Sharing; Savings Plan. **Special Programs:** Internships; Training Programs. **Corporate headquarters location:** Dallas TX. **Operations at this facility include:** Divisional Headquarters; Sales; Service. **Listed on:** New York Stock Exchange. **Number of employees at this location:** 8,000. **Number of employees nationwide:** 40,000.

STIDHAM TIRE COMPANY
3900 Whitetire Road, Landover MD 20785. 301/322-3200. **Contact:** Personnel Department. **Description:** Engaged in retail and wholesale tire sales at 15 area locations. **Corporate headquarters location:** This Location.

TRAK AUTO CORPORATION
3300 75th Avenue, Landover MD 20785. 301/731-1200. **Contact:** Personnel Manager. **Description:** Engaged in operating retail discount auto parts stores in the Washington, Baltimore, Richmond, Chicago, and Los Angeles areas. **Common positions include:** Accountant/Auditor; Computer Programmer; Draftsperson; Management Trainee; Systems Analyst. **Corporate headquarters location:** This Location. **Number of employees nationwide:** 2,168.

WOODWARD & LOTHROP INC.
1025 F Street NW, Washington DC 20013. 202/879-8000. **Contact:** Human Resources. **Description:** Operates a major department store.

Note: Because addresses and telephone numbers of smaller companies change rapidly, we recommend you call each company to verify the information below before inquiring about job opportunities. Mass mailings are not recommended.

Additional employers with under 250 employees:

VIDEO TAPE RENTAL

Erol's Video Inc.
3809 Mount Vernon Ave, Alexandria VA 22305-2410. 703/549-2121.

Erol's Video Inc.
6455 Dobbin Rd, Columbia MD 21045-5811. 410/740-0270.

Suncoast Motion Picture Company
White Flint Shopping Center, Kensington MD 20895. 301/881-8182.

Video World
207 Kings Hwy, Fredericksbrg VA 22405-2650. 703/372-4513.

RETAIL LUMBER AND BUILDING MATERIALS

Builders Square Main
4368 Brookfield Corporate Dr, Chantilly VA 22021. 703/802-1073.

Home Depot-Store 4605
2815 Merrilee Dr, Fairfax VA 22031-4409. 703/205-1245.

Smoot Lumber Co.
6295 Edsall Rd, Alexandria VA 22312-2617. 703/823-2100.

Alcan Building Products
1128 Wilso Dr, Baltimore MD 21223-3265. 410/646-4664.

Estate Garage Door Company
12100 Baltimore Ave, Beltsville MD 20705-1363. 301/210-1611.

Rollyson Aluminum Products
6850 Distribution Dr, Beltsville MD 20705-1403. 301/937-5898.

HARDWARE STORES

Stebbins Anderson
802 Kenilworth Dr, Baltimore MD 21204-2298. 410/823-6600.

RETAIL NURSERIES AND GARDEN SUPPLY STORES

Meadows Farms Nurseries
478 Jumpers Hole Rd, Severna Park MD 21146-1657. 410/544-0606.

DEPARTMENT STORES

C-Mart Inc.
1503 Rockspring Rd, Forest Hill MD 21050-2833.
410/879-7858.

Caldor Inc. District 17
6400 Rossville Blvd,
Baltimore MD 21237-2341.
410/682-4100.

Goldenberg Caplan Pierce
5810 Park Hts Ave,
Baltimore MD 21215-3932.
410/675-0300.

Leggett Inc. of Westminster
Cranberry Mall, Westminster MD 21157. 410/848-1200.

JCPenney Co. Inc.
2700 Potomac Mills Cir, Woodbridge VA 22192-4625. 703/494-0089.

Kmart Stores
209 Kentland Blvd,
Gaithersburg MD 20878-5446. 301/208-9091.

Kmart Stores
6000 Burke Commons Rd,
Burke VA 22015-2805.
703/764-2095.

Kmart Stores
7704 Richmond Hwy,
Alexandria VA 22306-2844.
703/799-0902.

Wal-Mart Discount Cities
950 Edwards Ferry Rd Ne,
Leesburg VA 22075-3324.
703/779-0102.

Ames Department Store
1060 Smallwood Dr, Waldorf MD 20603-4732. 301/645-8901.

Ames Department Stores
6751 Wilson Blvd, Falls Church VA 22044-3302.
703/534-3429.

Ames Department Store
514 Rhode Island Ave Ne, Washington DC 20002-1231. 202/635-6022.

Big Lots
2000 Plank Rd, Fredericksbrg VA 22401-5104. 703/374-1639.

Dollar Bills
2473 Frederick Ave,
Baltimore MD 21223-2856.
410/362-9242.

Caldor
Timonium Mall, Luthvle Timon MD 21093. 410/561-2056.

Marshalls
13007 Lee Jackson Memorial Hwy, Fairfax VA 22033-2001. 703/222-0976.

TJ Maxx
6140 Rose Hill Dr,
Alexandria VA 22310-1901.
703/719-6304.

American Tourister Factory Outlet
Chesapeake Village Outlet Cntr, Queenstown MD 21658. 410/827-4911.

Corning Revere Factory Store
68 Heather Ln, Perryville MD 21903-2507. 410/378-9391.

Libby Glass
595 Revell Hwy, Annapolis MD 21401. 410/757-6886.

Springmaid Wamsutta Factory Store
213 Chesapeake Village Rd, Queenstown MD 21658-1351. 410/827-4708.

Dollar Depot Inc.
237 Kentland Blvd,
Gaithersburg MD 20878-5446. 301/212-9647.

Dollar Tree
Capital Plaza, Hyattsville MD 20784. 301/322-4893.

All For One
Lake Forest Mall,
Gaithersburg MD 20877.
301/330-1680.

Crispies Coats
5300 Wisconsin Ave Nw,
Washington DC 20015-2013. 202/537-3741.

Dollar Do Ye
5422 Georgia Ave Nw,
Washington DC 20011-3910. 202/882-1133.

Family Dollars Stores
2197 Jefferson St,
Leonardtown MD 20650-3711. 301/475-7234.

Fantle's
12029 Georgia Ave, Silver Spring MD 20902-2003.
301/949-3571.

G C Murphy Co.
7448 Little River Tpke,
Annandale VA 22003-3013.
703/256-8030.

Leggett Department Store Inc.
8300 Sudley Rd, Manassas VA 22110-3458. 703/361-4181.

Morton's
Lexington & Howard Sts, Baltimore MD 21201.
410/783-7700.

Rite Aid Discount Centers
Fair Oaks Mall, Fairfax VA 22033. 703/591-0334.

Rite Aid Discount Centers
1841 Jefferson Davis Hwy, Arlington VA 22202-3502.
703/413-7993.

Ross Dress For Less
13065 Lee Jackson Memorial Hwy, Fairfax VA 22033-2001. 703/818-2180.

Rugbees Children's Wear
McKays Plaza, Charlott Hall MD 20622. 301/884-8774.

Sam's Club
610 N Frederick Ave,
Gaithersburg MD 20877-2529. 301/216-2550.

Sam's Club-Members Only
2700 N Salisbury Blvd,
Salisbury MD 21801-2143.
410/860-8466.

VARIETY STORES

Dollar Bills Discount
3563 Plank Rd, Fredericksbrg VA 22407-6800. 703/786-9342.

Dollar Tree
5115 Backlick Rd # A,
Annandale VA 22003-6051.
703/941-8920.

FW Woolworth Co.
11933 Reisterstown Rd,
Reisterstown MD 21136-3030. 410/833-1533.

GC Murphy Co. Stores
3411 Dundalk Ave, Baltimore MD 21222-5921. 410/284-4930.

Valu-Plus
3818 Eastern Ave, Baltimore MD 21224-4221. 410/732-6370.

MISC. GENERAL MERCHANDISE STORES

Service Merchandise
5562 Silver Hill Rd,
Forestville MD 20747-1100.
301/735-3094.

GROCERY STORES

Bon Foods
Triangle Plaza, Dumfries VA 22026. 703/385-9097.

Farm Fresh Supermarkets
3427 Clifton Ave, Baltimore MD 21216-2502. 410/624-1301.

Fresh Value Market
1609 Washington Plz N,
Reston VA 22090-4305.
703/471-0714.

Geroge's Foodland
11339 Liberty Rd, Frederick
MD 21701-2617. 410/795-2780.

Getty Mart
99 Manassas Dr, Manassas
Park VA 22111-2367.
703/361-6153.

Giant Food Inc.
1063 W Patrick St, Frederick
MD 21702-3903. 301/695-4420.

Goff's IGA Foodliner
124 N Main St, Berlin MD
21811-1045. 410/641-9055.

Kash & Karry Food Stores
6836 Reisterstown Rd,
Baltimore MD 21215-1476.
410/764-1529.

Magruder's Grocery
6936 Braddock Rd,
Annandale VA 22003-6036.
703/750-1266.

Pasadena Investment Corporation
8095A Edwin Raynor Blvd,
Pasadena MD 21122-6829.
410/255-0070.

Pop Shop Marts
7715 Westfield Rd,
Baltimore MD 21222-2133.
410/282-7678.

Safeway Stores #0007
3713 Lee Hwy, Arlington VA
22207-3720. 703/841-1155.

Save-A-Lot
5007 Ritchie Hwy, Baltimore
MD 21225-3062. 410/636-9805.

Shore Stop Food Stores
Rt 13A, Delmar MD 21875.
410/896-9106.

Stop Shop Save
770 W North Ave, Baltimore
MD 21217-4431. 410/225-7900.

Super Fresh
10320 Festival Ln, Manassas
VA 22110-3548. 703/335-1343.

Valu Food Supermarkets
7602 Belair Rd, Baltimore
MD 21236-4014. 410/661-6426.

Weis Markets
13866 Metro Tech Dr,
Chantilly VA 22021-3242.
703/266-0401.

High's Dairy Stores
10501 Courthouse Rd,
Fredericksbrg VA 22407-1611. 703/898-1687.

MISC. FOOD STORES

Dutterers of Manchester Corporation
2700 Lord Baltimore Dr,
Baltimore MD 21244-2657.
410/298-3663.

Omaha Steaks
560 N Frederick Ave,
Gaithersburg MD 20877-2504. 301/330-0778.

Colorado Prime Inc.
7600 Leesburg Pike # B,
Falls Church VA 22043-2004. 703/734-4809.

Godiva Chocolatier
1100 S Hayes St, Arlington
VA 22202-4907. 703/418-2270.

Mr Bulky's Treats & Gifts
Marley Station Mall, Glen
Burnie MD 21061. 410/768-1093.

Wawa Food Markets
2100 Creswell Rd, Bel Air
MD 21015-6502. 410/734-7096.

Wawa Food Markets
5134 Thunder Hill Rd,
Columbia MD 21045-1922.
410/995-0723.

Wawa Food Markets
7100 N Point Rd, Baltimore
MD 21219-1220. 410/477-1533.

Wawa Food Markets
1741 Elkton Rd, Elkton MD
21921-4129. 410/398-5152.

General Nutrition
Golden Ring Mall, Baltimore
MD 21237. 410/574-5822.

Forever Living Products
7411 Riggs Rd, Hyattsville
MD 20783-4246. 301/445-1256.

General Nutrition Centers
Liberty Court, Randallstown
MD 21133. 410/655-8735.

RETAIL BAKERIES

Chesapeake Bagel Bakery
6815 Old Dominion Dr, Mc
Lean VA 22101-3711.
703/506-0536.

Great American Cookie Company
Spotsylvania Mall,
Fredericksbrg VA 22401.
703/786-4222.

Mrs. Fields Cookies
Owings Mills Town Center,
Owings Mills MD 21117.
410/363-6082.

Schmidt Baking Co.
4425 Fitch Ave, Baltimore
MD 21236-3908. 410/882-9202.

Weis Markets
Colonial Bake Shop,
Manassas VA 22110.
703/590-0408.

Weis Markets Colonial Bake Shop
2 Old Camp Rd, Frederick
MD 21702-3740. 301/473-5303.

Swiss Pretzel Shop
Harford Mall, Bel Air MD
21014. 410/838-4450.
C Code: 54990100.

AUTO DEALERS

Austrian Motorcars
7020 Arlington Rd, Bethesda
MD 20814-5229. 301/986-8800.

Autohaus Tischer
3371 Fort Meade Rd, Laurel
MD 20724-2001. 301/498-7400.

Bob Davidson Ford
1845 E Joppa Rd, Baltimore
MD 21234-2794. 410/661-6400.

Davepyles Lincoln-Mercury
PO Box 605, Annandale VA
22003-0605. 703/750-2700.

Farrish Oldsmobile/Jeep/Subaru
9610 Lee Hwy, Fairfax VA
22031-2376. 703/273-0200.

Koons of Manassa
7105 Sudley Rd, Manassas
VA 22110-2636. 703/631-9500.

Lantzsh-Andreas Enterprises
8545 Leesburg Pike, Vienna
VA 22182-2203. 703/448-2222.

Marten's Volvo of Washington
4800 Wisconsin Ave Nw,
Washington DC 20016-4612. 202/537-3000.

O'Donnell Pontiac Inc.
Rte 29 & Rte 40, Ellicott City
MD 21043. 410/465-9100.

Rosenthal Chevrolet
3400 Columbia Pike,

Arlington VA 22204-4299.
703/920-8700.

Waldorf Toyota/Volvo
PO Box 739, Waldorf MD
20604-0739. 301/843-
3700.

Jerrys Chevrolet Geo and Oldsmobile
325 E Market St, Leesburg
VA 22075-4102. 703/589-
1902.

Radley Honda Chevrolet
3670 Jefferson Davis Hwy,
Fredericksbrg VA 22408-
4163. 703/898-4000.

Al Packer Ford Inc.
5665 Belair Rd, Baltimore
MD 21206-3693. 410/488-
5566.

Normandy Ford Inc.
8528 Baltimore National
Pike, Ellicott City MD 21043-
3385. 410/465-1300.

Sheehy Ford of Springfield
6727 Loisdale Rd, Springfield
VA 22150-1994. 703/922-
7900.

Brown's Honda City Honda
7160 Ritchie Hwy, Glen
Burnie MD 21061-2904.
410/553-8014.

Ourisman Honda Inc.
4800 Bethesda Ave,
Bethesda MD 20814-5247.
301/656-1000.

Rosenthal Honda Inc.
1580 Spring Hill Rd, Vienna
VA 22182-2205. 703/749-
6600.

Nationwide Mtr Sls Corporation Isuzu
2070 York Rd, Timonium MD
21093-4249. 410/561-
5900.

Rosenthal Automotive
1100 S Glebe Rd, Arlington
VA 22204-4309. 703/553-
6585.

Sport Jeep-Eagle
3271 Automobile Blvd, Silver
Spring MD 20904-4909.
301/890-7000.

Purvis Ford Inc.
3660 Jefferson Davis Hwy,
Fredericksbrg VA 22408-
4163. 703/898-3000.

Sheehy Nissan-Mitsubishi
9010 Liberia Ave, Manassas
VA 22110-5322. 703/631-
1966.

Saturn of Glen Burnie
Ritchie Hwy & Holsum Way,
Glen Burnie MD 21061.
410/766-1400.

C Earl Brown Inc.
11611 Hopewell Rd,
Hagerstown MD 21740-
2110. 301/582-2111.

Hinder Motors Inc.
117 S Philadelphia Blvd,
Aberdeen MD 21001-3205.
410/676-4855.

CONSUMER SUPPLY STORES

Salvo Auto Parts Inc.
14 Back River Neck Rd,
Baltimore MD 21221-3701.
410/682-2300.

Aberdeen Automotive Supply
524 S Philadelphia Blvd,
Aberdeen MD 21001-3405.
410/272-7110.

All Parts
254 Lee Hwy, Warrenton VA
22186-2501. 703/349-
9450.

Bel Air Auto Parts Inc.
418 N Main St, Bel Air MD
21014-3509. 410/893-
9546.

Fairfax Auto Parts Inc.
14154 Willard Rd # C,
Chantilly VA 22021-2976.
703/631-3800.

Hi Gear Discount Auto Parts
Spring Shopping Ctr,
Baltimore MD 21202.
410/256-2211.

Hi-Gear Discount Auto Parts
Bel Air Plaza, Bel Air MD
21014. 410/836-0120.

Hi-Gear Discount Auto Parts
Gunston Plaza Shopping
Center, Lorton VA 22079.
703/550-1447.

Hi-Gear Tire & Auto Supply
1281 Jefferson Davis Hwy,
Fredericksbrg VA 22401-
4415. 703/373-2277.

The Kunkel Service
908 Pulaski Hwy, Hvre De
Grace MD 21078-2602.
410/939-2300.

Western Auto
6724 Gov Ritchie Hwy, Glen
Burnie MD 21061. 410/768-
8890.

Ben Pilla Perform & Van Center
Arundel Village Plaza, Glen
Burnie MD 21061. 410/636-
6434.

NTW-National Tire Warehouse
6413 Old Alexandria Ferry
Rd, Clinton MD 20735-
1736. 301/856-4242.

Merchant's Tire & Auto Centers
13900 Lee Hwy, Centreville
VA 22020-2415. 703/631-
1025.

Merchant's Tire & Auto Centers
6609 Backlick Rd, Springfield
VA 22150-2702. 703/644-
4377.

Bogle Tire Co.
8827 Telegraph Rd # A,
Lorton VA 22079-1530.
703/550-9570.

Mr. Tire Auto Service Centers
7224 Ritchie Hwy, Glen
Burnie MD 21061-3039.
410/760-4377.

Anderson Tire Center
1600 Tidewater Trail,
Spotsylvania VA 22553.
703/373-0005.

Kimmel Tire & Auto Centers
8621 Baltimore National
Pike, Ellicott City MD 21043-
4114. 410/461-4941.

Mr. Tire Inc.
5603 Baltimore National
Pike, Catonsville MD 21228-
1402. 410/788-0377.

Speedy Muffler King
7600 Harford Rd, Baltimore
MD 21234-6402. 410/882-
4434.

BOAT DEALERS

U.S. Boat Marine Center
4955 Nicholson Ct,
Kensington MD 20895-
1004. 301/230-0945.

APPAREL STORES

American Eagle Outfitters
Marley Station Mall, Glen
Burnie MD 21061. 410/761-
7411.

Britches Great Outdoors
8300 Sudley Rd, Manassas
VA 22110-3458. 703/335-
5066.

Britches of Georgetowne
Gaithersburg Lakeforest Mall,
Gaithersburg MD 20877.
301/869-0100.

Cavalier Men's Shop
1345 University Blvd E,
Hyattsville MD 20783-4616.
301/431-1800.

Essex Co.
7540 Washington Blvd,
Elkridge MD 21227-6406.
410/799-4900.

J Riggings Inc.
Wheaton Plaza, Wheaton MD 20902. 301/949-6778.

Knot Crazy
1100 S Hayes St, Arlington VA 22202-4907. 703/418-0078.

Long Rap Inc.
1420 Wisconsin Ave Nw, Washington DC 20007-2827. 202/337-6610.

Steven-Windsor
2762 Duke St, Alexandria VA 22314-4511. 703/751-8844.

Tie Rack
1961 Chain Bridge Rd, Mc Lean VA 22102-4502. 703/790-5784.

Ziedler & Ziedler
Tyson's Corner Center, Mc Lean VA 22101. 703/448-8376.

Ann Taylor Clothing
Owings Mills Town Center, Owings Mills MD 21117. 410/363-0354.

Carole Little
Chesapeake Village, Queenstown MD 21658. 410/827-7746.

Cato Fashions-Cato Plus
White Marlin Mall, Ocean City MD 21842. 410/213-2120.

Christie's Fashions
6200 Annapolis Rd, Hyattsville MD 20784-1319. 301/773-0216.

County Seat Store
St Charles Town Center, Waldorf MD 20603. 301/645-0741.

Dress Barns
1239 Jefferson Davis Hwy, Fredericksbrg VA 22401-4415. 703/899-0593.

The Limited Express
11929 Market St, Reston VA 22090-5615. 703/904-9245.

Fashion Bug
4200 Baltimore National Pike, Ellicott City MD 21042. 410/461-6741.

Jones New York Factory Store
68 Heather Ln, Perryville MD 21903-2507. 410/642-0140.

The Limited Express
Galleria At Tysons II, Mc Lean VA 22102. 703/556-7895.

Marianne
50 Harundale Mall, Glen Burnie MD 21061. 410/766-4013.

Mondi International
1768 M International Dr, Mc Lean VA 22102. 703/448-8095.

The Answer
Loehmanns Plaza Shopping Cente, Falls Church VA 22042. 703/573-0485.

The Dress Barn
6435 Dobbin Rd, Columbia MD 21045-5821. 301/596-6384.

Up Against The Wall
St Charles Town Center, Waldorf MD 20603. 301/870-4373.

The Van Metre Companies
5252 Lyngate Ct, Burke VA 22015-1688. 703/425-2600.

Barbizon Lingerie
Chesapeake Village Outlet Cntr, Queenstown MD 21658. 410/827-7654.

Cacique
The Galleria, Mc Lean VA 22102. 703/448-1663.

Cacique
Tysons Corner Center, Mc Lean VA 22102. 703/893-1130.

Victoria's Secret
St Charles Town Center, Waldorf MD 20603. 301/705-8088.

Carter's Childrenswear
Eastern Shore Factory Stores, Chester MD 21619. 410/643-4003.

Gapkids
Springfield Mall, Springfield VA 22150. 703/971-8446.

Hess Shoes
7243 Ambassador Rd, Baltimore MD 21244-2710. 410/298-5555.

Kobacker Co./Fashion East
8360 Rt 3 Md, Millersville MD 21108. 410/987-0010.

Super Shoe Stores
PO Box 239, Cumberland MD 21501-0239. 301/759-4300.

Lady Foot Locker
7900 Ritchie Hwy, Glen Burnie MD 21061-0355. 410/760-9160.

Brown Shoes
305 Chesapeake Village Rd, Queenstown MD 21658-1352. 410/827-5644.

Jarman Shoe Stores
Tysons Corner Shopping Center, Mc Lean VA 22102. 703/893-5587.

Jarman Shoe Stores
Landover Mall, Landover MD 20785. 301/322-5293.

Kids Footlocker
2103 Brightseat Rd, Landover MD 20785-3601. 301/322-8604.

Parade of Shoes
9256 Old Keene Mill Rd, Burke VA 22015-4201. 703/912-6944.

Rack Room Shoes
896 Largo Center Dr, Hyattsville MD 20785-3705. 301/808-3496.

Rack Room Shoes
Montgomery Village Plaza, Gaithersburg MD 20877. 301/590-8705.

County Seat Stores
2001 International Dr, Mc Lean VA 22102-3909. 703/893-7296.

Galt Sand Company
307 Chesapeake Village Rd, Queenstown MD 21658-1352. 410/827-5200.

Going To The Game
7101 Democracy Blvd, Bethesda MD 20817-1018. 301/299-9739.

T Shirt People Factory Outlet
1800 Woodlawn Dr, Baltimore MD 21207-4007. 410/265-7140.

Pelle Cuir
2001 International Dr # 2, Mc Lean VA 22102-3909. 703/847-8550.

FURNITURE STORES

Danker Furniture
10670 Lee Hwy, Fairfax VA 22030-4310. 703/691-4333.

Door Store Inc.
3140 M St Nw, Washington DC 20007-3704. 202/333-8170.

Jennifer Convertibles
585 New Ordinance Rd, Glen Burnie MD 21060. 410/766-0675.

Jennifer Convertibles
1809 Reisterstown Rd,

Pikesville MD 21208-6329.
410/484-4790.

Mastercraft Interiors
6800 Distribution Dr,
Beltsville MD 20705-1400.
301/595-4422.

The Bombay Company
8300 Sudley Rd, Manassas
VA 22110-3458. 703/335-5542.

The Pine Factory Ltd.
Marley Station, Glen Burnie
MD 21061. 410/761-2044.

The Rowe Showplace
8344 Leesburg Pike, Vienna
VA 22182-2401. 703/821-7693.

Mattress Discounters
6728 Ritchie Hwy, Glen
Burnie MD 21061-2319.
410/761-5270.

Mattress Discounters
1409 Merritt Blvd, Baltimore
MD 21222-2111. 410/284-0242.

Mattress Discounters
1010 Smallwood Dr, Waldorf
MD 20603-4758. 301/645-6323.

Mattress Discounters
6476 Dobbin Center Way,
Columbia MD 21045-5842.
410/730-0040.

Mattress Discounters
9540 Old Keene Mill Rd,
Springfield VA 22015-4208.
703/912-7284.

Mattress Discounters
14017 Lee Jackson
Memorial Hig, Chantilly VA
22021-1601. 703/803-6978.

Select Comfort Air Sleeper
Tysons Corner Center, Mc
Lean VA 22102. 703/760-0401.

Kitchen Warehouse
13875 Smoketown Rd,
Woodbridge VA 22192-4206. 703/670-9884.

Moores Lumber and Building Supply
119 South Blvd, Salisbury
MD 21801-6464. 410/742-7134.

Burlington Coat Factory
3524 S Jefferson St, Falls
Church VA 22041-3119.
703/379-7878.

Offenbacher Pool 'N Patio
11213 Lee Hwy # G, Fairfax
VA 22030-5608. 703/591-9840.

MISC. HOME FURNISHINGS STORES

Carpet Fair Inc.
7100 Rutherford Rd,
Baltimore MD 21244-2747.
410/298-5800.

Floors Inc.
1775 Brightseat Rd,
Landover MD 20785-3767.
301/772-5800.

Choice Home & Design Center
Bright Acres Ctr E, Owings
MD 20736. 410/257-3838.

Kitchen Bazaar
1098 Taft St, Rockville MD
20850-1308. 301/424-4880.

Lechters
Owings Mills Town Center,
Owings Mills MD 21117.
410/363-4818.

Kitchen Bazaar
Galleria At Tysons II, Mc
Lean VA 22102. 703/883-1313.

Lite House Ltd.
6381 Old Branch Ave,
Temple Hills MD 20748-2619. 301/449-3900.

Linen Locker & More
10040 Baltimore National
Pike, Ellicott City MD 21042-3612. 410/461-3665.

CONSUMER ELECTRONICS STORES

Bryn Mawr Stereo
Merritt Blvd & Holabird Av,
Baltimore MD 21222.
410/284-4625.

Impulse
2001 International Dr, Mc
Lean VA 22102-3909.
703/893-4664.

COMPUTER AND SOFTWARE STORES

Bull
9810 Patuxent Woods Dr
Ste C, Columbia MD 21046-1577. 410/290-8390.

Clinton Computers
7475 Old Alexandria Ferry
Rd, Clinton MD 20735-1834. 301/599-9555.

Computer City Supercenter
50 W Ridgely Rd, Timonium
MD 21093-5112. 410/560-6930.

Computerland
202 Perry Pky, Gaithersburg
MD 20877-2172. 301/670-4031.

ECS Composites Inc.
5336 Tarkington Pl,
Columbia MD 21044-5406.
410/730-1144.

Frederick Computers Plus
5726 Industry Ln, Frederick
MD 21701-5134. 301/694-8884.

Next Computer Inc.
1650 Tysons Blvd, Mc Lean
VA 22102-3915. 703/506-3940.

Tandem Computers Incorporated
10700 Parkridge Blvd,
Reston VA 22091-5429.
703/476-0550.

Babbages Software
7958 Tysons Corner Ctr # L,
Mc Lean VA 22102-4500.
703/760-8973.

Computer City Supercenter
597 E Ordnance Rd, Glen
Burnie MD 21060-6555.
410/508-3865.

Computer City Supercenter
52 W Ridgely Rd, Timonium
MD 21093-5112. 410/560-3930.

Dunn & Bradstreet Software Service
3141 Fairview Park Dr, Falls
Church VA 22042-4507.
703/849-9700.

Electronics Boutique
179 Rt 450 & 178,
Annapolis MD 21401.
410/224-4220.

One Call Concepts
7223 Parkway Dr, Hanover
MD 21076-1337. 410/712-0082.

Rapid Systems Solutions
11201 Joan Marie Ct,
Clarksville MD 21029-1806.
301/317-4912.

Babbage's Software
Cranberry Mall, Westminster
MD 21157. 410/876-8835.

Software Etc.
Galleria At Tysons II, Mc
Lean VA 22102. 703/821-2043.

RECORD AND PRERECORDED TAPE STORES

Suncoast Motion Picture Company
8300 Sudley Rd, Manassas
VA 22110-3458. 703/369-9468.

Suncoast Motion Picture Company
Ballston Commons Mall,

Arlington VA 22203.
703/516-4527.

Record Town
Owings Mills Town Center,
Owings Mills MD 21117.
410/363-8471.

Record Town
5748 Baltimore National
Pike, Catonsville MD 21228-
1306. 410/719-7684.

Record World
8300 Sudley Rd, Manassas
VA 22110-3458. 703/368-
3485.

Wee Three Record Shops
Tysons Corner Shopping
Center, Mc Lean VA 22102.
703/893-5300.

MUSICAL INSTRUMENT STORES

Music & Arts Center Inc.
12312 Wilkins Ave, Rockville
MD 20852-1828. 301/881-
7760.

DRUG STORES

Discount Drugs Wisconsin Inc.
5100 Wisconsin Ave Nw,
Washington DC 20016-
4119. 202/363-3466.

Discount Drugs Wisconsin Inc.
4945 Wyaconda Rd,
Rockville MD 20852-2443.
301/230-8930.

CVS Pharmacy
6516 Landover Rd, Landover
MD 20785-1445. 301/773-
3355.

Giant Discount Drug
Tollgate Shopping Ctr, Bel
Air MD 21014. 410/879-
7121.

Giant Discount Drug
9200 Baltimore National
Pike, Ellicott City MD 21042-
2615. 410/465-5683.

Giant Discount Drug
8665 Philadelphia Rd,
Baltimore MD 21237-3020.
410/574-4766.

Rite Aid Pharmacies
Hampshire Langley Shopng
Ctr, Laurel MD 20723.
301/439-4400.

Rite Aid Pharmacies
Alameda Shopping Ctr,
Baltimore MD 21239.
410/532-3490.

Klein's Super Thrift Markets
Beards Hill Plaza, Aberdeen
MD 21001. 410/272-3101.

Peoples Drug Stores
425 N Washington St,
Leonardtown MD 20650-
3838. 301/475-8917.

Safeway Inc.
10000 Baltimore National
Pike, Ellicott City MD 21042-
3612. 410/750-3002.

Safeway Supermarkets
415 14th St Se, Washington
DC 20003-3002. 202/547-
4350.

Safeway Supermarkets
3838 Howard Ave,
Kensington MD 20895-
2402. 301/929-0733.

Safeway Supermarkets
9596 Old Keene Mill Rd,
Burke VA 22015-4208.
703/451-5566.

Giant Food Inc.
Leesburg Plaza, Leesburg VA
22075. 703/771-9518.

Giant Food Inc.
Mapledale Plaza, Woodbridge
VA 22193. 703/590-1700.

Neighborcare
4801 Dorsey Hall Dr Ste
108, Ellicott City MD 21042-
7749. 410/715-1000.

White Shield Pharmacy
231 Tippin Dr, Thurmont MD
21788-3211. 301/271-
1111.

LIQUOR STORES

Rodman's Gourmet & Beer
5120 Nicholson Ln,
Kensington MD 20895-
1046. 301/881-6253.

USED MERCHANDISE STORES

Village Economy Stores
5202 Baltimore National
Pike, Baltimore MD 21229-
1022. 410/744-6070.

SPORTING GOODS STORES

Athletic Attic
Spotsylvania Mall,
Fredericksbrg VA 22407.
703/786-8444.

Bicycle Exchange Inc.
4307 Wheeler Ave,
Alexandria VA 22304-6416.
703/461-9696.

Britches of Georgetowne
Arlington Fashion Center,
Arlington VA 22202.
703/415-2300.

Champs Sport Shops
Hunt Valley Mall, Cockys Ht
Vly MD 21030. 410/771-
9300.

Champs Sports
Lakeforest Mall, Gaithersburg
MD 20877. 301/921-4691.

Champs Sports
1961 Chain Bridge Rd, Mc
Lean VA 22102-4502.
703/821-5039.

Famous Footwear
Montgomery Village Plaza
Off P, Gaithersburg MD
20879. 301/330-2950.

Famous Footwear
Piney Narrows Rd, Chester
MD 21619. 410/643-6070.

Foot Locker
Fair Oaks Mall Store 7298,
Fairfax VA 22030. 703/273-
9667.

Hermans World of Sporting Goods
10776 Sudley Manor Dr,
Manassas VA 22110-2833.
703/369-5052.

Hermans World of Sporting Goods
6787 Springfield Mall,
Springfield VA 22150-1704.
703/971-8303.

Marvins Sport City
Cranberry Mall, Westminster
MD 21157. 410/876-0666.

Rudo Sports Inc.
6708 White Stone Rd,
Baltimore MD 21207-4102.
410/298-6618.

Ocean City Marina
Dorchester St & Bay, Ocean
City MD 21842. 410/289-
6188.

Tackle Crafters Inc.
28 Bonbon Ct, Reisterstown
MD 21136-1706. 410/833-
8568.

Toys R Us
8449 Leesburg Pike, Vienna
VA 22182-2404. 703/893-
2223.

BOOKSTORES

Brentano's Bookstore
Tyson's Corner, Mc Lean VA
22102. 703/760-8956.

Encore Books
Park Plaza, Severna Park MD
21146. 410/544-0717.

STATIONERY STORES

Signature Shoppe
Montgomery Mall, Bethesda
MD 20817. 301/365-2612.

Office Depot Inc.
1991 Chain Bridge Rd, Mc

Lean VA 22102-4407.
703/821-8371.

Staples Inc-Region 4
9470 Arlington Blvd, Fairfax
VA 22031-2402. 703/591-7287.

JEWELRY STORES

Best Jewelry
Spotsylvania Mall,
Fredericksbrg VA 22407.
703/786-5160.

Evans Jewelers Inc.
13055 Lee Jackson
Memorial Hwy, Fairfax VA
22033-2001. 703/817-1700.

Littman Jewelers
Eastpoint Mall, Baltimore MD
21224. 410/284-1272.

Melart Jewelers
Landover Mall, Hyattsville
MD 20785. 301/772-7377.

Melart Jewelers
8700 Georgia Ave Fl 5,
Silver Spring MD 20910-3614. 301/587-6880.

S & N Katz
Harford Mall, Bel Air MD
21014. 410/879-1885.

Service Merchandise Co.
9041 Snowden River Pky,
Columbia MD 21046-1657.
410/312-4932.

Shaw's Jeweler's
Spotsylvania Mall,
Fredericksbrg VA 22401.
703/786-4200.

Shaw's Jewelers
Montgomery Mall, Bethesda
MD 20817. 301/365-2609.

HOBBY, TOY, AND GAME SHOPS

Frank's Nursery & Crafts
7928 Eastern Ave, Baltimore
MD 21224-2125. 410/284-1202.

Frank's Nursery & Crafts
13770 Smoketown Rd,
Woodbridge VA 22192-4205. 703/494-7115.

Frank's Nursery & Crafts
1257 Jefferson Davis Hwy,
Fredericksbrg VA 22401-4415. 703/371-3232.

Imaginarium Inc.
1961 Chain Bridge Rd, Mc
Lean VA 22102-4502.
703/847-0011.

Kay-Bee Toys
Montgomery Mall, Bethesda
MD 20817. 301/469-6199.

Kay-Bee Toys
Spotsylvania Mall,
Fredericksbrg VA 22401.
703/786-6620.

CAMERA AND PHOTOGRAPHIC SUPPLY STORES

Ritz Camera Center
8300 Sudley Rd, Manassas
VA 22110-3458. 703/368-7676.

Ritz Camera One Hour Photo
600 King St, Alexandria VA
22314-3106. 703/683-1194.

GIFT, NOVELTY, AND SOUVENIR SHOPS

Balloon Man
12113 Rockville Pike,
Rockville MD 20852-1605.
301/770-7640.

Pam's Hallmark Shoppe
St Charles Towne Plaza,
Waldorf MD 20603.
301/705-9727.

The Pampered Party
Gateway Village Shopping
Cente, Fredericksbrg VA
22401. 703/373-2806.

B Dalton Bookseller
Hunt Valley Mall, Cockys Ht
Vly MD 21030. 410/771-6830.

Banner Management
443 N Frederick Ave,
Gaithersburg MD 20877-2405. 301/670-4140.

Books-A-Million
Potomac Mills Outlet,
Woodbridge VA 22192.
703/490-3809.

Crabtree & Evelyn Ltd.
1100 S Hayes St, Arlington
VA 22202-4907. 703/415-2232.

Crate & Barrell
Tysons Corner Center, Mc
Lean VA 22102. 703/847-8555.

Dollar Bills
6220 Central Ave, Capital
Hts MD 20743-6128.
301/336-5417.

Earthtones
40 Church Rd # R, Arnold
MD 21012-2314. 410/757-1247.

Elson's News & Gifts
Radisson Mark Hotel,
Alexandria VA 22311.
703/998-7575.

Natural Wonders
825 Dulaney Valley Rd,
Baltimore MD 21204-1010.
410/337-8727.

Persnickety
7974 Tysons Corner Ctr, Mc
Lean VA 22102-4500.
703/760-8996.

The San Francisco Music Box Company
Landmark Center, Annandale
VA 22003. 703/941-0813.

The San Francisco Music Box Company
Tyson's Corner Center, Mc
Lean VA 22102. 703/442-6607.

The Museum Company
1100 S Hayes St, Arlington
VA 22202-4907. 703/415-3838.

Things Remembered
St Charles Town Center,
Waldorf MD 20603.
301/932-4790.

LUGGAGE AND LEATHER GOODS STORES

Georgetown Leather Design
Lake Forest Mall,
Gaithersburg MD 20877.
301/990-2556.

Tuerkes
10640 Iron Bridge Rd,
Jessup MD 20794-9496.
410/792-7470.

Hamilton Luggage & Handbags
8661 Colesville Rd, Silver
Spring MD 20910-3924.
301/587-4982.

Hamilton Luggage & Handbags
2700 Potomac Mills Cir,
Woodbridge VA 22192-4625. 703/491-8241.

Travel 2000 Inc.
701 Russell Ave,
Gaithersburg MD 20877-2612. 301/975-0147.

SEWING SUPPLIES STORES

House of Fabrics
872 Largo Center Dr,
Hyattsville MD 20785-3705.
301/350-4640.

Jo-Ann Fabric & Crafts
9978 York Rd, Cockys Ht
Vly MD 21030-3401.
410/628-0805.

Total Crafts
Parkville Shopping Cntr,
Baltimore MD 21234.
410/444-4500.

Yarns Etcetera
215 King St, Alexandria VA

22314-3209. 703/548-3508.

Total Crafts
Price Club Plaza, Glen Burnie MD 21061. 410/766-2224.

CATALOG AND MAIL-ORDER HOUSES

Roar Music Inc.
2 Wisconsin Cir Ste 560, Chevy Chase MD 20815-7003. 301/657-8300.

Seabury & Smith
1255 23rd St NW Ste 300, Washington DC 20037-1125. 202/296-8030.

Wellington Jewels
4850 Connecticut Ave Nw, Washington DC 20008-5941. 202/244-1422.

FUEL DEALERS

House Warmers Diamond Grier Oil
N Philadelphia Blvd, Aberdeen MD 21001. 410/575-6572.

Commonwealth Propane
2014 Lafayette Blvd # C, Fredericksbrg VA 22401-2226. 703/898-0357.

FLORISTS

Flowers By Montgomery Wards
105 N Main St, Bel Air MD 21014-3539. 410/838-6832.

Meadows Farms Nurseries Inc.
1021 Norwood Rd, Silver Spring MD 20905-3897. 301/924-1515.

OPTICAL GOODS STORES

Lenscrafters
Landover Mall, Hyattsville MD 20785. 301/322-5515.

MISC. RETAIL STORES

The Nature Company
301 Light St, Baltimore MD 21202-1037. 410/576-0909.

Beltone Hearing Aid Center
148 E Franklin St, Hagerstown MD 21740-4906. 301/733-2205.

Miracle Ear
200 Defense Hwy, Annapolis MD 21401. 410/266-9442.

Pettrax
Wheaton Plaza Shopping Center, Wheaton MD 20902. 301/942-8833.

Petco
6394 Springfield Plz, Springfield VA 22150-3431. 703/866-1100.

Beauty Outlet
971 Beards Hill Rd, Aberdeen MD 21001-1782. 410/575-7177.

Sally Beauty Supply
514 Reisterstown Rd, Pikesville MD 21208-5339. 410/486-9581.

The Cosmetic Center
9679 Lost Knife Rd, Gaithersburg MD 20877-2622. 301/926-0500.

Total Crafts Stores
9230 Old Keene Mill Rd # B, Burke VA 22015-4201. 703/440-0556.

Total Crafts Stores
9528 Main St, Fairfax VA 22031-4031. 703/978-0400.

Ferguson Enterprises
4430 Beech Rd, Temple Hills MD 20748-6702. 301/899-8683.

Ferguson Enterprises
814 N Main St, Culpeper VA 22701-2212. 703/825-6969.

Schumacher & Seiler
2109 Bel Air Rd, Fallston MD 21047-2719. 410/879-3131.

Sun Gear
825 Dulaney Valley Rd, Baltimore MD 21204-1010. 410/337-9217.

For more information on career opportunities in retail:

Associations

INTERNATIONAL ASSOCIATION OF CHAIN STORES
3800 Moor Place, Alexandria VA 22305. 703/549-4525.

INTERNATIONAL COUNCIL OF SHOPPING CENTERS
665 Fifth Avenue, New York NY 10022. 212/421-8181. Offers conventions, research, education, a variety of publications, and awards programs.

NATIONAL AUTOMOTIVE DEALERS ASSOCIATION
8400 Westpark Drive, McLean VA 22102. 703/821-7000.

NATIONAL INDEPENDENT AUTOMOTIVE DEALERS ASSOCIATION
2521 Brown Boulevard, Suite 100, Arlington TX 76006. 817/640-3838.

NATIONAL RETAIL FEDERATION
325 7th Street NW, Suite 1000, Washington DC 20004. 202/783-7971. Provides information services, industry outlooks, and a variety of educational opportunities and publications.

Directories

AUTOMOTIVE NEWS MARKET DATA BOOK
Automotive News, Crain Communication, 1400 Woodbridge Avenue, Detroit MI 48207-3187. 313/446-6000.

STONE, CLAY, GLASS AND CONCRETE PRODUCTS

Growth in stone, clay, glass, concrete and related materials is closely tied to the success of the construction industry. On one hand, analysts believe that the fortunes of the construction industry should remain solid in the short-term, despite the added pressure of higher interest rates and an economy that has begun to cool from its torrid pace of growth in 1994 and early 1995. On the other, the longer-term forecast is for much slower growth, since infrastructure construction is dependent on shrinking local government budgets. All in all, the stone, clay, glass and concrete industry should see revenue growth of about 1 to 2 percent annually.

THE ARUNDEL CORPORATION
P.O. Box 5000, Sparks Glenco MD 21152-5000. 410/329-5000. **Contact:** Human Resources. **Description:** Mines quarries for building materials.

CARR-LOWREY GLASS COMPANY
2201 Kloman Street, Baltimore MD 21230. 410/347-8800. **Contact:** Thierry Bernard, President. **Description:** Produces glass bottles, glass jars, and is engaged in the labeling and decorating of glass products. A division of Anchor-Hocking Corporation (Lancaster, OH), which produces a wide variety of glassware, commercial and institutional chinaware; decorative and convenience hardware; glass containers, and metal and plastic closures. **Corporate headquarters location:** This Location.

GENERAL DYNAMICS CORPORATION
3190 Fairview Park Drive, Falls Church VA 22042-4523. 703/876-3000. **Contact:** Human Resources. **Description:** A producer of nuclear submarines and land systems. The company has two main divisions. The Electric Boat Division designs and builds nuclear submarines, including the Seawolf class attack submarine and the New Attack submarine due to go into production in 1998. The Land Systems Division designs and builds armored vehicles, such as the M1 Series of battle tanks, for the U.S. Army, the U.S. Marine Corps, and a number of international customers. The company has submarine manufacturing facilities in New Jersey, Connecticut, South Carolina, and Rhode Island and tank production facilities in Ohio and Michigan. The company also has coal mining operations located primarily in central Illinois, provides ship management services for the U.S. government on prepositioning and ready reserve ships, and leases liquefied natural gas tankers. **Common positions include:** Accountant/Auditor; Secretary. **Educational backgrounds include:** Accounting; Business Administration; Finance. **Benefits:** Dental Insurance; Disability Coverage; Life Insurance; Medical Insurance; Pension Plan; Profit Sharing; Savings Plan. **Corporate headquarters location:** This Location. **Other U.S. locations:** CT; IL; MI; NJ; OH; RI; SC. **Listed on:** New York Stock Exchange. **Number of employees at this location:** 60. **Number of employees nationwide:** 25,000.

GENSTAR STONE PRODUCTS COMPANY
Executive Plaza IV, 11350 McCormick Road, Hunt Valley MD 21031. **Contact:** Manager/Personnel Administration. **Description:** Produces crushed stone, gravel, sand, and similar products.

LAFARGE CORPORATION
11130 Sunrise Valley Drive, Suite 300, Reston VA 22091. 703/264-3600. **Contact:** Human Resources. **Description:** Lafarge produces cement, concrete, aggregates, and related products in the United States and in Canada through its subsidiary, Lafarge Canada Inc. The company operates 15 full-production cement plants and 420 construction materials facilities. Subsidiary Systech Environmental Corporation is a processor and recycler of industrial waste products into fuel for the cement kilns.

NOTE: Lafarge Corporation does not hire at this location, except for local administrative positions. **Listed on:** New York Stock Exchange.

NATIONAL GYPSUM COMPANY
2301 South Newkirk Street, Baltimore MD 21224. 410/631-4900. **Contact:** Sue Tyber, Personnel Director. **Description:** Manufactures gypsum wallboard and joint compounds. An integrated, diversified manufacturer of quality products for building, construction, and shelter markets. **Common positions include:** Blue-Collar Worker Supervisor; Buyer; Department Manager; General Manager; Human Resources Specialist; Operations/Production Manager; Quality Control Supervisor. **Educational backgrounds include:** Business Administration. **Benefits:** Dental Insurance; Disability Coverage; Employee Discounts; Life Insurance; Medical Insurance; Pension Plan; Savings Plan; Tuition Assistance. **Operations at this facility include:** Manufacturing.

OLD CASTLE, INC.
3299 K Street, Suite 402, Washington DC 20007. 202/625-2122. **Contact:** Human Resources. **Description:** The company produces aggregate, asphalt, ready mix concrete, and prestress concrete for road and bridge construction. **Corporate headquarters location:** Dublin, Ireland. **Parent company:** CRH plc.

PRICE BROTHERS CO.
P.O. Box 33, Perryman MD 21130. 410/272-8003. **Contact:** Karen George, Personnel Manager. **Description:** Produces concrete pressure pipe. Nationally, the company operates in three industry segments: Utility Construction; Non-residential Building; and Industrial. Pressure Pipe Division manufactures reinforced pipe (this facility), sold to the electric power, sewer, water utility, and other large-scale industrial markets. **Common positions include:** Civil Engineer; Department Manager; Operations/Production Manager. **Educational backgrounds include:** Business Administration; Engineering. **Benefits:** Dental Insurance; Disability Coverage; Life Insurance; Medical Insurance; Profit Sharing; Savings Plan; Tuition Assistance. **Operations at this facility include:** Manufacturing.

SIVACO
NATIONAL WIRE PRODUCTS CORPORATION
8203 Fischer Road, Baltimore MD 21222-8909. 410/477-1700. **Contact:** Personnel Administrator. **Description:** Produces concrete reinforcement products. **Common positions include:** Accountant/Auditor; Blue-Collar Worker Supervisor; Computer Programmer; Credit Manager; Draftsperson; Human Resources Specialist; Industrial Engineer; Manufacturer's/Wholesaler's Sales Rep. **Educational backgrounds include:** Accounting; Business Administration. **Benefits:** Disability Coverage; Life Insurance; Medical Insurance; Pension Plan. **Corporate headquarters location:** This Location. **Operations at this facility include:** Administration; Manufacturing; Sales.

VULCAN MATERIALS COMPANY
P.O. Box 509, Manassas VA 22110. 703/368-3135. **Contact:** Robin Hollyfield, Plant Clerk. **Description:** Produces crushed stone for construction applications. Nationally, the company is a multi-industry firm operating in three business segments. **Listed on:** New York Stock Exchange.

Note: Because addresses and telephone numbers of smaller companies change rapidly, we recommend you call each company to verify the information below before inquiring about job opportunities. Mass mailings are not recommended.

Additional employers with under 250 employees:

ASPHALT

APAC-Virginia Inc.
8738 Vulcan Ln, Manassas VA 22110-3951. 703/968-6370.

Tamko Asphalt Products
4500 Tamko Dr, Frederick MD 21701-8327. 301/694-7611.

CRUSHED AND BROKEN STONE

Browning's Deep Creek Quarry
Rt 219, Oakland MD 21550. 301/387-9390.

Chantilly Crushed Stone
RR 50, Fairfax VA 22033-9850. 703/471-4461.

GLASS AND GLASS PRODUCTS

Wheaton Tubing Products
Airport Dr, Easton MD 21601. 410/822-7191.

CEMENT

Essroc Materials Inc.
4120 Buckeystown Pike, Frederick MD 21701-7502. 301/662-8244.

Stone, Clay, Glass and Concrete Products/285

TILE

Cushwa Brick Inc.
15718 Clear Spring Rd # 160, Williamsport MD 21795-1009. 301/223-7700.

Glen-Gery Corporation
9905 Godwin Dr, Manassas VA 22111-4920. 703/368-3178.

CONCRETE, GYPSUM, AND PLASTER PRODUCTS

Betco Block & Products
5291 Wellington Rd, Gainesville VA 22065-1616. 703/754-9009.

Chaney Enterprises LP
PO Box 548, Waldorf MD 20604-0548. 301/843-6101.

Arban & Carosi Inc.
13800 Dawson Beach Rd, Woodbridge VA 22191-1497. 703/491-5121.

Exposaic Industries Inc. of VA
4717 Massaponax Church Rd, Fredericksbrg VA 22408-8751. 703/898-1221.

Strescon Industries
3501 Sinclair Ln, Baltimore MD 21213-2037. 410/327-7703.

Falcon Concrete Corporation
8115 Mims St, Lorton VA 22079-2412. 703/550-6163.

Phoenix OMC
PO Box 676, Frederick MD 21705-0676. 301/663-3151.

NON-CLAY REFRACTORIES

Lehigh Portland Cement
117 N Main St, Union Bridge MD 21791-9101. 410/775-1000.

For more information on career opportunities in stone, clay, glass and concrete products:

Associations

THE AMERICAN CERAMIC SOCIETY
735 Ceramic Place, Westerville OH 43081. 614/890-4700. Offers a variety of publications, meetings, information, and educational services. Also operates Ceramic Futures, an employment service with a resume database.

NATIONAL GLASS ASSOCIATION
8200 Greensboro Drive, Suite 802, McLean VA 22102. 703/442-4890.

Magazines

GLASS MAGAZINE
National Glass Association, 8200 Greensboro Drive, McLean VA 22102. 703/442-4890.

ROCK PRODUCTS
MacLean Hunter Publishing Co., 29 North Wacker Drive, Chicago IL 60606. 312/726-2805.

TRANSPORTATION

According to Labor Department estimates the number of jobs in the air transportation industry will increase faster than average. Passenger and cargo traffic should increase in response to a rise in population, incomes and business activity. Employment in other air transport activities will also increase as more aircraft are purchased for business, agriculture and recreation. Despite this expected growth, jobseekers should expect strong competition as the number of applicants for airline jobs exceeds the number of jobs available. Not only are airline jobs highly sought after, but the industry has been going through a period of consolidation, and today more and more of the business is concentrated with a handful of the major carriers, such as American, Delta, and USAir.

In the trucking and warehousing industry, the number of jobs created is very closely related to the health of the national economy. Competition in the industry is intense, both among truckers and with the railroads. Trucking companies compete by slashing rates or offering more customized service. Motor carriers must quote rates high enough to cover costs but low enough to remain competitive. Still, job opportunities for truckers are expected to be good. In some areas, companies have had trouble recruiting well-trained drivers. Although some routes have switched to intermodal transportation and recent downturns in the economy have eased some driver shortages, turnover is relatively high. That should ensure a steady supply of jobs.

On the railroads, the use of both freight and passenger rail will climb. And according to the U.S. Commerce Department, increased trade and stronger freight rates should help the performance of U.S. flag liner companies operating in the Asian markets. Domestic use of water transportation should also increase, especially between Alaska and the lower 48 states.

A.C.T.S. INC.
P.O. Box 28741, BWI Airport MD 21240. 717/854-8554. **Contact:** Human Resources. **Description:** An air transportation company.

ATLANTIC COAST AIRLINES, INC.
One Export Drive, Sterling VA 20164. 703/406-6500. **Contact:** Human Resources. **Description:** Atlantic Coast Airlines provides scheduled air transportation services. **Number of employees at this location:** 1,505.

BETHSHIP SPARROWS POINT SHIPYARD
Bethship Sparrows Point Shipyard, Baltimore MD 21219. 410/388-6759. **Fax:** 410/388-4560. **Contact:** Stephen F. Sullivan, Human Resources Manager. **Description:** BethShip Sparrows Point Shipyard is primarily in the ship repair business. The company converts, repairs, services all types of commercial and naval ships, and manufactures industrial products. **Common positions include:** Blue-Collar Worker Supervisor; Cost Estimator; Electrical/Electronics Engineer; Human Resources Specialist; Industrial Engineer; Industrial Production Manager; Management Trainee; Mechanical Engineer; Structural Engineer. **Educational backgrounds include:** Engineering. **Benefits:** 401K; Dental Insurance; Disability Coverage; Life Insurance; Medical Insurance; Pension Plan; Profit Sharing; Savings Plan; Tuition Assistance. **Special Programs:** Internships. **Corporate headquarters location:** Bethlehem PA. **Parent**

company: Bethlehem Steel Corporation. **Operations at this facility include:** Administration; Manufacturing; Sales; Service. **Listed on:** New York Stock Exchange. **Number of employees at this location:** 2,000. **Number of employees nationwide:** 25,000.

CSX TRANSPORTATION INC.
100 North Charles Street, One Charles Center, Baltimore MD 21201-3802. 410/237-2000. **Contact:** Human Resources Department. **Description:** A railroad transportation company.

DOGGETT ENTERPRISES, INC.
719 10th Street NW, Washington DC 20001. 202/638-2770. **Contact:** Ernest L. Bryant, II, Director of Operations. **Description:** Owns, manages, and operates area parking facilities. **Common positions include:** Blue-Collar Worker Supervisor; Cashier; Management Trainee; Parking Attendant. **Benefits:** Bonus Award/Plan; Disability Coverage; Life Insurance; Medical Insurance. **Corporate headquarters location:** This Location. **Operations at this facility include:** Service.

NATIONAL RAILROAD PASSENGER CORPORATION
60 Massachusetts Avenue Northeast, Washington DC 20002. 202/906-3000. **Contact:** Human Resources. **Description:** National Railroad Passenger Corporation is a subsidiary of Amtrak, the passenger railroad which makes almost 22 million trips per year to over 500 destinations in 45 states. Amtrak provides commuter service under contract in seven metropolitan areas, and dispatches trains and maintains the rail infrastructure in the northeast region to support Amtrak trains, commuter and freight trains. Amtrak also transports mail between U.S. postal facilities and packages between Amtrak stations. **Parent company:** Amtrak.

PRESTON TRUCKING COMPANY, INC.
151 Easton Boulevard, Preston MD 21655-9751. 410/673-7151. **Contact:** Human Resources. **Description:** Yellow Corporation is a holding company whose subsidiaries offer customers an array of high-service, value-added transportation products. Preston Trucking Company provides regional less-than-truckload services in the upper Midwest and Northeast. A network of 71 facilities throughout this geographic region is operated by 5,900 employees who focus on one and two-day service. Yellow's other subsidiaries included Yellow Freight System, Inc., the corporation's largest subsidiary providing less-than-truckload services; Saia Motor Freight Line, Inc., also providing less-than-truckload services; CSI/Reeves, Inc., a specialty carrier providing transportation, warehousing and distribution services to the carpet and floor industry; Westex, Inc., formerly Johnson's Freightlines, an acquisition providing less-than-truckload services; Yellow Logistics Services, Inc., offering a full range of integrated logistic management services; and Yellow Technology Services, Inc., ensuring that the operating companies have access to advanced information systems. **Corporate headquarters location:** This Location. **Parent company:** Yellow Corporation.

SECURITY STORAGE COMPANY OF WASHINGTON
1701 Florida Avenue NW, Washington DC 20009-2697. 202/234-5600. **Contact:** Conrad S. Reid, Executive Vice President. **Description:** A moving and storage firm, providing the following services: general storage, cold storage, freight forwarding, moving and packing, international trading services, and related insurance services. **Common positions include:** Accountant/Auditor; Administrator; Blue-Collar Worker Supervisor; Branch Manager; Claim Representative; Computer Programmer; Customer Service Representative; Department Manager; Management Trainee; Operations/Production Manager; Quality Control Supervisor; Transportation/Traffic Specialist. **Educational backgrounds include:** Accounting; Business Administration; Computer Science; Finance; Marketing. **Benefits:** Dental Insurance; Disability Coverage; Employee Discounts; Life Insurance; Medical Insurance; Pension Plan; Stock Option; Tuition Assistance. **Corporate headquarters location:** This Location. **Operations at this facility include:** Sales; Service. **Number of employees at this location:** 160.

SWATH OCEAN INTERNATIONAL
4061 Powder Mill Road, Calverton MD 20705. 301/595-9850. **Contact:** Human Resources. **Description:** A ship building and repairing company. **NOTE:** This company does not accept unsolicited resumes. Jobseekers should only apply for advertised openings.

UNC INC.
175 Admiral Cochrane Drive, Annapolis MD 21401-7307. 410/266-7333. **Contact:** Human Resources. **Description:** UNC is an aviation business that includes the manufacturing and remanufacturing of engine and aircraft components, the overhaul of aircraft accessories, aircraft engines and industrial gas turbines, and providing aircraft maintenance and pilot training contract services. UNC's organization is divided into five divisions. Engine Overhaul is comprised of three operations which perform turbine engine overhaul repair and parts provisioning for business aviation and helicopter operators, regional airlines and land based industrial turbine operators. Component Services provides a range of repair, remanufacturing and overhaul services to the aviation industry. The Manufacturing Division supplies turbine engine and airframe component parts for the prime engine and aircraft original equipment manufacturers and the military. Aviation Services provides aircraft maintenance, overhaul, logistics support and aviation training services to government agencies. UNC International Division crosses all areas of UNC's business.

USAIR GROUP, INC.
2345 Crystal Drive, Arlington VA 22227. 703/418-7000. **Recorded Jobline:** 703/418-7499. **Contact:** John P. Frestel, Jr., Senior Vice President of Human Resources. **Description:** A transportation holding company with regional, national, and international scheduled air services and express cargo operations. Principal subsidiary USAir offers service to 155 cities in the U.S., Canada, the Bahamas, Bermuda, Puerto Rico, the Virgin Islands, France, and Germany. Primary hubs are in Charlotte, Pittsburgh, Baltimore/Washington, and Philadelphia. **Other subsidiaries include:** USAir Express, USAir Florida Shuttle, and regional carriers Allegheny Commuter Airlines, Piedmont Airlines, and Jetstream International. **Corporate headquarters location:** This Location. **Listed on:** New York Stock Exchange.

VINNELL CORPORATION
12150 Easy Monument Drive #800, Fairfax VA 22033-4053. 703/385-4544. **Contact:** Human Resources. **Description:** An arranger of transportation of freight and cargo. **Number of employees at this location:** 1,000.

WORLDCORP INC.
13873 Park Center Rd Ste 490, Herndon VA 22071-3223. 703/834-9200. **Description:** WorldCorp is the parent company for World Airways, an airline.

Note: Because addresses and telephone numbers of smaller companies change rapidly, we recommend you call each company to verify the information below before inquiring about job opportunities. Mass mailings are not recommended.

Additional employers with under 250 employees:

SHIP/BOAT BUILDING AND REPAIRING

Blohm & Voss
5828 Glen Forest Dr, Falls Church VA 22041-2513.
703/845-5679.

Ingalls Shipbuilding
1725 Jeff Davis Hwy, Arlington VA 22202.
703/418-0300.

Jonathan Corporation
10205 Colvin Run Rd, Great Falls VA 22066-1833.
703/759-6400.

Kerney Ship Repair
2027 Bear Ridge Rd, Baltimore MD 21222-5742.
410/477-0681.

National Steel & Shipbuilding
2301 Jefferson Davis Hwy,
Arlington VA 22202-3820.
703/418-1195.

Bayliner Marine Corp.
2305 Northwood Dr, Salisbury MD 21801-7808.
410/546-4656.

Bayliner Marine Corp.
11100 P P G Rd S E, Cumberland MD 21502.
301/759-9460.

TRANSPORTATION EQUIPMENT

Oceaneering Technologies
501 Prince Georges Blvd, Uppr Marlboro MD 20772-7415. 301/249-3300.

LOCAL AND INTERURBAN PASSENGER TRANSIT

Trailways Bus Terminal
Rte 50 & Bucktown Rd, Cambridge MD 21613.
410/228-4626.

Red Top Cab
3251 Washington Blvd, Arlington VA 22201-4415.
703/525-0900.

Eyre Bus Service Inc.
PO Box 239, Glenelg MD 21737-0239. 410/442-1330.

TRUCKING

Bobs Transport & Stage
820 Oldham St, Baltimore MD 21224-4535. 410/285-6586.

Colonial Storage Company
9900 Fallard Ct, Uppr Marlboro MD 20772-6724.
301/856-6500.

Evans Century Express
1205 68th St, Baltimore MD 21237-2516. 410/866-9512.

Landstar System Inc.
6225 Brandon Ave, Springfield VA 22150-2519. 703/912-6808.

Leaseway Motorcroft Transprt Co.
Broening Hwy & Cardiff, Baltimore MD 21224. 410/631-5500.

New England Motor Freight Inc.
3600 Georgetown Rd, Baltimore MD 21227. 410/247-1886.

O'Brien Trucking
1238 Pleasant Valley Dr, Baltimore MD 21228-2649. 410/247-5064.

Overnite Transportation
6571 Washington Blvd, Baltimore MD 21227-5533. 410/796-8550.

Paris Foods Corporation
Route 50, Trappe MD 21673. 410/476-3185.

Pitt Ohio Express Inc.
2300 Eskow Ave, Baltimore MD 21227-4728. 410/247-1001.

Pruitt Trucking
2200 Broening Hwy, Baltimore MD 21224-6623. 410/633-2600.

Ranger Transportation
1205 68th St, Baltimore MD 21237-2516. 410/276-7540.

Robin Express Transfer
8224 Bletzer Rd, Baltimore MD 21222-2827. 410/477-1733.

Suggs Transportation Service Inc.
9015 Woodyard Rd Ste 207, Clinton MD 20735-4209. 301/868-7271.

Wilson Trucking Corporation
RR 17, Fredericksbrg VA 22407-9817. 703/373-6011.

Sea-Gal Express Inc.
4th & D Sts, Dundalk MD 21222. 410/282-2455.

Charlton Brothers Trnsprtn Co. Inc.
552 Jefferson St, Hagerstown MD 21740-5058. 301/733-2180.

DMT Trucking Inc.
1200 Chesapeake Ave, Baltimore MD 21226-1000. 410/355-6060.

Gold Line
5500 Tuxedo Rd, Hyattsville MD 20781-1314. 202/479-5972.

Colonial Storage Co.
4500 Southgate Pl, Chantilly VA 22021-1714. 703/802-3416.

Graebel Movers International Inc.
7426 Alban Station Blvd, Springfield VA 22150-2323. 703/644-3524.

Greenwoods Transfer & Storage Co.
821 Howard Rd Se, Washington DC 20020-5805. 202/678-8900.

Interstate Moving Systems Inc.
3901 Ironwood Pl, Landover MD 20785-2314. 301/773-3555.

Park Moving & Storage
1537 S Philadelphia Blvd, Aberdeen MD 21001-3916. 410/272-4466.

Paxton Van Lines Inc.
5300 Port Royal Rd, Springfield VA 22151-2112. 703/321-7600.

COURIER SERVICES

Washington Express Services Inc.
8541 Piney Branch Rd # A, Silver Spring MD 20901-3920. 301/650-5350.

WAREHOUSING AND STORAGE

GATX Logistics Inc.
8901 Snowden River Pky, Columbia MD 21046-1673. 410/312-2710.

Midas International
6930 San Tomas Rd, Baltimore MD 21227-6227. 410/796-4510.

Vault The Secure Self Storage
35 S Dove St, Alexandria VA 22314-4603. 703/684-7684.

Trans-Port Services
2700 Broening Hwy, Baltimore MD 21222-4102. 410/284-6214.

MARINE CARGO HANDLING

Clark Maryland Terminals
Dundalk Marine Terminal, Baltimore MD 21222. 410/282-6944.

AIR TRANSPORTATION AND SERVICES

Aeroflot Airlines
Dulles International Airport, Washington DC 20041. 703/661-8082.

British Airway
600 W Service Rd, Washington DC 20041. 703/661-4546.

British Airways
Dulles International Airport, Washington DC 20041. 703/661-8909.

Continental Airlines
National Airport, Washington DC 20001. 703/419-1013.

Delta Air Lines Inc.
1302 Concourse Dr, Linthicum Hts MD 21090-1000. 410/859-3100.

Icelandair
PO Box 18508, Baltimore MD 21240-8508. 410/859-2670.

Official Airlines Guides
Dulles International Airport, Washington DC 20041. 703/661-8914.

Republic Air Travel
30 E St Sw, Washington DC 20001. 202/347-6911.

Taca International Airlines
Dulles International Airport, Washington DC 20041. 703/661-6571.

Tennessee Airways
International Airport, Washington DC 20041. 703/661-8168.

Trans World Airlines
Washington National Airport, Washington DC 20001. 703/419-4425.

Trans World Airlines
Dulles Internatl Airpt, Washington DC 20041. 703/661-8637.

West Air Airlines
Dulles International Airport, Washington DC 20041. 703/661-6920.

JJ &W Aircraft Services
18450 Showalter Rd Ste 105, Hagerstown MD 21742-1372. 301/739-2159.

Duncan Avionics
Washington National Airport, Washington DC 20001. 703/419-5100.

PASSENGER TRANSPORTATION ARRANGEMENT SERVICES

Omega World Travel
3102 Omega Office Park,
Fairfax VA 22031-2400.
703/820-7171.

Omega World Travel
5203 Leesburg Pike Ste 2,
Falls Church VA 22041-3401. 703/998-7171.

Travel Destinations
110 Painters Mill Rd, Owings Mills MD 21117-4911.
410/363-3111.

Travel Services Group
1500 King St, Alexandria VA 22314-2730. 703/684-2777.

US Travel
4200 Wilson Blvd, Arlington VA 22203-1800. 703/524-9600.

VIP Travel Agency
450 W Broad St Ste 117,
Falls Church VA 22046-3318. 703/534-3377.

Ober United Travel Agency
4407 Willard Ave, Chevy Chase MD 20815-3649.
301/654-9325.

Travel One
8840 Stanford Blvd,
Columbia MD 21045-5852.
410/290-1990.

PACKING AND CRATING

Azar Storage
1799 Margaret Ave,
Annapolis MD 21401-4106.
301/261-1450.

Smith's Moving & Storage Co.
19020 Woodfield Rd,
Gaithersburg MD 20879-4799. 301/565-9000.

For more information on career opportunities in transportation:

Associations

AIR TRANSPORT ASSOCIATION OF AMERICA
1301 Pennsylvania Avenue NW, Suite 1100, Washington DC 20004. 202/626-4000.

AMERICAN BUREAU OF SHIPPING
2 World Trade Center, 106th Floor, New York NY 10048. 212/839-5000.

AMERICAN MARITIME ASSOCIATION
380 Madison Avenue, 17th Floor, New York NY 10017. 212/557-9520. A trade association which offers collection and bargaining services.

AMERICAN SOCIETY OF TRAVEL AGENTS
1101 King Street, Suite 200, Alexandria VA 22314. 703/739-2782. For information, send a SASE with $.75 postage to the attention of the Fulfillment Department.

AMERICAN TRUCKING ASSOCIATION
2200 Mill Road, Alexandria VA 22314-4677. 703/838-1700.

ASSOCIATION OF AMERICAN RAILROADS
50 F Street NW, Washington DC 20001. 202/639-2100.

FUTURE AVIATION PROFESSIONALS OF AMERICA
4959 Massachusetts Boulevard, Atlanta GA 30337. 404/997-8097. Publishes monthly newsletter which monitors the job market for flying jobs; a pilot employment guide, outlining what is required to become a pilot; and a directory of aviation employers.

INSTITUTE OF TRANSPORTATION ENGINEERS
525 School Street SW, Suite 410, Washington DC 20024-2797. 202/554-8050. Scientific and educational association, providing for professional development of members and others.

MARINE TECHNOLOGY SOCIETY
1828 L Street NW, Suite 906, Washington DC 20036. 202/775-5966.

NATIONAL MARINE MANUFACTURERS ASSOCIATION
401 North Michigan Avenue, Suite 1150, Chicago IL 60611. 312/836-4747. A partnership of three manufacturer groups: The National Association of Boat Manufacturers; The Association of Marine Engine Manufacturers; and The National Association of Marine Products & Services. Subscription to job listing publication is available for a fee.

NATIONAL MOTOR FREIGHT TRAFFIC ASSOCIATION
2200 Mill Road, Alexandria VA 22314-4654. 703/838-1810. Works towards the improvement and advancement of the interests and welfare of motor common carriers.

NATIONAL TANK TRUCK CARRIERS
2200 Mill Road, Alexandria VA 22314. 703/838-1700. A trade association representing and promoting the interests of the highway bulk transportation community.

Directories

MOODY'S TRANSPORTATION MANUAL
Moody's Investors Service, Inc., 99 Church Street, New York NY 10007. 212/553-0300. $12.95 per year with weekly updates.

NATIONAL TANK TRUCK CARRIER DIRECTORY
2200 Mill Road, Alexandria VA 22314. 703/838-1700.

OFFICIAL MOTOR FREIGHT GUIDE
1700 West Courtland Street, Chicago IL 60622. 312/278-2454.

Magazines

AMERICAN SHIPPER
P.O. Box 4728, Jacksonville FL 32201. 904/355-2601. Monthly.

FLEET OWNER
707 Westchester Avenue, White Plains NY 10604-3102. 914/949-8500.

HEAVY DUTY TRUCKING
Newport Communications, P.O. Box W, Newport Beach CA 92658. 714/261-1636.

ITE JOURNAL
Institute of Transportation Engineers, 525

School Street SW, Suite 410, Washington DC 20024-2797. 202/554-8050. One year subscription (12 issues): $50.

MARINE DIGEST AND TRANSPORTATION NEWS
P.O. Box 3905, Seattle WA 98124.
206/682-3607.

SHIPPING DIGEST
51 Madison Avenue, New York NY 10010.
212/689-4411.

TRAFFIC WORLD MAGAZINE
741 National Press Building, Washington DC 20045. 202/383-6140.

TRANSPORT TOPICS
2200 Mill Road, Alexandria VA 22314.
703/838-1772.

UTILITIES: ELECTRIC, GAS AND SANITATION

With deregulation looming closer and closer, utilities are adjusting by cutting costs and providing better service. This is a good sign for the industry but a bad sign for jobseekers as employment should remain just about flat. Job prospects in the utilities industry are probably best with large electric utilities, water supply facilities, and sanitary services right now. The most common positions with public utilities are precision production workers and operators, fabricators, and laborers.

AES CORPORATION
1001 North 19th Street, Arlington VA 22209. 703/522-1315. **Contact:** Joan Halbert, Administrative Assistant to the President. **Description:** This supplier of electricity to public utilities and steam to industrial companies is a developer and operator of electric generating facilities.

BALTIMORE GAS & ELECTRIC COMPANY
Charles Center, P.O. Box 1475, Baltimore MD 21203. 410/783-5920. **Contact:** Employment Representative. **Description:** Baltimore Gas & Electric is a provider of gas and electricity to 2.6 million customers in Maryland. BGE combines a core utility business (electric and gas) with diversified, non-utility operations including Constellation Holdings, a holding company for energy and environmental projects; real estate management and development; health care; investments; and other financial services. Employing 8,100 full-time workers as Maryland's ninth largest employer, BGE earned combined revenues of $2.8 billion in 1994. BGE home products include home appliances, electronics, replacement windows and doors, kitchen remodeling, installation of commercial and residential heating and air conditioning systems, and plumbing services. BGE also offers repair service and service contracts for appliances, electronics, and heating and cooling equipment. **Common positions include:** Accountant/Auditor; Electrical/Electronics Engineer; Mechanical Engineer; Nuclear Engineer. **Listed on:** New York Stock Exchange.

CHOPTANK ELECTRIC COOPERATIVE, INC.
P.O. Box 430, Denton MD 21629. 410/479-0380. **Contact:** Personnel. **Description:** An electric utility.

DELMARVA POWER & LIGHT/MD-VA
P.O. Box 1739, Salisbury MD 21802. 410/749-6111. **Contact:** Human Resources Department. **Description:** An electric company.

POTOMAC EDISON COMPANY
10435 Downsville Pike, Hagerstown MD 21740. 301/790-3400. **Contact:** Kevin E. Buhrman, Coordinator, Placement & Affirmative Action. **Description:** The Potomac Edison Company is an electric utility servicing an area of about 7,300 square miles in portions of Maryland, Virginia, and West Virginia. The company is a wholly-owned subsidiary of Allegheny Power System, Inc. and is a part of the Allegheny Power integrated electric utility system, which also includes Monongahela Power Company and West Penn Power Company. The operating companies of Allegheny Power are engaged in the production, transmission, distribution, and sale of electricity. **Parent company:** Allegheny Power System, Incorporated. **Number of employees nationwide:** 1,100.

POTOMAC ELECTRIC POWER COMPANY
1900 Pennsylvania Avenue NW, Washington DC 20068. 202/872-2100. **Contact:** Employment. **Description:** PEPCO is an investor-owned electric utility serving the electricity needs of 1.9 million people in the Washington metropolitan area. PEPCO's 640-square-mile service territory includes the District of Columbia and major portions

of Montgomery and Prince George's Counties in Maryland. PEPCO also sells electricity at wholesale to Southern Maryland Electric Cooperative.

STEUART PETROLEUM COMPANY
4646 40th Street NW, Washington DC 20016. 202/537-8900. **Contact:** Prescilla Altmann, Human Resources Manager. **Description:** An area fuel distributor, operating a home heating fuel distributorship, and service stations at several area locations.

SYNERGICS
191 Main Street, Annapolis MD 21401. 301/268-8820. **Contact:** Human Resources. **Description:** A developer, builder, owner, and operator of independent power generating plants, with emphasis on hydroelectric power.

WASHINGTON GAS LIGHT COMPANY
6801 Industrial Road, Springfield VA 22151. 703/750-5576. **Contact:** Jerri Harris, Manager/Employment and Equal Opportunity Programs. **Description:** Engaged in the purchase, sale, and distribution of natural gas in metropolitan Washington DC, including portions of Maryland and Virginia, through seven operating subsidiaries. Total population of service area exceeds three million. Equal Opportunity Employer. **Common positions include:** Accountant/Auditor; Blue-Collar Worker Supervisor; Civil Engineer; Computer Programmer; Customer Service Representative; Department Manager; Draftsperson; Electrical/Electronics Engineer; Financial Analyst; Human Resources Specialist; Mechanical Engineer. **Educational backgrounds include:** Accounting; Business Administration; Computer Science; Economics; Engineering; Finance; Marketing. **Benefits:** Dental Insurance; Disability Coverage; Employee Discounts; Life Insurance; Medical Insurance; Pension Plan; Savings Plan; Tuition Assistance. **Special Programs:** Internships; Training Programs. **Corporate headquarters location:** This Location. **Listed on:** New York Stock Exchange.

WASHINGTON SUBURBAN SANITARY COMMISSION
14501 Sweitzer Lane, Laurel MD 20707. 301/206-8678. **Contact:** John E. Prather, Senior Personnel Specialist. **Description:** In operation for more than 70 years. Responsible for the design, development, maintenance, and operation of the public water supply and sanitary sewerage systems for a 1,000-square-mile area, embracing Montgomery and Prince George's Counties. Also has a substantial responsibility for the regulation of plumbing in the suburban Maryland area. **Common positions include:** Accountant/Auditor; Attorney; Biological Scientist/Biochemist; Buyer; Chemist; Civil Engineer; Claim Representative; Computer Programmer; Corrosion Engineer; Customer Service Representative; Draftsperson; Electrical/Electronics Engineer; Financial Analyst; Human Resources Specialist; Industrial Engineer; Mechanical Engineer; Public Relations Specialist; Purchasing Agent and Manager; Quality Control Supervisor; Systems Analyst; Tax Specialist. **Educational backgrounds include:** Accounting; Business Administration; Chemistry; Computer Science; Engineering; Mathematics. **Benefits:** Daycare Assistance; Dental Insurance; Disability Coverage; Leave Time; Life Insurance; Medical Insurance; Pension Plan; Savings Plan; Tuition Assistance. **Corporate headquarters location:** This Location. **Operations at this facility include:** Administration; Research and Development; Service.

Note: Because addresses and telephone numbers of smaller companies change rapidly, we recommend you call each company to verify the information below before inquiring about job opportunities. Mass mailings are not recommended.

Additional employers with under 250 employees:

ELECTRIC SERVICES

City of Hagerstown Light Dept.
425 E Baltimore St, Hagerstown MD 21740-6105. 301/790-2600.

G & G Electrical Company
1401 Columbia Rd Nw, Washington DC 20009-4764. 202/986-5579.

G & R Electric Co.
17028 Old Baltimore Rd, Olney MD 20832-2410. 301/774-5550.

Good Housekeeping Electric
11222 Old Baltimore Pike, Beltsville MD 20705-2010. 301/572-2300.

Liberty Electric Service
10720 Main St, Fairfax VA 22030-3712. 703/273-3427.

Northern VA Electric Cooperative
5399 Wellington Rd, Gainesville VA 22065-1616. 703/754-6700.

Northern VA Electric Cooperative
349 E Market St, Leesburg VA 22075-4102. 703/777-2041.

Rappahannock Electric Cooperative
PO Box 7388, Fredericksbrg VA 22404-7388. 703/898-8500.

Southern MD Electr. Coop. Inc.
Hwy 231, Hughesville MD 20637. 301/274-3111.

Star Electric Co. Inc.
8900 Greenwood Pl, Savage MD 20763-9727. 301/725-4660.

Sun-Light Electric Co.
Southern Business Park, La Plata MD 20646. 301/934-2001.

Thurmont Municipal Light Company
10 Frederick Rd, Thurmont MD 21788-1809. 301/271-7872.

Wisconsin Electric Power Company
900 2nd St Ne, Washington DC 20002-3557. 202/408-1605.

Benning Road Generating Station
3400 Benning Rd Ne, Washington DC 20019-1503. 202/388-2501.

CP Crane Generating Station
PO Box 1475, Baltimore MD 21203-1475. 410/682-9701.

Dickerson Generating Station
21200 Martinsburg Rd, Dickerson MD 20842-9406. 301/428-7425.

Potomac River Generating Station
1400 N Royal St, Alexandria VA 22314-1111. 703/838-3721.

GAS UTILITY SERVICES

Liberty Gas Inc.
Acton Ln, Waldorf MD 20601. 301/645-2357.

For more information on career opportunities in the utilities industry:

Associations

AMERICAN PUBLIC GAS ASSOCIATION
Lee Highway, Suite 102, Fairfax VA 22030. 703/352-3890. Publishes a weekly newsletter.

AMERICAN PUBLIC POWER ASSOCIATION (APPA)
2301 M Street NW, Washington DC 20037. 202/467-2970. Represents publicly-owned utilities. Provides many services including: government relations, educational programs, and industry-related information publications.

AMERICAN WATER WORKS ASSOCIATION
6666 West Quincy Drive, Denver CO 80235. 303/794-7711.

NATIONAL RURAL ELECTRIC COOPERATIVE ASSOCIATION
1800 Massachusetts Avenue NW, Washington DC 20036. 202/857-9500.

Directories

MOODY'S PUBLIC UTILITY MANUAL
Moody's Investors Service, Inc., 99 Church Street, New York NY 10007. 212/553-0300. Annually available at libraries.

Magazines

PUBLIC POWER
2301 M Street NW, Washington DC 20037. 202/467-2900.

GOVERNMENT JOBS

WORKING FOR THE FEDERAL GOVERNMENT

IMPORTANT NOTE: *Since application procedures for federal jobs may vary from city to city and may change as new legislation is passed, please contact the Federal Job Information Center nearest the location you would like to work to find out about specific paths to employment in that area. Check the government listings section of your phone directory for contact information.*

Perhaps the most stable industry of all, the federal government is by far the nation's largest employer. More than 300,000 people each year are hired to work in a variety of government jobs, and for the most part, if a career exists in private business, someone somewhere has the same career working for the federal government. There are federal jobs in more than 200 career fields across the country and around the world from which to choose.

For instance, if you are interested in finance, you can sign on with the nation's largest bank. Science and technology? Naturally, the government runs a number of renowned laboratories, medical facilities, and sophisticated computer systems, all of which need workers to operate them. If you have an interest in protecting the public, becoming a federal law enforcement officer might be for you. Working for Uncle Sam certainly has its added advantages. As a federal employee, you can change jobs, offices, and agencies and still retain your benefits and service years.

Federal Pay Systems

The federal government has several different pay systems, the largest of which is called the General Schedule (GS). It covers most white-collar jobs and consists of 15 numerical grade levels and their corresponding salaries. The higher the GS number, the higher the pay level. Under this system, specific jobs, such as engineers, accountants, and nurses, have special salary rates. However, not all jobs in the federal service fall under the GS pay system. The Federal Wage Grade (WG) pay system covers blue-collar jobs in apprentice and journeyman trade and craft occupations, e.g., electricians, mechanics, plumbers, carpenters, trades-helpers, etc. And the Senior Executive Schedule (ES) covers high-level managerial and supervisory positions in the federal government's Senior Executive Service (SES).

The General Schedule

How do you know where you would fit in the GS pay system, the largest of the schedules? Eligibility for federal jobs is determined by your education and/or work experience. With a high school degree or three months of general experience, you'll usually qualify for GS-2 grade level positions. To qualify for the GS-5 or GS-7 grade levels in professional and administrative jobs, you need a bachelor's degree or three years of increasingly responsible work experience after high school. If you have an undergraduate grade point average of 3.0 or higher, or membership in an academic honor society, you may qualify for the GS-7 grade level. Applicants with master's degrees are eligible for the GS-9 grade level, and those with doctoral degrees may be considered at the GS-11 level.

Career Ladders and Promotions

Grade levels for professional and administrative positions under the GS pay system increase first in two-grade intervals (i.e., GS-5,7,9, and 11) and then in 1-grade intervals (i.e., GS-12, 13, 14, and 15). Many federal jobs offer a "career ladder" of promotion potential. For example, an entry-level position's career ladder might go from GS-5 to GS-11. This means that an employee in that job could be promoted from GS-5 to 7 to 9 to 11, after performing successfully for at least one year at each level. Each grade increase typically means a salary increase of several thousand dollars. A summary of the current GS pay scales appears at the end of this chapter.

Benefits

The federal government offers benefits such as life insurance, retirement plans, a variety of health insurance plans, and paid leave. New employees earn 13 days of annual leave and 13 days of sick leave, and are also paid for 10 national holidays. Many federal agencies also offer a number of special benefits, including child care arrangements, credit unions, fitness centers, and recreational activities.

Work Schedules

Another benefit of a federal job is that federal employees are not always limited to a traditional work schedule. You may be able to work a part-time, flexible, or alternate work schedule. The flextime approach, for example, allows you to have flexibility in your work schedule while still working a 40-hour work week.

Age/Citizenship Requirements

The standard age for starting a permanent job is 18. For some fields, such as law enforcement, there are higher age requirements for applicants. With few exceptions, federal employees must be U.S. citizens. However, some non-citizens may be selected for certain positions under special circumstances. Contact individual agencies to find out about such opportunities.

Equal Opportunity

The federal government is an Equal Opportunity Employer. Hiring and advancement are based on qualifications and performance regardless of race, color, religion, gender, age, national origin, political views, or disability.

Competitive Versus Excepted Services

The information in this chapter covers jobs in the federal competitive service, in which applicants compete for jobs based on a written exam and/or an evaluation of their education and work experience. However, in the case of jobs such as lawyer and chaplain, and for jobs with some government agencies, such as the Central Intelligence Agency and the General Accounting Office, hiring authorities are "excepted" from these procedures. Excepted agencies each have their own hiring methods, and should be contacted individually.

The Facts on Government Job Openings

The U.S. Office of Personnel Management (OPM) is the government agency that is responsible for all hiring of competitive service jobs. The OPM is headquartered in Washington, but it also has five regional offices and a number of service centers around the country. These offices are responsible for conducting OPM functions such as recruitment and job information in their location.

If you're looking for a job in Washington itself, the Washington Area Service Center (WASC) has the information you need. Contact WASC's Federal Job Information Center (FJIC) in the OPM's headquarters building. The address is 1900 E Street NW, Washington, DC. If you are looking for a federal job outside of Washington, contact the FJIC nearest you.

At your local FJIC, you can get information about federal jobs, and any forms and application materials you need. Job vacancies are advertised at the FJIC in a weekly publication called the Federal Job Opportunities Listing (FJOL). The FJOL advertises positions that are open and tells you who to call for additional information. The FJOL is also posted in state employment service offices.

To get information on jobs in Washington over the phone, you can use the FJIC's automated telephone line, touch computer screens, or talk directly with an information specialist who can tell you more about federal employment opportunities and application procedures. The Washington FJIC is open Monday through Friday from 8 a.m. to 4 p.m., Eastern time. The automated telephone line, 202/606-2700, provides job information 24 hours a day, seven days a week. It offers a menu of recorded information, including job vacancy listings. You can request applications and other forms on this line and talk to an information specialist during business hours about your specific questions.

How to Apply for Federal Jobs in Washington

Agencies in the Washington, DC metropolitan area fill their vacancies in a variety of ways, sometimes independently from OPM. For many federal jobs, you must apply directly for vacancies advertised by agencies. For others, you must take an entry-level test. The first step is to find out which of the following procedures is the right one for your field. Contact your local FJIC for specifics.

The SF-171

The Standard Form 171 (SF-171) is the application form used in applying for most federal government jobs. The SF-171 provides an overview of your educational and work history and highlights your skills and disabilities. Federal employers use the SF-171 to determine your eligibility for a position. You can get SF-171s at the FJIC, or at most federal agencies.

Clerical and Administrative Support Test

Many applicants refer to the Federal Clerical and Administrative Support test as the "Civil Service Exam." There is a mistaken impression that this test is required for all federal jobs. The test, which you can take at the FJIC, covers 64 different occupations at the GS-2 through GS-4 levels. Applicants can obtain sample test materials and the testing schedule from the FJIC. Applicants who get a passing score on the exam should attach a copy of their notice of results to their SF-171 and apply directly to agencies. The test is a good vehicle for recent high school graduates who are interested in beginning their federal careers.

Administrative Careers with America

The Administrative Careers with America (ACWA) tests cover entry-level professional and administrative positions in more than 100 occupations at the GS-5 and GS-7 levels. ACWA includes six groups of occupations, each requiring a separate written test. Applicants who pass an ACWA test will be placed (in score order) on a list for federal agencies to use when hiring. Agencies who have vacancies request names of the top scoring applicants from these lists, and contact them directly. In the Washington, DC metropolitan area, the ACWA tests are offered on a walk-in basis.

The ACWA test groups are:

- Health, Safety, and Environmental (Group 1)
- Writing and Public Information (Group 2)
- Business, Finance, and Management (Group 3)
- Personnel, Administration, and Computer (Group 4)
- Benefits Review, Tax, and Legal (Group 5)
- Law Enforcement and Investigation (Group 6)

There also is a seventh group of ACWA occupations for which there is no test. To apply for these positions, you must show that you have the required number of academic credits in the field for which you are applying. Group 7 occupations include archaeology, environment, social science, international relations, and others.

For information about ACWA testing schedules, sample test booklets, or application information for Group 7 occupations, you should call or visit the local FJIC. This is an important step because testing schedules and test availability may change.

Bilingual/Bicultural Provision

If you can show fluency in the Spanish language or are very knowledgeable about Hispanic culture, you may be hired under this provision if you pass an ACWA exam or qualify for Group 7 positions. Contact individual agencies to find out about these opportunities.

Shared Case Examining

In Washington, DC, many federal jobs are filled through "shared case examining" procedures. This means that agencies initially recruit and screen applications before sending them to OPM for final evaluation. OPM identifies the best qualified applicants and sends a list of these candidates back to the agency making the final selection. These jobs are typically in the financial, administrative, social, and physical sciences occupations (e.g., psychologists, economists, public affairs specialists, physicists, program analysts, etc.).

Job vacancies are advertised individually in the FJOL. Each job listing gives the title, grade, career ladder, and location of the position. You should call the contact number listed there to receive a vacancy announcement that will describe the position and application procedures in detail. If you have applied for a vacancy and have questions about the status of your application, you should contact the personnel office of the agency to which you sent your application, not OPM. *Note:* Senior executive positions and many wage grade positions are hired through this process as well. While wage grade positions are advertised in the FJOL, OPM publishes a separate SES Vacancy Listing that is available at the FJIC.

Delegated Examining

For occupations that are located primarily in one agency, the agency may be authorized to advertise, evaluate, and hire applicants independently from OPM. The Federal Aviation Administration (FAA), for example, uses this authority for air traffic controller jobs. The FJIC has information about which agencies have this "delegated examining authority" for certain occupations. You should contact agencies directly to apply for these positions.

Direct Hire Authority

For occupations where there are critical shortages, such as nurses and engineers, OPM has authorized agencies to use a "direct hire" approach to secure qualified applicants. *Best bets:* computer, mathematics, engineering, and some health occupations. Contact agency personnel offices directly if you are applying for a shortage occupation.

"Registers" and the Role of OPM

For a few occupations, such as accountant/auditor (GS-5/7/9) and biological sciences (GS-5/7), as well as some wage grade positions, OPM maintains "registers of eligible" or lists of qualified applicants. Agencies who have vacancies request the best qualified applicants from these lists and contact them directly. To apply for jobs filled this way, you will need to get additional application forms from the local FJIC and return them along with your SF-171 to the specified OPM office.

If you receive a notice that you are eligible, your name will be placed on a register and agencies will contact you directly if they have a vacancy. OPM will only accept applications for registers when there is a demand for the particular occupation in question, so find out from the local FJIC if the register you want is "open" before applying.

Job Information Sources

Here is a brief summary of the most important sources of information on federal jobs:

Federal Career Directory: This comprehensive resource guide profiles approximately 176 federal agencies and departments, and includes information on typical entry level jobs, personnel contacts, and student employment programs. Included are chapters on "How to Look for and Apply for a Government Job" and "Agency and Department Hiring by College Major." The Directory is available at college placement offices throughout the country.

X-118 Handbook: By applying the qualification standards outlined in this handbook, personnel officers determine if an applicant will qualify for a particular position. If you are interested in learning more about the required qualifications for an occupation, you can find this handbook in OPM's library, as well as at some public and university libraries and agency personnel offices.

General Employment Seminar: The Washington Area Service Center offers a General Employment Seminar at OPM on the first Tuesday of every month at 3 p.m. in room 1441 of its headquarters at 1900 E Street in Washington. This seminar will take you step-by-step through the federal employment process and provide you with informational tools that will start you off right! This is a walk-in seminar that usually lasts one hour and includes a tour of the FJIC facilities.

Federal Personnel Directory: The FJIC publishes a directory listing of personnel offices from local federal agencies. Each listing includes the mailing address and telephone number of the personnel office, as well as any job vacancy phone lines the agency might offer. You can use this to contact agencies where you want to explore opportunities.

Overseas Jobs: If you are interested in working in the Atlantic overseas area, contact the FJIC for a listing of current job vacancies.

Other Avenues to Employment
Presidential Management Intern Programs: If you've recently finished graduate school and have a strong interest in public management, you might want to consider the prestigious Presidential Management Intern (PMI) Program, which begins at GS-9 level with career ladders to GS-12. You must apply for this two-year program during your final year of studies and be nominated by your school. If you would like more information, contact the dean of your graduate school, your career services department, or the FJIC to get a copy of the application packet, which is available each year in September.

Military Service and Veterans Programs: Your military service may count as general or specialized experience when applying for civilian positions. Also, as a veteran, you might receive preference over a non-veteran when looking for a federal job. If you're qualified for the position you want, Veterans Preference will add either five or ten points to the numerical evaluation of your application. Qualified Vietnam vets, and other vets with a compensable disability of 30 percent or more, may be hired directly by agencies. The Veterans Programs Coordinator at individual federal agencies can provide program details and information on eligibility requirements. The Washington area FJIC also has a veteran's employment counselor who can be reached at 202/606-1848.

Employment of People With Disabilities: The federal government actively promotes the employment of people with disabilities through selective placement procedures. This assistance includes individual job counseling, special testing for visually- and hearing-impaired applicants, and referral to agency coordinators for selective placement. Special accommodations such as interpreters, readers, and restructured work sites can also be provided for the disabled. Contact the Selective Placement Coordinator at the agency where you wish to work or your state Office of Vocational Rehabilitation for more information. Washington's FJIC has a selective placement counselor who can be reached at 202/606-1848, as well as through Telecommunications Device for the Deaf (TDD) at 202/606-0591.

Student Employment Programs: The federal government also offers a variety of student employment programs to high school, undergraduate, and graduate students who are at least 16 years old and have U.S. citizenship. A government internship can be a great opportunity to gain experience. Decide which of the following programs is right for you and then contact your school's career placement center for more details.

- *Federal Cooperative Education Programs*

High school, undergraduate, graduate, vocational, and community college students enrolled at least part-time can work a parallel or alternate work/study schedule in the field of their interest. Benefits include salary, annual leave, sick leave, health and life insurance, and retirement plans. Often a "co-op" position can be converted into a permanent position upon graduation.

- *Summer Employment Programs*

Summer employees are hired to fill a variety of positions from office support to professional, between May 13 and September 30 every year. Summer employees earn salaries based on their education and experience. Vacancies are advertised annually in Summer Job Opportunities Announcement No. 414, available the last week of December at the FJIC.

- *Stay In School Program*

This program provides an opportunity for full-time high school, vocational, community college, or undergraduate students to work in order to resume or continue their education. Students work a maximum of 20 hours per week during school and full-time while on school breaks. The local state employment service office must certify that students meet the financial need criteria. Benefits include salary, annual leave, and sick leave. Agencies recruit candidates directly from schools and local state employment service offices.

- *Summer Aid*

Through this program, the federal government employs economically disadvantaged youths, who earn the federal minimum wage. The local state employment service office must certify that candidates meet the financial need criteria.

- *Student Volunteer Service*

High school undergraduate, graduate, or vocational students who are enrolled at least part-time can gain experience through this "internship" opportunity in a field related to their academic/career interest. In many cases, you can earn academic credit for your internship. Students should contact agency personnel offices directly to inquire about opportunities.

- *Federal Junior Fellowship*

This career-related work/study program helps to expose high school seniors who have a strong academic record and are planning to attend a higher education program to public service careers. Benefits includes salary, annual leave, sick leave, health and life insurance, and retirement plans. Students must be nominated during their senior year by their school and the local state employment service office must certify that they meet financial need criteria.

Federal Job Application Checklist
Here's a reference list of major steps to help you start your job search process:

1. Attend the General Employment seminar.
2. Call or visit your local FJIC to find out which application process you should follow.
3. Get the appropriate forms from the FJIC. If you will be taking a test, you should get the testing schedule and the sample test booklet. If you are applying for positions filled through a register, make sure you get the appropriate supplemental forms. Consult the FJOL if you are applying directly for a vacancy announced by an agency. You must call the contact person listed for each vacancy, and request a copy of the vacancy announcement for that position. The name, phone number, and job announcement number will be given in the position listing.

When filling out your SF-171, type or print clearly. Describe your work experience, education, training, and accomplishments. Create a master copy of your SF-171, leaving blank the job number and the signature block, and make several photocopies to use when applying for jobs. You can add an additional information sheet if necessary when applying for specific jobs. Several commercial SF-171 software programs are now available to make the process easier.

In your SF-171, address the specific "Knowledge, Skills, and Abilities" (KSAs) outlined in the vacancy announcement. Because KSAs are necessary for successful performance on the job, they are used to evaluate qualified applicants. Remember to include your volunteer work as work experience.
4. Mail or deliver your application to the office designated on the vacancy announcement or information materials.

To check on the status of your application, contact the personnel office of the hiring agency.

Glossary of Federal Terms
These are some of the terms you are likely to hear as you go through the application process:

CAREER CONDITIONAL STATUS — An employee who has served for less than three consecutive years in the federal government in a permanent position.

CAREER LADDER — The promotion potential of a federal job.

CAREER STATUS — An employee who has served for at least three consecutive years in the federal government in a permanent position.

CERTIFICATE — A ranked list of eligible applicants used by agency managers in selecting a candidate to fill a position.

INTERN PROGRAM (also "management trainee program") — Many agencies hire entry-level (GS-5/7) candidates in professional and administrative occupations for these one-to-three year full-time training programs, which offer rotational and career development opportunities. Contact agencies directly to find out about these programs.

MERIT PROMOTION — Opportunities for current federal employees to be promoted within the federal government's competitive service.

PROBATIONARY PERIOD — A trial period of one year that new employees serve. During this time a probationary employee may be dismissed without formal procedures.

RATING AND RANKING — The processes by which an agency numerically evaluates the candidates for a job and ranks them in score-order, after which a selection is made from the most qualified candidates.

REGISTERS — Lists of qualified applicants for specific occupations or positions, maintained by OPM, for use by agencies in filling vacancies.

REINSTATEMENT ELIGIBILITY — Provision allowing former federal employees to apply for federal jobs that are open to "status" employees. These former employees must have at least three consecutive years of service, or reapply within three years of leaving federal service, or qualify for veteran preference.

STATUS EMPLOYEE — An employee who has eligibility to apply for other federal positions based on current federal service or reinstatement eligibility.

Starting Salaries Under the General Schedule

Grade	Annual	Hourly	Biweekly
GS-01	$11,903	$5.70	$456.00
GS-02	$13,382	$6.41	$512.80
GS-03	$14,603	$7.00	$560.00
GS-04	$16,393	$7.85	$628.00

GS-05	$18,340	$8.79	$703.00
GS-06	$20,443	$9.80	$784.00
GS-07	$22,717	$10.89	$871.20
GS-08	$25,159	$12.06	$964.80
GS-09	$27,789	$13.32	$1065.60
GS-10	$30,603	$14.66	$1172.80
GS-11	$33,623	$16.11	$1288.80
GS-12	$40,298	$19.31	$1544.80
GS-13	$47,920	$22.96	$1836.80
GS-14	$56,627	$27.13	$2170.40
GS-15	$66,609	$31.92	$2553.60

Job Search Outlook: The Federal Government

Little or no change is expected in the overall level of federal government employment through the next decade. Where the jobs are, on the other hand, is changing. Defense Department jobs, which currently make up half of all federal jobs—are on the decline because of budget cuts and the disappearance of the Soviet threat. Hardest hit among Defense Department workers will be blue-collar workers. Three out of every four blue-collar workers in the federal government are employed by Defense, and while total employment of these workers may not be reduced with mass layoffs, their numbers will shrink by attrition. As a group, though, all other federal agencies will be adding more workers.

The reasons for rising and falling federal government employment are unique. Unlike any other employer in the nation, the government's payroll budget is determined by Congress and the President prior to each fiscal year, which runs from October 1 through September 30 of the following fiscal year. Whether operating at a surplus or a deficit, the federal government generally sticks to its payroll budget. As a result, federal employment is not affected by regular cycles in the economy, and employment levels tend to be relatively stable in the short run.

On the other hand, political changes can make staffing levels much more uncertain in the long run. Since each administration has different priorities, that could mean more hiring is done for some programs and less is done for others. Layoffs, called "reductions in force" in federal government language, do happen, but they're uncommon and generally affect relatively few workers.

Competition is intense for many federal jobs, especially during tough times when workers look for the stability of federal government jobs. For nurses and engineers, though, the prospects look good.

EMPLOYMENT SERVICES

TEMPORARY SERVICES AND EMPLOYMENT AGENCIES OF THE DISTRICT OF COLUMBIA

NOTE: *While every effort is made to keep the addresses and phone numbers of these companies up-to-date, employment services often move or change hands and are therefore more difficult to track. Please notify the publisher if you find any discrepancies.*

ADMIN ASSISTANCE
1350 Connecticut Avenue NW, Suite 1050, Washington DC 20036. 202/496-0300. **Contact:** Helen Hopkins, Manager. Temporary Agency. **Specializes in the areas of:** Legal Secretarial; Office Support. **Positions commonly filled include:** Administrator; Clerk; Legal Secretary; Paralegal; Receptionist; Secretary; Typist/Word Processor.

STAFF BUILDERS INC. OF WASHINGTON, DC
810 First Street NE, Suite 410, Washington DC 20002. 202/682-2200. **Contact:** Manager. Temporary Agency. **Positions commonly filled include:** Accountant/Auditor; Administrative Assistant; Administrative Worker/Clerk; Bookkeeper; Clerk; Computer Operator; Computer Programmer; Customer Service Representative; Data Entry Clerk; Driver; EDP Specialist; Factory Worker; Health Services Worker; Legal Secretary; Light Industrial Worker; Medical Secretary; Nurse; Public Relations Specialist; Receptionist; Sales Representative; Secretary; Stenographer; Technician; Typist/Word Processor. Company pays fee. **Number of placements per year:** 1000+.

NANCY ALLEN ASSOCIATES, INC.
1000 16th Street NW, Suite 501, Washington DC 20036. 202/467-4100. **Contact:** Polly Frye, Manager. Employment Agency. **Specializes in the areas of:** Legal; Office Support. **Positions commonly filled include:** Attorney; Management; Secretary; Typist/Word Processor.

ATLAS PERSONNEL AGENCY
1129 20th Street NW, Suite 400, Washington DC 20036. 202/293-7210. **Contact:** Manager. Employment Agency. **Specializes in the areas of:** Non-Specialized. **Positions commonly filled include:** Accountant/Auditor; Administrative Assistant; Bank Officer/Manager; Bookkeeper; Clerk; Credit Manager; Customer Service Representative; Data Entry Clerk; Financial Analyst; Legal Secretary; Medical Secretary; Receptionist; Secretary; Stenographer; Typist/Word Processor. Company pays fee. **Number of placements per year:** 200 - 499.

C ASSOCIATES
1619 G Street SE, Washington DC 20003-3132. 202/544-0821. **Fax:** 202/547-8357. **Contact:** John Capozzi, Jr., CPC. Employment Agency. **Specializes in the areas of:** Computer Science/Software.

MEDICAL PERSONNEL SERVICES, INC.
1707 L Street, Suite 250, Washington DC 20036. 202/466-2955. **Contact:** Janet Cline Patrick, President. Employment Agency. **Specializes in the areas of:** Health/Medical. **Positions commonly filled include:** Medical Secretary; Nurse.

POSITIONS INC.
1730 K Street NW, Suite 907, Washington DC 20006. 202/659-9270. **Fax:** 202/659-9245. **Contact:** Ellen Andrews, Manager. Employment Agency. **Specializes in the areas of:** Administration/MIS/EDP; Office Support. **Positions commonly filled include:** Administrator; Clerk; Management; Receptionist; Secretary; Typist/Word Processor.

DON RICHARD ASSOCIATES OF WASHINGTON, DC
1717 K Street NW, Suite 1000, Washington DC 20006. 202/463-7210. **Fax:** 202/331-9743. **Contact:** Mark Strassman, Manager. Employment Agency. **Specializes in the areas of:** Accounting/Auditing; Computer Science/Software; Finance; Temporary Assignments.

SIGMAN & SUMMERFIELD ASSOCIATES, INC.
1120 Connecticut Avenue NW, Suite 270, Washington DC 20036. 202/785-9044. **Fax:** 202/331-0375. **Contact:** Katheleijne Zambrowicz, Partner. Employment Agency. **Specializes in the areas of:** Administration/MIS/EDP; Legal; Non-Profit; Personnel/Labor

Relations; Secretarial. **Positions commonly filled include:** Administrative Assistant; Administrative Services Manager; Clerical Supervisor; Paralegal; Secretary. Company pays fee. **Number of placements per year:** 1 - 49.

SNELLING PERSONNEL
1612 K Street NW, Suite 308, Washington DC 20006. 202/223-3540. **Fax:** 202/872-1967. **Contact:** Sherry Jones, Manager. Employment Agency. **Specializes in the areas of:** Bookkeeping; Clerical; Hotel/Restaurant; Legal; Office Support. **Positions commonly filled include:** Administrative Worker/Clerk; Clerk; Management; Receptionist; Secretary; Typist/Word Processor.

TANGENT CORPORATION
1901 L Street NW, Suite 705, Washington DC 20036. 202/331-9484. **Contact:** Fran D'Ooge, President. Employment Agency. **Specializes in the areas of:** Administration/MIS/EDP; Government; Personnel/Labor Relations; Secretarial. **Positions commonly filled include:** Human Resources Specialist. Company pays fee. **Number of placements per year:** 100 - 199.

TRIFAX CORPORATION
4121 Minnesota Avenue NE, Washington DC 20019. 202/388-6000. **Fax:** 202/388-6001. **Contact:** Ruth Ledbetter, Executive Vice President. Employment Agency. **Specializes in the areas of:** Health/Medical; Personnel/Labor Relations. **Positions commonly filled include:** Administrative Assistant; Clerk; Data Entry Clerk; Marketing Specialist; Medical Secretary; Nurse; Social Worker; Typist/Word Processor. **Number of placements per year:** 50 - 99.

TEMPORARY SERVICES AND EMPLOYMENT AGENCIES OF MARYLAND

ADIA PERSONNEL SERVICES
300 East Lombard Street, Suite 935, Baltimore MD 21202. 410/837-2444. **Contact:** Branch Manager. Temporary Agency. **Specializes in the areas of:** Accounting/Auditing; Communications; Data Processing; General Labor; Secretarial; Word Processing. Company pays fee.

ECCO STAFFING SERVICES
1923 York Road, Timonium MD 21093. 410/561-0700. **Contact:** Manager. Temporary Agency. **Specializes in the areas of:** Non-Specialized. **Positions commonly filled include:** Accountant/Auditor; Administrative Assistant; Bookkeeper; Clerk; Computer Operator; Computer Programmer; Customer Service Representative; Data Entry Clerk; Draftsperson; Driver; EDP Specialist; Factory Worker; Health Services Worker; Legal Secretary; Light Industrial Worker; Medical Secretary; Nurse; Public Relations Specialist; Receptionist; Sales Representative; Secretary; Stenographer; Technician; Typist/Word Processor. Company pays fee. **Number of placements per year:** 1000+.

IDEAL DESIGN, INC.
2215-B Defense Highway, Crofton MD 21114. 410/721-1061. **Contact:** William Bomar, President. Temporary Agency. **Specializes in the areas of:** Technical and Scientific. **Positions commonly filled include:** Aerospace Engineer; Civil Engineer; Computer Programmer; Data Entry Clerk; Draftsperson; EDP Specialist; Electrical/Electronics Engineer; Industrial Designer; Systems Analyst; Technical Writer/Editor. **Number of placements per year:** 1 - 49.

INTERIM PERSONNEL
102 West Pennsylvania Avenue, Suite 204, Towson MD 21204. 410/828-8071. **Contact:** Manager. Temporary Agency. **Positions commonly filled include:** Assembly Worker; Bookkeeper; Clerk; Computer Operator; Customer Service Representative; Data Entry Clerk; Draftsperson; Factory Worker; Legal Secretary; Light Industrial Worker; Medical Secretary; Receptionist; Secretary; Stenographer; Technician; Typist/Word Processor. Company pays fee. **Number of placements per year:** 1000+.

MICRO/TEMPS AND EDP/TEMPS
A TECHNICAL AID COMPANY
7500 Greenway Center Drive, Greenbelt MD 20770. 301/474-9063. **Contact:** Manager. Temporary Agency. **Specializes in the areas of:** Administration/MIS/EDP; Computer Science/Software; Engineering; Technical and Scientific. **Positions commonly filled include:** Communications Engineer; Computer Operator; Computer Programmer; Design Engineer; EDP Specialist; MIS Specialist; Software Engineer; Systems Analyst; Systems Engineer; Technical Writer/Editor. Company pays fee. **Number of placements per year:** 1000+.

STAFF BUILDERS, INC. OF MARYLAND
1501 South Edgewood Street, Suite D, Baltimore MD 21227. 410/525-3000. **Contact:** Manager. Temporary Agency. **Positions commonly filled include:** Accountant/Auditor; Administrative Assistant; Bookkeeper; Clerk; Computer Operator; Computer Programmer; Customer Service Representative; Data Entry Clerk; Draftsperson; Driver; EDP Specialist; Factory Worker; Health Services Worker; Legal Secretary; Light Industrial Worker; Medical Secretary; Nurse; Public Relations Specialist; Receptionist; Sales Representative; Secretary; Stenographer; Technician; Typist/Word Processor. Company pays fee. **Number of placements per year:** 1000+.

STAFF BUILDERS, INC. OF MARYLAND
10227 Wincopin Circle, Columbia MD 21044. 401/992-1940. **Contact:** Manager. Temporary Agency. **Specializes in the areas of:** Non-Specialized. **Positions commonly filled include:** Accountant/Auditor; Administrative Assistant; Bookkeeper; Clerk; Computer Operator; Computer Programmer; Customer Service Representative; Data Entry Clerk; Draftsperson; Driver; EDP Specialist; Factory Worker; Health Services Worker; Legal Secretary; Light Industrial Worker; Medical Secretary; Nurse; Public Relations Specialist; Receptionist; Sales Representative; Secretary; Stenographer; Technician; Typist/Word Processor. Company pays fee. **Number of placements per year:** 1000+.

TAC/TEMPS, INC. OF MARYLAND
7500 Greenway Center Drive, Suite 330, Greenville MD 20770. 301/963-9590. **Contact:** Manager. Temporary Agency. **Specializes in the areas of:** Accounting/Auditing; Advertising; Banking; Clerical; Education; Finance; Health/Medical; Insurance; Legal; Manufacturing; Non-Profit; Personnel/Labor Relations; Printing/Publishing; Sales and Marketing; Transportation. **Positions commonly filled include:** Bookkeeper; Clerk; Data Entry Clerk; Driver; Factory Worker; Legal Secretary; Light Industrial Worker; Medical Secretary; Receptionist; Secretary; Typist/Word Processor. Company pays fee. **Number of placements per year:** 1000+.

TECH/AID OF MARYLAND
7000 Security Boulevard, Suite 108, Baltimore MD 21244. 410/597-9550. **Contact:** Manager. Temporary Agency. **Specializes in the areas of:** Architecture/Construction/Real Estate; Cable TV; Computer Hardware/Software; Engineering; Manufacturing; Technical and Scientific. **Positions commonly filled include:** Aerospace Engineer; Architect; Buyer; Ceramics Engineer; Chemical Engineer; Civil Engineer; Draftsperson; Electrical/Electronics Engineer; Estimator; Industrial Designer; Industrial Engineer; Mechanical Engineer; Metallurgical Engineer; Mining Engineer; Operations/Production Manager; Petroleum Engineer; Purchasing Agent and Manager; Quality Control Supervisor; Technical Writer/Editor; Technician. Company pays fee. **Number of placements per year:** 1000+.

TELESEC TEMPORARY PERSONNEL, INC.
10408 Montgomery Avenue, Kensington MD 20895. 301/949-3110. **Contact:** Recruiting Coordinator. Temporary Agency. **Specializes in the areas of:** Construction; Engineering; Health/Medical. **Positions commonly filled include:** Administrative Assistant; Bookkeeper; Claim Representative; Clerk; Customer Service Representative; Legal Secretary; Librarian; Library Technician; Light Industrial Worker; Medical Secretary; Receptionist; Secretary; Stenographer; Typist/Word Processor.

ADMIN PERSONNEL
1112 Wayne Avenue, Silver Springs MD 20910. 301/565-3900. **Contact:** Robert L. McDermott, Owner. Employment Agency. **Specializes in the areas of:** Accounting/Auditing; Administration/MIS/EDP; Banking; Clerical; Computer Hardware/Software; Finance; Mortgage; Sales and Marketing. **Positions commonly filled include:** Accountant/Auditor; Administrative Assistant; Administrative Worker/Clerk; Bank Officer/Manager; Bookkeeper; Clerk; Computer Operator; Computer Programmer; Credit Manager; Customer Service Representative; Data Entry Clerk; EDP Specialist;

Legal Secretary; Medical Secretary; Receptionist; Sales Associate; Sales Representative; Secretary; Stenographer; Typist/Word Processor. Company pays fee. **Number of placements per year:** 500 - 999.

ATLAS PERSONNEL AGENCY
11820 Parklawn Drive, Suite 330, Rockville MD 20852. 301/984-8075. **Contact:** Manager. Employment Agency. **Specializes in the areas of:** Non-Specialized. **Positions commonly filled include:** Accountant/Auditor; Administrative Assistant; Bank Officer/Manager; Bookkeeper; Clerk; Credit Manager; Customer Service Representative; Data Entry Clerk; Financial Analyst; Legal Secretary; Medical Secretary; Receptionist; Secretary; Stenographer; Typist/Word Processor. Company pays fee. **Number of placements per year:** 200 - 499.

CAREER BYTE, INC.
8604 Second Avenue, Suite 160, Silver Springs MD 20910. 301/587-5626. **Fax:** 301/587-0323. **Contact:** Carl Hollenbach, President. Employment Agency. **Specializes in the areas of:** Computer Science/Software. **Positions commonly filled include:** Computer Programmer; Computer Systems Analyst; Software Engineer. Company pays fee. **Number of placements per year:** 50 - 99.

CAREERS III, INC.
9039 Shady Grove Court, Gaithersburg MD 20877. 301/977-7000. **Contact:** Pat Busbice, President. Employment Agency. **Specializes in the areas of:** Clerical. **Positions commonly filled include:** Administrative Assistant; Bookkeeper; Clerk; Customer Service Representative; Data Entry Clerk; Legal Secretary; Medical Secretary; Receptionist; Secretary; Stenographer; Technical Writer/Editor; Typist/Word Processor. Company pays fee. **Number of placements per year:** 200 - 499.

CEMCON INTERNATIONAL INC.
1517 Reistertown Road, Suite 205, Baltimore MD 21208. 410/653-9121. **Fax:** 410/653-8864. **Contact:** Lee Rudolph, General Manager. Employment Agency. **Specializes in the areas of:** Engineering; Manufacturing. **Positions commonly filled include:** Chemical Engineer; Civil Engineer; Electrical/Electronics Engineer; Mechanical Engineer; Mining Engineer. **Number of placements per year:** 50 - 99.

CONTEMPORARY FAMILY CARE SERVICES, INC.
CHEVY CHASE BABYSITTERS
9222 Woodland Drive, Silver Springs MD 20910. 301/587-0135. **Contact:** Manager. Employment Agency. **Specializes in the areas of:** Childcare, In-Home; Elderly. **Positions commonly filled include:** Child Care Director. **Number of placements per year:** 1000 + .

DUNHILL OF ROCKVILLE, INC.
414 Hungerford Drive, Suite 252, Rockville MD 20850. 301/654-2115. **Contact:** Gordon Powers, President. Employment Agency. **Specializes in the areas of:** Accounting/Auditing; Banking; Clerical; Finance. **Positions commonly filled include:** Accountant/Auditor; Bank Officer/Manager; Bookkeeper; Financial Analyst; Legal Secretary; Medical Secretary; Purchasing Agent and Manager; Receptionist; Secretary; Statistician; Stenographer; Typist/Word Processor. Company pays fee. **Number of placements per year:** 1 - 49.

A.G. FISHKIN AND ASSOCIATES, INC.
P.O. Box 34413, Bethesda MD 20827. 301/770-4944. **Contact:** Ms. W.W. Coppedge, Director of Research. Employment Agency. **Specializes in the areas of:** Administration/ MIS/EDP; Computer Hardware/Software; Technical and Scientific; Telecommunications. **Positions commonly filled include:** Computer Programmer; Electrical/Electronics Engineer; Management Analyst/Consultant; Sales Representative; Systems Analyst. Company pays fee.

J.R. ASSOCIATES
152 Rollins Avenue, Suite 200, Rockville MD 20852. 301/984-8885. **Contact:** Daniel Keller, President. Employment Agency. **Specializes in the areas of:** Administration/MIS/EDP; Computer Hardware/Software; Engineering; Sales and Marketing; Technical and Scientific. **Positions commonly filled include:** Computer Programmer; Computer Systems Analyst; Data Analyst; EDP Specialist; Financial Analyst; Marketing Specialist; MIS Specialist; Sales Engineer; Sales Representative; Telecommunications Analyst. Company pays fee. **Number of placements per year:** 50 - 99.

TOM McCALL & ASSOCIATES
819 Munsey Building, Baltimore MD 21202. 410/539-0700. **Contact:** Charley Greene, Manager. Employment Agency. **Specializes in the areas of:** General Management; Personnel/Labor Relations; Sales and Marketing. **Positions commonly filled include:** General Manager; Human Resources Specialist. Company pays fee. **Number of placements per year:** 100 - 199.

OPPORTUNITY SEARCH INC.
3404 Dartmoor Lane, Olney MD 20832. 301/924-4741. **Fax:** 301/924-1318. **Contact:** Marc Tappis, President. Employment Agency. **Specializes in the areas of:** Computer Science/Software; Engineering. **Positions commonly filled include:** Computer Programmer; Computer Systems Analyst; Electrical/Electronics Engineer; Software Engineer. Company pays fee. **Number of placements per year:** 1 - 49.

SNELLING PERSONNEL
20 South Charles Street, Fourth Floor, Sun Life Building, Baltimore MD 21201. 410/528-9400. **Contact:** Manager. Employment Agency. **Positions commonly filled include:** Accountant/Auditor; Actuary; Administrative Assistant; Aerospace Engineer; Architect; Attorney; Bank Officer/Manager; Biomedical Engineer; Bookkeeper; Buyer; Ceramics Engineer; Chemical Engineer; Claim Representative; Clerk; Credit Manager; Customer Service Representative; Data Entry Clerk; Draftsperson; Electrical/Electronics Engineer; Electronics Technician; Financial Analyst; General Manager; Human Resources Specialist; Industrial Designer; Industrial Engineer; Insurance Agent/Broker; Legal Secretary; Marketing Specialist; Mechanical Engineer; Medical Secretary; Metallurgical Engineer; Operations/Production Manager; Physicist/Astronomer; Purchasing Agent and Manager; Quality Control Supervisor; Receptionist; Sales Manager; Sales Representative; Secretary; Stenographer; Technical Writer/Editor; Technician; Typist/Word Processor. Company pays fee. **Number of placements per year:** 100 - 199.

TECHNICAL PROFESSIONAL SEARCH GROUP
1305 Warwick Drive, Lutherville MD 21093. 410/296-4944. **Fax:** 410/321-4834. **Contact:** Dan Jones, Senior Consultant. Employment Agency. **Specializes in the areas of:** Communications; Computer Hardware/Software.

TRI-SERV INC.
P.O. Box 644, Hunt Valley MD 21030. 410/561-1740. **Contact:** Walter J. Braczynski, President. Employment Agency. **Specializes in the areas of:** Computer Hardware/Software; Engineering; Technical and Scientific. **Positions commonly filled include:** Aerospace Engineer; Ceramics Engineer; Chemical Engineer; Chemist; Civil Engineer; Computer Operator; Computer Programmer; Draftsperson; Electrical/Electronics Engineer; Industrial Engineer; Mechanical Engineer; Operations/Production Manager; Quality Control Supervisor; Systems Analyst; Technical Writer/Editor; Technician. Company pays fee. **Number of placements per year:** 100 - 199.

TEMPORARY SERVICES AND EMPLOYMENT AGENCIES OF VIRGINIA

ACCOUNTEMPS
1100 Wilson Boulevard, Suite 900, Arlington VA 22209. 703/243-3600. **Contact:** Ellen. Temporary Agency. **Specializes in the areas of:** Accounting/Auditing.

ADIA TEMPORARY SERVICES
45 West Boscawen, Winchester VA 22601. 703/667-1916. **Contact:** C. Lynn Weakley, Jr., Owner/Manager. Temporary Agency. **Specializes in the areas of:** Non-Specialized. **Positions commonly filled include:** Administrative Assistant; Advertising Clerk; Bookkeeper; Clerk; Computer Operator; Computer Programmer; Construction Trade Worker; Customer Service Representative; Data Entry Clerk; Draftsperson; EDP Specialist; Factory Worker; Human Resources Specialist; Laboratory Technician; Legal Secretary; Light Industrial Worker; Medical Secretary; Nurse; Quality Assurance Engineer; Receptionist; Secretary; Technician; Typist/Word Processor. Company pays fee. **Number of placements per year:** 200 - 499.

EDP/TEMPS OF VIRGINIA
2095 Chain Bridge Road, Vienna VA 22182. 703/893-2400. **Contact:** Manager. Temporary Agency. **Specializes in the areas of:** Accounting/Auditing; Administration/MIS/EDP; Banking; Computer Hardware/Software; Engineering; Finance; Insurance; Manufacturing; Non-Profit; Personnel/Labor Relations; Printing/Publishing; Technical and Scientific. **Positions commonly filled include:** Computer Operator; Computer Programmer; EDP Specialist; MIS Specialist; Systems Analyst; Technical Writer/Editor. Company pays fee. **Number of placements per year:** 1000+.

MANPOWER TEMPORARY SERVICES OF VIENNA
8280 Greensboro Drive, McLean VA 22102. 703/821-0101. **Contact:** Recruitment. Temporary Agency. **Specializes in the areas of:** Clerical; Personnel/Labor Relations; Word Processing. **Positions commonly filled include:** Administrative Assistant; Bookkeeper; Clerk; Customer Service Representative; Data Entry Clerk; Legal Secretary; Secretary; Stenographer; Technical Writer/Editor; Typist/Word Processor. Company pays fee. **Number of placements per year:** 1000+.

TAC/TEMPS INC. OF THE DISTRICT OF COLUMBIA
1700 North Moore Street, Suite 1225, Arlington VA 22209. 703/522-4988. **Contact:** Manager. Temporary Agency. **Specializes in the areas of:** Accounting/Auditing; Advertising; Banking; Clerical; Education; Finance; Health/Medical; Insurance; Legal; Manufacturing; Non-Profit; Personnel/Labor Relations; Printing/Publishing; Sales and Marketing; Transportation. **Positions commonly filled include:** Bookkeeper; Clerk; Data Entry Clerk; Driver; Factory Worker; Legal Secretary; Light Industrial Worker; Medical Secretary; Receptionist; Secretary; Typist/Word Processor. Company pays fee. **Number of placements per year:** 1000+.

TAC/TEMPS, INC. OF VIRGINIA
2095 Chain Bridge Road, Vienna VA 22182. 703/893-5260. **Contact:** Manager. Temporary Agency. **Specializes in the areas of:** Accounting/Auditing; Advertising; Banking; Clerical; Education; Finance; Health/Medical; Insurance; Legal; Manufacturing; Non-Profit; Personnel/Labor Relations; Printing/Publishing; Sales and Marketing; Transportation. **Positions commonly filled include:** Bookkeeper; Clerk; Data Entry Clerk; Driver; Factory Worker; Legal Secretary; Light Industrial Worker; Medical Secretary; Receptionist; Secretary; Typist/Word Processor. Company pays fee. **Number of placements per year:** 1000+.

TECH/AID OF VIRGINIA
2095 Chain Bridge Road, Suite 300, Vienna VA 22182. 703/893-6444. **Contact:** Manager. Temporary Agency. **Specializes in the areas of:** Architecture/Construction/Real Estate; Cable TV; Computer Hardware/Software; Engineering; Manufacturing; Technical and Scientific. **Positions commonly filled include:** Aerospace Engineer; Architect; Buyer; Ceramics Engineer; Chemical Engineer; Civil Engineer; Draftsperson; Electrical/Electronics Engineer; Estimator; Industrial Designer; Industrial Engineer; Manufacturing Engineer; Mechanical Engineer; Metallurgical Engineer; Mining Engineer; Operations/Production Manager; Petroleum Engineer; Purchasing Agent and Manager; Quality Control Supervisor; Technical Writer/Editor; Technician. Company pays fee. **Number of placements per year:** 1000+.

TELESEC TEMPORARY PERSONNEL OF FALLS CHURCH
6245 Leesburg Pike, Suite 305, Falls Church VA 22044. 703/237-8001. **Contact:** Manager. Temporary Agency. **Specializes in the areas of:** Non-Specialized. **Positions commonly filled include:** Administrative Assistant; Bookkeeper; Claim Representative; Customer Service Representative; Legal Secretary; Librarian; Library Technician; Light Industrial Worker; Medical Secretary; Receptionist; Secretary; Stenographer; Typist/Word Processor.

AMERICAN TECHNICAL RESOURCES
1651 Old Meadow Road, Sixth Floor, McLean VA 22102-4308. 703/917-7800. **Contact:** Jim Hollister, Manager of Technical Recruiting. Employment Agency. **Specializes in the areas of:** Administration/MIS/EDP; Computer Hardware/Software; Defense Industry; Engineering; Military; Technical and Scientific. **Positions commonly filled include:** Account Executive; Computer Operator; Computer Programmer; Computer Scientist; Customer Service Representative; Database Management Specialist; Electrical/Electronics Engineer; MIS Specialist; Operations/Production Manager; Software Engineer; Systems Analyst; Technical Writer/Editor. Company pays fee. **Number of placements per year:** 200 - 499.

CORE PERSONNEL
8201 Greensborough Drive, Suite 100, McLean VA 22102. 703/556-9610. **Contact:** Harvey Silver, President. Employment Agency. **Specializes in the areas of:** Computer Hardware/Software. **Positions commonly filled include:** Administrative Assistant; Clerk; Computer Programmer; Customer Service Representative; EDP Specialist; Legal Secretary; Medical Secretary; Receptionist; Sales Representative; Secretary; Stenographer; Systems Analyst; Typist/Word Processor. Company pays fee.

CAROL DAY & ASSOCIATES
2105 Electric Road SW, Roanoke VA 24018. 703/989-2831. **Contact:** Human Resources. Employment Agency. **Positions commonly filled include:** Chemical Engineer; Customer Service Representative; Electrical/Electronics Engineer; Insurance Agent/Broker; Management Trainee; Manufacturer's/Wholesaler's Sales Rep.; Mechanical Engineer; Restaurant/Food Service Manager. Company pays fee. **Number of placements per year:** 50 - 99.

HALBRECHT & COMPANY, INC.
10195 Main Street, Suite L, Fairfax VA 22031. 703/359-2880. **Contact:** Thomas Maltby, Vice President. Employment Agency. **Specializes in the areas of:** Administration/MIS/EDP; Computer Hardware/Software; Technical and Scientific. **Positions commonly filled include:** Actuary; Computer Programmer; EDP Specialist; Electrical/Electronics Engineer; Financial Analyst; Management Analyst/Consultant; Petroleum Engineer; Statistician; Systems Analyst. Company pays fee.

ROBERT HALF INTERNATIONAL
1100 Wilson Boulevard, Suite 900, Arlington VA 22209. 703/243-3600. **Contact:** Manager. Employment Agency. **Specializes in the areas of:** Accounting/Auditing. **Positions commonly filled include:** Accountant/Auditor; Bookkeeper; Data Entry Clerk; EDP Specialist; Financial Analyst. Company pays fee. **Number of placements per year:** 200 - 499.

PAT MURPHY ASSOCIATES
2009 North 14th Street, Suite 301, Arlington VA 22201. 703/522-4441. **Fax:** 703/522-4456. **Contact:** Pat Murphy, Owner. Employment Agency. **Specializes in the areas of:** Accounting/Auditing; Administration/MIS/EDP; Legal; Non-Profit; Personnel/Labor Relations; Retail; Sales and Marketing; Secretarial. **Positions commonly filled include:** Accountant/Auditor; Administrative Services Manager; Advertising Clerk; Biological Scientist/Biochemist; Buyer; Chemist; Clerical Supervisor; Customer Service Representative; Services Sales Representative.

PAE PLACEMENT
1601 North Kent Street, Suite 900, Arlington VA 22209. 703/243-6464. **Fax:** 703/243-5607. **Contact:** Manager. Employment Agency. **Specializes in the areas of:** Bilingual; International Executives.

PAUL-TITTLE ASSOCIATES, INC.
1485 Chain Bridge Road, Suite 304, McLean VA 22101-4501. 703/442-0500. **Fax:** 703/893-3871. **Contact:** Burt Heacock, Senior Vice President. Employment Agency. **Specializes in the areas of:** Computer Science/Software; Electronics; Engineering; Sales and Marketing; Telecommunications.

POTOMAC PERSONNEL
1640 Kings Street, Suite A, Alexandria VA 22314. 703/549-5055. **Contact:** Traci Hill, Branch Manager. Employment Agency. **Specializes in the areas of:** Clerical; Personnel/Labor Relations. **Positions commonly filled include:** Administrative Assistant; Bookkeeper; Clerk; Computer Operator; Data Entry Clerk; Legal Secretary; Medical Secretary; Receptionist; Secretary; Stenographer; Typist/Word Processor. Company pays fee.

PROFESSIONAL CAREER CONSULTANTS
319 William Street, Fredericksburg VA 22401. 703/371-8608. **Fax:** 703/371-0764. **Contact:** Christine Garber, Manager. Employment Agency. **Specializes in the areas of:** Insurance.

SNELLING PERSONNEL SERVICES
45 West Boscawen Street, Winchester VA 22601-4750. 703/667-1911. **Fax:** 703/667-0505. **Contact:** C. Lynn Weakley, Jr., Owner/Manager. Employment Agency. **Specializes in the areas of:** Accounting/Auditing; Administration/MIS/EDP; Art/Design; Banking; Education; Engineering; Food Industry; Health/Medical; Legal; Manufacturing;

Personnel/Labor Relations; Printing/Publishing; Retail; Sales and Marketing; Secretarial; Technical and Scientific. **Positions commonly filled include:** Accountant/Auditor; Administrative Services Manager; Aerospace Engineer; Attorney; Bank Officer/Manager; Branch Manager; Buyer; Ceramics Engineer; Chemical Engineer; Civil Engineer; Electrical/Electronics Engineer; Health Services Manager; Hotel Manager/Assistant Manager; Human Resources Specialist; Industrial Engineer; Industrial Production Manager; Library Technician; Management Trainee; Manufacturer's/Wholesaler's Sales Rep.; Materials Engineer; Mechanical Engineer; Metallurgical Engineer; Occupational Therapist; Paralegal; Purchasing Agent and Manager; Registered Nurse; Respiratory Therapist; Services Sales Representative; Teacher; Wholesale and Retail Buyer. **Number of placements per year:** 100 - 199.

TEAM PLACEMENT SERVICE, INC.
5113 Leesburg Pike, Suite 510, Falls Church VA 22041. 703/820-8618. **Contact:** Betty Peebles, Manager. Employment Agency. **Specializes in the areas of:** Health/Medical.

VANTAGE PERSONNEL, INC.
2300 Clarendon Boulevard, Suite 1109, Arlington VA 22201. 703/247-4100. **Fax:** 703/247-4102. **Contact:** Mary Ann Wilkinson, CPC, President. Employment Agency. **Specializes in the areas of:** Administration/MIS/EDP; Computer Science/Software; Office Support; Telecommunications. **Positions commonly filled include:** Administrator; Management; Secretary; Typist/Word Processor.

BILL YOUNG & ASSOCIATES
8550 Arlington Boulevard, Suite 202, Fairfax VA 22031. 703/573-0200. **Fax:** 703/573-3612. **Contact:** Bill Young, Owner. Employment Agency. **Specializes in the areas of:** Administration/MIS/EDP; Computer Science/Software; Electronics; Engineering; Manufacturing; Packaging; Telecommunications.

EXECUTIVE SEARCH FIRMS OF THE DISTRICT OF COLUMBIA

THE PERSONNEL INSTITUTE
1000 Connecticut Avenue NW, Suite 1108, Washington DC 20036. 202/223-4911. **Contact:** Dr. William E. Stuart, President. Executive Search Firm. **Specializes in the areas of:** Computer Hardware/Software; Engineering; Manufacturing; MIS/EDP; Technical and Scientific. **Positions commonly filled include:** Aerospace Engineer; Bank Officer/Manager; Biological Scientist/Biochemist; Biomedical Engineer; Computer Programmer; EDP Specialist; Industrial Designer; Industrial Engineer; Marketing Specialist; Mechanical Engineer; MIS Specialist; Operations/Production Manager; Physicist/Astronomer; Quality Control Supervisor; Systems Analyst. Company pays fee. **Number of placements per year:** 200 - 499.

EXECUTIVE SEARCH FIRMS OF MARYLAND

ACADEMY GRADUATES CAREER CONSULTANTS
250 Oak Court, Severna Park MD 21146-3140. 410/544-6687. **Contact:** Tom Karpick, President. Executive Search Firm. **Specializes in the areas of:** Administration/MIS/EDP; Architecture/Construction/Real Estate; Computer Science/Software; Engineering; General Management; Industrial; Manufacturing; Technical and Scientific. **Positions commonly filled include:** Administrative Services Manager; Aerospace Engineer; Bank Officer/Manager; Branch Manager; Civil Engineer; Computer Systems Analyst; Construction Contractor and Manager; Electrical/Electronics Engineer; General Manager; Industrial Engineer; Industrial Production Manager; Management Analyst/Consultant; Management Trainee; Mechanical Engineer; Metallurgical Engineer; Meteorologist; Nuclear Engineer; Operations/Production Manager; Quality Control Supervisor; Software Engineer; Structural Engineer. Company pays fee. **Number of placements per year:** 1 - 49.

Employment Services/317

CAPLAN ASSOCIATES
28 Allegheny Avenue #600, Baltimore MD 21204. 410/821-9351. **Fax:** 410/583-1901. **Contact:** Robert Caplan, President. Executive Search Firm. **Specializes in the areas of:** Accounting/Auditing; Finance; Health/Medical; Manufacturing; Personnel/Labor Relations; Sales and Marketing. **Positions commonly filled include:** Accountant/Auditor; Attorney; Budget Analyst; Cost Estimator; Credit Manager; Health Services Manager; Manufacturer's/Wholesaler's Sales Rep.; Purchasing Agent and Manager; Services Sales Representative. Company pays fee. **Number of placements per year:** 50 - 99.

COMPUTER MANAGEMENT INC.
809 Glen Eagle Court, Suite 205, Towson MD 21286. 410/583-0050. **Fax:** 410/494-9410. **Contact:** Janet Miller, Recruiter. Executive Search Firm. **Specializes in the areas of:** Computer Operations; Information Systems. **Positions commonly filled include:** Computer Programmer; Computer Systems Analyst; Network Engineer; Software Engineer. Company pays fee. **Number of placements per year:** 1 - 49.

CROSS COUNTRY CONSULTANTS, INC.
111 Warren Road, Suite 4B, Hunt Valley MD 21030. 410/666-1100. **Contact:** Scott Gottesfeld, President. Executive Search Firm. **Specializes in the areas of:** Accounting/Auditing; Engineering; Finance. **Number of placements per year:** 50 - 99.

DUNHILL PERSONNEL OF BEL AIR
P.O. Box 267, Bel Air MD 21014-0267. 410/836-0952. **Fax:** 410/836-0953. **Contact:** John Banister, President. Executive Search Firm. **Specializes in the areas of:** Health/ Medical; Pharmaceutical. **Positions commonly filled include:** Medical Technologist; Pharmacist; Physical Therapist. Company pays fee. **Number of placements per year:** 1 - 49.

FALLSTAFF SEARCH
111 Warren Road, Suite 4B, Hunt Valley MD 21030. 410/666-1100. **Fax:** 410/666-1119. **Contact:** Office Manager. Executive Search Firm. **Specializes in the areas of:** Health/Medical; Sales and Marketing. **Positions commonly filled include:** Biomedical Engineer; Chemical Engineer; Civil Engineer; Property and Real Estate Manager. **Number of placements per year:** 100 - 199.

FUTURES, INC.
Oxford Building, 8600 LaSalle Road, Suite 615, Baltimore MD 21286. 410/337-2001. **Contact:** Daniel Otakie, C.P.C., President. Executive Search Firm. **Specializes in the areas of:** Accounting/Auditing; Administration/MIS/EDP; Architecture/Construction/Real Estate; Banking; Computer Hardware/Software; Engineering; Fashion; Finance; Food Industry; General Management; Health/Medical; Insurance; Legal; Manufacturing; Personnel/Labor Relations; Retail; Sales and Marketing; Technical and Scientific; Transportation. **Positions commonly filled include:** Accountant/Auditor; Administrative Assistant; Aerospace Engineer; Architect; Biological Scientist/Biochemist; Biomedical Engineer; Bookkeeper; Buyer; Ceramics Engineer; Chemical Engineer; Chemist; Civil Engineer; Claim Representative; Computer Programmer; Customer Service Representative; Draftsperson; EDP Specialist; Electrical/Electronics Engineer; Hotel Manager/Assistant Manager; Industrial Designer; Industrial Engineer; Legal Secretary; Manufacturing Engineer; Mechanical Engineer; Medical Secretary; Metallurgical Engineer; MIS Specialist; Nurse; Purchasing Agent and Manager; Quality Control Supervisor; Sales Representative; Software Engineer; Systems Analyst; Technical Writer/Editor; Typist/Word Processor. Company pays fee.

MEI/RETAIL PLACEMENT ASSOCIATES
6001 Montrose Road, Suite 702, Rockville MD 20852. 301/231-8150. **Fax:** 301/881-2918. **Contact:** Mark Suss, President. Executive Search Firm. **Specializes in the areas of:** Advertising; Retail. **Positions commonly filled include:** Branch Manager; Buyer; District Manager; General Manager; Human Resources Specialist; Operations/Production Manager; Store Manager; Wholesale and Retail Buyer. Company pays fee. **Number of placements per year:** 50 - 99.

MANAGEMENT RECRUITERS
1100 Wayne Avenue, Suite 710, Silver Springs MD 20910. 301/589-5400. **Fax:** 301/589-3033. **Contact:** Manager. Executive Search Firm. **Specializes in the areas of:** Accounting/Auditing; Administration/MIS/EDP; Advertising; Architecture/Construction/Real Estate; Banking; Chemical; Communications; Computer Hardware/Software; Design; Electrical; Engineering; Finance; Food Industry; General Management; Health/Medical; Insurance; Legal; Manufacturing; Operations Management; Personnel/

Labor Relations; Pharmaceutical; Printing/Publishing; Procurement; Retail; Sales and Marketing; Technical and Scientific; Textiles; Transportation.

MANAGEMENT RECRUITERS OF ANNAPOLIS
2083 West Street, Suite 5A, Annapolis MD 21401-3030. 410/841-6600. **Contact:** John Czajkowski, Manager. Executive Search Firm. **Specializes in the areas of:** Accounting/Auditing; Administration/MIS/EDP; Advertising; Architecture/Construction/Real Estate; Banking; Chemical; Communications; Computer Hardware/Software; Design; Electrical; Engineering; Finance; Food Industry; General Management; Health/Medical; Insurance; Legal; Manufacturing; Operations Management; Personnel/Labor Relations; Pharmaceutical; Printing/Publishing; Procurement; Retail; Sales and Marketing; Technical and Scientific; Textiles; Transportation.

MANAGEMENT RECRUITERS OF BALTIMORE
d.b.a. COMPUSEARCH OF BALTIMORE
9515 Deereco Road, Suite 801, Timonium MD 21093. 410/252-6616. **Fax:** 410/252-7076. **Contact:** Ken Davis, General Manager. Executive Search Firm. **Specializes in the areas of:** Accounting/Auditing; Administration/MIS/EDP; Advertising; Architecture/Construction/Real Estate; Banking; Chemical; Communications; Computer Hardware/Software; Design; Electrical; Engineering; Finance; Food Industry; General Management; Health/Medical; Insurance; Legal; Manufacturing; Operations Management; Personnel/Labor Relations; Pharmaceutical; Printing/Publishing; Procurement; Retail; Sales and Marketing; Technical and Scientific; Textiles; Transportation. **Positions commonly filled include:** Accountant/Auditor; Aerospace Engineer; Bank Officer/Manager; Biological Scientist/Biochemist; Biomedical Engineer; Chemical Engineer; Civil Engineer; Claim Representative; Clerical Supervisor; Computer Programmer; Computer Systems Analyst; Credit Manager; Customer Service Representative; Electrical/Electronics Engineer; Financial Analyst; Industrial Engineer; Industrial Production Manager; Insurance Agent/Broker; Mechanical Engineer; Operations/Production Manager; Paralegal; Quality Control Supervisor; Securities Sales Rep. Company pays fee. **Number of placements per year:** 200 - 499.

MANAGEMENT RECRUITERS OF FREDERICK
d.b.a. OFFICEMATES5 OF BALTIMORE
201 Thomas Johnson Drive, Suite 202, Frederick MD 21702. 301/663-0600. **Fax:** 301/663-0454. **Contact:** Ms. Pat Webb, Owner/Manager. Executive Search Firm. **Specializes in the areas of:** Accounting/Auditing; Administration/MIS/EDP; Advertising; Architecture/Construction/Real Estate; Banking; Chemical; Communications; Computer Hardware/Software; Design; Electrical; Engineering; Finance; Food Industry; General Management; Health/Medical; Insurance; Legal; Manufacturing; Operations Management; Personnel/Labor Relations; Pharmaceutical; Printing/Publishing; Procurement; Retail; Sales and Marketing; Technical and Scientific; Textiles; Transportation.

PROFESSIONAL PERSONNEL SERVICES
1420 East Joppa Road, Towson MD 21286. 410/823-5630. **Fax:** 410/821-9423. **Contact:** Neal Fisher, President. Executive Search Firm. **Specializes in the areas of:** Computer Science/Software. **Positions commonly filled include:** Computer Programmer; Computer Systems Analyst. Company pays fee. **Number of placements per year:** 1 - 49.

QUEST SYSTEMS, INC.
4701 Sangamore Road, Bethesda MD 20816. 301/229-4200. **Contact:** Tom Carter, Manager. Executive Search Firm. **Specializes in the areas of:** Computer Hardware/Software. **Positions commonly filled include:** Computer Programmer; EDP Specialist; MIS Specialist; Recruiter; Software Engineer; Systems Analyst. Company pays fee. **Number of placements per year:** 1000+.

SALES CONSULTANTS OF BALTIMORE CITY
575 South Charles Street, Suite 401, Baltimore MD 21201. 410/727-5750. **Fax:** 410/727-1253. **Contact:** Steven Braun, President. Executive Search Firm. **Specializes in the areas of:** Advertising; Computer Hardware/Software; Fashion; Food Industry; General Management; Health/Medical; Industrial; Insurance; Manufacturing; Personnel/Labor Relations; Printing/Publishing; Retail; Secretarial; Technical and Scientific; Transportation. **Positions commonly filled include:** Administrative Assistant; Bookkeeper; Buyer; Claim Representative; Credit Manager; Customer Service Representative; Data Entry Clerk; EDP Specialist; Electrical/Electronics Engineer; Legal Secretary; Marketing Specialist; Medical Secretary; MIS Specialist; Nurse; Public Relations Specialist; Purchasing Agent and Manager; Receptionist; Recruiter; Sales

Representative; Secretary; Software Engineer; Systems Analyst; Typist/Word Processor. Company pays fee. **Number of placements per year:** 100 - 199.

SALES CONSULTANTS OF COLUMBIA
10320 Little Patuxent Parkway, Suite 511, Columbia MD 21044. 410/992-4900. **Fax:** 410/992-4905. **Contact:** David Rubin, General Manager. Executive Search Firm. **Specializes in the areas of:** Computer Hardware/Software; Datacommunications; Engineering; Sales and Marketing; Telecommunications. **Positions commonly filled include:** Sales Representative; Telecommunications Analyst. Company pays fee. **Number of placements per year:** 1 - 49.

SALES CONSULTANTS OF PRINCE GEORGES COUNTY
7515 Annapolis Road, Suite 404, Hyattsville MD 20784. 301/731-4200. **Contact:** Tom Hummel, Manager. Executive Search Firm. **Specializes in the areas of:** Accounting/Auditing; Administration/MIS/EDP; Advertising; Architecture/Construction/ Real Estate; Banking; Chemical; Communications; Computer Hardware/Software; Design; Electrical; Engineering; Finance; Food Industry; General Management; Health/ Medical; Insurance; Legal; Manufacturing; Operations Management; Personnel/Labor Relations; Pharmaceutical; Printing/Publishing; Procurement; Retail; Sales and Marketing; Technical and Scientific; Textiles; Transportation.

SALES CONSULTANTS OF ROCKVILLE
1395 Piccard Drive, Suite 330, Rockville MD 20850. 301/417-9100. **Fax:** 301/417-0101. **Contact:** Brian Hoffman, General Manager. Executive Search Firm. **Specializes in the areas of:** Communications; General Management; Mortgage; Sales and Marketing. **Positions commonly filled include:** Bank Officer/Manager; Electrical/ Electronics Engineer; General Manager; Management Analyst/Consultant.

TECHNICAL TALENT LOCATORS LTD.
8850 Stanford Boulevard, Suite 3400, Columbia MD 21045. 410/995-6051. **Fax:** 410/995-6281. **Contact:** Jim Garrett, Operations Manager. Executive Search Firm. **Specializes in the areas of:** Computer Science/Software; Engineering; Technical and Scientific. **Positions commonly filled include:** Computer Programmer; Computer Systems Analyst; Draftsperson; Electrical/Electronics Engineer; Software Engineer; Technical Writer/Editor. Company pays fee. **Number of placements per year:** 50 - 99.

WHITE RIDGELY & ASSOCIATES, INC.
2201 Old Court Road, Baltimore MD 21208. 410/296-1900. **Contact:** Manager. Executive Search Firm. **Specializes in the areas of:** Accounting/Auditing; Administration/MIS/EDP; Banking; Finance; Health/Medical; Insurance; Personnel/Labor Relations; Sales and Marketing. **Number of placements per year:** 50 - 99.

EXECUTIVE SEARCH FIRMS OF VIRGINIA

ABILITY RESOURCES, INC.
716 Church Street, Alexandria VA 22314. 703/548-6400. **Contact:** Noel L. Ruppert, President. Executive Search Firm. **Specializes in the areas of:** Administration/MIS/EDP; Computer Science/Software; Defense Industry; Economics; Engineering; Finance; General Management; Non-Profit; Personnel/Labor Relations; Sales and Marketing; Technical and Scientific. **Positions commonly filled include:** Accountant/Auditor; Administrative Services Manager; Computer Programmer; Computer Systems Analyst; Economist/Market Research Analyst; Engineer; Financial Analyst; General Manager; Management Analyst/Consultant; Mathematician; Operations/Production Manager; Public Relations Specialist; Statistician; Technical Writer/Editor. Company pays fee. **Number of placements per year:** 1 - 49.

DONMAC ASSOCIATES
P.O. Box 2541, Reston VA 22090. 703/620-2866. **Fax:** 703/620-2867. **Contact:** Connie Andersen, President. Executive Search Firm. **Specializes in the areas of:** Computer Science/Software. **Positions commonly filled include:** Computer Programmer; Computer Systems Analyst; Electrical/Electronics Engineer; Software Engineer. Company pays fee. **Number of placements per year:** 50 - 99.

EXECUTIVE RECRUITERS FAIRFAX
1907 Clarks Glen Place, Vienna VA 22182. 703/556-9580. **Contact:** Joe Segal, President. Executive Search Firm. **Specializes in the areas of:** Food Industry; Hotel/Restaurant. **Positions commonly filled include:** Hotel Manager/Assistant Manager; Restaurant/Food Service Manager. Company pays fee. **Number of placements per year:** 50 - 99.

MANAGEMENT RECRUITERS OF ALEXANDRIA
2121 Eisenhower, Suite 200, Alexandria VA 22314-1361. 703/548-9040. **Contact:** Michael Prentiss, Manager. Executive Search Firm. **Specializes in the areas of:** Accounting/Auditing; Administration/MIS/EDP; Advertising; Architecture/Construction/Real Estate; Banking; Communications; Computer Hardware/Software; Design; Electrical; Engineering; Finance; Food Industry; General Management; Health/Medical; Insurance; Legal; Manufacturing; Operations Management; Personnel/Labor Relations; Printing/Publishing; Procurement; Retail; Sales and Marketing; Technical and Scientific; Textiles; Transportation.

MANAGEMENT RECRUITERS OF LEESBURG
44084 Riverside Parkway, Suite 170, Leesburg VA 22075-5102. 703/729-5600. **Contact:** Account Executive. Executive Search Firm. **Specializes in the areas of:** Engineering; Health/Medical. **Positions commonly filled include:** Chemical Engineer.

MANAGEMENT RECRUITERS OF MANASSAS
8807 Sudley Road, Suite 208, Manassas VA 22110-4719. 703/330-1830. **Contact:** Professional Placement. Executive Search Firm. **Specializes in the areas of:** Accounting/Auditing; Administration/MIS/EDP; Advertising; Architecture/Construction/Real Estate; Banking; Communications; Computer Hardware/Software; Design; Electrical; Engineering; Finance; Food Industry; General Management; Health/Medical; Insurance; Legal; Manufacturing; Operations Management; Personnel/Labor Relations; Printing/Publishing; Procurement; Retail; Sales and Marketing; Technical and Scientific; Textiles; Transportation.

MANAGEMENT RECRUITERS OF McLEAN
Suite 325, 1568 Spring Hill Road, McLean VA 22102. 703/442-4842. **Contact:** Howard Reitkopp, Manager. Executive Search Firm. **Specializes in the areas of:** Accounting/Auditing; Administration/MIS/EDP; Advertising; Architecture/Construction/Real Estate; Banking; Communications; Computer Hardware/Software; Design; Electrical; Engineering; Finance; Food Industry; General Management; Health/Medical; Insurance; Legal; Manufacturing; Operations Management; Personnel/Labor Relations; Printing/Publishing; Procurement; Retail; Sales and Marketing; Technical and Scientific; Textiles; Transportation.

SOURCE SERVICES
8614 Westwood Center Drive, Suite 750, Vienna VA 22182. 703/790-5610. **Contact:** Manager. Executive Search Firm. **Specializes in the areas of:** Computer Science/Software.

RESUME AND CAREER COUNSELING SERVICES OF THE DISTRICT OF COLUMBIA

BLACKWELL AND ASSOCIATES
626 A Street SE, Capitol Hill, Washington DC 20003. 202/546-6835. **Fax:** 202/543-8393. **Contact:** Mary Ann Blackwell, President and Executive Director. Career/Outplacement Counseling.

RESUME AND CAREER COUNSELING SERVICES OF MARYLAND

SAMUEL R. BLATE ASSOCIATES
10331 Watkins Mill Drive, Gaithersburg MD 20879-2935. 301/840-2248. **Contact:** Samuel R. Blate, President. Career/Outplacement Counseling.

THE RESUME PLACE
310 Frederick Road, Baltimore MD 21228. 410/744-4324. **Contact:** Kathy Troutman, General Manager. Career/Outplacement Counseling.

RESUME AND CAREER COUNSELING SERVICES OF VIRGINIA

ACTION RESUMES
RUTKALS RESUMES
218 Light Road, Winchester VA 22603. 703/888-3790. **Contact:** Mike Rutkals, Owner. Career/Outplacement Counseling.

ERICH NORD ASSOCIATES
6801 Whittier Avenue, McLean VA 22101. 703/556-9505. **Contact:** Joan Wikstrom, Principal. Career/Outplacement Counseling.

INDEX OF PRIMARY EMPLOYERS

NOTE: *Below is an alphabetical index of primary employer listings included in this book. Those employers in each industry that fall under the headings "Additional employers" are not indexed here.*

A

AAI CORPORATION, 164
A.C.T.S. INC., 286
AEPA ARCHITECTS ENGINEERS, 75
AES CORPORATION, 292
AT&T (AMERICAN TELEPHONE & TELEGRAPH), 134
AT&T COMMUNICATIONS, INC., 134
AW INDUSTRIES, 234
ABERDEEN PROVING GROUNDS, 191
ABRAMSON ERLICH MANES, 64
ABSTRACT JANITORIAL SERVICES, 110
THE ACACIA GROUP, 178
ACE-FEDERAL REPORTERS, INC., 110
ACTION, 122
THE ADAMS EXPRESS COMPANY, 178
ADIA INFORMATION TECHNOLOGIES, 56
AEGON USA, INC., 226
AEROSPACE INDUSTRIES ASSOCIATION OF AMERICA, 68
AFRO AMERICAN NEWSPAPERS INC., 252
AGORA, INC., 252
AIRFLOW COMPANY, 238
ALBAN TRACTOR COMPANY, INC., 270
ALEXANDRIA HOSPITAL, 202
ALEXANDRIA, CITY OF, 191
ALFATECH CORPORATION, 110
ALLEGANY TECHNOLOGY, 238
ALLEN FAMILY FOODS INCORPORATED, 184
ALLIANT TECHSYSTEMS INC., 164
ALLIED ADVERTISING, 64
ALLIED RESEARCH CORPORATION, 238
ALLIEDSIGNAL AEROSPACE, 134
ALLIEDSIGNAL TECHNICAL SERVICES CORPORATION, 75
ALLSTATE INSURANCE COMPANY, 227
ALPHA INDUSTRIES INC., 71
AMECOM, 164
AMERICA ONLINE INC., 134
THE AMERICAN ASSOCIATION, 110
AMERICAN ASSOCIATION OF UNIVERSITY WOMEN, 111
AMERICAN BUSING ASSOCIATION, 111
THE AMERICAN CAFE, 218
AMERICAN COUNCIL OF LIFE INSURANCE, 111
AMERICAN COUNCIL OF THE BLIND, 122
AMERICAN CREDIT INDEMNITY COMPANY, 227
AMERICAN FEDERATION OF STATE, COUNTY, 111
AMERICAN HEALTHCARE ASSOCIATION, 111
AMERICAN INSTITUTE OF C.P.A.S, 56
AMERICAN MANAGEMENT SYSTEMS INC., 144
AMERICAN MEDICAL LABORATORIES, INC., 104
AMERICAN PETROLEUM INSTITUTE (API), 111
AMERICAN POSTAL WORKERS UNION, 111
AMERICAN PRESS, INC., 253
AMERICAN PSYCHOLOGICAL ASSOCIATION, 112
AMERICAN SYMPHONY ORCHESTRA LEAGUE, 85
AMERICAN TRADING & PRODUCTION CORP., 238
AMERICAN TRUCKING ASSOCIATIONS, 112
THE AMERICAN UNIVERSITY, 156
AMERICAN WOODMARK CORPORATION, 234
AMERIDITA, 144
AMSPICE INC./BALTIMORE SPICE COMPANY, 184

AMTOTE INTERNATIONAL, INC., 165
ANALYSAS CORPORATION, 172
ARTHUR ANDERSEN & COMPANY, 56, 57
ANGELS FOOD MARKET, INC., 270
ANSER (ANALYTIC SERVICES INC.), 104
ANSTEC, INCORPORATED, 144
APPLIED BIOSCIENCE INTERNATIONAL, 104
APPLIED GRAPHICS TECHNOLOGIES, 253
ARBITRON COMPANY, 64, 135
ARENA STAGE, 85
ARINC RESEARCH CORPORATION, 57
ARITEC INC., 57
ARLINGTON COUNTY, 191
ARLTEC INC., 218
ARMS CONTROL ASSOCIATION, 112
ARNOLD & PORTER, 231
ARONSON, FETRIDGE & WIEGLE, 57
THE ARUNDEL CORPORATION, 283
ANNE ARUNDEL MEDICAL CENTER, 202
ASPEN CORPORATION, 112
ASPEN SYSTEMS CORPORATION, 112
ASSATEAGUE ISLAND NATIONAL SEASHORE, 85
ATEC ASSOCIATES, INC., 75
ATLANTIC COAST AIRLINES, INC., 286
ATLANTIC RESEARCH CORPORATION, 239
ATLAS MACHINE & IRON WORKS INC., 175
AUTO TRADER, 253
AUTOMATA, INC., 165
AUTOMATED SCIENCES GROUP, INC., 172
AUTOMOTIVE INDUSTRIES, INC., 90
AVEMCO CORPORATION, 227

B

BDM INTERNATIONAL, INC., 145
BTG, INC., 145
BAGEL MASTER, INC., 184
MICHAEL BAKER JR., INC., 75
BALMAR PRINTING AND GRAPHICS, INC., 253
BALTIMORE, CITY OF, 191
BALTIMORE AIRCOIL COMPANY, 75
BALTIMORE COUNTY, 192
BALTIMORE COUNTY PUBLIC SCHOOLS, 156
BALTIMORE GAS & ELECTRIC COMPANY, 292
BALTIMORE HOUSING AUTHORITY, 192
BALTIMORE LIFE INSURANCE COMPANY, 227
BALTIMORE PUBLIC WORKS BUREAU, 192
BALTIMORE SIGN COMPANY, 64
THE BALTIMORE SUN, 253
BANCTEC SYSTEMS, 145
JOSEPH A. BANK CLOTHIERS INC., 272
BANNER AEROSPACE, INC., 68
BANNER LIFE INSURANCE COMPANY, 227
BARBER & ROSS COMPANY, 75
BARRE-NATIONAL INC., 104
BARTON-COTTON INC., 253
BASICS & METRO FOOD MARKETS, 270
BATA SHOE COMPANY, INC., 71

Index/325

BAUSCH & LOMB, 202
BEATTY, SATCHELL COMPANY, 57
BECTON DICKINSON DIAG. INSTRUMENT SYST., 203
BECTON DICKINSON MICROBIOLOGY SYSTEMS, 105
THE BELKO CORPORATION, 126
BELL ATLANTIC, 135
BELL ATLANTIC MARYLAND, 135
BELL'S PAPER RECYCLING COMPANY, 249
BEST PRODUCTS COMPANY, 270
BETHESDA MARRIOTT HOTELS, 219
BETHSHIP SPARROWS, 286
BIOSPHERICS INC., 172
BIOWHITTAKER, INC., 105
BLACK & DECKER, 234
BLACK ENTERTAINMENT TELEVISION, 135
BLAKE CONSTRUCTION COMPANY, 76
BLUE CROSS & BLUE SHIELD, 228
BLUE CROSS & BLUE SHIELD OF MARYLAND, 227
B'NAI B'RITH INTERNATIONAL, 122
BOARD OF GOVERNORS OF FEDERAL RESERVE SYST., 192
BOAT AMERICA CORPORATION, 112
BOLLING FEDERAL CREDIT UNION, 178
BON SECOURS HOSPITAL, 203
BOOZ-ALLEN & HAMILTON, INC., 57
BOWIE STATE UNIVERSITY, 156
BOWL AMERICA INC., 85
BRESLER & REINER INC., 265
BRITISH AEROSPACE, 68
THE BROOKINGS INSTITUTION, 113
ALEX BROWN & SONS INCORPORATED, 178
PAUL BROWNER, CHARTERED, 58
BRUBACH CORPORATION, 253
BUREAU OF BROADCASTING, 136
BUREAU OF ENGRAVING AND PRINTING, 253
THE BUREAU OF NATIONAL AFFAIRS, INC., 254

C

CACI, INC., 145
CBS NEWS/WASHINGTON OFFICE, 136
CNN AMERICA INC., 136
CSX TRANSPORTATION INC., 287
CABLE AND WIRELESS, INC., 136
CABLE TELEVISION OF MONTGOMERY, 136
CADMUS JOURNAL SERVICES, INC., 254
CALVERT GROUP, 178
CANTEEN CORPORATION, 219
CAPITAL CITIES/ABC, 136
CAPITAL GAZETTE NEWSPAPERS INC., 255
CAPITOL HILTON, 219
DALE CARNEGIE LEADERSHIP INSTITUTE, 156
CARR REAL ESTATE SERVICES, 265
CARR-LOWREY GLASS COMPANY, 283
CARROLL COUNTY GENERAL HOSPITAL, 203
CARROLL COUNTY TIMES, 255
CARROLLTON BANK, 93
CASUAL CORNER, 270
CATER AIR INTERNATIONAL CORPORATION, 185
THE CATHOLIC UNIVERSITY OF AMERICA, 156
CECO CONCRETE CONSTRUCTION, 76
THE CELLO CHEMICAL COMPANY, 126
CENTER FOR STRATEGIC & INT'L STUDIES, 113
CENTRAL INTELLIGENCE AGENCY, 192
CENTURY ENGINEERING, INC., 76
CERNER CORPORATION, 145

CHARTER MEDICAL CORPORATION, 203
CHASE MANAHATTAN BANK OF MARYLAND, 93
CHEMETALS, INC., 126
CHESAPEAKE & OHIO CANAL NAT'L HISTORIC PARK, 122
CHESAPEAKE BAY SEAFOOD HOUSE, 219
CHESAPEAKE FIBER PACKAGING CORPORATION, 249
CHESAPEAKE PAPERBOARD COMPANY, 249
CHILD WELFARE LEAGUE OF AMERICA, 122
CHILDREN'S NATIONAL MEDICAL CENTER, 204
THE CHIMES, INC., 122
CHOICE HOTELS INTERNATIONAL, 219
CHOPTANK ELECTRIC COOPERATIVE, INC., 292
CITIBANK, 93
CITIZENS BANCORP, 94
CITIZENS BANK OF MARYLAND, 94
CITIZENS NATIONAL BANK, 94
J.L. CLARK MANUFACTURING COMPANY, INC., 239
CLENDENIN BROTHERS, INC., 175
CLIFTON GUNDERSON & COMPANY, 58
CLOVERLAND FARMS DAIRY, INC., 185
COLUMBIA FIRST BANK, 94
COLUMBIA HOSPITAL FOR WOMEN MEDICAL CTR, 204
COLUMBIA RESEARCH CORPORATION, 105
COLUMBIA SPECIALTY COMPANY, INC., 175
COMMERCIAL CREDIT, 94
COMMODITY FUTURES TRADING COMMISSION, 179
COMMUNICATIONS SATELLITE CORPORATION, 136
COMMUNICATIONS WORKERS OF AMERICA, 113
COMMUNITY COLLEGE OF BALTIMORE, 157
COMNET CORPORATION, 146
COMPLETE BUILDING SERVICES INC., 76
COMPUCARE COMPANY, 146
COMPUTER DATA SYSTEMS, INC., 146
COMPUTER SCIENCE CORPORATION, 146
COMPUTER SCIENCES CORPORATION, 146, 147
COMSAT CORPORATION, 136
COMSYS TECHNICAL SERVICES INC., 147
CONAGRA, INC., 185
CONGRESSIONAL QUARTERLY, 255
CONSTAR INTERNATIONAL, 127
COOPERATIVE HOUSING FOUNDATION, 265
COOPERS & LYBRAND, 58
COPPIN STATE COLLEGE, 157
CORNING-HAZLETON, INC., 105
CORT FURNITURE RENTAL, 113
THE COSMETIC CENTER, 271
COUNTY COMMISSION ON AGING, 123
COVINGTON & BURLINGTON, 231
CRAFTSMAN PRESS, INC., 255
CRAY COMMUNICATIONS, 147
CRESTAR BANK, 94
CROWN BOOKS, 271
CROWN CENTRAL PETROLEUM, 247
CYTEC ENGINEERED MATERIALS, 105

D

DC CHARTERED HEALTH PLAN, 228
DCS CORPORATION, 165
DAKA FOOD SERVICE MANAGEMENT, INC., 219
DANAHER CORPORATION, 239
C.R. DANIELS, INC., 69
DAVENPORT INSULATION INC., 76
DAVID-EDWARD LTD., 235
DAVIS & HEMPHILL, INC., 239

DAVISON CHEMICAL DIVISION, 127
DEFENSE INTELLIGENCE AGENCY (DAH), 198
DEFENSE LOGISTICS AGENCY ADMIN. SUPPORT CTR, 192
DELEX SYSTEMS INC., 147
DELMARVA POWER & LIGHT/MD-VA, 292
DELOITTE & TOUCHE, 58
DEMOCRATIC NATIONAL COMMITTEE, 192
DENRO INC., 137
DERWOOD INVESTMENT CORPORATION, 179
DEVLIN LUMBER & SUPPLY CORPORATION, 271
DEWBERRY & DAVIS, 76
DIAMOND PRESS, 255
DIGITAL EQUIPMENT CORPORATION, 147
DIGITAL SYSTEMS CORPORATION, 147
DISCLOSURE INC., 113
DISTRICT PHOTO, INC., 271
DOGGETT ENTERPRISES, INC., 287
DOMINO SUGAR CORPORATION, 185
DOMINO'S TEAM WASHINGTON, INC., 219
THE DONOHOE COMPANIES, INC., 76
DOW JONES & COMPANY, 255
DRESSER INDUSTRIES INC., 90
THE DRIGGS CORPORATION, 77
DRUG ENFORCEMENT ADMINISTRATION, 192
DRYDEN OIL COMPANY, 247
DUPONT PLAZA HOTEL, 219
DURON PAINTS & WALL COVERINGS, 127
DYNALECTRIC COMPANY, 165
DYNCORP, 165

E

E-SYSTEMS/MELPAR DIVISION, 165
E.A. LABORATORIES, 106
EG&G PRESSURE SCIENCE, INC., 239
E.I.L. INSTRUMENTS, INC., 165
EARLE PALMER BROWN, 64
ECHELON SERVICE COMPANY, 113
EDISON ELECTRIC INSTITUTE, 114
EDITORS PRESS, INC., 255
EISNER & ASSOCIATES, INC., 65
ELLICOTT MACHINE CORPORATION, 239
EMBASSY DAIRY, 185
ENDEAVOR FOODS, INC., 219
ENGLISH AMERICAN TAILORING COMPANY, 71
THE ENGLISH COMPANY, 220
ENSCO INC., 166
ENTERPRISE LEASING COMPANY, 90
ENVIRONMENTAL ELEMENTS CORPORATION, 173
ENVIRONMENTAL PROTECTION AGENCY, 193
ENVIRONMENTAL TECHNOLOGIES GROUP, INC., 173
ERNST & YOUNG, 58
ESSEX COMMUNITY COLLEGE, 157
EVAPO, INC., 239
EXECUTIVE OFFICE OF THE PRESIDENT, 193
EXPORT-IMPORT BANK OF THE UNITED STATES, 94

F

FMC CORPORATION, 127
FAIRCHILD INDUSTRIES INC., 240
FAIRCHILD SPACE & DEFENSE CORPORATION, 69
FAIRFAX, CITY OF, 193
FAIRFAX COUNTY, 193
FALLS CHURCH, CITY OF, 193

FALLSTON GENERAL HOSPITAL, 204
FAMILY AND CHILD SERVICES OF WASHINGTON, DC, 123
FANNIE MAE, 179
FARBOIL COMPANY, 128
FARM CREDIT ADMINISTRATION, 193
FARMER AND MECHANICS NATIONAL BANK, 95
FAWN PLASTICS COMPANY, INC., 128
FEDERAL BUREAU OF INVESTIGATION, 194
FEDERAL COMMUNICATIONS COMMISSION, 194
FEDERAL DATA CORPORATION, 148
FEDERAL DEPOSIT INSURANCE CORPORATION (FDIC), 194
FEDERAL EMERGENCY MANAGEMENT AGENCY, 194
FEDERAL HOME LOAN MORTGAGE CORPORATION, 179
FEDERAL REALTY INVESTMENT TRUST, 265
FEDERAL TRADE COMMISSION, 194
FERTILIZER INSTITUTE, 114
FIDELITY & DEPOSIT COMPANY OF MARYLAND, 179
FIRST AMERICAN BANK SHARES, 95
FIRST FIDELITY BANK, 95
FIRST MARYLAND BANCORP, 95
FIRST NATIONAL BANK OF MARYLAND, 95
FIRST VIRGINIA BANKS INC., 95
P. FLANIGAN & SONS INC., 77
FLEETWOOD TRAVEL TRAILERS, 90
FOGARTY INTERNATIONAL CENTER, 106
FOREIGN POLICY MAGAZINE, 256
FORT MYER CONSTRUCTION CORPORATION, 77
FRANKLIN SQUARE HOSPITAL CENTER, 204
FREDERICK TRADING COMPANY, 240
FRIENDS OF THE NATIONAL ZOO (FONZ), 85
FUSION SYSTEMS CORPORATION, 240

G

GAF BUILDING MATERIALS CORPORATION, 240
GBS CORPORATION, 58
GM HUGHES NETWORK SYSTEMS, 137
GTE GOVERNMENT SYSTEMS, 137
GTSI, 148
GANNETT COMPANY, INC., 256
GARAMOND, INC., 256
GARDEN STATE TANNING, 90
GARLOCK MEMORIAL CONVALESCENT HOME, 204
GARRETT COUNTY MEMORIAL HOSPITAL, 204
GENERAL ACCOUNTING OFFICE, 59
GENERAL DYNAMICS CORPORATION, 283
GENERAL ELECTRIC INFORMATION SERVICES, 114
GENERAL MAINTENANCE SERVICE COMPANY, INC., 114
GENERAL MOTORS/TRUCK & BUS GROUP, 90
GENERAL PHYSICS CORPORATION, 114
GENERAL RESEARCH CORPORATION, 106
GENERAL SCIENCES CORPORATION, 148
GENESIS HEALTH VENTURES, 204
GENESYS CORPORATION, 271
GENICOM CORPORATION, 148
GENSTAR STONE PRODUCTS COMPANY, 283
GEORGE MASON UNIVERSITY, 157
GEORGE WASHINGTON UNIVERSITY, 157
GEORGE WASHINGTON UNIVERSITY HOSPITAL, 204
GEORGETOWN UNIVERSITY, 157
GNOSSOS SOFTWARE INC., 148
GOLDBERG, MARCHESANO, KOHLMAN, 65
GOVERNMENT TECHNOLOGY SERVICES INC., 149
W.R. GRACE & COMPANY, 128
GRANT THORNTON, 59

GREATER LAUREL REGIONAL HOSPITAL, 205
GREATER SOUTHEAST COMMUNITY HOSPITAL, 205
GREEN SPRING DAIRY, 185
GRIFFITH CONSUMERS COMPANY, 271
GROUP 1 SOFTWARE, INC., 149
GUEST SERVICES, 220

H

HFSI, 149
HADRON INC., 77
HALIFAX CORPORATION, 166
HALIBURTON/NUS ENVIRONMENTAL CORPORATION, 77
HAMILTON & SPIEGEL, INC., 77
JOHN H. HAMPSHIRE INC., 77
HARFORD MEMORIAL HOSPITAL, 205
HARFORD MUTUAL INSURANCE COMPANY, 228
HARITON, MANCUSO & JONES, P.C., 59
HARMAN INTERNATIONAL INDUSTRIES, INC., 240
HARTFORD COURTS, 194
HARTZ & COMPANY, INC., 72
HEAD SKI & SPORTSWEAR, INC., 271
HEALTH CARE MANAGEMENT CORPORATION, 205
HEALTHCARE AUTOMATION, 115
HECHINGER STORES COMPANY, 271
THE HECHT COMPANY, 272
HEDWIN CORPORATION, 128
HEINEMANN PRODUCTS, 166
HEKIMIAN LABORATORIES INC., 149
HELIX HEALTH SYSTEM, 205
HERNDON, CITY OF, 194
C. WILLIAM HETZER, INC., 266
HEWLETT-PACKARD COMPANY, 167
HIGH'S OF BALTIMORE, 185
HILL AND KNOWLTON, 65
HIT OR MISS, INC., 272
HOGAN & HARTSON, 231
HOLIDAY INN CROWNE PLAZA, 220
HOLLADAY CORPORATION, 266
HOLY CROSS HOSPITAL, 205
HOMECALL INCORPORATED, 205
HOPPMANN CORPORATION, 240
HORNING BROTHERS, 77
HOTEL HARRINGTON, 220
HOTEL WASHINGTON, 220
HOUSEHOLD BANK, 95
HOWARD COUNTY, 194
HOWARD COUNTY GENERAL HOSPITAL, 206
HOWARD UNIVERSITY, 157
HOWRY & SIMON, 231
HUB FURNITURE, 272
J.M. HUBER CORPORATION, 128
HUMANA GROUP HEALTH PLAN, 206
HYATT REGENCY BALTIMORE INNER HARBOR, 220
HYATT REGENCY BETHESDA, 220
HYATT REGENCY CRYSTAL CITY-NAT'L AIRPORT, 220
HYATT REGENCY WASHINGTON ON CAPITOL HILL, 220
HYDRO THERM INC., 241
THE GEORGE HYMAN CONSTRUCTION COMPANY, 77

I

IBM CORPORATION, 150
ICF INTERNATIONAL, INC., 173
IIT RESEARCH INSTITUTE, 106

IDEAS, INC., 241
IMAGE DYNAMICS, INC., 65
INDEPENDENT CAN COMPANY, 175
INOVA HEALTH SYSTEMS, INC., 206
INSTITUTE OF MEDICINE, 206
INTEGRATED HEALTH SERVICES, INC., 206
INTELSAT, 137
INTER-AMERICAN DEVELOPMENT BANK, 96
INT'L ASSOC. OF CHIEFS OF POLICE, 115
INT'L BRAILLE & TECHNOLOGY CTR FOR THE BLIND, 123
INT'L BROTHERHOOD OF ELECTRICAL WORKERS, 115
INT'L BROTHERHOOD OF TEAMSTERS, 115
INT'L BUSINESS & ECONOMIC RESEARCH CORP., 115
INT'L MEDICAL NEWS GROUP, 256
INT'L MONETARY FUND, 194
INT'L PAPER, 128
INT'L RESEARCH INSTITUTE, 150
INT'L UNION OF ELEC. ROAD MACHINERY WORKERS, 115
INT'L VOLUNTARY SERVICES, INC., 123
INTERSOLV, 150
INTERSTATE GENERAL COMPANY, L.P., 266
I.C. ISAACS & COMPANY, 72

J

JP FOODSERVICE, 185
JAMES MADISON UNIVERSITY, 157
JOHNS HOPKINS HOSPITAL, 206
JOHNS HOPKINS UNIVERSITY, 106
THE JOHNS HOPKINS UNIVERSITY PRESS, 256
JOHNSTON, LEMON & COMPANY INC., 179
JONES, DAY, REAVIS & POGUE, 231
JUDD'S INCORPORATED, 256

K

KCI TECHNOLOGIES, 77
KPMG PEAT MARWICK, 59
KAMANITZ UHLFELDER PERMISON, 59
HENRY J. KAUFMAN AND ASSOCIATES, INC., 65
KAYDON RING & SEAL INC., 167
KELLY-SPRINGFIELD TIRE COMPANY, 128
C.M. KEMP MANUFACTURING COMPANY, 241
KENFAIR MANUFACTURING COMPANY, 235
KENNEDY KRIEGER INSTITUTE, 206
KENNETH LEVENTHAL & COMPANY, 59
KETEMA INC., 128
THE KIPLINGER WASHINGTON EDITOR INC., 257
JOHN J. KIRLIN, INC., 78
KOP-FLEX, INC., 241
THE KRONHEIM COMPANY, 185

L

LAFARGE CORPORATION, 283
LANDMARK COMMUNITY NEWSPAPERS OF MD, 257
C.J. LANGENFELDER & SONS, INC., 78
LEGENT CORPORATION, 150
LEGG MASON, 179
LEHMAN BROTHERS, 180
LERNER PROCESSING LABS, 257
LEVER BROTHERS COMPANY, 129
LEVI STRAUSS & COMPANY, 72
LIBERTY FABRICS INC., 72
LIBRARY OF CONGRESS, 195

LIFE TECHNOLOGIES, INC., 106
LIGICON SYSTEM CORPORATION, 150
ARTHUR D. LITTLE, INC., 59
LOCKHEED MARTIN CORPORATION, 69
LONDON FOG INDUSTRIES, 72
LORAL ADVANCED PROJECTS, 167
LORAL AEROSYS, 69
LORAL WESTERN DEVELOPMENT LABS, 167
LORD & TAYLOR, 272
LOUDOUN COUNTY, 195
LOUDOUN MUTUAL INSURANCE COMPANY, 228
LOYOLA CAPITAL CORPORATION, 96
LOYOLA FEDERAL SAVINGS BANK, 96
LUCAS INDUSTRIES INC., 167
JOHN D. LUCAS PRINTING COMPANY, 257
LUSKIN INC., 272

M

MCI COMMUNICATIONS CORPORATION, 137
MD INDIVIDUAL PRACTICE ASSOCIATION, 207
MACK TRUCKS INC., 91
MAINSTREAM, INC., 115
MANOR HEALTHCARE CORPORATION, 207
MANUGISTICS, INC., 150
R. MARINUCCI & SONS, 78
MARKEL CORPORATION, 228
MARRIOTT INTERNATIONAL, 221
MARRIOTT METRO CENTER, 221
MARS SUPERMARKETS, INC., 272
MARS, INC., 185
MARTIN MARIETTA CORPORATION, 69
MARTIN MARIETTA LABORATORIES, 106
MARYLAND, STATE OF, 195
MARYLAND FEDERAL SAVINGS & LOAN ASSOCIATION, 96
MARYLAND INDEPENDENT NEWSPAPERS, 257
MARYLAND INSURANCE GROUP, 228
MARYLAND NATIONAL BANK/MNC FINANCIAL, 96
MARYLAND NATIONAL MORTGAGE COMPANY, 96
MARYLAND RIBBON COMPANY, 235
MARYLAND SPECIALTY WIRE COMPANY, 175
MARYLAND DEPT. OF HEALTH & MENTAL HYGIENE, 195
MAXIMA CORPORATION, 151
McARDLE PRINTING COMPANY, INC., 258
McCORMICK & COMPANY, 129, 185, 186
McDONALD'S CORPORATION, 221
McGRAW-HILL INC., 258
McGREGOR PRINTING CORPORATION, 258
MCLEAN HILTON AT TYSON'S CORNER, 221
MEDLANTIC HEALTHCARE GROUP, 207
MEMTEC AMERICA CORPORATION, 241
MERCANTILE BANCSHARES CORPORATION, 96
MERCER MANAGEMENT CONSULTING, 60
MERCY MEDICAL CENTER, 207
MERILLAT INDUSTRIES, INC., 249
MERRILL LYNCH, 180
MERRY-GO-ROUND ENTERPRISES, 272
METROPOLITAN WASHINGTON, 195
METTIKI COAL CORPORATION, 247
R.E. MICHEL COMPANY INC., 241
MICROBIOLOGICAL ASSOCIATES INC., 107
MICROS SYSTEMS, INC., 151
MID ATLANTIC MEDICAL SERVICES, INC., 208
MILLER & LONG COMPANY, INC., 78

MINE SAFETY APPLIANCES COMPANY, 241
MINITECH, 167
MITCHELL/TITUS & CO., 60
MOBIL CORPORATION, 247
MONARCH AVALON, 258
MONTGOMERY COLLEGE, 158
MONTGOMERY COMMUNITY TELEVISION, 138
MONTGOMERY COUNTY COMMUNITY CORRECTIONS, 123
MONTGOMERY GENERAL HOSPITAL, 208
MONTGOMERY WARD, 273
MONUMENTAL LIFE INSURANCE COMPANY, 228
MORGAN STATE UNIVERSITY, 158
MOTOROLA COMMUNICATIONS & ELECTRONICS, 167
MURRY'S INC., 186

N

NYMA, INC., 151
NATIONAL 4-H COUNCIL, 124
NATIONAL ACADEMY OF SCIENCES, 107
NATIONAL AERONAUTICS & SPACE ADMINISTRATION, 69
NATIONAL ALLIANCE FOR THE MENTALLY ILL, 123
NATIONAL ALLIANCE OF BUSINESS, 115
NATIONAL AQUARIUM IN BALTIMORE, 86
NATIONAL ASSOCIATION OF BLACK ACCOUNTANTS, 115
NATIONAL ASSOCIATION OF LIFE UNDERWRITERS, 116
NATIONAL ASSOCIATION OF MANUFACTURERS, 116
NATIONAL ASSOCIATION OF SECURITIES DEALERS, 180
NATIONAL CANCER INSTITUTE, 208
NATIONAL CENTER FOR PUBLIC POLICY RESEARCH, 116
NATIONAL CORP. FOR HOUSING PARTNERSHIPS, 266
NATIONAL EDUCATION ASSOCIATION (NEA), 116
NATIONAL ENDOWMENT FOR THE ARTS, 86
NATIONAL ENDOWMENT FOR THE HUMANITIES, 86
NATIONAL FEDERATION OF THE BLIND, 123
NATIONAL FRUIT PRODUCT CO., INC., 186
NATIONAL GEOGRAPHIC SOCIETY, 258
NATIONAL GYPSUM COMPANY, 284
NATIONAL JOURNAL, 258
THE NATIONAL LEARNING CENTER, 158
NATIONAL MUSEUM OF AFRICAN ART, 86
NATIONAL MUSEUM OF AMERICAN HISTORY, 86
NATIONAL PUBLIC RADIO, 138
NATIONAL RAILROAD PASSENGER CORPORATION, 287
NATIONAL REHABILITATION HOSPITAL, 208
NATIONAL RIFLE ASSOCIATION OF AMERICA, 116
NATIONAL RURAL ELECTRIC, 116
NATIONAL SCIENCE FOUNDATION, 195
NATIONAL TRUST FOR HISTORIC PRESERVATION, 117
NATIONAL WILDLIFE FEDERATION, 173
NATIONS SECURITIES, 97
NATIONSBANK, 97
NATIONSBANK CORPORATION, 97
NATIVE AMERICAN CONSULTANTS INC., 60
NAVAL RESEARCH LABORATORIES, 195
NAVY FEDERAL CREDIT UNION, 97
THE NELSON COMPANY, 249
NEWSPAPER ASSOCIATION OF AMERICA, 117
NILES BARTON & WILMER, 231
NORTH ARUNDEL HOSPITAL, 208
NORTHERN VIRGINIA COMMUNITY COLLEGE, 158
NORTHERN VIRGINIA DOCTORS HOSPITAL, 208
NORTHWEST HOSPITAL CENTER, 209

O

O'SULLIVAN CORPORATION, 129
OFFICE OF THE COMPTROLLER OF THE CURRENCY, 196
OGDEN PROFESSSIONIAL SERVICES, 117
THE OIL DAILY COMPANY, 258
OLD CASTLE, INC., 284
OMNI INNER HARBOR HOTEL, 221
OMNI SERVICES, INC., 117
OMNI SHOREHAM HOTEL, 221
OPTIC GRAPHICS, INC., 258
ORACLE COMPLEX SYSTEMS CORPORATION, 151
ORBITAL SCIENCES CORPORATION, 69
OVERSEAS PRIVATE INVESTMENT CORP., 196
OXFORD DEVELOPMENT CORPORATION, 180

P

PHH CORPORATION, 117
PRC, INC., 151
PACIFIC SCIENTIFIC COMPANY, 242
THE PALMER NATIONAL BANK, 97
PAN AMERICAN HEALTH ORGANIZATION, 118
PENRIL DATACOMM NETWORKS, 138
PENSION BENEFIT GUARANTEE CORP., 60
PEOPLE SECURITY, 228
PERDUE FARMS, INC., 186
PHILIPS TECHNOLOGY/AIRPAX CORP., 168
PHILLIPS FLAGSHIP RESTAURANT, 221
PHYSICIANS MEMORIAL HOSPITAL, 209
PIERCE ASSOCIATES, 78
PLAYTIME, 86
POLY-SEAL CORPORATION, 129
DOUGLAS PORETZ LTD., 78
PORTER/NOVELLI, 65
POST-NEWSWEEK STATIONS, INC., 138
POSTAL RATE COMMISSION, 196
POTOMAC EDISON COMPANY, 292
POTOMAC ELECTRIC POWER COMPANY, 292
PREMIER MANAGEMENT GROUP, INC., 266
PRESTON TRUCKING COMPANY, INC., 287
PRICE BROTHERS CO., 284
PRICE WATERHOUSE, 60
PROCTER AND GAMBLE, 235
PROGRAM RESOURCES INC., 107
PROVIDENCE HOSPITAL, 209
PROVIDENT BANK OF MARYLAND, 97
PULSE, INC., 242
PULSECOM/A SUBSIDIARY OF HUBBELL, INC., 138

Q

QUANTA SYSTEMS CORPORATION, 78
QUEBECOR PRINTING, 259
QUEBECOR PRINTING INCORPORATED, 259
QUES TECH, INC., 151
QUEST INTERNATIONAL FLAVORING, 187

R

RJO ENTERPRISES, 168
RACAL AVIONICS INC., 138
RACAL COMMUNICATIONS, INC., 139
RACAL HEALTH & SAFETY, INC., 242
RACAL-GUARDATA, INC., 139
RADIO FREE EUROPE/RADIO LIBERTY, INC., 139
RADISSON PLAZA HOTEL AT MARK CENTER, 221
RAMADA HOTEL TYSON'S, 221
RAMADA PLAZA HOTEL, 221
RANDOM HOUSE INC., 259
RELIABLE STORES INC., 273
REPUBLIC ENGINEERED STEELS, 176
REPUBLICAN NATIONAL COMMITTEE, 196
RESOURCE CONSULTANTS, INC. (RCI), 242
REYNOLDS & REYNOLDS, 152
RIGGS NATIONAL CORPORATION, 97
RINGLING BROS., 86
ROCCO INC., 187
ROCK CREEK FOUNDATION, 124
ROCKINGHAM MEMORIAL HOSPITAL, 209
RODMAN DISCOUNT FOOD & DRUG, 273
THE ROUSE COMPANY, 266
ROY ROGERS RESTAURANTS, 221
RUBBERMAID COMMERCIAL PRODUCTS, INC., 130
RUST ENVIRONMENTAL & INFRASTRUCTURE, 78
RYAN HOMES, INC., 78
THE RYLAND GROUP, INC., 78

S

SCM CHEMICALS INC., 130
SFA DATACOMM, INC., 139
SFA, INC., 152
STV GROUP, 79
A.J. SACKETT & SONS COMPANY, 79
SAFEWAY, INC., 273
ST. JOSEPH MEDICAL CENTER, 210
SAKS FIFTH AVENUE, 273
SALISBURY TECHNOLOGIES, LLC, 139
SAUL'S LITHOGRAPH COMPANY INC., 259
SCHLUMBERGER MALCO, INC, 130
THE SCHWAB COMPANY, 73
SCIENCE APPLICATIONS INTERNATIONAL CORP., 107
SEARS, ROEBUCK & COMPANY, 273
SECURITY PACIFIC FINANCE, 180
SECURITY STORAGE COMPANY OF WASHINGTON, 287
THE SENTINEL NEWSPAPERS, 259
SERVICE AMERICA CORPORATION, 222
SHEPPARD PRATT HEALTH SYSTEM, 210
SHERATON INNER HARBOR HOTEL, 222
SHERATON PREMIERE AT TYSON'S CORNER, 222
SHERATON WASHINGTON HOTEL, 222
SHERATON/CARLTON HOTEL, 222
SHERWIN WILLIAMS COMPANY, 130
SHOWELL FARMS, INC., 187
SIBLEY MEMORIAL HOSPITAL, 210
SIGNET BANK, 98
SIVACO, 284
SMELKINSON SYSCO, 187
THE SMITH COMPANY, 65
SMITHFIELD PACKAGING COMPANY, 187
SMITHSONIAN ENVIRONMENTAL RESEARCH CTR, 173
SMITHSONIAN INSTITUTION, 86
SMITHSONIAN INSTITUTION PRESS, 259
SMITHY BRAEDON COMPANY, 266
SOFTWARE AG OF NORTH AMERICA, 152
SOLAREX CORPORATION, 248
SOLO CUP COMPANY, 250
THOMAS SOMERVILLE CO., 235
SOUTHERN MARYLAND OIL, 248

SOUTHLAND CORPORATION, 274
SPRINT INTERNATIONAL, 139
STANLEY ACQUISITION CORPORATION, 235
STATISTICA, 152
STEGMAN & COMPANY, 60
STEPTOE & JOHNSON, 231
STEUART PETROLEUM COMPANY, 293
STIDHAM TIRE COMPANY, 274
KIRK STIEFF COMPANY, 235
STOUFFER HARBORPLACE HOTEL, 222
STROMBERG SHEET METAL WORKS, 176
STUDENT LOAN MARKETING ASSOCIATION, 180
SURVIVAL TECHNOLOGY, INC., 210
SWATH OCEAN INTERNATIONAL, 287
SWEETHEART CUP CORPORATION, 235
SYNERGICS, 293

T

TRESP ASSOCIATES, INCORPORATED, 152
TRW SYSTEMS, 91
TATE ACCESS FLOORS, INC., 243
TECHNICAL & MANAGEMENT SERVICES CORP., 139
TEKTRONIX INC., 168
TELECOMMUNICATIONS TECHNIQUES CORP., 140
TELEDYNE, 70
TELOS CORPORATION, 152
THIOKOL CORPORATION, 243
THOMPSON STEEL COMPANY INC., 176
TILT, 87
TIME-LIFE INC., 259
CHARLES H. TOMPKINS COMPANY, 79
TOWSON STATE UNIVERSITY, 158
TRACOR APPLIED SCIENCES INC., 168
TRAK AUTO CORPORATION, 274
TRANS-TECH INC./ALPHA INDUSTRIES INC., 168
THE TRAVELERS, INC., 180
TRIANGLE PACIFIC BUILDING PRODUCTS, 243
TRULAND SYSTEMS CORPORATION, 79

U

UNC INC., 288
USA TODAY, 260
USAIR GROUP, INC., 288
U.S. CAN COMPANY, 176
U.S. CHAMBER OF COMMERCE, 196
U.S. COURTS, 198
U.S. DEPT. OF AGRICULTURE, 198
U.S. DEPT. OF COMMERCE, 198
U.S. DEPT. OF DEFENSE, 198
U.S. DEPT. OF ENERGY, 198
U.S. DEPT. OF HEALTH & HUMAN SERVICES, 198, 199
U.S. DEPT. OF HOUSING AND URBAN DEVELOPMENT, 199
U.S. DEPT. OF JUSTICE, 199
U.S. DEPT. OF LABOR, 199
U.S. DEPT. OF NAVY, 200
U.S. DEPT. OF STATE, 200
U.S. DEPT. OF THE AIR FORCE, 200
U.S. DEPT. OF THE ARMY, 200
U.S. DEPT. OF THE INTERIOR, 200
U.S. DEPT. OF THE NAVY, 199
U.S. DEPT. OF THE TREASURY, 200
U.S. DEPT. OF TRANSPORTATION, 200
U.S. DEPT. OF VET. AFFAIRS MEDICAL CTR, 210, 211

U.S. HEALTH INCORPORATED, 87
U.S. MERIT SYSTEMS PROTECTION BOARD, 197
U.S. NAVY CIVIL ENGINEER CORPS (CEC), 197
U.S. NEWS & WORLD REPORT, 259
U.S. PATENT AND TRADEMARK OFFICE, 197
U.S. POSTAL SERVICE, 197
UNITED MINE WORKERS OF AMERICA, 118
UNITED PRESS INTERNATIONAL, 260
UNITED STATES FIDELITY & GUARANTY CORP., 229
UNITED STATES GYPSUM COMPANY, 79
UNITED STATES INFORMATION AGENCY, 201
UNITED STATES SENATE, 201
UNITED WAY OF AMERICA, 124
UNIVERSITY OF MARYLAND, 158, 211
UNIVERSITY OF MARYLAND AT BALTIMORE, 159
UNIVERSITY OF MARYLAND AT COLLEGE PARK, 159
UNIVERSITY OF MARYLAND BALTIMORE COUNTY, 159
UNIVERSITY OF THE DISTRICT OF COLUMBIA, 159

V

VSE CORPORATION, 60
THE VALSPAR CORPORATION, 130
VIE DE FRANCE CORPORATION, 187
VINNELL CORPORATION, 288
VIRGINIA BAPTIST HOMES, 266
VISITING NURSE ASSOCIATION OF WASHINGTON DC, 211
VISTA CHEMICALS COMPANY, 131
VITRO CORPORATION, 153
VULCAN HART PMI, 243
VULCAN MATERIALS COMPANY, 284

W, X, Y, Z

WBAL-TV, 140
WDCA-TV, 140
WJLA-TV, 140
WLR FOODS, 187
W.R.C. NBC NEWS, 140
WTTG FOX TELEVISION STATIONS, 140
THE WALTERS GALLERY, 87
H. WARSHOW & SONS INC., 73
WASHINGTON BUSINESS JOURNAL, 260
WASHINGTON COUNTY HOSPITAL ASSOCIATION, 211
WASHINGTON DC RENAISSANCE HOTEL, 222
WASHINGTON GAS LIGHT COMPANY, 293
WASHINGTON HILTON AND TOWERS, 222
WASHINGTON HOSPITAL CENTER, 211
THE WASHINGTON POST CO., 260
WASHINGTON SUBURBAN SANITARY COMMISSION, 293
THE WASHINGTON TIMES, 260
WASHINGTONIAN MAGAZINE, 261
WAVERLY, INC., 261
WELLS ALUMINUM CORPORATION, 176
WESTINGHOUSE ELECTRIC CORPORATION, 169
WESTVACO CORPORATION, 250
WHITING-TURNER CONTRACTING COMPANY, 79
WILLARD INTER-CONTINENTAL, 222
M.S. WILLETT, INC., 243
WILLIAMS INDUSTRIES INC., 79
WOODEN & BENSON, 60
WOODWARD & LOTHROP INC., 274
WORLD BANK GROUP, 98
WORLDCORP INC., 288
XEROX CORPORATION, 243

Your Job Hunt
Your Feedback

Comments, questions, or suggestions? We want to hear from you. Please complete this questionnaire and mail it to:

The JobBank Staff
Adams Media Corporation
260 Center Street
Holbrook, MA 02343

Did this book provide helpful advice and valuable information which you used in your job search? Was the information easy to access?

Recommendations for improvements. How could we improve this book to help in your job search? No suggestion is too small or too large.

Would you recommend this book to a friend beginning a job hunt?

Name:

Occupation:

Which JobBank did you use?

Address:

Daytime phone:

Other Books by Adams Publishing

The Adams Jobs Almanac, 1996. (Editors of Adams Publishing)

Updated annually, *The Adams Jobs Almanac, 1996* includes names and addresses of over 7,500 leading employers; information on which jobs each company commonly fills; industry forecasts and geographical cross-references; a close look at over 40 popular professions; a detailed forecast of 21st-century careers; and advice on preparing resumes and standing out at interviews. 5 1/2" x 8 1/2", 928 pages, paperback, $15.95.

The Adams Cover Letter Almanac. (Editors of Adams Publishing)

The Adams Cover Letter Almanac is the most detailed cover letter resource in print, containing over 600 cover letters used by real people to win real jobs. It features complete information on all types of letters, including networking, "cold," broadcast, and follow-up. In addition to advice on how to avoid fatal cover letter mistakes, the book includes strategies for people changing careers, relocating, recovering from layoff, and more. 5 1/2" x 8 1/2", 736 pages, paperback, $10.95.

The Adams Resume Almanac. (Editors of Adams Publishing)

This almanac features detailed information on resume development and layout, a review of the pros and cons of the various formats, an exhaustive look at the strategies that will definitely get a resume noticed, and 600 sample resumes in dozens of career categories. *The Adams Resume Almanac* is the most comprehensive, thoroughly researched resume guide ever published. 5 1/2" x 8 1/2", 768 pages, paperback, $10.95.

The JobBank Series. (Editors of Adams Publishing)

There are now 20 local *JobBank* books, each providing extensive, up-to-date employment information on hundreds of the largest employers in each job market. Recommended as an excellent place to begin your job search by *The New York Times, The Los Angeles Times, The Boston Globe, The Chicago Tribune,* and many other publications, *JobBank* books have been used by hundreds of thousands of people to find jobs. Editions available:

The Atlanta JobBank—The Boston JobBank—The Carolina JobBank—The Chicago JobBank—The Dallas-Ft. Worth JobBank—The Denver JobBank—The Detroit JobBank—The Florida JobBank—The Houston JobBank—The Los Angeles JobBank—The Minneapolis-St. Paul JobBank—The Metropolitan New York JobBank—The Ohio JobBank—The Greater Philadelphia JobBank—The Phoenix JobBank—The St. Louis JobBank—The San Francisco JobBank—The Seattle JobBank—The Tennessee JobBank—The Metropolitan Washington JobBank

Each *JobBank* book is 6" x 9 1/4", at least 320 pages, paperback, $15.95.

Available Wherever Books Are Sold

If you cannot find these titles at your favorite retail outlet, you may order them directly from the publisher. BY PHONE: Call 1-800-872-5627 (in Massachusetts 617-767-8100). We accept Visa, Mastercard, and American Express. $4.50 will be added to your total order for shipping and handling. BY MAIL: Write out the full title of the books you'd like to order and send payment, including $4.50 for shipping and handling to: Adams Publishing, 260 Center Street, Holbrook, MA 02343. 30-day money-back guarantee.

Adams Software

Adams JobBank

Leads job hunters directly to potential job opportunities at 14,000 U.S. corporations and employment services!

Pinpoint potential employers by state, industry, or positions commonly offered. Then review employer profiles that typically include contact name, phone number, address, company description, common professional positions, educational backgrounds sought, and even fringe benefits offered.

You have access to:
- 10,000 employer listings
- 1,900 recorded job lines
- 300 profiles of fast-growing firms
- 1,100 executive search firms
- 1,100 employment agencies

Automatically create personalized cover letters and use the resume program to produce professional-quality resumes. Keep track of it all with the built-in contact log. Available for Windows on disk.

Adams Resumes & Cover Letters Software

This package can virtually write your resumes and cover letters for you. You can choose suggested phrases and paragraphs, or customize one of the 1,200 sample resumes and cover letters provided. Available for Windows on disk.

Adams Job Interview Pro CD-Rom

This CD-Rom product lets you watch, listen, and respond to hundreds of tough interview questions. There are three full job interviews that you can watch and ask questions about, and twenty-three tutorials that allow you to master the fine points of job interviewing. *Adams Job Interview Pro* features Peter Veruki, one of the world's top experts on job interviewing. Available for Windows CD-Rom and Mac CD-Rom.

Adams JobBank Online

Explore current job opportunities with top employers nationwide. Listings typically include company background, benefits, contact person, and training programs. In addition, you can get answers to your career and job-search questions from nationally recognized experts by visiting the Job Hunting Conferences; review cutting-edge career articles, book excerpts, and software; and get valuable tips on networking, interview preparation, and career management. The online software is free (regular phone charges apply) with the purchase of this book—please mail this page. Shipping and handling costs are $5.95.

Available Wherever Software Is Sold

If you cannot find these software titles at your favorite retail outlet, you may order them directly from the publisher. Call for price information. BY PHONE: Call 1-800-872-5627 (in Massachusetts 617-767-8100). We accept Visa, Mastercard, and American Express. $4.50 will be added to your total order for shipping and handling ($5.95 for *Adams JobBank Online*). BY MAIL: Write out the full title of the software you'd like to order and send payment, including $4.50 ($5.95 for *Adams JobBank Online*) for shipping and handling to: Adams Publishing, 260 Center Street, Holbrook, MA 02343. 30-day money-back guarantee.

Visit our home page at http://www.adamsonline.com